THE CZECHOSLOVAK CONTRIBUTION
TO WORLD CULTURE

THE CZECHOSLOVAK CONTRIBUTION TO WORLD CULTURE

edited by

MILOSLAV RECHCIGL, JR.

*Published under the auspices of the
Czechoslovak Society of Arts and Sciences in America, Inc.*

by

MOUTON & CO
THE HAGUE/LONDON/PARIS
1964

© Copyright Mouton & Co., Publishers, The Hague, The Netherlands.

No part of this book may be translated or reproduced in any form, by print, photoprint, microfilm, or any other means, without written permission from the publisher.

Printed in the Netherlands by Mouton & Co., Printers, The Hague.

Table of Contents*

RENÉ WELLEK
Foreword 11

MILOSLAV RECHCIGL, JR.
Preface 13

Literature and Literary Criticism

RENÉ WELLEK
Recent Czech Literary History and Criticism* 17

JIŘÍ ŠKVOR
Humanistic and Democratic Thought in Czech Literature* . . 29

GEORGE PISTORIUS
Two Paradoxes of Czech Literary Evolution* 39

JURAJ SLÁVIK
One Hundred and Twenty Years of Slovak Literary Language . 44

RUDOLF STURM
Czech Opinion of America in the Mid-Nineteenth Century* . . 51

WILLIAM E. HARKINS
The Real Legacy of Karel Čapek* 60

JAROSLAV DRESLER
Čapek and Communism 68

PETER DEMETZ
The Art of Jan Čep* 76

* The papers presented at the First Congress of the Czechoslovak Society of Arts and Sciences in America are marked with an asterisk.

JAN TUMLÍŘ
Traditions of Czech Literature and the Writer in Exile*   83

Linguistics

HENRY KUČERA
The Czech Contribution to Modern Linguistics*   93

LADISLAV MATĚJKA
Moravian Codification of the First Slavic Literary Language* . 105

ANGELIKA K. CARDEW
The Influence of John of Neumarkt* 112

Music and Fine Arts

KAREL B. JIRÁK
Music in Czechoslovakia* 119

EDITH VOGL GARRETT
The Influence of 18th Century Czech Composers on the Development of Classical Music* 134

MOJMÍR S. FRINTA
Czechoslovak Painting from its Beginning until the Second World War 141

MOJMÍR S. FRINTA
Illuminator Egregius Temporibus Wenceslai IV in Regno Bohemiae Florens* 156

JAROSLAV ŠEJNOHA
Frank Kupka (1871-1957)* 167

JAN ZACH
The Contribution of the Sculpture of Czechoslovakia to the World of Art* 175

History

MILIČ ČAPEK
The First Contact of Czechs with Western Civilization: The Mission of St. Amand in the 7th Century 183

JERZY ZABORSKI
Dynamics of the Spatial Concept of Czechoslovakia: Persistence of Regional Consciousness and Unity over the Span of Thirteen Centuries 202

HOWARD KAMINSKY
The Religion of Hussite Tabor* 210

FREDERICK G. HEYMANN
George of Poděbrady's Plan for an International Peace League 224

JOSEPH S. ROUČEK and GEORGE WASKOWICH
The Development of Czechoslovak Historical Writing. 245

THEODORE PROCHÁZKA
Jaroslav Goll and his Historical School* 258

LUDVÍK NĚMEC
The Success of Professor Dvorník's Research in the Vindication of the Patriarch Photius* 262

Political Science and Philosophy

VÁCLÁV BENEŠ
Background of Czechoslovak Democracy 267

EDWARD TÁBORSKÝ
Political Science in Czechoslovakia 277

ERAZIM V. KOHÁK
Masaryk and Plato in the 20th Century 283

Sociology

OTAKAR MACHOTKA
The Character of Czech Scholarship: a Contribution to the Sociology of Knowledge* 297

JAN HAJDA
The Role of the Intelligentsia in the Development of the Czechoslovak Society* 307

JOSEPH S. ROUČEK
    The Development of Sociology in Czechoslovakia before World War II 313

JIŘÍ NEHNĚVAJSA
    Anticipated Changes in Czechoslovakia* 319

Economics

JAROSLAV GEORGE POLACH
    Teleological Construction of Economics: Professor Karel Engliš' Contribution to Economic Thought* 329

ANTHONY CEKOTA
    Tomáš Bat'a – Pioneer of Self-Government in Industry* 342

LADISLAV K. FEIERABEND
    Czechoslovak Grain Monopoly System* 350

V. E. ANDIC
    Economic and Social Structure of Czechoslovak Society between the Two Wars 359

JAN MICHAL
    Problems of Measuring Industrial Output in Czechoslovakia* . 373

Law

JAROSLAV NĚMEC
    The Origins and Development of the Study of History of Law in the Territory of Czechoslovakia (1775-1939) 381

VRATISLAV BUŠEK
    The Czechoslovak Constitutions of 1920, 1948, and 1960* . . . 396

ADOLF PROCHÁZKA
    The Brno School of Jurisprudence* 405

JOHN G. LEXA
    Election Laws and Democratic Government* 414

JAROSLAV JÍRA
    Some Criminological and Socio-Political Aspects of Czechoslovak Pre-Communist and Communist Legislation on Abortion* . . . 425

Science and Technology

KAREL HUJER
The Purkinje Effect in the Evolution of Scientific Thought* . . 449

JOSEF BROŽEK
Jindřich Matiegka and the Anthropometric Approach to the Study of Body Composition* 458

WALTER REDISCH
The Czechoslovak Contribution to the Change in Concept of Circulation of the Blood* 462

JAROSLAV NĚMEC
Prokop Waldfogel of Prague and the 15th Century Printers of the Kingdom of Bohemia* 471

JOSEPH Z. SCHNEIDER
Czechoslovak Engineering until the Second World War 477

MILOŠ ŠEBOR
Five Centuries of Czech Geography, Exploration, and Cartography: Comments on Major Trends and Present Status* . . . 482

Czechs and Slovaks Abroad

MATTHEW SPINKA
The Present Day Significance of John A. Comenius. 493

M. NORMA SVEJDA
Augustine Heřman of Bohemia Manor*. 500

T. D. STEWART
Aleš Hrdlička, Pioneer American Physical Anthropologist* . . 505

JOHN M. SKŘIVÁNEK
The Czechs in Texas*. 510

MILIČ KYBAL
Czechs and Slovaks in Latin America* 516

V. E. ANDIC
Trends in Czech and Slovak Economic Enterprise in the New World* 523

VOJTĚCH N. DUBEN
Czech and Slovak Press outside Czechoslovakia 528

VLASTA VRÁZ
Early Czech Journalism in the United States* 546

Bibliography

MILOSLAV RECHCIGL, JR.
Czechoslovakia and its Arts and Sciences: A Selective Bibliography in the Western European Languages 555

Contributors to this Volume 635

Index 653

Foreword

The Czechoslovak Society of Arts and Sciences in America is a young organization: it was founded in 1960 (after three years of preparation), mainly on the initiative of the famous mathematician, Václav Hlavatý, of Indiana University, who became its first President. The Society aims to bring together all Czech and Slovak intellectuals scattered today all over the world as well as other scholars interested in things Czechoslovak. It is completely unpolitical as it welcomes scholars and scientists of all persuasions and views as far as they are able to speak freely in the free world. It is completely independent as it draws its only financial support from the voluntary contributions of its members. Today the society has over 600 members, mainly in the United States and Canada, but also in many European countries and in other continents. College teachers, scientists, writers, artists, constitute the bulk of the membership, but anybody is welcome as an Associate member who is seriously interested in promoting its aims.

Obviously the first aim of the Society is help its own members to know each other and to support their activities. The Society has been publishing a monthly bulletin, *Zprávy SVU*, in Czech and Slovak, which is meant to be mainly informative. It has set up Working Groups in the main centers, New York, Washington, Toronto, Montreal, etc., which make social contacts among the members easier and arrange for lectures and discussions. It is beginning to support publication in Czech: the first number of a quarterly called *Proměny* ("Transformations") has just appeared. The Society has collected a small library and archive in Washington and is preparing a "Who's Who" among Czechoslovak Intellectuals Abroad which would be much more than a mere address book.

But the second task of the Society is the most important for the outsider. We want to speak to the world: not only about ourselves and the work of the members but on behalf of the great Czechoslovak cultural tradition which has again been interrupted by the events of 1948. The

Society wants to help in keeping alive and making the world aware of the Czechoslovak cultural tradition which dates back to the beginnings of Christianity and has consistently upheld the ideals of humanity. The great names of Jan Hus, Jan Amos Komenský (Comenius) and T. G. Masaryk are sufficient evidence that the Czechoslovak peoples were and are a part of the Western tradition. The first Congress, attended by over 200 members, held in Washington in April 1962 elaborated this theme, and we hope that the 2nd Congress, which will convene at New York City on September 11-12, 1964, will again testify to the vitality of the Czechoslovak tradition in the free world. This volume, is we hope, a good beginning.

January, 1964

RENÉ WELLEK
President,
Czechoslovak Society of
Arts and Sciences
in America

Preface

This volume, *The Czechoslovak Contribution to World Culture*, comprises primarily the papers presented at the First Congress of the Czechoslovak Society of Arts and Sciences in America, Inc. This Congress, the first of its kind in scope and presentation, was held April 20-22, 1962, at the Statler-Hilton Hotel in Washington, D. C.

The primary purpose of the Congress was to acquaint the international audience with the contributions of the Czechoslovak peoples to world culture in various fields of learning. The program covered a wide variety of topics, organized for the sake of convenience into eight separate sessions dealing, specifically, with: science, medicine and technology; fine arts; literature and literary criticism; linguistics and Slavistics; law and economics; sociology, theology, and philosophy; history and political science; and, finally, a session devoted to the accomplishments of Czechs and Slovaks abroad. Although there were also a few papers presented which dealt with the problems of today's Czechoslovakia, and several on topics unrelated to Czechoslovakia at all, except for the speaker's national background, most lectures were concerned with the past accomplishments of the Czechoslovak peoples. Short summaries of all papers presented are available in the *Abstracts* (Washington and New York, 1962), which were published by the Society at the time of the First Congress.

In order to achieve uniformity and harmony in the material covered in this volume, representatives of the Society, in conjunction with the publisher, agreed to include only selected papers which either have a direct bearing on our central theme, as expressed in the title of this book, or which are in some way related to Czechoslovakia. It was further decided to include in the book additional contributions on topics which were not covered at the Congress, to the extent that space would permit. Although it is not claimed that all principal achievements of the Czechoslovak peoples have received the coverage they deserve, or (in some cases) that they have even been mentioned, we hope that the supplementary essays in certain less fully-covered areas will increase the usefulness of the book. The addition of seventeen new papers brings the total to 57. The eight original sections have been completely rearranged, and three new sections added (including an extensive bibliography).

This is the first book of its kind in the English language, and those responsible for its conception and production hope that it will find a sympathetic audience among both students and scholars of Slavic studies in general, and studies of Czechoslovakia in particular. The title of the book, as well as the scope of the program of the Society's First Congress, was prompted by the Czech book of similar title, *Co daly naše země Evropě a lidstvu*[1] (ed. by V. Mathesius), which was published in Prague by Evropský literární klub in 1939, and by Sfinx, Bohumil Janda in 1940.

The editor wants to express his profound appreciation to all those who made the existence of this volume possible, both fellow-members and friends of the Society. His special gratitude is extended to Prof. Vratislav Bušek, Prof. Václav Hlavatý, Prof. Karel B. Jirák, Dr. Jaroslav Němec, and Prof. René Wellek for their wise counsel in preparing and organizing the program of the First Congress of the Czechoslovak Society of Arts and Sciences in America. He wants further to express his gratitude to the following scientists and scholars for their help in the reading, critical evaluation and selection of the manuscripts. They include, in alphabetical order: Josef Anderle, V. E. Andic, Antonín Basch, Vratislav Bušek, Josef Čada, Milič Čapek, Ivo Ducháček, Francis Dvorník, Jana Feierabend, Philipp Frank, Mojmír Frinta, Jan Hajda, Ervin Hexner, Frederick G. Heymann, Václav Hlavatý, Milo P. Hnilička, Karel B. Jirák, Bruno Kisch, Jiří Kolaja, Ferdinand Kolegar, Henry Kučera, John G. Lexa, Otakar Machotka, Ladislav Matějka, Frank Meissner, Jan V. Mládek, Jiří Nehněvajsa, Jaroslav Němec, V. N. Nevlud, Otakar Odložilík, Leopold Pospíšil, Jaroslav J. Pelikán, Jaroslav G. Polach, Theodore Procházka, George J. Staller, Ernest Šturc, Rudolf Sturm, Edward Táborský, Kurt Wehle, and René Wellek. Of these, Prof. Wellek and Dr. Němec were especially helpful. Special thanks are also offered Ann R. Lindsay for her skillful job in the editing of the manuscripts for English style and idiom. Last, but not least, sincere thanks are extended to Eva Rechcigl and Paul J. Edwards for their assistance in the preparation of the index and the editing of the authors' *Curricula vitae*.

MILOSLAV RECHCIGL, JR.

[1] "What Our Country Contributed to Europe and Humanity".

LITERATURE AND LITERARY CRITICISM

Recent Czech Literary History and Criticism

RENÉ WELLEK

In an article, "Modern Czech Criticism and Literary Scholarship", *Harvard Slavic Studies*, Vol. II, published in 1954 (but written in 1953 before the death of Stalin) I painted a somewhat nostalgic picture of Czech literary scholarship and criticism between the two world wars. I argued that there was an almost unique collaboration between scholarship and criticism, that "their critics were professors, and professors critics", and I described great men such as F. X. Šalda, Arne Novák, and Otokar Fischer as representing this ideal union of scholarship and criticism. I sketched also the teachings of Czech "structuralism", the slogan of a group of scholars within the Prague Linguistic Circle who developed and modified the teachings of the Russian Formalist movement. I glanced sadly at the havoc wrought by the Nazi occupation and the uncertainties and hesitations of the brief breathing spell between 1945 and the Communist takeover in 1948. I gloomily accepted the end of all independent scholarship and criticism. I knew that a dreary uniformity, with all results fixed in advance, had been imposed. "Criticism", I concluded, "as an act of understanding and free judgment is dead" (p. 357). I was dismayed at the general paralysis of even Marxist scholarship and criticism at that time. I complained that no systematic reinterpretation of the Czech literary tradition had been attempted. The pall of fear hung heavily over the land.

Some nine years have gone by and one must conclude that the basic situation, the complete dominance of the Marxist dogma, has not changed. Still, some of my reflections and predictions are outdated or rather we are confronted with new developments which deserve serious consideration. At least, we face now a new large production of books of literary scholarship and criticism which do attempt to carry out the large scale Marxist revision of literary history absent in 1953. I shall not attempt to explain the reasons for the change. I don't believe one can speak of a "thaw" or of revisionism in literary history and criticism in the sense in which one can speak of a shortlived loosening after 1956 in creative writing. The image of the "thaw" is accurate only if we interpret it literally as a freezing out, a freeing of energies, and not in any way as a warming up toward the West or a return to Western ideas. We are confronted rather with a consolidation of the ideology and methodology which seems the result of a long period of incubation and accumulation.

What has happened is precisely what I had missed in 1953: there is now a systematic Marxist interpretation of the history of Czech literature, while before that time there were only blueprints, programmatic pronouncements, brief outlines. I refer primarily to the two stout volumes (529 and 685 pages respectively) of *The History of Czech Literature* (*Dějiny české literatury*) published by the Czech Academy in 1959-60 under the general editorship of Jan Mukařovský, but largely written by two men, Josef Hrabák on Old Czech literature and Felix Vodička on the literature of the early 19th century. The two volumes trace the history of Czech literature from the beginnings to about 1862, the death of Božena Němcová. But I should not like to limit myself to reporting about the representative collective effort of the Academy. Much light is thrown on the situation by more specialized books such as a collection of programmatic articles by Jan Mukařovský (*Z české literatury*, 1961), or by a book on Vladislav Vančura by Milan Kundera (*Umění románu*, 1961). These books are concerned only with Czech literature, but the Marxist point of view has been also applied to Western literatures, and there are several books which I should like to discuss partly because they are symptomatic and partly because their themes make the discussion comprehensible to those who are not acquainted with Czech literature. I'll mention a book on Béranger by Jan Otokar Fischer (1957, available also in an East German translation, 1960), a book by Václav Černý on *The People and Literature in the Middle Ages* (1958), a book by Zdeněk Stříbrný on *Shakespeare's History Plays* (1959) and a little collective volume on *European Literatures*, 1945-1958, edited by Zdeněk Vančura (1959).

It will not surprise us that all this production moves rigidly within the circle of the accepted ideas of Marxist criticism and the general dogma of Socialist realism. Especially the programmatic pronouncements of Jan Mukařovský and the introduction to the first volume of the Academy *History* violently insist on the complete break with all *bourgeois* scholarship and criticism: its objectivity, its diversity, its supposed formalism, idealism, relativism, etc. Literature must be interpreted as a reflection of the social and economic evolution of society, of the class-struggle, and must be judged according to the position it assumes in this scheme of progress. Every work of literature is judged according to its contribution to the cause of progress – progress toward the Communist ideal. The whole of history and particularly Czech history is seen as a single process in which dark forces wage a losing battle against the light: oddly enough the nearer we get to our time the more does white turn into pink and red. All this is of course well known from Russian Marxist criticism and from the powerful writings of the Hungarian Georg Lukács.

What seems to me peculiar to the recent Czech theories is rather the insistence on the criterion of "popularity" (*lidovost*), a term which is hard to translate into English as it does not quite mean popularity, or folksiness or nationality. In practice, it achieves a dangerously plausible though very limited perspective. All Czech history (and literary history) is viewed from the point of view of the "people", i.e. in older times of the peasant masses, and all literature is judged by asking whether it "correctly" depicts the social situation of the masses, sympathizes with their plight, is addressed to them as readers, comprehensible to them and hence draws on the methods of folk-literature and folklore. Mukařovský makes a rather clumsy attempt to reconcile this purely ideological criterion with an aesthetic standard. He demands bluntly that "we must rank and judge works of art according to their relation to the struggle for justice", and this criterion, he asserts. "agrees, on the whole, with that of artistic perfection" (*loc. cit.* p. 28). One cannot help smiling at the little loophole he left for himself in the words "on the whole". Mukařovský, in his heyday, was a militant formalist, and used to admire *avant-garde* obscure poetry. He must know even now that there were great artists in history who have not contributed noticeably to the class struggle, are not easily comprehensible to the masses and are not inspired by folklore. Still, we hear from Mukařovský, of all people, that "the most popular authors are the greatest authors" (*ibid.*, p. 30) and that "a work that is alien to the people, ceases to be a work of art" (*ibid.*, p. 45). Mukařovský now rejects his earlier historical relativism. He now knows that the only "correct" method is that of dialectical materialism, and that literary scholarship has only one aim: "to help in the building of socialism" (*ibid.*, pp. 56, 234). The complete subservience to immediate political ends could not be proclaimed more openly and complacently.

But fortunately an investigation of the actual books produced somewhat mitigates the impression of a purely utilitarian dogmatism. Many of these writers, while undoubtedly orthodox in their professions, have preserved some regard for the evidence of their senses: for the facts of history and the appeal to their aesthetic sensibility. The two-volume

History of Czech Literature was obviously scrutinized with great care for any deviations and relapses and is thus the most rigid and also the dullest of the books under survey. It has even the petty features of Communist pedantry. Dates after Christ are referred to as "according to the new calendar". Quotations marks are put around such words as "martyrs". Certain scholars such as Roman Jakobson, Father Dvorník, and myself are on a blacklist: we have become "no-persons" from Orwell's *1984*. A harmless paper of mine on "Mácha and English Literature" is referred to, however, but without any indication of its authorship. We are merely, in the passive voice, told that "Mácha's relations to English literature are revised critically". The same has happened to Roman Jakobson several times (cf. Vol. II, 455; cf. on R. Jakobson II, 456, 565). But these are little things. More serious is the proclaimed playing-down of Western influences or the preposterous statement made elsewhere by Mukařovský that "Russian influences on Czech literature were stronger than all Western influences combined" (*Z české literatury*, p. 230). The mere fact that one can hardly speak of Russsian influences on Czech literature before the 19th century should suffice to refute this absurdity.

But the worst is of course not simple omissions or silence, but the way the essential tone and nature of Czech intellectual and literary history are falsified by the deliberate blindness to the tremendous all-absorbing interest in religion dominating older Czech literature. Not that the authors of the *History* can ignore the fact: they have to talk about saints' legends, liturgical plays, the chalice of the Hussites, the Bohemian Brethren, Bible translations, and the *Net of Faith*. But on every point they try to translate and actually to evaporate religious issues into social questions and to consider the reluctantly admitted dominance of religious themes, for instance, in Hussite literature "an optical illusion" (Vol, I, 188).

In general, the authors operate with the extremely broad and vague concepts of Marxist history: "feudalism" which may mean anything from the authority of the oldest Czech pre-Christian prince to Austrian bureaucracy in the later 19th century, and "bourgeoisie" which may mean anybody from medieval artisan and merchant to a modern intellectual who is not a Marxist. With the usual sleight of hand, "progress" can be found anywhere as things change at all times. Even Kosmas in the 11th century was "progressive" though he wrote in Latin for the clergy and supported the centralizing policy of the dynasty (Vol, I, 80). When it suits the purposes of the authors, works and figures are judged without regard to their historical context, anachronistically. Thus they lecture Chelčický for his pacifism which they consider a "tragic error" (Vol. I, 278) and, of course, all baroque poetry is condemned for bad taste and mysticism because it was produced by Catholics during the Counter-Reformation.

One should admit that the general scheme works much better when applied to the early nineteenth century. The role of religion did diminish perceptibly, and the influence of folklore on Czech literature, particularly on writers such as Čelakovský, Erben and Němcová, was crucial and almost all-pervasive. The discussions of the Czech Revival are instructive and illuminating if we manage to ignore such meaningless statements as that "Dobrovský's attitude toward scholarship and life was the consequence of freer production relations" (Vol. II, 103).

Zdeněk Nejedlý's article "The Communists are the Heirs of the Great Traditions of the Czech Nation" (1947), set the pattern, but even the authors of the first volume cannot hide the fervid religious motivation of men such as Hus, Chelčický, Blahoslav and Komenský, and the authors of the second volume must admit that Havlíček attacked communism, and that Mácha was an individualist and dark pessimist. In theory the authors have to exalt popular literature against what they term "exclusive" art. They should prefer the folksy *Legend of St. Procopius* to the exquisite and precious *Legend of St. Catharine*. But they have to admit that the *Legend of St. Catharine* contains "one of the most beautiful passages of our ancient poetry" (Vol. I, 131): the symbolic interpretation of the colors which appeared on the body of the martyred saint. One wonders what happened to realism, enlightenment and social progress. Though a desperate effort is made to make Mácha a revolutionary (and not merely a rebel), even V. Štěpánek, the author of the section, has to speak of his individualism, his pessimism, his inner division. It is almost pitiful to observe the writer of the section on Erben (Karel Dvořák) trying to justify Erben's use of myth by quoting Marx (Vol. II, 558) or to make something positive out of Erben's belief in fate or resignation. It is comforting to know that people even in Czechoslovakia cannot quite deny evidence which stares in their faces though we might reflect that precisely the undeniable learning contained in these volumes makes them much more insidious and dangerous. The student is apt to swallow the ideology along with the abundant information.

The very same conceptions permeate the books on foreign literatures. It is sad to open a book, *People and Literature in the Middle Ages*, by Václav Černý, a man who spent five years in a labor camp for his outspoken anti-Communist stand before 1948, and hear him talk about literature as "the superstructure reflecting economic-material conditions", quoting Engels and asking constantly the one leading question: whether a medieval author was "progressive" or not. Černý's book – as the criticism it received in Czechoslovakia sensed quite rightly – has actually only a thin Marxist veneer. It excerpts Henri Pirenne's *Economic and Social History of Europe* to establish the obligatory background but otherwise studies learnedly and sensibly such good old questions as folk poetry and its influence on court poetry, the role of the minstrels and the wandering scholars, the picture which we can form of peasants' life and peasants' misery from medieval sources, and finally asks the question whether there were authors who doubted the social basis of medieval society. Černý singles out the *Roman de la Rose* for a passage in the continuation by Jean de Meung which sounds to him revolutionary for its condemnation of social stratification and oppression (cf. pp. 253 ff.) though it is obviously only a paraphrase of classical commonplaces derived from Ovid and Lucretius about the golden age: a document in the history of primitivism. Černý's book is a learned miscellany of information grouped around the concept of popular art in the Middle Ages. A man who used to write on Romantic titanism, the Baroque and existentialism had to find refuge in the distant past and even there has to make his gestures of submission to the ideology.

A book such as Jan Otokar Fischer's attempt to exalt Béranger, the 19th-century political *chansonnier*, shows how the ideology would work if applied rigidly to modern Western literature. Béranger assumes an enormous importance for his social comments and his social sympathies, and also his art is defended as truly popular. Unfortunately, Fischer cannot refute the judgment of all modern French critics and readers sensitive to poetry, that Béranger was simply a bad poet, a sentimental and witty rhymester of hardly any artistic value. Fischer's book belongs to a whole group of attempts, in Russia and East Germany, to rescue and to blow up the reputation of mediocre 19th century writers merely because their political sympathies were on what the Communists consider the right side. French Communists have unearthed poets of the Commune, and also in Czech literature feeble attempts are being made to uncover political poets or rather versifiers of the 1848 revolution. The excessive praise suddenly lavished on such a naive, folksy and sentimental dramatist and novelist as Josef Kajetan Tyl also reflects this desperate search for a "usable past", for a respectable ancestry. There is inverted snobbery in the whole anxiety to establish a pedigree for oneself. On the one hand the Marxists proclaim the complete break with the past, and exalt the height of the mountain from which they look down on those still struggling in the plain and on the other hand, they try to find precursors, prophets or presumed sympathizers everywhere in the past, even at the expense of ignoring the context or large parts of a man's work. Thus Tyl, who wrote mawkish stories and fairy-tales, must be made out to be democratic and realistic because he sympathized with the 1848 revolution and did use local color details.

This separation into sheep (capitalist, bourgeois) and goat (progresssive or, better, Communist) – or is it the other way round? surely Capitalists can't be sheep? or can Communists be? – is also the only criterion which permeates an encyclopedic survey of *European Literatures between 1945 and 1958* edited by Zdeněk Vančura. The booklet cannot be taken seriously as scholarship: it provides largely a list of names and titles with brief comment which one can predict in almost every instance, once we know the point of view. T. S. Eliot, Aldous Huxley, Orwell, Maugham, Auden, are all disparaged. Camus is called a reactionary, much more pessimistic and inhuman than Sartre (p. 192), Stefan George is denounced as a forerunner of the Nazis (p. 139), Croce is most unjustly called "the second defence line of Fascism" (p. 210), and, of course, the very existence of the "sadly notorious" Pasternak is deplored as a misfortune (p. 47). Still, there are some signs of the Thaw in the book. It was, we are told, "incorrect" of Zhdanov to suppress Zoshchenko and Akhmatova and the struggle against cosmopolitanism in Russia was overdone (p. 41). Oddly enough, one author finds some positive values in Modernism introduced into Yugoslavia (pp. 103-4), and the account of West German literature, though hardly more than a list of names and titles, is studiously restrained and, shall we say, "objective".

But in the discussion of Czech literature the triumph of the party spirit, the unification of all literary life, is hailed as a great achievement, and in the section on Soviet literature the fictitious hero of a novel by Anatoli Kuznetsov even "arrives at the recognition of the Socialist essence of all events" (p. 48). Not only in this booklet but elsewhere in this literature we constantly encounter one strange feature of Communist ideology: the assumption – apparently held almost unconsciously – that they inhabit paradise, that all contradictions and conflicts of older societies are now resolved and that what they say about the West and the past has no bearing on their own society and age. Thus in a readable and perceptive book on the novelist Vladislav Vančura, its author, Milan Kundera, complains that "the bourgeois world is not a poetic world" (p. 180) and that "the division of labor has destroyed the possibility of developing the whole man" (p. 196). He never asks the obvious question whether the Communist world is so particularly poetic (it seemed to me, and many others, even drabber than the West) or whether the division of labor has been abolished behind the Iron Curtain. There is a constant celebration of the glories of Soviet literature which is supposedly on a different and higher plane than all preceding literatures, but we are never really told in what this superiority consists except in the correct ideology. The same is true of recent Czech literary production. When Mukařovský discusses current Czech literature he hems and haws with embarrassment, praises good intentions, correct ideology, but even he cannot pretend that any of the novels he singles out are even moderately successful works of art. Oddly enough, he praises a Slovak novel by Vladimir Mináč, *The Living and the Dead* (*Živí a mrtví*) for its final scene in which the hero recognizes his responsibility for everybody (*loc. cit.*, p. 87). Mukařovský does not know or does not want to tell us that the whole scene turns around a quotation from Dostoevsky. It is the teaching of Markel, in the *Brothers Karamazov*, expounded by the monk Zosima. It is not Communist ideology as Mukařovský pretends, but very old Christianity.

Still, talent, learning, insight are not entirely extinct in Czechoslovakia even in literary history. A younger man, Zdeněk Stříbrný, has written a good book on *Shakespeare's History Plays* (1959). It has also the basic Marxist slant, but it applies the scheme with some subtlety and some regard for the actual text. Stříbrný pursues the theme of Shakespeare's understanding of the process of history – conceived not merely as the wheel of fortune, the fall of princes, the mirror for magistrates, as it has been done before – but rather of Shakespeare's grasp of "the stream of time", the necessities brought about by changing circumstances, "the rough torrent of occasion" (cf. p. 252). Stříbrný uses the insight into the possible contradictions between theory and practice, conscious intention and actual accomplishment which was elaborated in a well-known letter by Engels on Balzac, but was of course known to many critics before. Stříbrný admits that Shakespeare was a fervent supporter of the Elizabethan monarchy and that he condemned revolution and civil war, but he argues that Shakespeare enters sympathetically into the minds and hearts of all kinds of people, that he can give expression to an almost elemental popular feeling against war, oppression and the privileges of the feudal upper crust. I am not convinced by his out-and-out defense of Falstaff and his condemnation of Falstaff's dismissal, but even here he is at least in good company. The book stands out among the publications I have discussed mainly because the author displays a genuine sensitivity to poetry and to poetic language and does analyze quite a few characters such as King Richard II with a proper regard for Shakespeare's insight into complexities and ambiguities of character undreamt of before his time. There is much truth in the conclusion that Shakespeare's peculiar greatness lies in his successfully fusing the traditions of the Renaissance with those of popular art and feeling rooted in the Middle Ages. Ultimately, Stříbrný lends support to the old idea of Shakespeare's universality and also his representativeness for the whole English nation united in the support of a popular monarch against the common enemy, Spain. Stříbrný's book occasionally lapses into Marxist jargon (which is, however, studiously kept out of the English summary), particularly when he quotes quite unoriginal Russian scholars, but taken as a whole, the book seems to me a fine example of genuine humanistic scholarship. It gives some hope that even under the dreary uniformity imposed by the ruling ideology some life of the mind can continue.

I have on purpose ignored the day-by-day debate in the Czech literary press and refused to engage in following the sinuosities of the party-line. I wanted to examine what seem to me the more permanent products of the system. One must, I think, recognize the attractions of Marxist criticism. Many people like to have their minds made up for them, not only in the satellite countries. Marxism provides a ready-made scheme both of historical explanation and of evaluation. It combines history and criticism, a point Mukařovský makes several times concealing the fact that there are many other such combinations. The historical explanation offered by Marxism has strangely enough managed to absorb all other and many older attempts to describe literary history in terms of social change. While it would be foolish to deny the close interrelations between society and literature, the particular solution offered by Marxism which makes literature dependent on economic change is surely the most tenuous and the least convincing in detail. The actual relations with specific economic factors are most difficult to establish and the whole concept of causation is most elusive in the life of the mind. I don't believe that anybody has yet succeeded in proving that because of certain events either in history or in literature there must have followed another specific event. We can see – and that has been seen, of course, long before Marxism – that literature reflects the conditions of chivalry or the dominance of the clergy or of a particular court, but one cannot prove that the Florentine burghers "caused" Dante, or that the Russian landowning aristocracy had to produce Turgenev or Tolstoy. The Marxist causal explanation necessarily leads to historical relativism and even fatalism. Events – even literary events – are completely determined and thus every work of art has its historical place and historical justification. But man cannot accept complete relativism: he has to distinguish between the good and the bad and he does so in ethics, politics, scholarship as well as in the arts. Marxism recognizes this, but imposes a criterion of judgment from the outside of literature: it completely ignores the nature of art and asks purely ideological questions about the content, the idea of a work of art which is judged by purely utilitarian terms, from a narrow contemporary perspective. The descriptive, historistic side of Marxism clashes violently with its prescriptive, evaluative side. The very term "socialist realism" reveals the contradiction: it asks the writer to depict reality as it is, objectively, realistically and at the same time it asks him *not* to depict it realistically but with his mind on the future society, socialistically, propagandistically. The naive, evaluative criterion of "progressiveness" appeals to many as it is easy to apply and flatters the self-complacency of the convinced Marxist. It allows him to look down at even the greatest men of the past who at most saw only glimmerings of the light. But Marxism totally obscures the main issue of literary criticism: the attempt to arrive at an aesthetic judgment. It labels all aesthetic judgment simply "formalist". But this of course is an insidious misunderstanding: an aesthetic judgment is concerned with the total meaning of a work of art, with its aesthetic effect which is dependent on a union of content and form. Content in a work of art is by no means mere ideology: it includes the whole world of the artist: his special creation of characters, events, moods, feelings which are not formal in the sense of verse-form or composition or diction, but make up a totality so deeply integrated that we cannot judge a work of art by isolating its social truth alone. Marxism encourages the confusion of reality and fiction, the ignoring of the obvious ontological gap between art and life, the fallacy of the aesthetics of realism with its idea of a slice of life. It denies what is most creative in man, his imagination, man's defiance of time and destiny, his victory over impermanence and transience, realitivity and history accomplished in the great achievements of the arts, in music, in painting and poetry.

The system was imported to Czechoslovakia from Russia, but in the version used there, a skilful attempt is made to appeal to the combination of nationalism and socialism which is particularly successful among the satellites. Nobody can deny that Czech history has a long tradition of nationalist feeling (just as any other nation) and that in Czech history the national struggle was associated with the rise of the peasant masses and the petty *bourgeoisie*. Nor can one deny the strong anti-Catholic strain in Czech history. But it is a complete falsification of history to make these traditions, nationalism, social discontent, and anti-clericalism, lead up to Soviet-style communism. The anti-Catholic revolt in Hussitism and the Union of the Bohemian Brethren was religious in inspiration, motivation and aim and the nationalism of the Revival was idealist and spiritual, centered around the concept of the "spirit of the nation", its mission within a final vision of humanity. The social aspirations of the Czech masses and later of the small *bourgeoisie* and even the proletariat (which can hardly be spoken of as a class before the very late 19th century) were not at all like the Communist collective farms or the regimented labor of the present regime. The basic liberalism and humanism, the basic democracy (in the Western sense and not in the topsy-turvy language of the cold-war ideology) is denied and distorted in the Marxist conception. The distortion of history is only one side of the picture. The other is the corruption of art, the imposition of bad taste, false aesthetic concepts, and purely ideological criteria of free creation. My review of these books may have shown that individuals have preserved a sense of fact and history, some taste and sensibility. They prove that the sense of truth and beauty cannot be entirely eradicated. They are eloquent testimony to the constancy of human nature. But they rather accentuate the dreary schematism imposed on them, the apparatus of concepts weighing on literary scholarship, history and criticism as it lies heavily on the nation in every aspect of its life. A radical change for the better can come only with a complete change in the political situation.

Here, in the free world, we thus have a special obligation and function to fulfill: to correct the distortions of Communist ideology and to preserve the traditions of the nation violently interrupted by the advent of Communism. The Czechoslovak Society of Arts and Sciences in America will try to contribute to this effort and I hope that this congress will be the first, and not the worst, example of our endeavor.

BOOKS DISCUSSED

Dějiny české literatury, Hlavní redaktor Jan Mukařovský, 2 vols. (Praha, Nakladatelství Československé akademie věd, 1959, 1960).
Václav Černý, *Lid a literatura ve středověku, zvláště v románských zemích* (Praha, Nakladatelství Československé akademie věd, 1958).
Milan Kundera, *Umění románu: Cesta Vladislava Vančury za velkou epikou* (Praha, Československý spisovatel, 1961).
Evropské literatury 1945-1958. Napsal kolektiv autorů za vedení Zdeňka Vančury (Praha, Orbis, 1959).

Zdeněk Stříbrný, *Shakespearovy historické hry* (Praha, Nakladatelství Československé akademie věd, 1959).

Jan O. Fischer, *Pierre-Jean de Béranger: Werk und Wirkung*. Aus dem Tschechischen übertragen von Richard Messer (Berlin, Rütten und Loening, 1960). (The Czech original was not accessible.)

Humanistic and Democratic Thought in Czech Literature

JIŘÍ ŠKVOR

Space permits only a brief consideration of my chosen theme, "Humanistic and Democratic Thought in Czech Literature". I selected this topic in order to refute the assertion of the Czechoslovak Communists that they and only they have created all the conditions necessary for an intensive cultural life; that they alone are "the heirs of the best Czechoslovak traditions", including the humanistic and democratic.

I shall trace humanistic and democratic thought mainly as seen in the literature of the Czech Middle Ages, in order to stress the ancient tradition of these two central themes.

The dawn of Czech cultural and political life is directly connected with the introduction of Christianity – a typical manifestation of humanism – in the middle of the 9th century. From the very beginning, the ideological foundation of Czech spiritual life was national and humanistic. The unique results of the activities of SS. Cyril and Methodius prove that the adoption of Christianity in those lands which now comprise Czechoslovakia cemented the religious, cultural and political aspirations of the people.

The enthusiasm of the people who gathered to hear the words of our Lord preached in the Old Slavic language was one of the first Czech cultural and national manifestations not only in "Great Moravia" but also in subsequent state and ecclesiastical formations.

The first Czech literary monuments, which dealt with the lives of the first Czech martyr-humanitarians – St. Ludmila and St. Wenceslas – very clearly manifest humanistic, Christian and national thought. The establishment of the Prague bishopric (in 973) also had an extraordinary influence on the entire Czech spiritual life.

In the oldest Czech religious songs (for instance, in the song "Hospodine, pomiluj ny" [Lord, have mercy upon us] which originated probably in the 9th century, and also in the *Pražské zlomky hlaholské* [Prague Fragments] from the 10th or 11th century), the anonymous authors ask for "bestowal of peace and abundance upon all the people".

"The Cosmas Chronicle of Bohemia" (written in Latin in the first quarter of the 12th century) combines the idea of Czech nationalism with the idea of humanity. The "Cosmas Chronicle" praises Prince Břetislav I for resisting intimidation at the Emperor's court and for abducting Jitka to avoid the humiliation of the Emperor's refusal. Similarly, an anonymous "Chronicle" written in the 12th century by "a Monk from Sázava" expresses the hope that by the mercy of God and the merits of the holy martyrs for Christ, St. Václav and St. Vojtěch (Adalbert) the country of the Czech people will not be given into the hands of foreigners.

The first Czech saints, as described in anonymous Czech legends of the 13th and 14th centuries, were not only intercessors at the throne of our Lord, but also courageous political spokesmen. (In one of the legends, for example, St. Ludmila is desribed as "the Lord's gift to the whole Czech nation", the "morning star" and "the spring primrose". The first Czech bishop-martyr, St. Vojtěch, is called "the Lord's warrior" and a "Slav".)

In the period of the reign of the last Přemyslides, when the influence of German colonists greatly threatened the Czech nation, humanistic and national ideas were strengthened by pronounced patriotic thought. In the Czech "Alexandreis" (1172) we read: "The Germans, who are only guests in Bohemia, are trying to exterminate the whole Czech race, so that even if by the grace of God the Bridge of Prague is saved from destruction, there will not be a single Czech left to cross it". ("Němci, již sú zde hoscie, chtie doždati, by na mostě Praze, jehož bóh snad nechá(!), nebude viděti Čecha, i mohlo by se brž státi, by jich nebylo nevídati".) The hero of this anonymous epic in ten cantos is a Christian knight, renowned for his humanity and courage, whose deeds are highly reminiscent of the feats of the Czech king Přemysl Otakar II. The nation in the Czech "Alexandreis" is represented by a group of the lower nobility and common folk.

Humanistic, Christian and patriotic ideas are also present in "Dalimil's Chronicle", which dates from the first third of the 14th century. This chronicle is the first to have been written in Czech, and its author, who was probably a member of the lower Czech aristocracy, writes enthusiastically of "justice and humanity", expresses his love of the Czech tongue and the Czech land. (Dalimil reports that Princess Libuše said: "If a foreigner rules you, your language shall not last long, – "Bude-li vám cizozemec vlásti, nebude moci váš jazyk dlouho trvati".)

In the first codified laws of Bohemia, such as "Rožmberk's Book" (*Kniha Rožmberská*), dating from the second half of the 14th century, and "An Exposition of Bohemian Law" (*Výklad na právo země české*) by Ondřej z Dubé, corporal punishment is recommended only for "rebels, traitors and thieves" but not for "humble folk".

During the 13th and 14th centuries, under the influence of numerous religious sects which advocated reform of existing conditions in both ecclesiastical and secular life, the ground was being prepared for the Hussite reformation. The Hussite movement was the strongest and most typical manifestation of revival tendencies in the spirit of Czech democracy. Even before this reformation, however, the spirit of patriotic democratization can be observed in the activities of Konrád Waldhauser, Jan Milíč z Kroměříže, Matěj z Janova, Tomáš Štítný ze Štítného, and others, who are called the "predecessors of Jan Hus".

Ranconis ab Ericinio, one of the foremost professors at the University of Paris, wrote this note of praise about Jan Milíč z Kroměříže: "Omne quidquid ego pro sermone faciendo viris literatis et illuminatis vix in uno mense comprehendere possum, Milicius vero tantum una hora suo studio comprehendit". ("When it takes me a month to convey my convictions to intelligent and cultivated men, Milicius, by his enthusiasm and capabilities, can comprehend my meaning in a single hour".)

The principal polemical works of John Hus, especially *De Ecclesia*, *Postilla* and the "Exposition of the Creed" (*Výklad víry*), were the basis for the reformation not only of the church but also of the whole Bohemian, and, to a certain extent, European society. The Hussite reformation was also a strong democratic and national movement. The Czech Diet in its "Four Articles of Prague" (*Čtyři artikule pražské*) demanded from the German Emperor Sigismund "freedom of the Lord's Law", i.e. freedom of the religious faith, and the precedence of the Czech tongue over the German, the main cultural and political demand of the Czech nobility.

In the middle of the 14th century, Tomáš Štítný ze Štítného wrote for his children "The Six Treatises on General Christian Matters" (*Knížky šestery o obecných věcech křestanských*). Štítný hardly could have foreseen their ultimate general educational, humanistic and Christian application.

The activities of Jan Hus, Petr Chelčický, and, later, of Jan Amos Komenský (Comenius) enlarged the idea of Christianity and national humanity by a democratic concept of God, Church and State. In the medieval society of those times this Czech democratic concept was a truly revolutionary element.

The principal themes of the Czech Reformation were based on Christ, liberty, brotherhood, and peace. These themes may be found in the program of the "Unity of the Brethren" ("Unitas Fratrum"), founded in 1457. The founders of the "Unity" were Petr Chelčický – the peasant-theologian – and Brother Rokycana, who were disturbed by the intellectual instability and even more by the moral standards then prevailing. The unrest expressed by the "Czech Brethren" was not only intellectual. It was also an unrest of conscience. For this reason, they sought to cast off the old standards and seek the standards which prevailed during the early days of Christianity.

In his polemical treatise, "On the Three Classes" (*O trojím lidu*), Petr Chelčický rejects social discrimination and emphasizes the idea of democracy. Chelčický wrote: "If the common people are indeed a part of Christ's Body, peasants and shepherds should be the most honored since they are the humblest". ("Je-li pak lid obecný opravdu částí Těla Kristova, tehdy sedláky, pastýře a chodce mají v najvěčší čest míti, ješto najmenší sú v uobci".) For Petr Chelčický, all Christian doctrine was a "joyful message of the Gospel".

In the "Quarrel of Truth with Falsehood" (*Hádání pravdy a lži*), written by Ctibor Tovačovský z Cimburka, the idea of human justice and democracy is also strikingly evident. ("He who lives in Christ, should walk where He walked ... do not love evil and do not do it onto others ... praise God, do not praise yourself." – "Kdož v Kristu přebývá, má též tudy choditi, kudy jest On chodil, ... křivdy nemilovati, ani žádnému ji nečiniti ... ne své, ale Stvořitele chvály hleděti".)

With the danger of Germanization growing in Bohemia, the humanistic, democratic and patriotic idea was embodied in many an apology and "praise" of the Czech tongue. Among the oldest is the introduction to the translation of "On the Amendment of the Fallen" (*O napravení padlého*) by St. Jan Zlatoústý (John Chrysostom). This "introduction", written in 1495 by the Czech lawyer, Vitorin Kornel ze Všehrd, says: "Let the others write new books in Latin, adding thus new water to the Roman sea; I shall translate good old books into the Czech tongue, thus making the poor richer."

A particular aspect of Czech spiritual life is the manifestation of humanistic and democratic thought throughout the Renaissance era. Toward the end of the 15th century and later, a whole series of allegoric works emerged. In these allegories, the critical spirit of the Czech Reformation met a happier Hellenic-Renaissance conception. The Czech literature of those times, striving to free itself from the captivity of mediaeval scholasticism by the revival of ancient and Christian ideals, was frequently a significant fusion of the ideas held by the Czech Brethren with humanistic ideas. West European humanism had already penetrated into Bohemia during the reign of Charles IV, where it was absorbed and molded in a special Czech manner.

Under the influence of the Czech Reformation, a whole series of new copies and translations of the Bible were made, such as the "Bible Svatováclavská", "Drážďanská", "Olomoucká", and others. Humanistic and democratic ideas are also noticeable in the work of the "Unitas Fratrum" bishop Jan Blahoslav. His work, *Summa quaedam brevissima*, contributed greatly to the understanding of the history of the Czech Reformation. Blahoslav's translation of the New Testament from Greek into Czech prepared the way for the publication of the famous "Bible Kralická," one of the most important Czech literary achievements of the second half of the 16th century.

The peak of the humanistic, democratic and educational endeavours of the Czech spiritual reformation were the works of Jan Amos Komenský (Comenius), who saw Christianity as a supreme moral force bringing men together as brothers, regardless of the differences among the various sects and the many conflicts among states and politicians. To spread his convictions, Komenský originated a new approach to education. In fact, he went so far as to draft a new, practical plan to be followed by teachers throughout the world. Its aim was to make man aware of his relationship with God and of the need to practice the eternal virtues of love, charity and understanding.

In the 16th and early 17th centuries, when tension between Catholicism and Protestantism reached its climax in Bohemia, a series of works were produced representing the "Golden Era of Czech literature". These works, too, contained humanistic, democratic and patriotic ideas, and, popularized by Daniel Adam z Veleslavína, Jiří Melantrich and others, educated the broad masses of the Czech nation. "Dictionaries" by Veleslavín, his "Historical Calendars", his *Politica Historica*, are interesting sociological and economic studies of those times. Travel books such as "The Adventures of Václav Vratislav z Mitrovic" and tales of Krištof Harant z Polžic a Bezdružic, introduced foreign lands to Czech readers.

The participation of the common people in the development of Czech literature at that time coincided with the increased literary use of the Czech language in contemporary works. Václav Písecký compares the "finesse and brightness" ("světlost a lepotu") of the Greek and Czech languages. Jan Vodňanský in his "Lactifer" states: "The Czech tongue is not at all as narrow and as rough as it seems to many". ("Jazyk český není tak úzký ani tak nehladký, jakož se některým zdá".) Such praise prepared the ground for the famous official "Defences" of the Czech literary languages. The most important was that by the Czech Jesuit priest, Bohuslav Balbín, entitled *Dissertatio apologetica pro lingua slavonica, praecipue bohemica*.

In connection with Bohuslav Balbín, we should note that the era of the so called "Counter-Reformation" also brought an enrichment of Czech spiritual life. It should be stressed that during the period which Alois Jirásek called "darkness" ("Temno"), many a representative of the Roman Catholic Church acted in a traditional humanistic-democratic manner, thus helping the Czech nation to bear the burden of Germanization and of social oppression.

In the late 18th and early 19th centuries, the humanistic concept of the nation found a sympathetic response in Bohemia. The achievements of English Deists, French Encyclopedists and German Rationalists influenced Czech cultural and economic life somewhat later. They contributed to the abolition of serfdom (1781) and this gave rise to the more active participation of the Czech people in the national cultural life. When, in 1769, a "learned society" was founded in Prague (renamed in 1790 "The Royal Bohemian Learned Society" – "Královská česká společnost nauk"), Czech intellectuals had a permanent base from which to develop their cultural activities.

Almost all Czech and Slovak men of learning and science (Dobrovský, Jungmann, Šafařík, Kollár, Palacký, Pelcl, Palkovič, Bernolák and many others) came from the common people, and this left a certain imprint on their humanistic, democratic and patriotic outlook. In 1775, the representatives of Czech cultural life established a chair of Czech language and literature at the University of Vienna. Josef Dobrovský took advantage of the visit paid by Emperor Leopold II to the Royal Bohemian Learned Society in 1791 to bring to the ruler's attention the importance of Czech popular support for the stability of his throne.

We should not forget that the German language was still used by the majority of Czech intellectuals; that Dobrovský wrote (in 1792) his *Geschichte der böhmischen Sprache und Literatur* in German; that Puchmajer entitled the introduction to his "Collection of Czech Verses" (*Sebrání českých veršů*) "the voice crying in the wilderness".

Cultural works produced by Czech intellectuals under the influence of the modern Western outlook on State, Church and the people (as described in the works of Voltaire, Montesquieu, Rousseau, Locke, Herder and Kant) received assistance which underlined and stressed the cult of the individual, national, and democratic tradition. The French Revolution and Napoleon's march through Europe furthered Czech nationalism and Panslavism. Classical antiquity and Herder's humanity were merged in the didactic efforts of Jungmann, Šafařík, Kollár and others. (In *Krok*, a magazine published by Presl, Jungmann wrote: "It is not the mountains, castles, strong weapons, riches of nature, agricultural and industrial skill that make a nation, but above all the free cultivation of arts and sciences, which weld the educated and uneducated classes of a nation together.")

Kollár's *Slávy dcera* ("Daughter of Sláva") is another unique synthesis of humanistic, national and pan-Slavic characteristics, both spiritual and physical. National and humanistic ideals were expanded by Jan Kollár into a universal ideal of mankind.

The Romantic era, with its cult of the individual, nature and the humble people, stressed even more the humanistic and democratic idea in Czech literature. The literary output of the foremost Czech romantics, (F. L. Čelakovský, K. J. Erben, K. H. Mácha and others) showed clearly that the authors were typical representatives of the common people. In 1848 the "Spring of Nations" year, the "All-Slavic Congress" assembled in Prague. The humanistic and national character of Czech literature was further developed during that year by a clearly formulated element of a political nature. F. L. Rieger stressed that the Slavic people comprised more than half the population of the Austro-Hungarian monarchy. The scholarly and artistic works of František Palacký, Karel Havlíček Borovský, Jan Neruda and Svatopluk Čech were in complete accord with humanistic, national and democratic ideas. The influence of Western thought which clearly manifested itself in 1848 helped the Czechs to understand the true meaning of Nation, State and Patriotism.

Karel Havlíček Borovský emphasized that the nation is not created for the despotism of the ruler. Božena Němcová placed the future of the nation into the hands of a type of educated woman and mother. The poets Neruda and Hálek emphasized humanism and nationalism as the pillars of the spiritual life of the people. Karolina Světlá thought the "preaching of truth to be the main mission of the Czech writer". Holeček, Heyduk, Sládek, Herben, Nováková and many others saw in the humble people, especially peasants and workers, the source of national revival. Thomas Garrigue Masaryk felt the existence of some kind of "invisible church", a society of individuals, strenuously endeavoring to fulfill the national and universal ideals.

Similar ideas may be found in the works of Sova, the brothers Mrštík,

Durych, Křička, Toman, Bezruč, the brothers Čapek, Zahradníček, Čep, and many others. Some of these authors were born in the Christian, humanistic and democratic tradition; others attained these ideals through conviction. In the old as well as in modern Czech literature we can find hardly a single outstanding author who did not accept humanistic and democratic thought as a foundation of his philosophical outlook.

The Czech people attained Masaryk's ideal of "humanistic democracy" in a millenium of natural and organic development. Worldly and ecclesiastical rulers condemned the Czech nation as "heretic and disobedient". For 300 years the Czech spirit was enslaved by German hierarchy and aristocracy. During this long period, it was the small people in the cities and on the farms ("misera plebs contribuens") who remained spiritually "Czech". These humble people, always religious and democratic, bided their time to shake off the foreign, undemocratic and inhuman yoke.

After 1848, the new generation of Czech poets, accepted the democratic and humanistic program as their ideal. The scholarly and political works of Thomas Garrigue Masaryk purified this democratic and national program, liberated it from romantic tendencies, and imbued it with clear political concepts.

The fatal "February, 1948" was not a climax to, but a violent interruption of, this development. The Czechoslovak Communists are not – as they try to portray themselves – "heirs of the best Czechoslovak tradition". They do not struggle for "the soul of the nation": on the contrary, they avoid meeting it.

It has been said: "Whatever grows – cries not." And the soul of the Czech nation, alive in Czech literature, "grows and cries not". It grows in the calm of the Czech fields, over the rooftops of old Prague, in the studies of silenced intellectuals – of those who "stayed faithful". It grew, and will continue to grow out of its own strength, out of its own genius.

I will conclude with two ideas best expressed in the words of Josef Čapek and F. X. Šalda. First, I quote Josef Čapek: "They shall claim that they are the tongue and the arms of the people, that they are its plenipotentiaries; but those who suffer under them, those whom they strike with an iron fist, those upon whom they trample with their boots – these are the nation. However, in a nation, there always is something that will remain when the vermin is gone, something that cannot be stamped out, cannot be smothered: *moral strength*."

F. X. Šalda, reflecting on the spirit of the nation, said: "In great and crucial times, the nation is endowed with a deeper instinct of wisdom than is its transient government. This is so, because the soul of the nation is not its tongue, its art or church, its economic or cultural institutions, not even its race. These are all merely external and transient characteristics, not the essence. The soul of the nation is an imperceptible creative force – moral and ideal."

And today we can look at the forces around us and ask ourselves: "Who would dare, who would permanently be able, to enslave and destroy the humanistic and democratic soul of this nation?"

A. *The Sources Used*:

Bartoš, F. M., *Bojovníci a mučedníci* (Prague, 1939).
Bílý, František, *Od kolébky našeho obrození* (Prague, 1904).
Coster-Colin, Goldring, Guarnieri-Huebner-Rutte, *Nové evropské umění a básnictví* (Prague, 1923).
Denis, Ernest, *La Bohème depuis la Montagne-Blanche* (Paris, 1930).
——, *Huss et la guerre des Hussites* (Paris, 1878).
Fischer, Otokar,*Slovo a svět* (Prague, 1937).
Flajšhans, Václav, *Nejstarší památky jazyka a písemnictví českého* (Prague, 1903).
Götz, František, *Tvář století* (Prague, 1930).
——, *Osudná česká otázka* (Prague, 1934).
Hájek, Jiří, *Literatura a život* (Praha, 1955).
Harkins, W. E., *Anthology of Czech Literature* (New York, 1953).
Horák, Jiří, *Z dějin literatur slovanských* (Prague, 1948).
Hromádka-Hrubý-Pražák-Peroutka, *At the Cross-Roads of Europe* (Prague, 1938).
Chudoba, František, *A Short Survey of Czech Literature* (London, 1924).
Jakubec, Jan, *Dějiny literatury české* (Prague, 1911).
Jelínek, Hanuš, *La littérature tchèque contemporaine* (Paris, 1912).
Jirát, Vojtěch, *Lyrika českého obrození*, Anthology (Prague, 1940).
Kalista, Zdeněk *České baroko* (Prague, 1940).
Krofta, Kamil, *John Hus* (Cambridge, 1936).
Kunc, Jaroslav, *Slovník soudobých českých spisovatelů*, Vol. 1, 2 (Prague, 1946).
Leger, Louis, *La renaissance tchèque au dix-neuvième siècle* (Paris, 1911).
Lützow, count Franz, *Bohemia* (Prague, 1939).
Máchal, Jan, *Slovanské literatury*, Vols. 1-3 (Prague, 1929).
Machonin, S., *Slovo k naší současné poesii* (Prague, 1955).
Mathesius, Vilém, *Co daly naše země Evropě a lidstvu* (Prague, 1939).
Novák, Arne, *Stručné dějiny české literatury* (Olomouc, 1936).
——, *Myšlenky a spisovatelé* (Prague, 1913).
Novotný, M., *Letáky z roku 1848* (Prague, 1948).
Palacký, František, *Z dějin národu českého* (Prague, 1957).
Pražák, Albert, *Národ se bránil* (Prague, 1946).
——, *Duch naší obrozenské literatury* (Prague, 1938).
Salzmann, Zdeněk, *Czech Literature before Hus*, Manuscript, Sedona, 1961.
Sezima, K. – Veselý, A., *Výbor z krásné prózy československé* (Prague, 1932).
Sezima, Karel, *Podobizny a reliefy* (Prague, 1927).
Součková, Milada, *The Czech Romantics* (The Hague, 1958).
Šalda, F. X., *Kritické projevy*, Vols. X, XI (Prague, 1957).
——, *Moderní literatura česká* (Prague, 1920).
Václavek, Bedřich, *Písemnictví a lidová tradice* (Prague, 1947).

Vlček, Jaroslav, *Dějiny české literatury*. Vols. 1-2 (Prague, 1951).
Watson-Seton, R. W., *A History of the Czechs and Slovaks* (London, 1943).

B. The Sources Consulted:

Bartoš, F. M., *Husitství a cizina* (Prague, 1931).
Bitnar, Vilém, *O českém baroku slovesném* (Prague, 1932).
Brandl, V. (ed.), *Spisy Karla staršího z Žerotína* (Prague, 1926).
Čapek, J. B., *Profil české poesie a prosy od r. 1918* (Prague, 1947).
Dějiny české literatury, ed. by Josef Hrabák (Prague, 1959).
Dvě legendy z doby Karlovy, ed. Hrabák a Vážný (Prague, 1959).
Diamond, William, *Czechoslovakia between East and West* (London, 1947).
Ginzel, J. A., *Cyrill und Method* (Vienna, 1861).
Helfert, J. A., *Mistr Jan Hus aneb Počátkové církevního rozdvojení v Čechách* (Prague, 1857).
Hrejsa, F., *Dějiny křestanství v Československu* (Prague, 1947-50).
Kalivoda, R., *Husitská ideologie* (Prague, 1961).
Kopecký, F., *Eucharistická křížová cesta v duchu sv. Václava* (Chicago, 1933).
Král, Josef, *O prosodii české* (Prague, 1923).
Krofta, Kamil, *Bohemia to the Extinction of the Přemyslides* (New York, 1929).
——, *Bohemia in the Fifteenth Century* (New York, 1936).
Kybal, V., *Drobné spisy historické* (Prague, 1915).
Malý, J., *Vlastenecký slovník historický* (Prague, 1877).
Masaryk, T. G., *L'Idéal d'humanité* (Paris, 1930).
Müller-Bartoš, *Dějiny Jednoty bratrské* (Prague, 1923).
Novotný, K., *Bible, pramen křestanského náboženství* (Prague, 1926).
Osuský, St., *Úloha Československa v Europe* (London, 1955).
Pekař, Josef, *Dějiny československé pro nejvyšší třídy škol* (Prague, 1937).
Polišenský, J. V., *History of Czechoslovakia in Outline* (Prague, 1948).
Pražák, Albert, *Míza stromu* (Prague, 1940).
Vlček, Jaroslav, *Kapitoly z dějin české literatury* (Prague, 1952).

C. Direct Quotations:

Václav Kopecký, *Rudé Právo* (Daily News), Praha, 9.5.1958.
Jaroslav Vlček, *Dějiny české literatury*, Vol. 1 (Praha, 1951), p. 24.
Albert Pražák, *Národ se bránil* (Praha, 1946), p. 19.
Jaroslav Vlček, *Dějiny české literatury* (Praha, 1951), p. 42.
Ibidem, p. 58.
R. W. Seton-Watson, *History of the Czechs and Slovaks* (London, 1943), p. 62.
Jaroslav Vlček, *Dějiny české literatury*, vol. I (Praha, 1951), p. 147.
Ibidem, p. 154
Ibidem, 179-180.
Albert Pražák, *Národ se bránil* (Praha, 1946), p. 31.
Jaroslav Vlček, *Dějiny české literatury*, Vol. I (Praha, 1951), p. 280.
Albert Pražák, *Národ se bránil* (Praha, 1946), p. 33.
Hanuš Jelínek, *La littérature tchèque contemporaine* (Paris, 1911).
Albert Pražák, *Národ se bránil* (Praha, 1946), p. 230.
Hanuš Jelínek, *La littérature tchèque contemporaine* (Paris, 1911).
Our Voices, Weekly, Toronto, October, 1961.
Ibidem.

Two Paradoxes of Czech Literary Evolution

GEORGE PISTORIUS

It is not because I have a taste for paradoxes that I have entitled my paper "Two paradoxes of Czech literary evolution". I realize how dangerous such a penchant might be in studies as complicated as those involving the factors which determine a literary tradition. I have not invented these paradoxes; I have touched upon them while trying to answer the following question, which is essentially a statement of fact: Why hasn't Czech literature become an integral part of universal literature yet? On the one hand, one could even say that the literatures of other small European nations such as Denmark, Portugal, Sweden, Norway, Holland, etc., have all attained a degree of universality which is less debatable than that of the Czech literature. On the other hand, one must confess that as far as universal prestige is concerned, Czech literature remains behind not only literary theory and criticism, which have a broad and important influence, but also other domains of the Czech "esprit". It certainly has not a degree of universality comparable with that of Czech music or at least a part of Czech science.

I wonder if you were as surprised as I was when I opened the second edition of the famous *History of Bohemian Literature* by Count Lützow published in London in 1907. Here we learn in a single line that K. H. Mácha was one of the "minor poets of Bohemia" (p. 404) and that he "imitated Byron". It is even more shocking to find that the founder and the greatest genius of Czech poetry is associated with a rather heterogeneous group of 5 poets, of whom F. J. Rubeš is one. Rubeš is the author of the famous song, "I am Czech, who is more?" and his place in real Czech literature could be subject to question. It is even more astonishing because this edition of Lützow appeared in 1907, the same year as the first critical edition of the complete works of Mácha (Jaroslav Vlček's edition).

This small item concerning Mácha's posthumous destiny outside his native country helps to give us an instantaneous image of the fate of

Czech literary universality: on one hand Mácha is reduced to being a simple imitator of Byron, and on the other, he is nothing but a cold university subject, a person who remains poorly known, which is even something worse than being unknown for a poet, and all of this even by the specialist.

It is not that the absolute value of Czech work has not withstood transportation beyond the frontier of its native land in the sense that it has not withstood comparison with other poets of European romanticism. No, it is rather that an unsuspected change takes place in this work the moment it is transferred from one context to another.

It seems to me that this phenomenon cannot be explained by simple exterior circumstances. What is coming into play here is rather the intrinsic qualities of Czech literature.

While trying to avoid as much as possible using a purely causal or finalist type of argument, which is always dangerous, I would like to point out briefly three characteristic traits of the Czech literary tradition. They are, of course, essential and while they contradict each other frequently, they determine the character of Czech literature. But the only point which interests us here is the obstacle which they present to access to Czech literature in the world community.

First we should enumerate these three traits:

1. The function of promoting national emancipation with which Czech literature has been burdened and often overburdened in a permanent and even exclusive fashion from the very beginning.

2. The Czech literary language, the rapid evolution of which was almost parallel with that of Czech literature, developed in such a direction that it was a question less of saying things than of creating an autonomous impression of beauty by sounds and words.

3. The great receptivity, that is, the passive universality which consisted of an extraordinary and quasi-permanent disposition to receive impulses from outside.

As far as the first item is concerned, it is only too well known. It is a matter of something more than national inspiration. This was formulated in an exact manner by J. Mukařovský when he explained to the first Congress of Czech Writers (1946) the degree to which Czech literature was bound and garrotted by other demands of national life which Mukařovský called at that time "an abnormal state of these functions". It is impossible not to see how this emancipative national function *was substituted directly* for an aesthetic function. In regard to Mácha, Tyl asked, "Why is it that among us, when *one needs especially to speak to the nation,* a young man must occupy himself with an execution?" The example is clear: according to the literary critic the poem is bad as a poem, that is, in its only aesthetic function, because it completely neglected the national function!

Second, the evolution of the Czech language was extremely rapid and precipitous; a language thus undergoing a permanent transformation, always in motion, offers to literature – almost imposes on it – the task of discovering the unique sources of its aesthetic functions. Such a flexible language lends itself to everything: literary art could find there an infinite number of procedures. Not being able to lean on any rigid system that it could accept or violate, it constantly contributes to the language by new inventions, the aesthetic value of which is of very short duration. Why? Neologisms are quickly worn out and soon become part of the living language, and literature only has to reinvent them and to renew them ceaselessly.

Such a language is rich in stylistic potential rather than already existing stylistic procedures, and draws literature, especially poetry, towards the pole of art for art's sake.

We now state the first paradox: Czech literature produced in the course of the last 150 years is a literature in which, on the one hand, the extra-literary function is primary, a literature in which the patriotic idea has been elevated above all other aesthetic principles. On the other hand however, it is a literature in which, especially during the last 40 years, the search for the stylistic values of sounds, words and syntactic structures replaces the search for ideas. In the context of every other literary tradition these two self-contradictory tendencies would exclude each other. In the Czech context they were condemned to coexistence in spite of everything. But the direct reflection of such a situation on the universal intelligibility of Czech literature is certainly negative. On one hand the patriotic idea which penetrates it like gangrene (because it frequently goes as far as stylistic procedures) weakens its universal range and renders it incomprehensible. On the other hand the specific system of its aesthetic functions renders it untranslatable. (Therefore Mácha never appeared to foreign readers except as an imitator of the Byronic style.)

Third, we get to the last characteristic, namely, passive universalism. As far back as 1892, F. X. Šalda said (in his article, "The role of translation in national literature"): "No other European literature has been so nourished by foreign blood as our own." The fact that from the advent of the symbolist school Czech literature developed in company with other European poetry, following the rhythm of Western thought, is without doubt a strong positive feature in itself, yet, paradoxically, it was also a negative feature.

a) Such receptivity enriches the literature which receives foreign inspiration only if that literature has enough energy and time to transform what is received and to convert it into the expression of its own intrinsic values. But Czech literature lacked these. It was overburdened, as we have seen, by its patriotic emancipative function. It did not have the time to re-create the influences which were received and transpose them into a system of its own values. The result was that the originality of Czech literature suffered. Nothing endangers aspirations toward universalism more than the lack of originality.

b) The second aspect of this passive universality goes back to the Czech reader and his particular social characteristics. We have often congratulated ourselves on the popular nature of those new segments of the population who have participated as consumers in the renaissance of Czech literature.

But this public, in its social capacity, has imposed upon the new literature a certain number of limitations. Among these is the fact that bodies of European literature were undeniably modified when they came into contact with Czech literature. Neither Molière nor Schiller nor Shakespeare were played in the Czech theater at the end of the 18th century. Rather they were represented by vulgarized adaptations which were almost always distorted. European literature (for a long time and almost exclusively) entered into Czech consciousness in the pitiful form of Volksbücher (chap-books). Even in 1863, the date of the first translation of *Don Quixote*, and extremely late compared to the date of reception of Cervantes in other European countries, a *chef d'œuvre* of world literature had its first impact on the Czech public in a mutilated and abbreviated form for popular reading. The behaviour of the reader, who is, of course, conditioned by social and psychological factors, is partly responsible for the quality of literary production; by influencing literature and asking from it not so much originality as mechanical transposition, the reader also participates in the paradox. Briefly it could be defined thus: the greater the passive universality of Czech literature, the more limited was its active universality.

We now come to the end and also to a conclusion, or, at least, a provisionary conclusion. It seems to us that what one may call the fate of a national literature in the world depends less than is often supposed on outside circumstances, and that one can find the true causes of the fate by examining its intrinsic qualities.

By the word "qualities" we do not wish to express value judgements. Rather we mean the essential characteristics of the literature. In order to show how this value within a literature has nothing to do with the absolute, or world, value, I quote, finally, a single Czech example: One of the greatest acts of Czech literature was realized quite suddenly at the beginning of its modern period, namely, the poetic translation by J. Jungmann of *Atala* in 1805. We know that this was, without exaggeration, a gigantic enterprise. The translator had to create a completely new vocabulary, one which did not exist at all before his time, an entire system of poetic prose. Can one try to give back to Europe this act of courage which in the frame of its own literature has a pre-eminent position because it has for fifty years determined the evolution of Czech prose in a decisive fashion? Would it make sense to translate this work in order to obtain something which Europe already has, that is, Chateaubriand? Here we find an example of the pathetic fate of Czech literature. Its greatest values remain silent for other people.

BIBLIOGRAPHY

A History of Bohemian Literature, by Count Lützow. First edition appeared in 1899. (New impression: London, Heinemann, 1907).

"First critical edition of the Complete Works of Mácha...", *Sebrané spisy Karla Hynka Máchy*. 2 vols. In: *Čeští spisovatelé 19. století*. Ed. Jaroslav Vlček (Prague, Laichter, 1906-1907).

The quoted article by Jan Mukařovský, "Zúčtování a výhledy", is to be found in the second edition of *Kapitoly z české poetiky*, I (Prague, Svoboda, 1948), pp. 235-244. This article was read before the Congress of Czech Writers, Prague, June 1946.

Josef Kajetán Tyl, "Pohled na literaturu nejnovější", in *Květy* (literary journal published in Prague in the XIXth century), III, 21 August 1836, pp. 57-58.

F. X. Šalda, "Překlad v národní literatuře" ("The role of translation in national literature"), *Literární listy*, XIV (1892), pp. 1-4, 27-28, 48-51. Reprinted in F. X. Šalda, *Juvenilie* (Prague, 1925) and in *Kritické Projevy*, I, 1892-1893. Ed. J. Pistorius and F. Vodička (Prague, Melantrich, 1949), pp. 139-155.

The title in Czech of the quoted translation of *Don Quixote*: *Bláznivý rytíř. Kratochvilné čtení pro lid. Dle španělského románu Don Quixote de la Mancha vzdělal a vydal Josef Pečírka* (Prague, 1864).

The translations of Josef Jungmann (1773-1847) were an exceptional achievement, if one considers that they were written at the very start of the revival of the Czech language and literature. Of all his translations, that of Chateaubriand's *Atala*, which determined the evolution of Czech prose, is probably the most important. Jungmann also translated Milton's *Paradise Lost*, Gray's *Elegy Written in a Country Churchyard*, Goethe's *Hermann und Dorothea*, and poems by Schiller.

One Hundred and Twenty Years of Slovak Literary Language

JURAJ SLÁVIK

The Slovaks, who represent the ethnographic center of the Slavic world, were already leading a literary life in the 8th or 9th century. Some pagan songs were preserved, and during the period of the Great Moravian empire in the ninth century the Greek Christian missionaries, Constantine and Methodius, created a literary language, the so-called Glagolitic language – in which they wrote liturgical and canonical books and tractates. By the tenth century, the Slovaks, like other Central European peoples, wrote in Latin; after the Hussite movement, the literary language of Slovakia was Czech. By the 18th century, Latin had become interlaced with Czech literary expressions – even in popular literature written in local Slovak dialects. It is true that some of the Slovak writers had used a Western dialect of the Slovak language from the beginning of the 19th century, and, that a great poet, Ján Hollý, wrote his epic poems on the ancient history of the Slovaks, published from 1824 to 1846, in this language. However, most Slovak writers until the 1840's continued to write in Czech, even though Slovak words and expressions were intermingled with the Czech literary language.

A school of Slovak writers developed under the strong influence of L'udovít Štúr, and by the 1840's the Slovak reading public had adopted the Slovak literary language, basically a dialect from central Slovakia, essentially as it is used today. We certainly can say that Slovak literature is a child of the West, of Western tendencies and currents, of Western ideas. The Slovak literary language of today, created by the generation of L'udovít Štúr, Michal Miloslav Hodža and Jozef Miloslav Hurban, is only about 120 years old. It is, therefore, one of the youngest European literary languages. It is certainly a miracle, and a proof of the great vitality of the Slovak nation, that Slovak literature had not only reached the literary level of other small nations, but indeed had even overtaken some of them. From its very beginning Slovak literature was constantly influenced by the currents of world literature. Even when they had spread to the East also, these currents of Romanticism, Realism, Naturalism, etc., came to Slovakia by way of the West. It is not my purpose to write about the ideas of the Reformation or the Age of Enlightenment, which came to Slovakia via our common literature with the Czechs. But in the 1840's, when Ľudovít Štúr, Jozef Miloslav Hurban and Michal Miloslav Hodža introduced the new Slovak literary language to Slovakia, the Romantic school was the leading literary movement in Slovakia. Romanticism came into being at the end of the 18th century, and reached full maturity in France in the 1820's with the works of Lamartine, Béranger, Hugo, Musset, George Sand, Dumas père, etc. The influence of Goethe, Schiller, Byron and Walter Scott was also notable. As early as the 1820's, the poetry of Ján Kollár (who was still writing in Czech) was influenced by Romanticism. His epic poem *Slávy Dcera* ("The Daughter of Sláva") published in 1824, became the literary trademark of the movement called "Panslavism".

The main poets of the Štúr school – Andrej Sládkovič, Samo Chalupka, Janko Kráľ, Ján Botto – as well as the founders of the Slovak literary language – Hodža, Hurban and Štúr – became the chief representatives of the Romantic school in Slovakia. The novelists of the period, Janko Kalinčiak, Jozef Miloslav Hurban and the dramatic writer, Ján Chalupka, also show Romantic characteristics in their work.

From its very beginning Slovak literature showed strong nationalistic tendencies. Hegel, the German philosopher, pointed the way to Slovak folk-lore, and as is common in most nations that are not free and independent, the Slovaks also exalted the ideals of freedom and independence in their literature. This national revival received its most idealistic expression in the poetry of Sládkovič, Botto and Kráľ. The latter two poets glorified Jánošík, the Slovak Robin Hood who became a symbol of freedom and a fighter for liberty and against foreign feudalism in Slovak literature. I should like to point out that our neighbours, the Poles, later had an outstanding poet and novelist, Kazimierz Przerwa-Tetmajer, who also immortalized Jánošík.

The literary school of Realism, which was influenced by Balzac and Stendhal and which culminated in the works of Trollope, Thackeray, Dickens, Mark Twain and Whitman, had developed in France into naturalism of the novels of Flaubert, the Goncourt brothers, Daudet, Maupassant and Zola. These had a strong influence on Slovak literature. Kalinčiak, in his novel, *Reštaurácia*, foreshadowed the forerunner of Realism. Pavel Országh-Hviezdoslav, the greatest of all Slovak poets, although basically an idealist, showed typical realism in his epic poems as well as in most of his lyric poetry and in his drama, "Herodes and Herodias". Hviezdoslav translated into Slovak the representative works of such poets as Shakespeare, Goethe, Schiller, Mickiewicz, Slowacki, Pushkin, Lermontov, Arany, Petőfi and Madách. Among these were *Hamlet, A Midsummer Night's Dream, Faust, Boris Godunov, The Demon, The Crimean Sonnets, the Ballads of Arany*, and *The Tragedy of Man*, by Madách. This demonstrated how strongly he was influenced by or in constant touch with the great works of all nations.

This applies also to the outstanding Slovak novelist, Dr. Matej Bencúr, better known under his pen name, Martin Kukučin; he wrote his humorous novels and short stories chiefly under the influence of Western writers, an influence transmitted to him by way of Czech literature, but also under the influence of the Russians Gogol and Tolstoy. Only Svetozár Hurban-Vajanský, the third poet and novelist of the great epoch of Slovak literature before World War I, was a disciple of Turgenev, closely followed the evolution of Russian literature, and was an admirer and follower of the Russian Slavophiles.

Realism remained the main literary current until and after the liberation of the first World War, especially in the novels of Jozef Gregor-Tajovský, Janko Jesenský and the three well-known women writers, Terezia Vansová, Elena Maróthy-Šoltésová and, the most important, Božena Slančíková-Timrava.

In poetry, however, Symbolism led to the evolution of the most outstanding modern Slovak poet, Ján Botto, who wrote under the pen name of Ivan Krasko, and his contemporaries, Vladimír Roy and Martin Rázus. Krasko was influenced by the Czech Symbolist poets, Hlaváček and Sova, but he also knew modern poets such as Verlaine, Mallarmé, Baudelaire and many others. He was also influenced by the German poets Richard Dehmel and Stephan George. His friends, Roy and Rázus, translated the poetry of Endre Ady from the Hungarian, and Krasko himself translated verses of Eminescu and Goga from the Rumanian.

The Écoles Litteraires of the post-Symbolistic era, such as Dadaisme, the Unanimisme of Jules Romains and Georges Duhamel, Futurisme, Traditionalisme, Intimisme, Néo-Classicisme etc., also had their followers in Slovakia; Slovak poetry was also influenced by the Czech Ruralists, Regionalists and Catholic Modernists. André Breton's Surréalisme, in particular, acquired many followers. It has survived up to the present and the followers of this poetic expression are still trying hard to be understood and turn themselves into social realists according to the Communist doctrine. The same is true of the former Catholic Modernists, the Subjectivists and the Impressionists. I could cite dozens of those poets who were disciples of Claudel, Duhamel, Valéry, Paul Eluard, Philip Soupalt, Guillaume Appollinaire, and other French and German poets who tried to introduce into Slovak literature all the tendencies which had originated in the West and found this way into Czech and Slovak literature. Even those poets and ideologists who introduced socialistic and communistic tendencies into Slovak literature, especially poetry, through the magazine *Dav*, the so-called "Davists" – Clementis, Novomeský, Okáli, Poničan, have had to learn their lesson anew, providing they were not executed, but merely imprisoned. Nevertheless such Communist poets and writers as Novomeský and Horváth learned more from the West than from the East.

Milo Urban, the most outstanding Slovak novelist of the post-World War I era, who manifested strong Slovak separatist tendencies, recanted only recently and is now publishing his new novel in the spirit of Socialist realism.

I would like to stress again that Slovak literature, even when formally separated from Czech literature, remains ideologically closely connected with it, its currents, tendencies and forms of expression, and through Czech literature, with Western ideological and formal evolution.

After World War I, political tendencies became stronger than ideological literary trends and currents. Militant, separatist nationalism, inspired by hatred, developed under the influence of separatist political trends. On the other hand, these trends were opposed by patriotic Czechoslovak tendencies and by some Communist inclinations. This was especially true during the era of the so-called Slovak state, when many literary figures became adherents of totalitarianism. But even in these circumstances, the impulse to opposition and the belief in freedom and independence survived. Independent writers published many valuable works during World War II, and a clandestine literature developed which found its way even to exiles in France and Great Britain.

We Slovaks participated in three exiles, and the traditional Slovak literature remained alive during all three. During World War I, many prominent Slovak writers were active in the fight against the Germans and the Habsburgs, and also against the Communists in Russia and Siberia. Jozef Gregor-Tajovský, a novelist and dramatic writer, and Janko Jesenský, a novelist and poet and a member of the Czechoslovak Council who wrote revolutionary verses (many of them anti-Communist), were the most outstanding writers in the Czechoslovak legions in Siberia.

During World War II, there were Slovak writers in exile in Paris and

London. The poet, Janko Jesenský, who was living at home in Slovakia provided the greatest amount of help in the fight against Nazism and Slovak totalitarian tendencies by sending his political satirical verses to us in Paris and London. I should like to quote from a booklet I published in 1947, entitled "Poetry of the Resistance Movement of the Czechs and Slovaks Abroad".[1]

"Slovak participation in the poetry of the Resistance was smaller both in its extent and in its diversity than the Czech participation. Nevertheless, thanks to Janko Jesenský, Slovak poetry abroad was much more effective because of its martial spirit and by its warlike readiness. Janko Jesenský, a legionnaire and a poet of our first fight for freedom, a historical annalist and a critic of our free life in the Czechoslovak republic, grew in this new fight for freedom into a great fighter by his pen – into a bard such as no other nation had in this struggle. Beginning with the year 1938 no one reacted more violently or fundamentally against the perversion and treason of the 'ignoble self-appointed saviours' than this man, old in years, yet a young man and a hero in spirit. Janko Jesenský became the Slovak conscience and no one carried the title of 'Poet Laureate' after the liberation with such authority.

His poetry, a unique document of a great age, was not written to be locked away. Rather, he wrote it at home, in the fighting underground, and his poetry circulated in copies or was smuggled abroad to come to the hearing of all faithful fighters for freedom on the program of the B.B.C., 'The Voice of Free Czechoslovakia'. And of course nobody at home doubted whose word was spoken and also printed in our publications abroad. The style of Janko Jesenský was so characteristic that no one could have mistaken its identity, not even the officials of the puppet Slovak Government. They could not have missed recognising that the strongest sentences I read on my broadcasts home were from the pen of this poet, who was living among them in Bratislava and saw all that was going on at home. And yet – no one dared lay a hand on this 'prophet'."

In the present Czechoslovak exiled community, Slovak literary participation is less significant. Only a very few critics and writers are among us. I should now like to quote from my introduction to a book of selections from the poetry of Janko Jesenský, published anonymously during World War II in London.

"Slovak poets are marching with heads high toward the future. Their

---

[1] Juraj Slávik, *Odbojová poezia Čechov a Slovákov v zahraničí* ("Poetry of the Resistance Movement of the Czechs and Slovaks Abroad"), published by the New York Daily, 1947.

verses express the conscience of the nation, they express poetically what the great majority of Slovaks feel. They set ringing the tocsin to warn the pilgrims who are making their way through a winding maze, the paths of which vanish over a precipice. Let us send out into the world this poetic star of Bethlehem – to lead the people at home and everywhere in the world to a new Bethlehem, where freedom and salvation will again be born."[2]

The Slovak writers at home in Slovakia are, for the most part, true to the tradition of their famous predecessors. Many of them refuse or are unable to publish, and are again writing clandestinely. The revolt against slavery and violation of the free mind is very much alive.

Communist Slovakia has not produced outstanding Slovak poets. The Slovak Academician František Votruba, who was an outstanding literary critic and historian already before World War I, and who had to recant and become a Marxist and a Communist, writes of the young poets of Communist Slovakia:

"If we look at the activity of the young poets, we are surprised first of all by their lack of responsibility, by the way they are sending their poetry into the world... poems, verses, which are not mature, and in the first place over-expressed, written in superlatives from the first word, starting in fortissimo, so that they are unable to maintain the tone... And another misery: How many verses are being rushed into the publishing houses or magazines which have been created 'in a cold way'? They were not created by an intensively strained imagination, by a deeply felt sentiment, by an honest effort to achieve a clean and faultless form. There is in our poetry a want of shyness, of an essential modesty. And do not forget: A respect and love are due to the native language..."[3]

But I do not doubt that Slovak literature will again be valuable and that Slovak poets and writers will be the leaders of the nation. I would like therefore to finish with a quotation from the "Robbers Song", by Martin Rázus:

> Let the hills and forest ring,
> Warning whistles pierce the air.
> Let the mountains flame at night
> High above the Tatry there.

---

[2] *Pred Ohnivým drakom. Z básní odbojného Slovenska* ("In front of the fiery dragon. From the verses of revolutionary Slovakia") (London, Unwin Brothers Limited, 1914).
[3] Akademik František Votruba, *Vybrané spisy*, II: *Cesta slovenskej poezie* ("Selected Works, II: The Way of Slovak Poetry") Slovak publishing of the belles-lettres (Bratislava, 1955).

Hej, my Juro Jánošík:
We'll yet set the world aright.[4]

GENERAL BIBLIOGRAPHY

Jaroslav Vlček, *Dejiny Literatúry Slovenskej* ("A History of Slovak Literature"), 3rd edition. Turč. Sv. Martin; published by Matica Slovenská (1933).

Štefan Krčméry, *Stopät'desiat' rokov Slovenskej literatúry* ("One Hundred Fifty Years of Slovak Literature"). Turč. Sv Martin (1943).

Andrej Mráz, *Dejiny Slovenskej Litiratúry* ("A History of Slovak Literature") (Bratislava, 1948).

Dejiny Slovenskej Literatúry ("A History of Slovak Literature"). Chief Editor Univ. Prof. Dr. Milan Pišút. Edition Osveta (Bratislava, 1960).

---

[4] Translation of Ivan J. Kramoris, *An Anthology of Slovak Poetry* (Obrana Press Inc., 1947).

Czech Opinion of America in the Mid-Nineteenth Century

RUDOLF STURM

The revolutionary year 1848 marked for the Czechs, besides its tremendous political meaning, the beginnning of a flow of information, in comparison to the pre-1848 sparsity, about life in America. It showed itself in fiction and non-fiction, especially in the Czech press. The nature of the material also changed considerably. Betweeen 1800 and 1848, we see in Czech literature historical descriptions of the discovery of America and the Indians, sentimental "American" love stories, and Benjamin Franklin's educational and ethical essays. These American works were translated into Czech mostly from the German.

In the late eighteen-forties, this type of literature was replaced mainly by newspaper articles discussing American democracy and the liberal regime of the United States. The most outspoken voice of all was that of Karel Havlíček Borovský, who, in his *Národní noviny*, and later in *Slovan*, wrote a number of editorials and informative articles on the American way of life, before he was silenced by the Austrian police. In nearly every issue Havlíček also published news items from the United States, commenting favorably on its constitution, democratic organization of state and local governments, and separation of church and state. He frowned upon only one thing: the institution of Negro slavery.

Havlíček paid particular attention to the right of citizens to conduct their own affairs, as evidenced in their self-government. He often quoted Alexis de Tocqueville's *De la Démocratie en Amérique* and his descriptions of the functioning of local administrations. In the article, "On Communal Administration in the United States",[1] Havlíček evaluated public institutions in Massachusetts, using de Tocqueville's information; he stressed the importance of town meetings and praised the appointment of town officials by election. In a similar article entitled "The Citizens' Autonomy",[2] he pointed out that only those states which had a liberal constitu-

---

[1] "O zřízení obecním v USA", *Slovan*, May-July, 1850, 332-5.
[2] "Samospráva občanská", *ibidem*, 177.

tion could avoid a revolution, and gave as an example the United States, "where all citizens share in the government, making an overthrow of the government by force and violence impossible".[3] Writing about Millard Fillmore, the then new President of the United States, Havlíček said: "The most important thing is that only his own intellectual striving opened to the former draper's apprentice the way to such a high office."[4]

In a series of three articles on Benjamin Franklin's life and policies, he called Franklin "the worthiest son of mankind, the chief supporter of progress among his fellow citizens".[5] Commenting on the situation in India, Havlíček wrote that the English government in India was only temporary and that there was no doubt that the same thing would happen to the "haughty English rulers" in India as had happened to them at the end of the eighteenth century in America, and that "India is awaiting its Franklin and Washington to become its liberators from the terrible yoke of the British rule".[6] Remarkable foresight, indeed, to prophesy the work of Mahatma Gandhi a century in advance.

Commenting on freedom of the press in the United States, Havlíček wrote: "In the Republic of the U.S.A. all newspaper correspondents enjoy the privilege of free mail. That government, as we can see, does not fear the newspapers as some other governments do. And while in our country the authorities think of nothing but how they can smother and weaken the public press, in the New World they support it as much as they can".[7] The American Declaration of Independence was also published in Havlíček's newspaper for the first time in Czech translation.[8]

Havlíček's views on America – and because of his great prestige there can be no doubt that these were also the opinions of most Czechs in the eighteen-fifties – were summarized in an article on free production and free business, published in *Slovan* in 1851 and later reprinted in Havlíček's *Epistles from Kutná Hora*. In it, he wrote about the wealth and happiness of all the classes in the United States, coming to this conclusion:

Where did this general prosperity originate, this miraculous growth of the American nation? Nowhere else than in general freedom, in genuine legality. Everybody works for himself there, no one takes away a part of the proceeds of his endeavor. Everybody chooses and pursues, without any limitation, the profession for which he feels ability and inclination. No law, no authorities limit

[3] All translations are mine.
[4] *Ibidem*, 781.
[5] "Franklin a jeho politika", *ibidem*, 714 ff.
[6] *Ibidem*, 295.
[7] *Ibidem*, 915.
[8] In the article "Anglicko a jeho osady", August-September, 1850, 1064-8.

him in that. All talents and endeavors are appreciated there and nobody is ashamed to work. Hence comes happiness and the growth of the United States for the general welfare of all. And even more remarkable is the fact that constant peace and the greatest security of person and property reign in that country and, although the least peaceful people from the whole world converge there; although they can preach there absolutely freely even the most harmful doctrines; although the followers of some hundred different religions live side by side there; and although there is no standing army there, no police, no informers, still they have no revolution, no fight of citizens among themselves, no insurrection, no conspiracy! All this is the result of true freedom and legality![9]

Although Havlíček had a very positive attitude toward the United States, he nevertheless kept an open mind in judging it and did not hesitate to criticize it. For instance, in "The Union of North America", a study of American history, geography, population and public administration, he listed "the lack of national history and of the past" as the main shortcomings of the United States, and reached the following conclusion:

There is no nation in America and therefore no love for the fatherland. The past is lacking and hence also the lack of motives for great and noble acts, for self-sacrifice and devotion. And lastly, sentiment and poetry are absent from life there. Everything breathes with prosaic character and materialism.[10]

An altogether biased opinion of the United States was held by Josef Kajetán Tyl, a noted Czech playwright and author of historical novels. In *The Forest Fairy*,[11] subtitled a "magic play", Tyl wrote unfavorably about conditions in America, describing a group of Czech villagers who emigrate to America, lured by enthusiastic news about gold in California and an easy life. But after unpleasant experiences with hypocritical Quakers and hostile Indians they return home, happy to be back in the Czech town again. Tyl was known as an intransigent patriot who disliked seeing so many Czechs leave the country to seek a better living abroad, and this may have been his way of fighting it. It is also possible that at the same time he wanted to contradict Havlíček's favorable descriptions of the United States, because the two writers were not on friendly terms. In 1845, Havlíček published a devastating review of Tyl's novella, *The*

---

[9] "Svobodný výrob a svobodný obchod", *Epištoly kutnohorské a vybrané články politické* (Prague, 1906), 137-8.
[10] "Soustátí severní Ameriky", *Slovan*, May-July, 1850, 535. It is interesting to note in this connection the opinion of Thomas G. Masaryk about "American materialism". He agreed in principle with Havlíček, as most Czechs did, but added that, while in America people chase after the dollar, "we in Europe chase after the penny". (See Karel Čapek, *Hovory s T.G.M.*, Prague, 1946, 171.)
[11] *Lesní panna* (Prague, 1850).

Last Czech, castigating its over-sentimentality and "weeping patriotism"; hence Tyl's dislike for Havlíček.[12]

It should be said here that Tyl's critical attitude toward emigration is generally in accord with Czech literary attitudes toward this problem. A little later in this study, we shall see it once more in the tragic end of the imaginary New Bohemia on the Mississippi. We see it again and again in the works of Svatopluk Čech, Josef Václav Sládek, Karel Klostermann, Karel Václav Rais, Antal Stašek, Alois Jirásek, and even in the stories of the contemporary Czech writers Zdeněk Němeček and Egon Hostovský. Their emigrant and exile heroes either return home because they are unable to forget their native land and can find neither happiness nor prosperity abroad, or, if they stay in the foreign country, they are frustrated and suffer in numerous ways.

Be it as it may, Tyl's severe criticism of America was itself an isolated case in post-1848 Bohemia. All other books and periodicals dealing with America voiced a nostalgic longing for freedom such as they saw in the United States, emphasizing that country's liberal traditions and democratic institutions. Even such a non-political magazine as *The Journal of the Czech Museum* carried an article "On the Political Effects of the Decentralization of Government in America", which was a translation of excerpts from de Tocqueville's *De la Démocratie en Amérique.* The 16-page study opened with the assertion that administrative centralism is harmful, and the translator, Josef Jireček, said in a footnote to that sentence: "If I am not mistaken, the words with which de Tocqueville opens this chapter are fully valid also in our country".[13]

Books on the United States as well as works of American writers in Czech translation continued to flow in ever-greater numbers into the hands of the Czech reading public. The year 1852 saw the publication in Prague of two American books: Cooper's *The Last of the Mohicans* and Franklin's *Autobiography.*[14] During the next two years, *Uncle Tom's Cabin* was published in two different translations in Prague and Brno, thus increasing the Czechs' dislike for America's mistreatment of the Negroes. The Prague translation appeared in 1853 under the title, *Uncle Tom, or Slavery in Free America.*[15] The name of the translator was omitted. This was only one year after the book had been published in the

[12] M. Hýsek, *J. K. Tyl* (Prague, 1926), *passim.*
[13] "O politických aučincích decentralisace spráwní w Americe", *Časopis Českého musea,* III (1849), 133 ff.
[14] *Poslední Mohykán,* J. Vojáček, tr., and *Benjamin Franklin: Jeho životopis a jeho pravidla.* No translator listed.
[15] *Strejček Tom, čili: Otroctví ve svobodné Americe.*

United States. The Brno rendition, in 1854, *Uncle Thomas, or Pictures from the Life of Black Slaves in America*,[16] was done by František Matouš Klácel, who himself went to the United States subsequently, and lived there for fifteen years until his death. Klácel, like Havlíček, was conversant with American affairs and shared his knowledge of American culture as early as 1849 with Božena Němcová, the noted Czech woman writer of that time.[17]

Washington Irving, introduced to the Czechs in the eighteen-thirties, remained on the book market through the fifties. In 1853, Irving's *History of the Life and Voyages of Christopher Columbus* and *Mahomet and His Successor* were published separately in Prague in the translations of František Doucha and František Ladislav Rieger, respectively.[18] Also in the fifties, Jakub Malý reprinted his translations of Irving's *Rip van Winkel*, *The Alhambra*, and a few of Irving's minor works, all of these first published in Czech in the thirties. By this time Malý was the main propagator in Bohemia-Moravia of foreign authors and books on foreign countries. From 1853 to 1855, he published in Prague a six-volume history of America,[19] the first four volumes being an adaptation and compilation of various historical works by Irving and William H. Prescott, the fifth and sixth volumes, his own work.

In 1854, a short novel, *Libuse in America*,[20] appeared in the collected works of Josef Jiří Kolár. It had been published originally in 1842 in German under the title *Libusa am Mississippi*. Kolár himself termed it a "fantastic novel" about Henry Klen, an imagenary Czech emigrant who, because he rendered good service to Congress in the Revolutionary War, later was awarded a large section of land on the banks of the Mississippi. He intended to people it with other Czechs and establish a new Bohemia there, but he died prematurely. His daughter Molly, nicknamed Libuše after the legendary foundress of Prague, carried out her father's plans. The New Bohemia flourished under Libuše's rule for some time, until one day, through the betrayal of a money-hungry Negro and the savagery of a tribe of Indians, the settlement was destroyed and its inhabitants all killed.

During the fifties, American poetry was introduced for the first time into Bohemia. Longfellow's poems, "The Open Window", "Excelsior", "The

---

[16] *Strýc Tomáš, aneb: Obrazy ze života černých otroků v Americe.*
[17] *Božena Němcová* (Prague, 1920), 3rd ed., 129.
[18] *Život a plavby Kr. Kolumba* and *Život Mohamedův.*
[19] *Amerika od časů svého odkrytí až do nejnovější doby.*
[20] *Libuše v Americe* (Prague, 1854).

Arrow and the Song", and "To an Old Danish Song-Book", were published in the translations of Josef R. Čejka.[21] In 1856, portions of Edgar Allan Poe's poetry were translated by Edmund Kaizl.[22] Both translators were minor literary figures, and there is no evidence that either Longfellow or Poe influenced Czech poetry.

Beginning in 1860, the first modern Czech encyclopedia, *Slovník naučný*, was published in Prague under the editorship of F. L. Rieger and J. Malý. It contained numerous entries on the United States, its culture, politics, and economy. As was to be expected, *Slovník* devoted more space to the Slavic areas than to the Anglo-Saxon world. For instance, the main entry on Poland occupied ninety pages and on Russia, three hundred and forty-four pages, while the entry entitled "The United States of North America" covered only fifty-two pages. Nevertheless, the encyclopedia was, in the sixties, the most important source of information on America. In almost every general entry, whether it was "Banks" or "Coffee", "Linguistics" or "Slavery", there was always some material on the United States.

As in other writings of the decade following 1848, in *Slovník*, too, stress was laid on the democratic traditions of the United States and the freedom and independence of its citizens. The Czech immigrants in America received considerable attention. The Civil War, which was in progress at the time of the publication of the encyclopedia, accounted for an unusual number of entries concerning America. A few examples will suffice to illustrate how *Slovník naučný*, following the pattern set by Karel Havlíček, contrasted the freedom in America with the oppression in Bohemia and Moravia.

An article on American churches opened as follows:

In no other country are there so many and such varied political parties and religious groups as in North America. But in no other land, again, are there so many pious minds, so much respect for faith and its performance, so much earnestness and effective charity as here.[23]

The author of the article listed the following reasons for his statement: complete freedom of conscience, equality of all churches, and the fact that each society and church rules and administers itself and expects no support from the government. It was obvious that Rieger, an important

---

[21] "Otevřené okno", "Excelsior", Šíp a píseň", and "Na starý dánský zpěvník", *Časopis Českého musea*, I (1855), 24 ff.
[22] In *Lumír*, 1856, 1049.
[23] "Americké sekty a spolky křesťanské", *Slovník naučný*, I (1860), 174.

cultural and political figure, not daring to deplore openly the lack of freedom in his own country and the subservience of the Church to the hated Hapsburgs, hid in such praise of America the nostalgic question: "Why cannot similar conditions also prevail in Bohemia?"

Even in the biographical notes on Thaddeus Kosciusko and Louis Kossuth, the encyclopedia underlined their connection with the United States; in Kosciusko's case, his military career in America and his collaboration with George Washington were described in detail.[24] Kossuth's biography stressed the enthusiastic reception which the people of the United States gave the Hungarian rebel when he landed in New York in 1851.[25]

Another example of the *Slovník* editors' predilection for the United States and the favorable role they assigned to all things American is clear from the fact that even Karel Havlíček's biography in the encyclopedia mentioned that Czechs in America printed his picture for themselves in their new country. It was hardly accidental, in the early sixties, that this connection – although somewhat far-fetched – was created between Havlíček and the United States.[26]

Indicative of Czech opinion of the United States in mid-century were the comments of Božena Němcová and Josef Václav Frič, two leading writers of the period. In 1856, Němcová wrote to her son Karel: "In America, there are many Czechs, and thus it is also our country, because people of our language and our customs live there". And a few sentences later in the same letter she said:

You write that I always was against emigrating to America. Yes, and I still am in the case of those who are lured there by gold or by things which they can have here too. But if one is driven from here by such a thing as we are, that is another story. In this case we would not be helped if we go to Hungary.[27]

Němcová obviously tried to say that she would not go to the United States to make money, but only to escape the atmosphere of fear and police persecution to which she and her husband were subjected. Only recently another significant letter by Němcová, dated in 1856 and addressed to a Czech immigrant in Texas, was unearthed from the papers of an old settler and published in New York. In this letter Němcová wrote of the "great

---

[24] *Ibidem*, IV (1863-5), 846.
[25] *Ibidem*, 863.
[26] *Ibidem*, III (1862-3), 680.
[27] *Sebrané spisy B. Němcové. Korrespondence* (Prague, 1914), II, 241.

funeral" of Karel Havlíček, complained of her family's difficult financial situation, and then:

Forgive me that I am complaining to you so much about the unfortunate conditions in Bohemia, but I trust you greatly, and also want you to know how lucky you are that you have escaped from such a situation. Yours was a fortunate step, and as long as I live I shall regret that at the time of your departure I also did not decide to emigrate. My husband, too, was then willing to go. Had I done so, I would have spared myself many a bitter day, and would have set myself free from these miserable conditions.[28]

In 1858, Němcová wrote to Alois Vojtěch Šembera, a Czech literary historian and philologist: "It seems to me that at the end I shall have no choice but to accept the offer and go to America as a teacher in the Czech colony in Viscounsin, although I cannot get used to that idea."[29] It is not known who in "Viscounsin" made the offer to Němcová, nor is it known that the Czech settlers there were then so numerous as to need a Czech teacher for their children. In any case, she did not go, but died four years later in Bohemia, poor and desolate, at the age of forty-two. Her letters show, however, how the Czech colonies in the United States haunted the minds of the people in Bohemia and Moravia, although – or perhaps because – their importance and numbers were exaggerated.

Frič also was unable to "get used" to the idea of going to America. In Deess, Hungary, where he was interned for his anti-Austrian activities, he wrote in 1858 a petition to the Police Minister in which he asked to be released from confinement and permitted to emigrate to the United States. He later said of this in his memoirs:

I only simulated my yearning for America and my European ennui in order to more easily achieve my purpose. [In actuality, Frič wanted to go, not to faraway America, but to Germany, where he hoped to continue his activities against the Hapsburgs.] Knowing that my letters, no matter where sent, were carefully examined, I spoke even in them always of America. Also, I ordered a map of the United States and babbled in English all the time. With the District Attorney, in whom I feigned confidence, I talked about American laws.... Back in Prague, people of course thought that I had lost my mind, raving suddenly for America where, according to my father's judgement and warning, only feelingless profiteers can thrive.[30]

---

[28] *Litera* (New York, Fall 1955), No. 1.
[29] *Sebrané spisy B. Němcové. Korrespondence* (Prague, 1920), III, 22 f.
[30] *Paměti Josefa V. Friče* (Prague, 1887), IV, 503-4.

Such, then, was the image of America in the minds of the Czech people in the mid-nineteenth century. America was, for them, overwhelmingly, a land of freedom and abundance. Criticism was directed mainly at the inequality of white and Negro, and at the business-like aspects of American society. A century later, the same praise and the same criticism still prevail among the Czechs.

The Real Legacy of Karel Čapek

WILLIAM E. HARKINS

Karel Čapek's world reputation rests today primarily on his utopian dramas and novels and his science fiction. To the ordinary reader he is known only as the author of the play about robots, *R.U.R.*, *The Insect Comedy*, and *The War with the Newts*, but not very much else. His fantastic play, *The Makropulos Secret*, was recently revived in New York with great success. And if Čapek has been influential in world literature, one must admit that it has been primarily as a writer of utopian and science fiction.

We may grant that in fact the themes of Čapek's scientific fantasies are significant and striking. His prophetic anticipation in *Factory for the Absolute* and *Krakatit* of later developments in the field of atomic energy was brilliant. Especially successful was his masterly choice of the robot as a symbol in *R.U.R.* The robot stands as a complex expressionistic symbol of both the power of the machine to free man from toil, thus bringing utopia, and the danger that, in removing the element of conflict from human life, a mechanized civilization may in turn dehumanize man, may "robotize" him. This fusion of two meanings in a single symbol was an inspired act of artistic compression; viewed purely as symbolism, *R.U.R.*, for all its faults, is a masterpiece of the expressionistic drama. Moreover, the symbol is a thoroughly dramatic one: the actors who portrayed robots in the first Prague production were able to express eloquently the idea of a mechanized humanity by their stiffness of movement and gait.

Yet, in spite of all their apparent modernity, the scientific fantasies of Čapek strike us today as dated. The warnings against the dangers of a technological civilization sounded in *R.U.R.* or *Factory for the Absolute* seem almost irrelevant for our own age. For the machine has not freed man from conflict; rather, it has brought new conflicts of its own, not the least of which is that of atomic fission. Nor is our machine paradise free from toil, and perhaps no one is busier than the family which dwells in the modern American suburban utopia.

The question of the value of Čapek's scientific fantasies as art leads us to the more general question of the value of all science fiction as art. To pose the question is in part to suggest the answer. Though science fiction has been a tremendously popular and vital literary form, it is a form which, like the detective story, has always remained on the periphery of literature. And, just as with the detective story and its inevitable puzzle, the failure of science fiction derives from the fact that it is a dehumanized form of literature, that it has little or nothing to do with man himself. Man is first and foremost a creature who loves and hates, who is born and dies, and only secondarily a creature who may fly through outer space or travel to the depth of the oceans. The world of science is ultimately unsuitable subject matter for a great literature, because science has no immediate or compulsive symbolic significance for man's spirit and his fundamental needs. This is true in spite of the fact that science and technology satisfy certain of those needs, such as food and clothing. The link between science and its technological products is a purely rational one which can hardly appeal to the creative imagination. The work of science and its effects on human life are the proper subject matter of philosophy or sociology, but not of literature, which is concerned with less rational symbols. Science is not directly involved with any of what we might call the "eternal themes" of literature: the quest for God, the good, self-realization, love, happiness, freedom, the relation of the individual to society, the revolt of youth against age, etc.

Of course it is true that the world of science may serve as a source of irrational and moving symbols which are capable of appealing to our imagination and becoming art. And so science has actually been used by the surrealists in their painting and literature. One thinks of Nezval's long poem, *Edison*, for example. But this surrealistic use goes beyond science itself, and is not what we usually mean by science fiction.

But are not Čapek's expressionist symbols – robots, newts, insects – just such irrational expressive symbols of eternal literary themes, of man's eternal needs? Čapek wrote of *R.U.R.* that he conceived the play as a eulogy to man, that he wanted to view human life in retrospect and say, as his character Hallemeier does in the play, "It was a great thing to be a man." And Čapek comments: "Technology, progress, ideals, faith – all these were rather only illustrations of humanity than the sense of the play."[1] And to the extent that this idea of man's passing from the earth is realized in *R.U.R.*, the play is great. But one must add that this note of

---

[1] "Ještě R. U. R.", *Jeviště*, 2 (1921), 8.

eulogy is not the principal one and not the final one. *R.U.R.* is a failure, as critics as different as the Czech Václav Černý, and the American Kenneth Burke, have claimed,[2] and the author himself once admitted to Dorothy Thompson that it was the worst of all his plays, one which he no longer wished to see on the stage, and did not see again until he was trapped in a small Czech provincial town by the manager of the local theater.[3]

The same is true of *The Makropulos Secret*. This play achieves greatness at those moments when it gives us an insight into the horror and tedium of the life of Elena Makropulos, who has used an elixir to prolong her existence because she is afraid of death. The horror of death is an eternal literary theme. But Čapek, the philosophical relativist, finds death to be a good thing; as he and his brother had remarked rather bathetically in *The Insect Comedy*: "Jeden se narodí a jeden umře, a pořád je lidí dost" (One is born and one dies, and always there are people enough). Čapek fails to see the tragedy of individual death; if society is immortal, still the individual must die, and the immortality of society is no sure compensation for one's own death. In *The Makropulos Secret* Čapek is preoccupied with a philosophical concern lest longer life constitute a burden for man, but he overlooks a gripping, "eternal" theme of literature: the tragedy of individual death.

The finest of Čapek's fantasies is doubtless his novel, *War with the Newts*. But it is hardly a fantasy of science. One must distinguish clearly between science fiction and the classical genre of the utopian novel. In the utopian novel, science may serve to transplant man to a strange world or to travel ahead or backward in time; the journey, however, is no mere flight of fancy, but a means of revealing to the reader the vices of his own world all the more sharply and objectively. This is the classical technique of Swift's great satire, *Gulliver's Travels*, and in fact *The War with the Newts* is far more like Swift than H. G. Wells.[4]

Secondly, Čapek's utopian works are vitiated by that very philosophy of relativism which he preached so ardently in the early 1920's. Unlike Maeterlinck or Pirandello, who perceived that the relativism of each man's isolated truth involved individual man in tragic isolation, Čapek tried to believe that life could be enriched by a multiplicity of truths. Yet meta-

---

[2] See Václav Černý, *Karel Čapek* (Prague, 1936), p. 13 ff.; Kenneth Burke, *Counter-Statement* (New York, 1931), pp. 49-50.
[3] Interview with Dorothy Thompson, *New York Post*, Feb. 23, 1925.
[4] Bohuslava Bradbrook, *Karel Čapek and the Western World*. Unpublished master's essay, Oxford University, 1958, p. 77.

physical relativism could only imply ethical relativism: if each man has his own truth, then each man's conduct is also somehow right. Quite this far Čapek was not prepared to go; he was too idealistic and sensitive to moral issues, and such a philosophy would have involved the world in an ethical anarchy as total as the ethical anarchy which he sees resulting from absolutism in *Factory for the Absolute*. Ethical relativism could serve to justify all forms of political expediency; it is perhaps no accident that Čapek abandoned relativism and undertook a new search for absolutes just at the end of his life, at a time when it was necessary to strengthen the Czechoslovak will to resist Nazi aggression. The truth of relativism would imply that fascism was somehow "just as right" as democracy.

Among Čapek's works it is his most ardent defenses of relativism, such as *Factory for the Absolute* or *Adam the Creator*, which are the worst artistic failures. If the search for the Absolute is one of literature's eternal themes, the defense of relativism is not. There is an almost unbelievable bathetic quality in the final scene of *Factory for the Absolute*, in which some of the leading characters gather in a tavern to eat sausages and sauerkraut and drink beer and discuss the triumph of the relativist philosophy. And it was only when Čapek, like his contemporary Pirandello, could grasp the tragedy of relativist existence, the existential anxiety to which it exposed the individual, that he could achieve greatness. This discovery came, almost belatedly, with the first novel of his trilogy, *Hordubal*.

The real legacy of Karel Čapek is political. Such a statement may come as a surprise, for at first sight Čapek's political accomplishments seem rather slight. His articles on political questions, collected in *O věcech obecných, čili ZOON POLITIKON*, are on the whole rather undistinguished and uninteresting; an exception might be made only for the eloquent "Proč nejsem komunistou" (Why I am not a Communist), and for one or two articles such as "Betlém" (Bethlehem) and "O malých poměrech" (On a Small Scale), in which he finds fault with those of his countrymen who apologize for all Czechoslovak shortcomings by pointing to the small scale of Czechoslovak life. (In a healthy regionalism and localism Čapek sees the roots of a vigorous culture, not a weak one.) If Čapek's political theorizing is mildly interesting, his practical action in the field of politics was to prove less successful. The attempt to found a Czechoslovak Labor Party – Strana práce – in the mid-1920's, an attempt which he actively supported, was a disastrous failure, and his noble efforts to stiffen the resistance of his country against Nazi Germany were rendered futile by the betrayal of Czechoslovakia by her allies.

Čapek's whole relation to politics and political thought was confused and in a sense contradictory, and for this reason, too, it may seem strange to call his real legacy political. In the recently published second part of her reminiscences of her two uncles, the Brothers Čapek, Helena Koželuhová characterizes Karel as rather less interested in politics and public life than in other matters, but still interested in them as he was interested in everything.[5] The portrait she gives of the brothers is perhaps oversimplified; in her book they appear as political neutrals for whom neutralism and lack of political identification is something quite normal. This characterization no doubt conforms most closely to Karel in earlier life, but one can hardly reconcile it with his later activity as supporter of the Strana práce, biographer of Masaryk, president of the Czech P.E.N. club, opponent of Communism, or critic and foe of Nazism. Still one must confess that in fact there was a streak of political neutralism in Čapek, and a generous one; his view of life is deeply esthetic, and he celebrates life as good as much because of its beauty and variety as for its moral perfectibility. Čapek the hobbyist, the gardener, the European traveller, photographer, collector of exotic phonograph records, the patient observer of nature who could spend an entire journey by rail in winter observing the formation of "ice flowers" on the windows of the railroad car – this Čapek was an esthete first and foremost, and political man only second.

Conventionally, Čapek has been celebrated as a great democrat, and such he no doubt was, but his faith in democracy was not unlimited; at times he seems inclined to a degree of individualism which can hardly be reconciled with democracy, and which one might best describe as anarchist. Čapek himself used the latter term to S.K. Neumann when he said, "I think that I am almost an anarchist, that that is only another name for my individualism, and I think that you will understand it in that sense as opposed to collectivism."[6] Critics such as Václav Černý have long ago pointed out the deep-seated conflicts in Čapek between an optimistic and a pessimistic view of life, between faith in the collective and fear lest its power destroy the individual. In none of Čapek's works where destruction threatens man – in *R.U.R.*, *Factory for the Absolute*, *Krakatit*, *Adam the Creator*, or *The War with the Newts* – does democracy intervene to save man from destruction. As late as in his drama *The White Plague* (1937), Čapek expresses his distrust of the masses, so easily misled by demagogues. And it is the democratic colossi of the Western World who

[5] Helena Koželuhová, *Čapci očima rodiny*, Vol. II (Hamburg, 1961), p. 51 ff.
[6] Quoted in Ivan Klíma, *Karel Čapek* (Prague, 1962), p. 18.

are a principal target of his satire in *The War with the Newts*. Čapek's democracy may seem in the last analysis to be little more than an acceptance of the least of all possible evils.

Yet in the trilogy of three novels, *Hordubal, Meteor*, and *An Ordinary Life*, Čapek has laid down a philosophical foundation for democracy which is well-nigh unique in modern literature. The trilogy was Čapek's masterpiece, free from the artistic defects and shallow relativism typical of his writing of the 1920's. Professor René Wellek has described the trilogy as "one of the most successful attempts at a philosophical novel in any language", and so indeed it is.

From a philosophical point of view, Čapek's trilogy has been analyzed from two standpoints, first, as a study of how man apprehends truth; in the trilogy, Čapek moves from a relativist epistemology to a more sophisticated perspectivism: he finds that the different views of reality which individual men obtain are analogous to the different perspectives which may be joined together to depict truth. Thus the divergent accounts of the unknown victim of the plane crash in *Meteor* may be combined to produce human truth, if not the truth of one human being's life. This epistemological or noetic theme is joined to a metaphysical one: the analysis of the nature of individual man. Less appreciated in the trilogy is the fact that in dealing with the question of the nature of individual existence, Čapek has also faced the question of the individual's relation to society, for the individual can be defined completely only if his relation to society is also defined. In the trilogy, Čapek has answered this question of the individual's relation to society in a positive, democratic spirit. In doing so he has indicated the possibility of an escape for modern man from the existential prison of individualism, and laid down at least the foundation of an acceptable philosophy of democracy. The success of his achievement is almost unique in an age when literature is largely devoted to the expression of scepticism or despair, particularly in dealing with the individual's relation to the world or to society.

The tripartite division of the trilogy suggests the triad formula of dialectic: thesis, antithesis, and synthesis. The first novel of the trilogy, *Hordubal*, is our thesis: all men are separate and distinct, and no man can know the truth of another man's life. The police and court can convict Hordubal's murderers, but they cannot understand the depth of Hordubal's pathetic love for Polana. Hordubal is a figure of isolation rendered tragic by the incommunicability of his deepest feelings. His friendship with animals is sensitively treated by Čapek in order to underscore the pathos of his inability to communicate his feelings to his fellow men. In this novel Čapek has finally realized that the relativism of truths which he had earlier celebrated as a positive good would in fact doom the individual to the prison of self, and each man's truth would remain forever mute, incommunicable. This pessimistic implication of relativism underlies the tragedy of the novel's leading character, and finds its tragic expression in the closing sentence: "The heart of Juraj Hordubal was lost somewhere and never buried."

Meteor is the antithesis. Granted that the "detectives" of the novel – the two doctors, the nurse, the writer and the clairvoyant – who try to reconstruct the life of the unknown victim of the plane crash can only speculate concerning his past. Still, because they are human, they can understand the essence of humanity, of what it is to be a man. They cannot know what has happened in a man's life, but they can know what a man is capable of experiencing, just because he is a man. The clairvoyant of the novel expresses it in an eloquent image comparing man's life to the cycle which water undergoes in its passage from sea to sky and back via the earth to the sea again. Just so, man's life always remains human, no matter what particular form it may take. Life, then, is simply the totality of what is possible to life, and a single life is the potentiality of experiencing all events which are possible. Thus an individual man may transcend his isolation and come to a sympathetic understanding of his fellows, for his experience is also theirs.

An Ordinary Life is the synthesis of the trilogy. A retired railway official writes the story of his life. At first it seems a quiet, simple, good, and contented life, in everything, a quite "ordinary life". But then, from some subconscious depth, forgotten voices remind him of suppressed longings and experiences; the "ordinary man" he has become is only one of a diversity of persons which existed within him. He concludes that perhaps each man has the potentiality of becoming all men, but must necessarily restrict himself in development to realizing only certain potentialities. And so the plurality of men in external society corresponds to the plurality of personalities within each man. We are given a basis for understanding the truth of another man's life; we may know other men, for we ourselves are potentially like them. Each man is a microcosm which mirrors all human society. "Have you ever seen anyone, brother, who couldn't be *your brother*?" one of the inner group of voices asks the "ordinary man". And Čapek comments in the epilogue to the novel that "this is just the reason why we can know and understand plurality, because we ourselves are such a plurality".

Thus a firm foundation is laid down for the brotherhood and equality of all men. The individual is no prisoner of existential isolation; within him are resources for bridging the gap which seems to separate him from other men. He can know them as aspects of himself and hence he can accept them.

Perhaps Čapek would have gone on to develop his ideas on social democracy further. But the times were against him. The creative freedom and calm which he had enjoyed while composing the trilogy were cut off by the spectre of the rise of Nazi Germany and the threat of war. Paradoxically, it may have been the need to oppose Nazism which turned his attention from the problem of democracy as such; his energies had to be devoted to the attack on fascism, and the superiority of democracy had in a sense to be taken for granted.

But one more concept was added to Čapek's theory of democracy. In *The First Rescue Party* we have a novel of heroism and the need to defend society in the face of a common danger. The novel is an allegory of democratic society defending itself heroically against aggression. The rescue brigade succeeds because of its democratic cooperation, just as democracy is justified in using the political powers of social organization to defend itself against aggression. As the Czech critic Oldřich Králík has recently pointed out, *The First Rescue Party* makes what is in a sense the obverse of the point of *An Ordinary Life*. In the earlier novel one man proves to contain many different personalities. In *The First Rescue Party* a number of individuals merge together into a single group which has its own spirit and distinct personality.[7] The two novels, taken together, supply a humanistic foundation for a philosophy of democracy.

More than this Čapek was not destined to accomplish. The tragedy of his homeland and his premature death cut short the philosophical and creative development of a great writer, a profound thinker, and a great human spirit.

---

[7] O. Králík, "Čapkova První parta", *Nový život*, No. 12 (1958), pp. 924-25.

Čapek and Communism

JAROSLAV DRESLER

As a philosophic disciple of American pragmatism and an enthusiastic admirer of England, its way of life, its humor, its modern literature, and finally, as one thoroughly conversant with French literature and especially its poetry, Karel Čapek clashed early and quite logically with the Communist movement which had begun to develop in Czechoslovakia shortly after World War I. Čapek was a democrat of Western vintage, and in Communism he came against a doctrine fundamentally foreign to his thinking. Čapek engaged the Communists in frequent journalistic polemics and articles. Unfortunately, this original source material is not easily accessible today for critical evaluation. All newspapers and periodicals which appeared in print during the First Republic are available in present-day Czechoslovakia only upon receipt of the special permission granted to no one but accredited Communist historians. And nowhere in all of Western Europe can one find complete files of the newspapers and periodicals published in Czechoslovakia between 1918 and 1938.

Fortunately, there are two timely essays in some of Čapek's published works which, in spite of their fragmentary and unorganized form, express the author's basic views. These early opinions have assumed a permanency, and even though they had to be modified to some extent under varying conditions, Čapek defended them to the very end. The first of these essays, "Why I Am Not a Communist", ranks high among those of the author's works which are forbidden reading in Czechoslovakia. Among other such interdicted articles is the author's dissertation on American pragmatism which appeared in book form in 1917 as *Pragmatism, or the Philosophy of the Practical Life*. Other forbidden Čapek reading material is a collection of short essays, and his *Conversations with T. G. Masaryk*, which covers the period from 1928 to 1935. Čapek's "Why I Am Not a Communist" was published in the fall of 1924 in the weekly *Přítomnost* and the author included it in a collection of political essays and feuilletons, published in 1932 as *On Matters of Universal Interest; or, Zoon Politikon*. Although most of Čapek's works have been translated into many languages, as far as is known this particular collection appeared only in several Czech editions, while the essay dealing with the author's views on Communism appeared only once in a German publication. Hence it is advantageous that we quote extensively from the article "Why I Am Not a Communist".

From today's viewpoint, it may appear that in his analysis of Communism Čapek is rather superficial. However, it must be borne in mind that when it was written in 1924, the international Communist movement was just embarking upon its historic journey. Čapek had no way of knowing, then, what direction Communism would later take. It appears that he sensed some of the fundamental features of Communism intuitively rather than on the basis of direct experience. Even in his criticism of Communism Čapek was influenced predominantly by the attitudes of American pragmatism. He writes:

Why am I not a Communist? This question has been asked suddenly by people who were formerly inclined to do most anything else but playing at politics. It is certain that none among them would ask, "Why am I not an Agrarian?" or "Why am I not a Social Democrat?" Not to be an Agrarian does not necessarily mean that one must have a specific opinion or a vital belief; but not to be a Communist definitely means being a non-Communist; not to be a Communist is not merely a viewpoint, but a definite credo.

For me personally this question has been one of relief; because I felt an urgent necessity not to merely engage in newspaper polemics with Communism, but to defend myself against the fact that I am not a Communist and can never be one. It would be much easier for me if I were a Communist. Then I could live under the assumption that I was contributing most incisively toward reforming the world; I could assume that I was on the side of the poor against the rich, taking sides with the hungry against the moneybags; I would know then what opinions to entertain, what I should hate and what I should disregard. Instead, I stand here naked in a field of thorns; empty-handed, not shielded by any doctrine, aware of my helplessness toward helping the world and often not knowing how to defend my own conscience. If my heart is on the side of the poor, why in the world am I not a Communist?

Because I am on the side of the poor. The bourgeoisie which cannot or does not want to help is alien to me; but equally alien to my feelings is Communism, which waves the banners of revolution instead of help... The last word of Communism is to rule, not to save; its great motto is Power, not Aid... To feed a poor man with promises is equivalent to robbing him. Perhaps he finds living a bit easier if he is being taunted with pictures of fat geese within reach; but on the practical side it is just as true today as it was a hundred years ago that a sparrow in one's hand is better than a pigeon sitting atop a government building and that a fire in one's hearth is better than a red rooster perched upon a palace roof; and incidentally, we have far fewer palaces than could be believed by a man upon whom they have forced class consciousness in place of his eyes. What to do then? As far as I am concerned I do not console myself with the word "evolution"; it is my belief that poverty is the only condition upon this earth that does not evolve, but rather grows chaotically. But it is not possible to postpone the settlement of the problem of the poor till some other future order. If they are to be helped at all, we must begin to do so today. There is of course the question of whether our present-day world has sufficient moral means to offer such aid. Communism says No; hence it is this negation with which we disagree.

The strangest and most inhuman feature of Communism is its peculiar form of glumness. The worse, the better; if a bicyclist accidentally knocks down an old deaf woman, it is seized upon as evidence of the decadence of our present order; if a machinist lets his fingers be caught in a gear-train, it was not the gears that crushed his fingers, but the capitalists, and what's more, they did so with bloodthirsty thrills.

The hearts of all people who, for one reason or another, are not Communists are beastly and revolting, like a boil; there is not a single stitch of goodness in the entire social system today, and what there is, is bad.... Inhospitable and inhuman is the climate of Communism; there is no midway temperature between the frigid bourgeoisie and the fire of revolution. There is nothing to which a proletarian may devote himself with uninterrupted pleasure. As far as I am concerned, I do not believe it is my habit to paint the world in especially rosy hues, but whenever I kick against the inhuman negation and tragedy of Communism, I feel like shouting my angry protest that it is not true, and that in reality it does not look as painted. ... Hatred, ignorance, basic distrust, this is the psychological world of Communism; a medical diagnosis would label it pathological negativism... The world today does not need hatred; it needs good will, willingness, harmony, and cooperation; it needs a kindlier moral climate; I think that with a bit of ordinary love and kindness we could still perform miracles...

Immediately after the Communist putsch in Czechoslovakia in February 1948, the publishing of Čapek's books was strictly forbidden and most of his books were withdrawn from open shelves in the public libraries. It was not till 1953 that Čapek was again "discovered" by the Soviet literary critics in Moscow, and since then Čapek has been again published even in Prague. The prelude to this reversal was a lecture by Olga Scheinpflug, Čapek's widow, delivered in March 1953 in the auditorium of Prague's Municipal Library. The immense success of this lecture brought about its repetition several times in various sections of Prague. Immediately, the National Theater presented Čapek's "Mother", and there followed an era during which Čapek was being "re-evaluated" and "re-interpreted". At first the emphasis was mainly on pointing out the anti-Nazi character of Čapek's last plays, dating from the late thirties, but later Čapek's earlier plays were being analyzed and given meanings definitely in conflict with the author's intent. Thus Čapek's "The White Plague", which is clearly a protest against dictatorships in general and Nazism in particular, was staged in Bratislava several years ago, when it was presented with an anti-American bias. For instance, the dictator, who is the leading character in this play and was definitely intended by Čapek to portray Hitler, appeared in the re-interpreted version in Bratislava as a caricature of President Eisenhower, The second article dealing with Communism, which the author inserted subsequently into one of his published books, was written by Karel Čapek in 1925 under the title "Proletarian Art". It appeared in book form in 1931 in a collection of essays entitled, *Marsyas; or, On the Fringe of Literature*. As far as we know, this book has not appeared in any other language. Seven years after the first World War and eight years after the Bolshevik revolution, when Čapek began to be interested in Communist art, the so-called "socialist realism" was as yet an unknown concept. Stalin had still not gained complete control of the government in the Soviet Union, and likewise, Zhdanov was then a little-known propagandist still in the background. Communist art was only in a cautious, experimental stage within Soviet Russia. One group of the contemporary artists followed the trend of Western modernism, especially futurism, abstractionism, and constructivism, while others carried on the tradition of Gorki and forged ahead with the banners of proletarian art. In Czechoslovakia, the group calling itself the "Devětsil" and the poets rallied under the banners of Western constructivism, cubism and, later yet, surrealism and both Western and Soviet futurism, while only a few individuals fought for proletarian art. Čapek entered into these disputes with a brief commentary more on the level of an intellectual joke than a serious theory of art, and of the yet-unborn and unbaptized socialist realism. In the preface to his article, "Proletarian Art", Čapek writes:

Perhaps I have erred in this matter as in many other problems; but I must admit that I was expecting something. That I envisioned the ascension of new people with a new imagination and new concepts, with primitive, inexhaustible potential and strong productivity. Not that I expected any miracles; but I did expect at least some form of loosening up. Or at least a trickle of a stream, not overflowing, but genuinely new and struggling out of the soil ... the new soil of the proletariat. They used to say that a new proletarian culture is coming, a culture is coming, a culture that would throw the contemporary bourgeoisie culture into a rubbish heap; it went so far as to assert that it is here already, and that while these lines are being written, the revolution in art is being enacted. If it were only so!

Čapek followed carefully the prevalent bombastic declarations of the Communist theorists in asserting that Communism would give birth to an entirely new type of art, and their conceited claims that this would be a higher form of art, truly popular, democratic, and more genuine than the so-called bourgeois art. Following this exceptionally brief and general preface, so typical of Čapek, he approaches the core of more specific material and writes:

I do not intend to speak of the artistic quality of what is being offered under the label of Communist art. There are some very promising, as well as totally useless, examples being offered, just as would be true of Catholic art or any other art. All I want to be assured of is its proletarian quality. Proletarian art can mean: 1) art created by proletarians, 2) created about the proletariat, 3) created for the proletariat, or, finally, 4) carried on in the spirit motivating the world profession of proletarianism, such as its collectivism, its revolutionary trends, its internationalism, and so forth. Accepting this minimum theoretical assumption, let us set out in quest of proletarian art.

Let us look at art created by proletarians. Julius Bab undertook this task literally, and attempted to collect poetry written by workingmen. There is not too much of it. Nine-tenths of it is formal poetry derived from bourgeois romanticists. In its contents it indulges in outbursts of political programs, and is unique perhaps only in that it was written by workingmen instead of people who had more or less struggled through their high school years.

Čapek's assertion is correct. Even though, during the following decades, Communist literary historians rummaged through all available archives, they were unable to discover any true "workingman's poetry". What Čapek originally felt only intuitively was confirmed by later historical research. The working classes did not create any worthwhile popular poetry which could compare favorably with the popular poetry of the baroque era, or the type that appeared later in the rural areas of Central and Western Europe. Of further interest also is his assertion of the relationship between the bourgeois romanticists and the proletarian poets. The following facts were not known to Čapek at the time, because only later research revealed them: specifically, that young Karl Marx and Friedrich Engels, who began to write revolutionary verses at the outset of their careers, were originally worshipful followers of the most extreme German bourgeois romantics and nationalists. In another part of the article Čapek deals with that art which would take a proletarian and his life as its theme:

Hence it does not seem that this would be something entirely new and unusual. Nor does it appear that our contemporary literature is rushing into this with rolled-up sleeves. It would be good for life and for literature if we did have, for instance, a novel about some machinist as powerful as the *Iliad*, or an epic poem about a weaver as entrancing as some novel about a beautiful, truly great actress. There is much yet to be discovered about life and work. But this cannot be forced out by any political program.

How little Čapek had erred in this particular criticism is best attested to by the many conferences, programs and manifestoes of Communist writers, some of which have remained merely on paper, while others have resulted in a rash of "literary" publications about "literature". Čapek condemns this nonsensical effort to stamp out at all costs novels about the Communist type of heroes and builders, and though his criticism is handled in a humorous vein it is nevertheless very telling:

When all is said and done, literature dealing with the working people is no more a form of proletarian literature, than, for instance, is a story about a princess a typical portrayal of a aristocratic society.

After this Čapek delves into the problem of proletarian art for the proletariat:

It appears that this phase has created and is still creating the greatest amount of misunderstanding. Usually this term applies to a form of literature thickly larded with revolutionary tendencies. In this form of literature the demands upon art are nominal. Likewise, there is very little consideration for the reader himself. For the greater part it is constant rehashing of certain political contentions, presented in an entertaining form, unfortunately, as a rule, not too amusing. I do not reject with any sense of physical revulsion the use of tendentious material in art; but I think that as far as using such material is concerned, truly genuine poets precede their era and do not trot noisily after its passing. True art can do anything; it can conjure up fairies in the forests and angels among people, but it can never stoop to lies. It cannot distort what is, to serve a purpose not its own. This is of course an old garment, but even the loudest, most vulgar new necktie will not render this garment useless. Art for the good of a political party is not in itself art for the people. It remains proletarian art only in the sense that its form and styling inspires ideological words, by means of which we usually designate the revolutionary movement of the proletariat. Some poets actually think that they are participating in a world revolution if, for instance, they can create chaotic disorder in the typographical arrangement of their poems. In this there is much wishfulness, but also a great deal of naiveté. The suppression of punctuation marks may be fairly amusing, especially for one who is doing the suppressing, but somehow it has no effect upon the situation of the masses. And as far as the literary interests of the proletariat itself are concerned, I believe that the majority still sticks to the periods and commas in their usual place. ... Often, when I read a new book, I am taken aback when I think how narrow is the reading circle to which it is directed. The old books were directed to a larger number of readers, and the earliest literature spoke to the greatest number, to princes as well as to goat-herds.

I want to be sincere; I want to admit that I too expect art to be to some degree a pastime, or, let us say, some form of pleasure. I also know that it has other, loftier, more mysterious functions. But this is not its only goal. It must have been the mission of the primitive claw-type axe to contribute to the instrumental progress of man and to some day render testimony to man's beginning. But its more immediate and actual purpose was to kill a wolf or a bear. Likewise the actual purpose of art is to kill boredom, melancholy, and the greyness of life. If it can do more than this, so much the better, but if it fails to do this it is a poor ineffective clawhatchet because it will not protect us against the monsters that are devouring us.

Both of Čapek's articles from which we have quoted dictated the tone of Communist literary criticism of his novels and plays up to his death in 1938. The Czechoslovak Communist literary critics saw in Čapek a representative of the ruling bourgeoisie, a defender of philosophic relativism, and a thinker who, in contrast to Marx, was firmly convinced of the unchangeability of social conditions. They accused him of near-earthiness, of escapism to the realm of metaphysics, and of futile humanitarianism. During the years 1945 to 1948, the Communists, for purely tactical reasons, labelled Čapek a "fighter against fascism". However, from 1948 to 1954, as stated above, he was relegated to the limbo of forbidden authors, and it was not until after several of his works had been published in Moscow that they were mercifully readmitted by the Czechoslovak Communists. An attempt to explain this vacillation of the Communists' literary judgment of Čapek was made by Václav Kopecký, an old-guard Czechoslovak Communist, when he spoke before the Central Committee of the Communist Party in June 1957:

... Karel Čapek was indeed a great writer, but it was thus more painful for us Communists, that with his pen, as journalist and publicist, Karel Čapek for many years during the First Republic directed his attacks not to the right against the Czechoslovak bourgeoisie, but to the left against us Communists. With his so-called witty style Karel Čapek insulted and ridiculed us, only to realize later, during the era of the Hitler menace, that we, the Communists, were the nation's best patriots, and that in the revolutionary struggle we are striving for a free country and a happier national life. At one time, I told Mrs. Scheinpflug, Čapek's widow, that she need not fear that we would allow Karel Čapek's words to be forgotten. But I told her that it would take time to destroy all memories of Karel Čapek's anti-Communist writings and his relations with representatives of the Czechoslovak bourgeoisie. Today the majority of those who read his literary work no longer associate them with such brief political aberrations.

Kopecký's assertion that during the time of Hitler's menace Čapek adopted an affirmative stand on Communism is a part of today's often-repeated legend. It is true that from 1933 to his death Čapek no longer engaged in polemics with the Communists, but this was not because he had made peace with the Communists and their ideology. At the instigation of several democratic journalists, shortly after Hitler's seizure of power in Germany, there began a series of regular, informal gatherings of the leading representatives of the democratic Czechoslovak press. Their purpose was to plan unified action against Nazism, and, above all, to prevent the democratic press from wasting its energies in useless polemic squabbles among themselves. The first of these meetings was called by Karel Čapek and F. X. Šalda, the literary critic, and almost without exception they were continued in Čapek's house each Thursday. With the consent of both Šalda and Čapek, it was decided to exclude from these gatherings not only representatives of the Henlein press and the extreme right, but also those representing the Communist press. Hence, it is clear that Karel Čapek was not reconciled with the Communists even during the last days of his life. He merely maintained toward them an attitude based on the principle that during a period of danger it is not judicious to split one's strength; that is why he stopped his polemics against the Communists.

Statements to the contrary which are now appearing in the Communist press are not based on truth. Even shortly before his death, Čapek did not surrender the ideals held in his youth. The fact that Čapek's works are being published today in almost all Communist countries, including Red China, merely shows that Communism has not brought forth any literature, either qualitatively or quantitatively, to satisfy its readers. That is why today they must reach out for works of non-Communists and anti-Communists like Karel Čapek, and, in their prologues and epilogues, deliberately falsify the author's political profile.

The Art of Jan Čep

PETER DEMETZ

Among the exiled writers, Egon Hostovský and Jan Čep represent central interests of modern Czech prose. Hostovský probes the selfconscious sufferings of the alienated intellectual in a sterile society; Jan Čep opens the more consoling view of a rustic counter-world, of hills, forests, and meandering rivers which, in their calm and translucence, seem mirrors of eternity. To say that Jan Čep works within the European tradition of the *roman champêtre*, or the rustic story (introduced to Bohemia by Božena Němcová), does not imply that he belongs to the past: Čep uses a tradition without being its slave. Perhaps one should not forget that in Czechoslovakia, Hungary, and other Central and East European countries, the rustic novel possesses a dignity of its own. In these countries with their age-old peasant *substratum*, the rustic novel does not constitute merely one of the possible modes of realism which may, or may not, compete with the historical narrative or the novel of manners; it is not, as in France or England, one of the potential tributaries adding its waters to the great realistic stream. In countries with substantial agricultural civilizations, late-born and tenuously developing middle classes, and an aristocracy often belonging to a different linguistic sphere, the rustic story has come to articulate the once inarticulate, to loosen the nation's tongue, to rediscover, in a serious mode, the dignity of a people long excluded from literary consideration by inherited esthetic norms. In this sense we are entitled to say that Božena Němcová, by introducing the interests of George Sand and Berthold Auerbach to Bohemia, made the Czech nation speak modern prose; perhaps it is even more important that she gave to Czech literary development a substance and a continuity rare in neighboring European literatures. Yet it is impossible to ignore the fact that the heritage of the *roman champêtre* has been particularly susceptible to perversion: in concentrating on the provincial, it may ossify into a *ruralism* of anti- or un-liberal inclinations foreign to the Czech mind; and because of its elements of philosophical naturalism, or mere biologism, it may become (as we have seen in Germany) an easy prey for the political manipulators of a fascist blood-and-soil literature or, as happened during the Stalinist winter in Soviet Russia, fall victim to the functionaries of Socialist Realism.

If a writer like Jan Čep has never submitted to perverting temptations, it is not because of his rigid traditionalism; it is rather because he transcended the world of the rustic story and created, from the inherited materials, an artistic world of consistent colors, structures, and metaphysical principles. Jan Čep's artistic universe is, I believe, dominated by a hidden clash between a realistic technique and a burning religious belief. Čep recreates the landscapes of realism, but they are illuminated by a *tremendum et fascinans* flowing from other than purely physical sources. As a Christian writer, Čep seizes upon the epic world of naturalism to demonstrate its glory as well as its deficiencies; the world as he creates it in his novels is nothing if not a *závdavek věčnosti*, a promise of eternity.

In Čep's early prose we discover sketches of almost impressionistic lightness and brevity. But Čep is not interested in changing moods or in an ephemeral play of light and shade; he is fascinated by particular moments of human experience. He observes the sudden, unexpected, breathtaking fragment of time, the split second in which man faces, for the first time, a remote image, a reflex of the other, the hidden dimension of his universe; a window or a door opens, a yellow leaf tumbles from a nut tree, and suddenly his meditative heroes are aware of the spaces beyond, of their transience thirsting for eternity. It would be unfair to term these moments, singled out by the younger writer, *epiphanies*, or, in modern existentialist terminology, *border situations*. An epiphany carries the shock of a direct revelation of divinity that would crush Čep's brooding pilgrims and pensive boys; much less could one speak of an existentialist "border situation" because what is discovered in these rare moments is not brutal nothingness, not the radical negation of being, but, on the contrary, that supreme mode of existence which is plenitude, harmony, and radiance.

In *Zeměžluč*, Čep's first collection of short stories, we encounter boys and old men experiencing their first discovery of infinity. While building a toy house in the loneliness of an exuberant garden, little Jeník suddenly looks up to the clouds and is seized by a sweet realization of the immense spaces beyond the grass and the trees, Or an old man watches the animals grazing; around him the landscape of his life unfolds, the hills and forests of his childhood. Yet suddenly he shudders; he has the feeling that the clouds above are stained by a strange blackness and that the path through the fields suddenly moves "like a snake before it disappears behind the rocks." Although the landscape immediately takes on its well-known shape again, old Vrána has become aware of an ominous power beyond his ken.

These moments of sudden awareness continue to fascinate Čep throughout his artistic maturing; they dominate his earlier prose and they are present, as characteristic episodes, in his later stories. Tomáš Suchomel, in *Polní tráva* (1946), has his experience no less than little Jeník, in *Domek* (1926): Tomáš Suchomel, too, feels the overpowering presence of something he cannot fully explain. "There are things in the world which we do not see and usually do not feel. We pass by as if they were cracks in the rocks or trees in a forest. But sometimes it happens that we step over a forbidden threshold..."

To suggest the suddenness of the moment and the infinity it opens up, Čep relies on a constellation of metaphors and motifs that recur with revealing regularity; whenever they emerge, they tend to confirm the exceptional importance of the moment and suggest the second of discovery as a first stage in the progress toward sharpened "metaphysical" sensibilities. Jan Čep again and again uses the simile of a draft, or a sudden gust of wind blowing from unknown spaces: *průvan přicházející z neznámého*, or *strašlivý průvan, jako dechnutí nesmírného prostoru...* To characterize the suddenness, Čep speaks of the crack of a whip: *jako svihnutí biče*, or, sometimes, an image of Biblical connotations appears: the clouds are torn asunder, and above them opens a *trhlina*, an abyss.

These images of the terrible draft from the unknown, the crack of the whip, and the abyss suggest Čep's idea of time and eternity as coexisting spaces or landscapes penetrating one another. The trouble is that man, because of his limited view, cannot easily survey the intertwined countries; he prefers to see and to set boundaries where there is constant flow, transition, analogy. This is the reason why young Čep constantly returns to scenes of death and dying. He does not merely follow the demands of a traditional poor-house naturalism that prefers to shock the reader with the stench of *les misérables*; to Čep's mind, even the poorest peasant and shepherd, created in the image of God, may hope to have in death his supreme moment of discovery. *Trhlina*, the gap, opens like a wide door, and man, with a consciousness finely honed by approaching death, recognizes the secret parallelism of time and eternity, the two spaces in which he has unsuspectingly lived from his very first day. It is not hard to see that moments of anticipation and recurrent death scenes are intimately related to each other. The hour of death, as recorded in *Husopas, Samo-*

mluva, Děravý plášť', Člověk na silnici, Oldřich Babor, Elegie, Rozárka Lukášová, fulfils the promise of the anticipatory moment; death confirms man's earlier discoveries, rewards hope, reveals to the inarticulate peasants, children, and women an overwhelming reality. "Her eyes turned into stone, charmed by a spectacle that no man could see and stay alive. The other space, the presence of which had filled her entire short life with a curious sadness, absorbed her. But to those who remained, her dead face again suggested an ambivalent smile which does not betray its secret."

One of Čep's earliest stories is called *Dvojí Domov*, the twofold homeland. It suggests the central metaphor which expresses the substance of Čep's metaphysical and Christian commitment. Time, with its narrow limits and its material restrictions, corresponds to what people mistakenly call their *real* home: villages, fields, the Moravian hills, and the slow Morava river. Infinity crystallizes in the other space, the other homeland, pure and calm; a landscape whose presence people feel in unique moments and enter only at the hour of death. In Jan Čep's artistic universe the two countries of man coexist; living in one, man also unknowingly exists in the other; and moving among the living, we are constantly moving among the dead who are around us. Again and again, Čep's characters feel, or believe they feel, the presence of the dead: *měl pocit jakoby za ním někdo stal... někdy se bál otočit*; day and night, the two worlds face each other, even at high noon: *v pravé poledne, kdy se znenadání protnou dráhy světa našeho a jejich*. Here it is quite evident how radically Čep differs from the ruralists who are satisfied to accept landscape and soil as absolute and final values that fully determine human dimensions – to Čep, the *real* landscape merely hides the invisible landscape of infinity, and he cannot praise his central figures more than to say of them, as he does of Oldřich Babor, that they recognize the signs of the dead; that they can 'read' the landscape, the hieroglyphics of the fields and the patterns of the roads betraying the presence of earlier generations who have receded into pure invisibility. *Kolik rukou, které hnětly tuto hlínu?*

It is easy to misunderstand Jan Čep and to interpret his loving images of the Moravian hill and river country as an expression of a traditional patriotism cherishing the homeland, the soil, the chain of generations, above all else. But this is to misconstrue the artist's belief as well as his metaphors. Čep makes it quite clear that in the *Dvojí Domov*, man's fundamental loyalty is to his *první domov*, his first home, that is, to transcendence. Once man has come close enough to feel the charms of his supernatural home, he will never be satisfied with the blessings of the natural world: *sen o prvním domově, neustále pociťěný, ji zanechal v duši tesknotu do smrti otevřenou*. This is the reason why all of Čep's major figures feel, at one point or another, the sadness of the *anima naturaliter christiana*. The key phrases with which Čep suggests the essential core of humanity consistently point to sadness, brooding, the thirst of the soul: *prudká lítost nad čímsi nevyplněným a nedokončeným ... nevýslovný smutek ...drásavá tesknota ... nevyslovitelná úzkost*. Tomáš Suchomel, Čep's most convincing figure, represents the basic paradox: the sheer physical weight of a peasant's existence, yet a life driven on by inexplicable desire that only slowly articulates; a life longing from its second home for its first unchanging one: "The old man had to admit to himself that he had always lived in a kind of expectation, as if the horizons of a new landscape today or tomorrow would open up before him; as if he should encounter somebody dear and rare who would feel the impulse of his restless longings." Incapable of metaphysical speculations, the old man (one thinks of Gerhart Hauptmann's *Fuhrmann Henschel*) increasingly feels what Christian theology may term the fundamental realization of the incompleteness of human life: *ta touha po otevření nových obzorů*.

In Čep's epic world, much as in Maxim Gorki's related universe, the restless, the wanderers, and the pilgrims suggest the essential image of man. Inexplicable desires drive these people from their homes on the road; and even when they suddenly settle down, when they age, they feel again an instinctive urge that forces them to roam the country. If Gorki had a particular liking for the *bossjak*, the holy picaro who wanders through old Russia, Jan Čep has his own *putovatelé* who run away from their farms and long for distant lands. There is Cyril Nedoma, whose very name suggests the "unhoused man"; there is old Hanýsek, who prefers alien shelters to his own house; there is, in a comic variation of the motif, indefatigable Uncle Dodor who from the hills of Moravia longs for the vineyards of Hungary, and one day simply disappears; there are Josef Brach, Oldřich Babor, and Jakob Lešek; and, of course, Tomáš Suchomel, who cannot stay home, but again and again sets out on his pilgrimages through the Moravian and the Czech countryside as if his thirst for eternity really could be quenched here and now. Man is *quasi peregrinus*: he may, as Suchomel, believe that his restlessness is a secret vice or curse, yet it is, we are inclined to believe, his hidden strength and virtue because it separates him from the insensitive hoarders of goods, the easily satisfied, those chained to their second home by their property, by soil and matter. Clearly those who wander *quasi peregrini* are the truly free, because they are not yet completely enchained by the *natura naturata*, but keep their feet and eyes searching for the *natura naturans*.

The Art of Jan Čep

Inevitably, in this world of the *peregrini*, religious pilgrimages appear as a motif of central implications. Three times in Čep's prose, a *pout'* [pilgrimage] emerges as a decisive event: in the short story of the same title (1934), in *Svatojanská pout'*, and in *Polní tráva* (1946). Throughout the years, the motif retains its unaltered charm. Again, one could remark that Čep merely follows the traditions of the Czech folklore tale which, as in Božena Němcová's *Babička*, always had a marked tendency to recall the exciting colors, sounds, and movements of fairs and folk gatherings. But within the context of Čep's universe, the *pout'* is of much more than folklore interest. In each case Čep is deliberately slow in preparing the stage; he describes the exhausting procession through the forests and fields; surveys the Holy Mountain, the goal of the pilgrimage, from afar; speaks of the renewed vigor of the pilgrims; accompanies them on their difficult ascent; admires the sudden opening of the cathedral doors, the frankincense, the light from the distant altar, the glorious radiance of the shrine. At this point, his narrative tends to change (as one could easily demonstrate by structural analysis) into a poetic hymn and a prayer confirming rare illumination and bliss – pilgrims, it seems, may experience, at least from afar, what to other people is given only in the moment of death. Čep's peasant pilgrimage is a *typos*, a symbolical anticipation of man's salvation, in the theological sense. As man ascends to the mountain church and kneels down upon the stones to adore the Mother of Christ, he acts out – a living emblem, as it were – his own future, the coming metamorphosis of his world. Perhaps it would be revealing to compare the different use of the pilgrimage motif by Božena Němcová and Jan Čep. In the world of *Babička*, dominated by folklore interests, humanism, and anticipations of Darwin, the pilgrimage sets the scene for homely details of peasant life; the metaphysical relevance of the pilgrimage seems neglected, and the church ritual, as so often in *Babička*, appears but briefly and on the periphery of the writer's narrative interests. To Božena Němcová, man's second home clearly takes precedence over his first one; in Čep's stories, the narrative resolutely aims at the essential meaning of the Church ritual as a promise enacted here and now.

My attempt to delineate Jan Čep's image of man tends to neglect his developing art, but I hope I have at least implied something of the narrative structures and motifs which he frequently uses. In his early work, Čep concentrated on the brief image of the supreme moment of discovery or death; later, he came to prefer the long, dense story that unfolds a fate told or remembered in its full biographical continuity. It is curious to see that Čep hardly ever deviated from the linear narrative, from relating the story of the individual in the strict sense of the word. He never surveys the interaction of a circle of persons or a group; he never develops intricate plots or intensely complex actions; and he never, at least not in the core of his work, discusses ideological or philosophical problems in the essayistic manner of the experimental novel. These are limitations at once fruitful, characteristic, and inevitable. Clearly, the Christian writer prefers to choose a narrative structure singling out the individual and his unique fate – if Čep's art has a certain monological character, if much of it is a *samomluva* (to quote the title of one of his stories), we should add that within his Christian world, the other, the gently answering, voice speaks a language that surpasses man's perception. In art, Čep leads us to believe, we can hear only the human side of the dialogue between man and God.

But Jan Čep developed in more than one way. In his early prose, the symbolist impact of Zeyer and Březina emerges from this concentration of imagery; and conceits reminiscent of Vladislav Vančura abound. Often the rustic narrative seems interrupted by invocations whose function one may doubt; they are poetry in their own right, but are not necessarily in their proper place. I think that an incisive change occurs in Čep's first *récits* in the thirties: there, as, for instance, in *Zápisky Jiljího Klena*, the story is told by an individual narrator and Čep cannot escape the need to control his language according to the voice and the horizon of the speaker. Metaphors and conceits almost disappear, and the technique of the dramatized first-person narrrator contributes to artistic purification. Čep's artistic development leads from a bold and metaphoric to a simple and translucent narrative – but it is not the simplicity of a naive mind that confronts us. Flaubert once remarked that he felt devoured by metaphors and that he had to fight the pressing tide of images. The poet Čep may have fought similar secret battles. Čep's Christian humility of language – corresponding to his image of man and his *dvojí domov* – derives, one suspects, from a craftmanship in which artistic self-discipline and renunciation are imperceptibly combined.

BIBLIOGRAPHICAL NOTE

Jan Čep, born December 31, 1902, Myšlechovice, Moravia, escaped in 1949 from Communist Czechoslovakia, and now resides in Paris.

Main publications: *Dvojí domov* (1926), *Vigilie* (1928), *Děravý plášť* (1934), *Hranice stínu* (1935), *Modrá a zlatá* (1938), *Sestra úzkost* (1944), *O lidský svět* (1953).

Articles on Jan Čep: Karel Sezima in *Mlází*, 1936; René Wellek in *Columbia Dictionary of Modern European Literature* (1947).

Traditions of Czech Literature and the Writer in Exile

JAN TUMLÍŘ

It fills me with emotion to think of the occasion – the years behind us of our exile – and to realize that I am somehow called to account for our accomplishments. It is difficult for me to speak about the literary achievements of the exiled Czech writers for many reasons. Above all, I cannot be objective. To me, their books are not finished works to be judged; they are projections of a situation which I share and which continues to confuse me. I propose therefore to talk about this situation. Discussing the problems with which the exiled Czech writers have to contend, I shall concentrate on their fight with certain traditions established in Czech literature. It may be a way to appraise what they have done thus far.

I

The writer draws sustenance for his work from words and phrases freely flowing past his ears in the daily life of his people. Fragments of conversation, words, and voices which accidentally meet in the distracted ear, may create a verbal gesture which becomes an important stimulus when the work slackens. In another situation, the expression of a vague worry or desire overheard in a crowd may become the needed corrective or signpost to the writer's thought. There are innumerable ways, often so subtle as to go unnoticed, in which society aids its writer in shaping his work. This sustenance, this helpful context, is lost to the exiled writer. Plucked out of the seminal stream of daily speech, his work loses some of its immediacy, carries more strain.

The isolation in which the exiled writer works is doubly serious; he especially needs the stimuli and correctives and signposts which his native society offers. He drifts in a maelstrom of moods; he knows well how easily they grow to a feverish pitch in his isolation and how often – for sometimes ridiculous reasons – they suddenly change. He writes and the very newness (to him) of the things which he describes fills him with enthusiasm – but the moment he encounters the slightest difficulty, the novelty may change into strangeness and throw him into despair. He may sometimes even feel heroic, "proudly maintaining his lonely truth" – yet the slightest change in the physical atmosphere, the first breath of spring, a wisp of fog winding through the dusk, an elusive waft of a long forgotten smell, can bring a piercing nostalgia upon him in which the lost home appears the only true security and never to be regained. If moods are important to the writer, and if they are so unreliable here, what remains?

I can illustrate these remarks by a curious phenomenon which you may at first think funny. It is a fact that a large part, perhaps the better part, of exile literature is oral literature. The number of stories I have heard, some of them first-rate, that were never written! Or the manuscripts which read so disappointingly after one had been *told* the story and still remembered the excitement of the oral narrative! I have often felt, coming from Germany to visit friends in Paris, that there was something in the Parisian atmosphere that acted as a catalyst to writing, letting almost any small occurrence crystallize into a story, almost without effort. Today I realize that most of us have had the same experience, and that it was not the other city and its atmosphere, but the physical presence of a listener, which made the difference. We have now our little "inside history" of exile literature, and one of its episodes recalls that well-known incident between Scott Fitzgerald and Hemingway, when the former sighed, "The rich are different from us", the latter answering. "Sure, they've got more money". With the same dreamy look which must have been Fitzgerald's at the moment of his remark, one of our writers said some years ago in Paris, "You know, I often feel that memory is a fantastic novel". Whereupon his friend remarked sceptically, "Except that a novel must have two hard covers and several hundred pages of print between them". In both cases the sceptics stole the show. But to me, each of the contradicting views seems to have a validity of its own, and the tension between them characterizes the literature in question.

II

When history moves too fast, when events threaten to overwhelm us, and moods begin to cramp our reason and will, we almost instinctively turn to reading history. Our writers, too, have been preoccupied with history.

Discussion of our national literary and other traditions has been continuous ever since that spring of 1948. It is remarkable that the exiled poets and novelists spend so much time writing essays on tradition instead of writing more poems and novels. But this is understandable, for they question, in this debate, mainly those traditional concepts which made Czech creative writing so closely dependent on its social context, on the presence of the "living language" about which I spoke earlier.

There are many valid traditions in our literature. There is the tradition of compassionate understanding for the simple and the poor, for the common man of the people. In its purest, this quality is far removed from the Russian "narodnikism" – from any tendency to deify the people as such. On the contrary, it is a power and a compulsion to individualize, to see the individual, however humble, in his own right. It might be also described negatively as the absence of the outwardly remarkable, immediately captivating, characters from our fiction. There are few geniuses, adventurers, noblemen, millionaires or daemonic criminals in our novels. And if Karel Čapek describes an epoch-making inventor, he typically treats him as a very plain man whose genius is just an additional, almost accidental, quality. In the best works of this tradition, most notably in the work of Božena Němcová, the life of the simple people is rich in its immediacy, yet also clearly seen in its moral perspective.

Then there is the tradition of what we like to call our "peasant realism". It is best manifested in literary regionalism, in the effort to express the spirit of a certain region, in its landscape and people. It requires the writer to explore his subject to the tiniest detail, to identify himself with it for his whole life. The corollary of this way of work is a certain distrust of abstractions, a need to translate each generalization into the physical terms of one's own intimately known environment.

And there is a third tradition which, at least superficially, contradicts the preceding one. It is an urge to transcend the limitations of geography and language, to participate really and fully in Europe and the world, to seek solutions to our national problems in the open world. This tradition is best symbolized by Comenius.

In an essay, written a few years ago, Jiří Pistorius analyzed yet another complex of traditions. These derive from the fact that since its "reawakening" in the early 19th century, our literature has been heavily burdened with extraneous social functions. Indeed, our literary scholars have come to speak of the "permanently unnatural state of literary functions". As one of these extra-literary functions in the wake of the European enlightenment, our literature had to unify and develop the grammatical rules of the Czech language, and to build its vocabulary. Actually, this development has never ceased; to this day, the language and the literature have grown in close dependence on each other.

Their mutual relation is, as far as I know, unique. For literature, the language has become the object of supreme loyalty. In no other literature are there so many poems devoted to the language. The poets address the language, converse with it, view it as enbodying the wisdom of the generations, and believe that in the process of literary creation the language thinks by itself. (I myself believe this, but only in the sense that God helps those who help themselves.)

As for the effects of continuous linguistic innovation on the literary standards, I am inclined to agree with Pistorius that they were positively harmful. Various explanations are given for the lack of classicism in our literary history. The linguistic preoccupation of the writers may be another. The language was in a state of constant flux, and therefore could never crystallize into an order within which the sensual, the emotional, and the intellectual could perfectly merge. Baumgarter's classical requirement of the "perfectly sensuous speech" – *der vollkommen sinnlichen Rede* – could never be fulfilled because the writers relied for their main effect on the rational pleasure which we feel at an unexpected, yet somehow logical, deviation from the linguistic norm.

III

I do not want to suggest that the difficulty experienced by the exiled writers was the main cause of this debate. To create such an impression would be unjust. If the whole concception of literature which these writers brought with themselves into exile was in doubt, it was due to a weightier reason.

This conception emerged in the great outburst of literary creativity which the Czech countries experienced, in consonance with the rest of the world, after the First World War. What we have observed over the past years, from across the Iron Curtain, is the final disintegration of the literary impetus of that era. In fact, this impetus destroyed itself in and through the works of the very authors who some thirty years ago had formed the avant-garde of the modern movement. But the exiled writers, too, have been a part of that movement. Let us therefore see how the various features of the Czech literary tradition combined in recent decades.

Our first distinct literary movement after World War I was the so-called "proletarian poetry". One aspect of this poetry, it seems to me, has not yet been fully appreciated: its *formal austerity*, which was not a sign of spiritual poverty, but rather a reflection of an inner balance. It was an authentic expression of a new outlook, wide of scope and of remarkable internal consistency, with no contradiction between thought and feeling. This poetry did not seek to record directly the state of the writer's soul; it was "objective", often epic and dramatic. It always contained a message, but rarely indulged in mere political agitation. It was concerned with a new way of life. The group disintegrated in about 1924, apparently for political reasons, but it is clear in retrospect that there were deeper forces at work. The growing influence of the West prepared the ground for another sweeping change of poetic style. In the debates of the transition period, the proletarian poetry was criticized mainly for its sentimentality, though not always justly. It is striking that its formal aspects, the discipline, the striving toward what I should call "the architectonic in poetry", were never mentioned.

The new style which captured the literary scene was called "Poetism". A product of both of Dada and Surrealism, it relied fully on free association of words. Words were juggled and balanced like colorful balls and balloons for their vague and fleeting sensual effect; indeed, balls and balloons, juggling, *escamotage*, the variety show, and the circus became the key words and topics of this poetry. Another recurring theme was the yearning for exotic countries, for the tropics – a feeling that comes to every circus spectator. Indeed, one poet of the group, a former member of the proletarian school, literally followed his *rêve exotique* and went to Java, returning with a book of poems called "With The Ship Transporting Tea and Coffee..." He committed suicide in 1951, one of the most celebrated writers of the Communist regime.

In poetism, Czech poetry finally achieved that stage of modernity where words and images no longer conveyed coherent meaning, but, rather, carried their own poetic charge. Each word thus became an end in itself. You may notice that this conception of poetry ideally corresponds to that fateful proclivity of the Czech writer to engage in purely linguistic adventure. Given the tradition, the influence of poetism was bound to be great. We like to think of a poem as of a defiant attempt to seize a truth from the chaos of the world. Under the influence of poetism, this conception of a poem changed. It became an attempt to capture, not truth, but poetic effect.

Poetism, for all its exuberance, was the product of an intellectual, even ideological, crisis. The chase after the colorful shadows of words was clearly an escape. The writer's intellectual responsibilities had become too heavy in a world whose traditions seemed to have perished in the war, and in which even the stop-gap certainty of world revolution was beginning to dissolve. Events in the Soviet Union had begun to deviate incomprehensibly from the blueprint of the prophets.

But the writers who in 1926 espoused poetism had been supporting proletarian poetry only a few years ago. They still considered themselves involved, and the first *Manifesto of Poetism* contains a rather pathetic attempt to prove their social involvement. In this document the new poetry presented itself as a kind of public utility, serving to provide a refreshing bath for the tired senses of the city dweller. The works of the individual poets abound in similar attempts at self-justification. The literature developed a "bad conscience".

We may understand, therefore, why the teaching of Rosa Luxemburg was so eagerly accepted at that time by the East-Central European leftist intelligentsia. One of her important tenets was that the workingman's movement was endowed with a natural impulse toward revolution and liberty – that the working class possesses a special instinct which unerringly leads it, even under the most complex and confusing circumstances, towards the promised land of universal brotherhood. The original, sincere unity of belief was still a part of the writers' ties with the workers. But it now became tinged with a new craving for intellectual security. As Surrealism further undermined their belief in their own reason, the writers began to use the working class as a symbol of truth. The traditional faith in the innate goodness and wisdom of the simple man was perverted into something dangerous: a subconscious reverence for the mass.

IV

It cannot have escaped your attention that, even in its crisis, Czech literature participates in a wider development. All modern literature, and modern art in general, has been marked by a similar dissociation between thought, feeling, and sensual perception. The most telling symptom of this sickness is artistic specialization, the ever-increasing emphasis on the purely formal, technical aspects of the *métier*. How many novels have appeared, after Gide's *The Counterfeiters*, of which the protagonist is – a novel! In poetry, there has been almost total agreement with T. S. Eliot's dictum that *thought* does not belong in a poem, which is concerned only with the "poetic equivalent" of thought. Tutored by the New Criticism, the younger poets speak proudly of poetry which has only now emerged from the stage of alchemy into that of science, and they produce a flood of works in which the dazzle of technical effect obliterates all vision.

The comparison of alchemy and science may be worth developing a little further. The notion of "pure essences" which the various schools of modern art are trying to transmit is clearly of scientific origin. The arts have attempted to develop their own "laboratory methods" to distill the pure essence of thought, faith, feeling, or perception, with the result that thought was soon swallowed up by sensations, while faith was absent, and feeling inarticulate. Czech literature is only one of many examples of art losing its autonomy in this process. Has it not struck you that the more abstract, the more exclusively self-concerned, art becomes, the more readily it yields to purposeful, often outright, commercial exploitation? The precious insights of the abstract painters indeed influence the masses today – but in the form of bookbinding, carpet designs, layouts of the big picture magazines. The exciting musical experiments of the *avant-garde* of yesterday, for example, the Parisian Six, have been channelled into scores accompanying the movies, have become the music which moves you although you do not consciously hear it. And the lyrical essences distilled by modern poetry? Today they are the editorial of a Communist newspaper, but also the hypnotic speech of the ad-man. "In this friendly, freedom-loving land of ours – Schlitz beer belongs." Had they hired Verlaine, he could not have done it better. Wherever you are manipulated, influenced subconsciously, you may find the techniques of modern art at work.

Today's best artists and writers realize that they are themselves responsible. It is the responsibility of the creator to endow his work with a sense so unique, with a meaning so distinct and an emotion so pervasive, that it shall remain incorruptible.

Boris Pasternak, talking to a foreign journalist in 1957, was surprisingly disparaging of his own poetry. "Trifles", he said, "too fragmentary and personal to render the sense of human experience." Distrusting the merely lyrical, the vaguely exciting, he chose the form of a novel to express what he felt most urgently. Ignazio Silone, whose voice seems to gain still more warmth in its increasing weariness... They all talk about the same thing.

To return to the exiled Czech writers, I hope to have shown that it was a certain conception of literature, prevalent in Prague at a certain time, which threatened to make writing impossible for them once they had left Prague. As writers, they were in danger of becoming incommunicado.

But I have also tried to show that the problem of communication has become central for all serious literature of our time.

In this sense, then, their exile is an advantage. It has forced them to make the distinction between the durable and the short-lived in their tradition, or, more exactly, between the vital tradition of Czech literature and a flat literary convention.

Their situation has also helped by removing most of the temptations to which the Czech writer so easily falls prey. The linguistic experiment and innovation must of necessity cease in exile; when you live part of your time in a foreign language, writing in your own becomes more difficult, but must also be much more precise. Furthermore, the traditional tendency to exaggerate the political aspect of literature loses much of its danger in exile. Without a mass audience you are automatically at one remove from the political, which is a very much healthier position.

Thus, too, the traditional interest in the simple and humble man, the compassion and understanding which Czech literature extends to him, are now rid of their political emphasis. We know now that no people, no class, is politically infallible or has a unique mission. Once deemed the natural source of all virtue, wisdom, and nobility, people today seem almost accidental by-products of their industrial system. But are they therefore less worthy of sympathy? Sometimes I think that Camus, Pasternak, and Silone have been rare and lonely writers precisely because, in this age of anxiety, true compassion is rare. It should come naturally, however, to writers who grew in the tradition of Božena Němcová. Yes, I believe that the exile writers have something to offer.

I am glad to see how their latest work broadens in scope and develops a directness which is, in itself, a victory over their isolation. They are few, of course, and cannot alone redeem Czech literature. That will require a national effort. From the national standpoint, the merit of the exile writers lies in the fact that they brought into the open the causes which made recent Czech literature a prisoner of its own rhetoric, walled off even from its national context. It seems that the younger writers in Prague have lately been concerned with the same problems. For them our experience may be of value. If it becomes, at some future date, a basis for our discussion with them – that, I think, will be the most valuable contribution of our exile literature.

LINGUISTICS

The Czech Contribution to Modern Linguistics

HENRY KUČERA

In the late 1920's and during the 1930's, Prague was among the principal centers of language study in the world. It was in Prague that some of the basic theoretical and methodological postulates of modern linguistic science were formulated, and where important linguistic literature was published. The Prague Linguistic Circle, which was the center of these activities, was not, of course, an exclusively Czech phenomenon. Its membership was, rather, cosmopolitan, its orientation international; its founders were a Czech and an exiled Russian. But this character of the group, which certainly was the antithesis of parochialism, was in itself a function of the general atmosphere of Czechoslovakia after World War I. There seems to have been at that time in Prague an openness to outside influences and a willingness to receive them, but, at the same time, a spirit of critical examination of all that was happening in European culture, and an eagerness to offer original contributions. In this context, the Prague Linguistic Circle and its character were by no means accidental.

But there were also deeper roots of language studies in Czechoslovakia which undoubtedly contributed to the growth of the Prague linguistic school. Any discussion of the Czech contribution to modern linguistics is inextricably bound with this older tradition of language studies, principally of the Czech language and its related Slavic tongues, a tradition which may have received its original stimulus as far back as in the Cyrillo-Methodian period of Greater Moravia. Although some of these aspects of Czech philological scholarship are discussed in other papers in this volume, it may be perhaps appropriate to mention some of this traditional background, at least briefly, in order to place the discussion in a better perspective.

Prince Rostislav's call for Christian missionaries from Constantinople may have been a skillful move of political tactics in the relatively simple spectrum of power distribution in 9th century Europe. For the Slavic peoples, however, this move had a lasting cultural effect. For the Eastern and Southern Slavs, the importance of this development is obvious; in the case of the Czechs and the Slovaks, it is much more subtle, but nevertheless substantial. Constantine and Methodius brought to Moravia not only Christianity, but also the first Slavic literary language, the first Slavic alphabet, and the first literature. They also brought with them the advocacy of the rightful place of the vernacular in church services and affairs which they vigorously defended in Rome. Political and cultural developments in the Czechoslovak territory soon interrupted the Church Slavonic liturgical and literary tradition. Nevertheless, much of it remained; primary among these lasting effects was the realization that the national language was a suitable and dignified instrument for even the highest purposes, for religious literary expression. So the seeds of national consciousness and respect for the Slavic vernacular were sown. Subsequent Czech history shows that the seed had fallen on fertile ground, indeed. It is evident not only in the remarkable development of literature in the Czech language in the 14th century, but also in the strong emphasis on the national element in the Czech Reformation movement. It was thus not incongruous that the religious reformer, Jan Hus, paid so much attention to the Czech language, creating a new orthography for it and elevating the dialect of Prague to the status of a new literary medium. And again, at the end of the 18th and in the 19th century, the period of the so-called Czech National Revival, when the nation made a determined effort to emancipate itself from German tutelage and to reestablish its sense of vitality, cohesiveness, and a more promising national future, studies of the Czech language and its relationship to other Slavic tongues were at the center of the movement's effort. Philological and literary research was, after all, one of the main interests of the first of these national emancipators, Josef Dobrovský. Even when he wrote about the Czech language and literature in Latin or in German, his intention – to raise the prestige of his mother tongue and make it the basis for a new national culture – was always clearly evident. The philological and literary orientation of the National Revival was carried on by Jungmann, Šafařík, and others to whom the continued life of the nation often appeared synonymous with the survival of the national language.

Somerset Maugham, in his *Writer's Notebook*, has a few recollections of his contact with Czechs during World War I. Their patriotism, he says, filled him with amazement. "It is a passion so single and so devouring", writes Maugham, "that it leaves room for no others."[1] While this may be

---

[1] W. Somerset Maugham, *A Writer's Notebook* (New York, 1949), p. 149.

a somewhat exaggerated view, the fact is that the Czechs and the Slovaks have been, and have had to be, almost continuously preoccupied during their difficult history with the ultimate problem of their national existence; the native language, as the prerequisite and symbol of this existence, understandably became also something of a passion. Thus, in the final analysis, the reasons for the philological interest of the Czechs may be geographic and historical; a look at the map of Europe gives one a view of Bohemia that is like a ship's bow heading into a German sea. But whatever may have motivated the intense interest in language and language studies, the ground was certainly well prepared, by the turn of this century, for a further development of linguistics in the country. Moreover, with independence in 1918, both Czech and Slovak literature and scholarship could turn their attention from questions of national identity to problems of a more universal nature; the 1920's were a period of internationalism and experimentation. Thus, in addition to the traditional interest in language studies, the cultural crosswinds blowing through Prague furnished the second impetus.

In 1926, the birth year of the Prague Linguistic Circle, the field of language studies everywhere was ready for a new methodology and new approaches. The 19th century in linguistics had been, in a sense, an age of discovery. The discovery that languages as far distant as those of India and Western Europe are genetically related, having come presumably from a single common ancestor, was naturally an exciting realization. So was the discovery of regular phonetic correspondences, the so-called phonetic laws of the neo-grammarians, and the whole notion that older stages and extinct ancestors of languages, even if unknown from written sources, can be reconstructed on the basis of these observations. But by being an age of discovery, the 19th century in linguistics was also primarily a period of empiricism, of attempts to uncover new items of information and new links between languages, to fill in new pieces in the genealogical mosaic of speech families. When the century of discovery was nearing its end, the need arose for a shift from the empirical to a theoretical and methodological approach. The awareness grew that language investigation had to be more than a mere collection of primarily historical facts and observations, however fascinating they may be; that language is a system of symbols, a highly intricate and structured system, and that further insight into language operation and development can be gained only from pursuing this notion of the systematic organization of language. And so the third impetus to the formation of the Prague linguistic school was supplied.

Aside from traditions and impetuses, people and accidental occurrences also played their role in the pre-history and history of the Prague Linguistic Circle. One of these necessary conditions was the personality of Vilém Mathesius, the first professor of English philology at Charles University in Prague, a linguist of great originality, and a capable organizer who grew up in the Czech philological tradition and who, because of his specialty, was at the same time in active contact with the Anglo-Saxon world. And the necessary historical incident was supplied by the arrival in Prague, in July of 1920, of a young Russian emigré, Roman Jakobson, who was well acquainted with the new linguistic ideas at Moscow University and who himself proved to have a remarkable talent for identifying and dissecting the basic problems of the emerging science of language. The first meeting of the Prague Linguistic Circle took place on October 6, 1926.[2] As if in anticipation of the future international character of the group, the occasion for the first meeting was a lecture by a visiting German linguist, Dr. Henrik Becker, who was interested in the formation and codification of literary languages in the smaller nations of Europe. Besides Becker, Mathesius, and Jakobson, only three other people were present at that time. But interest grew rapidly, and the activities of the Circle began to multiply. Without wanting to overemphasize the cosmopolitan nature of the group, I still think that it is important to realize this if one wishes to gain a good understanding of the wide impact of the Circle and a true appreciation for Prague's role as a center of modern linguistics. It is thus, perhaps, worth mentioning that during the first two years of the Circle's existence, lectures at its Prague meetings were delivered by eight Czechs, five Russians, two Frenchmen, and a German.

A further stimulus to the activities of the Circle was the convocation of the First International Congress of Linguists at The Hague in 1928. The organizers of the Congress formulated six important questions of modern linguistics to which answers were solicited from the participants and then submitted to the Congress. The crucial topic among these questions was the search for the best method for the complete analysis of languages in their grammatical aspects. Of the thirteen responses on this subject, nine came from the members of the Prague Linguistic Circle. The Congress in The Hague also witnessed a rapprochement of the Prague and Geneva schools of linguistics, which together submitted a formulation of

---

[2] An account of the history of the Prague Linguistic Circle during its first decade was given by V. Mathesius in "Deset let pražského linguistického kroužku", *Slovo a slovesnost*, 2 (1936), pp. 137-145.

linguistic postulates which the Congress accepted without opposition.

The next ten years witnessed vigorous activity on the part of the Prague group, both at international congresses and in publishing. The first congress of Slavists took place in Prague in 1929, and the Circle issued, on this occasion, the first two volumes of its *Travaux du Cercle Linguistique de Prague*. In 1930, again in Prague, the Circle organized the International Phonological Conference, at which linguists from eight countries participated. The conference was in preparation for the next International Congress of Linguists in Geneva the following year, at which phonology was to be the main subject of discussion. During the 1930's, the activities of the Circle and the participation of its members in international linguistic life were so numerous that only a few of them can be mentioned. The ideas and the members of the group had a significant impact, for example, on the Third Linguistic Congress in Rome in 1933, the Second Slavic Congress in Warsaw in 1934, the Phonetic Congresses in Amsterdam in 1932 and in London in 1935. Aside from the volumes of the *Travaux*, which appeared at irregular intervals,[3] the Circle began issuing, in 1935, its periodical, *Slovo a slovesnost*, which, with the exception of a few years of interruption during and after World War II, has been published ever since.

The European crisis of the late 1930's gradually changed the character of Prague from a city which had been at the center of European culture and scholarship to a dismayed capital of a dismembered country, soon to be occupied by the German armies. The Prague Linguistic Circle suffered both from this tragedy and from some severe personal losses. Nicholas Trubetzkoy, one of the group's most original and prolific members, died in Vienna in 1938. Jakobson left Czechoslovakia shortly after the Nazi occupation and went first to Scandinavia and later to America, never to return to Prague permanently. Mathesius lived through the war, but died at its very conclusion on April 12, 1945, in Prague. Others left or perished, and the contacts were interrupted. Those members of the Circle who remained and survived the war had only a brief breathing spell before 1948, which was not long enough to reestablish the eminence of the Circle in international linguistics, even if the personalities and the intellectual force still had been available. The events of 1948 eventually resulted not only in a complete decline of the Circle itself, but even in the rejection of some of its valuable contributions by the political authorities in Czechoslovakia, as well as by some Czech linguists themselves.

---

[3] Altogether eight volumes of the *Travaux* were published between 1929 and 1939.

It would not be appropriate, in a paper of this kind, to go into technical details of the linguistic theories and methodologies of the Prague Linguistic Circle. Nevertheless, some of the essential concepts need summarizing. I shall attempt to do so, being fully aware that summarizing so conceptually complex a body of ideas and the contributions of so many scholars can be only a very imperfect undertaking. Neither can it be entirely original, since this has been done effectively by some of the principal members of the Circle themselves. Jakobson, writing in the *Ottův slovník naučný*, saw the Circle's main task as the "investigation of linguistic facts from the point of view of their function, and from the point of view of their relationship to language as an integral, systematic structure."[4] The emphasis is here on the concept of language as a structure, that is, as an organized set of symbols, each of which, in relation to other symbols, fulfils definite functions; these functionally delimited symbols are then hierarchically ordered into increasingly more complex configurations. Language thus is not viewed as a collection of sounds, words, or phrases or other linguistic elements, but, rather, as a structure built in a complex manner from these elements, very much as a building cannot be defined as a collection of bricks, but must be described in terms of its design, architecture, and purpose. It is because of this emphasis on linguistic structure that the term "structural linguistics" is frequently used to describe this approach. Perhaps one clarification is needed: I do not want to imply that the Prague Linguistic Circle was the first or the only group which advanced the notion of language as a structure. These concepts were contributed by many men in various countries; one can find them in the works of the pioneering Pole, Baudouin de Courtenay, of the Swiss professor Ferdinand de Saussure, who taught courses in general linguistics at the University of Geneva between 1906 and 1911, and whose ideas were published only posthumously, thanks to the efforts of his students who put their lecture notes together, or of the American linguist and anthropologist Edward Sapir, who had already published his basic and still very widely used treatise, *Language*, in 1921. In the Prague Circle, however, structural linguistics found a well organized and vigorous school. It provided a forum for the exchange of opinions, a stage for the development of concepts and formulations, and a center of publishing activity. These were some of the reasons why the impact of the Circle has been so pronounced in almost every country where this field of scholarship is pursued.

[4] Roman Jakobson, "Pražský linguistický kroužek", in *Ottův slovník naučný nové doby, Dodatky*, 5 (Prague, 1938).

It is natural that a view of language with a focus on the structural features of the linguistic code will attempt, in the analysis of the structure, to proceed from the basic level to the higher levels of language components. From this comes the dominant interest in phonology, the study of the functionally relevant properties of sounds, and of their distribution and organization in the speech sequence. The Prague school probably paid more attention to phonology than to all other levels of linguistic analysis combined; such interest, too, reflected the general tendencies of structural linguistics during the 1930's. I would like, for this reason, to dwell briefly on some of the principal aspects of the phonological theories and methodology of the Prague school. In the fourth volume of the *Travaux*, published in 1931 on the occasion of the International Phonological Conference held in Prague, the Circle proposed a standardized phonological terminology and definitions of basic phonological concepts.[5] This dictionary of terms and definitions gives an instructive insight into the principal methodological and theoretical notions of the Circle as they had been developed by that time. Phonology is there defined as that branch of linguistics which deals with the phonic phenomena from the point of view of their function in language; phonetics, on the other hand, is explicitly described as an *auxiliary* discipline of linguistics which deals with the linguistically relevant phonic phenomena from the point of view of their production and perception. The French linguist Tesnière, in his remarks regarding the proposed definitions, objected to this relegation of phonetics to the role of an auxiliary discipline. It is interesting to note, however, that the Prague school, although making such a hierarchical distinction of these two disciplines according to the functional criterion, never did evolve its phonological theory toward a fictionalist or algebraic model, as happened with some other modern linguists (Twaddell, the Copenhagen school). The Prague school defined the phoneme as a phonological unit not divisible any further into smaller and simpler phonological units. The actual physical reality underlying the concept of a phoneme is introduced into the definition by the requirement that all members of a phoneme have common acoustic and motor characteristics which differentiate them from all other sounds. This reliance on the phonic reality of the speech event is apparent not only in Trubetzkoy's later major work, *Grundzüge der Phonologie*,[6] but also in the phonological theory

---

[5] "Projet de terminologie phonologique standardisée", *Travaux*, 4 (Prague, 1931).
[6] Trubetzkoy's *Grundzüge der Phonologie* appeared originally as *Travaux*, 7 (Prague, 1939).

developed more recently in America by Jakobson and his collaborators in the so-called distinctive feature analysis.[7]

The Prague school paid considerable attention to what it called the correlational properties of phonemes. This notion, too, is later developed further in Trubetzkoy's work and, in a more sophisticated form, in Jakobson's distinctive feature model. In the Prague terminology, a correlational property is the opposition of the presence versus the absence of a certain phonic characteristic which can differentiate several pairs of phonemes in the language – as quantity differentiates, for example, the five pairs of vowel phonemes in Czech. This correlational property is conceived as an abstraction deduced from all the particular pairs which are found in such opposition. The phonic characteristic which, in opposition to the absence of such characteristic, forms the correlational property, is known as the mark of correlation; and the series of phonemes characterized by the presence of the mark constitute the marked correlative series, their opposites, the unmarked correlative series. The concepts of the archiphoneme and of the neutralization of phonemic oppositions, two concepts often considered with skepticism by American linguists, follow logically from the notion of correlation. The archiphoneme is an abstraction consisting of all those elements which two or more correlated phonemes have in common, such as the dental stop articulation of the Czech /t/ and /d/. In some languages, the voiced-vs.-voiceless feature which distinguishes such pairs as /t/ and /d/ may be, in certain positions, phonologically irrelevant, as it is in Czech at the end of a word. In such cases, a normally contrastive correlational property no longer results in a phonological contrast; Trubetzkoy then speaks of the "Aufhebung" or neutralization of the opposition. Some American linguists prefer different procedures to analyze such situations, speaking, for example, as Hockett does, of "partial complementation", and viewing neutralization and archiphonemes with skepticism because "they confuse the facts without adding anything."[8] Martin Joos dismisses these concepts of the Prague school as "obfuscation."[9] Without wanting to go into a detailed disputation, my personal impression is that the matter can hardly be bypassed so lightly, and that the Prague school, in this respect also, has offered a valuable analytical procedure.

[7] Cf. R. Jakobson, C. G. M. Fant, M. Halle, *Preliminaries to Speech Analysis* (Cambridge, Massachusetts Institute of Technology, 1952, 1955 and 1961); and R. Jakobson and M. Halle, *Fundamentals of Language* (The Hague, 1956).
[8] Charles F. Hockett, "A System of Descriptive Phonology", as reprinted in *Reading in Linguistics*, M. Joos, ed. (Washington, 1957), p. 101.
[9] *Ibid.*, p. 419.

The Prague school's awareness of the hierarchical organization and interrelationship of different linguistic levels is apparent in its differentiation of phonology into word-phonology and syntax-phonology; the former is defined as the investigation of phonic differences which are capable of distinguishing the meaning of words, the latter deals with phonic differences which delimit words in strings and distinguish the meaning of phrases. The concept of a morphoneme, which was recently reintroduced in this country as a basic unit of analysis by Morris Halle in his book on the *Sound Pattern of Russian*,[10] is defined in the *Travaux* dictionary in terms of the membership of the morphological alternation series.

There are many studies by the members and affiliates of the Prague Circle which apply these theoretical concepts and procedures in concrete analysis; perhaps a few should be briefly mentioned here. Some of the studies of Mathesius, dealing largely with problems of Czech and English, have been collected in the posthumous volume *Čeština a obecný jazykozpyt* (Czech and General Linguistics).[11]

Jakobson contributed, almost at the very beginning of the publishing activity of the Circle, his well-known study *Remarques sur l'évolution phonologique du russe comparé à celle des autres langues slaves*, in the second volume of the *Travaux*; this he followed by several studies in the *Travaux* and in *Slovo a slovesnost*, as well as in numerous other publications.

Bohumil Trnka, like Mathesius, generally drew upon English and Czech for his material, and contributed, aside from more specialized studies, (for example, his inquiry into the phonology of English)[12] a brief treatise on *General Laws of Phonemic Combinations* which, in my opinion, offers some valuable insight into a little-explored area of phonology.[13] The famous work of Nicholas Trubetzkoy, *Grundzüge der Phonologie*, which appeared originally as volume seven of the *Travaux* is, of course, one of the principal contributions of the Prague school.

Phonology, while perhaps the principal preoccupation, was not the only branch of linguistics which the Circle investigated. In view of the emphasis on the formulation of theory and methodology which characterizes the Prague school, it is not surprising to see that some of the basic concepts and procedures which I mentioned here in connection with phonology find a reflection also on other levels of analysis. This is true,

---

[10] Morris Halle, *The Sound Pattern of Russian* (The Hague, 1959).
[11] Vilém Mathesius, *Čeština a obecný jazykozpyt* (Prague, 1947).
[12] B. Trnka, *A Phonological Analysis of Present-Day Standard English* (Prague, 1935).
[13] In *Travaux*, 6 (Prague, 1936), pp. 57-62.

of course, of the more general principles, such as the stress on the functional role of linguistic elements and on the analysis of language as a structure. But it is also true of more detailed notions. In morphology, one has to remember only the well-known study by Jakobson, *Beitrag zur allgemeinen Kasuslehre*, published in volume six of the *Travaux*, in which the Russian case system is viewed in its total meaning (*Gesamtbedeutung*) and in which the aim is the discovery of morphological correlations which constitute the modern Russian declension, and the identification of the marked members of such correlations.[14]

Syntax, too, has been dealt with by members of the Circle, although less intensively. Perhaps Trnkas's study *On the Syntax of the English Verb from Caxton to Dryden*, published as volume three of the *Travaux*, should be mentioned.

Because of its emphasis on the function of linguistic elements, the Prague school rather naturally found an interest in the literary and poetic functions of language. Much work was done in the Circle on the nature of poetic language, its differentiation from ordinary communicational language, and the mutual influence of these two functionally distinct codes on each other. One of the early and most active members of the Prague Circle was the literary aesthetician, Jan Mukařovský, and among the Circle's most prominent members was the well-known literary scholar, René Wellek. Unfortunately, space and subject limitations will not allow me to go into this aspect of the Circle's activity which, too, had a world-wide influence.

Perhaps one other matter should be mentioned which has a place in a volume dealing with Czechoslovak culture. Although the Circle had an international character and membership, the very fact that its seat was in Prague focused much of its members' attention on the analysis of the Czech language, and involved the Circle also in the whole question of Czech language standards. In this last respect, the Circle's effect on the linguistic life in Czechoslovakia was quite dramatic. In 1931, the respected Czech philologist, Josef Zubatý, who had been editor of the periodical, *Naše řeč* (Our Speech), died, and Jiří Haller became his successor. *Naše řeč* had always viewed it as its task to determine the Czech language standard and had a tradition of moderate linguistic purism. With the advent of Haller to the editorship, the purism became militant. Mathesius, when writing about the event, rather colorfully describes Haller as one "who with the pedantry of a true epigone, began to dispense puristic reprimands

---

[14] *Travaux*, 6 (Prague, 1936), pp. 240-288.

to all sides."[15] All of this created something of an uproar among Czech writers and poets, and a vigorous controversy between them and *Naše řeč*. The Circle eventually stepped in with a defense of what might be called the doctrine of good usage as the basis of the standard literary language, and with an emphasis on the functionality of linguistic expression. The intervention in the controversy took the form of five lectures delivered by Mathesius, Havránek, Jakobson, Mukařovský, and Weingart, reviewing the whole question of standardization of the literary language, the matter of linguistic purism, the functional distinction between communicational language and the language of poetry, and the matter of standard pronunciation. The lectures, which aroused considerable interest even among the general public, were later published in the collection, *Spisovná čeština a jazyková kultura* (Literary Czech and Linguistic Culture).[16]

The members of the Circle also played an important role in the preparation of those volumes of *Československá vlastivěda* which dealt with language, i.e., volume three, published in 1934, and the special volume of series two, published in 1936. The study by Bohuslav Havránek of Czech and Moravian dialects, and other treatises in these volumes are still standard references for a scientific study of the Czech language.

The strength of the Prague Linguistic Circle was its international character and orientation, a natural outgrowth of the general atmosphere of Prague in those days;[17] in that respect, post-1948 Czech linguistics is the exact opposite. It has been marked by politically conditioned dogmatism and the unavoidable stagnation during the last years of Stalinism. It has been also marked by increasing Soviet-bloc parochialism which was so characteristic of Stalinist thinking, and by the fear of true internationalism which so paradoxically has become one of the phobias of Communism. The early 1950's in Czech linguistics make a rather sad story and I don't propose to dwell on them in any detail. It should be said, however, that the attack on some of the basic principles of the Prague school, and consequently the attack on many of the generally accepted concepts of modern linguistics, was waged especially fiercely in Prague, where the statues of Stalin seem to have been built bigger and the denunciations pronounced more loudly. The attack on formalism, cosmo-

---

[15] *Slovo a slovesnost*, 2 (1936).
[16] *Spisovná čeština a jazyková kultura* (Prague, 1932).
[17] A good insight into the conceptual and terminological framework of the Prague school is also provided by the recently published *Dictionnaire de linguistique de l'École de Prague*, edited by Josef Vachek in collaboration with Josef Dubský (Utrecht, 1960).

politanism, and all the other supposed sins of the structuralist school were led primarily by politicians, but, unfortunately, echoed also by some linguists; among them, the most prominently heard were one old man, now dead, František Trávníček, and one young one, Petr Sgall, who so appropriately made his main attack on structural linguistics in the political magazine, *Tvorba*. If one leafs through *Slovo a slovesnost* during the late 40's and early 50's, one comes across some rather symbolic things. In the first issue of 1948, for example, one finds the leading article written by Ivan Ivanovich Meshchaninov, the prominent disciple of Marr's "new language theory", which was a teaching so absurd that some two years later it was officially denounced even in the Soviet Union. And the second number of *Slovo a slovesnost* of 1950 devotes the first 14 pages to a discourse by that most famous linguist himself, Joseph V. Stalin.

It is not my purpose here to assign blame for this state of affairs. The linguists perhaps bear some of the guilt, but surely not the bulk of it. The situation in Czech linguistics has improved somewhat since the death of Stalin, and here is now at least some contact between Prague and the Western centers of linguistic research. Allow me to say, however, that the history of the Prague Linguistic Circle seems to me still a significant, even if at the present time inapplicable, guide-line for the future. Prague, being located physically at the crossroads of Europe, has to be there again intellectually and culturally also, before one can hope that it will contribute to contemporary culture and scholarship anything comparable in significance to what the Prague Linguistic Circle contributed between the two World Wars.

Moravian Codification of the First Slavic Literary Language

LADISLAV MATĚJKA

1. Great Moravia, the first Slavic dynastic state in Central Europe, was established in the 9th century. It included Moravia and Slovakia, and in the period of its widest expansion, it influenced Bohemia and probably also a part of Poland and the Western Ukraine. In 863, Great Moravia, tied politically to Byzantium, received two Byzantine missionaries, Constantine, later given the monastic name Cyril, and his elder brother Methodius. The highly reputed interpreter of these historical events, Francis Dvornik, calls the alliance of the Moravian prince with the Byzantine emperor a brilliant "stroke of diplomacy".[1] He indicates that the political and cultural emancipation of the semi-barbarian Slavic state in Central Europe was achieved by a shrewd balancing between Eastern and Western Christian cultural centers, or, more specifically, among Byzantium, Rome, and the Frankish heirs of the Carolingian Empire. For a time Great Moravia succeeded in playing a more or less independent role in the European structure, in spite of her strong Frankish environment. During this period, the first Slavic literary school was established, using Constantine's new alphabet, ingeniously adapted to the Slavic sound pattern and later called Glagolitic. Translations from Greek and Latin, together with the original literary productivity of the Moravian school, substantially contributed to the codification of the first Slavic literary language, known as Old Church Slavonic; the Moravian school founded the tradition which directly or indirectly influenced the formation of most of the Slavic literary languages.

2. The Byzantine Christian mission did not represent the very first attempt to evangelize the Slavic-speaking population in Europe. As far as we know, however, none of the previous attempts were made by Slavic-speaking missionaries. Among other obstacles faced by the Frankish,

---

[1] Francis Dvornik, *The Slavs, Their Early History and Civilization* (Boston, 1956), p. 82.

Irish, Greek, and Roman missions were difficulties in verbal communication with the Slavic pagans, not to mention the very important fact that most of the Western missionaries insisted on the Latin liturgy as a matter of policy. Constantine's biography, one of the original literary contributions of the Moravian school, emphasizes the message of the Moravian prince Rastislav to the Byzantine Emperor:[2] "Our people have rejected paganism and obey the laws of Christianity; however, we have no teacher who can interpret the true Christian faith to us in our language so that other countries, seeing this, would imitate us. Therefore send us, oh ruler, such a bishop and teacher, for from you good law always comes to all lands." *A Life of Methodius*, ascribed to Clement, the very prominent writer of the Moravian school, reports Rastislav's message as follows:[3] "Many Christian teachers have come to us, from Italy, from Greece, and from Germany, teaching us differently. But we Slavs are simple people, and we have no one who could instruct us in truth and talk sense..." Then the biographer continues: "The emperor Michael said to Constantine: 'Do you hear this speech, philosopher? For no one but you can do this... Take your brother, the abbot Methodius, and go there. For you are Thessalonians, and the Thessalonians all speak pure Slavic [*Solunjane v'si čisto Slověn'sky besědujǫt*]. Then God revealed to the Philosopher the Slavic writing [*slověn'sky knigy*], and having without delay constructed letters and composed the text, he set out for Moravia, taking Methodius with him."

Thus the Moravian Lives of the Slavic Apostles, together with other historical sources, indicate that Constantine and Methodius were speakers of a Slavic dialect used in their birthplace, Thessaloniki, in Northern Greece. This knowledge of a South Slavic dialect belonging to the Macedonian area qualified them for the evangelization of the Western Slavs, who certainly must have spoken a different dialect. There is no scientific method of reconstructing 9th century Slavic dialects to ascertain the degree of mutual understanding between a Macedonian and a Moravian speaker. On the other hand, linguistic analysis of the available information strongly indicates that in the 9th century a speaker of Macedonian had far better chances for using his dialectal code in lingual communication in Great Moravia than someone speaking Bavarian, Irish, or Latin. It is even possible that an educated Macedonian speaker was better off at that time in Great Moravia than, for example, a speaker of Rusnjak might be today, communicating in his Ukrainian dialect with someone using one

[2] *Żywoty Konstantyna i Metodego*, ed. T. Lehr-Spławiński (Poznań, 1959), p. 65.
[3] *Ibid.*, p. 107.

of the Eastern Ukrainian dialects, since the Ukrainian dialects have been exposed to diverse cultural influences for centuries. In the 9th century a vigorous differentiation of Slavic dialects was only beginning. Hence the dispatching in 863 of two Macedonian speakers to the Moravians who wished to be taught in their own language was probably quite justified by actual linguistic conditions.

3. The historical sources[4] lead us to assume that Constantine and Methodius spent approximately one year in preparing for their mission, Constantine composing his alphabet, and both of them working on the first translations of the liturgical texts. In this period Constantine probably began to translate the Evangeliarium, a selection from the New Testament starting with the Gospel according to St. John. Thus it may well be that the first line translated from the Bible into Slavic was: "In the beginning was the Word, and the Word was with God, and the Word was God (Iskoni bě slovo [i] slovo bě u B[og]a i B[og]" bě slovo".[5] Nevertheless, the literary activity of the Byzantine missionaries was not fully developed until they reached their destination. In Great Moravia, the translations included the four Gospels, an essential part of the Old Testament, the Psalter, and various liturgical texts. Although during the preparatory period between 862-863, Constantine and Methodius used only Greek sources and depended chiefly on the Macedonian dialect, in Great Moravia they and their pupils started to utilize Latin models as well, and Western Slavic features began to manifest themselves in the formation of the literary language. Moreover, the Moravian literary school obviously took advantage of the partial achievements of the earlier Christian missions, adapting to the Slavic formula mostly Latin and Old High German models needed for the Confession, and other fundamental Christian rites which could not entirely avoid using a vernacular. Words like *oplat"*, *m'še, papež'*,[6] were most probably used by the Western Slavs before the Byzantine mission. The Old High German text also served as a model for the oldest Western Slavic version of the Lord's Prayer; through it the

---

[4] *Ibid.*
[5] *Evangeliarium Assemani*, ed. J. Kurz (Praha, 1955), p. 2.
[6] Rajko Nahtigal, *Starocerkvenoslovanske študije* (Ljubljana, 1936). Cf. Karel Horálek, "K otázce lexikálních bohemismů v staroslověnských památkách", *Slovanské studie*, Sbírka statí, věnovaných prelátu univ. prof. dr. Josefu Vajsovi k uctění jeho životního díla (Praha, 1948), pp. 115-119; V. F. Mareš, "Drevneslavjanskij literaturnyj jazyk v velikomoravskom gosudarstve", *Voprosy jazykoznanija*, 2 (Moskva, 1961), pp. 12-23; A. Isačenko, "Nachträgliche Bemerkungen zur Frage der ältesten deutschslavischen literarischen Beziehungen", *Zeitschrift für sl. Phil.*, XIX (1947).

Old High German concept of "daily bread", "broot emizzigaz", "always existing", probably influenced Constantine's translation of this prayer in the New Testament, in spite of the fact that the Old High German "daily bread" deviates from the Byzantine "bread preserving the human existence".[7] The Moravian school obviously respected the established Christian nomenclature and, to some degree, the proto-Czech *usus loquendi*. Thus the codification of Old Church Slavonic was determined by more than one Slavic dialect and more than one European language; it was elaborated into a literary language which could convert all Slavic peoples and express the most subtle messages of the highly refined Greek and Latin. For a time, at least, historical circumstances and the location of Great Moravia on the border between the Western Latin and the Eastern Byzantine civilizations furnished very favorable conditions for this ambitious plan.

4. It is possible that Constantine's original intention was to establish a *liturgical language* for the Slavic Church; such a language could actually serve its purpose without being fully understood; a lack of complete understanding might even constitute a special value of a *liturgical language*. St. Jerome, the translator of the Vulgate, is known for his conviction that everything in the Scriptures, including the word-order, must remain a mystery. Old Church Slavonic, as it developed in Great Moravia, however, cannot be properly classified as a *liturgical language*. Even in the early years of the Byzantine mission, Old Church Slavonic in Great Moravia was probably used for a translation of the judicial law for laymen (*Zakon sudnyj ljudem*), a law collection of the Emperor-iconoclast, Leo the Isaurian. Quite recently, Josef Vašica pointed out the linguistic relationship between *Zakon sudnyj ljudem* and the second homily in the *Glagolita Clozianus*.[8] This homily, called by Vaillant "Method's homily", is, according to Vašica and Grivec, an exhortation of Methodius to the princes, reminding them of their obligation to act in accordance with Christian law. The homily, which seems to have been an original work of Methodius in Old Church Slavonic, contains a strong attack on paganism, particularly polygamy; it may well have increased the tension between Prince Svatopluk and Archbishop Methodius.

---

[7] Josef Cibulka, "Epioysios – nasǫšt'nyi – quotidianus – vezdejší", *Slavia*, XXV, 3 (Praha, 1956), pp. 406-415.

[8] Josef Vašica, "Origine cyrillo-méthodienne du plus ancien code slave dit 'Zakon sudnyj ljudem'", *Byzantinoslavica*, XII (Praha, 1951), pp. 154-174; "Jazyková povaha 'Zakona sudného ljudem'", *Slavia*, XXVII, 4 (Praha, 1958).

Josef Vašica concludes that the Moravian school also translated into Old Church Slavonic the *Nomokanon*, based on John Scholastik's canonical collection, *Synagoga*, and preserved in the 13th-century Russian copy known as *Ustjužskaja kormčaja*.[9] Vašica's conclusion recently received unexpected support by the discovery of a few Slavic glosses in a Latin judicial codex from the second part of the 9th century. These glosses annotate a legal passage in a manner which corresponds surprisingly to the *Ustjužskaja kormčaja*. According to current opinion, these glosses were engraved by a stylus into the parchment around 880 and, consequently, represent the oldest datable Old Church Slavonic text. Curiously enough, they are neither in Glagolitic nor in Cyrillic, but in Latin characters. They were analyzed in 1952 by W. Lettenbauer,[10] and are known in the literature as Emmeram's glosses because the codex was stored in the monastery of St. Emmeram in Regensburg.

These glosses dramatically illuminate Methodius' struggles on behalf of his mission during the period when his only supporters were the Roman Popes acting as a third power between the Eastern Byzantine and Western Carolingian Empires. Emmeram's glosses were found in a canonical collection assembled by the Greco-Roman clergy in Ravenna around 867. This judicial codex, with its Greco-Roman background, may well have been presented to Archbishop Methodius by Pope John VIII as a symbolic gift to emphasize his direct dependency on Roman jurisdiction, and his autonomous status vis-à-vis the Frankish clergy. The Slavic glosses annotate a passage which defines the rights of a bishop. The passage was probably quoted in a legal dispute, and the Slavic glosses based on the Old Church Slavonic *Nomokanon* were appended for the convenience of those not trained in the Glagolitic writing. Many questions about Emmeram's glosses still remain unanswered. Nevertheless, the glosses strongly support the assumption that Old Church Slavonic was used in Methodius' own diocese, in Great Moravia, and among Panonian Slavs, Slovenians, and Croats for legal matters. In this context, of course, Old Church Slavonic did not serve as a liturgical language.

5. Roman Jakobson, the most prominent contemporary expert on the Moravian period of Old Church Slavonic, has demonstrated[11] in his bril-

---

[9] Josef Vašica, "Metodějův překlad nomokanonu", *Slavia*, XXIV, 1 (Praha, 1955).
[10] Wilhelm Lettenbauer, "Eine lateinische Kanonessammlung in Mähren im 9. Jahrhundert", *Orientalia Christiana Periodica*, XVII (1952).
[11] Roman Jakobson, "St. Constantine's Prologue to the Gospels", *St. Vladimir Seminary Quarterly*, Summer 1954; "The Kernel of Comparative Slavic Literature",

liant contributions that Old Church Slavonic was also used from the very beginning for poetic purposes. According to Roman Jakobson, Constantine's remarkable prologue in verse to the translation of the Gospels is the first Czechoslovak poem. It glorifies the introduction into the Church of the vernacular instead of the incomprehensible languages, and preaches the equality of peoples:

>...Now hear with your understanding,
> Since you have learned to hear, Slavic people,
> Hear the word, for it came from God...
>...Slyšite nyně ot" svoego uma
> slyšaste ubo, slovenstii narodi
> slyšite slovo bo ot" Boga bo priide...

The *Prologue* is organized into twelve-syllable lines, with the obvious pattern of a caesura after the fifth syllable (74.5%) or the seventh syllable (25.5%). This type of versification indicates a Byzantine poetic erudition; the Byzantine models, however, cannot satisfactorily explain the frequent etymological figures, the alliterations, and various types of sound repetitions, e.g.,

Se s"byst" sę v" sedmyi věk" s' (This came to pass in this seventh millenium).

Many subtle poetic devices can also be found in the Kiev Leaflets, the oldest preserved Slavic manuscript, a tenth-century copy of an Old Church Slavonic translation of the Latin Mass formulary. Some parts of the Kiev Leaflets correspond, word for word, to the Sacramentarium of St. Gregory the Great, particularly the version preserved in a Paduan manuscript of the 7th century. In spite of the very close relationship of some passages, the Kiev Leaflets clearly deviate by frequent alliterations completely lacking in the Latin text, e.g.,

Priimi gi prosim" t prinos" s' prineseny tebě (suscipe quaesumus domine hostiam ...).

Miloš Weingart even found some rhymes in the Kiev Leaflets, and Roman Jakobson has pointed out the presence of etymological figures and traces of syllabism.

Some scholars ascribe the Kiev Leaflets to Constantine himself. It is evident that the author followed a Latin model, at the same time, however, utilizing Old Church Slavonic in such a way that the receiver's attention

---

Harvard Slavic Studies, I (1953); "Český podíl na církevněslovanské kultuře", *Co daly naše země Evropě a lidstvu*, I (Praha, 1939); *Moudrost starých Čechů* (New York, 1943).

is concentrated not only on the message, but on the language itself. Thus, the relationship among the words receives greater emphasis than is grammatically required. Such a focusing on the conveying means is one of the essential characteristics of a language used for poetic purposes.

6. Old Church Slavonic as it developed during the Great Moravian period was a literary language capable of being fully used for literature. It was artificial, as any literary language must be, particularly one used in an area of high dialectal differentiation. It was far closer to some Slavic dialects than to others, and it was obviously more understandable to better educated speakers than to the less educated. Its relationship to several Slavic dialects, as well as the Greco-Latin influence on its development, are reflected in its structure.

7. The activity of the Byzantine mission in Great Moravia lasted from 863 until 885, when it was suppressed by the Franks after the death of Methodius. It continued, however, in other Slavic countries, particularly Bulgaria and Bohemia. In the Czech principality in Bohemia, the tradition of the first Slavic literary language persisted until the end of the 11th century.

Original works of this period include the "Lives of St. Wenceslas" and his Grandmother Ludmilla, and the spiritual song, *Gospodi pomilui ny* (Lord, Have Mercy on Us).

The sophisticated tradition of Old Church Slavonic declined in Bohemia during the eleventh century, but in influenced, directly or indirectly, the formation of other Slavic literary languages. Some features in the oldest Russian manuscripts from the eleventh century could hardly be explained without acknowledgment of the Western Slavic contribution. This is true, for example, of the beautiful lyric composition, *Kanon" stgo Vjačeslava* appearing in the *Služebnyja minei* from 1095 to 1097. In this text appear several lexical and syntactical features known from the Kiev Leaflets; it also includes some of their poetic devices, such as alliteration and paronomasia:

> *Tělo tvoje stoe, blžne, priim" Prag" d'n's'*
> *prexval'n" ti grad" i pridiv'naja čjudesa mirovi*
> *prov"zvěščaet', prěv"znoša.*
> O Blessed, your holy body which was received today by
> Prague, your illustrious city, proclaims to the world
> your wondrous miracles, glorifying Christ forever.

The Influence of John of Neumarkt

ANGELIKA K. CARDEW

It is a well established fact that John of Neumarkt[1] exerted a great deal of influence upon his contemporaries. What is not as well established or examined, if we except his political influence, is the "how" and "why".

John of Neumarkt is usually referred to as having had great influence upon the standardization of the German language, upon the *Ackermann aus Boehmen*, and the first German Humanists. Let us examine his claim to nationality (as we know it), and what his aims in language were; I shall not dispute, but, rather, emphasize his achievements.

It cannot be said that John of Neumarkt was a "comet from nowhere". He was not a creative spirit, but a kind of a scholar, a teacher. By studying the period closely, we can see that the circle of John or Neumarkt closely resembled an "ivory tower" or a closed society.

Among his collaborators were Nicholas of Kroměříž and Paul of Jenštein, the brother of John Očko of Vlašim and father of the third archbishop, John of Jenštein. We also find John of Humpolec, an apparent protégé of the chancellor, and Notarius Otto, author of *Chronica Ecclesiae Pragensis*. Others were Notarius of the Chancellery Matthew of Cracow, the author of *De conflictu rationis* and *De Arte Moriendi*, and Milič of Kroměříž, the scribe and official who turned preacher of fiery eloquence. If John accepted these men, and even befriended them, we know that they must have been of the highest caliber, since he would not tolerate any inferior performance. To support this inference, we know that he had the scribe Elis driven from Kroměříž because of careless work on the copy of *De Gestis Domini* by Simon de Cassia (1348). We also know of his efforts to clarify the legal language of the *Codex Caroli*.

John is well known as an avid collector of manuscripts and manuscript copies, and as an investigator of translations and translator in his own right. Among the notable manuscript copies and translations are the

[1] Known also as John of Středa and Johannes Noviforensis.

Policraticus of John of Salesbury, *Questiones* of Buridan, and his own translation of *Soliloquiae*, etc.

The chief influences upon John of Neumarkt include the rhetorical treatise of Galfred de Vinsalvo, *Poetria Nova* (Patrologia, Migne), which might account for his rather bombastic style. That it is a work which was familiar to Bohemia we know, since Heinrich Hainburg (another stylist) quotes him upon the death of Přemysl Otakar II, and its influences upon *Plankty Magdaleny* had been established.[2] We know that the author of *Ars Dictandi*, Henricus de Isernia, was influenced by Ovid[3] and had a school of rhetoric in Prague.[4] Another influence prevalent at the time was that of Johannes de Garlandia (*De Musica, De ritmis, De trimitate Ecclesiae*). Let us add the influence of Italy and Petrarca, and we have about 75% of the make-up of John of Neumarkt. Therefore, his style and interests were not highly original.

Yet what is unique is the force by which he influenced a local group, and imparted to them such a standard of style that the prayers of Milič could be confused with his own.[5]

Not only the scribes were influenced by him. John of Jenštein's *Book of Dialogues* is dedicated to John of Neumarkt; and in the *Codex Epistolaris*, we find what has been called a touching lament upon the death of John of Neumarkt. Even the letters of the *Codex* show the prevalent rhetorical "Formulae" and the influence of John of Neumarkt, although Jenštein's style is a little simpler and a little different, probably due to the difference in date.

The consolation Jenštein finds in his lament is not "gratia dei deorum", but the fact that John of Neumarkt left all his books behind. In style, he does use a few of the stock phrases his master might have admired, and the technique of gradation of tropisms. However, the letter has a genuine ring.

Some of the letters of John of Neumarkt have that same genuine ring, not the judicial and business letters, but those concerned with literature and language.

I shall now quote from a letter by John of Neumarkt written to Emperor Charles IV: "Nam et ibi sunt philosophiae naturalis ac loycae termini et exquisita vocabula theologica et magnae retionis profunditas, ut nedum *intellectus mei parvitas*, immo vix sancti Hieronimi grata facun-

---

[2] Vilikosky, p. 386.
[3] *Ibid.*, p. 170.
[4] Černý, p. 244.
[5] *Analecta hymnica medii aevi*; Dreves-Blume; Klapper; Vilikovský, p. 112.

dia ad interpretandum eam sufficeret, etiam si permissione divina adhuc in carne persisteret et eandem *ad nobilem linguam Sclavonicam producere niteretur*" (italics mine). Translated, this reads: parvitas intellectus mei... would try to extend to the noble Slavic language ... If we follow his complaint further, we find "incompta verba linguae Teutonicae etc." Johannes is complaining about the slow progress of his translation of Hieronymus. (In German, the *extant* text.)

As we know,[6] Charles IV speaks of Czech as the sweet and smooth native language, and we know that Czech was called Charles" "lingua naturalis – lingua bohemica". Although the reference in the document for Emaus was called an *Arenga*[7], and this is defined as "preface to capture the benevolence and made as an ornament", the letter of John is no *Arenga*.

Another fact worth mentioning is that after the death of Conrad Waldhauser, Milič of Kroměříž adds German to his Latin (for clergy and and clerics) and Czech sermons for the people. Jenštein, too, knew all three languages. What can we deduce from these simple facts? That the culture bearers, and even the reformers (at least those influenced by our chancellor), were trilingual.

This seems to have been the main cultural accomplishment of the circle of John of Neumarkt. I might claim that the *Arenga* preceding the *Ackermann aus Boehmen* (Hueber emendation) has something to do with this topic. We find there: "Epistola oblata petro rothers civi pragensis cum libello ackerman de *novo dictato*" (italics mine). Do we translate *de novo* as "recently" or "anew"? I maintain that it should be the latter. We know that the author, John of Teplá (*et aliae*), was a protégé of John of Jenštein, and was acquainted with the sermons of Milič and Hus. It has been established that the author of *Ackermann aus Boehmen* borrowed whole passages from John of Neumarkt. Since the *Ackermann aus Boehmen* has a Czech successor in *Tkadleček*, it would not be wrong to assume that there might have been a Latin predecessor. This was very often the case in that "Mutual Translation" society. Even from the text of Ackermann we can assume that the author was familiar with the vernacular.

What, then, is the influence of John of Neumarkt? What did he contribute to Western culture?

As far as style and translation efforts are concerned, he clearly influenced all the leading spirits of his time and place – John of Jenštein, Milič of

---

[6] Werunsky, I, 443 et al.
[7] Werunsky, *ibidem* (I, 443 ff.).

Kroměříž, John of Teplá, *et al.* What was this contribution? The introduction of tri-lingualism and all the connotations inherent in that fact – not literary humanism – but humanism.

SELECTED BIBLIOGRAPHY

Guido M. Dreves, S. J., and Blume, S. J., *Lateinische Hymnen* (Leipzig 1909).
——, *Analecta Hymnica* (Leipzig, 1886).
Jan Vilikovský, *Písemnictví Českého Středověku* (Prague, 1948).
Václav Černý, *Středověká Lyrika* (Prague, 1947).
Zdeněk Nejedlý, *Dějiny Predhusitského Zpěvu* (Prague, 1904).
Franz Bäuml, *Rhetorical Devices in Ackermann von Boehmen* (U. of Cal., 1960).
Konrad Burdach, *Vom Mittelalter zur Renaissaince* (Halle, 1893).
Cancellaria: Caroli IV.
   Johanni de Jenzenstein
   Ernesti
   Johanni Noviforensis
Archiv für Österreichische Geschichte, Vols. 53, 55, 60, 61, 68.
Briefe des Johannes von Neumarkt, ed. P. Piur (Berlin, 1937).
Scriptores rerum Germaniae, M G M.
Patrologia: Mign.
Joseph Klapper, *Gebete des Hofkanzlers Johanes von Neumarkt* (Berlin, 1935).
Emil Werunsky, *Kaiser Karl IV. und Seine Zeit* (Prague, 1900).
Ludwig Rockinger, *Briefsteller und Formelbucher* (New York, 1961).
Jaroslav Vlček, *Dějiny Literatury České*, I (Prague, 2 editions).

MUSIC AND FINE ARTS

Music in Czechoslovakia

KAREL B. JIRÁK

The peoples of Czechoslovakia, especially the Czechs or, in the now outmoded terminology, the Bohemians, have long been recognized for their musical gifts. "Every Czech a musician" was a famous slogan, and the great English music historian, Dr. Charles Burney (1726-1814), who, in 1772, traveled in Central Europe, collecting materials for his *General History of Music*, wrote this in his travelog[1]: "I had frequently been told, that the Bohemians were the most musical people of Germany [sic!], or, perhaps, of all Europe; and an eminent German composer, now in London, had declared to me, that if they enjoyed the same advantages as the Italians, they would excel them. I crossed the whole Kingdom of Bohemia from south to north; and being very assiduous in my enquiries, how the common people learned music, I found out at length, that, not only in every large town, but in all villages, where there is a reading and writing school, children of both sexes are taught music." He describes then how he found the music instruction in the little town of Čáslav (45 miles S.E. of Prague): "The organist and cantor M. Johann Dulsick (?), and the first violin of the parish church, M. Martin Kruch, who are likewise the two school-masters, gave me all the satisfaction I required. I went into the school, which was full of children of both sexes, from six to ten or eleven years old, who were reading, writing, playing on violins, hautbois and bassoons, and other instruments. The organist had in a small room of his home four clavichords, with little boys practising on them all: his son of nine years old, was a very good performer." Dr. Burney further describes that the school-master later, in the church, played for him an admirable "voluntary" (prelude) on the organ, and an "extempore fugue, upon a new and pleasing subject, in a very masterly manner; and I think him one

---

[1] *The Present State of Music in Germany, the Netherlands and United Provinces* (London, 1775), Newly edited by Percy A. Scholes as *An 18th Century Musical Tour in Central Europe and Netherlands* (London, Oxford University Press, 1959). Cf. Chapter X, p. 131-132.

of the best performers on the organ, which I heard throughout my journey."

This was, of course, in the 18th century, when all Europe was flooded with Czech musicians, so that "Bohemia" was sometimes called "the music conservatory of Europe". (The real Conservatory of Music was founded in Prague in 1811 as the first school of this kind in Central Europe – before Vienna and Leipzig.) The Czech musicians abroad were emigrants from their then-impoverished country. They were good technicians who fertilized the musical life in foreign lands, without, however, demonstrating much originality. Indeed, some of them were little more than vagrant, half-educated musicians, although others occasionally were first rate virtuosi who became real assets to their adopted countries.

Even as late as the 19th century there was widespread conviction that the Czechs were merely good players or interpreters, but not real, creative artists. An argument on this subject among admirers of Liszt in Weimar allegedly stimulated Smetana to the resolution that he would show the world how good and independent Czech music could be.

One aspect of the proverbial Czech, Moravian, Silesian, and Slovak musicality has received universal recognition; it is the multitude of extraordinarily beautiful folksongs, recorded and still partly living in all four regions of the country. Each has its distinctive characteristics, from the Western type of musical formulation in Bohemia to the more Eastern type in Eastern Moravia and Slovakia. Such differences are quite natural in a country that lies at the crossroads of Europe, West to East. The number of Czechoslovak folksongs recorded in the archives of the Czechoslovak State Institute of Folklore goes into the tens of thousands, and is still only partly published. (The official count in 1948 was over 25 thousand.)

The origins of music in what is now Czechoslovakia are lost in the darkness of the Middle Ages. According to the most recent studies, there was some Byzantine influence in the church of the Great Moravian Empire (830-906), which is natural when we know that this part of the country was Christianized by the brothers, SS. Cyril and Methodius, who came from the Greek town of Saloniki. Literary research has proved that the words of the oldest spiritual hymn, "Hospodine, pomiluj ny" (Lord have Mercy Upon Us), the first religious song composed in Central Europe, were composed according to the rules of the Old Slavic liturgy. Thus we know that this song, which is still sung, incidentally, in Czechoslovak churches, was definitely written before the beginning of the 11th century, when the influence of the Byzantine church was succeeded by that of the church of Rome.

After the fall of the Great Moravian Empire, efforts to standardize the liturgy directed Czech musical attention toward the West, to which it remained oriented. To the end of the 12th century, European music was entirely governed by the monodic principle – unison singing – which in Bohemia encouraged only the composing of folk hymns to be sung at religious services, and, later, of secular art songs, both based on the Gregorian chant in all its forms. Among the most important songs of this period are "Svatý Václave" (a hymn invoking St. Wenceslas, Patron Saint of the country) and "Jezu Kriste, ščedrý kněže" (Jesus Christ, Our Generous Lord) from the first half of the 14th century. These songs are much simpler than analogous contemporary hymns in France; the monodic principle, with its simplicity, was retained in Bohemia long after the music of Western Europe had already adopted the polyphonic style in the so-called Ars Nova and Netherland Schools. Even in the first half of the 15th century, Jan Hus and his followers, the Hussites, stuck to the old monodic style when the West was already stirring with the beginnings of polyphonic music. The reason, of course, was mainly religious. The Hussites were strictly opposed to all luxuries, ornate ecclesiastic regalia, and also, unfortunately, to the liturgical art music. This delayed the development of music in Czech lands for at least two centuries. One compensation, however, was the heritage of religious hymns of such greatness and vigor that their influence was long felt in neighboring lands·

The Hussite hymns are basically folk songs, simple, but full of melodious strength, just as the Hussite movement itself was strong. The most famous of the hymns, "Ktož jsú Boží bojovníci" (All Ye Warriors of Lord) allegedly turned the crusaders sent against the Hussites into panic flight even before the battle. A romanticized form of this song is conspicuous in the works of Smetana and Dvořák as, symbol of the glorious past.

The influence of the Hussite hymns is clearly evidenced in later Lutheran chorals composed in Germany. In Czech music, the hymns were an important influence from the 15th to the 18th century, their most recent descendants being the hymns of the Bohemian or "Moravian" Brethren which later became the Herrenhut hymns and were brought to the so-called "Moravian" settlements in America. These Czech religious folk songs are quite distinct from German, French, or Italian religious songs as a lasting monument of the Czech creative spirit.

Secular music did not develop in Czechoslovakia until the end of the 14th century, when the name of Magister Záviš appears. His music, even though marked by personal melodious originality, is inferior to contemporary "lays" of other countries. The new music of the 15th and 16th centuries penetrated rather slowly into the Czech lands, because the

Hussite movement, with its unfortunate political and economical consequences, limited contact with contemporary music of other European nations. The polyphonic system first reached Bohemia toward the end of the 15th century, during the reconstruction period under King George of Poděbrady (1458-71), and after the ascension of the Hapsburgs to the Bohemian throne in 1526. At that time, new contacts with the Netherlands brought new music. Musical fraternities were organized (so-called "Literátská bratrstva"), usually connected with some church, but still rather conservative in upholding the old traditions of church singing within the principles of the new style. We may see their high standards in the still-extant, handwritten hymnals of the 15th and 16th centuries. Beside these more or less religious organizations, there were also private orchestras. The best were the royal orchestras of Ferdinand I and Maxmilian II (between 1526 and 1564) in Prague, but many other good ones were organized by members of the nobility, such as the Rožmberk orchestra in Český Krumlov. During the reign of Rudolph II (1575-1612) Prague was a center of European musical life, and the home of masters like Philip de Monte, Charles Luyton, Jacques Regnard, Jacobus Handel-Gallus, and others. Such unusually propitious conditions could not leave Czech music untouched. The major composers who accepted the new polyphonic style were Jan Trojan Turnovský, Jiří Rychnovský, and Christoph Harant of Polžice, the latter a nobleman who subsequently became one of the insurgent generals against the Hapsburgs and was beheaded in the mass execution in front of the Prague City Hall in 1621.

The suppression of this uprising and the ensuing Thirty Year's War were another obstacle in the progress of Czech music. The Hapsburg court was moved from Prague to Vienna, and the military catastrophe of the Battle of the White Mountain which destroyed Czech political independence dealt a mortal blow to cultural life in Bohemia. The ensuing period of wars, confiscations, oppression and general impoverishment hardly encouraged the development of musical arts. Thus, the early Baroque period, when the new style (the "stile rappresentativo") was created, and a new form, the opera, was born, saw the Czech lands half dead, suffering under oppression and under the blows of counter-reformation. Czech aristocracy and intelligentia, belonging either to the Unity of Bohemian (Moravian) Brethren or to the Lutherans, were exiled or executed. The last bishop of the Bohemian Brethren, Jan Amos Comemius (also a good musician), wrote his famous pedagogical works in foreign countries and died in Holland. Czech lands were a cultural desert. Nothing of musical significance appeared there for a long time.

Recovery was slow. Meanwhile, Baroque music, both Catholic (in Italy and France) and Protestant (in North Germany), flourished elsewhere. The first Czech master of Baroque music was the half-legendary Bohuslav Černohorský (1648-1742), allegedly the teacher of Giuseppe Tartini and Chr. W. Gluck, in whose learned fugues there are interludes which resound with folkloristic melodies. Unfortunately only a few are preserved. The Dresden court conductor, Jan Dismas Zelenka (1679-1745), one of the first famous emigrant musicians, has often been compared with Joh. Seb. Bach, his contemporary. Zelenka did not forget his Czech descent, for he wrote a St. Wenceslas oratorio. Francis Tůma (1704-1774), a famous contrapuntist, and Černohorský's pupil, Jan Zach (1699-1773), one of the early representatives of the new instrumental style, besides Joseph Seeger (1716-1782), a famed organist and teacher, also belong to the first wave of Czech musical emigrants.

In the mid-eighteenth century a new change occurred in music: the transition from the solemn Baroque style to classicism, in a sort of stenographic abbreviation, from Bach to Mozart. The transitional period between these styles is crowded with Czech composers, so-called "Kleinmeisters" or "lesser masters", who contributed, stone by stone, brick by brick, to the monumental development of what is today known as musical classicism, the foundation of our present-day music. In this era there was a remarkable outburst of musical talent in Bohemia and Moravia, based, indubitably, on the natural gift of the Czech people for music, especially instrumental music, and on the generally high standards of popular music education, as described in the book by Charles Burney mentioned previously. Unfortunately, most of these gifted musicians felt it necessary to emigrate from their native country because of the provincialism which prevailed there after the imperial court was transferred to Vienna. Most of the remaining Czech aristocracy also went to Vienna, where they, too, played an important role in the music life of that capital. The premiere of Beethoven's "Eroica" symphony, for instance, took place in the Vienna palace of the Czech Princess Lobkowicz; most of Beethoven's supporters and patrons were Bohemian aristocrats, and his circle of friends included many musicians of Czech origin.

Miss Vogl-Garrett's article (see p. 134 of the present book) deals with this important phase of Czech music. Therefore, we will mention only the most important names, such as George Benda (1715-1795) in Germany, whom the young Mozart admired and whose best works are comparable with those of Beethoven's middle period; the famous operatic composer, Joseph Mysliveček-Venatorini (1737-1781), the "divine Bohemian", also greatly admired by Mozart; and the enormously important group of Mannheim musicians, headed by Jan Václav Stamitz (1717-1757) from Bohemia and Fr. X. Richter (1709-1789) from Moravia, who initiated a new style in instrumental music. The latter were both, in their younger days, connected with a humble conductor of Count Questenberg's orchestra in the Jaroměřice castle in Moravia, Francis Václav Míča (1694-1744), who composed many oratorios and operas, some based on Czech texts, and who seems to be among the first to use the new orchestral style in his overtures.

Let us not exaggerate the significance of all these "lesser masters". They did not create the new style; they were precursors, not accomplishers, and even though some of them were very successful in their time, sometimes even more successful than such masters as Mozart and Beethoven, they are all but forgotten today, and live chiefly in doctoral dissertations and music dictionaries.

Only a few of them stayed at home. Among these, the most influential was Francis Xaver Brixi (1732-1771), the music director of the St. Vitus cathedral in Prague, a prolific composer of more than 440 works for the church. His music has a spontaneous, melodious character and a clear harmony, without the serious monumentality of the Baroque style, and prepared his country for its enthusiastic acceptance of Mozart, who was so rudely rejected in his beloved Vienna and best understood in Prague. The incomparable success of his "Marriage of Figaro" and "Don Giovanni" in Prague was a landmark in the history of Czech music, which was long influenced by Mozart. Later, in the 19th century, this predilection for Mozart became almost a handicap to the new trends which appeared in the dawn of romanticism.

An intelligent, yet stubborn, guardian of the Mozart tradition in Prague was Václav Jan Tomášek (1774-1850), for many years the "music pope" of Prague. To him, Beethoven was "too modern", yet even he was not left untouched by the new style, especially in his piano "Eclogues" and in his songs, some of them to the words of the so-called "Královédvorský" manuscript. They are unmistakably romantic.

During Tomášek's life, an enormous change occurred in the spiritual life of the Czech nation. The White Mountain disaster in 1621, with its economic and cultural consequences, and the Hapsburg-Viennese centralization of power, together with the ever-increasing Germanization, had all but destroyed the Czech nationality in the Austrian monarchy. Toward the end of the 18th century, practically only peasants still spoke Czech. Secondary and higher education were available only in the German language. Then, suddenly, and ironically enough, under the influence of the German Herderian humanitarianism, the Czech renascence began. A sense of national pride began to spread and within a few decades, almost a new nation was reborn in the heart of Europe.

During the transitional period, those patriots who wanted to create a new Czech cultural life bore a heavy load. The intelligentsia, educated perforce in German schools, had essentially to relearn their own language. German historians never fail to stress the fact that even Smetana as an adult had to learn Czech spelling. They do not feel that it was rather the Germanophile regime's, not Smetana's, shame, because in Smetana's youth no schools in the Czech language, above primitive level, were permitted.

The Czech "national school" of music started rather modestly with songs in folk style written by Jan Jakub Ryba (1765-1815), who also wrote a Christmas mass, based on Czech carols, which is still the delight of Czech Cristmas programs; choral works in similar manner were composed by Alois Jelen (1801-1857). Soon enough, in 1886, the first Czech opera, "Drátenik" (The Tinker), was produced by Francis Škroup (1801-1862), and won enthusiastic acclaim. Škroup's music, of course, shows the influence of the early romantic and German operas; his later works were mostly failures. However, he deserves to be remembered as the composer of the Czech national anthem, "Kde domov můj" (Where is my home?). Also important were choruses in folkloristic style written by the Moravian priest, Pavel Křížkovský (1820-1885).

The first real genius of Czech music was Bedřich (Frederick) Smetana (1824-1884), whose name will always be associated immediately with his comic opera, "The Bartered Bride" (1866), a world-renowned masterpiece. This opera, however, is only a lucky, almost marginal, stroke of genius. Smetana has a far greater significance for Czech music. He singlehandedly created Czech opera (both tragic and comic), the new Czech symphonic music (especially in his monumental cycle, "My Country") and laid a foundation for the development of characteristically Czech chamber music, piano, and vocal literature. His artistic standards were very high. He demolished the amateurish notion that a national music means imitations of folk songs. He violently opposed such concepts and actually never quoted any folk tunes (except in arrangements of folk dances); in "The Bartered Bride" there is not a single melody that is not his own. And yet every Czech recognizes in this music his own soul and spirit. This phenomenon is hard to describe: Smetana's music bears the stamp of his own personality, yet it has a mysterious, almost subliminal, tie with the Czech national spirit. Smetana's personal fate was extremely unhappy. He wrote the last three of his eight operas, the "My Country" cycle, and 2 quartets in total deafness, and died in an insane asylum.

Luckily, another great Czech composer was born very soon after Smetana: Antonín Dvořák (1841-1904). In 1884, in the very year of Smetana's death, Dvořák's oratorios and symphonies were triumphantly received, under Dvořák's own direction, in England. Dvořák is more famous abroad than Smetana, because his style is more international, based more on the principles of classicism. He wrote nine symphonies and a stately number of significant chamber music works, as well as nine operas and several great oratorios, some of which were composed directly for big choral festivals in England. His fame started with his colorful Slavic Dances and Rhapsodies, but he was soon recognized as one of the leading European composers, especially in the field of symphonic and chamber music. In 1892 he was invited, as a world celebrity, to become the director of a new, important institution in New York, the National Conservatory; he spent three years in the United States as a teacher of young American composers. He advised them to use the American folk idiom, especially Negro spirituals and certain Indian rhythms, as the basis for a body of new American music. These ideas were not widely accepted by the American musicians, chiefly because of prejudices, but at least Dvořák gave the Americans, who had up to that time been educated principally in Germany or by German professors, the first powerful impulse to create a new, independent American style in music. More important for Dvořák was, of course, the new impressions received in this country, which left an unmistakable imprint on his own music. Some of his most famous works, the "New World" symphony, the "American" quartet, the Cello Concerto and the "Biblical Songs", were written in America.

After three years in America, Dvořák's homesickness drew him back to his beloved country, where he resumed professorship at the Prague conservatory, giving his country a galaxy of young composers who, in their turn, have dominated Czech music as the famous "Dvořák School" for at least 50 years.

This brief article does not permit us to go deeper into the life of Smetana and Dvořák, nor to analyze their artistic relationship.[2] However, with these two composers, the existence of a special Czech school of music as a historic entity was firmly established. Their contemporaries and followers

[2] This was attempted in my study *Antonín Dvořák* (New York, Czechoslovak Society of Arts and Sciences in America, 1961).

included many good, or even outstanding, composers, of whom we can mention only a few.

The third major composer who was active during Smetana's and Dvořák's lifetime, was Zdeněk Fibich (1850-1900), a Schumannesque romantic dreamer productive in all branches of music. He composed one of the most imposing tragic operas of Czech musical literature, the "Bride of Messina" (based on Schiller's fatalistic drama), but his most valuable contributions to world music were his melodramas, or recitations with accompanying music. This form, first brought into being by J. J. Rousseau, was cultivated in the 18th century by the aforementioned Czech émigré, Fr. Benda, and later, intermittently, by some romantic composers. Of these, Zdeněk Fibich is by far the most important, because he succeeded, as no one before him, in bringing poetry, recitation, and the sound of music into accord so that each retained its own importance, yet contributed to the total effect. After several concert melodramas, Fibich wrote as his culminating effort a melodramatic trilogy, "Hippodamia", based on a dramatic poem by the great Czech poet Jaroslav Vrchlický. This monumental drama with continuous musical accompaniment was not only influenced by the form of Wagner's tetralogy, "The Ring of the Nibelung", but was hailed by some writers as the final perfection of Wagner's dramatic principles. It was a gallant experiment, historically a positive contribution to the development of dramatic music, but it remained without lasting consequence, although the principle of melodramatic recitation appears again, intermittently, in some modern operas, such as "Wozzeck" by Alban Berg. Furthermore, Fibich was, like Dvořák, a successful teacher, and his best pupil, Otakar Ostrčil (1879-1935), later became not only one of the most distinguished modern Czech composers, but also an outstanding conductor of the Czech National Opera between the two World Wars.

Two composers followed very closely the great triad of Smetana, Dvořák, and Fibich, at least chronologically. One was Jos. Bohuslav Foerster (1859-1951), a fine lyricist, composer of five symphonies, cantatas, and several operas, who never became much known outside of Czechoslovakia, but was the beloved master of many younger musicians, including the present writer. Foerster's best known contributions to Czech modern music was in the field of choral literature. In particular, his choruses for men's voices raised the artistic level of Czech choral singing and it is with his compositions that the famous Czech choral organizations have been winning highest awards in many international singing contests.

The other master, born only 13 years after Dvořák, Leoš Janáček (1854-1928), is Foerster's antipode. Foerster was a traditionally minded lyricist, Janáček a violent non-conformist. For a very long time he was unrecognized at home, much less known abroad. In 1916, when he was 54 years old, his opera "Jenufa" was successfully performed in Prague and soon after in Vienna; from there it started its glorious journey into the whole world. This belated success so stimulated the aging composer that he wrote, in the 12 years that remained of his life, five more operas, a sinfonietta, chamber music works, two short piano concertos, a Slavonic Mass, and many smaller works. He is the first great composer of Czechoslovakia born in Moravia, which folkloristically lies farther to the East than Bohemia. Janáček himself was much interested in Moravian folklore, and certainly his "Jenufa" and other works show its strong influence. But it would be a mistake to consider folklore his only inspiration. He was far too great a composer for this. There is also another inspiration in Janáček's music: his love of Russian music, especially that of Mussorgsky. But the most important role in his increasing success was played by his own strikingly original personality. He was, so to speak, a lone wolf of Czech music, without predecessors and actually without successors, because none of his numerous pupils followed his whimsical, sometimes odd, ways of expression; perhaps they are inimitable. Although Janáček has been dead for over 30 years, he is now being discovered in one country after another, and his fame is constantly growing, especially in England and Germany.

During the long years when Janáček lived undiscovered and unrecognized, a host of Dvořák's pupils dominated Czech music. Among them the most influential were Vítězslav Novák (1870-1949) and Josef Suk (1874-1935), Dvořák's own son-in-law. Both departed, in time, from the path of Dvořák's neo-romanticism into the all-powerful realm of the early 20th-century's impressionism, even in its modified, Slavic form. Both of them contributed greatly to the modernization of Czech music; Suk cultivated mainly instrumental forms, while Novák's larger output embraces both instrumental and vocal forms, including cantatas and operas. Although their works compare favorably with, and rather surpass, the works of many other composers of their time abroad, they remained almost unknown in America. Suk is more fortunate, because at least his melodious String Serenade, his Fantasy for Violin and Orchestra, and some of his violin pieces are occasionally performed, but not, unfortunately, his symphony and his symphonic poems. Novák's music, however, remains almost unknown. Perhaps it is because impressionism now is "deader than dead" and the general trend is away from profound programs of symphonic poems. But history changes continuously; what was dead yesterday is very much alive today, and so maybe the world will discover one day the wonderful music of both Novák and Suk.

Vítězslav Novák was for almost five decades the most sought-after teacher of composition. His position in Prague was comparable to that of the aforementioned "music pope" of Prague, J. V. Tomášek, more than 100 years before. The number of his pupils is unbelievable; hardly any musician of the younger generation, including this author,[3] did not go, some time or other, through his school. It is impossible to enumerate them. One facet of Novák's activity is, however, of the utmost importance. Although born in Southern Bohemia, he acquired in his early manhood a special fondness for Moravian and Slovak folklore. He not only became a real expert in this field, but also wrote a substantial part of his compositions in a deliberately Moravian style, a rare case of acquiring a regional character, not by birth, but by choice. Thus, quite logically, Novák has become, since the incorporation of Slovakia into the new Czechoslovak republic, the beloved teacher of Slovak musicians. We have not yet mentioned Slovak music in this study at all, for the simple reason that no genuinely Slovak art music existed until 1918. Only in the Czechoslovak republic did the Slovak young musicians find an opportunity to cultivate their rich musical folklore and to forge with it a new Slovak branch of Czechoslovak music. In this process, Vítězslav Novák was enormously helpful. There is now a host of contemporary Slovak composers of middle age or younger, most of whom were Novák's pupils. If we mention only those who contributed to the world musical scene, we must cite Eugen Suchoň (born 1908), who has won some international success, especially with his opera *Krútňava* ("The Whirlpool"), which was performed in Germany and elsewhere.

Among Novák's pupils there was also a daring extremist who is invariably mentioned in all handbooks on modern music: Alois Hába (born 1898), the protagonist of the "quarter-tone music", who tries to write music not only based on new sounds derived from the splitting of chro-

---

[3] Karel Boleslav Jirák, composer, conductor, writer, educator. Since 1947 Chairman of Theory Department, Chicago Musical College of Roosevelt University. Compositions: opera, "Woman and God", orchestral works (5 symphonies), chamber music (10 sonatas, 7 string quartets, etc.), cantatas, piano music, over 100 songs, etc. Books: *Musical Forms*, in Czech, 5th edition (Praha, Hudební Matice, 1946); in Serbian (Belgrade, Prosveta, 1948), Biographies of W. A. Mozart, pianist Jan Heřman and Zd. Fibich (Prague, Orbis, 1947 and 1948); *Antonín Dvořák*, in English (New York, Czechoslovak Society of Arts and Sciences in America, 1961).

maticism, but also in a new, so-called "athematic style" that rejects the whole historic past, in which music was based on repeating and developing musical themes. Like many other modernists, Hába, an old Communist, hoped that the new political régime would support his revolutionary ideas. In the beginning, it seemed that he would succeed. He was promptly made the director of the second opera house in Prague, and his first production was a quarter-tone opera of his own, "The Mother". However, the régime soon imposed strict limitations on such "decadent bourgeois" excesses. Whereas the democratic Czechoslovak republic gave Hába a chair at the Prague State Conservatory to teach quarter-tone composition, and appropriated funds to build new quarter-tone pianos and other instruments needed for performance of his music, quarter-tone music is now banished as imcompatible with the new realism in art, and Alois Hába is now a frustrated man.

Of the younger composers now active in Czechoslovakia – and there are hosts of them – I can only state that none of them has become really known abroad. Many of them are certainly gifted musicians, like Iša Krejčí (born 1904), Miloslav Kabeláč (born 1908), and Klement Slavický (born 1910) – all three, incidentally, this writer's former students at the Prague Conservatory – but none of them has won a decisive success abroad. Renowned successors of the Novák-Suk generation seem to be the Novák pupil, Ladislav Vycpálek, a fine lyricist often given to ascetic mysticism (and also the author of a Psalm cantata dedicated to the memory of T. G. Masaryk, written, of course, before the last war), and Jaroslav Křička, who won considerable international success with his opera, "The Ghost in the Castle" (with the text of this Society's honorary member Dr. Jan Lowenbach). Both Vycpálek and Křička were born in 1882 and celebrated their 80th birthdays in 1962.

The composer who in the last decades most successfully represented the Czech music abroad, was an artist who somehow does not fit into any category of Czech music as I have described them. He is Bohuslav Martinů (1890-1959), the most admired Czech composer in exile. He had a very checkered career, starting as an undisciplined youth who failed at the Prague Conservatory, could learn nothing from Josef Suk or, later, from Albert Roussel in Paris, and who in spite of it moved to uncontested world fame. He emigrated long before the war, in 1923, to Paris, where he was first influenced by Stravinsky and the Group of Six. He passed through a period of constructivism and neoclassicism, briefly trying some jazz. For a long time his favorite style was a modern version of concerto grosso, but in his later years he returned more and more to the native sources of

Czech music, even to its folklore. He went through many phases; there is even a surrealist opera among his compositions, "Juliette", with a libretto by the French surrealist poet, Georges Neveux, as well as adaptations of Czech and Moravian folksongs, ballets, symphonies, concertos, and chamber music. His output was enormous, written during the last years on commission in America. He came to America during the last war, after the fall of France, settled there, and became an American citizen. Although he was appointed professor of composition at the Academy of Musical Arts in Prague in 1947, he resisted the call to return to his native country and never went back. During the last years of his life he lived in Europe and died in Switzerland. Since his death, his compositions have not been as frequently performed as during his lifetime, probably because the steady flow of new works has ceased. Yet his music is still in high esteem. After a recent performance of his Sixth Symphony by the Boston Symphony Orchestra, conducted by Martinů's friend, Charles Munch, the critic of *The New York Times* wrote a few lines which summarize quite well the impressions made by his later compositions: "Like many of the late composer's works, it is full of reminiscences of other music, stylistic references that run the gamut from Brahms to impressionism to Stravinsky. It is often mysterious, sometimes commonplace, usually colorful; it is romantic, vital, inconsistent, odd, assertive. It is all these things and more; yet somehow everything is managed together in a work that has very much his own kind of statement and personality."[4] These lines could serve as a motto on the title page of all Martinů's compositions. Yet Martinů was, undoubtedly, the most successful Czech composer on the world scene in our time, and his contribution to world music can be compared, at a certain distance, with that of Antonín Dvořák.

In this brief survey we were unable to mention the high standards of Czechoslovak performing artists, some of whom have attained world fame, whether they where violinists (the name of Jan Kubelík is still in world's memory), pianists, conductors, or singers. (Of these, the still unforgettable Emmy Destinn and the tenor Karel Burian belonged to the stars of the Metropolitan Opera in New York.) The recent death of the brillant Czech conductor Václav Talich, "the Toscanini of the Slavic world", reminded the connoisseurs of his own contribution to the art of conducting, not only in Czechoslovakia but also abroad.

Among the Czech musicians living abroad in a self-imposed exile, the most successful are the distinguished conductor and composer Rafael

---

[4] Eric Salzman in *The New York Times*, Feb. 25, 1962.

Kubelík (b. in 1914, son of the world-famous violinist), the brilliant pianist Rudolf Firkušný (b. 1912), and two young composers: Oskar Morawetz (b. 1917) in Toronto, Ont., and Karel Husa (b. 1921), of Cornell University, renowned also as a conductor.

Today's music life in Czechoslovakia enjoys very high technical standards under the present régime. At least ten state-supported symphony orchestras and about twenty year-round opera houses compare with the best institutions of any other country. In an official Czech music almanac for 1960, nearly 300 composers of all kinds are listed, beside almost 200 musicologists and music critics. Economically, the composers are reportedly pretty well off, provided they write in the style of the approved Socialist realism. Radical excesses or deviations are frowned upon, so that all contemporary Czech music brought to the attention of the Western world is invariably labeled "conservative".

This has been a sort of survey, a bird's-eye view, of how much Czechoslovakia has contributed to the world musical scene. With all modesty it can be said that it is a fairly sizable contribution that compares favorably with that of much larger nations.

BIBLIOGRAPHY

Czech Music (General)

Zdeněk Nejedlý, *Dějiny české hudby* ("The History of Czech Music") (Praha, Hejda & Tuček, 1903). Out of print.
Vladimír Helfert, *Česká hudební tvořivost před Smetanou* ("Czech Creative Music before Smetana") (Praha, Kmen, 1935). Out of print.
——, Erich Steinhard, *Geschichte der Musik in der Tschechoslovakischen Republik. – Histoire de la musique dans la République Tchécoslovaque* (Praha, Orbis, 1936). Out of print.
"Hudba v Československu", soubor statí v VIII. díle *Československé vlastivědy*, redaktor Jan Branberger (Praha, Sfinx, Janda, 1935). ("Music in Czechoslovakia", in volume VIII of the *Československá vlastivěda*). Out of print.
An Informative Book on Czechoslovak Music in English, French and Russian (Prague, Orbis, 1936).

Different Historical Periods:

Zdeněk Nejedlý, *Dějiny předhusitského zpěvu v Čechách* ("The History of Czech Song in Bohemia before the Hussite Wars") (Praha, Král. česká společnost nauk, 1904). Out of print.
——, *Počátky husitského zpěvu* ("The Early Stages of Hussite Song") Praha, Král. česká společnost nauk, 1907). Out of print.

——, *Dějiny husitského zpěvu za válek husitských* ("The History of Hussite Song in Wartime") (Praha, Král. česká společnost nauk, 1913). Out of print.

Dobroslav Orel, *Počátky uměleho vícehlasu v Čechách* ("The Beginning of Polyphony in Bohemia") (Bratislava, Filozofická fakulta, 1922). Out of print.

Hubert Doležil, *Česka píseň reformační a vývoj protestantského chorálu* ("Czech Reformation Song and the Development of the Protestant Choral") (Praha, Sfinx, 1939). Out of print.

Vladimír Helfert, *Dvůr Rudolfův, Dvorská kapela* ("The Court of Rudolph II, His Court Orchestra") (Praha, Sfinx, 1939). Out of print.

——, *Hudební barok na českých zámcích* ("Baroque Music in Czech Castles") (Praha, Čes. Akademie věd a umění, 1916). Out of print.

——, *Hudba na jaroměřiokěm zámku* ("Music at the Jaroměřice Castle") (Praha, Čes. Akademie věd a umění, 1925). Out of print.

Jan Racek, *Duch českého hudebního baroku* ("The Spirit of Czech Baroque Music") (Brno, Akord, 1940).

——, *Italská monodie z doby raného baroku v Čechách* ("Italian Monody of the Early Baroque Period in Bohemia") (Olomouc, Velehrad, 1945).

Alois Hnilička, *Portréty starých českých mistrů* ("Portraits of Old Czech Masters") (Praha, Borový, 1922). Out of print.

——, *Profily české hudby z prvé poloviny 19. století* ("Profiles of Czech Music of the First Half of the 19th Century") (Praha, Borový, 1924). Out of print.

Zdeněk Nejedlý, *Bedřich Smetana*, I-IV (Praha, Hudební Matice, 1924-33). Unfinished.

Mirko Očadlík, *Tvůrce české moderní hudby, B. Smetana* ("Smetana, Father of Modern Czech Music") (Praha, Práce, 1945).

Otakar Šourek, *Antonín Dvořák, život a dílo*, I-IV ("A. Dvořák, His Life and Work") (Praha, Hudební Matice, 1922-33).

Alec Robertson, *Ant. Dvořák* (New York, Pellegrini & Gudahy Inc., 1949).

Josef Bartoš, *Zdeněk Fibich* (Praha, Zlatoroh, 1914). Out of print.

K. B. Jirák, *Zdeněk Fibich* (Praha, Orbis, 1947).

Bohumír Štědroň, *Leoš Janáček, Letters and Reminiscences* (Prague, Artia, 1955).

——, *The Work of Leoš Janáček* (Praha, Library of the Hudební Rozhledy, 1959). In English.

Miloš Šafránek, *Bohuslav Martinů* (Praha, Stát. hud, nakladatelství, 1961).

Czechoslovak Music, I: *Bohemia and Moravia* (Prague, Orbis, 1948). Almanac of articles; in English.

Czechoslovak Music (Prague, Orbis, 1946). In English; articles by Vlad. Helfert, Jos. Plavec, Jiří Dostál, Ferd. Pujman, et al.).

The Influence of 18th Century Czech Composers on the Development of Classical Music

EDITH VOGL GARRETT

Despite the widespread musical culture which astonished travelers to Bohemia in the 18th century, Prague was fast losing its position of musical ascendency. For, with wealth, patronage, and power vested almost exclusively in Teutonic hands, and the seat of government shifted to Vienna, the nobility who as patrons of the arts had helped to make Prague the center of European music, followed the court to the Austrian capital. They chose prosperity rather than the inevitable poverty they would face by remaining in Prague; there could be little thought of patriotism. Consequently, in the words of a Czech historian, "almost all the musical sources which welled up from the soil of Bohemia sped by the shortest course to join the mainstream of the world's music". The best chances for success lay in exchanging nationality for universal citizenship. In the eighteenth-century composers whose names took on the etymological coloring of the land in which the exiled chanced to have settled, we will see a solid array of musical talent and industry, great executive ability, pedagogic gifts of the highest order, and occasional flashes of inspiration which, under happier conditions, might have developed into something even more potent.

As a result of the Counter Reformation, under the rule of Charles VI, everyone registered as Brethren or Protestant was considered a criminal. This was another reason that entire families of composers migrated out of Bohemia. The Benda family, for example, went to Berlin, for just these reasons of religion. The chief centers of this musical migration were in Germany, France, Italy, and Vienna.

From the musical point of view, the two most important cities in 18th-century Germany were Mannheim and Berlin. Mannheim had a predominantly French culture, as Voltaire often visited there. This was the only place where there was a court orchestra, since the orchestra had been more fully developed in the French courts some decades earlier by the composer Lully. Other German courts indulged predominantly in opera. Mannheim's orchestra in the mid-18th century was the best in Europe. It consisted of 22 violins, 4 violas, 4 violoncellos, 2 double basses, 2 clarinets, 2 oboes, 2 hunting horns, 2 trumpets, and 2 tympani.

The most important Bohemian composer at Mannheim was Jan Václav Stamic (Johann Stamitz), 1717-61, the son of a great cantor in Německý Brod (Deutschbrod), who had come originally from what is now Yugoslavia. Because of the name of his birthplace, Stamic was called by the Germans, *Boemus Teutobrodensis*.[1] In 1741, he went to Frankfurt, then to Mannheim the following year, in the service of Carl Theodore, the Elector of Pfalzbayern (Bavarian Palatinate). Carl Theodore had a beautiful baroque theater, and was himself a skilled musician. Stamic joined the orchestra in 1745, and soon became its conductor. He inaugurated at Mannheim an entirely novel style of orchestral music and orchestral performance, which laid the foundation for the Viennese classical school at the time when the tradition of baroque music had reached its culmination in the late works of Bach and Handel.

Conspicuous features of the new style are: melodic prominence of the violins in an essentially homophonic, non-contrapuntal texture; abandonment of imitation and fugal style; presto character of the quick movements; use of orchestral effects such as tremolos and broken chords in quick notes; dynamic devices used as a structural principle, e.g., extended crescendos, unexpected fortes, and general rests. The new musical subjects rise quickly over a wide range, usually in triadic arpeggios. One of the most significant innovations, however, was the replacement of the thorough bass accompaniment with written-out orchestral parts. When the harpsichord, which used to fill in the chords and otherwise implied harmonic foundation, was eliminated, the orchestra, so to speak, "lost its pedals". It was necessary to find a new means of completing the harmonic texture, and this function was transferred to the woodwind instruments, especially the horns, which now had a very prominent position in the overall structure.

Stamic composed 50 symphonies. The first movements are mostly in sonata form with two contrasting themes. The 3-part form of the first movement (A-B-A) is related to the Neapolitan *da capo* aria. In Stamic's compositions the development section of the sonata form is usually confined to a few sequences, and is immediately followed by the recapitula-

---

[1] German musicologists (e.g. K. M. Komma in *Das Böhmische Musikantentum*, Kassel, 1960) are trying to prove that Stamic was a German. However, the newly discovered personal documents (testaments of his father and his brother, all written in Czech) demonstrate sufficiently that his original nationality was Czech.

tion. The second movement is usually slow, in a 2- or 3-part form, sometimes with variations. The third movement is a minuet with trio; the closing movement either is in a rondo-like form or approaches sonata form.

Stamic's formal scheme for a four-movement symphony was preserved up to the time of Beethoven, and thus Stamic is, if not the inventor, at least one of the pioneers of the classical forms in European instrumental music. Not only did Stamic foster the growth of a conscious feeling for formal design, but he also created hospitable conditions for a new and colorful sound of the orchestral ensemble. It was at his suggestion that, as early as 1748, horns were introduced into the Paris orchestra.

Stamic exerted a strong influence on the melodic language of the Viennese classical school by introducing a melodic line based on Italian models, but also derived from Czech folk motives. In quick outer movements the melody is often playful and abounding in embellishments; in slow movements it widens out into a broad, pathetic *cantilena*. So-called melodic sighs, which are actually suspensions in seconds, are common. Appoggiaturas, acciaccaturas, and gruppettos, so significant in the language of Caldara and Conti, also occur frequently. Instrumental compositions characterized by a merry, creative atmosphere, optimistic cheerfulness, and a warm, lyrical melodic line – all of these qualities are also typical of the earlier and later Viennese classical style.

An example of his symphonic writing is his Symphony in A major, called the "Spring" Symphony (1754). This work expressed the mood of spring, a swift upsurge of excitement, joy, and enthusiasm. In the subsidiary theme of the first movement there is an imitation of bird calls. This descriptive method made an entirely novel impression, for in Stamic's work, it sprang from an authentic and real source, a truly spring-like and natural mood.

The work of Jan Václav Stamic was continued by his two sons, Karl (1745-1801) and Johann Anton (1754-1809). The elder son studied in Mannheim, his birthplace. He studied violin with Cannabich and composition with Holzbauer. Later he became second violinist in the orchestra. Johann Anton was more conscious of his Czech background, and his works show more of the style derived from the Czech folk idiom. He was employed in the Paris orchestra.

Among the other Czech composers who went to the Mannheim court were František Xaver Richter (1709-89), a Moravian by birth, whose works have an affinity with, and similarity to, those of Haydn and Mozart, and Antonín Fils (1730-60), a pupil of Jan Václav Stamic. The sound and dynamic elements in his scores (e.g., his concerto in D major for flute and orchestra) bear testimony to the application of a new principle of composition, which presented European music with so many creative stimuli and gave rise to the great epoch of musical classicism. It is significant that Mozart visited Mannheim twice – once as a child, in 1762, and again in 1771, at which time he met all the personnel of the orchestra, and studied many of the novel techniques. This second trip was very important in the development of Mozart's symphonic writing.

The musical scene in eighteenth-century Berlin furnishes us with an example of an entire family from Bohemia which became absorbed, for the reasons we have mentioned, into the ranks of German musicians: the Benda family might be called the Bach family of Bohemia.

The first was Jan Jiří Benda (1685-1757), whose wife was a member of another musician's family, Brixi. Benda combined the occupations of weaver and local musician in the villages of Staré and Nové Benátky. His four sons and one daughter all distinguished themselves in the musical profession, and in at least two instances passed their talent on to a third generation.

František, the oldest son, was a choir boy in Prague, and later entered the Jesuit Gymnasium, where humanistic studies were paramount. He turned Lutheran, and went with the Elector to Vienna, Breslau, Warsaw, and Dresden. From 1740 on, he was concert master to King Frederick II. He played the violin like a magician, and composed mainly for that instrument. He wrote an autobiography, which included accounts of all his family. Two of his sons followed in his footsteps: Friedrich Wilhelm Heinrich (1754-1814) was a member of the court band and a composer of operas, oratorios, and instrumental works; Carl Hermann Heinrich (1748-1836) was an esteemed violinist.

The weaver's second son, Johann (1715-1752), spent all his life in Germany. He joined František in Berlin and also became a member of Frederick the Great's orchestra.

The youngest son, Joseph (1724-1804), was a violinist in the service of Friedrich Wilhelm II, and lived in Berlin, where his son Ernst (1747-85) was also a professional musician who helped to introduce amateur concerts in the Prussian capital.

Anna Franziska (1726-80) was a well-known singer, who married the German composer Reichardt in 1779.

The most important figure was the third son, Jiří Antonín, "Georg", who made a European reputation as the most successful composer if not inventor of the modern melodrama, i.e., recitation accompanied by orchestral music.[2] He spent most of his life in Gotha, a part of Thuringia, a province with a rich atmosphere and heritage. The Masonic order had spread in northern and central Germany. He absorbed many of its concepts, in addition to the philosophical thoughts of Voltaire and Rousseau.

In Gotha, Georg Benda's duties consisted of supervision of the music in church and in the court theater. In addition, he found time for creative work in chamber music, church music, and dramatic compositions. He found Italian music superficial and opposed everything he had acquired in his solid German education. On the other hand, ambition spurred him on to achieve success in the theater; his first stage was Munich.

A chain of unexpected events now led to Benda's opportunity to do something great and new for dramatic art. In 1774, the Duke of Weimar's castle, including the theater, was destroyed by fire. The actors suddenly found themselves without employment, and the Duchess of Weimar wrote to the Duke of Gotha asking his assistence for the homeless company. An invitation to the ducal palace theater of Gotha was gratefully accepted. Among the company were Johann Christian Brandes and his wife; it was for Brandes that Benda gave up his post at Gotha and wrote his melodramas, "Ariadne auf Naxos" and "Medea".

Benda did much to prepare the way for the culmination of classicism as typified by the work of Beethoven. The new methods of composition are evident not only in his cantatas and dramatic works, where he conveys an intensity of expression and a sense of tragic pathos in the spirit of Gluck's reforms, but also in his instrumental music, where he achieves a masterly combination of profound thoughtfulness with his typically Czech musical talent. His individual and melodious style grew from the folk elements of his native land, which helped to form his musical speech. His "Singspiels" influenced the development of Hiller's style. Benda is considered the precursor of Beethoven's classicism.

For reasons of space, we can mention only briefly composers who emigrated to other countries. The most important composers who went to Paris include Antonin Rejcha (1770-1836), the successor of Cherubini at the Paris Conservatory and composer of numerous woodwind ensemble works which are as popular today as then; he was a progressive composer whose works helped to open the way for Romanticism. Another was Jan Václav Stich, known as Giovanni Punto (1746-1803), a virtuoso horn player for whom Mozart wrote his Sinfonia Concertante for winds

[2] It was actually J. J. Rousseau who wrote the first melodrama (*Pygmalion*) in 1772, two years before Benda's first "duodrama" "Ariadne in Naxos".

and orchestra, and of whom Mozart said: "Punto bläst magnifique".

Only one Czech composer made a success in Italy writing operas; this was Josef Mysliveček (1737-81), a friend of the Mozart family, who greatly influenced Mozart's style. Indeed, his renown prepared the ground for Mozart's success in Prague, five years after Mysliveček's death. It is well known that the "Marriage of Figaro" was not as successful in Vienna at its first performance as it became in Prague. This is because Mysliveček's musical language was recognized in his native Bohemia, and therefore Mozart's style was more familiar in Prague. It was as a result of the "Figaro" success in Prague in 1786 that "Don Giovanni" was commissioned and premiered the following year in the Bohemian capital.

Vienna attracted most of the composers who were seeking steady employment, such as František Tůma (1704-74), Florian Leopold Gassmann (1729-74),[3] Jan Křtitel Vaňhal (1739-1813), and Leopold Koželuh (1747-1818), the latter best known now for his arrangements of Scottish folk songs for the Edinburgh publisher George Thomson. František Krommer-Kramář (1759-1831) is noteworthy for the distinctly Czech flavor of his melodic idiom, expecially in his oboe and clarinet concertos. Space does not permit us to enumerate and evaluate all the excellent Czech composers who settled around the Vienna court.

One of the composers who did not leave his native land was František Václav Míča (1694-1744), who held the position of both musician and valet to Count Questenberg in Jaroměřice (Moravia). These dual occupations were an economic custom at the small courts in the 18th century. Antonio Caldara, the second court conductor, and composer of 87 operas at the Viennese court when Joh. Josef Fux ruled the musical taste of Vienna, was a frequent guest in Jaroměřice, and we find mutual influence between Caldara's and Míča's dramatic style. There has been some confusion as to whether certain works were composed by him or by his nephew, František Adam Míča (1746-1811), a Viennese civil servant, for whom music was an avocation, but who earned the respect and admiration even of Mozart.

The influence of the Czech composers on the classical style of Gluck, Haydn, and Mozart persisted in later generations: as an example, we need only cite the influence of Tomášek, Voříšek, and Dusík on the young Beethoven.

Charles Burney, the 18th century English music historian, called

---

[3] Gassmann, a native of Most (Brüx) in Northern Bohemia, was a Bohemian of German nationality.

Bohemia "the Music Conservatory of Europe". This continuous contribution to musical composition and performance all over the world throughout the centuries exists in our own time as well, and let us hope that music, the universal language, will enlighten our musicians everywhere.

SELECTED BIBLIOGRAPHY

Richard Batka, *Geschichte der Musik in Böhmen* (Prague, 1906).
Charles Burney, *The Present State of Music in Germany, the Netherlands and United Provinces* (London, 1773-75).
Vladimír Helfert-Erich Steinhard, *Geschichte der Musik in der Tschechoslowakischen Republik* (Prague, 1936).
Musica Antiqua Bohemica (Publication of Early Czech Music) (Prague, Artia).
Zdeněk Nejedlý, *Dějiny české hudby* (Prague, 1903).
Rosa Newmarch, *The Music of Czechoslovakia* (Oxford, 1943).
Jaroslav Pohanka, *Dějiny české hudby v příkladech* (Prague, 1957).
Jan Racek, *Česká hudba od nejstarších dob do počatku 19. století* (Prague, 1958).
Jan Němeček, *Nastín České hudby XVIII. století* (Prague, 1955).
Jaroslav Čeleda, *Josef Mysliveček* (Prague, 1946).
Maurice Emmanuel, *Antonín Reicha* (Paris, 1937).

Czechoslovak Painting from its Beginning until the Second World War

MOJMÍR S. FRINTA

The task of surveying and evaluating Czechoslovak painting in this present brief form is a difficult and involved one. The main problem is to steer a course honorably between Scylla and Charybdis, i.e., on one hand, to avoid the piling up of names and monuments, and on the other hand, not to fall prey to generalizations in an effort to achieve a synthesis.

Yet a still greater problem is to establish the scope of the artistic manifestations to be included, a problem based on the varying definitions of Czechoslovak art. For the very word "Czechoslovak" loses its meaning more and more as we go back into the years before the nineteenth century. Its Czech and Slovak components must be viewed separately in the more remote past because they evolved under different historical and cultural conditions, first in the Bohemian and Hungarian kingdoms, and then as parts of Austria and Hungary. We have to decide whether Czechoslovak painting means for us all art created in the present territory of Czechoslovakia, or only that for which the native Czech and Slovak artists were responsible. And what about German nationals native there? Imported works of art are, of course, automatically left out, but we must decide for ourselves: what about the imported artists themselves? Foreign-sounding names appear often in the documents, and here we are free to make a more subtle – and tricky – differentiation between those who settled there and became "acclimatized", and the pure, unassimilated foreigners. And what criteria are we going to follow in dealing with anonymous paintings, murals, and manuscript illuminations?

The separation of artists of Czech and German nationalities was rigidly observed in most writings only after the revolutionary era of 1848. With each period the criteria differ: in the Middle Ages, the internationalism of the monastic orders which stood in the forefront of artistic production gave to nationality a more or less geographic content. The elevation of Prague to the status of capital of the Holy Roman Empire further reduced the importance and relevancy of nationality in art, in our modern sense.

We may wonder whether the word "Bohemian" should not be used instead of "Czech", to avoid any arguments about particular national claims.

Prudence and a certain elasticity of mind are required in order to strike a balance between stressing the fruits of Czech genius regardless of where they ripened, and stressing the formative and inspirational powers of the *genius loci*. The first approach justifies, for example, the inclusion of two eminent emigrant-artists of the Baroque period – the graphic artist Václav (Wenceslaus) Hollar, who settled in Western Europe, and the portraitist Jan Kupecký, active in Germany and Austria. By the same token, František (François) Kupka, living in Paris, must be mentioned in the history of Czechoslovak art.

On the other hand, the second viewpoint entitles us to speak of Gothic mural paintings at Karlstein, by Nicholas Wurmser of Strassburg, of the Baroque sculptures of the Brokoffs, the paintings of the present-day Willy Nowak, and some works of the half-Czech Oskar Kokoschka produced during his Prague period. We are aware of the subjectivity of such criteria for selecting artists. These same criteria, however, have been applied in other studies of the world history of art, with such examples as Veit Stoss (Wit Stwosz), Claude Lorrain, Vincent Van Gogh, Pablo Picasso, Walter Gropius, Amadeo Modigliani, and many other emigrants and bi-nationals.

Our earliest examples of painting in Czechoslovakia belong to the mural painting and manuscript illumination of the Romanesque period. There, the fruitful interplay with the chief European trends can be well observed. The art of painting attained a higher level of quality and sophistication that the contemporaneous sculpture. It is particularly in the chief work, the *Vyšehrad Codex* (the Coronation Evangeliary of King Vratislav), sumptuously illuminated in about 1085, that the Prague production equals the European level. Bavarian influences and, possibly, those of Lower Saxony may be recognized there. In the course of its subsequent development, the school assimilated characteristics of the schools of Salzburg, Cologne, and the Valley of the Meuse, yet never degenerated into a dependent art devoid of originality. The thirteenth century is marked by an intense interest in Byzantine expressive forms as manifested in the "zig-zag" style. Bohemia ceased her chief dependence for inspiration on Western styles and favored those of Northern Italy (Padua, Venice). This phenomenon is well illustrated in the similarity of monumental spirit in the illuminations of the Sedlec Antiphonary (middle of the thirteenth century) to the style and decorative motifs of the Paduan school (Givanni da Gaibano) and the wall paintings on the North shore of the Adriatic and Jugoslavia.

The number of preserved Romanesque mural paintings is small, and probably the best among them, those decorating important churches in larger centers, perished with the buildings. Two ensembles, however, an extensive cycle depicting the genealogy of the Přemyslids in the rotunda in Znojmo (1134), and the frescoes in St. Clement's in Stará Boleslav (third quarter of the twelfth century), testify to the quality of the monumental painting in Bohemia and Moravia which influenced even the manuscript illumination. The subsequent, more Southern orientation may be perceived in fragmentary lay paintings from a Prague house, in their relation to such murals as those in the cathedral of Aquileia.

It is only shortly before the end of the thirteenth century that the Romanesque vocabulary of forms is replaced by the Gothic. The earliest example from the realm of murals exists in the decoration of the Church of the Virgin's Nativity in Písek. The wall paintings of the first half of the 14th century generally are still below the high level of European production, but qualitative progress may be seen in such large cycles as those in the house of the Knights of St. John in Strakonice, and even more in the Castles Houska and Jindřichův Hradec (1338). Unfortunately, the legend of St. George, as depicted in the latter, is disfigured by repainting, but we glimpse the quality of this Western-oriented style in a country church in Křeč near Jihlava. Again, it is difficult to evaluate properly the early Gothic frescoes, because the undoubtedly more mature and accomplished works in larger centers have disappeared. A considerable proportion of those preserved are only rustic offsprings in country churches.

All these mural paintings owe much to the style that evolved in Bohemian manuscript illumination, which was in close contact with the progressive art of the West, mainly the French-English schools. We find Western parallels for the group of manuscripts which Queen Elizabeth Rejčka commissioned around 1320, as well as for the expressive illuminations in the Passionary of Abbess Cunegonde (ca. 1320), some of which attain an almost unparalleled intensity of feeling, and for the linear style of the Velislav Bible (ca. 1340). Religious orders played an important role in transmitting these influences, and many of the early illuminators were probably members of some order. (On the other hand, we do know the names of two Romanesque lay painters, Hildebert and Everwin.) It appears that lay painters took over the production in the studios formed in the towns when a great surge of artistic activity took place under the Luxemburg dynasty.

The second half of the 14th century marks the culmination of Czech mediaeval art. It is the time when Bohemia was no longer receiving outside influences, but had become one of the focal centers of European art. With the coronation of Charles IV, Prague became the capital of the Holy Roman Empire, and indigenous artists, as well as foreigners (e.g., Wurmser of Strassburg, Tomaso da Modena), who flocked to the Court, were busy producing panel paintings and illuminated manuscripts – an impressive number of them – although a mere fraction of the former wealth has been preserved. Bohemian production attained great fame because of the exquisiteness of style and form, and many products were exported. Influence radiating from Bohemia not only reached neighboring countries, but can be detected also as far as in Northwestern Europe.

The Franco-Gothic style prevailing in Europe in the first half of the 14th century undoubtedly contributed much to the formation of the original style of the Bohemian school around 1350. But the Bohemian artists had begun also to be interested in Italian ideas of form, such as spatial relationship, architectural representation, modelling of volumes, and intricacy of color. The Sienese concept exerted far greater impact than did the Florentine art, and examples of Simone Martini's and Lorenzetti's art may be recognized in Bohemian panel painting more readily than the more monumental and severe art of Giotto.

The truly Bohemian school was initiated by the creative genius of an anonymous master called after the Cistercian monastery of Vyšší Brod (Hohenfurt), where the panels, once forming a large retable, have been preserved. His art, which is dated ca. 1350, shows a great step forward from the style of the Austrian panels at the Klosterneuburg monastery. His style, also apparent in the painted Madonnas of Zbraslav, Veveří, and Kladsko, was carried to Silesia and East Prussia.

Quite a different artistic ideal from that of the Master of the Vyšší Brod was embodied in the paintings of Master Theodoric. As the painter of the court of Emperor Charles IV, he decorated the Holy Cross Chapel at Karlstein Castle sometime before 1367. His powerful and highly personal forms emphasize the volume, unlike the earlier linear trend, and epitomize the "Soft Style" at its best. Though likely autochthonous, the possibility of the origins of Theodoric's art in the region of the lower Rhine can not be wholly discarded as fantastic. Theodoric's followers continued his style in Prague (the votive panel of Očko of Vlašim, the Mühlhausen retable) and abroad (the altarpiece from Tirol Castle, murals in Niepołomice in S. Poland, and in Levoča, Slovakia). Master Bertram of Minden, active in Hamburg, whose art is strikingly similar to that of Theodoric, perhaps spent his apprenticeship in Prague. However, the relationship of various paintings done in the Soft Style throughout Europe is quite complex, and a certain universalism of artistic ideas within the German Empire and Netherlands provinces could account for the affinity of works of this stylistic trend. A few English manuscripts and mural paintings (cf. fragments in the London Tower) show us that the style spread even further West. It might have been carried there by Netherland or North German artists, or, perhaps, directly from Bohemia on the occasion of the marriage of Anne, daughter of Charles IV, to King Richard I in 1382.

North Italian, mainly Bolognese, illumination style was amalgamated with the Western-inspired style in the Prague ateliers. Most notable is the *Liber viaticus* of John of Středa (Neumarkt), after 1360 – which belongs to the highest achievements of the period in all of Europe; John of Opava, who in 1368 wrote and illuminated an Evangeliary, derived from the circle of Bishop John of Středa. In the last quarter of the century, art stagnated into a coarser and less idealistic style. The prolific illuminators of the Court of King Wenceslaus IV excelled more, perhaps, in the sumptuous and original foliage decor of the borders than in the painted scenes themselves.

The third great personality, as we follow the apogee of Bohemian panel painting, is the Master of Třeboň (Wittingau), named after a town in South Bohemia in which the panels have been preserved. His scenes have a great dramatic power heightened by a technique of chromatic *chiaroscuro*. His noble art is one of the starting points for the "Beautiful Style" which swept from its cradle in Bohemia through the whole of Central Europe up to the Rhine. Both painting and sculpture of the period around 1400 followed the esthetic and formal principles of this courtly, refined style. Its salient creations are the so-called Beautiful Madonnas, painted (the St. Vitus' Madonna) and sculptured (the Krumlov Madonna), and the statues of the Pietà. The Beautiful Style may be viewed as part of a broad European movement which, shortly after the blossoming of the Beautiful Style in Central Europe, culminated in the West in the International Style. The Beautiful Style flourished especially in Austria, Bavaria, Silesia, and Prussia, as well as in Bohemia. Its enchanting quality is particularly appealing in the miniatures of the Missal of Zbyněk of Hasenburg, Archbishop of Prague (1409). Along with this highly decorative, lyrical style, which tended to become manneristic and precious, a more sober and realistic style appeared in Bohemia in the early 15th century, introduced by the Master of the Gerona Martyrology. This innovator collaborated in 1402 on the Bible of Conrad of Vechta. His progressive style betrays affinity with the rapidly ascending Lower Rhenish and Netherlandish painting. His impact may be ascertained also in the panel painting of the first quarter of the 15th century in Bohemia, Moravia, and Silesia (the Master of the Rajhrad altarpiece). Another of the fine artists schooled in Bohemia, Nicholas of Brno, became the chief illuminator at the ducal court in Vienna in the first decade of the century. The expansion of Bohemian art abroad may be related to the suspected emigration of leading artists which started, perhaps as early as 1400, when Prague lost its importance and prestige after ceasing to be the capital of the Holy Roman Empire. It is an axiom that the highest forms of art may be created when the optimal spiritual, cultural, political, and economic conditions exist simultaneously, but they may occasionally survive in a sublime form for a time, beyond the highest point of intellectual and material concentration.

The final blow to the Bohemian art of this epoch was dealt by the Hussite revolutionary uprising; the artists lost their patronage, which had come from the losing party, and, in fact, their *raison d'être*, as well. Surviving activity was extremely meager and lacking in creative originality; better conditions for the continuation of the art production existed only in Southern Bohemia under the powerful lords of Rožmberg (Rosenberg). It was indeed a sad retreat from the glory which was never again to be fully retrieved. The lag was most acute in the second third of the 15th century, when Bohemia was sealed off from contacts with outside art, which meanwhile made great advances toward realism. With the easing of the tension, some contacts were renewed. But in a reversal of direction, Bohemia, which had previously generated new ideas and disseminated them, began to accept influences from neighboring countries as it had done before the great surge under the Luxemburg dynasty. The influence of Flemish painting, which became dominant in the West, was never felt directly, and reached Bohemia only through the intermediaries of its German adaptations. In the last third of the century, German painting became increasingly important for Bohemian art. But with the notable exceptions of the wall paintings in St. Barbara's in Kutná Hora (the Smíškovská Chapel), The Master of the Puchner altarpiece from 1482, and Master I. W., active in the first quarter of the 16th century, Bohemian art of the Late Gothic seldom reached higher quality. Cologne influences recognizable in the Puchner alterpiece were succeeded by strong dependence on Lucas Cranach's paintings.

Monuments of mediaeval paintings in Slovakia consist of murals, supplemented by panel paintings at the end of the fourteenth century. No real school of illumination existed in Slovakia: later examples are influenced by Bohemian art by way of Vienna. As had not been the case in Bohemia, Italian influences were strong even in early times (*vide* murals in Dravce from the middle of the 13th century, then in Žehra and Švábovce). The Italianate trend persisted in the frescoes of the 14th century (Svinica), inspired by the actual presence of Italian painters, as we see in the paintings in Sazdice near Levice. Side by side, murals in the Western-inspired style exist in Slovakia (Velká Lomnica, Krušovce), and toward the end of the century, the connection with the style emanating from Bohemia may be recognized (Levoča, Biacovce, Zemianská Ludrová). Models in the Beautiful Style were utilized for the murals in Poniky near Zvolen, and in the cathedral in Košice from the first part of the 15th century. The panels from Hronský Sv. Beňadik must be linked with Bohemian painting.

This duality of inspiration is quite unique in Central Europe, and may be, perhaps, explained by two strata of patronage: on the one hand, the element of German colonists in the Spiš district and in the mining towns of Central Slovakia who favored the Western and Bohemian styles, and on the other hand, the higher clergy and nobles who propagated the Italian taste prevailing in Hungary. A number of large Late Gothic altarpieces are preserved which owe much to German painting (Lipt. Sv. Mikuláš, Matejovce).

Renaissance art took hold very late in the countries north of the Alps – and Bohemia was not an exception – when Italian craftsmen were summoned by the rulers and nobility to decorate their castles and palaces. Their works never went beyond the level of mere craftsman decoration, and hardly anything is worth mentioning. The forms elaborated by German Renaissance painters in Nuremberg and Augsburg were better understood by the native artists (murals in St. Wenceslaus' Chapel in the Prague Cathedral). Much of the mural decoration was based, quite uninspiredly, on models from woodcuts and engravings. The Renaissance lasted in Bohemian lands for about one century, from 1520 to 1620. The artistic concentration at the court of Emperor Rudolf II was only ephemeral, and this community of foreign artists dispersed after his death in 1614 (Hans von Aachen, B. Spranger).

After the defeat at the White Mountain near Prague in 1620, the country was laid wide open to the Counter-Reformation movement, of which the Baroque style was the chief vehicle for indoctrination by means of art. The first outstanding personality after a prolongated period of stagnation was Karel Škréta. During his long stay in Italy, he gained a first-hand knowledge of the *tenebroso* concept of Caravaggio in the works of his followers (Strozzi), as well as the academic style of the Carracci. The multiple influences are still to be recognized in his St. Wenceslaus cycle. Yet some of his portraits betray the more Northern sense of realism gained in his schooling with the Rudolfine artists.

The generation of the early eighteenth century were great decorators of theatrical, and sometimes magniloquent, style as they adhered to the grandiose manner of the Italian Baroque. They painted large altarpieces and decorated ceilings à la Pozzo, or, later, Piazzetta, in the monastery, town, and pilgrimage churches which vied mutually with new embellishments. Ecstatic visions are often the themes of large canvases of Peter Brandl, painted for churches in Prague, Svatá Hora, Skalka, Doksany, Litoměřice between 1697 and 1735. Another great Baroque Czech painter is Václav Vavřinec Rainer, who painted altarpieces and murals in the Prague churches and in N. W. Bohemia for the Cistercians in Osek near Duchcov (1719), and later for the Benedictines in Broumov. He worked in Lower Austria, where he painted frescoes in 1723 in the monastery in Gaming. Artists moved around according to their commissions; thus, outsiders were also active in Bohemian lands. (F. A. Maulbertsch, an Austrian, but native of Swabia, painted frescoes in the castle in Kroměříž and, church in Brno-Královo Pole.) Others, such as Michael Willman and Francis Xaver Palko, might also be mentioned. The exquisite portraitist Jan Kupecký, emigrated from Bohemia and was active in Austria and Bavaria.

The importance of Rococo painting in Bohemia recedes into the background after the spectacular fireworks of the Baroque. Truly delightful touches of Rococo spirit exist, nevertheless, in the little genre pictures of Norbert Grund (fl. second third of the 18th century), which evoke the atmosphere of Watteau, Pater, and Fragonard.

Czech art hit a new low in the rationalistic, workaday atmosphere under Emperor Joseph II, but the creativity had already begun to taper off around 1760. The stagnation and artistic sterility caused great concern to a group of influential people, mostly from among the nobility, and their effort to revitalize the degenerating spirit in the arts resulted in the establishment of an academy in Prague in 1800. Yet this did not improve the situation, since the indigenous tradition had been extinguished in the 18th century, and there was nothing of the decorative splendor of the late Venetians, nothing comparable to the charms of the English portraiture, nor to the psychological penetration of Goya and the realism of Chardin, which paved the road to the modern art. The teaching of the Prague

Academy in the first decades of its existence produced nothing but an eclectic art ranging from a cool Nazarene classicism lacking all pictorial quality to a sentimental romanticism (František Tkadlík, Christian Ruben, Karel Postl). Alpine romanticism was dear to August Piepenhagen, who came from Germany in his early age. The exceptions were the landscapes of Antonín Mánes and portraits of Antonín Machek, who endeavored to penetrate deeper into the reality of the represented subjects.

The exquisite talent of the slightly younger Josef Navrátil brought him far beyond the epigone landscapes of Postl, his teacher at the Academy. His great decorative abilities are apparent in wall paintings such as those in the Liběchov Castle and later, in the fifties, in the large vedutas in the castle at Velké Jirny. His prominent sensitivity is revealed in the delightfully colored genre details and in the little still-life pictures.

It was not until the period of Josef Mánes, son of Antonín Mánes, that the new Czech art got its genius. He was able to imbue his art with a truly Czech ideal based on the patriotic convictions of the Romantics (Kollár), who believed in the integrity and greatness of the nation. Czech and Slovak peasants incarnate his human ideal, treated, not in a dry, archaeological, or descriptive manner, but in a fresh and immediate representation in which he was aided by a colorist's instinct for the sensual charm of color (e.g. the Red Parasol). The ill-famed Manuscript of Dvůr Králové inspired Mánes in 1857-59 to a series of illustrations exalting the fictive deeds of Slav antiquity. The Labors of the Months painted by him in 1865-6 in the medallions of the famous horologe on the Old Town Hall in Prague are performed by members of a healthy Czech peasant race of the past.

We may regard Mikoláš Aleš as Mánes' follower, as one who likewise devoted his art to the noble theme of national consciousness. The dawn of Czech culture inspired *Vlast*, his winning project of a cycle of monumental compositions destined to decorate the foyer of the new National Theatre. Deprived unjustly of the opportunity actually to execute these monumental paintings, Aleš put all his talent into countles drawings and illustrations, and renounced all painting. Czech antiquity was also the subject of early paintings by Jaroslav Čermák, who then, under the influence of Décamps, became interested in more exotic subjects and turned his attention to the portrayal of the heroism and suffering of Yugoslav people. In the same way, other Czech painters devoted their talents to the people and nature of Eastern Europe; Čeněk Melka worked in Transsylvania, and O. Mrkvička in Bulgaria.

Landscape painting was a favorite preoccupation of many Czech painters, who pursued its transformation from romantic to realistic landscape on the foundations laid by Antonín Mánes. The atmospheric landscapes of Adolf Kosárek excelled among the works of such contemporaries as Bedřich Havránek, Alois Bubák, and Hugo Ullík, but he unfortunately died at the age of twenty-nine. To this generation of pioneers of modern art belonged another artist to whom a fulfilment of his promising work was likewise denied, namely, Karel Purkyně. His scenes and boldly-painted still lives are dominated by a realistic preoccupation to which he was introduced during his stay in France. His powerful style further reflects his interest in Titian, Rubens, and the Dutch masters. Similar realistic interests were shared by his contemporaries Soběslav Pinkas and Karel Barvitius, who likewise made their exodus to France for the teaching of the new French school headed by Courbet and Millet. The sojourn of Antonín Chittussi in France was also beneficial to his talent: his landscapes, under the influence of the Barbizon School and, perhaps, of Eugène Boudin, often achieve a surprisingly modern effect. On the other hand, the influence of the Vienna and Munich schools in the forest scenes of Julius Mařák, seascapes of Beneš Knüpfer, and landscapes of Hanuš Schweiger retain a traditional, heavier, and more romantic mood. A romantically tinted realism also permeates the landscapes of the nineteenth century Slovak painters Fr. Klimkovič, Ladislav Medňanský, and Ludovít Čordák.

More academic and traditional forms prevailed among the painters of the so-called Generation of the National Theatre, who excelled in allegorical painting (Vojtěch Hynais, František Ženíšek, Josef Tulka, Václav Brožík). Brožík is a Czech counterpart of Munkaczy, Piloty, and Matejko in the field of historical painting (*vide* his monumental canvases in the Old Town Hall in Prague). More conservatively conceived form would continue to be the basic *credo* of a whole line of Czech painters, as almost always happens in the art history of every nation (Luděk Marold, Alfons Mucha, Max Švabinský, Stretti-Zamponi, etc.).

Meanwhile, the glorious era of the Impressionistic conquests in France was almost over; only then did their impact become a matter of course in Prague circles. Impressionism became very popular, however, after the start of the 20th century, and remained so with many landscapists for a long time (Kaván, Hudeček, Panuška, Lolek, Kalvoda, Kuba, Blažíček, Lebeda, Radimský). Among the early adherents, we should mention Miloš Jiránek and Jindřich Prucha, but mainly Antonín Slovíček, all three dead prematurely. Slavíček's view of hilly Kameničky and majestic Prague reveals him as a great painter.

Compared with the Impressionistic movement, the post-Impressionistic developments in France likewise did not have an immediate repercussion in Prague, and the vital importance of Van Gogh, Gauguin, and Cézanne was recognized only by the next generation of artists.

Art Nouveau and Symbolism were the expression of the *fin de siècle* spirit in Western capitals as well as in Vienna and Prague (Alfons Mucha). Czech artists did not delay in joining this movement, embracing, as it did, more than a mere painting trend. Lyrical mood and fondness for dreams in the symbolic paintings of Jan Preisler compared favorably in their freshness and fullnes of life (triptych Spring) to the anemic life of the Symbolist, Puvis de Chavannes. Some of his works are closer to the forceful expression of Edvard Munch, though without the element of morbidity. Czech Expressionism owes enough to the Norwegian master, and in various ramifications it became one of the chief constituents of modern Czech painting (Josef Čapek). It still is, since it is more a state of mind than a doctrinary trend, unlike the programs of some modern movements (the Baroque type of Jan Bauch or the more introvert type of Rudolf Kremlička and Karel Černý).

The twentieth century is marked by a great diversification of points of views in European production, and this development is readily reflected in Czech and Slovak painting. There were some who, believing in the traditional values, achieved excellence by adhering to this *credo*. Here we should consider the long and fruitful career of Max Švabinský, graphic artist and painter of a bucolic and sensual vision of the world, and the works of most of the teachers at the Academy of Fine Arts (Otakar Nejedlý, Vratislav Nechleba). More decisive, however, for the shaping of artistic life were the more radical and daring spirits. Czech painters were in contact with, and responded to, almost all European movements, and it would not be difficult to find adherents to any of the "-isms" of every shade of expression. This is even more remarkable for the years before World War I, if one realizes that Prague was forced to occupy the definitely secondary place of a provincial center in the Austro-Hungarian Empire.

The younger generation endeavored enthusiastically to enter into close communion with the international avant-garde in painting. A great event for Prague was the exhibition of Edvard Munch (and that of Rodin) and the "opening of the windows into Europe" by the art periodical, *Volné Směry* ("Free Trends"), published by a newly founded association of artists called *Mánes*. Young progressive artists formed groups such as the *Devětsil* and the *Osma* (the Eight). The associations, *Mánes* and *Umělecká Beseda*, were to become pillars of all important artistic happenings. *Hollar* grouped the graphic artists, and *Myslbek* the more traditional artists.

The news of the Cubist movement made a great impact on the young people. One of the apostles of this new art, Bohumil Kubišta, had a chance to study it at first hand in Paris. Many others who later acquired diverging artistic identities started to paint in the Cubist style, e.g., Václav Špála, Josef Čapek, Vincenc Beneš, Antonín Procházka, and the spiritual leader of the group *Osma*, Emil Filla. He was the only one to remain faithful to Cubism throughout his life, in conformance with the evolution within Picasso's art. Špála evolved his own distinct style from his Cubist beginnings, while for others Cubism was just a transitory stage of testing its principles. Many artists ventured a trip to Paris in seeking the French formal innovations before and after the war. There were no such contacts with Italian Futurists, and thus their elaboration did not receive any considerable Czech response.

Paris was the Mecca of modern art – and all of France along with it. The Czech artistic colony in France was quite large; Otakar Kubín (Coubine), a painter of delicate lyrical mood, settled in Southern France. The solitary pursuit of his own ideal toward a symbolism expressed in simplified, abstracted forms led one of the members of the *Osma*, Jan Zrzavý, to settle in the severe and harsh terrain of Brittany. In Paris, František Kupka was in 1909 among the very first to conceive completely abstract paintings.

Surrealism reacted against the doctrinary discipline of Cubism, but sometimes fell prey to an over-literary content. This danger was escaped in the dreamy visions of Josef Šíma, another Parisian *habitué*. Štyrský and Toyen loyally utilized all the sanctioned and internationally recognized paraphernalia of the Surrealist style.

Many of the Czechoslovak artists convey in their works poetic qualities and a pronounced lyricism which may also be recognized as a salient feature of many monuments of the past. (Attempts have been made to see this quality as a national characteristic for Czechoslovak and all of Slavic art.) Essentially lyrical are the noble figural compositions of Rudolf Kremlička and Karel Černý, and the refined gouaches of Bedřich Vaníček. Civil poetry of the humble suburbs is evoked in the pictures of F. Gross and F. Hudeček. It is plausible to suggest that the pervasive, warm sentiment of lyricism is hardly compatible with the cooly precise, constructivist approach of a Mondriaan, nor with the gruesome distortion and brutal pathos of the German Expressionists. Yet the decorative possibilities of evolving Cubism were exploited, for example, by Pravoslav and Jan Kotíks and, of course, E. Filla.

Czech landscape and cityscape were portrayed from various points of view, ranging from Fauvism and Expressionistic dramatic mood to a measured, quiet, and lyrical tenderness: we see these various approaches in the palpitating canvases by Vincenc Beneš and Bohumír Dvorský, the monumental stretches of fields by Václav Rabas, and fishing scenes by Jan Kojan: a light, almost Japanese touch in the temperas of Vojtěch Sedláček, the tinge of humor in the genre landscapes of Vlastimil Rada, the taciturn landscapes of V. V. Novák and Jan Zrzavý. Czechoslovak folklore depicted in the South Moravian scenes by Joža Úprka in the previous generation continues to be of interest to Josef Lada, Karel Svolinský, Jiří Trnka, and Antonín Strnadel, both in paintings and drawings.

Slovak folk art, still more alive than in Bohemia, is the source of inspiration to Ludo Fulla. His original approach was lately internationally acclaimed. Other interesting Slovak painters who catch with verve all the pathos of the Slovak countryside are Bedrich Hoffstädter, Ján Želibský, Martin Benka, and Janko Alexy.

The younger generation before the Second World War was more interested in recording their own inner reflections and interests, often psychologically oriented, than in forming a collective, homogeneous, and more universal style. They were concerned with the mysteries of the human soul and existence more than with any constructivist and formal solution. The strange and remote life of the circus performers, fascinating figures like Don Quixote and Paganini, enchanted František Tichý. The tragedies and nostalgia of the life and world of the theatre intrigued Josef Liesler and Arnošt Paderlík and appeared in the enigmatic scenes of Cyprián Majerník and the dreamy portraits of Vladimír Sychra. Bizarre and obsolete machines and gadgets in the little pictures of Kamil Lhoták evoked the nostalgic poetry of an era past and never to return. Though the impact of psychoanalysis can not be denied, there might be something more to it: these associations may have represented, perhaps, less escapism than a presentiment, and reaction to the thickening, ominous atmosphere before the impending national catastrophe.

With the tragic events which caused the end of the first Czechoslovak republic, the ruthless Nazi control systematically strangled creative *élan* and freedom, and marked the closing of a chapter in Czechoslovak art.

SELECTED BIBLIOGRAPHY

J. Květ and H. Swarzenski, *Czechoslovakia. Romanesque and Gothic Illuminated Manuscripts* (= Unesco World Art Series, (1959).
J. Mašín, *Románská nástěnná malba v Čechách a na Maravě* (Prague, 1954).
J. Pešina and others, *Gotická nástěnná malba v zemích českých*, I: 1300-1350 (Prague, 1958).
A. Boeckler, "Zur Böhmischen Buchkunst des 12. Jahrhunderts", *Konsthistorisk Tidskrift*, XXII (Stockholm, 1953).
J. Květ, *Italské vlivy na pozdně románskou knižní malbu v Čechách* (Prague, 1927).
——, *Iluminátoři královny Rejčky* (Prague, 1929).
J. Friedl, *Hildebert a Everwin* (Prague, 1927).
A. Matějček, *Le Passionaire de l'abbesse Cunégonde* (Prague, 1922).
——, *Velislavova bible* (Prague, 1926).
A. Friedl, *Magister Theodoricus* (Prague, Artia, n.d.).
——, *Mistr Karlštejnské Apokalypsy* (Prague, 1950).
A. Matějček, *Czech Gothic Painting 1350-1450* (Prague, 1950).
J. Dupont, *Gothic Painting* (= *The Great Centuries of Painting*) (1954).
A. Stange, *Deutsche Malerei der Gotik*, vols. I, II, IX (Berlin).
[Catalogue], *L'art ancien en Tchécoslovaquie* (Paris, 1957).
J. Krofta, *Mistr breviře Jana ze Středy* (Prague, Prameny, 1940).
E. Trenkler, *Das Evangeliar des Johannes von Troppau* (Klagenfurt, 1948).
O. Kletzl, "Studien zur Böhmischen Buchmalerei", *Marburger Jahrbuch für Kunstwissenschaft*, 1933, pp. 1-76.
Z. Drobná, *Gothic Drawing* (Prague, Artia, n.d.).
J. von Schlosser, "Die Bilderhandschriften Könings Wenzel I", *Jahrbuch der Kunsthistorischen Sammlungen*, 1893, pp. 214-317.
L. Vermeiren, "La bible de Wenceslas du Musée Plantin-Moretus à Anvers", *De Gulden Passer*, 1953, pp. 191-229.
O. Pächt, "A Bohemian Martyrology", *The Burlington Magazine*, 1938, pp. 192-204.
H. Jerchel, "Das Hasenburgische Missale von 1409, die Wenzelswerkstatt und die Mettener Malereien von 1414", *Zeitschrift des Deutschen Vereins für Kunstwissenschaft*, 1937, pp. 218-242.
V. Denkstein and F. Matouš, *Gothic Art of Southern Bohemia* (Prague, Artia, 1955).
J. Pešina, "Nový pokus o revisi dějin českého malířství 15. století", *Umění*, 1960, pp. 109-134.
J. Pešina, *Painting of the Gothic and Renaissance Periods, 1450-1550* (Prague, Artia, n.d.).
P. Kropáček, *Malířství doby Husitské* (Prague, 1946).
V. Dvořáková, J. Krása and K. Stejskal, "Zpráva o průzkumu středověkých nástěnných maleb na Slovensku", *Umění*, 1961, pp. 197-206. 257-275.
O. Schürer and E. Wiese, *Deutsche Kunst in der Zips* (Brno, 1938).
J. Neumann, *Malířství XVII. století v Čechách* (Prague, 1951).
Vl. Novotný, "V. V. Rainer", *Umění*, XIII, XIV (1941-42).
J. Urzidil, *Wenceslaus Hollar, der Kupferstecher des Barocks* (Vienna, 1936).
F. Dvořák, *Kupecký, der grosse Porträtmaler des Barocks* (Prague, Artia, 1956).
J. Loriš, *Česká barokní kresba* (Prague).
J. Paur, *Josef Mánes* (Prague).
J. Neumann, *České malířství XIX.století* (= *Národní Galerie*, Vol. II) (Prague, 1952).
V. Novotný, *České malířství XIX.století*, vol. III (Prague, 1954)
V. V. Štech, and V. Hnízdo, *Wandmalereien des Biedermeiers. Ein Werk Josef Navrátils* (Prague, Artia, 1958).
L. Halasová and V.V. Štech, *Adolf Kosárek* (Prague, 1959).

A. Matějček, *Mikoláš Aleš. Malířská tvorba* (Prague, 1954).
V. Volavka, *Purkyně* (Prague).
M. Míčko and E. Svoboda, *Národní divadlo a jeho výtvarníci* (Prague, 1952).
F. V. Mokrý, *Jaroslav Čermák* (Prague, 1953).
K. Novotný, *A. Chittussi* (Prague, Prameny, 1939).
J. B. Svrček, *Miloš Jiránek* (Prague, 1932).
V. V. Štech, *Antonín Slavíček* (Prague, 1947).
J. Pečírka, *Jan Preisler* (Prague, Prameny, 1940).
J. Květ, *Max Švabinský, der grosse tschechische Maler und Graphiker* (Prague, Artia, 1960).
Ch. Kunstler, *Coubine* (Paris, 1929).
D. Plichta, *The Modern Symbolist. The Painter Jan Zrzavý* (Prague, Artia,).
J. Kotalík, "Moderní československé malířství", *Československo*, II (1947), pp. 129-207.
M. Lamač, *Contemporary Art in Czechoslovakia* (Prague, 1958).

Illuminator Egregius Temporibus Wenceslai IV in Regno Bohemiae Florens

MOJMÍR S. FRINTA

My title is not intended to impose a barrier of learned pretentiousness. I merely wish, by using Latin, to convey the mood in which the illuminators' work was carried on in the period of our concern. The mediaeval master-illuminators were well versed in Latin, as we know from the marginal instructions for illuminators written in Latin in two great Bohemian bibles of the period. These glosses were later erased when the miniature had been executed.

Bohemian manuscript illumination of the second half of the fourteenth century is universally valued as an important manifestation of European painting of the Gothic period. Manuscripts from the 'sixties from the circle of Jan of Středa, chancellor to Emperor Charles IV, are rightly recognized as artistically nobler than those illuminated for King Wenceslaus IV during the last two decades of the century. The importance of the latter lies mainly in their original and highly imaginative acanthus decoration luxuriously filling the margins.

However, it became the custom for art-historians to evaluate the last phase of this magnificent surge of Bohemian mediaeval painting as a somewhat stagnant art, showing no signs of progress toward realism in tune with contemporary achievements in Western Europe and Italy.[1]

---

[1] In the latter part of the 14th century, Czech art achieved international recognition, and we may learn from various documents about the exporting of Bohemian works of art. Among earlier examples are the Evangeliary of Johannes of Opava, dated 1368, and the Mühlhausen retable painted in 1385 in Prague. Manuscripts copied abroad, such as one written in 1397 in the Austrian monastery at Mauerbach, were brought to Bohemia to be illuminated. Two records document the exportation of Czech sculpture: one from 1400 states that the Great Master of the Teutonic Knights had installed in the chapel of Marienburg a sculpture brought in from Bohemia. A document about the import of a Bohemian Pietà to Strasbourg in 1404 is well known in the literature. The heyday of the Bohemian genius was marked by the expansion of the so-called "Beautiful Style" throughout Central Europe. Even the powerful Italian tradition was not entirely impervious to the charms of this style, as may be seen in the "Beautiful Madonna" by Michele Giambono in Rome, or Stefano da Zevio's pictures in Verona.

I hope to show in this paper that such an appraisal is not entirely valid. It is my aim to single out the works of an excellent painter, active in Bohemian territory from about 1400 to 1420, who rivalled in excellence the contemporary Franco-Flemish artists. I believe that the task of identifying marked creative talents in the complex artistic production of the time by recognizing their distinctive idioms and individual characteristics becomes important whenever we are faced with some innovation or impulse which changed the existing trend of art production.

A number of manuscripts originating in Bohemia at that time contain illuminations which reveal a great artistic personality, mingled though they are with miniatures of lesser quality and divergent style. Their author was an artist of great sensitivity and intellect, as well as an accomplished draftsman preoccupied with the perfection and accuracy of drawing.

It is a little sad that not one of the manuscripts containing the Master's miniatures remains in its country of origin. All known manuscripts reached their present repositories in Austria, Hungary, Belgium, Spain, and the United States through more or less unknown channels.

We see this artist's early style in the illuminations in the second half of the first volume of a Latin bible now in the Museum Plantin Moretus in Antwerp (M 15.1). The two-volume manuscript was commissioned by Conrad of Vechta, Master of the Mint to the Czech king Wenceslaus IV; the text was completed in 1402, according to the *explicit*. Previous research (Chytil, Matějček, Vermeiren) has determined the general extent of our master's participation, which totals about forty miniatures.[2] The last fifteen scenes are of extraordinary importance to our study, because they provide us with some clues to the essential characteristics of the Master. They are unfinished, and the masterful underdrawing is therefore visible. Some portions of these scenes, such as patterned background, simple terrain, architecture, clusters of trees, and, occasionally, subordinate figures were already executed in paint and must be assumed for

---

Bohemian artists were active in neighboring countries in ever-increasing numbers; this might have become a real exodus with the subsequent unrest and, finally, the outburst of the Hussite Wars. It is quite possible that the Master of the Gerona Martyrology at that time exchanged his diminishing opportunities in the Bohemian kingdom for more promising patronage abroad.

[2] Karel Chytil in *Památky Archeologické*, XVIII (Prague, 1885), pp. 311-16; Antonín Matějček, "Bible mincmistra Konráda z Vechty", *Umění*, Prague 1936, and "La bible du frappeur de monnaie Konrad de Vechta", *Les arts plastiques*, Bruxelles, Sept.-Oct. 1950, pp. 275-282: Louise Vermeiren, "La bible de Wenceslas du Musée Plantin-Moretus à Anvers", *De Gulden Passer*, Antwerp, 1953, pp. 191-229.

various reasons to be the work of an assistant. The difference in the two renderings of the trees – one intense, dramatic, and more real, the other conventional and summary – may well illustrate the unequal capacities of the two painters. The assistant's contribution may be conjectured in subordinate areas of other scenes, as well, such as "Samson Destroying the palace". On the other hand, "Gideon's Fleece" is entirely from the hand of the Master.

The Master created in his paintings his own race of people, as leading artists always do by projecting their concepts of humanity and ideals of physical beauty into specific physiognomies. His people are endowed with great dignity and nobility; the realism which marks their serious faces with intense, searching looks never descends into vulgarity or caricature. There is an air of mystery about them, modified, in the negative characters, into fierceness or mischief. The men wear heavy, dark beards and their features are slightly Semitic. This is in accord with a basic desire for veracity which was then beginning to appear in European art. The women's faces are less individualized, and in their pleasant, regular features we see a tendency toward greater idealization.

The artist created not only physiognomies, but also a color gamut of his own. Its originality may be perceived best in the unusual color harmonies of the patterned background. Highly saturated colors are, on the whole, more favored than the pale tones. The colors, black, cocoa, aubergine, mauve, and Venetian red, are enhanced by golden rinceaux or phoenixes. On the other hand, lighter colors such as salmon, old rose, pale buff, and creamy raspberry form the ground for the sumptuous, multicolored ornaments usually based on a rhombic system. These patterns were a complete innovation indecorative lay-outs of the period.

The color harmony, usually cool, is carefully premeditated for each individual composition. Subtle and refined gamuts are played throughout the scenes by the elaboration of the half-tones. Gray of different hues becomes an important factor in harmonizing the tones. There is no longer the flowering-carpet effect or the mosaic-like distribution of suave colors typical of Bohemian production in the last quarter of the century, such as the Wenceslaus Bible.[3]

The Master achieved a *chiaroscuro* effect by gradually deepening color values into definite zones. The terrain becomes progressively darker

---

[3] Vienna, National Library Cod. 2759-63. Julius von Schlosser, "Die Bilderhandschriften Königs Wenzel I", *Jahrbuch der Kunsthistorischen Sammlungen* ..., XIV (1893), pp. 214-317.

Illuminator Egregius Temporibus Wenceslai IV Florens 159

toward the horizon. If a light shape is surrounded by an equally light area, an adjustment is made by darkening its border zone to define more clearly the enclosed shape. This can be seen particularly well around the head of Gideon (fol. 143r).

The Master already showed promise of excellence in the Antwerp Bible. We may observe the evolution of his art in the illuminations of a sumptuous martyrology which is preserved in the Diocesan Museum in Gerona. Professor Otto Pächt discussed its history in the *Burlington Magazine*, 1938.[4]

The origin of this luxurious manuscript is unknown, but from the presence of certain specific saints, a Silesian, or, possibly, a Moravian monastery may be suggested as its destination. It is not dated, but from the monogram "W" of King Wenceslaus which occurs twice – once surmounted with a crown – the date of 1419 may implied as *terminus ante quem*, and probably not the immediately preceding years. Pächt recognized three hands involved in the 705 illuminations, and delineated the extent of each artist's participation. A minute analysis brings a more subtle differentiation and suggests a greater number of participants. We are concerned here only with the sixty miniatures executed in the style of our master, whom I propose to call the Master of the Gerona Martyrology, because Barcelona, the designation introduced by Pächt, was associated with the manuscript's history only fleetingly. Our master was undoubtedly the leader who designed the decorative lay-out of the pages consisting of simple scenes enclosed in medallions, three to six to a page, connected with acanthus vines.

All the tendencies apparent in the Antwerp miniatures assert themselves now in an even more pronounced form. His art is more mature; traditional elements are almost gone. The distant architectural elements grow more realistic and reach the level of the earlier style of the Limbourg brothers.

A close scrutiny, however, of these sixty seemingly homogeneous pages uncovers a difference in the canon of proportions, the expressive power of faces and forms, the use of color, and the ornamentation. Even granting a change in personal style, it is difficult to reconcile these differences with a single personality.

I believe that they were painted by three artists working intimately in an almost identical style, and even jointly on certain pages, so that their respective portions can be distinguished only with the greatest difficulty.

---

[4] "A Bohemian Martyrology", pp. 192-204.

The master who worked on the first pages of this group used more attenuated figures with sharp features and strongly modelled shapes. His conventional rendering of the architecture seems more archaic; he was, perhaps, the oldest. His art is intense, and its dramatic quality is heightened by a strong *chiaroscuro* treatment.

The next master preferred round physiognomies and less emphatically shaded draperies. He is more progressive in the greater realism of his figures and architecture. The general mood is more lyrical, and therefore more in accord with the Bohemian tradition. A salient feature of their art is the precision of form which is achieved by their technical virtuosity. The modelling is extremely supple, and the convincing rendition of difficult postures and gestures show, an advance in understanding of the human body. The final statement of the outlines is achieved in the second master's miniatures by silverpoint-line drawn over the paint. This precision procedure is unlike the outlines drawn by previous Bohemian illuminators with brush in brown color. This technique was also shared by the master's intimate associates.

This third associate illuminated the last portion of the group of sixty pages. His art is less refined than that of the other two artists. The shapes are less exacting, less anatomical, and the principle of light and dark is not of primary importance. For example, in the "Seven Sleepers of Ephesus" we may observe the more amorphous shapes and flimsier drawing of the stick-like trees. The difference between his artistic temperament and that of the other two may be recognized also in the foliate decor. The third master C used uncomplicated, two-dimensional patterns of scanty acanthus leaves, carefully outlined with silverpoint and rather symmetrically organized, contrasting with the more powerful foliate patterns of Masters A and B. By the latter two, the coiling stems and curling leaves roll in an involved three-dimensional design, strongly modelled. The highly imaginative and original spirit of Master A is revealed by one intriguing and unique feature in his more turbulent flow of vegetation: the stalks, leaves, and serpent-like tendrils at places transform themselves mysteriously into strange shapes evoking dragons' bodies. This metamorphosis is totally unlike the traditional concept of monsters growing out of the foliage as if grafted onto them. On the contrary, the floral forms, without ever losing their vegetal characteristics, here merely paraphrase stretching members and sinuously twisting tremendous necks. This ambiguity of form is a sign of its creator's intellectually involved mind, and is a predecessor of the surrealistic point of view. (Let us remember the weird world of Max Ernst!)

In the same studio was illuminated the Sedlec Antiphonary, which is perhaps slightly later than the martyrology. The manuscript itself no longer exists, and only eight single miniatures in the Budapest Museum of Fine Arts were thought to have survived in addition to the three in the manuscript's portion which was preserved until World War II in the monastery at Nová Říše.[5] Their authors again are not easy to distinguish, and at least three painters seem to have been involved. The best of the miniatures, those of "St. Benedict Giving the Rules of his Order to the Monks" and "The Dream of Jacob", are probably by Master B, while Master C is the most likely author of the "Maries at the Tomb" and "Christ's Entry into Jerusalem". "The Annunciation" and "Philip and James" may have been by an assistant to Master C who followed scrupulously the idioms of the latter and is betrayed chiefly by somewhat inferior workmanship.

To this ensemble must be added a miniature representing a Trinity which is in the Rosenwald Collection at the National Gallery of Art in Washington. A qualitative wavering of its execution may be explained by assigning it to Master C, with the exception of the two heads which seem to be by Master B. It is very likely that this miniature was cut out of the Sedlec Antiphonary and therefore ought to be dated 1414, from the evidence of the *explicit* in that portion of the manuscript which was earlier preserved at Nová Říše.

A gradual in the Cantonal Library in Lucerne was donated to an unknown monastery by a nobleman named Andrew. The title page, which represents *molendarium hostiae* (mill for holy wafers), is unquestionably by Master A, as is evident from the typology, decoration, and high quality of execution. The weird, sinister monsters familiar to us from the margins of the Antwerp Bible and the Gerona Martyrology are present once more as hallmarks of the ingenuity of Master A. The remaining historiated initials are by less noteworthy assistants.[6]

To complete the survey of the illuminations which issued from the Master's studio, the Annunciation miniature in an antiphonary in the

---

[5] Edith Hoffmann, "Cseh miniatürök a Szépmüveszeti Múzeumban", *Az Országos Magyar Szépmüvészeti Evkönyvei*, I (1918), pp. 49-74; Zoroslava Drobná, "Les huit miniatures tchèques de Budapest", *Bulletin du Musée National Hongrois des Beaux-Arts*, 11 (1957), pp. 28-50.

[6] Dr. Josef Schmid, *Schöne Miniaturen aus Handschriften der Kantonsbibliothek Luzern*, I (Lucerne, 1941), pls. 35-41. He assigned the gradual to French-Alsatian production of the first quarter of the 15th century. The correct association was, however, perceived by Jaroslav Pešina, "Nový pokus o revisi dějin českého malířství 15. století", *Umění*, 1960, p. 117.

Brno Library must be mentioned.[7] It seems to show a particularly clear connection with the progressive Western style. Two illuminations in a cantionale in Vienna National Library (Ms. ser. nov. 4642), the Resurrection and the Last Supper, are from the assistants' hands. Furthermore, four miniatures in two Czech bibles were executed by the members of the Master's studio. The Nativity and "Moses Talking to God" are in the Boskovice Bible in the Olomouc Study Library; they follow the figural style of Master C and may conceivably be by him. One miniature, close to Master's A style, in the Olomouc Bible of 1417 further testifies that the Master's studio produced work for the Czech nobility as well as for the king and ecclesiastic patrons.

Probably contemporary with the Gerona manuscript is a missal of the Prague chapter in the Vienna Library (Cod. 1850).[8] It may be dated rather soon after 1411. Its illuminations are joined, being by the associates identified in the Martyrology, with the Master's atelier, which strengthens the assumption that the atelier was located in Prague. The Zodiac medallions at the beginning of the missal are by Master A.

At the beginning of the first volume of the so-called Korczek Bible in Vienna (Cod. 1169), there are three illuminations which are related in a puzzlingly close way to the miniatures of Masters A and B.[9] Because of the pervasive similarity in the canon and physiognomies of the figures, in the modelling, coloring, and general mood, it may be suggested that the Creation scenes and the two St. Jerome miniatures constitute perhaps the earliest works of Master A, since the bible is dated 1400 by an inscription in its second volume, which is in the library in Karlsruhe. The acanthus foliage here is strongly modelled, as if chiselled out in an extraordinary, bold design.

The progressive character of the Master's work is analogous in many respects to the realistic orientation of the contemporary Franco-Flemish *foyer*. Thus, we may suppose that some kind of contact or confrontation took place. The Master's sense of realism seems, however, to have been focused on the human representation, its anatomy and naturalistic modelling. At this stage of his evolution he is less interested than his Franco-Flemish contemporaries in the natural setting. Instead, he tends to render

---

[7] Josef Krása, "K článku o českých gotických miniaturách v Budapešti", *Umění*, 1959, p. 169f.

[8] Catalogue of the exhibition held in 1962 at the Kunsthistorisches Museum in Vienna, *Europäische Kunst um 1400*, No. 178.

[9] Kurt Holter, "Die Korczek-Bibel der Nationalbibliothek in Wien", *Die Graphischen Künste*, N.F., 3, figs. 8, 9, p. 88f.

the terrain and architecture in a summary, synthetic, and often chiefly decorative way. His greater breadth is likewise reflected in a sparser use of various anecdotal accessories. All this may well be compared with the concepts prevailing in Italian painting. Italianate is also a linear decor on the inner circumference of some medallions. North Italian influence can not be excluded.

In Bohemian art, we may find precedents for some of the stylistic features in the Master's work. Close ties exist with the art of the Třeboň Master. The latter belongs to an earlier phase of artistic evolution, and it may be suggested that perhaps our master was at one time a pupil of the Třeboň Master. *Chiaroscuro* was for both artists a salient, expressive vehicle invoking an atmosphere of enchantment. One may also compare the facial types of both masters. There is an affinity in the seriousness and nobility of their countenances. However, the Gerona Master has progressed further toward individualization and realism.

The stylistic similarities are not confined only to manuscript illumination. The Master's style has a strong affinity with the panel of St. Vitus' Madonna.[10] By its execution, the painting stands quite apart from the entire Bohemian production. X-rays reveal technical characteristics, such as the absence of incised underdrawing, which must be explained either as its author's absolute freedom from the indigenous painting practices, or as a result of his transferring the technique of illumination to another medium. The association of the panel with the sphere of the Master's art may carry further implications as to his identity. It has been suggested that the St. Vitus' Madonna was painted by the famous Panici-Junkers, artists active in the *entourage* of King Wenceslaus IV.[11] If we accept this assumption, then we may conclude that the three prominent illuminators distinguishable in the Gerona manuscript are the three Panici brothers – Janko, Petr, and Václav – who died before 1435. The problem of echoes of Western forms in these illuminations would then be less puzzling, because it is easily conceivable that the Panici had the opportunity of first-hand knowledge of other artistic foyers.

I am inclined to consider two drawings, i.e., the busts of the Virgin and the angel, in the Fogg Art Museum in Cambridge, Mass., as belonging not merely to the sphere of Bohemian art, but actually to the orbit of the Gerona Master.[12] A typological and morphological analysis points in

---

[10] Antonín Matějček, *Czech Gothic Painting 1350-1450* (Prague, 1950), pl. 142.
[11] Albert Kutal, "O mistru Krumlovské Madony", *Umění*, 1957, p. 63, note 72.
[12] Z. Drobná, *Gothic Drawing* (Prague, n.d.), pls. 81f.; Catalogue of the exhibition

this direction. I feel that these drawings should be directly linked to the painted portrait of Emperor Sigismund in the Vienna Kunsthistorisches Museum, and I propose Master B as the author of the portrait.[13]

The prestige of the revolutionary art of the Gerona Master must have been considerable, and his distinctive types, colors, and ornamentation made a distinct impression on contemporary Bohemian manuscript and panel painting. His influence was felt in Silesia, Austria, and South Germany. Some of the figural types in the Book of John Mandeville in the British Museum even suggest that a follower of the Master may have emigrated to the West, perhaps after the outbreak of the Hussite Wars.[14]

The fact that the specific types of the Gerona Master can be found in the Bohemian panel painting of the first quarter of the fifteenth century encourages the assumption that he and his associates were also panel painters, and thus supports the attribution proposed in this paper. His types are echoed in some of the apostles in the cycle from the Capuchine monastery in Prague, and in the Christ of the Roudnice retable. These types appear also on South Bohemian panels such as in the Reininghaus, Zátoň, and Hýrov retables, and in the half-figures on the frame of the Vyšší Brod Madonna. A direct relationship between the Gerona Master and the Master of the Rajhrad altarpiece must have existed. The physiognomies in the altarpiece, which probably was destined for Olomouc, especially recall those by Master C and his assistant. Additional Moravian paintings which reveal the influence of the Master's prototypes are the panel from Náměšť and St. James' altarpiece. A close analogy, again to Master C, exists in the figures of a Crucifixion in the Berlin Museum (unfortunately of unknown provenance).[15]

However, the closest parallel to the physiognomies of the Master exists in the Dormition panel from Langendorf in Silesia (now in the Muzeum Sląski in Wróclaw).[16] Its stylistic relationship to the Rajhrad retable is clear, and in view of its outstanding quality, the attribution to Master C himself may be surmised. In any case, some member of the Gerona

---

The International Style held in the Fall 1962 at the Walters Art Gallery in Baltimore, No. 5.
[13] Niccolo Rasmo, "Il ritratto di Sigismondo", *Cultura Atesina*, 1955, pp. 11-16.
[14] George F. Warner, *The Buke of John Maundeuill* (London, The Roxburghe Club, 1889).
[15] All above-mentioned panel paintings, mostly in the National Gallery in Prague, are reproduced in A. Matějček, *op. cit.*, pls. 159, 161, 166, 173, 176, 178, 181-192, 204, 205, 208, 216-227, 246-260.
[16] Heinz Braune and Erich Wiese, *Schlesische Malerei und Plastik des Mittelalters* (Leipzig, 1929), No. 174, pl. 173f: Matějček, *op. cit.*, pl. 147.

Master's studio must have been active in Silesia, because the typological influence is recognizable in the retable from Rauske near Strzygow and in the Crucifixion in a bible from 1427, once in the Municipal Library in Wróclaw (R 162).[17]

The characteristic acanthus style conceived by the Master was imitated by inferior followers in such work as the Litoměřice-Třeboň Bible from 1411-1414. This style appears in Austria after 1420 in the illuminations of several Klosterneuburg manuscripts done by Nicholas of Brno and his collaborators, Michael and Vitus (a large antiphonary and a *Catena* Cod. 37). It was used subsequently in Austria by the "Albrechts Miniator" and "Martinus Opifex", and in Salzburg by the illuminator of the Grillinger Bible (1428-1430).[18] The sharp acanthus foliage based on the Master's prototypes was perpetuated in Central European manuscripts far into the third quarter of the fifteenth century.

His figural style was imitated, as well; however, it lost much of its elegance in the subsequent miniature production at Prague, curtailed by the political situation, such as in the Bible of Queen Christina (the Vatican Library) and the bible cod. 1181 in Vienna dating from 1443. Closer to his style is a picture of a Madonna with Saints, painted on parchment, now in the Ferdinandeum in Innsbruck.[19] It is probably by one of the Master's associates. The parallel expressive means of style in this little picture and in Franco-Flemish painting may be demonstrated by comparing the bust of God with that in the Martyrdom of St. Denis, by Jean Malouel (Louvre).

Yet the Master's leap toward realism was not extended, in Bohemia, by consecutive steps which would have led to a new era of painting. He stands alone, and the examples just referred to are imitations of some of his novel elements rather than a further evolution. It may be that some of the key works are lost, but it may also be that his art was not understood by the average painter. Many of them, and precisely the best artists who used to work for sophisticated patrons, must have left the country at the time of the Hussite upheaval. It is quite possible that the Master of the Gerona Martyrology was one of those who sought a more promising and stable patronage abroad.

---

[17] Stanislawa Sawicka, *Straty wojenne zbiorow polskich w dziedzinie rekopisów iluminowanych* (Warsaw, 1952), No. 196, pl. CXVIII. The bible was destroyed in World War II.

[18] Karl Oettinger, "Der Illuminator Nikolaus", *Jahrbuch der preussischen Kunstsammlungen*, 45 (1933), p. 221ff: Alfred Stage, *Deutsche Malerei der Gotik*, X, fig. 8; vol. XI, figs. 73, 74, 77-79.

[19] Exhibition catalogue *Da Altichiero a Pisanello*, Verona, 1958, p. 33f., pl. XLVI.

Nothing is certain, but it is tempting to think of the court of Wenceslaus' half-brother, Sigismund, as the haven for the Master and his associates, especially if our attribution of the Emperor's portrait is accepted. Be it as it may, we know of none of the Master's paintings in Bohemia which would have followed his illuminations from the Wenceslavian period.

Frank Kupka (1871-1957)

JAROSLAV ŠEJNOHA

The discoveries and revolutions in the artistic world of the past hundred years have been as decisive and numerous as the technological changes which have brought about the extraordinary progress of our time. The triumph of science has had one obvious result: man, never too sure of his future, has remained under the spell of his own seemingly unlimited possibilities.

When he has found time at all to turn his attention away from the world of science, in order to take stock of the latest aesthetic developments, it was only to manifest his disapproval by abuse and ridicule. Artistic changes always appear in opposition to the taste of society and the established authorities. The ever-growing number of commercial art galleries must not deceive us. The vast majority of modern works of art are bought as the result of snobbery on the part of people who wish to be up-to-date. At the same time, there is, of course, the desire to invest one's money cleverly, in accordance with the dictates of official art criticism, which, in turn, frequently amounts to no more than prepaid publicity. And thus the public buys works which for some time have ceased to be modern. They are fashionable, no more. Without exaggeration, it can be said that the public of our time is the chief enemy of all truly aesthetic creations.

On the other hand, the greater public sinks deeper and deeper into a comfortable uniformity; guided only by its laziness of thought, it prefers the brutal vulgarity of television and colour photography to true works of art. The same public, when it demands that the artist become more intelligible, is actually demanding that the artist conform to lower standards, that the artist himself annihilate his artistic expression. In short, it demands the end of art. This malady is not new, but it has now become so widespread as to be almost stifling.

We may recall the ridicule, indignation, and scandals which so long pursued the paintings of the Impressionists. As late as 1900, the President of the French Republic, during a visit to the Grande Exposition, found his way to the gallery of Impressionist paintings barred by an Academician of repute: "Do not go beyond this point, Monsieur le Président. You would only see the shame of France". Later, when it became known that Rodin had decided to bequeath to France the contents of his studio, a veritable storm of indignation arose among the "Immortals" of the Institut.

Let us not speak of what happened outside France, but let us remain in Paris – the Athens of our day. In 1912, two important paintings were exhibited in Paris at the Salon d'Automne: *La Fugue en deux couleurs* and *La Chromatique chaude*. As had happened so frequently with other masterpieces in the past, they were greeted with incomprehension and derision. The senior member of the Conseil Municipal of Paris lodged an official protest, and a deputy seconded him with a motion in Parliament. Neither of them realized that Frank Kupka, a Czech who had lived in Paris since 1894, had created in these two masterpieces what we call modern art, the art of our time.

What exactly had happened? One could say this was no more than the fulfilment of Rimbaud's perspicacious prediction: "Objects shall no longer be reproduced; instead, sensations shall be expressed through lines, colours, and schemes derived from the outside world, simplified and controlled: true magic".

The art of our time had been created.

If Frank Kupka had died before 1909, he would have been classed with the many Czechs for whom, during the time of the Austrian Empire, France had become the land of liberty and enlightenment. He would be considered one of the famous Parisian draughtsmen, like Steinlen, Villon, Juan Gris, etc., as an illustrator of books designed for bibliophiles. (I refer to such volumes as *Lysistratos*, *Prometheus*, *Les Erynnies*, and *The Song of Songs*.) He might possibly be remembered as the winner of the gold medal for painting at the World Fair in St. Louis in 1902, and, more probably, as one of the famous group of Fauves and Cubists of the Section d'Or. There the first Cubist team had appeared as a united front: Archipenko, Braque, Brancusi, Delaunay, Gleizes, Herbin, Kupka, Le Fauconnier, Léger, Lhote, Metzinger, Picabia, Picasso.

But at the moment that Cubism was at last accepted by the public and the battle won (or so it seemed) – at that very moment, Kupka abandoned his fellow-artists and, strongly attracted by the lure of a new vision, broke with a rich and beautiful past.

Frank Kupka may be compared to Cézanne, who had recognized the limitations of Impressionism and changed it to something more solid and enduring by giving back to painting its claim to form, volume and construction. In the same way Frank Kupka indicated the end of Cubism and its mechanical application by giving back to painting its claim to colour, rhythm, and poetry.

There are men among us, geniuses, who appear to have been chosen by destiny to overthrow those clay statues which we took for marble.

Kupka did not stop, once Fauvism and Cubism had been established. By his rebellion, he pointed instead to a new path. It is true, of course, that at this moment of general effervescence, Kupka was not an isolated phenomenon. A number of artists had contributed to this fundamental aesthetic revolution. In Moscow, Larionov published his manifesto, and abstraction appears in his paintings, just as in the paintings of Gontcharova and Malevitch. The cosmopolitan Kandinsky, on the other hand, remained an expressionist for several years more. Abstract art does, however, show its first manifestations simultaneously in the work of both Picabia and Mondrian. Among these first pioneers of modern art, Robert and Sonia Delaunay come closest to Kupka. But it should never be forgotten that memories of external reality were to haunt the paintings of all these artists for some time to come.

The paintings of Kupka, on the other hand, were absolute creations entirely independent of reality, by 1912 and even earlier. The Museum of Modern Art in New York and museums in Paris and Prague own a number of abstract works which Kupka had painted as early as 1909 and 1910.

Kupka gives us in these works representations of another reality which transcends the traditional reproduction or interpretation of natural forms. They are an absolute refusal to recognize the existence of external reality, they are the result of the penetration into a purely poetical world, they are the *declaration of the supremacy of purely spiritual values*.

Kupka stated, and even engraved, his credo in his album of woodcuts, *Quatre histoires de blanc et noir*, where we find these words: "The work of art being in itself an abstract reality demands to be formed by elements of inventions." And also: "Either the artist betrays his artistic vision in order not to betray the model or he deforms the model in order to come closer to the true aspect of his vision", and he adds: "If this is so, why use a model at all?" These words indicate a total break with the past. They show us the essence of the plastic arts in the purest state. At the same time, they were an attempt to establish the supremacy of colour over the geometric apprehensions of Cubism.

Apollinaire confirmed, once again, the interdependence of the different domains of art when he labelled Kupka's art "Orphism", an allusion to the myth of Orpheus, the conqueror of night and the god of the underworld, the creator of music and poetry. Music and poetry at this moment manifested themselves everywhere. Despite the fact that the outbreak of the war in 1914 interrupted idealist speculations to a certain extent, Bourdelle, speaking of music as "a harmony of numbers", calls on his fellow sculptors: "You must explore and measure. You must become like compasses, like calculators. You must experience forms as a geometer would, you must become the *musicians of proportions*."

The example of Kupka's revolt against Cubism – imprisoned as Cubism had become in the rationalism of icy constructions – continued to influence others; Picasso, for instance, was helped to find the road towards colour, music, and poetry.

Many other artists have drawn from Kupka's new interpretation of painting. His influence in Paris was the outstanding and predominant force, especially from 1909 and 1914, although, of course, within a certain restricted circle of initiates.

As he refused to compromise in his art, no matter what the cost, so Kupka made no concessions in his private life. He withdrew his canvases on the eve of the opening of the largest exhibition of the Section d'Or held after World War I, because his fellow-artists, who had often told him that he was the keystone and leader of the group, hesitated to assign to his paintings the place of honour. By nature an indomitable creator, and at the same time a wayward artist, he gradually withdrew more and more into the isolation of his ivory tower, that now legendary retreat of the Ecole de Paris at Puteaux near the Rond Point de la Défense— and what a symbol! There, Kupka and his friend Jacques Villon had their studios side by side.

If the first important and original abstract works of the period from 1909 to 1914 were attacked and ridiculed by the public and orthodox critics, the years after the war witnessed a certain measure of comprehension and recognition. Alexandre Mercereau wrote in *Les Hommes du Jour* in November 1920: "Far from being buried, Kupka illuminates the crypt which one seems to have already decided to call his tomb".

On the occasion of the exhibition of Kupka's work in the Galerie Povolozky in 1921, when Louis Arnould-Gremilly gave a startlingly brilliant and bold speech, critics already spoke of Kupka's "superb compositions rich in colour", of "paintings which are like music, and recall the poetry of Mallarmé". They refer to his paintings as representations of invisible elements, of fluids, electricity, heat, and speak of "a marvellous splendour" and of "cosmic, almost religious paintings". In *The New York Times* (1913) we read: "Matisse, Van Gogh, Cézanne, Picasso, Kupka are the masters of the new age."

But all this did not prevent Kupka from retreating more and more into isolation. It is true that he was nominated professor at the Académie Supérieure des Beaux-Arts at Prague, but he maintained his residence in Paris. In fact, he assisted a large number of young artists who had come from Czechoslovakia to study in Paris, in order to introduce them as directly as possible into their new milieu. But he never ceased his research and never interrupted his impassioned work. Never did the fervour and lyrical impetus of this gentle dreamer of plastic forms and the play of hypothetical light slacken. Indeed, we owe to him a great many poems of the greatest purity. In the last letter which I received from him in Toronto, he told me that in spite of failing health, "I am still able to add something that is new".

He was a truly indomitable creator. He never worshipped the idol of publicity. Therefore, although well known to his fellow-artists and a certain number of initiates, he never attained world-wide celebrity. Of Kupka, one could say with Baudelaire that, having the wings of a giant, he was unable to walk on earth.

Abstract art is no longer modern. It is merely a fashion. Many painters of today whom we call modern would not even know the name of Kupka, that inventor who was so prodigiously in advance of his time and to whom they owe so much, since he was the first with the courage to conceive of painting divorced from subject-matter, as pure music for the eyes – which today is obviously nothing new.

The thousands of painters who today continue to paint in abstract style, not because of an inner necessity, not by a personal, logical evolution, or by rebellion against the style of yesterday, but only because there is a demand – these painters actually produce no more than ornaments or arabesques which could be cut from a canvas without destroying their quality and which are thus fit designs for linoleum or wall-paper. I would like them to study the paintings of Kupka which this innovator of genius created half a century ago. They would be surprised how little their work has advanced, even if they consider it *le dernier cri* of our time. They would see, if they are sentitive and sincere artists, that what they are trying to say, the problems they are trying to solve, and the territory they are trying to conquer, that all has already been said, has been solved, and has been conquered, long ago, and by a master. They do little more than repeat.

It would be reassuring if a visionary poet like Rimbaud might reveal to us a new manner of expression soon to be given to the artist of tomorrow.

If abstract art is in decline today, no more than a fad, this obviously does not lessen the greatness of its first creators, or certainly of Kupka, who was first among the first, just as today's followers of Impressionism in no way diminish the grandeur of Monet, Manet, and other 19th-century masters.

Fame, for Kupka, arrived only after his death.[1] Jean Cassou, in his superb and all-embracing work, *Panorama des Arts Plastiques Contemporains*, begins his essay on the School of Paris as follows: "1871: Frank Kupka born at Opočno, Czechoslovakia".

Four years ago, in 1958, the retrospective exhibition at the Musée d'Art Moderne in Paris (where the "Salle Kupka" is found) finally assigned to Kupka his place as the founder of modern art, the first of the early creators of abstract art, a place which has long been his due.

In the evolution of the plastic arts, Kupka appears like a strong searchlight which has suddenly illuminated the dark sky of Cubism – and in his paintings there is indeed light and fire everywhere! If Kupka's place in history can no longer be disputed, it should not be forgotten that this true classic of abstract art offers – through the probity of his disinterested life and the nobility of his solitary soul, as much as through the value, sincerity, and honesty of his work – the most splendid contribution in that Homeric battle being waged in our time by an intellectual minority against the rising tide of conventional uniformity which threatens that the human species may become so monotonous and so ugly that life no longer would appear worth living.

APPRAISALS

"Gil Blas":
"Le Salon d'Automne, dont l'ouverture est imminente, nous réserve quelques surprises. Les futuristes y ont, naturellement, fait des leurs. Par exemple, M. François Kupka, que le catalogue annonce né en Bohême, expose: 'Amorpha, chromatique chaude'. Et la vue de cette toile, composée d'arabesques futuristes échevelées, ne permet pas de même comprendre le sens de cette mystérieuse

---

[1] Kupka prices have already risen in the current art market. In Paris recently, a forger was caught who had painted about 100 pictures "signed" by Braque, Delaunay, Kupka, Picasso, and Pollock for various art galleries. This would no doubt have evoked an ironic smile from Kupka. But much more serious appreciation of his work appears elsewhere.

désignation. Nous connaissions la tisane chaude et la soupe au lait, mais la chromatique?" (*Echo*, 29 septembre 1912)

M. Claude:
"M. Kupka – qui se manifesta naguère dessinateur intelligent, artiste, lettré, d'invention riche et nombreuse – M. Kupka a tourné, lui, au 'sphérisme'. Ses deux envois 'Amorpha chromatique chaude' font penser aux tapis..."
(*Petit Parisien*, Septembre 1912)

Gustave Kahn:
"Un homme qui a montré beaucoup de talent, M. Kupka, déconcerte..."
(*Mercure de France*, Octobre 1912)

M. Vauxcelles:
"La salle XI déçoit. – Ce n'est que cela, les cubistes? – Oui, Madame. – Mais ce n'est rien! – Rien, Madame. – Qu'est-ce qu'une 'chromatique chaude?' – Demandez à M. Hourcade. – Qu'est-ce qu'une Amorpha? – Demandez à M. Roger Allard. – Mais ces deux littérateurs ont du talent, cependant? – Beaucoup de talent. – Alors? – Alors, Madame ils se f... de nous. – Si Dieu le Père avait créé le Monde 'cubique', la planète serait vraiment cocasse."
(*Gil Blas*, Octobre 1912)

W. Warshawsky:
"Matisse, Van Gogh, Cézanne, Picasso, Kupka are the masters of the new age...
There lives in Paris a painter by the name of François Kupka. He is of an entirely different school, known as the school of Orpheism. He seeks to produce the same impressions on the emotions that music inspires. In painting nature he will so swing his colors and forms about on the canvas as to convey the color feeling of a musical symphony. In painting a red rose he will feel the necessity of a blue or purple or green object in another part of the canvas to convey his emotion. He will therefore swing his colors into such forms as to produce the emotional effect he desires. The whole forms a beautiful, decorative, unified effect". (*The New York Times*, 1913)

A. Gybal:
"François Kupka continue son évolution...... Mais cette peinture est aussi toute force. Ces arabesques mouvementées, c'est le vent, c'est la flamme, c'est la foudre, ce sont les vagues, les gerbes des geysers, c'est le jaillissement des sources, c'est tout ce qui remue, grouille, tout ce qui palpite, c'est le dynamisme de la Nature!
Et c'est surtout la représentation des éléments invisibles, des fluides, de l'électricité, de la chaleur: c'est toute la vie, toute la pensée du monde – et même celle des hommes!" (*Le Journal du Peuple*, Juin 1921)

Alexandre Mercereau:
"... François Kupka n'honore pas seulement la Tchécoslovaquie, où il est né, et la France, qu'il habite, mais l'Art plastique tout entier".
(*Les Hommes du Jour*, Juin 1921)

BIBLIOGRAPHY

L. Arnould Grémilly, *Quelques peintres. Frank Kupka* (Collection d'art "*La Cible*") (Paris, 1922).
Frank Kupka, *Quatre histoires de blanc et noir* (Paris, 1926).
Charles Estienne, *L'Art abstrait est-il un Académisme?* (Collection Le Cavalier d'Epée) (Paris, 1950).
A. L. Channin, "The World of Art. Luminous Works of Kupka Shown at Carré Gallery", *The Compass*, May 13, 1951.
A Dictionary of Modern Painting (New York, Tudor Publishing Co., 1956).
Dictionary of Abstract Painting (New York, Tudor Publishing Co., 1957).
Lillian Lonngren, "Kupka: innovator of the abstract international style", *Art News*, New York, 1957.
Guy Habasque, "Kupka: trois ans après sa mort, la célébrité", *Connaissance des arts*, Paris, Juillet 1960.
Dora Vallier, "L'Art abstrait en Russie. Ses origines. Ses premières manifestations, 1910-1917", *Cahiers d'art*, Paris, 1960.
Joseph-Emile Muller, *La Peinture moderne de Manet à Mondrian*. Edited by Fernand Hazan (Paris, 1960).
Jean Cassou, *Panorama des arts plastiques contemporains* (Paris, Librairie Gallimard, 1960).

EXHIBITION CATALOGUES:

Louis Carré Gallery, New York, 1951.
Musée National d'Art Moderne, Paris, 1958.
Galerie Karl Flinger, Paris, 1960.
Galerie Charles Lienhard, Zurich, 1961.
Saidenberg Gallery, New York, 1962.

The Contribution of the Sculpture of Czechoslovakia to the World of Art

JAN ZACH

An historical survey of the art of sculpture in Czechoslovakia divides naturally into two parts: before and after the nineteenth century, that is, before and after Myslbek.

Though no one particular discipline can be considered the exclusive means of creative communication, sculpture is a conspicuous expression of a given period. That statement can be substantiated by the work of the sculptors and painters invited from Italy, France, Germany and other parts of Europe by the Czech kings to build and decorate churches and palaces during the time of the Kingdom of Bohemia.

In 1344 King Charles IV invited the French architect, Matthias d'Arras, to construct the Gothic cathedral of St. Vitus at Prague Castle. He and his company of French artists, masons and artisans gave an impetus to Czech art which produced an especially high quality of church decoration, altar pieces, cenotaphs and tombstones, as well as the masonry and woodcarving. The standard of decoration was further developed after the arrival of Peter Parler of Swabia, who took over the work of Matthias d'Arras when the latter died in 1352. In his book *Art and Architecture in Europe*, Antonín Matějček says:

Peter Parler, a native of Gmund in Swabia, who in 1352 took over the work of building St. Vitus's Cathedral, was not only an accomplished architect but also the most outstanding sculptor working in Bohemia at that time. He established a workshop in St. Vitus's....[1]

This may seem to suggest that there were no indigenous artists, but the case was rather the opposite. As Jaroslav Jira explained in his excellent article, *Czech Gothic Painting and Sculpture*[2]: There were many artists

---

[1] Antonin Matějček, *Art and Architecture in Europe* (London, Batchworth Press, 1960), p. 256.
[2] Jaroslav Jíra, "České Gotické Malířství a Sochařství", in *Sborník Sklizeň Svobodné Tvorby Č.* 1 (Červenec, 1958), ed. Robert Vlach, Bennett College, Greensboro, N.C., pp. 41, 42.

who were schooling themselves in their own milieu, but they were given no more credit than skilled craftsmen. Their fame is preserved in the records of the Professional Painters Brotherhood by their Christian names only, as, for example, Venceslaus, sculptor, or Ladyslaus, painter. This Brotherhood was founded in 1348 during the reign of Charles IV.

By establishing his workshop in Prague he gave a great boost to the art of sculpture of Bohemia. One result of this centralization of sculptors, masons and artisans was the creation of a truly Czech expression of the Virgin Mary known as Beautiful Madonna, which combined beauty of form and profundity of expression. A good example of these Beautiful Madonnas are the Krumlow Madonnas. Progressive development continued through the late Gothic and Renaissance periods, although Bohemia was being weakened by the Hussite wars. Here and there, woodcarvers and stone masons reached a high standard of skill in church decoration, but no sculptor of significance emerged during this time. However, sculptural "documents" of the period are found in castle architecture such as Křivoklát, Pernstein, or the lovely, old Gothic cathedral of Kutná Hora.

The Baroque style left a very deep impression on Bohemia. Sculpture reached a high degree of excellence, with carving maintaining its leading place. The development of illusionist trends led to the employment of a polychrome technique on woodcarving, with especially fine results. By the introduction of spiral movement within the design of Baroque sculpture, a new concept of action was achieved. The strong influence of the Italian sculptor Bernini was apparent.

Sculpture was carved in stone and modelled in stucco. The public squares and the Gothic Charles Bridge in Prague were transformed into Avenues of the Statues of Saints. Churches were ablaze with colored and gilded sculptures. Prague was transformed into a Baroque city of the character which that beautiful city bears yet today. Much of the early work was done by Italian artists, but by the end of the seventeenth century, the sculptor Brokoff established a workshop in Prague. Matějček says of this artist:

... J. Brokoff established a sculptors' workshop, which, under F. M. Brokoff, produced many of the statues of saints for the Charles Bridge and numerous other works of original design. One of Brokoff's co-workers was M. Braun, a master in expressing passionate pathos, sudden movement and excited postures, who pursued Bernini's concept of dynamic movement to its final limits. In his numerous monumental statues and sculptures for architecture, gardens and churches (St. Luitgarda on Charles Bridge, 1710, statues at Kuks, etc.), Braun

The Sculpture of Czechoslovakia

raised Prague sculpture to a level which often outshone the standard in the rest of Europe.[3]

All of these artists were forerunners of the nineteenth-century Czech Renaissance, when Josef Václav Myslbek became the pivot upon which the old tradition in sculpture turned to the new. His creative contemporaries include Smetana, Dvořák and Janáček in music; Josef Mánes, Mikoláš Aleš and Antonín Slavíček in painting; and A. Jirásek, Jungman, Šafařík, B. Němcová, Čech and Vrchlický in letters. They all worked hand in hand toward the monumental rebirth of Czechoslovak culture in that period.

J. V. Myslbek was born in 1844 and died in 1922. He was the great Czech sculptor of the 19th century, attaining for the Czechs the same importance that Rodin had for the French. His work was intensely national in feeling, expressing deep love for his country. His imagination had grown on tales of the heroic deeds of ancestors. He strove to create in sculpture, under the romantic influence of his time, those historical and religious images of which every Czech has heard. The provincial atmosphere of Prague limited this great genius to the type of descriptive realism which then prevailed throughout Central Europe. The same romantic idiom can be discerned in the music of Smetana and Dvořák.

Myslbek was a devout, religious man. His work was full of compassion, and his influence on Czech sculptors, immense. E. H. Ramsden says:

Nearly every artist of repute has either been trained in his studio or has come under his influence in one way or another, "being drawn, again and again, through the magnetism of his creative personality, to the master's works, no matter how far they may venture from his realistic monumentality".[4]

His foremost pupil, Jan Štursa, was a very fine modeller, his sense of movement defined by a flow of light over every part of the surface of his sculpture. He affected a whole succeeding generation of Czech sculptors.

After the first World War, the influence of the School of Paris was very strong in Central Europe. The impressionistic treatment of form and freedom of modelling characteristic of this school are evident in the work of Myslbek's pupils, in the work of Štursa's pupil, Lauda, as well as in the sculpture of Gutfround, Makovský, Dvořák, Kostka, Kubiček and others. The freshness of expression of the School of Paris fitted the new life

---

[3] Antonín Matějček, *Art and Architecture in Europe* (London, Batchworth Press, 1960), p. 454.
[4] E. H. Ramsden, *Twentieth Century Sculpture* (London, Pleiades Books, 1949), pp. 23, 24.

which sparked from the liberation of Czechoslovakia from the Austro-Hungarian Empire in 1918.

The philosophy of the Constructivists probably had the greatest impact on the culture of Czechoslovakia in the period between the two World Wars. The architect Pešánek was the most successful member of this group. His electric piano fountain executed for the Czech Pavillion at the Universal Exhibition in Paris in 1936 was a good example of the Constructivist movement.

There are many Czech sculptors today in different parts of the world; some are in England, having remained after World War II, of whom Veigl is the best known, and in Paris, there is Jan Vlach. But most of them took root in the United States. Some have achieved distinction in teaching, for instance, the sculptors Albin Polášek in Chicago, and George Leišner at Washington State University in Pullman. Mario Korbel is represented mostly in private collections; Louis Durchánek, of New York, is represented in the most significant collections and museums of the United States, including the Museum of Modern Art in New York City.

My own concern in sculpture is with the illumination of forms in space and with the utilization of the resultant shadows (whether created by solar or artificial light) as a plastic element of *equal importance* with the solid and negative volumes of the sculptural work.

In other words, whereas contemporary sculpture has, in the case of such artists as Moore and Zadkine, employed negative volume as integral parts of the sculptural work, I am striving to make the additional elements of shadow and time equal partners in sculptural content.

In the last eleven years the magnificent beaches of Oregon and Vancouver Island have exerted an increasingly strong influence on my ideas of sculptural form. The endless variety of shapes cast up by the sea – roots of trees, branch fragments, seaweed, natural rock formations – have impressed me with the immense vitality inherent in natural formations. They have clarified for me certain sculptural concepts of growth and movement through time, as expressed in the twisting and thrusting trunks and roots of trees. I am searching for an understanding of nature more closely in harmony with Einstein's vision – that of the space-time continuum.

In Czechoslovakia today the creative experimentation with plastic means which started after the 'twenties is almost totally paralyzed, and only some of us living abroad are carrying further the vanguard of research and experiment in the creative field. Only in the animated film and the art of puppetry does Czechoslovakia excel today. The painter

Jiří Trnka, pupil of the very fine graphic artist Kratochvíl, has brought the animated film and the art of puppetry to the highest degree of excellence in the world, yet he, as many other artists, is the product of the cultural dynamism which prevailed before the second World War.

History shows the concept of life and definition of beauty constantly changing with the development of the human mind and technology. When man reaches the conviction that he has found the "eternal truth," he declines into imitation and decadence. In art there is nothing final, only constant growth and progress which go hand in hand with all social and technical changes of human development. This constant growth and progress can happen only in a world of freedom of mind and creative expression.

HISTORY

The First Contact of Czechs with Western Civilization: The Mission of St. Amand in the 7th Century

MILIČ ČAPEK

1. INTRODUCTION

It is generally believed that the Slavic inhabitants of the present territory of Czechoslovakia did not come in contact with Christianity before the ninth century A. D. Three important dates are usually mentioned: the building of the first church in Nitra in 836, the baptism of fourteen Czech dukes at Regensburg in 845, and, finally, the mission of Cyril and Methodius to Moravia in 863. This view was held by both Czech and foreign historians; it can be found in the classical work of Palacký and it remained unchallenged despite the fact that some of Palacky's conclusions concerning the earliest centuries of Czech history have been revised. Thus it is hardly surprising that Ferdinand Hrejsa, in his *History of Christianity in Czechoslovakia*, published after the Second World War, did not depart from the traditional view.[1] The view that Christianity reached the regions of Czechs and Slovaks in the ninth century seemed natural, according to the available sources. It is the purpose of this study to point out that attentive reading and careful analysis of one or two documents strongly suggest the possibility of such contact no less than two centuries earlier, in the first half of the seventh century.

The document itself is fairly well known, although its true meaning, in my opinion, has not been understood; it is the Latin biography of St. Amand, apostle of Belgium and The Netherlands, who became the bishop of Maastricht and eventually retired to the Abbey of Elnon near Tournai, where he died around 675. We are not concerned here with his missionary activity among the Franks inhabiting the present territory of northern France, Belgium and The Netherlands; of direct interest is what his modern biographer, Edouard de Moreau, called "a strange chapter of St.

---

[1] F. Hrejsa, *Dějiny křestanství v Československu* (Praha, 1947), I, p. 15-17.

Amand's life": his missionary voyage to the Slavs "beyond the Danube".[2] The precise date of his voyage is, and probably will always remain, conjectural, but it is generally agreed that it took place around the year 630. The text of the biography states:

Audivit denique quod Sclavi, nimie errore decepti a diaboli laqueis tenerentur oppressi, maximeque martyrii palmam se adsequi posse confidens, *transfretato Danubio eadem circumiens loca* libera voce evangelium Christi gentibus praedicabat. Paucisque ex his in Christo regeneratis, videns etiam sibi minime adcrescere fructum et martyrium, quod semper quaerebat, minime adepturum, ad proprias reversus est oves... [Italics mine.][3]

All what we know about St. Amand's missionary trip is contained in this passage: its motive, an apostle's missionary zeal and desire for martyrdom, its limited duration, its little success and, finally, the single, and all too vague, indication of its geographical location. Obviously this area was somewhere "beyond the Danube", but where? According to the prevailing interpretation (the only one I know of) "behind the Danube" means "behind" relative to the area of St. Amand's previous activity – that is, Belgium. In other words, St. Amand crossed the Danube on his way from Belgium to the Slovenes of Carinthia.[4] I believe that there are solid reasons to regard this interpretation as highly artificial and strained, and that there is an alternative interpretation which is far more natural and whose probability is greatly increased by other circumstantial evidence.

2. THE IMPROBABILITY OF THE TRADITIONAL INTERPRETATION

Let us consider first the geographical reasons. It is true that the Danube flows "between" Belgium and Carinthia; in other words, that the bee-line joining Carinthia and the region where St. Amand dwelt prior to his

---

[2] Edouard de Moreau, *St. Amand, apôtre de la Belgique et du Nord de France*, Musaeum Lessianum, 1927, ch. IV ("Saint Amand chez les Slaves du sud").

[3] *Scriptores rerum Merovingiarum*, ed. by B. Krusch (Leipzig, 1910), V, p. 439-40; *Acta Sanctorum*, ed. by Ioannes Bollandius and Godefridus Henschenius, Februarius, Tomus I (Antverpiae, Anno MDCLVIII), p. 851.

F. W. Rettberg, *Kirchengeschichte Deutschlands* (Göttingen, 1846), II, p. 556; A. Hauck, *Kirchengeschichte Deutschlands* (Leipzig, 1887), I, 298; Gosse, "Essai sur St. Amand", *Revue de Gascogne*, X (1869), p. 333; E. de Moreau, *op. cit.*, ch. IV; Alois Huber, *Geschichte der Einführung und Verbreitung des Christenthums in Südostdeutschland*, IV, p. 159; O. Kämmel, *Die Entstehung des österreichischen Deutschtums* (Leipzig, 1879), p. 196; M. Büdinger, *Österreichische Geschichte* (Leipzig, 1858), p. 82.

trip crosses the Danube somewhere in the present territory of Würtemberg. This geographical truth is obvious to anyone looking at a modern map of Central Europe. Certainly this was the main reason why modern historians located St. Amand's missionary activity in Slovenia. But to presuppose such detailed geographical knowledge in an eighth century monk[5] is certainly an anachronism. The reason why the author of *Vita Sancti Amandi* even mentioned the Danube must have been different from that which may occur to the reader of a modern detailed map. *Either* he wanted to indicate the general direction of the route which the apostle followed in going to the Slavs, *or* he wanted to indicate the *final destination* of his trip, that is, the area in which he eventually preached the gospel.

If we consider the first alternative, we wonder why the author mentioned crossing the Danube at all. In its upper reaches the Danube is not sufficiently wide to be designated as an important landmark on the eastward route from Belgium to Carinthia. It would have been far more natural to mention crossing the Rhine,[6] which in its mid-section not only is wider than the upper Danube, but also flows from the South to the North, that is, perpendicular to the general direction of St. Amand's route. In ancient chronicles it was customary to mention the crossing of rivers only when they were notably large, and when they lay athwart the route so that their crossing was unavoidable. This would have been true of the Rhine and, to a lesser degree, of several southern tributaries of the Danube such as the Lech, the Isar, the Inn, which all lie "on the way to Carinthia" and which are not much different in width from the upper Danube. Unlike its southern tributaries, the Danube flows generally *eastward*, that is, parallel to the route of St. Amand; its crossing is certainly not necessary in going from Belgium to the Alps of Carinthia. Thus the choice of the upper Danube as an important landmark designating the direction of St. Amand's route to the Slovenes would have been very odd, both because of the direction of its flow and its relatively insignificant width.

The second interpretation, that the author wanted to indicate by his reference to the Danube *the final destination* of St. Amand's journey, is far more probable; but if we accept this, we must revise completely the traditional interpretation of this passage. According to the traditional, so far unchallenged, view, St. Amand crossed the Danube from the North to the South, that is, from the left to the right bank. Disregarding its *his-*

---

[5] According to E. de Moreau, the first Latin biography was written in the first half, probably in the first quarter, of the eighth century (*op. cit.*, pp. 50-51).
[6] This is what Bonaldus does in his commentary: "ultra Rhenum, Danubiumque profectus", *A. S.*, Feb., I, p. 828.

torical improbability (to be discussed below) this explanation would make sense only if the Slavs had been residing directly *behind the Danube* ("behind" in respect to Belgium), or at least, not far from it, somewhere in the southern part of Würtemberg or Bavaria. Now it is true that in the seventh century the Slovenes extended much farther West and North than now, but certainly not as far as the upper Danube in Bavaria or Würtemberg. They occupied, besides the whole of Carinthia and Styria, also the easternmost valleys of Tyrol, the southeastern corner of Salzburg, and the southern portion of Upper Austria as far as the Enns river. Between the Enns and Inn, there were only sparse settlements, while farther West there were only a few places where the Wends captured in war were settled in the midst of the compact Teutonic population. It is true that after Samo's victory over Dagobert, the Slavs pushed as far west as the Main and Radnitz River, where they remained for several centuries and were known as *Moinwinidi et Ratanzwinidi* (Wends of the Main and Radnitz R.). These settlements, however, were North of the Danube.[7] Had St. Amand been active among these westernmost Slavs, the expression "Danubio transfretato" would have been completely inappropriate, and the term "Rheno transfretato" far more natural. In any case this interpretation would require giving up the hypothesis of St. Amand's mission to the Slovenes, who certainly had not settled near that section of the Danube which St. Amand allegedly crossed.

3. THE NEW INTERPRETATION OF THE CRUCIAL TEXT

In the light of these negative conclusions, what is a correct, or, at least, more satisfactory interpretation of the crucial expression "Danubio transfretato"? The explanation offered below seems the most natural, and it may appear bold at first glance only because it differs from the previously accepted explanation. The essential features of the new hypothesis are here set forth.

On his way from Belgium to Central Europe St. Amand travelled by a more southerly route than has been believed until now; he thus reached the *right* bank of the Danube, not the left, or northern, bank, and crossed the river heading *north*. For reasons fully stated below, this crossing took place *approximately* in Upper Austria or Eastern Bavaria, i.e., in a sector limited by Regensburg in the West and the Enns River in

---

[7] Lubor Niederle, *Slovanské starožitnosti* (Praha, 1919), II, pp. 82-87.

the East; his apostolic mission was carried on among the Slavs then inhabiting the western and southern slopes of the Bohemian Forest (Šumava), who belonged ethnically to the Slavic population of the present territory of Bohemia and Moravia.

We stated the reasons why the designation of the Danube as a geographical landmark of St. Amand's route is unintelligible as long as we assume that he travelled to the Slovenes of Carinthia. Some additional historical arguments militate against the probability of this route. The route of a Christian apostle journeying south of the Danube through the still-pagan Bavaria to the Alps was risky enough, as the fate of St. Emmeram one century later clearly showed; the route through the wild and pagan regions north of the Danube, which (unlike Bavaria) had never been under lasting Roman rule, and which had hardly changed since the times of Tacitus, was certainly out of the question. It is much more probable that St. Amand chose a much safer route through the former Roman province of Raetia south of the Danube; it had for centuries been under the civilizing influence of the Romans and its still-usable network of Roman highways made it far more accessible.[8] Moreover, in Bavaria there were still some remnants of Roman Christians who had survived the barbarian invasions and on whose cooperation and advice St. Amand could count before he ventured into still wilder regions in the East. A similar southern route was taken by St. Columbanus shortly before St. Amand; he started from Burgundy and followed the course of the Rhine eastward along the present Swiss-German boundary up to Bregenz, where he paused to consider his missionary expedition to the Slavs. St. Columbanus himself did not realize the contemplated expedition, and it is uncertain whether any of his twelve companions did, but his plan illustrates the general historical pattern: the Christianizing influences always reached the Slavs of the Alps from the West, never from the North.

The northern boundary of the Slovenes was then approximately the Danube, which separated them from the Slavic ancestors of Czechs, and nothing would be more preposterous than to assume that St. Amand reached the Slovenians from this direction. Such an assumption implies that the apostle travelled, first, across the whole territory between the Rhine and Bohemia which began to be Christianized one full century later by St. Boniface, then through pagan Bohemia itself before reaching the Danube. Yet this fantastic hypothesis is implicitly postulated by those who claim that St. Amand crossed the Danube in the *southward*

---

[8] Alois Huber, *op. cit.*, III, I. Abhandlung ("Die Alten Römerstrassen als Substrat des Christianisierungsganges"), pp. 1-98, esp. pp. 10-19.

direction; for the only place where the Danube bounded the Slovene territory in the seventh century was where it separated them from the Czechs and Moravians. For a person not acquainted with history, it is difficult to visualize the contiguity of the Czechs and the Slovenes on the Danube as part of the compact bloc of Slavic population stretching from the Baltic shore to the northern corner of the Adriatic Sea. Yet this is unquestionable historical fact to any serious Slavic or German historian – the fact which explains the spectacular rise of the first Slavic Federation in Central Europe under the leadership of Samo. The map at the end of the third volume of Lubor Niederle's *Slovanské starožitnosti*, showing the early ethnographical boundaries of the Western Slavs in respect to both the Germans and the Southern Slavs makes this fact abundantly clear.

The same map shows even more graphically than other circumstantial evidence how incomparably more natural it is to believe that St. Amand crossed the Danube going northward to the Slavs. For while the Danube formed an approximate boundary between the Czechs and the Slovenes in the present territory of Lower, and in the eastern part of Upper, Austria, *farther west, in the foothills of the Bohemian Forest (between Regensburg in the West and the mouth of the Enns River in the East), it divided the Czechs from the Bavarians.* In other words, it formed the northern boundary of Bavaria and the southern territorial limit of the Slavic ancestors of the Czech population which was overflowing southward on the western and southern slopes of the Bohemian Forest. If St. Amand, as we suggest, crossed the Danube in this region on arriving from the South, the expression "Danubio transfretato", so absurd in any other interpretation, becomes entirely intelligible. I believe it becomes truly intelligible *only* in this interpretation. Not only was the Danube east from Regensburg sizeable enough to be designated as a conspicuous landmark, but it was also at that time the southern boundary of the Czech Slavs who were then residing literally behind it – "trans Danubium", as another early biographer of St. Amand says.[9] Let us survey all other additional evidence favoring this interpretation; despite its circumstantial character, its cumulative effect is quite impressive.

Another relatively early source of information about St. Amand's life is the Latin poem of Milo, a monk at the monastery of Elnon about two centuries later.[10] It was the monastery where St. Amand died and in which apparently the memory of his life and deeds, including his mis-

---

[9] *A. S.*, Feb., I, p. 855: "Deinde trans Danubium ad terras ubi Christus non nominabatur praedicare perrexit" (Alia vita Auctore Aquitano anonymo).
[10] *Poetae Latini aevi Carolini*, III, ed. by L. Traube (Berlin, 1896), esp. pp. 591-92.

sionary expedition to the Slavs, was kept alive. Its name was later changed to that of its founder, and even the present name of the locality, "St. Amand-les-Eaux", commemorates the seventh-century apostle. Milo lived between 809 and 872,[11] and the relevant passages in his poem unmistakably suggest the way in which "the crossing of the Danube" was understood in the monastic community which, by tradition and geography, stood closer to St. Amand's life than the modern historians. Let the text of the poem speak for itself. The author first refers to "the land of Slavs" as previously untouched by Christianity (v. 149-151):

> Te neque, apostolica numquam purgata securi
> Ac fidei sulcis ullo neque vomere culta,
> Pertransisse virum doleas, Sclavinia tellus...

Can these be the characteristics of the region *south of the Danube*, which used to be the Roman province of Noricum and later one of the earliest Christian dioceses? Even assuming that the memory of early Christianity faded during the seventh and eight centuries, when Noricum was devastated by the Avars, it must be remembered that Milo wrote in the *ninth* century, fifty years after the Avars had been decisively defeated and chased to the East by the armies of Charlemagne, while the Slovenes had been converted to Christianity a full century before. We know that the re-christianization of Noricum, *which was bounded by the Danube on the North*, revived the memory of the earliest Christian apostles St. Florian and St. Severinus, who were active there. But Milo's poem explicitly states that St. Amand ventured into a wild, unknown territory where *no* Christian missionary had ever dared to tread (vv. 180-188):

> Te quoque, sancte sator, dum nos comitamur euntem
> Atque tuum sequimur felicem carmine cursum,
> *Ignotum transimus iter* sermone meantes
> *Quo nullus missus milleno ex agmine Iesu*
> *Vivificam iecit cornu curvante sagittam.*
> Non Petrus, Paulus neque seminiverbius olim
> Propter opus solitum veraci errore vocatus,
> Nemo alius, validis quanquam confisus in armis,
> cuspidis eximium iactavit acumen in illam.
> [Italics mine.]

But even more definite are other passages in the poem which clearly support our theory about the apostle's *northward crossing* of the Danube (vv. 159-164):

[11] *Ibidem*, p. 557.

> ... Comperit adstrictos Sclavos errore inimici.
> Quo se martyrium pro Christo posse mereri
> Confidens sanctus *glacialem transiit Istrum,*
> Incipit et glebas durae perscindere terrae;
> Inde evangelii semen dispergit ubique
> Per loca perque domos, per rura et competa iactans.
>
> [Italics mine.]

Was the adjective "glacialis" accidentally chosen as a mere *epitheton ornans* without any geographical significance? Does not the choice of this adjective strongly suggest the connotation of a cold northern region which St. Amand was entering in crossing the Danube from the South? Does not the adjective describe rather accurately the banks of the Danube on the foothills of the Bohemian Forest or, even more accurately, the gorges through which the river flows in Upper Austria and the western part of Lower Austria? This interpretation is even more strongly suggested in another passage in which Milo expressed his amazement and admiration of the bravery and courage with which St. Amand ignored all the dangers of his trip to the *unknown* country where even his armed Frankish compatriots were not secure (vv. 194-200):

> Qualis forte tuam rexit constantia pectus?
> Qualis et invictum retinens audacia robur
> *Fecit in ignotam regionem* tendere gressum?
> *De qua pro donis veniebant vulnera Francis;*
> *Rex quibus armorum valido munimine septus*
> *Terga dabat fugiens Franco comitante feroce:*
> Tu socio sine per markas clusasque ruebas.
>
> [Italics mine.]

Edouard de Moreau, the modern biographer of St. Amand, following in this respect B. Krusch, the editor of *Scriptores Rerum Merovingiarum*, sees in the lines just quoted the allusion to the defeats which the armies of Louis the German suffered from Rostislav, the Duke of Great Moravia in the years 846 and 849. (This helped Traube approximately to determine the period 845-855 as that in which the poem was written.[12]) But it is equally possible that the author of the poem referred to the defeat of the Frankish king Dagobert in 631, and that the contemporary defeats of Louis the German merely made the recollection of Dagobert's defeat in Milo's mind more vivid.[13] In any case, whether Milo referred to the defeat of

---

[12] Ibidem, III, p. 557; *S. R. M.*, IV, p. 407.

[13] The phrase "De qua pro donis veniebant vulnera Francis" might have been an allusion to the murder of some Frankish merchants by the Slavs. This was one of the causes of the conflict between Dagobert and Samo (Fredegar's Chronicle, *S.R.M.*, II, 154).

Dagobert or the defeats of Louis the German, *there is no question that in either case the reference was made to the region north of the Danube.* This river in Milo's time was the southern boundary of the Moravian empire from Děvín (Theben) in the East as far west as the gorge of Wachau; in other words, in invading Great Moravia, Louis the German was moving to the northern bank of the Danube. On the other hand, although the exact location of Wogast, where Dagobert was defeated by Samo in 631, will probably remain forever uncertain, all historians think that it was somewhere *north* of the Danube. Thus the passage just quoted is another powerful argument in favor of revising the traditional interpretation of St. Amand's itinerary.

It would be otiose to speculate about the exact location of St. Amand's crossing of the Danube. No information about it is available. But it is possible to determine, broadly at least, *the stretch* of the river where the crossing took place without trying ambitiously to localize it exactly. Let us examine the reasons for our previously stated belief that this spot lies somewhere between Regensburg in the West and Lorch (the ancient Laureacum) in the East where the Enns River joins the Danube. In this respect Milo's allusion to the defeats of the Frankish armies, together with the general ethnographical conditions in the seventh century, are the most precious clues. From Regensburg, where it bends in the Southeast up to the mouth of the Enns River, the Danube runs near the slopes of the Bohemian Forest and, at the time of St. Amand's expedition, it constituted *approximately* the ethnic boundary between the Czechs and the Bavarians. East from the Enns river the Danube flowed through the compact Slavic territory roughly dividing the Czechs occupying the northern bank from the Slovenians residing on the southern bank. In other words, had St. Amand crossed the Danube farther east, he would have reached the compact Slavic settlements *before* reaching the Danube line; nothing of this kind is hinted at in any biography of St. Amand. As long as we take the only available historical sources seriously, we cannot escape the conclusion that the crossing occurred *west* of the Enns river, perhaps even west of the Inn river; for there were some sparse Slavic settlements even between the Inn and the Enns rivers. On the other hand, it is highly improbable that St. Amand crossed the Danube west, or at least far west, of Regensburg, unless we assume that he went preaching to the Slavs on the rivers Main and Radnitz. These Slavic settlements could have been reached far more directly by crossing the Rhine in the neighbourhood of the city of Worms (at that time already a seat of bishopric) without crossing the Danube.

4. THE EARLY ETHNOGRAPHIC CONDITIONS ON THE NORTHERN BANK OF THE DANUBE

It remains to show how and to what extent the northern bank of the Danube from Regensburg eastward was settled by the Slavs. Even a superficial glance at the present toponymy of the northeastern strip of Bavaria between the Danube and the Bohemian Forest will reveal now, thirteen centuries after St. Amand, some village names whose Slavic origin is obvious. Alois Huber lists in his detailed work no less than 46 "Wendish or Czechoslavic" names in the decanal district of Neunburg vorm Walde, Cham, Underviehtach in the diocese of Regensburg. Among them are: Grabitz, Köblitz, Kötzing, Kolmitz, Kulz, Lam, Premaischl, Rötz, Salliz, Wuritz and Zelz. To these he adds 21 other more germanized names such as Wenzenried and Windish Bergerndorf. Slavic names are rarer in the decanal districts of Regen, Schönberg, Waldkirchen, but even there Huber counts no less than 15 names, among which are Flainz (Flanitz), Leiflitz, Prag (!) and another Rötz. Even more significant are the names of mountains and brooks, because they usually reflect the oldest ethnographical conditions: Arber (Javor), Lusen (Luzný), Ossa (Osí) and Rachel (Roklan). These mountains are hard on the border, although Huber points out that Klein-Rachel lies deep in the interior. As far as the names of the brooks are concerned, Huber mentions that on the older maps they were purely Slavic ("rein-slavisch"); one of them, Flanitz, (from the Czech "Blatnice") gave its name to the hamlet mentioned above.[14] The perusal of some ancient archives fully confirms the conclusion suggested by the toponymy of the region. Both Lubor Niederle and Alois Huber mention King Arnulf's endowing chart of the year 896, referring to "the strangers and free Slavs" ("ad hospites pertinent et liberos Slavos") in the neighbourhood of the villages Pösing and Roding northeast of Regensburg. Niederle points out that the settlement of Pempling, as late as the twelfth century, was called Boem-villingen, while Huber stresses that the village *Böhmerbruck*, the ancient *Pons Bohemorum*, lies deeper in Bavarian territory than the German villages of Bruck near Nittenau, and Arnbruck near Javor (Arber). Niederle also stresses the fact that the political boundary of Bohemia, as late as the eleventh century, lay farther to the West and Southwest, as the founding charter of the bishopric of Prague clearly shows when it refers to the river Chuba (the

---

[14] A. Huber, *op. cit.*, IV, p. 89. Paul Müller in his dissertation thesis *Böhmerwald und seine Stellung in der Geschichte* (Strassburg, 1904), pp. 107-13, lists 129 names of Slavic origin on the Bavarian side of the Bohemian Forest.

present Kamb) in Bavaria.[15] Other evidence on this point is contained in biographies of the German hermit, Günther (in Czech: Vintíř), according to which he founded the monastery of Rinchnach *in Bohemia* ("in Poemia", or "in quodum saltu Boemico").[16] Today Rinchnach lies deep in Bavaria. Ernst Schwarz's recent post-war study showed the Slavic character of two settlements north-east of Regensburg, whose names today sound purely German: Appattzwing was *Abbatiwinidun* ("Wends of the Abbot") in 1031, and Wolferzwing, *Wolfartswinden* (Wends of Wolfart, their landlord) in 1325.[17]

Early ethnographical conditions on the southern slopes of the Bohemian Forest, that is, in the northern part of Upper Austria (between the Danube and the present Czechoslovak border), were not essentially different. Again the toponymy of the rivers and mountains bears clear traces of the original Slavic settlement. The present political boundary between Austria and Bohemia somehow obscures the fact that the Bohemian Forest, which today constitutes the boundary between Bavaria and Bohemia, extends much further southeastward through the territories of Upper and Lower Austria, as far as the Danube; in truth, the picturesque gorge of the Wachau is formed by the southernmost foothills of the Bohemian Forest and the northern promontories of the Alps. It is true that this Austrian section of the Bohemian Forest is now called *"Greinwald"*, but it has not been always so. Thus the charter of Räffelstatten, dated 906, regulating the commercial traffic on the Danube, grants the privilege of carrying trade on the river as far as the Bohemian Forest ("licentiam mercandi habent *ad silvam bohemicam*"). This is not the only trace of the original Czech population of the northern bank of the Danube. L. Niederle pointed out that when the *Annales Einhardi* describe the retreat of Charlemagne's army from Pannonia to Regensburg in 791 "per Behaimos," this expression should not be interpreted as "through Bohemia" in its present narrow sense, but as "through Bohemians residing on the northern bank of the Danube." O. Kämmel showed that the toponymy of the valley of Wachau is clearly Slavic, even though the original Slavic names are often distorted beyond recognition and only archival research enables us to identify them.[18]

---

[15] Niederle, III, p. 84; Huber, *ibidem*.
[16] *Monumenta Germaniae Historica*, SS XI, p. 383: "A beato Gunthario coenobium quoddam constructum est in Poemia", *Vita Guntheri eremiate*; *ibidem*, p. 277.
[17] E. Schwarz, "Die bayrische Landnahme um Regensburg im Spiegel der Völker- and Ortsnamen", in *Beiträge zur Namenforschung*, Bd. I (1949-50), p. 70.
[18] O. Kämmel, *Die Entstehung des österreichischen Deutschtums* (Leipzig, 1879), pp.

Farther west, in Upper Austria, not only there are clearly Slavic names of the mountain brooks north of the Danube, Sarming (Sabinicha 1037, from Slavic *Žabinica*) near Grein, Jaunitz (Iowerniz in 1142, from *Javornice*), Feistritz (*Bystřice*), Flanitz (*Blanice*), Granitz (*Granice*), but many of the originally Slavic settlements have been identified by the detailed studies of J. Strnadt, V, Hasenhöhrl and Lubor Niederle.[19] Strnadt counted no less than 175 Slavic names, too many to be listed here. Most conspicuous are: Zwettl (Světlá) on Gross-Rodl, Primislasdorf, Kulm (from *chlum*), Pregarten (from *pre-grad*), and all other names which contain the components Böhm-, Böhmisch or Wind-, Windisch, sometimes considerably deformed: Boheimschlag, Böhmdorf, Böhmsedt, Pehersdorf (Pehaimsdorf in 1303), Windekk, Winden, Wienerweg ("der Weg der Wenden" in Strnadt's interpretation), Windisch-Markt, (the former name of Freistadt, in Czech: Cáhlov), Holzwinden, and finally Abwinden on the Danube. Strnadt believes that the Slavs occupied these regions before the Bavarians in the fifth century, that is, two centuries before St. Amand's mission; according to him they constituted an independent *Župa*, ruled probably from the castle of Graz located near the angle between Gusen and Grosse Gusen, southeast of the present town of Gallneukirchen, where traces of the ancient Slavic fortifications are still discernible.[20] The original independence of the Trans-Danubian Slavs is made more probable by the explicit reference to "free Slavs" (Slavi liberi) between the rivers of Aist and Naarn in 853, while the Slavic landowners north of Linz are mentioned as late as 1111 and 1115. In 827, "Slavic witnesses" were mentioned at Puchenau north of Linz;[21] earlier, in 805, part of the famous "limes Sorabicus", that is, the military border established by Charlemagne against the Slavs, ran along the Danube from Laureacum (Lorch) at the mouth of the Enns up to Regensburg.[22] The poet Milo was born at about that time, and thus we can understand why to

---

172-73; 208; L. Niederle, "Jak daleko seděli Čechové na jih?", *Český časopis historický*, XV (1909), pp. 73-76; *Slovanské starožitnosti*, II, p. 354.

[19] Niederle, *op. cit.* 354-355; J. Strnadt, "Die freien Leute der alten Riedmark. Wenden- und Bajuwaren siedlung", *Archiv für österreichische Geschichte*, v. 104 (1915), pp. 499-539; V. Hasenhöhrl, "Deutschlands südostliche Marken", *Archiv für öst. Geschichte*, v. 92 (1882); O. Kämmel, *op. cit.*, pp. 171-2; the same author, "Die slavische Ortsnamen in nordlichen Theile Niederösterreichs", *Archiv für slav. Philogie*, VII (1884).

[20] J. Strnadt, *loc. cit.*, pp. 467-6; 506; 541-2. Cf. the plan of "the Wendish fortress at Graz", *ibid.*, p. 545. Strnadt's view that the Slavs north of the Danube were Slovenes was critized by Niederle, *Čes. Časopis Historicky*, XXIV, p. 349. Niederle points out that while the Danube was the northern boundary of the Slovenes, some Czech settlements were even on the southern bank. Cf. *Slov. starožitnosti*, II, 354; III, 212.

[21] Alois Huber, *op. cit.*, IV, 232, 253; O. Kämmel, *op. cit.*, pp. 170-171.

[22] L. Niederle, *op. cit.*, II, pp. 70-71.

The First Contact of Czechs with Western Civilization 195

him the name of the Danube meant the northern, cold boundary of the Empire which St. Amand crossed into an "unknown land". It is clear that the establishment of the military Frankish border between Regensburg and Enns in 805 merely confirmed the military and ethnical *status quo* which had existed two centuries before; for it was in the seventh century that the Slavic westward expansion reached its outermost limits.[23]

5. THE MOTIVES AND THE EFFECTS OF ST. AMAND'S MISSION

Historians often wonder about the possible motive of St. Amand's mission to the Slavs. What inspired him to travel so far to the East and to preach the gospel to the Slavs of the Danube when there were many pagan populations much closer?[24] His Latin biography seems to suggest that St. Amand, encouraged by the partial success of his missionary activity in Belgium, wanted to carry the gospel to other nations. Did he choose the Slavs because this mission seemed more dangerous and he desired martyrdom? Possibly; but this desire could have been satisfied among the pagans of Germany. Even Bavaria, which he had to cross, was still largely pagan in spite of its scattered remnants of Christianity. Sigismund Riezler, the historian of Bavaria, believes that St. Amand went to the Slavs, that is, beyond the limits of the Frankish empire, because he fell into disgrace with King Dagobert, whose loose moral life he severely censured.[25] Another interesting, though fanciful, conjecture was proffered by the seventeenth century editor of *Acta Sanctorum*, J. Bolland. As a Belgian, Bolland naturally wondered why the apostle of Belgium went so far to the East. Bolland was acquainted with the chronicle of Fredegar, which is nearly the only historical source about the Slavic king, Samo. Fredegar's statement that Samo was of Frankish origin clearly inspired Bolland's attempt to explain St. Amand's decision to go preaching to the Slavs. According to Bolland, St. Amand, hearing that the Slavs had elected his countryman Samo their king, decided to convert them to

---

[23] Nor should we forget that the notion of the Danube as the northernmost boundary of the civilization was, so to speak, inherited from Roman times, when the Danube was, first, the northern limit of the Empire and, later, the northern limit of early Christianity; the diocese of Noricum was bounded by the Danube.
[24] E. de Moreau, *op. cit.*, ch. IV, pp. 152-153.
[25] S. Riezler, *Geschichte Bayerns* (Gotha, 1878), I, p. 91, H. Pirenne, *Histoire de Belgique* (Bruxelles, 1902), I, 16, believes the very opposite was true: St. Amand discouraged by the lack of response in Belgium, looked for a more promising field of his missionary activity among "the Slavs of the Danube".

Christianity, and started his eastward journey equipped with the letters of recommendation from Samo's Frankish and already Christianized relatives! Bolland himself regarded this explanation as hypothetical; no historian, so far as I know, took it seriously, except Šafařík, who did not exclude the possibility that St. Amand's mission took place with the permission of Samo.[26] This would certainly explain the partial, though very limited, success of St. Amand's preaching, and especially his failure to secure a martyr's crown. But as no contact of St. Amand with Samo is documented, Bolland's story is merely an interesting, though not absurd, conjecture.

But in one respect Bolland's hypothesis had a lasting effect. At that time, historians placed the empire of Samo in *Caranthania* on the basis of a single sentence in the ninth century *Conversio Bagoariorum et Caranthanorum*: "Samo manens in Caranthanis". This, and the assumption of the contact between the Christian apostle and the Slavic king, obviously led Bolland to locate St. Amand's missionary activity south of the Danube, among the Slovenes in Carinthia. Today critical scholarship is fairly unanimous in locating the center of Samo's empire in Bohemia, even though the Slovenians of the Alps, in a loose sense, also belonged to it. Yet all church historians, so far as I know, continue to accept Bolland's hypothesis of St. Amand preaching in Carinthia, although they reject or ignore Bolland's main reason – the hypothesis of some connection between St. Amand and Samo![27] Today such a hypothesis would only strengthen our conclusion that St. Amand preached *north* of the Danube. But we believe that this conclusion is safe enough to be independent of any such unverified – and unverifiable – hypothesis.

In order to understand St. Amand's motives, we shall be on much safer ground if we consider historical facts only. Undoubtedly, missionary zeal,

---

[26] *Acta Sanctorum*, I, p. 828: "Regis Samonis notitia S. Amandus, instructus etiam fortasse litteris consanguineorum Regis, in eodem pago Sennonagi religione Christiana iam ante institutorum, ultra Rhenum, Danubiumque profectus est, estuans desiderio aut hanc gentem, eiusque Regem, ad fidem Christi adducendi, aut martyrii palmam consequendi." ("De S. Amando episcopo Traiectensi Elmone sive Amandopoli in Belgio Commentarius previus".) Cf. P. J. Šafařík, *Slovanské starožitnosti* (Praha, 1863), II, p. 337; F. Hrejsa, *op. cit.*, p. 12, believes that Samo was and remained a Christian; R. Barroux in his *Dagobert, roi des Francs* (Paris, 1938), p. 141 and E. De Moreau (*op. cit.*, p. 156) believe that he was a Christian originally, but became an apostate after becoming the king of Slavs.

[27] It is interesting that some authors, for instance, H. Pirenne (*op. cit.*, p. 16) and E. de Moreau (*op. cit.*, p. 157) arrived at virtually the same conclusion as I did when they wrote of St. Amand as preaching to "the Slavs of the Danube" instead claiming that he went to Carinthia and Carniole. About the Czech or semi-Czech character of the population on the banks of the Danube, cf. the reference to Niederle, notes 18 and 20.

the desire for martyrdom, and the desire to keep out of reach of the angered King Dagobert all played some part in his decision. But why did he choose the distant Slavs when so many Teutonic pagans were closer? Two historical facts may shed light on this point. First, the biography mentions the pilgrimage of young St. Amand to the grave of St. Martin at Tours. Was it this early visit that left a lasting impression on St. Amand's mind? For St. Martin was born in Pannonia, where he even temporarily returned for missionary purposes. Was it possible that St. Martin's mission to a remote land in the East became for St. Amand an ideal example which he wanted to imitate? The second fact is St. Columbanus' plan during his sojourn in Bregenz, to undertake a missionary expedition to the Slavs about two decades earlier. Evidently, St. Amand was not the first to think about converting the Slavs. The influence of St. Columbanus, who had founded the monastery at Luxeil in Burgundy, on French monastic life in the seventh century was great and extensive; St. Amand was certainly exposed to this influence.[28] The plan of St. Columbanus to preach to the Slavs hardly remained unknown to St. Amand. It is thus possible that St. Amand consciously followed in the footsteps of his Irish predecessor, perhaps even in a literal sense; in other words, that he went to Bregenz, thence crossing Bavaria en route to the Danube. Hypothetical as this itinerary is, it still is much more probable than the traditionally accepted northern route, with subsequent *southward* crossing of the Danube.

This leads us to the *effects* of St. Amand's journey. Its immediate result was small; the first biography explicitly states that only a few Slavs were converted. On the other hand, the mission was certainly not a complete failure. Šafařík's view that the mission was a partial success accords better with the testimony of the *Vita*. Nor should we overlook the important fact that St. Amand did not gain the martyr's crown of which he was dreaming. This indicates the absence of any resolutely hostile attitude among the Slavs to whom he was preaching. This is even more significant if we accept the usual dating of St. Amand's journey as around 630 – that is, when hostility between the Franks and the Slavs of Samo was just beginning, and when any missionary enterprise among Samo's subjects must have been especially dangerous.[29] As noted above, St. Emmeram was murdered in a Bavaria already partly Christianized, one century af-

---

[28] E. de Moreau, *op. cit.*, pp. 239-243. The author even admits the possibility that the visit of St. Columbanus at Tours coincided with the sojourn of St. Amand.

[29] This would be especially true if the journey of St. Amand took place *after* Dagobert's defeat by Samo, as E. de Moreau believes (*op. cit.*, p. 155).

ter St. Amand's mission. This shows clearly that the thesis of some German historians about the stubborn resistance of the Slavs to the civilizing influence of Christianity is nothing but a nationalistic prejudice or a racialist myth.[30]

In any case, the direct effect of St. Amand's mission north of the Danube was limited both in space and time. It would be otiose to speculate about how far north the first apostle of the Slavs went – hardly farther than southern Bohemia, assuming that he crossed the Bohemian Forest at all. Or perhaps the southern approaches to Moravia (i.e., northern Lower Austria today), if we interpret the relevant passage in Milo's poem as an allusion to the battlefields of Franks and Great Moravians. The expression "circumiens illa loca" can be interpreted quite broadly. Neither do we have illusions about the lasting character of even his few successful conversions. Yet it would be uncritical to exclude dogmatically the possibility that this early Christianizing mission left some trace. The following illustrates how careful we must be in this respect. We had mentioned that St. Columbanus planned to travel to the Slavs. Did one of his companions perhaps realize what he himself did not? Among his twelve companions was St. Gallus. J. Strnadt believes that the church of St. Gallus at Gallneukirchen in Upper Austria (significantly *north* of the Danube in the former Slavic territory) is very old, built probably not too long after the death of St. Gallus himself, in the middle of the seventh century.[31] This would have been during St. Amand's lifetime. In that case, the founding of the church would have been the fruit of some very early Christian mission in the early seventh century. Did St. Gallus himself go to preach beyond the Danube? Or was it a fruit of St. Amand's missionary activity inspired by St. Columbanus and his twelve apostles, including St. Gallus? Although we are treading on very uncertain ground, there is no question that the patronate of a church is an important historical clue to the date of its establishment.

6. EARLY CHRISTIANIZATION OF THE SLAVS ON THE UPPER DANUBE

The first known Christian apostles who appeared on the Upper Danube after St. Amand were St. Rupert and St. Emmeram, both countrymen of

---

[30] According to Alois Huber, the mission of St. Amand "wegen der Hartnäckigkeit der Slaven gänzlich misslungen ist" (*op. cit.*, III, p. 301); according to A. Hauck, *Kirchengeschichte Deutschlands*, I, 298, it was "fruchtlos".
[31] J. Strnadt, *loc. cit.*, p. 549.

St. Amand: the former was a member of the Merovingian dynasty, the latter came from Poitiers in France. This happened at the end of the seventh and the beginning of the eighth century. They both are regarded as the apostles of Bavaria; but as the area of their activity – Regensburg, Lorch, – was practically on the ethnic borderline, their contact with some Slavic population was inevitable.[32] St. Peter's Church, founded by St. Rupert on the ruins of the Roman Iuvavum, which subsequently became Salzburg, played a leading role in the conversion of the Slovenes and the Slavs of the Danube, while the monastery of St. Emmeram at Regensburg became the main focus of the missionary activity in the Bohemian Forest and later in Bohemia. It is natural that this missionary activity became systematic only when St. Boniface gave Bavaria the first ecclesiastic organization in 739. Four bishoprics were founded in that year: Salzburg, Regensburg, Lorch-Passau and Freisingen. Only a few years later the monastery at Nieder Altaich was founded, and its importance for the conversion of the Slavs of the Bohemian Forest ("Waldslaven" as called by Alois Huber) was hardly less than that of Regensburg. There is the documentary evidence that a monastic cell at Cham, located practically on the border of Bohemia, was in existence in 819; it was one among the first cells which appeared in the Bohemian Forest. The present toponymy of the region contains not only a number of names with the German ending -zell, but also some Slavic names which betray the same origin: Zelz (from "celica" – little cell), Sallitz, Sölling. That the Christianization of the Czech settlers did not necessarily mean their Germanization is evident from the patronate of St. Vitus in the churches at Kötzing and Tiefenbach, from the patronate of St. Wenceslaus at Schönsee; they were, in the words of the German historian, concessions made to the local Czech inhabitants.[33] In any case, there is no question that the baptism of fourteen Czech chieftains at Regensburg was merely the culmination of the long process by which Christianity began to penetrate into the southernmost Czech settlements in the Bohemian Forest in the seventh century.

A similar process was taking place farther south and southeast. The conversion of the Slovenes was achieved by Virgil, the Bishop of Salzburg in the second half of the eighth century. His successor, Bishop Arno, continued his work, and it was in his time that the memory of St. Amand was kept alive at Salzburg. This was certainly due to the fact that before coming to Salzburg Arno was at the abbey of Elnon in Belgium, where he undoubtedly became acquainted with the life and the deeds of St.

[32] Cf. Šafařík, *op. cit.*, II, p. 338.
[33] A. Huber, *op. cit.*, IV, p. 94.

Amand; it was there where he restored, according to Alcuin's testimony, St. Amand's grave. Apparently he did not forget the memory of the Belgian saint even after coming to Salzburg; on the contrary, as the modern biographer of St. Amand suspects, there was an additional reason for not forgetting it, because the diocese of Salzburg included the regions where St. Amand preached two centuries before.[34] It was only logical for Arno and his successors to regard themselves as the continuators in the missionary work of St. Amand. Although the missionary activity took place on either side of the Danube, that is, among the Slovenes and the Czechs, its results were first visible among the Slovenes of the Alps and south of the Danube, which were geographically closer to the center of the diocese. This was an additional reason why the memory of St. Amand became gradually associated with the conversion of the Slovenes only. But as the Slovenes in the eighth century extended as far north as the Danube, where they bordered on the Czechs (in truth, as Lubor Niederle showed, there was a mixed population even *south* of the Danube), the Christianization of Slovenes and the Czechs then inhabiting Upper Austria took place at the same time. Needless to repeat what had been already said about the Czech population in that area; let us mention only one significant fact – the presence of the Slavic (and undoubtedly Christian) witnesses called by the Bishop of Freisingen, Hitto, in 827 to fix the boundary of the estate belonging to the church at Puchenau north of the Danube. This church was already in existence as early as 811. Further east and *south of the Danube* the presence of Czech peasants is documented as late as *the end of the tenth century* at Perschling (834 Bersnicha from the Slavic "Breznica") while the church there was in existence in 834.[35] This indicates clearly the persistence of the Czech settlements on the Danube, as well as their early exposure to Christianizing influences. There is hardly any question that these Czech settlers were the descendants of those who were first touched by the Christian mission of St. Amand two centuries before.

Thus in a broader historical perspective, St. Amand's journey was something more than an isolated and curious event; it is the first recorded stage of the Christianization of Western Slavs. The most recent archeological evidence for the Iro-Scottish origins of Christianity on the present territory of Czechoslovakia fits into the general pattern outlined in this study: as stated above, St. Amand was probably inspired by the example

---

[34] E. de Moreau, *op. cit.*, pp. 159-60; Hauck, *Kirchengeschichte Deutschlands*, pp. 382-6.

[35] O. Kämmel, *op. cit.*, pp. 168, 170, 255-56.

of St. Columbanus and other Irish monks who daringly ventured into remote areas in their missionary expeditions. If Christianity, according to this recent evidence, began to be established in southern Moravia around 800 A.D.,[36] it is only natural to expect that the Slavic regions lying *on the route* to Moravia, along the northern banks of the Danube, were exposed to Christian influences much earlier. In this respect the present southern political boundary of Czechoslovakia anachronistically obscured to the majority of historians the crucial importance of the western and southern slopes of the Bohemian Forest, in spite of its early undeniably Slavic character. Whether we locate the area of St. Amand's activity in what is now Upper Austria, or farther west nearer to Regensburg, the conclusion remains the same: his mission was a first step in the general eastward movement of Christianity to Bohemia and Moravia.

There is even some deeper symbolic significance in this reconstruction of St. Amand's itinerary. His mission was obviously the first, fleeting contact of the Czechs with Western civilization and, more specifically, with Western Europe. It is significant that in view of St. Amand's origin and nationality, this first contact was *direct*, not mediated by the geographically closer Germans. This illustrates the general pattern of the history of Czechs and Slovaks: those moments of their history which were most significant and of which they are most proud are those which resulted from their renewed *direct* contacts with Western Europe. St. Amand and the early Christian missions, the movement of Cluny at the time of St. Adalbert, the founding of the University of Prague on the model of the University of Paris in the fourteenth century, the ideas of Wyclif at the time of Hus and, finally, Thomas G. Masaryk's responsiveness to the ideas of Western democracy, are different illustrations of the same basic pattern. Today, when this fact is deliberately obscured by unscrupulous propaganda, it is worth remembering.

---

[36] J. Böhm, "Deux églises datant de l'Empire de Grande Moravie découvertes en Tchécoslovaquie", *Byzantinoslavica*, XI (1950), pp. 207 f., especially pp. 219-20 about the evidence of Christian worship in Great Moravia in the eighth century.

Dynamics of the Spatial Concept of Czechoslovakia: Persistence of Regional Consciousness and Unity over the Span of Thirteen Centuries

JERZY ZABORSKI

> "Byl to velkorysý pokus o vytvoření obrovské slovanské říše."
> Dvorník on Greater Moravia[1]

During the latter part of the sixth century of our era, an Altaian nation, the Avars, was able to cross the Carpathians from its temporary stopping place, the Ukraine, and achieve dominance over the mid-Danubian basin. The Avars formed a complex society with a complex political organization. They did not rule their territorial holdings in the present meaning of the word, but organized them into one confederate, political unit, dominated by that nomadic nation, which had originated in Central Asia. In the Ukrainian country of the East Slavic Antes,[2] the Avars had already come in contact with Slavs and their civilization. At first, those contacts were limited strictly to military operations; later, together with the Sclavini of Dacia and the Antes, the Avars managed to subdue the northeastern regions of Balkanic and Danubian lands.[3]

However, the Slavic colonization of the cis-mountainous side of the Carpathian Arc[4] was not limited to the Moldavia-Wallachia lowland;

---

[1] Dvorník, F., "České pronikání na severovýchod", *Západo-Slovansky Vestnik*, Vol. III, No. 6 (London, 1942), p. 5. Translation of motto: "It was a broadly conceived plan of creating a great Slavic state."
[2] Dvornik, F., *The Making of Central and Eastern Europe* (London, The Polish Research Centre, 1949), pp. 277-297. Dvornik, F., *The Slavs, their Early History and Civilization* (Boston, American Academy of Arts and Sciences, 1956), pp. 3-45. – Dvornik, F., *The Slavs in European History and Civilization* (New Brunswick, Rutgers University Press, 1962). – Czekanowski, Jan, *Wstęp do historii Słowian*, 2d ed. (Poznań, Instytut Zachodni, 1957), pp. 206-210. – Lehr-Spławiński, Tadeusz, *Rozprawy i szkice z dziejów kultury Słowian* (Warsaw, Pax, 1954), pp. 15-48.
[3] Jażdżewski, Konrad, *Atlas to the Prehistory of the Slavs*, 2 vols. (Łódź, Societas Scientiarum Lodziensis, 1949), maps 13-15. – Labuda, Gerard, *Pierwsze państwo słowiańskie, Państwo Samona* (Poznań, Księgarnia Akademicka, 1949), pp. 148-193.
[4] A Mediterranean orientation was adopted for cis- and transmountainous designations on the basis of cultural seniority and the earliest scientific works produced in those lands.

on the contrary, the Danube-Tisa mesopotamia and the rest of the left-bank Pannonian Plain had already been under at least partial Slavic control since the early Roman period (0-200 A.D.), when the Slavs came through the Dukla and other mountain passes.[5]

At the same time other Slavs moved south across the Moravian Gate from their trans-Rudavan and trans-Sudetan cradle, and across the mountain ranges of the Rudaves and the Sudetes themselves, to reinforce the local Slavic population. This local Slavic population, living in the Czech Massif (from eastern Bavaria to Moravia), withstood numerous invasions by neighboring peoples after the decline of the Protoslavic Lusatian culture.[6] That movement toward the South accounted for the revival of Slavic settlements as far as the Danube in the Czech lands of Bohemia (including eastern Bavaria) and Moravia, where the river coincided with the borders of the Roman Empire.[7]

In the course of the sixth century, the Sclavini of Moldavia-Wallachia closed ranks, not only with the Slavs of the Tisa-Danube mesopotamia, but also with their Slavic kinsmen from the upper reaches of the Danube, who, under constantly increasing Teutonic pressure from the West, had followed the retreating borders of Roman domination into the remainder of the Pannonian Plain and the east Alpine region. In 548 they first reached the Adriatic coast.[8]

The Avars entered the Danubian and Balkan regions at that time. They established a symbiotic relation with the local populations, Slavs included, making them Avar tributaries. During the several decades, perhaps a generation, of Avar domination and occupation, the Slavs reinforced their holdings in the Danubian region and the Balkan Peninsula, either as settlers or as military support for the Avar Confederacy. In these ways, the Slavs reached the borders of the new Roman Empire, much less extensive than before. Beside the Slavs, however, there were many other nationalities in the Avar state, remnants of former inhabitants or wan-

---

[5] Jażdżewski, *op. cit.*, map 9.
[6] An extremely rich literature exists on this subject. The following are but a few selected titles: Kostrzewski, Józef, *Prasłowiańszczyzna* (Poznań, Księgarnia Akademicka, 1946). – Kostrzewski, Józef, *Pradzieje Polski* (Poznań, Księgarnia Akademicka, 1949). – Kostrzewski, Józef, *Wielkopolska w pradziejach* (Warsaw-Wrocław, Ossolineum, 1955). – Zaborski, Jerzy, review of Kostrzewski's *Wielkopolska w pradziejach*, in *Artibus Asiae*, Vol. XX, No. 2/3 (1957), p. 232. – Lehr-Spławiński, Tadeusz, *O pochodzeniu i praojczyźnie Słowian* (Poznań, Instytut Zachodni, 1946). – Filip, Jan, *Pradzieje Czechosłowacji* (Poznań, Instytut Zachodni, 1951), translated from the Czech by Józef Kostrzewski.
[7] Jażdżewski, *op. cit.*, maps 8-12.
[8] Labuda, *op. cit.*, p. 164.

derers who dwelt in this complex and culturally advanced Central European region.

The Avar-Slavic symbiotic relationship ended abruptly when the Byzantines were menaced by a new Persian danger. The Persians formed a coalition with the Avars, and Byzantium sought new allies. At the same time, people in the old Slavic region on the Danube, from the upper Vltava to the Morava River, and even further, in Slovakia, were growing restless under the cruel and much-resented Avar rule. Therefore, in about 623 A.D., when the Avars were involved in a controversy with Byzantium, and had even begun to make overtures to the previously hostile Franconian monarchy, the hard-pressed Slavs of Moravia (which then included today's Upper and Lower Austria) revolted against their occupiers.[9]

The uprising proved successful and the Czech lands of Moravia and Bohemia (which then included eastern Bavaria), and Slovakia, as well as Pannonia from the Drava River and Lake Balaton to the Danube, and the east Alpine region became free. There were other significant results of the war of 623-624. Some of the Slavs of the western and northern provinces of the now-defunct Avar Confederacy, and the adjacent northwestern periphery of those provinces, when aroused, took the opportunity to move away from their own Teutonic-threatened regions, and settled in large number in the thus-far thinly colonized area of their predecessors. Those Slavic pioneers gave birth to the national states of the Slovenes, Croats and Serbs in the eastern Alps and in present Yugoslavia.

During the brief period of the war itself and soon afterwards, those states paid allegiance to the capital of the Slavic nations which had been liberated from the Avar yoke. Soon, however, though they never regained their previous importance, the Avars managed to sever that Slavic alliance, separating Western from Southern Slavs and establishing brief control over the Sava-Drava interfluvium,[10] or today's Slavonia.

The area north of the new Yugoslav kingdoms and north of that interfluvium of the (soon to be independent) Slavic tribes is known in historiography as "Samo's State". After the liberation of 623-624, a monarch apparently was elected, in accord with Slavic political tradition. According to Professor Labuda's interpretations of Fredegar's Chronicle, he was of Gallo-Roman ancestry,[11] though other authors suggest a native ori-

---

[9] Ibid., pp. 262-284.
[10] Ibid., p. 292.
[11] Ibid., pp. 93-147. This and all other specific references pertaining to Samo and his state are based on Professor Labuda's researches, his interpretation of Fredegar's Chronicle and of other historical sources.

gin.[12] Samo must have rendered important services essential to the victory of the freedom-loving insurgents. This event – the election, and possibly even the coronation itself – almost certainly took place after the war for independence had been won, in about 625 A.D., as documented by sources which have since been painstakingly interpreted.[13]

Samo's State was organized as a confederacy of nations, like the state of the Avars or the adjacent confederacy of the Franks, who superimposed themselves on the Gallo-Roman population. There was a difference, however, between the former confederacies and the new state: the state of Samo was composed only of Slavic nations and was founded by the Slavs themselves. The attraction of the new state was so strong that the neighboring country of Lusatia soon joined the confederacy under the leadership of the Lusatian monarch Derwan, thus embarking on the long emotional and linguistic association with the Czechoslovak branch of the West Slavic ethnolinguistic family.[14]

According to this author's findings, the center of Samo's State must have been somewhere near modern Vienna; had it been located in the Bratislava area, it would have been too close to the Avars in the Tisa-Danube interfluvium.

Samo's State consisted mainly of a population tracing its lineage back to the archaeologically documented Protoslavic Lusatian culture (dating back at least to the Bronze Age, 1,800 – 700 B.C.), reinforced with later arrivals from trans-Rudavan, trans-Sudetan and trans-Carpathian Slavic populations. This state exerted considerable cultural and political influence on its neighbors.

The establishment of Samo's State had been prepared for over many generations: it finally came into being in 623 A.D., the founding date of a phenomenon known in the twentieth century as Czechoslovakia. Samo's State was thus the first incarnation of Czechoslovakia, which has the same outlook, is the same composite of nations, has the same rational approach to politics and socioeconomic problems, and possesses the amazing stability of a regional concept so characteristic of the 1340 years

---

[12] Palacký, F., *Geschichte von Böhmen* (Prague, 1836-1867), and "Über den Chronisten Fredegar und seine Nachrichten von Samo", *Jahrbücher des böhm. Museums für Natur-Landerkunde, Geschichte, Kunst und Literatur*, 1 (1827), pp. 387-413, suggest that Samo was of Slavic or Balto-Slavic origin. This author would also suggest a native origin, especially when Samo's name is compared with names of the Piast dynasty derived from the word for "earth" (Polish "ziemia", and the names: Ziemowit, Ziemomysł) and other similar Slavic names. The study requires a separate monograph.

[13] Labuda, *op. cit.*, pp. 289-290.

[14] Ibid., p. 281. Jażdżewski, *op. cit.*, map 16.

of Czechoslovakia's existence as an independent multi-national state.

Samo's State declined under Teutonic Franconian pressure, but flowered into new glory under the Mojmír dynasty a century and a half later, in the same Czechoslovak territory from eastern Bavaria (West and Southwest Bohemia), through northern Austria (South Moravia), to the vicinity of Tokaj on the Tisa, and Vyšehrad (just north of Budapest) on the Danube. The state's second phase, known in historiography as Greater Moravia, created new and even more extensive glory worthy of its predecessor. It was a period when adjacent countries received membership in the confederacy. Lusatia joined under its monarch Miliduch, heir of Derwan; also a large part of southern Poland, the Vistulan state, together with its ruler, joined in the Mojmír Confederacy of Greater Moravia.

During the first period of Czechoslovakia's existence (as Samo's State) Moravian influence was strongest. During the second period, that of the state of the Mojmírs, despite political continuity and probable dynastic ties to Samo,[15] dominance had shifted to Slovakia. The state was still known by the name of its original center, Moravia, but the capital and royal residence moved under Teutonic Franconian pressure, and after the withering of the Avar state, to Děvín near Bratislava on the lower course of the Morava.

This Slovak dominance during the second period of Czechoslovakia's being was also manifested by the importance of Nitra; it was, however, less important than when the confederate capital was further to the West, near Vienna. The additional argument for Slovak dominance over the Greater Moravian incarnation of Czechoslovakia is the very name of the state. The name implies continuity of political tradition, yet implies that its sphere of influence is much larger than originally, much broader than "Moravia" – so it became "Greater Moravia".[16]

Furthermore, in addition to the continuity of name, dynasty, confederate multi-national political organization, and the same region, Greater Moravia maintained its alliance with the Greeks. This alliance proved rewarding both politically and culturally for most of Europe. Thanks to the efforts of Cyril and Methodius, learned and dedicated missionaries from Constantinople who established Slavic rite and liturgy, Slavic church hierarchy, and – according to newest findings – a second European

---

[15] Labuda, *op. cit.*, pp. 294-295. – Czekanowski, *op. cit.*, pp. 287-288.
[16] Most outspoken on the subject is Professor Marek Korowicz, though other Polish historians and paleoanthropogeographers are in complete agreement that Greater Moravia was a Slovak-dominated state.

university,[17] and by the efforts of able and wise monarchs of Greater Moravia, the confederated countries accepted Christianity. And from the present region of Czechoslovakia, other Slavs, Balts, Hungarians and Scandinavians were converted to that faith over the following centuries.[18] Thanks to this Byzantine orientation, the Slavs obtained both of their alphabets, the Glagolitic and Cyrillic, their translations of the Scriptures, and their earliest documented written literary masterpieces authored by Cyril and Methodius, and their students.

When the Magyars caused the decline of the great state of Greater Moravia, the dominance of Bohemia begun. Libice of the Slavníks, closely connected with the Mojmírs, and Prague of the Přemyslides, who by that time had fully accepted Greater Moravia's heritage, were the original centers. The Bohemian influence, which first manifested itself in the tenth century, is still apparent there, more then a millenium later. Under the Přemyslides (nor should Slavník, Piast and Jagiellonian efforts be forgotten), the Bohemians, Moravians and Slovaks recreated the glory of Samo and the Mojmírs. It was only the German pressure of the late Middle Ages which relegated this third embodiment of Czechoslovakia to its decline. The spirit, however, survived, and a new fire was kindled. One has only to look at such events as the Czechoslovak participation in the Spring of Nations, the Panslavic Congress amidst the barricades of free Prague in 1848, or the founding of the Sokol movement by Miroslav Tyrš in 1861.

Half a century later the fourth phase of Czechoslovak existence emerged by the concerted effort of the Slovak and Czech nations with Štefanik, Kramář and Masaryk as leaders. This fourth phase, the Czechoslovakia of our times, was not very different from its predecessors. Its only failure was its lack of Samo's and the Mojmírs', the Slavníks', Piasts', Přemyslides' and the Jagiellonians' ambition to enlarge its area to include all Western Slavs within its limits – the objective of all Czechoslovak statesmen of the past thirteen centuries.

This objective was realized when, on the basis of the stated desire of the nations concerned, the Czechoslovak and Polish parliaments and

---

[17] Spławiński, *Rozprawy i szkice z dziejów kultury Słowian*, op. cit., p. 149-189. – Włodarski, S., "Apostołowie obrządku narodowego", *Posłannictwo*, Vol. XXIX, No. 8/9 (Warsaw, 1960), pp. 22-27. – Zaborski, Jerzy, *Ku syntezie cyrylometodejskiej* (in press).

[18] Gabriel, Astrik L., "The Conversion of Hungary to Christianity", *The Polish Review*, Vol. VI, No. 4 (New York, Polish Institute of Arts and Sciences in America, 1961), pp. 31-43. – Zaborski, Jerzy, *Przyjęcie chrześcijaństwa w Polsce* (in press).

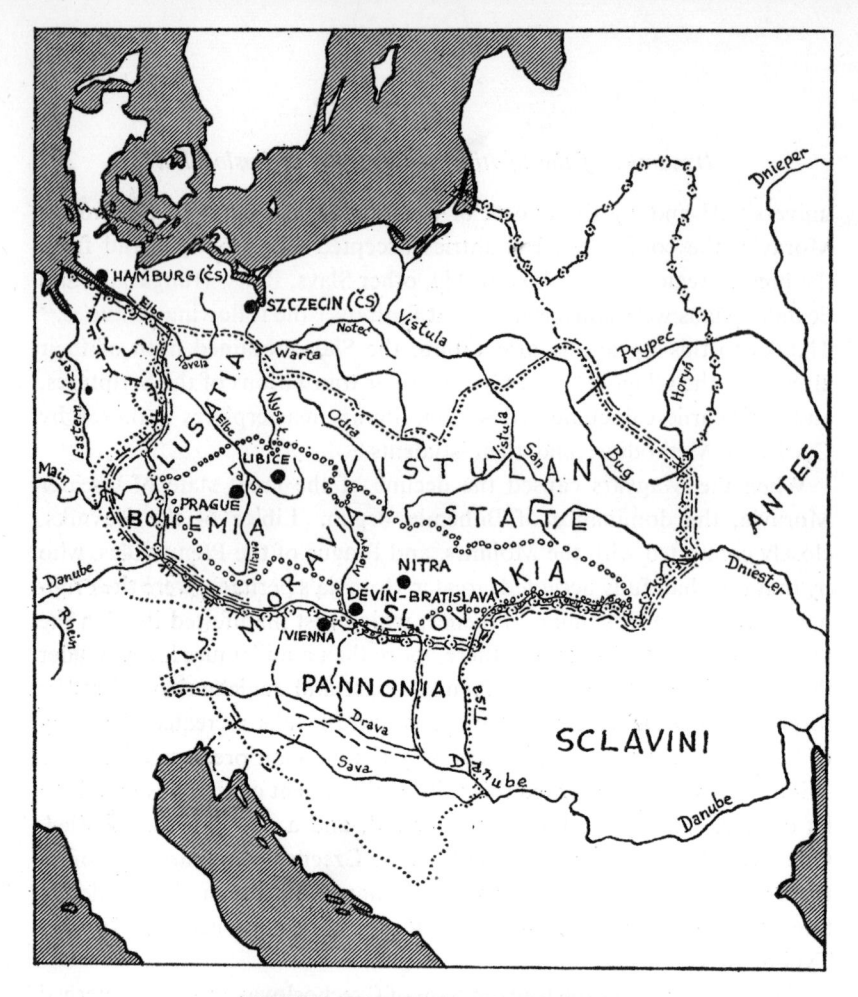

THIRTEEN CENTURIES OF CZECHOSLOVAKIA
Base map after Jażdżewski. (Scale 1:12,000,000)

Boundaries include maximal superimposed spatial distributions including military occupation and contemporary legal claims.

Legend:

Limes sorabicus – Easternmost boundary, Carolingian Empire, 9th-10th centuries, after Niederle.

First Phase: Samo's State, Moravian prevalence, 7th-8th centuries, modified after Labuda, and Jażdżewski.

Second Phase: Greater Moravia, Slovak prevalence, 8th-10th centuries, modified after Widajewicz, Jażdżewski, Nanke, Piotrowicz, and Semkowicz.

Third Phase: The Czech Crown, beginning of Bohemian prevalence, 10th-20th centuries, modified after Jażdżewski, Nanke, Piotrowicz, and Semkowicz.

Fourth Phase: Czechoslovak Republic.

Fifth Phase: Proposed Czechoslovak-Polish Confederation, after the Declaration of 11 November 1940, and Zaborski, Jerzy, "Zasławia".

(čs) Czechoslovak exterritorial port rights granted by the League of Nations.

governments announced a constitutional declaration promising a Czecho-slovak-Polish Confederation. The declaration was signed on November 11, 1940, by President Eduard Beneš and Prime Minister Władysław Sikorski. This Confederation was to be the fifth, glorious incarnation of Czechoslovakia – a West Slavic realm based on the spatial concepts called into being in 623 A.D., which withstood thirteen centuries of testing and is still valid as the corner-stone of a future peaceful Europe.[19]

Additional references cited in map legend

Niederle, Lubor, *Slovanské starožitnosti* (Prague, 1902-1924). – Nanke, Cz., Piotrowicz, L., and Semkowicz, Wl., *Mały atlas historyczny* (Wroclaw-Warsaw, Książnica-Atlas 1950). – Widajewicz, J., *Państwo Wiślan* (Kraków, Ossolineum, 1947).

---

[19] *Západo-Slovansky Vestnik*, Vol. I-III (London, 1940-1942). – Zaborski, Jerzy, "Zasławia", *Biuletyn Informacyjny*, Vol. I, No. 11 (London, Związek Polskich Ziem Zachodnich, November 1951), pp. 6-7; reprinted in *Czas*, Winnipeg, Dec. 1951.

The Religion of Hussite Tabor

HOWARD KAMINSKY

To the medievalist who has not studied the Hussite movement, Tabor stands above all for revolutionary fanaticism, for chiliasm, blind destructiveness, and, in the end, the excesses of Pikartism and Adamitism. It is probably no exaggeration to say that Tabor as a stable societal order, with its distinctive religion, is all but unknown to the non-specialist. In the last century, to be sure, such scholars as Hermann Haupt and Friedrich von Bezold drew attention to the "often underestimated religious content of the Taborite movement",[1] but their excellent work has not been continued – indeed, it was shoved brutally aside by the extraordinary influence of Johann Loserth's *Huss und Wiclif*, which focussed attention on the unoriginality of Hus's thought. In subsequent works, moreover, Loserth sought to extend his method of textual comparisons to Taborite theology, and show that it, too, was but the appropriation and working out of Wyclifism.[2] The Prague masters with whom the Taborites disputed were not quite so heavy-handed; they too recognized

---

[1] H. Haupt, "Waldensertum und Inquisition im südöstlichen Deutschland", *Deutsche Zeitschrift für Geschichtswissenschaft*, III (1890), 395; cf. F. Bezold, *Zur Geschichte des Hussitenthums* (Munich, 1874), p. 30: "Wir haben es hier ganz und gar nicht mit bibelfesten, aber sonst ungebildeten Leuten zu thun, sondern mit Männern, welche an Wissen und Schule den Pragern durchaus ebenbürtig sind." Among Czech scholars only Zdeněk Nejedlý has devoted a major work to the study of Tabor's religion: *Dějiny husitského zpěvu za válek husitských* (Prague, 1913); new printing as *Dějiny husitského zpěvu*, in six vols., of which vol. IV, *Táboři* (Prague, 1955), deals with our subject. Josef Pekař's *Žižka a jeho doba*, 4 vols. (Prague, 1927-1933), has much material on Taborite religion, *passim*, especially in Vol. I, but the discussion is neither systematic nor connected, and in any case is highly distorted by anti-Taborite bias. Relatively little attention is paid to the period after the early 1420's.

[2] J. Loserth, *Huss und Wiclif* (Munich-Berlin, 1884; 2d ed., 1925); for the alleged Wyclifism of the Taborites see his reviews of works by Haupt and W. Preger, in the *Göttingische gelehrte Anzeiger*, 1889, No. 12, pp. 475-504; 1891, No. 4, pp. 140-152; cf. also his appendices to *Huss und Wiclif*, both editions, and such articles as "Die Wiclif'sche Abendmahlslehre und ihre Aufnahme in Böhmen", *Mitteilungen des Vereins für Geschichte der Deutschen in Böhmen*, XXX (1892), 1-33; etc.

that to Tabor Wyclif was "pre omnibus nostris sufficientissimus",³ and Master John Příbram was fond of urging his opponents to pay due respect to Bohemia's own teacher, Matthew of Janov.⁴ At the same time, however, Příbram, along with Jakoubek of Stříbro, John Rokycana, and others with whom the Taborites argued, saw that Wyclifism was essentially an apparatus, used sometimes in a rather opportunistic fashion: what the Taborites really based their ideas on was something else, the exclusive authority of Scripture, interpreted by themselves.⁵ It is a tribute to the intellectual powers of Tabor's chief spokesman, her Bishop, Nicholas of Pelhřimov, that this potentially stultifying doctrine was in fact made to serve as the foundation of a highly developed and self-consistent theology, quite the equal of that of Prague.

The documents of this theological system are for the most part well-known, and the most important of them, Nicholas of Pelhřimov's majestic, indeed unique, work of documentary *Geistesgeschichte*, the "Chronicle Containing the Cause of the Priests of Tabor and the Attacks of the Prague Masters", has been in print for a century.⁶ Even earlier, the text forming the heart of this work, Nicholas's Taborite Confession of 1431, was recognized by Protestant historians as a gem of "sound doctrine" and published by them – once by Flacius Illyricus in 1568, and then by

---

[3] Thus, e.g., John Příbram wrote in the 1430's: "... a sanctis doctoribus auditum et animam contumaciter avertunt [*scil.*, the Taborites], dogmata Johannis Wiclef cunctis sanctis doctoribus preferunt, et hos qui Wiclef in placitis eorum non suscipiunt, odiunt, persecuntur, reppellunt, et minas eis mortis imponunt" ("Cum ab inicio", MS Prague Cathedral Chapter Library, D 47, f. 25; cf. F. M. Bartoš, *Literární činnost... M. Jana Příbrama...*, Prague, 1928, No. 24). Many other passages of similar import could be cited from the works of Příbram and Rokycana.

[4] E.g., in the work just cited, Příbram cited on his side "Magister Mathias dictus Parisiensis, quondam huic secte infideli non solum amabilis sed valde et solicite imitabilis" (f. 36). And in his "De ritibus misse", included in Nicholas of Pelhřimov's "Chronicle", ed. K. Höfler, *Geschichtschreiber der husitischen Bewegung in Böhmen*, II, *Fontes rerum austriacarum*, Erste Abt., VI (1865), p. 530f., Příbram wrote, after citing "venerabilis Magister Mathias Bohemus": "Utinam saltim hunc mellifluum Mathiam testem suscipiant fratres Thaborienses...."

[5] Příbram devoted a whole tractate to refuting Tabor's principle of the sole authority of Scripture: "Cum ab inicio" (see note 3 above). Cf. the passage from Rokycana cited below, *ad* note 19, from his "De septem culpis Taboritarum", MS Cathedral Chapter D 88, f. 199, and the passage on f. 264', where he supports his own attack on Tabor's rejection of the Doctors by citing an otherwise unknown tractate of Jakoubek of Stříbro in the same sense (See Bartoš, *Literární činnost M. Jana Rokycana*, Prague, 1928, No. 3; *Literární činnost M. Jakoubka ze Stříbra*, Prague, 1925, No. 91).

[6] Ed. K. Höfler, *op. cit.*, pp. 475-820. The edition is quite unscientific, but the text itself is not as corrupt as others published by Höfler, since he could use Josef Dobrovský's copy of the MS.

Balthasar Lydius in 1616.[7] Other texts of both Taborites and Praguers in the formative decade of the 1420's, with which we shall be most concerned, remain for the most part unpublished, but have been studied in manuscript, and used by scholars more than once.[8] Thus it is not claimed, for the present brief study, that any new evidence will be exploited, or that substantively new information will be provided about Tabor's doctrine; rather it is proposed to examine this doctrine as a system, and to interpret it as an ideology, in order to define its essential characteristics, its spirit, which may then be taken as the spirit of Tabor itself.

The man with whom we are chiefly concerned, Bishop Nicholas of Pelhřimov, was a stormy figure in his own day, and his career of leadership and controversy, along with his vigorous but nuanced personality, has its own fascination. His arch-antagonist, John Rokycana, called him a man of "wondrous inconsistency", and another opponent, Peter Chelčický, accused him outright of duplicity, of writing one thing and saying another.[9] But such was his function: he was elected bishop or "senior" in September 1420, a time when the new Taborite community still had to choose between the chiliast-Pikart permanent revolution and the norms of a stable society, and when, moreover, the very legitimacy of a stable society that would also claim to be evangelically Christian had to be defended against the point of view, expressed by Peter Chelčický, that truly

---

[7] Lydius's edition is the more generally used: *Waldensia*, I (Rotterdam, 1616), 1-303. In his *Catalogus testium veritatis* (1556), Flacius Illyricus mentions the Taborite Confession as being in his hands, and observes: "There is by far a better and purer understanding in that confession, on all matters of religion, than either Hus or Wyclif had" – in fact, he notes, it agrees wholly with "our doctrine" (ch. ccxlvii).

[8] The best guide to the sources is the work of F. M. Bartoš, both his innumerable articles and his catalogues of the works of Jakoubek, Rokycana, Příbram, and Payne (see above). The unpublished work of Nicholas of Pelhřimov urgently requires similar cataloguing; meanwhile the best survey, based in part on Bartoš's discoveries and identifications, is Bohuslav Souček's "Veritas super omnia. Z biblických studií a odkazu Mikuláše Biskupce z Pelhřimova", *Křestanská revue*, 1961, N. 6, *Theologická příloha*, pp. 73-90.

[9] Rokycana's verdict appears in his "Tractatus de existentia corporis Christi in sacramento", in Z. Nejedlý, *Prameny k synodám strany pražské a táborské v letech 1441-1444* (Prague, 1900), p. 138 ("Et nota istius Nicolai variabilitatem mirandam!"). Chelčický's statement ("...kdyz sem w twych pismiech ginak nalezl, nez sy ty mnie nayprwe wyznal...") is in his "Replika proti Biskupcovi", edd. J. Annenkov & V. Jagić, *Sbornik otdělenija russkago jazyka i slovesnosti Imperatorskoj akademij nauk*, LXVI (St. Petersburg, 1893), p. 413. (For Chelčický's works, etc., see the bibliography by Eduard Petrů, *Soupis díla Petra Chelčického a literatury o něm* (Prague, 1957).) Modern studies of Nicholas of Pelhřimov include F. M. Bartoš's "Mikuláš z Pelhřimova," *Světci a kacíři* (Prague, 1949), pp. 175-196, and Josef Pekař's chapter, "Mikuláš z Pelhřimova", in *Žižka a jeho doba*, I (Prague, 1927), pp. 125-138. Cf. also the essays published in the *Theologická příloha* cited in note 8 above.

to follow in the way of Jesus and the apostles meant to renounce any identification of the Christian religion with a social order based, as all social orders must be, on force.[10] Nicholas carried on the battle on both fronts, with great decisiveness; the Pikarts were attacked with the help of the Prague masters and driven out of Tabor, to be burnt in the hundreds by John Žižka. Chelčický's sectarianism was rejected in favor of the standard medieval doctrine, derived through Wyclif and shared by the Prague masters: that the Church Militant *was* the social order, with secular power exercising the Christian function of defending God's Law by force.[11] This concept of a Christian society was purely medieval, and the contending parties in Bohemia differed only in regard to the framework within which it would be realized: for the Romanists it was Europe, for the Praguers the nation, for the Taborites the congregational community.

But even while arguing with Chelčický and attacking the Pikarts, Nicholas had begun his disputations with the Masters of Prague, which lasted from 1420 to 1444, and in the course of which he was to bring the religious outlook of his community to the highest pitch of explicitness. His opponents were harsh in their judgements of his inadequacies – both Příbram and Rokycana called his arguments flimsy spider-webs, and both also affected contempt for his Latinity,[12] but we can dismiss these invidious opinions as the products not only of polemical passion, but also of the rather unattractive disdain of University masters for a man who did

---

[10] See Chelčický's "O boji duchovním" and "O trojím lidu", both published by K. Krofta (Prague, 1911). The best modern study of Chelčický's socio-political ideas is Peter Brock's chapter, "Peter Chelčický, Forerunner of the Unity", in *The Social and Political Doctrines of the Unity of Czech Brethren* (The Hague, 1957), pp. 25-69.
[11] In his "O trojím lidu", p. 163f., Chelčický tells how the Taborite priests cited this doctrine against him at a meeting in Taborite Písek in the first year of the war – probably in the second half of 1420.
[12] Příbram, "De ritibus misse", Höfler, II, 632 ("Nec mirum, quod aranea se putet ferrea nectere tenimenta"); Rokycana, "De septem culpis Taboritarum," MS D 88, f. 218 (Nicholas's arguments are "telas aranearum"). In this work, f. 265′, Rokycana criticizes the presumption of the Taborite priests, "quos videmus adeo diminutos, ut eciam neque gramatice congruum sciant proferre sermonem"; similar passages appear several times in the works of Rokycana and Příbram. Nicholas of Pelhřimov for his part asked the reader's pardon if the latter found, in the "Chronicle of the Priests of Tabor", "inurbane aliquid compositum", and he went on: "Et si alicui academicis studiis innutrito haec sua displiceret editio ob hoc forsitan, quia pedestri sermone incedens plus justo in eo rusticaverit, cuilibet tali editor notificat, quia probabilius est abscondita rusticando elucidare, quam aperta philosophando obnubilare..." (Höfler, II, 476). This modesty was in part a literary convention – and hence far from "rustic" – but also reflected the fact that while the Prague masters had a vested interest in making things complex, the Bishop of Tabor had every reason to insist on the utmost simplicity – it suited his arguments better. But in fact his works show much erudition and literary skill.

not have the degree – whom, in fact, the masters seem to have regarded as a particularly presumptuous ex-student. Fortunately they had no choice but to argue with him, and since Nicholas had enough confidence in the justice of his cause to put together in his Chronicle not only his works but those of the masters too, the modern reader can inspect the texts *in extenso* and, as Nicholas urged, make up his own mind who was right.[13] In the process, noting Nicholas's remarkable ability to combine authorities in a rigorously logical argument, the reader may wonder just what the Praguers found wanting in their opponent.

More serious were the criticisms of Nicholas's – and Tabor's – adherence to the norm of *scriptura sola*, and in particular the New Testament, Christ's Law *par excellence*.[14] Tabor really recognized nothing but this as in itself binding; the Fathers were admitted only insofar as they pronounced doctrines that were legitimately derived from Scripture, by which their works were to be judged, while the Church's tradition was similarly undercut, with the added point that most of what had been developed by the post-primitive Church was not only superfluous, but even harmful. In all points of ritual and observance the norm was the Primitive Church, which Nicholas generally understood in a restricted sense, as the Church whose rectors were the Apostles.[15] The Prague view was quite different;[16] the Primitive Church was to be used as a norm for devaluing such elements of Romanist practice as seemed unwholesome or illegitimate – the classic case was, of course, the rejection of Rome's practice of lay communion in only one kind – but other elements of the Roman tradition were to be preserved, if they served to promote or decorate the faith. Furthermore, after the Bible, the Four Doctors – Jerome, Ambrose, Augustine, and Gregory – and the Four Councils – Nicaea, Constantinople, Ephesus, and Chalcedon – were to be regarded as normative, especially when they were in mutual agreement. Nicholas had no trouble disposing of these authorities. Since the Council of Nicaea had approved of the clergy's endowment by Constantine, which neither

---

[13] Höfler, II, 477: "... quilibet causam sacerdotum Thaboriensium..., qui indifferenti oculo dicenda inspexerit, agnoscere poterit, et de parte alia magistrorum eorundem impugnationes, si verae sunt, judicare". As the work progressed, however, it became more and more a Taborite statement, with the opposing side's treatises only summarized or left out.

[14] Perhaps the best statement defining Tabor's norm of judgement is that which comes at the beginning of the Confession of 1431; see Höfler, II, 599-601.

[15] E.g., in the Confession (Höfler, II, 602): "... in fide et ritu et praxi primitivae ecclesiae, cujus rectores erant Apostoli..." Many other passages could be cited.

[16] See the Confession of 1431, Lydius, *op. cit.*, I, 90-108 – a detailed discussion of Rokycana's "fundamentum".

Prague nor Tabor approved of, the Four Councils were not so reliable.[17] And as for the Doctors: "If in any point of faith the Four Doctors speak unanimously and erroneously, then they are unanimously in error, and this is highly possible."[18] He went on to say: "We believe the Holy Doctors as they themselves want to be believed, that is, insofar as they base themselves truly in Scripture; for an argument taken solely from their testimony is not enough – they could all be deceived." At the same time, and this is perhaps the most significant point of all, "if by revelation... of Scripture, God should today grant a more potent understanding to someone, that man would be more to be believed than those Doctors." Tradition and human authority were for those who did not have direct contact with God; Tabor sought such contact by strict and exclusive adherence to God's Law, and lived in hope of an even more direct guidance. This hope, though for obvious reasons not stressed in the sources, was perhaps central to Tabor's religious spirit.

The defect of Tabor's position, however, was that it made real controversy all but impossible. John Rokycana tells us that when Nicholas was accused in the disputation of 1431 of having used Scripture falsely, by citing passages out of context, he replied, simply, "I take what I need" – *hoc recipio quod pro me valet* – a position that Rokycana branded as insane, and as barring the way to effective criticism of anyone. Even utraquism could be refuted in this way![19] John Příbram pushed the argument even further, in a tractate written expressly against Tabor's reliance on Scripture alone.[20] He, too, complained that the Taborites accepted no arguments from the Church's tradition, no proofs from the Holy Doctors, but only "naked Scripture", and that when this was cited against them, they twisted Scripture to their own false understanding". He believed that this principle was "undoubtedly the pestilential root and origin of all the errors and enormities currently produced by the Taborites", and he warned:

It this principle should establish itself in the hearts of men, it would allow thousands of the worst errors and heresies into the Church...
    How will the sacred order of the Church be stabilized if each single nation can choose its own teachers as it likes, without testing, approval, or authorization by the Church? Indeed, if this license be given to the world, in a short time doctrine

---

[17] *Ibid.*, p. 104f.
[18] Höfler, II, 578.
[19] "De septem culpis Taboritarum", MS D 88, f. 199.
[20] "Cum ab inicio", MS D 47, f. 1-40 (see above, note 3). The passages quoted here are on f. 1, f. 1′, 25.

will confound doctrine, nation will turn away from nation, and the common faith will stand in peril.

This was excellent prophecy, and we can understand why very soon after in the 1420's John Příbram turned from radicalism to conservatism and even reaction; more than any other Prague master, he felt the absolute need of the Church Universal, which could be only that of Rome, and his constant invocation of the authority of the Holy Roman Church is both striking and, given his own utraquism, amusing.[21] That he could cite even John Hus on his side may serve to remind us that none of the Prague masters, certainly not Hus, really came to grips with the problem of authority.[22]

But Tabor could also follow Hus, in his more radical passages, and, like him, combine Wyclif's doctrine of predestination with the visible criterion of good works to destroy the whole authority of Rome. As Příbram put it:[23]

They say that the Holy Church consists only of all those who are to be saved. And they add to this that if the pope and prelates are not of the number of those to be saved, they are not of the Holy Church and are not to be obeyed. And that they in fact are not of that number, the Taborites prove, according to Wyclif, on the basis of their works, and they say: Almost all of them are here-

---

[21] For Příbram's early anti-Romanism, see the fragment of his discussion "de ecclesia", MS Prague University Library, III A 18, f. 301′-303: thus, f. 303, "...patet quam horrenda heresis est preferre auctoritatem ecclesie alicuius post primitivam ecclesiam apostolorum, auctoritati ewangelii" – and this is directed explicitly against the Romanists, "volentes habere colorem pro iacticacione et magnificacione curie Romane supra Cristum". The MS attributes this bit to Příbram (cf. also Bartoš's discussion, Činnost Příbrama, p. 68f.); the text is in part identical with one surviving in Jakoubek's own hand (MS Prague University Library VIII E 7, f. 129) – one no doubt copied from the other, a frequent custom with Jakoubek and Příbram. In the 1420's, however, Příbram moved very far to the right, abandoning even Jakoubek's style of Wyclifism (see the discussion in Bartoš's Činnost Příbrama, pp. 61-62). References to the authority of the "ecclesia" and in a number of cases the "sancta romana ecclesia" (e.g., "Cum ab inicio", f. 10′) become more and more frequent. In this work he defines it as a duty of the faithful to accept, among other points, the "punctum ... de invariabili et firma adhesione et obediencia ecclesie sancte Romane" (f. 39′).

[22] The Czech tractate, "O poslušenství" (MS Vienna Nationalbibliothek 4314, f. 150; cf. Činnost Příbrama, No. 14), cites John Hus's questio against the Crusade of 1411 to show that Hus defined the Church as the congregation of the faithful, and specified its head was the Roman Church. On several occasions Příbram cites John Hus's adherence to the condemnation of Wyclif's articles by the Czech Nation of the University in 1408, a condemnation that was actually so conditional as to be worthless: cf. the discussion by Jan Sedlák, M. Jan Hus (Prague, 1915), p. 125f. It is noteworthy that just as Příbram strove to present an orthodox Roman Catholic Hus, so the Taborites tried to make Hus one of them – even to the point of saying that he had not believed in Purgatory (Confession of 1431, Lydius, op. cit., I, 46f., 293f.).

[23] "O poslušenství", f. 149.

tics, for they are simoniacs and concubinaries, they do not believe that the bread remains in the sacrament, they hold ecclesiastical endowments, and from their many works we can tell that they are not of the Holy Church. And so they deny them obedience....

To replace this authority Tabor offered ... itself "They regard *themselves* as the Holy Universal Church of all Christendom."[24] The point is of course overstated, for polemical purposes, but it points to a truth: Tabor attempted to revive the Primitive Church by strict obedience to its Law and by cutting away every doctrine and practice that stemmed from postprimitive times; thus Tabor *became* the Primitive Church, in a more than figurative sense, and could think of himself as entitled to enjoy the liberty, sovereignty, and power of judgement that pertained to the Body of Christ. As Nicholas put it on one occasion, the rulers of the Primitive Church "were *and are* the Apostles"[25] – history was overcome and the past lived again in the present. It was for this reason that Tabor refused to grant that harmless or decorous practices of the Roman tradition might be continued; for Christ had not instituted them and he would not have failed to do so if he had thought them beneficial. Therefore they must have been instituted by Antichrist.

These were the ideas that had originally called the Taborite community into being as a congregation of those who were willing to secede from the existing societal order and join the brethren in evangelical poverty – either having nothing to begin with, or having given their property over to the priests, to be used for the community.[26] At the same time, this com-

---

[24] *Loc. cit.*: "Ale sami sie magí za czierkwe s. obecznú wšeho krzestianstwa." And just as there were those in the time of St. Augustine who held that the One, Universal, Holy Church was not extended over the whole world, but only in Africa, so the Taborites held it was only in Bohemia ("yako nyňýe rzkú že gest toliko w Čzechach").

[25] Postil on Apokalypse, MS Vienna Nationalbibliothek 4520, f. 190' ("...statum ecclesie primitive cuius rectores erant et sunt apostoli"). For this work and its attribution to Nicholas, see F. M. Bartoš, "Táborské bratrstvo let 1425-1426 na soudě svého biskupa Mikuláše z Pelhřimova", *Časopis společnosti přátel starožitností českých*, XXIX (1921), 102-122; Bartoš's dating, in 1425-1426, may be a few years too early.

[26] For this development see my "Chiliasm and the Hussite Revolution", *Church History*, XXVI (1957), 43-71. In his recent monograph on *Tábor v husitském revolučním hnutí*, 2 vols. (Prague, 1952-1955), Josef Macek argues that the original Taborite community was essentially a grouping of the poor – those in both town and countryside, especially the latter, who had no property and had to live on wages; he derives Tabor's doctrines from this social composition. Since Macek is not interested in the doctrinal development of Tabor after the chiliast party had lost its power – he regards Nicholas of Pelhřimov as the ideologue of the "bourgeois opposition" – his work offers little for the present study, except the vigorous and often brilliant presentation of a theory about the nature of Tabor and, in consequence, the nature of Nicholas's work. Against this theory the present study seeks to find the social correlates of Taborite ideologies, not

munity was engaged in a real war to the death with the anti-Hussites, who, persecuting the imitators of the Primitive Church, could only be regarded as followers of Antichrist. Thus it was that the ideas of Prague's anti-Roman polemic took on a quite new value, as constituent principles of the new order: the Primitive Church was no longer just a criterion, but became a living model; predestinarian ecclesiology was not just a way of attacking the Roman hierarchy, but a psychological reality; the war with Antichrist was not a figure for the struggle against sin and corruption, but a real war in which people were killed. Even the overwhelming emphasis placed by Jakoubek on the cult of Christ in the eucharist – an emphasis that had given birth to utraquism – became something else, the point of departure for a completely new liturgy.[27] And as the congregation developed into a new social community, it freely solved its ecclesio-political problems in conformity with its own nature. The clergy had to be regulated, but there was no need to look to a higher authority: the brethren could imitate the Primitive Church and elect their own bishop or elder, Nicholas of Pelhřimov, who would later write, "until priests of Christ are elected by the people ... the Church cannot be purged of her vices".[28] This position contrasted with Prague's pathetic reliance on Archbishop Conrad for ordinations – Conrad, a time-serving simoniac, as the Taborites frequently observed, who did not even know the Ten Commandments.[29] The problem of maintenance of Christian order, with

---

in classes – the poor, the bourgeois opposition, etc. – but in the various forms of the Taborite movement, understood as a religious movement whose social dimension was simply the result of its existence in the social world. Thus the pursuit of sectarian ideals of perfection by withdrawal from established society found religious expression in ideas like those of Peter Chelčický; chiliast ideas expressed the outlook of the sectarian movement after it had been in existence for a time, and had thus taken on social reality – opposition to "the world" was transformed into a determination to create a separate world of perfection. But the realities of social existence made this sort of perfection impossible, and Nicholas of Pelhřimov expressed the point of view of those who accepted these realities, which were not radically different from those of outside society, but sought to adapt Taborite idealism to them, as a specifically *religious* program. Nicholas was a spokesman for the whole societal organism, not merely for those who were on top of it, and his thought can therefore be better understood as the creation of something new than as merely the formulation of a reaction against the poor. This at any rate is the presupposition of the present study, which would hardly be possible on the basis of Macek's class-analysis.

[27] Nejedlý, *Dějiny husitského zpěvu*, IV: *Táboři* (Prague, 1955), 177ff.
[28] Postil on Apocalypse, MS 4520, f. 197 (cited by Bartoš, "Táborské bratrstvo", p. 116, n. 4).
[29] *Loc. cit.*; cf. also the Confession of 1431, Lydius, I, 112f., 113f. (Höfler, II, 647). Ignorance of the Ten Commandments is asserted of bishops *like* Conrad, and should no doubt be understood as a rhetorical exaggeration.

repression of sinful behavior, was also solved in a congregational spirit; the commmunity had its secular magistrates, but beside them there stood the priests, who preached against sins and, when necessary, denounced sinners from the pulpit by name, so that the magistrates could put them in the stocks or take other punitive action.[30] The clergy exercised a similar function, according to Romanist theory, too, but there was a difference: at Tabor the clergy were not a corporate estate, but merely the spiritual rectors of a community that also had secular rectors; both came from the community and were part of it; their position was derived from their function, not vice versa.[31] And the primary aim of the rectors, at least in theory, was to purge the community of every taint of sin, everyone being in principle entitled to correct everyone else, with no distinction between spiritual and secular law. Nicholas's defense of this ideal, at the Council of Basel, against Aegidius Carlerius's orthodox argument that sinners may be tolerated if correcting them were too inconvenient or dangerous, clearly defines the difference between the spirit of Tabor and the spirit of the old order.[32]

[30] Postil on Apocalypse, MS 4520, f. 227 sq.: the proper relationship between the two powers is that the "status secularis audit spirituales viros, qui in malicia maturos et in operibus infructuosos demonstrant eis et publice quandoque denuncciant." Cf. Bartoš, "Táborské bratrstvo," p. 112. Chelčický's *O trojím lidu*, ed. Krofta, p. 153, contains a passage that must certainly be interpreted as a reference to actual Taborite practice – which, of course, Chelčický criticizes: "Weak is the preaching of Christ's priest who, unable to bring some people into Christ's justice through Scripture, calls upon power and announces their adultery, drunkenness, and other sins in the church, forces power to punish them, and believes that in so doing he is successful in his preaching..."

[31] Bartoš, "Táborské bratrstvo", p. 112f. has a number of pertinent passages from Nicholas's Postil on Apocalypse; more could be added, but in fact Nicholas's political thought was quite primitive and hardly deserves much attention. He always had in mind the reality of the Taborite community, which needed no elaborate legal system, but only the Law of Christ, "cum illa perfecte executa doceat rectissime, quomodo omnis injusticia debeat a Republica extirpari" (Confession of 1431, Lydius, I, 55f.). In fact the situation was more complex, since Tabor had laws of her own, ordinary human laws, but these could enter the theoretical structure only as implementing the Law of Christ, which was itself *sufficientissima*. On this basis there was no need to speculate about whether secular power had its sword from God or from the clergy; the answer was obvious: "... potestas secularis ... habet a domino gladium" (Postil on Apocalypse, MS 4520, f. 227). God's community was regulated by God's Law, implemented by God's ministers. But outside of this framework, even Hussite secular power was suspect: "Quis enim Imperator, quis rex, quis baro etc., non est bestialis, eciam satham, veritati dei contrarius? Nam eciam si inter illos quesierimus qui se dicunt pro lege pugnare, et ibi inveniemus bestialiter viventes et adversari legi domini" (*ibid.*, f. 253). See also the following note.

[32] Nicholas's first oration, in defense of the fourth Prague Article, on the punishment of public sins, is published by F. M. Bartoš, *Orationes*... (Tábor, 1935), pp. 3-32. Carlerius's reply is in Mansi, XXIX, 868-972; Nicholas's reply to that, in Bartoš, *op.*

If, then, we keep in mind *both* the ideal of regenerating the Primitive Church and the actual nature of the community striving for this ideal, we can understand Tabor's doctrines in terms of their inner necessity. Thus, while the debates with Prague over the vestments and rites of the mass seem often to be a kind of stubborn game played with authorities, we can readily understand why the Roman Mass, used by the Praguers with slight modifications, was impossible at Tabor. As Nicholas pointed out, it was too long to hold the laity's active interest, and was unintelligible to them because celebrated in Latin; its ornaments and décor distracted the people from exclusive attention to God, and its quality as a sacrifice that could be offered apart from lay communion tended to seduce the people into thinking that it was an act of merit just to look at a mass.[33] To Tabor, of course, the Eucharist was consecrated only for the purpose of communion, and everyone was expected to take it.[34] As for the priests, they complained that the Roman rite left too little time for preaching – Tabor favored long, didactic sermons – and that the missals available to them did not include scriptural texts for weekdays. Moreover, the Roman vestments were nothing but the imperial trappings given to Pope Silvester by Constantine, and were obviously unsuitable for priests who wished to be imitators of the apostles.[35] Tabor's own liturgy was both popular and simple, involving a minimum of preparatory and decorative prayers, and consisting essentially of consecration, communion, and preaching, in a liturgical structure that was composed not only of the priest's words and

---

cit., pp. 36-82; Carlerius's final reply, in Mansi, XXX, 388-456. Nicholas's formulation of the article in question was very broad: "Peccata mortalia publica, et quantum racionabiliter fieri potest, privata alieque deordinaciones, legi dei contrarie, in communitatibus christianorum et quolibet statu earundem debite iuxta dictamen divine legis per Christi fideles, tam spirituales quam seculares, prout congruit utrisque, sint cohibenda, corripienda, castiganda et pro posse ab eisdem propellenda" (Bartoš, *op. cit.*, p. 3). He went on to say that "corripere peccantes ... est omnium in omnes", "ex zelo caritatis", although officials had an additional obligation "ex officio prelacionis" (p. 6). In another passage he referred to the officials as "rectores spitituales et seculares" (p. 12). In the extreme case, when the rectors of both kinds were themselves sinful, "subditi fideles licite possunt illos vel crimina illorum caritative arguere, ypocrisim eorum detegere et eorum manifestis sceleribus eciam coram aliis publice contraire" (p. 14). For Nicholas's rejection of prudential considerations that would mitigate the force of his article, see, e.g., p. 43f., where the arguments for tolerating prostitution are crisply refuted.

[33] Höfler, II, 579ff.
[34] Nejedlý, *Dějiny husitského zpěvu*, IV (1955), 289 and *passim*.
[35] Höfler, II, 579ff. This interpretation of the Roman vestments was derived from Wyclif: Höfler, II, 555.

acts, but also of the congregation's hymns, sung at every step of the service.[36] Everything was, of course, in the vernacular.

We will also understand that when Nicholas of Pelhřimov wrote that the seven sacraments were to be observed in the manner of the Primitive Church, he had in mind a concept of the sacrament that was miles away from those of Rome and Prague. [37] In fact, we feel that he discussed the matter only because the polemic with Prague forced him to do so. As he observed, in regard to extreme unction, "those who are predestined will certainly be saved even if they never receive such unction".[38] And the sacraments, in general, were "useful and salubrious antidotes of souls", not necessary prerequisites of salvation.[39] The issue here was whether the confrontation between the Christian and God was to be mediated in any essential or necessary way by the authoritative Church, functioning as a kind of salvation machine. Nicholas's real feeling on this point comes through most clearly in his attack on the cult of saints, as practiced in the Prague and Roman faith:[40]

The masters wish to show the sufficiency of the saints, so that everyone may more freely and securely turn to them, for he has heard that they pay heed to our needs and have compassion for us and are solicitous for our welfare.... And the uneducated [simplices] can draw no other conclusion from all of this than that they are sure of their salvation if they diligently serve the saints, pray to them, fast to them, burn incense to them, and, on their feast-days, take up no sickle, axe, or other instrument of servile labor. But it is all right for them to take up a cup of wine or beer! Such doctrines are very harmful and enticing to men.

The Virgin Mary, in particular, was exalted in Prague-Roman religion, and adorned with such epithets as The Merciful, The Omnipotent, The Queen of Heaven, The Hope of Sinners; Nicholas remarked that "this magnification of her makes it seem to the uneducated, even to the greatest sinners among them, that no one will be damned, because The Hope of Sinners rules in heaven and is diligent on behalf of her clients."[41] Man confronts

---

[36] Nejedlý, *Dějiny husitského zpěvu*, IV (1955), 249ff.
[37] Höfler, II, 601f. Cf. also Nicholas's Postil on Apocalypse, MS 4520, f. 188', where he attacks those "qui sacramenta ecclesie, baptismum, confirmacionem sive manuum imposicionem, sacrosancte eucaristie [sic], penitenciam, ordinem, matrimonium, et infirmorum unccionem, in auctoritate sensuque Cristi et ritu primitive ecclesie non promovent."
[38] Confession of 1431, Lydius, I, 117.
[39] Höfler, II, 602.
[40] Höfler, II, 675 (Lydius, I, 199).
[41] Lydius, I, 234.

God and only God, and the matter of man's salvation falls entirely within this relationship:[42]

From his hidden judgements, God wishes to benefit some men and does not wish to benefit others; some he benefits without being asked, ... some he hears because he sees their future conversion; ... sometimes, moreover, he does not hear even his elect in their difficulties. And the saints are of no use in all these things, for they do not have the knowledge that God has of them. Therefore the function of interceding cannot well subsist in the saints, because they cannot have so great a knowledge of hearts, of predestination, and of the other differences among men, as God has.

The doctrine of Purgatory seemed to Nicholas to be another such comfortable way of humanizing the economy of salvation, and when the Prague masters argued that the doctrine was necessary because, among other things, it would be unjust if God allowed a bad man who repented just before dying to go to heaven at once, just like the good man, – Nicholas replied with the scornful remark: "God is accused of injustice if he does not act according to their confections."[43] More than once Nicholas stressed the point that "God may do as he likes", that such cases as that of Jacob and Esau, of the laborers in the vineyard, and of the thief on the cross, were not to be judged according to human norms.[44]

Tabor's faith was thus harsh and strenuous, the faith of saints, and Nicholas's sermons provide ample evidence of what we might in any case guess: as the years passed, and as the poor warriors of God became more or less prosperous citizens, enriched by booty and otherwise, as their "purses came to be stuffed with florins", the people who once were diligent in faith and warfare began to want to stay home in idleness, drinking and banqueting, instead of fasting, attending to their property, and even getting married.[45] Peter Chelčický had told the priests of Tabor that the way of Christ was the renunciation of this world, not the struggle to master it, that the world as a whole could never be Christian, and that the instruments of power and the worldly ideals of peace and secular justice could only interfere with the faith.[46] Nicholas had heard him and was

---

[42] Lydius, I, 205ff. (Höfler, II, 679f.).
[43] Lydius, I, 177-179 (Höfler, II, 662-664).
[44] Loc. cit.
[45] Postil on Apocalypse, MS 4520. f. 284 (cited by Bartoš, "Táborské bratrstvo", p. 113). For Tabor's passage to the ordinary life of a "craft-town" see J. Macek, op. cit., I, 345ff.
[46] This is the argument of Chelčický's O trojím lidu, passim. It is evident, and generally recognized by scholars, that this work was addressed to a Taborite; how closely it was related to Tabor's own doubts about the course she was taking in 1420ff., is

evidently strongly moved by him, but he, along with his colleagues, chose to attempt a work that was perhaps more admirable, and certainly more difficult than renunciation. His faith was both evangelical and apocalyptic, involving a belief not only in the perfection of the Primitive Church, but also in the urgency of reform, and in "God's vengeance and the secret coming of Christ."[47] It would be unjust to say that he failed – the Taborite system was still in force when George of Poděbrady conquered the town in 1452[48] – and such a verdict would be in large part irrelevant. What Tabor had done was to create a new societal form in which the absolute demands of the Christian faith and ethos could resonate with social and psychological realities, and thus create a new approach to the problem of civilization. South Bohemia is far away, but Massachusetts is close by, and the results of the Puritans' experiment in virtue and dedication should help us to appreciate the identical enterprise of the Taborites.

---

perhaps not as fully appreciated as it should be. I discuss the matter in a preface to an English translation of Chelčický's treatise that I hope to publish soon.

[47] Postil on Apocalypse, MS 4520, f. 244'. The passage is cited by Bartoš, "Táborské bratrstvo", p. 110, but misunderstood as an attack on the chiliasts: in fact, Nicholas was imbued with apocalyptic passion, and, as Amadeo Molnár has recently pointed out, the whole Taborite enterprise, both during and after the chiliast period, can be understood only in the light of its profoundly eschatological coloring ("Eschatologická naděje české reformace", *Od reformace k zítřku*, Prague, Kalich, 1956, p. 32 & *passim*).

[48] See my article, "Pius Aeneas among the Taborites", *Church History*, XXVIII (1959), 281-309, esp. pp. 288-294.

George of Poděbrady's Plan for an International Peace League

FREDERICK G. HEYMANN

At the time of this publication it is just 500 years since there was launched from the Chancery of the Czech king, George of Poděbrady, a plan that can, with much justification, be considered the first serious design for an International Peace Organization based on the free cooperation of sovereign states. As one of the most important contributions to advanced political thought coming out of late medieval Bohemia, this plan fully deserves a discussion of both its historic character and its systematic features.

In the spring and summer of the year 1462, George of Poděbrady, who four years earlier had been elected and crowned as King of Bohemia, experienced the first great crisis of his reign.[1] In the spring he had sent an embassy to Rome with a double purpose. The first was to bring to Pope Pius II the official "obedience" of the King, his family and his people. At the same time, the embassy, consisting of the King's foremost advisers, one a Catholic and the other an adherent of the Hussite-Utraquist reform church, was to ask the Pope for the confirmation of the Basel Compacts, the religious and church-political peace treaty which had put an end to the terrible Hussite Wars (1419-1436) and enabled the people of the Czech countries to live in relative religious peace, especially after the restoration of a strong government, first by George's regency (since 1452), and later by his kingship. There had been a time when Pius II (then, in 1455, still Bishop Enea Silvio de' Piccolomini) had strongly advocated this act of

---

[1] The most detailed and authentic treatment of the reign of George of Poděbrady, up to the year 1464, is Rudolf Urbánek's great work, *Věk poděbradský*, in 4 volumes (Prague, 1915-1962) (= part III of *České dějiny*, unfortunately unfinished and, owing to the author's recent death, hardly likely ever to be finished; quoted after this as Urbánek, *Věk*). For treatments in languages other than Czech, see the German edition of Palacký's *Geschichte von Böhmen*, vol. IV, several editions; Ernest Denis, *Georges de Podiébrod, Les Jagellons* (= *Fin de l'indépendance de Bohème*, I) (Paris, 1890), and A. Bachmann, *Böhmen und seine Nachbarländer unter Georg von Podiebrad, 1458-1461* (Prag, 1878), and the same author's *Deutsche Reichsgeschichte im Zeitalter Friedrich III und Max I*, 2 vols. (Leipzig, 1884 and 1894).

confirmation as the best way to overcome the religious split. Meanwhile, however, Pius, who considered himself the foremost expert in matters relating to Bohemia as to all of Central Europe, had changed his mind. Convinced that King George, if he but willed, could with relative ease overcome the dogmatic and, especially, the liturgical deviations of the strong Hussite majority of the Czechs, he had, after effectively supporting the King, put increasing pressure on him, expecting that this would induce George to liquidate the Utraquist Church, particularly its central symbol, the communion in both kinds, that is the offering of the chalice to laymen, granted to the Czechs by the Council of Basel. When King George, through his ambassadors, demanded confirmation instead of liquidation of this long-tolerated religious distinction, the Pope solemnly abrogated the Compacts and sent a legate to Prague demanding immediate and complete conformity with the Roman ritual. This ultimatum was later answered by the King with the declaration that he, his family and all those trusting his leadership would, in the future as in the past, live and die within the Compacts as granted by the Holy Council and as the only basis, in Bohemia, for the maintenance of domestic peace.[2] From now on the relationship between Pope and King, Rome and Prague, was one of steady and constantly sharpening ideological and political struggle. In general, the Curia was on the offensive, while the Czech King tried to defend himself, his nation and his religion against this renewed attack. As a good political strategist, however, George tried to counteract Papal diplomacy by seeking to ally himself with powers which he knew to have themselves strained relations with the Holy See. This was especially true of the two greatest Christian powers on the European continent. One was France, whose young King, Louis XI, felt betrayed by the Pope who had not paid (as Louis had expected) for the official abrogation of the Pragmatic Sanction of Bourges with his support of the claims of the Anjous in Naples, or, at least, with neutrality in their struggle with Ferrante of Aragon. The other was Poland, whose prolonged war with the Teutonic Knights in Prussia had found the Holy See consistently on the side of the Knights, to the point of threatening King Casimir IV and his chief advisers with church punishments if he did not cease to fight the semi-ecclesiastical Prussian state.

The rapprochement between King George and King Casimir seemed the most urgent of these two tasks, especially since, during the earlier years of George's reign, there had been frictions between the two rulers. Casi-

---

[2] See Urbánek, *Věk*, IV, 464-575; Palacký, *Geschichte*, IV, 215-254; and Bachmann, *Reichsgeschichte*, I, 193-209, 230-246.

mir, married to a sister of George's predecessor, Ladislav Posthumus, had, at the latter's death, claimed hereditary rights to the Bohemian crown in the name of his Queen; although he had not pursued this claim with great urgency it had, with other issues, prevented any real friendship or cooperation between the two kingdoms.[3] But a new approach was made during a solemn meeting of both rulers, which took place in the Silesian city of Glogau (Głogów) and lasted from May 18 to early June, 1462.[4]

Some of the foremost members of the high clergy and the aristocracy of both countries took part in the negotiations at Glogau. But among the advisors whom King George called on here there was, it seems, also a Frenchman called Antoine Marini, a citizen of Grenoble (if probably of Italian origin) who had gained King George's confidence especially as an economic expert, but who had also been consulted on matters of foreign policy because of his considerable acquaintance with conditions in Western and Southern Europe. He had lived not only in France, but also, for some time, in Venice as an active member of that great city-state's business community.[5]

Whether Marini had any part in the official negotiations at Glogau may be doubted, as his name has not been mentioned by the sources in this context. The negotiations themselves succeeded in eliminating all outstanding problems between the two Kingdoms. In particular, George agreed to forego, during his lifetime, all demands for the return of the Upper Silesian holdings now in Polish hands, especially the principalities of Oswiecim (Auschwitz) and Zator, while Casimir would do the same with claims on Queen Elizabeth's dowry based on the Bohemian inheritance from her mother. There was nothing unusual in the majority of the other clauses relating to the maintenance of peace: the promise not to

[3] The relations between the two rulers has been the subject of a monograph by Zd Tobolka, "Styky krále Jiřího z Poděbrad s králem polským Kazimírem", *Časopis matice moravské*, No. 22 (Brno, 1898), pp. 70-76, 163-175, 300-310, 373-384.
[4] About the meeting, see Długosz, *Opera omnia*, XIII (V) ed. Przezdziecki (Cracow, 1877), 343-345; Eschenloer, G., *Geschichte der Stadt Breslau*, ed. Kunisch, vol. I (Breslau, 1827), 188-190; *Scriptores rerum Silesiacarum* ed. Markgraf, X, 15, Chronicle of Glogau); also *ibid.*, XII, 78; finally M. Toeppen, *Acten der Ständetage Preussens*, V (Leipzig, 1886), 62-65. Modern treatments: Bachmann, *Reichsgeschichte*, I, 222-225; Tobolka, *op. cit.*, 163-165; and Urbánek, *Věk*, IV, 540-544.
[5] Marini has been the subject of a not inconsiderable literature. It is best listed bibliographically by Urbánek, *Věk*, IV, 214-215, nn. 246-251. Of special significance is N. Jorgas' sketch: "Un auteur de projects de croisades, Antoine Marini", in *Études d'histoire du moyen âge dédiées à G. Monod* (Paris, 1896), 445f. German historians, especially Bachmann and Voigt, have wrongly seen him as nothing but an irresponsible adventurer.

help the other party's enemies; an end to private feuding (with causes to be submitted to courts, or, if necessary, to a special commission to meet in January, 1463); the safeguarding of freedom and security of roads; and the prohibition of the issue of false or debased coins. But the most important issue was contained in the introduction, which emphasizes that, on the suggestion of King George, both rulers had resolved to help one another with all their power in case one of them should be threatened by the Turks. This, it is true, sounds rather vague and general, especially if it is realized that for geographical reasons alone the two realms were not – or not yet – exposed to an immediate attack by Ottoman forces, and that at the time in question, in the spring of 1462, the immediate threat was still to the Principality of Wallachia and the Kingdom of Bosnia. This situation left Hungary alone, of the three important eastern European powers, under some substantial pressure from the Southeast.

But the declaration was not really the reaction to an immediate military threat to one or the other of the contracting parties. Rather was its purpose – envisaged clearly by George – a twofold one. It was to establish a new, close relationship between the two West-Slav nations. But it was also to prepare the way for an unusual and daring scheme of international organization, one whose very daring, whose anachronistically advanced concept, reveals its historical interest as well as its main weakness: it was sure to shock, and it was likely to fail. But at the time, King George was not aware of its long-range hopelessness, and even if he had been, he might still, for other reasons, have chosen this course.

The first purpose – close cooperation in the terms of a truly functioning, truly reliable and lasting non-aggression pact, was of course the most important gain that historically resulted from the Glogau meeting for George and his Utraquist commonwealth in the tense situation in which he now had to operate. This value must be measured in the terms of the strong and, for a while, quite relentless pressure that was later put on Casimir to renew his claim to the Bohemian crown which Pius' successor, Paul II, especially would have been only too happy to bestow on the Polish ruler. It must be measured, furthermore, in terms of the impression which a falling-out of the greatest power of Eastern Europe with the Czech King would have made, especially among those German princes who for a while would sit on the fence in the great and prolonged struggle between Prague and Rome. Under such circumstances, the attempt of the Curia again to concentrate overwhelmingly strong forces against Hussite Bohemia might well have had far greater success than it actually attained.

There remains the question: why was it necessary for a treaty of friendship like the one concluded at Glogau to refer to the Turkish danger? The answer to this question reveals also the second purpose of the meeting – far more striking and, as such, far less successful than the first. For behind it stands the great plan for an organization of European princes and their states which is indeed an attempt by George to answer in a positive form the attack of the Curia against him.

It is clear that the plan for a league of Princes,[6] intended to maintain and guarantee the internal peace of Christian Europe and thus to enable the participants to stand up to the Turkish danger, was not, in all its complex details, a brain child of George alone. Usually Antoine Marini has been considered the man to be credited with the draft. It is true, as we shall see, that he, more than any other of King George's advisers or diplomats, was later charged with the presentation of the plan to various European courts, and we find several important similarities in a memorandum[7]

---

[6] The plan has been treated by a large number of historians, political scientist and students of law, in the framework of larger works as well as in monographs. Among the latter are: H. Markgraf, "Über Georgs von Podiebrad Project eines christlichen Fürstenbundes", *Historische Zeitschrift*, 21 (München, 1869), 257-304; E. Schwitzky, *Der Europäische Fürstenbund Georgs von Podiebrad* (= *Abhandlungen aus dem juristisch-staatswissenschaftlichen Seminar der Universität Marburg*, ed. Schücking, vol. 6) (Marburg, 1907); W. Weizsäcker, "Fürstenbund und Völkerbund", in *Prager juristische Zeitschrift*, X (1930), pp. 234-245; J. Kapras, *The Peace league of George Poděbrad, King of Bohemia* (= *The Czechoslovak Republic*, vol. II, part 5) (Prague, 1919); J. Kliment, *Svaz národu Jiřího z Poděbrad a idea jediné světovlády* (Prague, 1935); F. M. Bartoš, "Návrh Krále Jiřího na utvoření svazu evropských států", *Jihočeský sborník historický*, XII (Tábor, 1939), 65-82; J. Polišenský, "Problemy zahraniční politiky Jiřího z Poděbrad", *Acta Universitatis Palackianae Olomucensis*, Historica I (Olomouc, 1960), 107-125. A Polish contribution to the topic is J. Pogonowski's *Projekt związku wlaców króla Jerzego z Podiebrad* (Warsaw, 1932). The project is also discussed in considerable detail by Jacob ter Meulen in *Der Gedanke der internationalen Organization in seiner Entwickelung 1300-1800* (The Hague, 1917). In the more important standard works, the plan is treated by Palacký IV, 2. 209-212, (German 237-240), Bachmann, *Reichsgeschichte*, I, 214-218, and above all, Urbánek, *Věk*, IV, 580-599.

[7] The memorandum, as yet unprinted, had already been mentioned by Jorga in his sketch on Marini in *Études d'histoire du moyen âge dédiées à G. Monod* (Paris, 1896), on pp. 451-453. Urbánek, in *Věk*, IV, 585-589, gives an extended presentation of its content (details about the MS on p. 583, n. 25). Among the striking similarities between the memorandum and the final plan as we know it is a jeremiad about the decline of the Christian World that forms the introduction in both documents. Marini sees three possibilities for future development: either a return to the old status of a Christian Europe led by two powerful heads – Pope and Emperor – in purposive strength and unity; an alliance of all the great Christian lay princes; or the final destruction of Christianity. Despite a very sharp criticism of the errors and omissions of the lay princes who are so divided that the people have lost confidence, he sees real hope only in their alliance. But he goes into considerable detail in his criticism of the sins of clergy, princes and lawyers, of the corruption in ecclesiastical administration, and the sophisms and

which he is believed to have prepared shortly before the Glogau conference to be submitted there to both Kings. Thus it would seem most unlikely that he was not also, to a considerable extent, responsible for and instrumental in helping to draft the plan. Yet it seems doubtful, as has recently been pointed out,[8] that he had quite the legal training to work out, by himself, a plan like this in all its aspects, and there is no reason to assume that for an undertaking of such importance, once he had decided for it, George would not have drawn on the talent of two or more of the gifted minds at his disposal. With this in view, the suggestion that Martin Mair, the Bavarian lawyer and diplomat who had long fought for the plan of making George King of the Romans, had something to do with developing and writing the plan has much to recommend itself, though not to the extent where Mair alone could be considered as the author. Documents of such length and such wealth of ideas and constructive conceptions are rarely produced by only one mind. In this case, in particular, several of the guiding ideas may have come from George himself, whose helpers,

---

errors of the university teachers; and he castigates, among other things, the criminal selfishness which has induced Western people and traders who, blinded by monetary gains, were ready to help the Turks by delivering to them ships, guns and other means of waging war. He finally names five great nations which should form the backbone of the resistance to the Turks: Greeks, Germans, French, Italian and Spaniards. Despite the odd inclusion of the Greeks and the absence of the English, this point of Marini's memorandum, the final plan, distinctly shows its model: the Council of Constance. Here, indeed, appears a strange inconsistency: while no Slavic power is mentioned, Marini nevertheless appeals to the two Slavic rulers to organize the needed cooperation of the princes of the Christian nations of Europe. And he justifies his belief in their great European role with a prophecy which he claims he heard from Flavio Biondo, apostolic secretary since the time of Eugene IV and a close friend of Pope Pius, who, like others, considered Biondo (e.g. *Commentaries*, Smith College edition, XI, 766 f.) a distinguished historian of ancient Rome. Marini ends with the suggestion that the King should invite the rulers of France, Burgundy, Venice and Bavaria to a common meeting in Venice, the place to which Marini himself was soon to travel. The inclusion of Duke Louis of Bavaria, a rather petty prince in comparison with the others, makes one wonder whether Dr. Martin Mair, the Duke's chief councillor, had not already had some influence on the redaction of the memorandum.

[8] See F. M. Bartoš, whose contribution in *Jihočeský sborník historický*, XII (1939), 65ff. quoted above is mainly devoted to proving that the real author of the plan was Mair rather than Marini. Beside contributing to the general discussion of the project and helping to clarify its genesis, Bartoš has also, in an appendix to his article (pp. 74-81), presented the best text of the project known to me, superior to the older publications by Schwitzky and Kliment. (See the editorial notes by Bartoš, *op. cit.*, 81 and 82, and Urbánek *Věk* IV 580, n. 16.) Another text, until quite recently unknown, has been discovered in the archives of the Royal Polish Chancery, called *Metryka koronna*, volume XI, pp. 578-587. A publication of this text is imminent in Prague, but I have had no chance to see it. I understand that it does not give any essentially new or different versions of the text.

probably Mair at least as much as Marini, would then have provided most of the legal-historical knowledge, the sophisticated organization and the Latin diction.

It is quite impossible, however, to present anything like a proper history of the genesis of this earlier "grand design". Certain similarities to the much older plan of Pierre Dubois[9] may well be incidental, though perhaps the possibility cannot be completely excluded that the Frenchman Marini had some knowledge of it. One of the elements of the plan – the reorganization of Christian Europe for the task of an anti-Turkish crusade – was, of course, very much "in the air" at the time. We have only to think of Pope Pius' initiative in calling, quite early in his reign, the congress of princes to Mantua, as well as the many *Reichstage* called to deal with the same problem. The Mantuan Congress as well as the *Reichstage* were notoriously unsuccessful, and this in itself could well have taught a critical observer like George that the old conception of the defense of Christian Europe against the unbelievers, under the common leadership of Pope and Emperor, was now even less promising than it had been in centuries past, and should be replaced by something more effective. Modern commentators have mostly emphasized that George's plan put forward the idea of an organization of the temporal powers, in the form of national states, as against the previous expectation of ecclesiastical leadership. There is much truth in this, and to that extent the project is certainly far closer to the one developed by Sully a century and a half later than to Dubois' scheme presented a century and a half before. Yet the "secularization" of the idea of European organization in George's project is not yet complete, and the role of the Holy See in it not quite as negligible as is often claimed. This, at least, is true for the draft text that has come down to us in a couple of only slightly differing versions. Even so, the draft remains an instrument of a political trend directed largely against the Papacy and its leadership claims, since it contains important elements which the Papacy had all along resented, and no one, disavowing his own past, more than Pius II. These elements are derived from the Church Councils, especially those of Constance and Basel. While their main emphasis is organizational, this is enough to make the plan appear to belong to the very policy fought with such energy by Pope Pius in his bull "Execrabilis". And for the same reasons it would make the plan appear attractive in the eyes of all those opposed to that bull, first of all, presumably, the King of France, Louis XI, whose disappointment with

---

[9] Pierre Dubois, *De recuperatione terrae sanctae*, ed. Langlois (Paris, 1891). See also ter Meulen's evaluation in his work quoted above in n. 17, pp. 101 ff.

Pius' policy had long made him regret his concession regarding the Pragmatic Sanction of Bourges.

Attempts to date with some precision the genesis of the plan in its earlier phases met with difficulties. There are only a few clues, such as a letter from Marini to King George[10] in which he, as early as August 1461, thus before the outbreak of the crisis, pointed to Godfrey of Bouillon as a model for George's policy, and, more important, the memorandum mentioned above. Other than this, we have no clear indications of how the idea materialized. Yet it is quite likely that the substance had taken shape before, or took shape during the great meeting of the Kings at Glogau. Relatively soon thereafter, Antoine Marini went on to present the draft – in whatever stage of maturation it may then have been – to Venice. From our records, including the text of a letter from the Doge to King George dated August 9, 1462, it seems clear that in Venice Marini's diplomatic work, based on a program of close cooperation of the rulers of Bohemia, Hungary, France, Burgundy and the Republic of Venice, had made a good impression and would be supported.[11] The Venetians did, however, suggest that the Curia be given a more influential role, and they did not believe, or pretended they did not believe, that, merely because of the participation and expected leading role of the King of Bohemia, Pope Pius II would be reluctant to cooperate.

It is not very clear whether Marini, after his preliminary success in Venice, returned to Prague and stayed there through the autumn. This seems likely, however, since in this period, presumably, he had the opportunity to participate in further dicsussions of the plan. In any case he took it westward around the turn of the year,[12] visiting first the court of the Duke of Burgundy in Brussels, where, however, he seems to have found little encouragement. The fact that Duke Philip was included in Marini's itinerary had been presented as proof of the poor judgment of King

[10] See Palacký's publication in *Časopis českého Museum*, III (1828), pp. 21-24.
[11] See *Fontes rerum Austriacarum*, vol. 20, ed. Palacký (Vienna, 1860), 289f.
[12] It is generally taken for granted that at this stage of the negotiations, King Matthias of Hungary was entirely disregarded – a neglect which would reflect also on George's treatment of his son-in-law. There is, however, one source which makes it appear possible that, before his great Western trip, Marini had also visited Matthias, though perhaps without presenting his ideas to him fully. See the letter of Otto de Carretto, ambassador of the Duke of Milan at the papal court, written from Rome to Duke Francesco on January 13, 1463, concerning recent discussions with the Pope. In it Carretto mentions Marini as a French national who has not only (apparently recently) been in Hungary and Bohemia, but is now in France as an envoy of the King of Bohemia, as well as of the Kings of Hungary and Poland. See Pastor, *Geschichte der Päpste*, vol. II (Freiburg, 1904), documentary appendix pp. 736, 737. See also Urbánek *Věk*, IV, 592, n. 45.

George's diplomats, since the Duke was just then the object of lively wooing from both the Bavarian and Imperial parties in the Empire and would thus not be accessible to the Bohemian advances.[13] But it is difficult to see why a scheme of which the Wittelsbach party was at least well informed, and in which it might even have had a hand through Mair, should not include an attempt to gain the support of Burgundy, especially at a moment when the relationship between Burgundy and France seemed on the point of being mended. True, the court of Burgundy could not be expected to keep the matter hidden from the Curia, but at this time the Pope would have heard of it anyhow, if from no other sources than his intelligence service in Venice.[14]

In any case Brussels was only a stage on the way to Paris, and there Marini's reception was, at least by his own evaluation, as warm as that in Burgundy had been cool. King Louis found the plan worthy of energetic support, and the only regret the French uttered was that Marini did not have full power to conclude a formal treaty embodying all the points put forward by the Czech King's ambassador.[15]

Whether, and to what extent, French suggestions for changes of the scheme were advanced, and to what extent they were accepted, are matters of mere conjecture. It seems at least possible, however, that the discussion with the French helped to give the scheme that final shape in which we read it today, and that in this form it was then presented again, first to the Venetians,[16] and eventually also to other princes, including Matthias of Hungary.

What, then, was the scheme? The document, about 4000 words long, begins with a long preamble describing the misery to which the Turkish

---

[13] See Bachmann, *Reichsgeschichte*, I, 404, 405; Markgraf, *op. cit.*, 279, and Urbánek, *Věk*, IV, 593.

[14] Possibly Theodore de Lelli, Bishop of Feltre, who later became a prominent diplomat under Paul II. For information about his stay in Venice, see Jaochimsohn, *Gregor Heimburg* (Bamberg, 1891), p. 243.

[15] See the Venetian answer to the lost letter of Louis XI, in *Fontes rerum Austriacarum*, 20, 290-291. For another, more direct source, so far entirely unnoticed by all Czech or German historians, see King Louis' letter to Duke Philip the Good of Burgundy, in *Lettres de Louis XI, Roi de France*, ed. Vaesen et Charavay, vol. II (Paris, 1885), pp. 82-83.

[16] Bachmann (*Reichsgeschichte*, I, 406-407) sees a strong French influence upon the project, and assumes that it was, by the clever Frenchmen, "noch weiter zu ihrem Vorteile umgemodelt..." Details which are supposed to prove this are to be found in the footnotes on both pages. Urbánek clearly does not share this view, nor does he see the reaction of Louis in as positive a light as Bachmann, since he assumes, probably correctly, that under the influence of some of his clerical advisors the King was somewhat hesitant to assume a leading role in the scheme (pp. 599-600).

conquests had reduced the Christian world. Once, this world had embraced 117 flourishing realms, and had included even the tomb of the Savior. Of these realms, barely 16 were left since Mahomet had seduced the Arab people and his followers had overrun large parts of Africa and Asia. Even Greece and Constantinople had fallen. This dreadful collapse, the preamble says, is difficult to grasp, and is probably God's punishment for our sins. But nothing could please the Lord better than the urge to create peace and concord within, and to defend the Christian world on this earth against all its enemies. and especially against the infidels.

But since it seemed hopeless for any single nation to resist the Turkish power, all the Christian nations of Europe would have to unite in a perpetual union, in order to work with combined strength to drive the Turks from the soil of Europe. The main prerequisite for such a union, however, would be the creation of Christian peace within the Union and with other Christian nations. After this preamble – whose rather passionate language clearly tries to appeal to the emotions of those to whom it should have been adressed – there follows what might be called the constitution of the intended League of Princes – for despite the important role that the Republic of Venice is expected to play, even there, the Doge is referred to as one of the regional leaders of the league.[17] This Constitution is organized in about twenty-four paragraphs, of which the first four are actually numbered.[18] The following extract attempts to adhere to the logic rather than to the literal sequence of the draft.

The constitution, following the example of the Council of Constance (but also the much older examples of some great universities like Bologna, Paris and pre-Hussite Prague), divides Christian Europe into a small number of large "*nationes*", a term by no means identical with the modern usage of the word. This is most obvious in view of the fact that the King of France appears "together with the other kings and princes of Gaul;"

---

[17] In reference to Italy, however, alone of all nations or regions, there is also mention (in § 20) of the city states (*communitates*), especially necessary in view of the official structure of the Florentine state, where the factual rule of the Medici had not yet been recognized in any formal way.

[18] The original has no paragraph number beyond those first four, but all modern editors have, for good practical reasons, continued the numbering all through. Naturally there are differences, as the numbering is bound to be somewhat arbitrary. Thus Schwitzky counts only 21 whereas Kliment comes to 24. Bartoš follows Kliment's example. I have therefore quoted on the basis of these two publications. For readers to whom Schwitzky rather than Kliment and Bartoš may be accessible, I might mention that paragraphs 9-11 are listed as one paragraph, and paragraphs 17 and 18 again as only one by Schwitzky, so that from 10 on, his count lags by two figures, from 19 on, by three figures, behind the count used here. Markgraf, too, incidentally, used 24 paragraphs, but differs in detail from those of Kliment and Bartoš.

that no mention is made of the Holy Roman Emperor, but that there are several "Kings and princes of Germany", among these presumably all rulers of Central and East Central Europe, not only of Bohemia, but also of Poland and Hungary, neither of whom is expressly mentioned anywhere. In this sense it would be correct to speak of a regional rather than a national division of Europe. Beside the two regions mentioned before, there was the Italian, which was supposed to be under the political leadership of Venice, and finally, planned as a future addition, the kings and princes of Spain, clearly meaning the whole peninsula, under the leadership of the King of Castile, rather than Aragon, which, with its great Mediterranean empire and its strong navy, would have been better able to play a role in a common war against the Ottomans. Here, clearly, we find an expression of French interests which, as we know, were in sharp opposition to the Aragonese rule in Southern Italy.[19] Why the authors of this constitution neglected England it is difficult to say, though it would not be overly surprising to see the English Kingdom included in either *"Gallia"* or even in *"Germania"*. The latter region seems certainly likely to include Scandinavia, all the more since its ruler Christian I was, in any case, as Count of Holstein, a prince of the Empire. A clear delimitation between the member-"nations" is not recognizable, and the position of as important a border-state as Burgundy (probably within "Gallia") can only be guessed.

The three or four "nations" or regions – the term *"provinciae"* is also occasionally used – are supposed to operate as units within the league. The main organ of the league is a council of representatives or ambassadors of the princes who are members, variously called *"congregatio"*, *"collegium"*, *"corpus"* or even *"universitas"*, each "nation" or region holding but one vote. (§ 20) This is an arrangement which might well have caused difficulties if and when the total number of "nations" in the league would have reached four. There are no attempts to solve this problem on the international level, which is the more noticeable because the same problem is faced and at least partially solved in relation to those decisions within one nation or region on which the vote on the international level is based. Normally, each king or prince, whatever his general status and whatever the number of his representatives, is supposed to have but one vote, and if no unanimity can be achieved, the simple majority decides. If, however, the vote is evenly split the voices shall be weighed and those of the more important members (such as kings as against dukes or princes)

---

[19] See the remarks of Bachmann, *op. cit.*, 407, and Urbánek, *Věk*, IV, 598 n. 66.

shall prevail. But when the two sides remain numerically even, then the "nation" to which they belong loses, on the issue in question, its voice as against those of the other "nations".

The fact that, measured by the terms of the period, considerable care is given to the voting procedure shows that the author or authors intended to develop a congressional mechanism which could really function. This, indeed, was of central importance, since there was no other, higher central organ, and since the functions and powers of the only other body, the international court, were naturally more specialized and more limited than those of the general council.

Which were those functions and powers? They went very far indeed in determining the actions of the League and, therewith, of everyone of its members. In some ways those powers went farther than any of the two great modern experiments of international organization in the direction of a world government. Above all, it is up to the general assembly to maintain the peace between and within all the members of the League, a duty based on those rights which it derives from the solemn obligation of each member never under any circumstances to resort to the use of force against any other member (§§ 1 and 2). The League, again upon the decision of the assembly, will protect any of its members against attacks from outside, after first having made attempts at reconciliation through its own diplomats (§ 4). Since wars even between non-members are considered dangerous, the council will offer its services as arbitrator for settling major quarrels, but if this procedure should be unsuccessful, it will eventually use its own military power on the side of that power that itself has refrained from aggression and has been prepared to accept arbitration (§ 5). The power of the League, in an age in which the border between private feuds and international wars was still so fluid, was also supposed to include the quenching of such feuds. While acts of aggression in the form of feuds were, in the first place, to be punished severely by the local ruler, the latter was responsible for the maintenance of peace and order to the extent that he himself would be punished by the League for tolerating disturbance of the peace with the same punishments normally meted out to the delinquent (§§ 6-8).

Since the waging of individual wars or military actions of any size is completely outlawed, as a result of the basic obligations undertaken by any member (including new members whose accession had to be agreed to by the Council (§ 12)), the question remained of how and in what form he League would and could build up it own supranational military forces. h is is of course a problem that has plagued modern international bodies down to the United Nations. The constitution of the League devotes a number of paragraphs (§§ 13-18) to this difficult problem, and from them it appears (though not spelled out expressly) that the instrument of feudal levies, especially for the purpose of anti-Turkish crusades, is meant to be discarded. At least the fact that much emphasis is put on the financial aspect seems to indicate that the army to operate in the name of the League will consist essentially of mercenaries. Here, as in so many other aspects of the plan, we can see the attempt to move away from older time-worn patterns and accept instead the needs and trends of an economically and socially changing world.[20] There was to be a common tax rate to be applied for war, especially the war against the Turks, by all members of the League, and it would be allocated in a way which would fully consider each member's ability to pay. In all member states the clergy would be taxed one-tenth of its income, and other subjects three days of income as long as needed (§ 13). The League, furthermore, would have the right to coin its own currency (§ 16) for the purpose of paying the armed forces which were to be hired, owing to the orders given by the council, in the individual member states. The council would also determine the place and date of military action, the type and strength of the forces to be employed, (§ 14), and the ways in which they are to be provisioned (§ 15). Finally it would be up to the council to decide about and to administer territories conquered in a common war, the permanent security of the Christian world being the predominant consideration.

The second and only other organ[21] of the League was the international court. It is called variously *"parlamentum"*[22] and *"consistorium"* (both terms sometimes used together), occasionally also *"judicium"*. Its foremost tasks are judicial decisions on issues arising between member-states (§ 3) and in connection with deeds considered crimes against the peace of the land (§ 4). There is also a remarkable paragraph (§ 9) giving something like the philosophical basis for this new and – outside the ecclesiastical jurisdiction – unheard-of conception. It points out that there can be

---

[20] Here, presumably, in a field in which he was considered an expert and authority, Marini's ideas and suggestions must have prevailed against any competing ones.

[21] Urbánek (*op. cit.*, 599) assumes that beside the general assembly there was provision also for a narrower body of the greater princes, somewhat akin to the Security Council of the U.N. There are, however, only vague references to justify this assumption.

[22] As far as I can see, the term "parlamentum", in accordance, of course, with French medieval and modern pre-revolutionary terminology, is used only in relation to the international law court. Thus I am somewhat puzzled by Urbánek's consistent usage of the term for the League as such, the chapter in question being called "Plán o parlamentu". (Palacký had also used the term, but only occasionally.)

no international peace without justice, and essentially the justification for introducing a new law (*de naturae gremio nova jura producere*)[23] anticipates the Grotian conception of a natural law of the nations.

The international court itself would consist of one chief justice (*judex*) and an indefinite number of associate judges (*assessores*), all of them appointed by the council, but without any indications on how they were to be selected. Some emphasis is put on the need to give sentences which are clear, easily understandable, and in their implementation do not permit any subterfuges or prolonged and frustrating litigations (§ 10). The following paragraph (§ 11) reconfirms the emphasis on the complete authority of the court in all quarrels or differences between the member states.

It is toward the end that this document, thus far essentially devoted to the principles and the structure of the planned organization, becomes more concrete in the political and topical sense. And it is here that we find important historical clues as well.

The council of the League, says § 17, will meet for the first time on the Sunday Reminiscere (February 26) 1464 in the city of Basel, within the territory of the German nation, where it will reside for five years. After that, in 1469, it will move to a city in France, and still five years later to another city, this time in Italy.

The council, as we see in the same context, is considered essentially a judicial person, with its own coat of arms, its own seal, archives and treasury. It also has its own syndics, fiscal officers and other officials. This may sound as if here we even anticipate the modern conception of an international civil service, a conception, indeed, which is not too alien to the the time, having been approached both in the papal Curia and in the preceding organizations of the great church councils. The following paragraph (§ 18), however, states that the council of the League, during the five-year period during which it resides in one "nation", is supposed to appoint or elect most of its officials from the ranks of the peoples within that "nation". This, of course, tends to reduce the international character of the staff of the League in favor of a "national" character expected to change every five years.

The question arises – how far would this clause reach toward the top of the chain of command? Paragraph 17, in many ways the one that gives us the best historical clues, establishes the position of the head of the League (*unus praesidens pater et caput*), and with virtual unanimity it had been assumed by all the historians and political scientists who have

---

[23] P. 62 in Kliment's, p. 78 in Bartoš's text.

so far studied the document that it was King Louis XI who was meant immediately to fill this position.[24] But there are good reasons to disagree with this assumption, which is based mainly on guesswork and on what might be called the political logic of the situation, especially in its subsequent development. On the basis of paragraph 18, one would, indeed expect that the position of head of the League would, during the five-year period in which the League would reside in a city in "Gaul", fall to the French King as the leader and most powerful ruler of that region or nation. Similarly the Doge of Venice would take over the presidency of the League during the third period. But what of the first period? In this phase the League was supposed to have its headquarters in Basel, then a German Imperial city made famous by the long years of the Church Council and by the very recent establishment there (1460) of a university. Thus it would seem logical to make the leader of the "natio Germaniae" the head and "presiding father" of the League. But who is the leader? Under normal circumstances it would naturally be the Emperor of the Romans. Yet he is not even mentioned. Where the draft says "*nos, rex Franciae, una cum ceteris regibus et principibus Galliae*", and "*nos, Dux Venetiarum, una cum principus et communitatibus Italiae*", it says in the case of Central Europe, only "*nos vero reges et principes Germaniae*". What conclusion can we draw from this striking omission, and especially from the use of the plural in the term "kings"?

On the basis of what we know about his activities immediately preceding this period, as well as some intentions later expressed, of the man essentially responsible for the whole bold scheme the answer is not too difficult to find. King George had made a considerable effort to become King of the Romans – an elevation which would have given him the leading position in the Empire formally as well as factually. The recent events in the Empire (especially the battles of Seckenheim and Giengen which had made it clear to the Hohenzollern party that their freedom of movement definitely did not included a policy hostile to the King of Bohemia) had made George's politically dominant role in Central Europe clearer than even before. All this might have made him feel that the leading role in the League during the first phase of its existence by rights belonged to him. This position, if it really could be created, would serve him as well as the Roman kingship

---

[24] In view of the historical importance that the negotiations with Louis XI necessarily assumed in this connection, and on the basis of the decisive role he would have had to play in it simply in terms of political and military strength, this assumption certainly appeared most plausible. See Markgraf, *op. cit.*, 285, Bachmann, *op. cit.*, 405, Urbánek *Věk*, IV, 597.

would have served him – as Martin Mair in particular might well have told him. It would indeed check, in a truly effective way, the attempts of the Pope to isolate him and, if he did not capitulate, destroy him. If we accept the astute surmise that much of the structure and diction of the draft can be ascribed to Martin Mair, then the logic of this answer becomes even more forceful. It fits in well with the advice given to to King George by Mair upon the latter's return from Milan, as well as with later plans for George's role in a contemplated crusade against the Turks.[25] And if George expected or at least hoped, at the time of the conception of the scheme, that he himself would be president of the League during the decisive five years in question, then this explains with the greatest ease why the draft only dicusses the *"reges Germaniae"* without as much as mentioning the Emperor as one of them, and this at a time when, in general, George had reason to remain friendly with Frederick III, and when, indeed, he was soon going to save him from a situation of deadly peril. This assumption does not preclude the possibility that, if necessary for political reasons, George would eventually, perhaps even soon, be ready to cede the priority for the presidency of the League to Louis XI. This is, indeed, what George did when, in the summer of 1464, he sent Marini and the Utraquist Lord Albert Kostka of Postupice for further negotiations about the League to France.[26]

There is still another small riddle which is presumably solved by the assumption that George expected to become the first head of the League: the fact that of the two great powers then in steady contact with the Turks, only one, Venice, figures importantly in the draft, whereas the other, Hungary, is not mentioned. George, it seems, did not want to jeopardize his own role, in what would have been his own creation, by allowing his young, ambitious son-in-law, Matthias Corvinus, to compete with him. Venice, of course, was another matter, since Venice's contribution was bound to be, in the first place, that of a naval power. Though himself the ruler of a landlocked kingdom, George was clearly aware of the great role that naval power would have to play in any attempt at a really powerful undertaking of the Christian World against the explosive strength of the Crescent. And here, then, is one of the roles which the draft allotted to the man against whom, in several ways, the scheme is directed: the Pope.

---

[25] See, e.g. Mair's approaches to King George as summarized by Bartoš, *op. cit.*, 69-71. It seems to me that the very arguments Bartoš used for Mair's role in the scheme also support my thesis that, in the view of its author, no one but George himself was originally supposed to be the natural leader of the League in its decisive early years.
[26] See Urbánek, *Ve službách Jiříka krále* (Prague, 1940), pp. 1-30.

The references to him are essentially limited to one paragraph, if a very long one (§ 22). In it only two tasks are assigned to the Pope: first, that he should, by the issue of "authentic bulls" and under threat of "formidable punishments", enforce the prompt payment of the taxes without which the League could not possibly fulfill its function of defending the Christian World against the Turks, or for that matter any other function. Second, the Pope should call together a conference of the princes and cities of Italy and, again under the threat of heavy punishment, induce them to employ all their available naval strength to help the League in the struggle against the Turks.

The language used in relation to the Pope is full of those expressions of extreme devotion and veneration which were the style of the time. This is by no means astonishing since George himself, far from being a schismatic, still claimed to stay in the full unity of the Church, since most of his advisers, chief diplomats and secretaries were Catholics (almost the only exceptions being the brothers Kostka of Postupice), and since, of course, all the other princes who would have joined the League were Catholics, like the overwhelming majority of their subjects. Yet in spite of all these utterances of deep respect and veneration for the person and office of the Supreme Pontiff, the essentially anticurial character of the document is clearly beyond any doubt. Of the dominant role that the Papacy, and Pius II as much as or perhaps more than any of his predecessors since Eugen IV, had tried to play in facing the Turkish threat, only little is left in the project. The task allotted the Pope is strictly auxiliary. What Pius II had tried to do with conspicuous lack of success, during the months at Mantua – to rally around himself all the important princes of Christian Europe – King George's plan now tried to do on a permanent basis, without any direction from the Holy See, simply as the decision of those princes, based on clear reasoning and high resolve, to abolish war and organize perpetual peace between themselves as the only healthy basis for survival. And he expected to start this action in Basel, in a city whose very name in this situation had a symbolic sound, recalling the days when great assemblies of Christian statesmen and churchmen defied the Papal claim to absolute rule over the Christian World.

Though the need for defence, eventually even for the crusading offensive, against the Turks was to provide the strong inducement for princes and nations to join together, the vision behind the plan is not limited to an organization against anyone. Rather, it is rooted in the great human hope for peace on earth, based on justice for everyone and organized by those who would combine the will for peace with the strength and power to maintain it. While, in the five centuries that have elapsed since the great plan was conceived, the whole idea has often been thought utterly utopian, today we are perhaps more than ever ready for the understanding that pure, anarchic power struggle must lead to catastrophe. In this sense, then, George's League, as a bold image shaped in an early pioneering effort, merits a place of high honor in the history of the idea of organized peace, even though its actual historical role for his reign and his struggle with Rome was – except for the resulting friendship between George and Louis XI – of minor importance, and at the time achieved nothing at all for Christian Europe's struggle with the Turks.

The exception – George's friendship with Louis – was, however, far from unimportant. Added to his alliance with Poland, it gave him considerable support in Western Europe and certainly diminished the chances for the Papacy to push the German princes out of the neutrality that most of them would keep throughout the struggle. The development of closer Franco-Bohemian relations indeed continued as a important issue of George's foreign policy.

There remains the need to evaluate George's part in evolving the plan and the significance it has for the judgment of his historical role. We could, of course, try to be satisfied with the knowledge that the plan was evolved and presented under his name and under his authority, and this judgment, with the limited credit remaining for George, would fit the earlier assumption that the whole project was originally conceived, fully elaborated and brought to its final stage of presentation by one man only: Antoine Marini. As soon as we introduce one additional participant into our assumptions about the genesis of the plan – Martin Mair – we also have to assume some overall direction in its development for which no one can be credited except the King himself.

But perhaps we can be even more specific about George's part. There is at least one important element in the draft which shows rather distinctly his way of thinking. It is the emphasis on mediation and arbitration in international conflicts. George was often attacked, by contemporaries as well as by later historians, for his supposed faithlessness, for the fact that he usually did not go all-out in his support of an ally but left him, as it were, in mid-air just before that ally could achieve a decisive victory over his enemies. The claim as such is not without some mesaure of truth, and it may well be admitted that "Nibelungentreue", the willingness to stand and fall (especially to fall) with one's ally was not in George's program. We may go farther and state that he may have preferred, in that sphere of Europe's political geography which had much influence upon his own political status, the existence of princes and states none of whom would be too strong. It is a principle of politics later honored by the term "balance of power". Yet it would probably be a mistake to see in this policy nothing but the "selfish" seeking of strength for his own nation and throne at the cost of other states. It is certainly true – and eventually admitted even by his critics – that George disliked war, himself used it only reluctantly as a last resort in what seemed a political emergency, and above all never expected to wage it as an instrument of all-out destruction of the enemy. Rather was war, more than once, for him a quick way to nudge or push the other side to certain limited political concessions, or to deter him from going too far in certain political demands. In consequence, most of the wars in which he was involved were really "little wars", often ended by armistice before any real military action had properly started, except, of course, for the last period of his reign when war on a large scale was forced on him by his enemies. While he admitted by his actions that recourse to arms could no always be avoided, he was always at his best in manoeuvering toward rapprochement, and most in his element when peace was within reach and became the object of his political operations. This genuine love of peace as the most desirable state of affairs between people and between states did, indeed, impress his contemporaries to the extent that, even in the mid-sixties, already an object of Papal hostility and persecution, he was still the most acceptable international mediator and arbitrator in Central Europe. And it is this whole mentality that so clearly finds its expression in the great plan for a League of Princes.

Surely the idea of peace on earth as a thing to be desired is age-old, and had found many an expression deeper and more unconditional in some of the great literature of the earlier Middle Ages, for instance in the 19th book of St. Augustine's *City of God*. Yet outside the spheres of theology and philosophy, outside the already-moribund conception of a universal Roman Empire allied with a universal Roman Church, it would be difficult to find any previous document which not only expresses with such clear determination the need for peace on the widest possible scale, but also looks with such sober clarity for ways to achieve and maintain it, at first within Christendom and, hopefully, after the Turkish drive has been defeated, all over the known world. It is extremely difficult to decide whether and to what extent George's sponsorship and direction of the great peace plan contains conscious elements of the idea of ideological and political progress as against the essentially hopeless muddle which at his time dominated all other attempts at restoring to the Western world any sense of unity and concerted purpose. It remains remarkable that, pressed to the wall by the Pope's action, his most ambitious countering step took the form of so constructive and imaginative a project. To recognize and acknowledge this fact disposes, it seems to me, also of the reproach of insincerity or hypocrisy in this instance, or in George's policy in general.[27] It would be absurd to expect that he could have presented a project like this (or any other in later times) if it could not be expected to be also in the interest of the Czech realm. No attempt at strengthening the cooperative element in international relations was ever made by any statesman in any age who could not hope and assume that such a policy was also in the interest of his own people. Here as elsewhere we perceive King George's ability to identify himself and his immediate interests with those of a wider, greater community, wider and greater at this time than even the nation which he directed and served.

ADDENDUM

Since this study was written, the author has been given access to the earliest text of the basic document for the Leagues of Princes, which was only recently discovered in Poland, in the archives of the Royal Polish Chancery (*Metryka Koronna*, vol. XI, pp. 578-587). (I am specially indebted for this to Dr. Jiří Kejř of the Legal-Historical Institute of the Czechoslovak Academy of Science.) The differences between this text and earlier versions (e.g. the one published by Prof. F. M. Bartoš) are very small and have hardly any historical significance. There is, however, one interesting fact to be noted. It has to do with the beginning of the text which, in later versions, such as the one published by Kliment, reads "*Nos Georgius, Rex Bohemiae*", a version which already in the form published by Bartoš appeared as "*Nos A.B.C.*". The Polish text, as the oldest and most authentic version, confirm the correctness of the "*A.B.C.*" (The other form may result from a wrong reading of the three letters as R.B.G., for Rex Bohemiae Georgius.) The significance of this lies in the fact that in the form in which the Polish court retained this early and most authentic copy of the great plan was most likely the draft as worked out by diplomats of both nations, Bohemia as well as Poland, or at least as worked out by King George's experts (presumably Marini *and* Mair) and approved, as the basis for further procedure, by King Casimir and his advisers. There is then no room for A. Bachmann's assumption (see his

---

[27] See e.g. Bachmann, *Geschichte Böhmens*, II, 535: "nicht heiliger Eifer für den Glauben ...", or, more pronounced, Weizsäcker, *op. cit.*, 237. See the contrary in Kliment, *op. cit.*, 38f., and Urbánek *Věk*, IV, 594 n. 51.

Deutsche Reichsgeschichte, vol. I, 406) that the whole draft received the form known to us only by the negotiations conducted between Marini and Louis XI (or his advisers) early in 1464, for there is no substantial difference between the drafts preserved in Poland and those preserved in France. We have no trace at all of later textual developments resulting from French cooperation. It appears all the more likely that the plan must be considered as the result of close cooperation between the two West-Slavic Kingdoms, though the main credit of initiating and formulating it still belongs to King George and his advisers. See also the most recent Polish treatment: Roman Heck, "Czeski plan związku wladców europejskich z lat 1462-1464 i Polska", in *Studia z dziejów polskich i czeskoslowackich* I (Wrocław, 1960), 169 ff.

The Development of Czechoslovak Historical Writing

JOSEPH S. ROUČEK AND GEORGE WASKOWICH

The development of modern historical writing in Czechoslovakia is associated with the spread of complex social and political forces emanating not only from the scene with which it was directly concerned, but also those released by the general European stream of history of the 18th and 19th centuries. The lack of historical consciousness and the concept of a united Czechoslovakia is indicated by the fact that apparently no single work was devoted to such a concept before the 20th century. In the latter part of the 18th century separate works were written on the historical progress of parts of the Czech crown lands, but there was no synthesis of them all. The growth of such a concept was associated, on the one hand with the philosophical movements rooted in the 18th century, and on the other hand with the increase of general Slavonic consciousness.[1] The greatest names attached to the rise of the new Czech spirit are to be found in the field of *belles lettres*, and the philological works of such men as Jungmann and Dobrovský; in the field of Slavistics, Václav Fortunát Durych; in Slavonic antiquities, Pavel Josef Šafařík. In the field of historiography the name of František Palacký has dominated historical thinking and historical concepts to the present. A vastly intricate movement affecting not only Bohemia but the rest of the Slavonic world, and producing similar results in historical writing, was thus compounded of the residue of 18th century Enlightenment and 19th century Romanticism.

PALACKÝ

The problems of Czech history as seen and formulated by Palacký have produced an extensive literature and literally hundreds of polemical works

---

[1] Cf. Jan Jakubec, "Historical Studies" (in Czech), in *Literatura česká devatenctého stoleti* ("Czech Literature of the 19th Century") (Prague, Jan Laichter, 1911), I, 62ff.; cf. also: Jaroslaw Werstadt, *Legacy of History and Historians* (in Czech) (Prague, Historický Klub, 1948), 10ff.

dealing with the significance of certain key events.[2] Palacký's education included the reading of the works of the philosopher Kant, supplemented by the writings of the English historiographers, Robertson and Gibbon, as well as the German, Luden. However, Jan Heidler, in a penetrating article in the "Czech Historical Review" (*Český Časopis Historický*) has shown Palacký's indebtedness to Hegel, as well as the little he gleaned from Kant, in his effort to arrive at a developmental concept of history. On the other hand, Palacký's knowledge of Hume and Comte was limited.[3] It was, however, in the sphere of political planning that Palacký most reflects the Hegelian dialectic.[4]

Palacký's European outlook and his knowledge of the history of the Austrian Empire history enabled him to place the history of Bohemia-Moravia in the mainstream of mankind's development. History in the "highest sense" is the "teacher of life" and the ultimate court in which mankind is to be judged. The historian holds a most important office in the name of humanity: he is the servant of truth and justice. Thus it behooves him to plumb to the depths the historical forces and facts by means of which he reconstructs the past.[5] History is the expression of the "spirit of the world", a struggle of the spirit of man in his effort to conquer matter and thus more nearly approach God. Palacký's concept of the interplay of historical forces was dramatic and idealistic. The content of history reflects the continuous struggle of opposing elements: the individual in opposition to society, as well as to nature, science, antionality, law, the state, language, morality and religion. The ultimate aim of all this strife is to achieve the "Good, the True, and the Beautiful" in reaching for liberty and the realm of God. This serves not only for the individual, but for all history .[6] The historic dualistic struggle is reflected in the history of the Czech nation, not only by a *national* contest within the Slavonic world, but a *national* struggle with the German world. In the religious field, opposing forces are represented by the Roman "Universal" Church and the "Reformation", i.e., Catholicism and Protestantism.

---

[2] Cf. Joseph Fischer, *Myšlenka a dílo Františka Palackého* ("Ideas and Work of František Palacký") (Prague, Čin, 1926), 25 ff.
[3] Jan Heidler, "O vlivu Hegelismu na filosofii dějin a na politický program Františka Palackého" (The Influence of Hegelianism on World History and Political Program), in *Český Časopis Historický*, XVII (January-February, 1911), 5 ff. and 160 ff.; also: Josef Fischer, *op. cit.*, 153 ff., II, 36 ff.
[4] Jan Heidler, *op. cit.*, 5.
[5] Josef Fischer, *František Palacký, Od minulosti pro budoucnost* ("František Palacký: From the Past for the Future") (Prague, 1926), 6 ff.
[6] Josef Fischer, *op. cit.*, 152 ff.

These two forces have existed from earliest times in the development of Czech history. The religious struggle came to the fore in the days of Hus and remained a major factor until the disastrous Battle of the White Mountain.[7]

According to Palacký, the Slavs and the Germans, from the very beginning of their history, observed different principles in their ideas of the foundations of human society. While the Germans stressed power, the Slavs laid emphasis on voluntary and free agreement conditioned by the need for social solidarity. The Germans, primarily warriors and conquerors, founded their society on inequality, whereas the Slavs did not know or recognize difference of estate or inequality before the law.[8]

Palacký also propounded a rather romantic national character of the Slavs, but later revised his views on this point. No Slavonic people was originally enslaved or practised enslavement; none desired to enslave or conquer other peoples. If their love of liberty was sometimes punished by fearful consequences, it was because they did not understand the necessary conditions for the enjoyment of liberty.[9] These views, based on German Romanticism, especially on the philosophy of Herder, and the Polish and Czech Romanticists, no longer have any currency and are unable to stand up under historical criticism.

The Religious Significance of Czech History. Since all life, according to Palacký, is founded in struggle, it was not difficult for him to carry the idea of a Slavonic-German duel into the field of morals and religion. Both in his treatment of a Hussite movement and in his *Brief View of Czech History* (1861), this religious struggle becomes primarily a war between Slav and German.[10] In this respect Czech nationalism is not a new development, but a very old principle. Another facet is presented in the struggle between liberty of conscience and ecclesiastical absolutism, which is but another aspect of the duel between "democracy" and "aristocracy".[11] The Hussite Wars were the first of the great struggles in the realm of ideas which the Czech people were called upon to undertake. Czech his-

---

[7] Jaroslav Werstadt, *op. cit.*, 15; cf. also: Josef Fischer, *op. cit.*, 157-163.
[8] František Palacký, *Spisy drobné* ("Small Writings"), "Idea of an Austrian State", I, 262ff.
[9] František Palacký, *ibid.*, "The Struggle between Czechs and Germans", 323ff.; also: Josef Fischer, *op. cit.*, I, 158ff.
[10] Josef Fischer, *op. cit.*, I, 171; cf. also: Jaroslav Werstadt, *op. cit.*, 17; cf. also Josef Kalousek, "O vůdčích myšlenkách v historickém díle Palackého" (The Leading Ideas in Palacký's Historical Work), in *Památník Františka Palackého* ("Memorial Volume of František Palacký") (Prague, Matice Česká, 1898), 208ff.
[11] Jaroslav Werstadt, "The Philosophy of Czech History", in *Slavonic Review*, III, 9 (March, 1925), 543ff.

tory, however, presents an almost unbroken series of struggles in politics, nationalism and religion: struggles against absolutism in church and state, and against the development and growth of Germanic elements on Slavonic soil. We see here the historical method of Hegel: the resolution of two antagonistic forces into ultimate synthesis, which, in turn, calls into being another antagonistic force, to repeat the process.[12]

THE IMPORTANCE OF PALACKÝ FOR CZECH HISTORIOGRAPHY

František Palacký is not only the founder of modern, scientific Czech historical writing, but one of the builders and founders of the Czechoslovak state. Until recently, the views of Palacký were more or less faithfully reflected in those of the numerous successors who have carried on his work of historical investigation. His pupils have not, however, slavishly followed the master without criticism; these include Tomek, Kalousek, and Rezek, and, to some extent, Gindely. The foremost critic has been Josef Pekař, and Masaryk has, in his *Jan Hus, Světova revoluce* and in numerous passages of his *Karel Havlíček*, eloquently tried to show that the moral revolution of the Czech Brethren experienced a resurgence in the course of the revival of the national life of the Czechoslovak nation.[13]

Note also that Palacký's ideas were not independent of the romantic manuscript forgeries, particularly in regard to the part played by the Germans in Bohemia. His fascination for the past of his own people led him also to gloss over or "forget" certain historical realities and to conceive history mostly within the framework of his own tendency towards dramatics and idealism. He especially overstressed the concept that the content of history reflects the continuous struggle and byplay of opposing elements, reflected in his thesis that the history of the Czech nation is not only the national struggle within the Slavonic world but also a national struggle with Germandom. Not entirely without foundation were the criticisms leveled by the German critic, Höfler, that his *History of the Czech Nation* was in reality a history of the Hussite period, with a prologue and an epilogue. But we must keep in mind that Palacký saw in the Hussite period an epoch in which the Czechs attained the height of their national and

---

[12] Cf. Josef Fischer, *op cit.*, II, 37 ff.
[13] Cf. T. G. Masaryk, *Jan Hus* (Prague, Bursik and Kohout, 1925), 16, 62, 110 ff; cf. Masaryk, *Karel Havlíček* (Prague, Jan Laichter, 1920), 29 ff. are devoted to exposition of Palacky's theory of politics. Cf. also: *Česká otázka* ("The Czech Question") (Prague, Prokop, second edition, 1908), 31 ff. and passim.

religious development. Palacký visualized in this movement the realization of his ideals; the progress of history is the attainment of the good, the true, the right life toward the ideal of Humanity.[14]

VÁCLAV VLADIVOJ TOMEK

If the work of Palacký is to be viewed in proper perspective we must remember that the foremost task of the intellectual of his period, dominated by Romanticist ideas, was to awaken the nation to a new life. His successors built on this foundation, and their activities and works must be judged as a part of the *political* awakening which followed. In one way or another, these, his pupils, directly or indirectly reflected the method and the orientation of the master.[15]

The historian who stood nearest to him personally in methodology and orientation was Václav Vladivoj Tomek (1818-1905). While living with Palacký, he started his *Dějepis města Prahy* ("History of the Town of Prague"). The promise he showed as a young man was soon fulfilled in a series of articles based on historical research in the archives, the mysteries of which were explained to him by Palacký. Among his minor works was *Děje mocnářství rakouského* ("History of the Austrian Empire", 1845). In addition to numerous articles on the relations of Czechs and Germans up to the 15th century, he busied himself with his *Děje University pražské* ("History of the University of Prague", published in 1849 in two volumes); its German counterpart is the *Geschichte der Prager Universität*. Here Tomek showed the interconnection of the University's history, not only with the nation at large, but also with the main currents of European intellectual development. In the judgment of Pekař, this is one of the finest achievements of Czech historiography, despite the fact that it was never finished in the Czech version. The German account runs to 1848, but constitutes a sort of synopsis of what Tomek expected to do with the subject. Conversely his Czech history is

---

[14] Josef Pekař, "Dejěpisectví" (Historiography) in *Památník na oslavu 50 letého Panovnického jubilea* ("Memorial Volume in Celebration of the 50th Jubilee of the Lords") (Prague, Česká Akademie, 1898), 24; also: Pekař, *František Palacký* (Prague, Otto, Světova Knihovna, 1912), 91ff. See also: František Palacký, *Dějiny* ("History") (Prague, 1894), III, Book XII, 157ff, and the comparison drawn between Palacký and Michelet in Jaroslav Werstadt, *Politické dějepisectví XIX století a jeho čestí představitelé* ("Political Historiography of the 19th Century and its Czech Representatives") (Prague, Historical Club, 1920), 7ff. Critical evaluations of Palacký and of the whole idea of the Reformation were also published by F. M. Bartoš.

[15] Cf. Jaroslav Werstadt, *op. cit.*, 35ff.; Josef Pekař, *op. cit.*, 27ff.

not merely a pale reflection of his master; in his description of the Hussite movement he detours from Palacký by showing how it was intimately connected with the University. Tomek was not inclined by temperament to draw abstruse or abstract conclusions from the study of history. History, he wrote, must be the mirror held up to a nation to develop its self-understanding. While history's purpose is to instil a national consciousness, nevertheless too sanguine a reflection in the mirror leads to national vanity; if the picture is too dark, the people fail to draw lessons from their history. In any case the historian must be devoted to absolute truth, however difficult its reconciliation with national objectives.

The appointment of Lev Thun, who played a somewhat singular role in the Czech Revolution of 1848, to the post of Minister of Education in the Schwarzenberg Ministry presented an opportunity for the expansion of historical studies at Charles University. This task was assigned to Tomek, who was also to establish a historical seminar. Thus, in 1850, Tomek set out on a journey which took him to Paris, where he made copies of documents concerning the Council of Basel for Palacký, and visited the Ecole des Chartres; in Berlin he visited Pertz and Leopold van Ranke, and in Göttingen became acquainted with Waitz. On his return, after a short period of research in the Vienna archives, he was named a regular Professor of Austrian History at the Charles University and began to lecture in 1851, maintaining his post until he left in 1888 for reasons of health. It was a period of tremendous activity. During this time there appeared his *O právním poměru Čech k nekdější říši německé* ("Concerning the legal relationships of Bohemia to the former German Reich") (1857), containing his considered judgment that Bohemia had never been a feudality of the Reich. An even thornier question of historical research was undertaken in his *O starém rozdělení Čech na župy a pozdějším na kraje* ("Concerning the old division of Bohemia into counties and later into provinces") (1857-1858), in which he opposed Palacký and Jireček.

ANTONÍN GINDELY

Palacký chose Antonín Gindely (1829-1892) to assume the responsibility of continuing the *Dějiny*. The choice was probably made for a number of reasons: Palacký acknowledged Gindely's latent talent, and perhaps felt that he would most faithfully maintain the spirit of the *Dějiny*; or there may have been no alternative.

Gindely's concept of historical writing is best revealed in his voluminous correspondence with various contemporaries. Czech and German; namely, Palacký, Höfler, Baron von Helfert, and Chlumecký. Although he originally intended to study theology, his love for history, stimulated by his teacher at the gymnasium in Prague's Malá Strana, eventually triumphed. Later, at Charles University, Höfler turned to write an elaborate history of the Czech Brethren, but issued only a preliminary minor works, *Über die dogmatischen Ansichten der Böhmisch-Mährischen Brüder nebst einigen Notizen zur Geschichte ihrer Entstehung* (1854); he soon followed this with a study of Comenius, *Über des Johann Amos Comenius Leben und Wirksamkeit in der Fremde*. Gindely worked on a grand scale. His minor works were issued independently, but were intended to fit into a much larger conception of the religious history of Bohemia-Moravia. The aforementioned elaborate work, *Böhmen und Mähren im Zeitalter der Reformation*, was well on the way with the appearance of a first part in 1857-1858 of his *Geschichte der Böhmischen Brüder*; but only one other volume appeared, carrying the account to 1609; the third and final volume was never finished. Gindely's great knowledge of source materials resulted in his publication of the *Quellen zur Geschichte der Böhmischen Brüder*, and, in Czech, the *Dekrety Jednoty bratrské* ("The Decrees of Moravian Brotherhood") as an integral part of the *Old Memoirs of Czech History* (1865). In the first half of the sixties he busied himself with *Rudolf II und seine Zeit, 1600-1612*, based on a great deal of new material and revealing a grasp of not only the immediate Bohemian aspect of this period, but also its general European implications. He pursued the work in a spirit of "indiscriminate truth, which might perhaps hurt, but with which we must reconcile ourselves". In the early '70's he published his "Geschichte des Böhmischen Aufstandes" (*Dějiny českého povstání*), subsequently embodied in his best known work, *Geschichte des dreissigjahrigen Krieges*. (The English version is a translation by Andrew Ten Eyck.) One of his latest works, the *Geschichte der Gegenreformation in Böhmen* (A History of Counter-Reformation in Bohemia), was published in 1894, but had no Czech counterpart. Beside many articles, he also wrote a number of general European history works in a popular vein which were translated into other Central European languages. After the division of Prague University, Gindely more and more allied himself with the German side.[16] Thus the promise of holding to the Palacký line was not fulfilled.

---

[16] J. Pekař, *op. cit.*, passim; also: Werstadt, *op. cit.*, 52ff.; Josef Šusta, "Tchécoslovaquie", in *Histoire et historiens depuis cinquante ans* (Paris, Felix Alcan, 1927), 421.

JOSEF KALOUSEK

Like Tomek, Josef Kalousek lived and worked in Palacký's home; but unlike Tomek, Kalousek eventually specialized in the field of legal history. It was his lot to become not only Palacký's defender on many counts, but also the corrector of some of his errors. Kalousek (1838-1916), however, differed from both Palacký and Tomek in that his work was most clearly oriented to national interest and liberal principles.

His most important study, *Česke státní právo* ("Bohemian State Rights"), originally published in 1871, proved to have so much vitality that a second edition appeared in 1892. His work coincided, therefore, with the intensification of Czech and Hapsburg strife and threw a searchlight on Bohemian legal development both before and after the White Mountain. While Tomek also busied himself with similar questions, credit for the most fruitful work, in terms of thoroughness of legal and historical interpretation, belongs without question to Kalousek, whose work dealt with the years from Charlemagne to the revolutionary period of 1848. It reflects the firm opposition of the author to *centralism* and *bureaucracy*; conversely, he emphasizes the principle of autonomy as a basic constituent element of his creed of liberalism. He delineated this creed in a pamphlet entitled "Co jest liberálnost?" (What is Liberalism?) It is apparent that his liberalism was closely associated with his nationalism. Kalousek's concentration on the secular aspect of the Czech national struggle led him eventually to neglect an aspect emphasized in the work of Palacký and other historians; namely the *religious* stream of Czech history. Thus Kalousek's emphasis on national self-preservation, organic development, and regulated progress preclude the use of the weapons of revolution and social disturbance.[17]

Kalousek's early training as a journalist stood him in good stead during his many polemical contests with his contemporaries. He defended Palacký's treatment of King Přemysl Otakar II, which had been attacked by the German historian O. Lorenz, and came to the rescue of Charles IV, whose "nationality" had been questioned by Loserth. He differed with Jireček, Tomek and Palacký concerning the administrative division of the church in Bohemia. In 1878, on the 500th anniversary of the death of Charles IV, Kalousek published a biography, *Karel IV, Otec Vlasti* ("Charles IV, Father of his Country"). One of his great projects, for which he gathered enormous amounts of material, dealt with the *History*

---

[17] Jaroslav Werstadt, *Politické dějepisectví, op. cit.*, 57ff.

of the Peasants in Bohemia, but he never finished it. Among the lost causes which he defended, we may mention the famous forgeries by Václav Hanka, the *Královedvorský rukopis* ("Königinhofer Handschrift"). In celebration of the 25th year of Alexander II's rule in Russia, he published a work called *Origins of the Russian State* (1880). He also wrote a short biography of Palacký, and edited the speeches and writings of F. L. Rieger. To the *Památník*, which was issued to celebrate the 100th anniversary of Palacký's birth in 1898, he contributed a noteworthy article, "O vůdčích myšlenkách v historickém díle Fr. Palackého" (The Leading Ideas in the Historical Work of Fr. Palacký).

ANTONÍN REZEK

A noteworthy pupil of Tomek was Antonín Rezek (1853-1909), who was in turn the teacher of Josef Pekař. He succeeded Tomek as Professor of Austrian History at Charles University. Hoping to accomplish what Gindely had failed to do, namely, to carry on the work of Palacký, he published a series of works on Ferdinand I, beginning with the *Zvolení Ferdinanda I. za krále českého* ("The Election of Ferdinand I as Czech King", 1877); a German version, based a number of expanded essays, appeared as *Geschichte Ferdinands I. in Böhmen*. Thereafter he authored a large number of monographs in this rather narrow and highly specialized field. Of his more general works, the unfinished *Dějiny prostonárodního hnutí náboženského v Čechách* ("History of popular religious movements in Bohemia") is of special interest. Rezek's treatment of this difficult subject was inspired by the work of Macaulay and an interest in the development of Scottish religious history, it proved a real contribution to Czech cultural history. The thorny topic of the Bohemian Counter-Reformation was treated in a volume which appeared in 1890, *Dějiny Čech a Moravy za Ferdinanda III. až do konce třicetileté války*, (1637-1648 ("The History of Bohemia and Moravia in the Time of Ferdinand III to the End of the Thirty Year War"). Two years later there appeared his *Dějiny Čech a Moravy v nové době* ("History of Bohemia and Moravia in Modern Times"), which he dedicated to Tomek; not only was it based on new materials, but it also was conceived on the broadest possible cultural and social foundation.

Bohemia's historical studies received quite an impetus when Rezek founded, in 1893, the first Czech historical review, *Sborník Historický* ("Historical Review"). Although it lasted only four years, its excellent editorial policy paved the way for *Český Časopis Historický* ("Czech Historical Review"), which Rezek edited with the help of Jaroslav Goll until 1897. Except for certain critical periods like the recent German occupation, this journal managed to appear mostly regularly thereafter. Its title remained the same until around 1941; after a pause of several years, it was replaced by the *Československý Časopis Historický* ("Czechoslovak Historical Review").

THOMAS G. MASARYK

Czech historiography in the latter nineteenth and early twentieth century was dominated to a remarkable degree for over four decades by the ideas of Thomas G. Masaryk (1850-1937), for many years Professor at Charles University, and later Czechoslovakia's foremost statesman. Indeed, he might be called the most influential philosopher of history in Bohemia during his time. In contrast to Goll, for example, whose basic approach is difficult to apprehend, Masaryk's writings are replete with profound, readily discernible reflections on the course of Czech development.[18]

Masaryk started to specialize in sociology, but soon transferred his interest to the formulation of historical and political theories, especially in their application to the events and problems then facing his nation.[19] In this he differed fundamentally from earlier Czech political thinkers who tended to take a historical approach, and for whom historical experience alone was a valid guide to future courses. Thus he differed with Kalousek on Czech "liberalism", and with Rieger on the character of the "states' rights" program; the historians in turn criticised Masaryk's

---

[18] The most recent study of Masaryk's work by a historian is Jaroslav Papoušek, "T. G. Masaryk a Československé dějepisectví" (T. G. Masaryk and Czechoslovak Historiography), in *Český Časopis Historický*, XIIV (1938), 2ff.

[19] Masaryk's writings are too numerous to be listed here. However, a work by Karel Čapek, *Mlčení s T. G. Masarykem* ("Silences with T. G. Masaryk") (Prague, Čin, 1935), 27-31, contains a valuable and complete bibliography of Masaryk's works. There have been numerous studies of Masaryk's ideas. For summaries available in English, see: Joseph S. Rouček, "Czechoslovak Sociology", 717-731, in George Gurvitch and Wilbert E. Moore, eds., *Twentieth Century Sociology* (New York, Philosophical Library, 1945); C. J. C. Street, *Thomas Masaryk of Czechoslovakia* (New York, Dodd, Mead and Co., 1930); E. Ludwig, *Defender of Democracy, Masaryk of Czechoslovakia* (New York, Robert M. McBride, 1936); Karel Čapek, *President Masaryk Tells His Story* (New York, G. P. Putnam's Sons, 1935). Masaryk's own ideas are partially set forth in his magnum opus *The Spirit of Russia* (New York, Macmillan Co., 1919 and 1956), 2 vols., in *The Making of a State* (New York, Frederick Stokes, 1927), and in his privately published *The New Europe* (1918).

philosophy of history as being insufficiently grounded in the facts of Czech history, and questioned his methodology as applied to history. He agreed, however, with Goll on the need for precise facts in history, and shared his dislike for superficial generalizations. Goll felt that history should or could be studied for history's sake, but to Masaryk history was a preparation for life, not a surprising view considering his active disposition and the nature of the era in which he lived. Thus it is important to keep in mind Masaryk's political activities to evaluate his historical judgments properly. His writings reflected Czech (and, subsequently, Czechoslovak) national and political conditions. He believed with Palacký that "whosoever does not understand contemporary social life, cannot understand old or older societies."[20] Masaryk's approach to history was eminently pragmatic. He contended that any "historian must understand the content of the subject about which he writes, for history is still the history of something. Development is not the development of something empty. He must know the content (*Podstata*) of this or that science which history studies, the basis of art, of political institutions, etc. That mathematicians alone understand the history of mathematics, everyone will admit. What does a historian understand?"[21]

The Czech Provinces were under the domination of the Austro-Hungarian Monarchy before World War I, and Masaryk was interested in directing the nation's energies towards strengthening and enhancing the nationalistic ideal; everything in the field of national endeavor was to be measured by the standards of national utility. It is to his credit that he played a special role in the famous affair of the forgery of the old Czech manuscripts.[22] Prompted by the example of Macpherson and Chatterton in England, some romantic disciples of Dobrovský, Václav Hanka, J. Linda, and V. A. Svoboda, forged some old, presumably ninth, eleventh and thirteenth century manuscripts, and smuggled them into an ancient building in order to demonstrate that the Czechs had already developed a body of strong epic poetry at a time when their mighty German neighbors slept in barbaric ignorance. (Another of their "discoveries" was an even more daring falsification relative to the archaeological history and customs of the Slavs.) The picture they created of old Czech society not unnaturally evoked a great deal of national pride. But the

---

[20] Jaroslav Papoušek, *op. cit.*, 3.
[21] Quoted by Papoušek, *op. cit.*
[22] Josef Hanuš, "Padělky romantické družiny české" (Forgeries of the Czech Romantic Circles), Chapter 14, 829-987, in Jan Jakubec, *Literatura česká devatenáctého století* ("Czech Literature in the 19th Century").

criticisms by Masaryk (and the philologist Gebauer and the literary historian J. Máchal) destroyed any possibility that these documents were authentic, despite the blow to national pride. Masaryk claimed that false historicity should not be used to glorify the national past and that national greatness should be sought in the present rather than the past, since a nation with a great past, but a small present, could have but a small future. In addition, he stressed that history should be approached and examined in a *realistic* spirit, not in a mood of false romanticism which ignores the true greatness of the past. Masaryk's moral and religious approach was adapted from the philosophy of history of František Palacký, modified by his own studies.[23]

While Palacký viewed history as a struggle between two opposite principles (emphasizing the Protestant and liberal character of the Hussite movement in which he saw mirrored the world-wide struggle for freedom and democracy), Masaryk developed some of these ideas further by his insistence that the aims of the Czech people were also the aims of worldwide democracy. Thus, to Masaryk, "The Czech Question" was a universal question. The ideas of the Bohemian Reformation and Hussitism were basic to the rise of modern Europe and the French Revolution; therefore the struggle against Austria-Hungary (and later Germany) was also a struggle for democracy, since all of these involved the hope for a better world and closer human relationships among all peoples.

In view of the present influence of Soviet ideology on historiography in all parts of Eastern Europe, and the tendency in Czechoslovakia since 1948 to entrust the cultural development of the country to "Slavic" Russia, it is interesting to recall Masaryk's clearcut views on Czech Russophilism. In his younger days a movement developed which contended that the Church founded in Moravia by Sts. Cyril and Methodius was actually identical with the Eastern Orthodox Church, and that the Bohemian Reformation had a direct historical connection with that church. This movement therefore, led by Sladkovský, Rieger, Grégr and others, was dedicated to promoting the return of the Czechs, not to the creed of the Bohemian Brethren, but to the proto-Christian church of Cyril and Methodius, through the medium of Russian Orthodoxy. Masaryk pointed out, correctly, that the "Slav Apostles" had recognized the supremacy of the Roman Pontiff; and that the Great Schism had occurred *after* the completion of their work. Agreeing with Palacký, he insisted that

[23] Hans Kohn, "Roots of Czech Democracy", Chapter VI, 91-105, in R. J. Kerner, ed., *Czechoslovakia: Twenty Years of Independence* (Berkeley, Calif., University of California Press, 1940), is a valuable summary of Palacký's and Masaryk's basic ideas.

the Hussite movement did not stem from the Eastern Church, and contended further that the inner spirit and ritual of the Eastern Orthodox Church were alien to the essentially rational, contemplative, and educated Czechs. While Masaryk felt that Catholicism was unsuited to the Czech historic character, he was very strongly opposed to religious indifferentism and empty atheism.

Masaryk's opposition to any tendency to identify or merge the course of future Czech history with the development of Russia crystallized during and after World War I, when, seeking assistance from the Russians for the Czech cause, he became critical of the Czarist system and later the Soviet experiment. In his profound study of Russia, he came to regard Dostoevski as a true representative of the Russian spirit and the Russian revolution, rejected him, and regretted that the Russians had never come under the influence of Kant and his critical spirit. He was opposed to Slavophilism and rejected without reservation Lenin's revolution and the subsequent development of Bolshevism in theory and practice, finding in Leninism more of Bakunin than of Karl Marx. For Masaryk, individual initiative and the right to think for one's self were the indispensable foundations of political and intellectual life. He wished to strengthen European democracy among the Czechs, and he desired the Europeanization of Russia.[24]

Having analyzed Masaryk's historical philosophy, we find it easy to understand his leadership of the Czechoslovak revolutionary movement during World War I and the character of the influence he exerted on the course of political events as first President of the Czechoslovak Republic. One of his basic tenets was the pragmatic necessity to maintain a middle course between extreme individualism and extreme collectivism – the program of "critical realism".[25]

---

[24] Hans Kohn, "The Heritage of Masaryk", 70-73, in *The Annals of the American Academy of Political and Social Science*, CCLVIII (July, 1948).
[25] For an analysis of Masaryk's *Světová revoluce* ("World Revolution"), see: K. Vorovka, *Dvě studie o Masarykově filosofii* ("Two Studies of Masaryk's Philosophy") (Prague, Union of Czechoslovak Mathematicians and Physicists, 1926), 37ff. Masaryk's *The Spirit of Russia* was republished in New York (Macmillan, 1955), with two chapters by Jan Slavík.

Jaroslav Goll and his Historical School

THEODORE PROCHÁZKA

In his book on *History and Historians in the 19th Century*, the British historian George P. Gooch devotes one chapter to the historiography of minor nations. Starting with Czech historiography, he analyzes for five pages the work of František Palacký, author of the monumental history of the Czech people. Then he deals briefly with Václav Vladivoj Tomek, a conservative scholar of immense industry, and author of a twelve-volume *History of the City of Prague to 1603*. Another historian mentioned by Gooch is Antonin Gindely, known chiefly for his works on the Thirty Years' War, written mostly in German.

Of the vigorous development of Czech historiography after Palacký, Gooch says nothing, with the above exceptions. It is to this theme that I want to devote my lecture. I will, however, limit myself only to a few representative figures.

The founder of the modern Czech historical school was Jaroslav Goll. In 1876, when Palacký died, Goll was 30 years old. He had already been a lecturer for one year at Charles University in Prague; in 1885 he was appointed professor. After the romantic historiography represented primarily by Palacký, an era of scientific realism and positivism dawned in Czech historical research. Goll excelled above all in his teaching skill. As a teacher, he influenced the intellectual evolution of his nation more than as the author of several painstaking monographs, e.g., on the founder of the Unitas Fratrum, Petr Chelčický, or on the relations of Bohemia and Prussia in the Middle Ages. In contrast to Palacký's idealistic and romantic conceptions, Goll emphasized not only the purely political aspects of the past, but also economic and constitutional problems. At the same time, throughout his work he put the history of the Czech nation into the context of general historical trends in Europe, especially in Western Europe.

If this was a marked improvement over Palacký, there were also some drawbacks stemming from the nature of positivist scientism. Says one modern Czech historian: "If Palacký has a certain weakness as regards historical criticism, the weakness of positivist historiography is on the other hand a lack of philosophical conception, of philosophical spirit and erudition". And this weakness was apparent in the Department of History at Prague University even before World War II, though by then, a return to synthesis, based on philosophical concepts, was apparent among the younger generation of Czech historians.

Goll's real heir – as far as methods of historical research are concerned – was Václav Novotný (1869-1932), known especially for his monumental series on Czech history, České dějiny, to which he contributed almost four large volumes. He was a master of critical analysis, a true representative of positivist historiography. His Czech history, reaching to the second half of the 13th century – precisely to 1272 – is a masterpiece of analytical research, leaving no stone unturned and exhausting all problems of the mediaeval political history of the Czech State. Novotný also devoted attention to the religious history of mediaeval Bohemia. He wrote a book on the beginnings of religious reform in the 14th century, dealing with the forerunners of John Huss; in the early twenties he and another disciple of Goll, Vlastimil Kybal (1880-1958), wrote a comprehensive biography of Huss. In these works Novotný stressed the national originality of the Czech religious thinkers who, in spite of foreign influences, such as that of Wycliff, were rooted firmly in their native soil.

Another member of Goll's school, Josef Pekař (1870-1937), was certainly one of the most original representatives of the whole group. Pekař devoted his lifework to Czech history in all its epochs. He started his academic career with a monograph on Wallenstein. Later he studied the problems of early Czech history of the 10th century, then the social history of the 17th century, and after World War I he published a voluminous biography of John Žižka. His evaluation of the Hussite movement is opposite to that of Palacký. Pekař stresses its mediaeval character and thus deprives Hussitism of the universal groundbreaking character attributed to it by Palacký. Still later he enlarged and re-edited his book on Wallenstein. This revised version was translated into German shortly before his death. His interest in contemporary life and politics was expressed in several books on diverse topics such as agricultural reform in Czechoslovakia and the beginnings of World War I.

Pekař was by nature a conservative. Whereas Masaryk maintained that the leading idea of Czech history was religious, Pekař emphasized the idea of nationalism. The debate between these two schools of thought started before World War I, and it continued even after Masaryk returned to Prague as President-Liberator. It was a duel of two powerful minds, a conflict of two conceptions of national history, comparable perhaps to similar discussions in France about the true meaning and interpretation of the French Revolution.

While Pekař devoted his energy solely to Czech history, his younger colleague and friend Josef Šusta (1874-1945) had a more universal outlook, although he too specialized in Czech history, and in this he closely followed the example of his teacher. Šusta first published short articles dealing with the times of Přemysl Otakar II, and to this theme – Czech history at the end of the Přemyslid dynasty and the start of the Luxemburg, the latter half of the 13th century and the 14th century – he remained faithful throughout his life whenever he wrote on the history of his native country. His *Dvě knihy českých dějin* (Two Books of Czech History) are devoted to this period, depicting the profound economic changes brought about in Bohemia by the introduction of a stable silver currency, the groschen of Prague, thanks to the flourishing mines at Kutná Hora. Later Šusta expanded and completed this work as a section of the Czech history series initiated by Václav Novotný. Like his teacher Goll, he carefully places Czech history within the frame of general European history. The same may be said about his history of Europe and the world in the 19th century. Šusta modestly stated of this work that it was just a piece of popularization in which "you must not expect scholarly research", but in spite of his deprecatory statement, this ample work of 2,400 pages ranks high among similar works in world historical literature. Shortly before the outbreak of World War II, Šusta became editor-in-chief of a world history, the publication of which was, however, interrupted by the war and postwar vicissitudes.

The last Foreign Minister of pre-Munich Czechoslovakia, Kamil Krofta (1876-1945), was also a prominent representative of Goll's school. He produced several works on Czech religious history and a useful survey of the history of Czech peasantry. In 1939, shortly before the outbreak of the war, he published a general survey of Czechoslovak foreign policy before Munich and during the Sudeten crisis.

Here I might add a few words about Slavic studies. Among Goll's disciples, this task fell to Jaroslav Bidlo (1868-1937). Bidlo concentrated on Polish and Russian history, and also introduced Byzantine studies at Charles University.

The generation of Goll and his disciples devoted its chief efforts to the mediaeval history of Bohemia and the national catastrophe in the 17th century. Religious history was also studied very painstakingly. The history of the 19th century was explored more thoroughly only after World War I, when several young researchers specialized in this difficult field. This lag may be explained by the general inaccessibility of the archives of the old Austrian régime; not until after 1918 was it possible to study the political evolution of the immediate past on the basis of original documents, especially those preserved in Vienna. Several monographs were published on events of 1848, and historians devoted their attention to contemporary history, as well.

In 1918, when the independence of Czechoslovakia was proclaimed, Goll's disciples were at the height of their creative power. Several of them, however, left the academic world; Krofta and Kybal entered the diplomatic service and Šusta, in the early twenties, was Minister of Education. Goll himself lived until 1929, but his last book – about the Prussian wars of the 18th century – was published in 1915.

Toward the end of the period between the two World Wars, a younger generation of historians appeared, disciples of Pekař, Šusta and Novotný. Some of them, while still building on the traditions of positivist research, abandoned strict positivist doctrine and laid more stress on sociology and philosophy. After the reign of rigid specialization the trend toward synthetic treatment of history again set in. The German occupation and the advent of the Communist régime cut short this evolution. New people and new trends appeared, basically different from and opposed to the principles followed by Goll and his school.

BIBLIOGRAPHY

Goll-Šusta, *Posledních padesát let české práce dějepisné* (Prague, 1926), VII + 212 pp.
Novák, A., Grund, A., Havel, R., *Stručné dějiny literatury české* (Olomouc, 1946), III + 818 pp.
Odložilík, Otakar, "Husův životopisec" (About Václav Novotný) *Husův Lid*, XIII (Chicago, 1952), pp. 108-113.
Prokeš, Jaroslav, "Literatura dějepisná", *Československá vlastivěda*, X, *Osvěta* (Prague, 1931).
Entries: Goll Jaroslav, Novotný Václav, Pekař Josef, Šusta Josef, in *Ottův Slovník Naučný Nové Doby*.

The Success of Professor Dvorník's Research in the Vindication of the Patriarch Photius

(An Abstract of the Detailed Paper)

LUDVÍK NĚMEC

The personality of the Patriarch Photius (820-91) has attracted the attention of almost all Church historians ever since the Reformation, and their verdict has in most cases been unfavorable. The Christian West has branded him as one who disrupted Church unity and loosed the tragic forces of dissent and schism, while the East has continued to esteem him as a hero and saint.

In the course of his basic Slavic studies, Father Francis Dvorník's attention was drawn to this anomaly, and the research incorporated in the works, *Les Slaves, Byzanze et Rome au IXe Siècle* (Paris, 1926) and *Les Légendes de Constantin et de Méthode vues de Byzance* (Prague, 1933), brought him to a realization of the far-reaching influence of the Byzantine cultural renaissance in the Photian era. His combined scholarship, theology, history and Slavistics, directed toward Byzantology, centered around Photius as a fascinating enigma.

Photius' "wickedness", recounted in the *Annales Ecclesiastici* (1588-1601), the monumental work of Cardinal Caesar Baronius (1538-1607), was challenged by the Protestant historian M. Hancke in *De Byzantinarum Rerum Scriptoribus Graecis Liber* (Leipzig, 1677). However, his arguments did not prevail against the avalanche of dialectics that had poured from Baronius' pen, and in the controversy that ensued, Photius' name became a shibboleth which Catholic and Protestant historians flourished in each others' face.

Attempts at re-examination by the scholarly Cardinal J. Hergenroether in his work, *Photius, Patriarch von Konstantinopel, sein Leben, seine Schriften und das Griechische Schisma*, 3 vols. (Regensburg, 1861-9), appeared to clinch the Photian controversy so conclusively that it became the traditional view, and even the Orthodox felt uneasy about attempting to refute it, as may be seen in the works of the Russian historian, A. P. Lebedev. Only the comparatively unknown monk, Gerazim Yared, of Syriac origin, dared to write a refutation of the Cardinal's thesis in the *Chtenia* of the Theological Academy of Kiev (1872). In 1895, the French Jesuit, A. Lapôtre, ventured to mitigate the indictment against Photius, while the works of the critical Byzantinist, J. B. Bury, and the historians, E. Amann and Venance Grumel, were directed toward a reappraisal of the Patriarch. Recognizing that the history of the unfortunate Patriarch required review and the documents demanded reassessment, Dvorník proceeded to examine the collection of anti-Photian documents and pamphlets. He discovered that the sources on which the history of the second schism had been based were valueless, and his study, "Le Second schisme de Photios, une mystification historique", *Byzantion*, 8 (1933), 301-25, exposed the second rupture between Photius and Rome as a complete fallacy. This finding was confirmed by Father V. Grumel with his independent study, "Y eut-il un second Schisme de Photius?" in the *Revue des Sciences Philosophiques et Théologiques*, 12 (1933), 432-57, wherein he reached a similar conclusion. Following this breakthrough, Dvorník turned his attention to the oecumenicity of the Ignation Synod (869-70) as seen in Western medieval tradition, in his study, "L'Oecuménicité du huitième concile (869-70) dans la tradition occidentale du Moyen Âge", *Académie Royale de Belgigue*, 24 (1938), 445-87. In his effort to reassess Photius' character and career, he began a detailed consideration of the development of what may be called the Photian Legend in the Middle Ages.

As the results of his research clashed with conventional opinion, he presented them to the specialists in Byzantine history at the International Congresses of Byzantine Studies in Sofia (1934) and Rome (1936), introduced them in his lectures at the Royal Academy of Brussels and Athens (1938), and published numerous studies in various periodicals to test the arguments.

Finally all were embodied, together with new evidence and the necessary historical setting, in his book, *The Photian Schism: History and Legend* (Cambridge, 1948). Here he presented his findings in a new light favorable to the Patriarch. Father Dvorník then undertook to popularize this new concept, publishing short studies in different languages, such as "The Photian Schism in Western and Eastern Tradition", *Review of Politics*, 10 (1948), 310-31, in order to acquaint the general public with it and to prepare for its acceptance. His other works, *The Idea of Apostolicity in Byzantium and the Legend of the Apostle Andrew* (Cambridge, Mass., 1958) and *The Patriarch Photius in the light of Recent Research* (*Munich*, 1958), together with minor studies, clarified related problems. Thus the success of Dvorník's research vindicating the Patriarch Photius as an extraordinary scholar, statesman, and churchman, which was so well encompassed in his study, "Patriarch Photius, Scholar and Statesman", *Classical Folia*, 13 (1959), 3-18; 14 (1960), 3-22, rewrote a page of history to form a bridge of mutual East-West understanding, envisioning a reunion of their churches – a monumental contribution, indeed.

POLITICAL SCIENCE AND PHILOSOPHY

Background of Czechoslovak Democracy

VÁCLAV BENEŠ

After the First World War a number of democratic republics emerged in Central and Eastern Europe. Practices of Western democracy – parliamentary government, equality of citizens, and emphasis on civil and political rights – made their victorious entry into the area. But soon it became clear that almost all its nations lacked the ability to grasp the meaning of the great European tradition of spiritual and political liberty. One after another, they succumbed to the revived forces of European reaction. Only Czechoslovakia managed to maintain a system of government based on the combination of freedom and self-discipline.

What was the secret of this astounding success? Was it the fact that the Czech and Slovak peoples, having been deprived of most members of their aristocracy, founded their modern national existence on the concept of the common man? No doubt many Czech and Slovak national leaders were largely of peasant stock. Karel Čapek spoke of Czechoslovak democracy as "hereditary and inborn as the democracy of the American nation".[1] Czech egalitarianism alone, however, could have hardly explained the success of democracy. The absence of an aristocracy failed to save other nations from autocratic and dictatorial regimes, nor did its presence elsewhere prevent the establishment of successful systems of democratic government. As in Western Europe, in the Czech lands, too, the growth of liberal democracy was supported by a relatively strong middle class. But the political fortunes of Germany demonstrated that the middle classes did not necessarily guarantee the development and continued existence of democracy. It is obvious that the remarkable success of Czechoslovak democracy was caused by other factors. Of these, two seem to be of fundamental significance: (1) the development of an essentially

---

[1] Karel Čapek, "Introduction", *At the Crossroads of Europe* (Prague, Pen Club, 1938), p. 17.

democratic national ideology,[2] and (2) the modern political experience of the Czech people.

DEMOCRATIC IDEOLOGY

The pre-1918 political struggle of the Czechs against Austria-Hungary drew strength from a moral and political philosophy which earned for them an honorable place in European intellectual history, uniting their past with their present spiritual and political aspirations. The authors of this rather lofty ideology were two scholars who also became political leaders of their people. The historian, František Palacký, developed a dialectial law of contradiction, which he called "polarity", declaring it a characteristic feature of historical development. Polarity of Czech history, he held, resulted from the conflict of two philosophies of life: the Slavic one – peaceful, egalitarian, and based on primitive democracy; and the Germanic one, characterized by aggressive authoritarianism and aristocratism. This conflict marked all Czech history and found its strongest expression in the fifteenth century Hussite Revolution, which Palacký regarded as the first attack against both the spiritual absolutism of Rome and German feudalism. By revolting against these two major representatives of medieval autocracy, the Czechs became the torch-bearers of all subsequent liberal movements and precursors of modern democracy.[3] The religious zeal of the Hussites, like that of the Union of Bohemian Brethren, later was motivated by humanitarian concepts characteristic of the ancient Slavs. The combined Slavic and Reformation elements gave rise to a peculiarly Czech humanitarian ideal which, Palacký believed, emphasized moral perfection and intellectual excellence as the only safeguards of the national existence of his people.

The idealized notion of the Slavs accepted by Palacký was entirely due to the influence of Herder and his Slovak followers, Šafařík and Kollár. It did not survive the scrutiny of later historical research, but the analysis of Czech history as constant opposition between the democratic Czechs and the autocratic Germans played an important role in Czech modern political thinking. Palacký's re-discovery of the Hussite Reformation

---

[2] A very perceptive discussion of the ideological background of Czechoslovak democracy can be found in Hans Kohn's "The Historical Roots of Czech Democracy", in Robert J. Kerner, *Czechoslovakia: Twenty Years of Independence* (Berkeley-Los Angeles, University of California Press, 1940), pp. 91-105.

[3] A similar opinion was expressed by Arnold Toynbee in "The Revolutions We Are Living Through", *New York Times Magazine*, July 25, 1954, p. 44.

and its spiritual values left a permanent imprint on the Czech national consciousness. It lent them the self-confidence of those early fighters for the modern concept of freedom; it gave unity and purpose to their history, and associated them with all liberal and democratic movements in the world.

Thomas Masaryk, a disciple of Palacký, did not subscribe to his teacher's analysis of the Slav character. Nevertheless, he gave Palacký's central thesis new prominence by focusing his attention on the heritage of the Czech Reformation. Like Palacký he regarded the moral and political achievements of the Reformation period as the principal contribution of the Czechs to the spiritual growth of man. Above all, he expanded Palacký's humanitarian ideal into a full-fledged philosophy of life which combined an abstract belief in fundamental rights with practical concern for the social welfare of man. Masaryk believed that the main expression of Czech humanitarianism was a continuing struggle for the realization of true Christianity. It was in this sense that he regarded the *raison d'être* of the Czech nation as that of religion and humanity.[4]

The significance of Masaryk's and Palacký's philosophy consisted in the identification of the ideology of the Czech Reformation with the rise of modern Europe. For the spiritual movement, which started with Jan Hus and reached its highest expression in the Union of Bohemian Brethren, was not only concerned with the issue of freedom of conscience, but also contained rudimentary ideas of democratic equality. Masaryk offered the two primary elements of his and Palacký's philosophy – religious idealism and enlightened rationalism – as the basis of modern Czech and Slovak ideology and practice. The first, by its rigorous emphasis on moral perfection, would provide Czech democracy with a spiritual background and justification; the second, with its insistence on cultural progress and enlightenment, gave it a practical program of action.

Palacký's and Masaryk's influence on the moral and political consciousness of the Czechs and Slovaks was immense. Palacký's analysis of Czech history hastened the process of national rebirth, increasing the self-confidence of the broad masses of the people. Masaryk's direct influence in the period before the outbreak of the First World War was limited to a relatively small but intellectually alert group of followers. More important, however, was the indirect influence of the brilliant mind and compelling personality that mercilessly destroyed fashionable myths and

---

[4] To this problem Thomas Masaryk devoted a book bearing the significant title *Česká otázka* ("The Czech Question"), first published in 1894.

demolished the provincial outlook of his countrymen.[5] Palacký's and Masaryk's political philosophy and their essentially democratic and humanitarian concept of Czech national identity were by no means universally accepted. In particular, Masaryk's conviction that the question of religion and humanity represented Czech history's most decisive problems was rejected by many historians and political thinkers. Nationalism and the instinct of self-preservation, rather than the illusory idea of humanity, were considered the leading issues of the Czech past.[6] Nor can it be said that the majority of the Czech people were able fully to comprehend the lofty principle of Masaryk's political philosophy. In spite of its logic, it was too abstract and intellectual to be readily understood by the common man. Because of its moral rigidity and absolute nature, it was regarded as a remote goal rather than a concrete national and political program.

It was in the cataclysm of the world conflict that Thomas Masaryk was able to identify his political philosophy with that of the Czechoslovak nation. It became the foundation and the intellectual platform of the Czechoslovak struggle for liberation. The diplomatic and political victory of the First World War, crowned by the founding of an independent Czechoslovak state, seemed to confirm not only Masaryk's personal leadership, but also the validity of his political philosophy. Some of his prewar opponents were genuinely convinced; others were reduced to silence. Thus, while never entirely understood and frequently vilified, Masaryk's humanitarian ideology served as both justification and theoretical foundation of the post-1918 Czechoslovak democracy.[7]

---

[5] In 1886, Masaryk together with the linguist, J. Gebauer, and the historian, J. Goll, proved (to the dismay of most of the nation and a large part of the academic community) that the famous *Manuscripts* (of *Králové Dvůr* and *Zelená Hora*), generally regarded as evidence of ancient Czech culture antedating that of the Germans, were forgeries. In the year 1900 Masaryk intervened in the Polná trial of L. Hilsner, exploding the myth of ritual murder and its background of rabid anti-Semitism, thus incurring the wrath of reactionary and ultra-nationalist segments of Czech society.

[6] The main protagonist of this point of view was the noted Czech historian Josef Pekař.

[7] The political thinking of the Slovaks developed under different conditions. Throughout the nineteenth century they suffered national oppression which, after the establishment of the Dual Monarchy, changed to outright Magyarization. Traditionally, leadership in Slovakia was divided along religious lines. At first, it fell to the representatives of the Protestant minority who favored identification of the Czechs and Slovaks as one people, in both the political and ethnic sense. Later the Protestants became the core of the National Party which, until the end of the century, acted as the sole political spokesman for the Slovak people. The adoption in 1845 of a separate Slovak literary language and the weakening, especially after the 1867 *Ausgleich*, of political ties with the Czechs caused many members of the National Party to replace their pro-Czech sympathies with an intense Slavic sentiment and Russophilism. – The Catholics, who spoke for the

POLITICAL EXPERIENCE IN AUSTRIA-HUNGARY

There was another factor which decisively improved the Czech and Slovak chances not only to establish, but also to maintain a democratic system of government. This was the political experience they had acquired in their nineteenth century struggle for political emancipation in the Hapsburg Empire. From the moment it entered the political arena in 1848, the sights of the Czech nation were fixed upon democracy. In accord with the policy of Austroslavism, developed by František Palacký and almost unanimously accepted by the nation, the monarchy was to be changed into a free association of peoples organized on the basis of modern democracy, constitutional parliamentarianism, and recognizing the civil and political rights of the individual. The *Ausgleich* of 1867 shattered Palacký's hopes, but could not change the fundamental Austroslav inclination of Czech policy. The political tactics of the handful of Slovaks[8] allowed to take part in Hungarian political life followed essentially the same trend. They, too, worked for the idea of a federalization and democratization of Hungary, combining their efforts with those of other non-Magyar nationalities in the Eastern section of the monarchy. Thomas Masaryk, too, who later helped to destroy the Hapsburg Empire, started his political career by subscribing to the idea of a federalized Austria. The tenacity of Austroslavism as a political concept was demonstrated by the majority of Czech representatives in the Viennese Parliament, who, almost until

---

majority of the Slovak people, were handicapped by a late start and by lack of political consciousness of the masses to whom they directed their appeal. A few years before the First World War, when their leaders began to develop a political program, their ideology was very similar to that of the contemporary Catholic parties of Central Europe. It emphasized principles of Christian morality, combining them with concrete national and political demands. – Only a part of the Slovak national leadership, the so-called *Hlasists*, who derived their name from their literary review *Hlas*, subscribed to Thomas Masaryk's political and moral philosophy, considering it applicable to the Slovaks. Despite their energy and devotion, they were consciously supported by only a fraction of the Slovak people. They would hardly have been successful had it not been for developments during the First World War which vindicated their spiritual orientation and political program.

[8] C. J. C. Street in *Hungary and Democracy* (London, 1923), pp. 55-60, gives the following figures on the Slovak representation in the Lower House of the Hungarian Parliament: In the elections of 1869, 1875, 1878 and 1881 the Slovaks had no representation at all, all 58 seats being allotted to the Magyars. In 1872, 1905 and 1910, they received two seats each time. In 1901 the Slovaks had 4 and the Magyars 54 deputies from Slovak constituencies, and in 1907 they scored their greatest success, gaining 7 as compared with 51 seats. Quoted from Josef Lettrich, *History of Modern Slovakia* (New York, Praeger, 1955).

1917,[9] continued to believe in the possibility of a just Austria, certainly not motivated only by fear or political careerism.

Furthermore, the political methods of Austroslavism were fundamentally democratic. With a few notable exceptions, the great majority of Czech political leaders rejected violence as an instrument in their struggle for political emancipation. This was best expressed by Karel Havlíček, the journalistic interpreter and ardent defender of Palacký's program. In 1849, when the cause of Austrian federalism seemed irretrievably lost, he reiterated his belief that, sooner or later, Austria would have to become a "union of free nations of Central Europe". The political tactics that he recommended the Czechs follow was, perhaps, best summed up in the following statement:

... we must remain united in our opposition against the government, acting, however, within the rigid limits of law, fighting – as we have done until now – with spiritual and intellectual weapons when the material ones are lacking; at the same time, in our actions we must rely on genuine democracy which from the very beginning has been the essence of our national efforts. This is our task; in it alone shall we find our salvation.[10]

Thus the methods of Czech nationalism stemmed from belief in the ultimate effectiveness of negotiation and compromise, and consisted of slow but steady work for the improvement of the intellectual and material standards of the people. The motto of Karel Havlíček, "elsewhere men died for the honor and welfare of their nation, but we shall live and work for the same cause", was embraced by the entire nation. After the fall in 1860 of Bach's absolutism, the Czechs proved their ability to use the still inadequate liberties provided by the Austrian semi-constitutional regime for the advancement of their national cause. While continuing their endeavor to secure recognition of the traditional rights of the ancient Kingdom of Bohemia, they intensified their spiritual and cultural life. This was the period of the climax of the national revival which, in 1882, was inaugurated by the re-establishment of an independent Czech university in Prague. At the turn of the century the Czechs began to move into economic and financial positions in the monarchy. Introduction of modern methods of agriculture, as well as participation in industrial and economic activities, greatly increased their economic welfare. Practically all these achievements were gained by their own and cooperative

---

[9] See Ferdinand Peroutka, *Budování státu*, Vol. I (Praha, Borový, 1933), pp. 5-16.
[10] Karel Havlíček, "Naše úloha", *Národní noviny*, May 23, 1849, quoted from T. G. Masaryk, *Česká otázka* (Praha, Pokrok, 1908), p. 94.

action. Particularly in the cultural sphere the Czechs received practically no aid from the official authorities, but depended entirely on their devotion to the national cause and their native abilities. In many voluntary organizations – cultural, economic, gymnastic, and welfare – the people went through a practical school of democracy. Foremost among these organizations was the Sokol gymnastic movement which provided an outlet for the accumulated energies of the Czech people. The Sokol program, which combined the rationalism of the Enlightenment with the nineteenth-century idea of nationalism, was based on the spirit of brotherhood of all Czechs. Thus it could be identified with the cause of democracy.[11]

Unfortunately, the growing internal strength of the Czechs was accompanied by an increase of German nationalism, especially among the German minority in Bohemia. In the strife with the Germans, however, the Czechs were no longer defenseless; their main concern was the preservation of the Czech national domain in the Bohemian lands against further encroachments of Germanization. This led to their realization of the fundamental importance of every individual to the existence of the nation. Even the poorest and least important members of the national community were recognized as equal and fully entitled to the protection given by the national collective. This sentiment helped to provide a broad foundation for the acceptance of democratic theory and practice which came to be regarded as indispensable by the entire nation.

The Austrian rulers were unwilling to make substantial concessions to meet the national aspirations of the Czechs. But the degree of constitutionalism inaugurated after 1860 – despite the injustices and inadequacies of the Viennese régime – made possible a continuous growth of Czech cultural and economic life. These successes would have been impossible had it not been for the peculiar conditions in the Austrian half of the monarchy. Although it favored the German element, the Viennese government did not entirely escape the liberal trend of the times. Gradually, the Court and the dominant Germans were forced to grant greater politi-

---

[11] There were many other organizations which covered practically all aspects of Czech national life. Among those dedicated to the promotion of general cultural and literary activities perhaps the most important were the following: *Museum království českého* ("The Museum of the Kingdom of Bohemia"); *Česká Matice* ("Czech Foundation") for the publication of Czech books; *Sbor pro zřízení českého Národního divadla* (Society for the Building of the Czech national Theatre); and a large number of choral societies, headed by the Prague *Hlahol*. Of the economic organizations we should mention *Průmyslová jednota* (Industrial Union) and a host of loan associations, as well as numerous agricultural and artisans' co-operatives.

cal participation to the population, introducing a modicum of autonomy in local and provincial government and, in 1907, even universal suffrage. At the same time, an independent judiciary and a relatively efficient bureaucracy came into being. With a few notable exceptions, the Austrian rulers did not stoop to excessively brutal methods, their behavior being characterized by a tendency toward restraint and moderation. Of course, in the last analysis, Austria remained an autocratic state in which constitutionalism and parliamentarism were only half-heartedly accepted. Above all, through their unconcealed support of the Germans, the Court and the German aristocratic and bureaucratic elite élicited antagonism, especially among the Czechs. But the relatively moderate, liberalizing atmosphere of the Austrian half of the Empire enabled the individual nationalities to defend themselves effectively, if not always entirely successfully, against the Viennese challenge. The Hapsburg rule was sufficiently oppressive to serve as a constant stimulant to Czech nationalism, but too half-hearted to present an insurmountable obstacle to their cultural, economic, and (partly) political growth. Thus, Austria itself created a political climate which fully justified Czech endeavors to achieve national emancipation and independence within the framework of the monarchy.

The effect of the Czech political tactics was both positive and negative. More than any other nation of the Austrian Empire, the Czechs had managed to grasp the true meaning of democracy. It is paradoxical that exclusion from direct rule by the state in which they lived – the main source of Czech dissatisfaction – was not entirely without advantage. Left to themselves, the Czechs concentrated their efforts on improving their material and intellectual standards, practicing the art of self-government in their numerous national organizations. Democracy in the Czech lands became a way of life long before it was a political fact.

The insistence on non-violent political tactics had profound justification in the legacy of Czech national history. The over-cautious behaviour of the early nineteenth-century leaders was dictated by the over-all weakness, both numerical and cultural, of a nation which had almost miraculously escaped the tragic fate of national extinction.[12] In the early

---

[12] That the very existence of the Czech nation was in balance has been perhaps best demonstrated by the attitude of the first of the great revivalists, Josef Dobrovský. As late as 1810 he wrote to the Slovene scholar B. Kopitar: *Causa gentis nostrae, nisi Deus adjuvet, plane desperata est*. V. Jagic, *Briefwechsel zwischen Dobrovský und Kopitar 1808-1828* (1885), Dobrovský's letter of October 20, 1810, p. 173; quoted from A. Denis and Dr. Jindřich Vančura, *Čechy po Bílé Hoře* (Praha, Šimáček, 1911), Vol II-I, p. 100.

stages of national revival, caution and moderation, far from indicating a lack of stamina, became absolute necessities. The shadow of the seventeenth-century Battle of the White Mountain, in which Czech independence was lost, continued to haunt the subconscious mind of Czech national leaders, exerting a significant influence on their political thinking and actions. This tragic experience of the past reinforced their belief in moderation, rejection of all extremes, and calculated realism which endeavored to make best use of the available national resources. Revolution as a means of fulfilling Czech national aspirations was repudiated because it was in conflict not only with the tactics of Austroslavism, but also with modern Czech psychology. Only once, in the stormy year of 1848, a group of young radicals attempted a revolution.[13] Their action was repudiated by Palacký and practically all the national leaders.[14] Toward the end of the nineteenth century, voices were again heard pleading for more radical policies against Vienna. It was Thomas Masaryk who revealed the shallowness of this new radicalism. He condemned revolution as a "relic of the old regime", adding that "however imperfect our present parliamentarism may be ... it is good for those who can use it".[15]

But Masaryk realized the dangers for the national character of his people of a policy which *a limine* rejected the use of force. There were situations, he declared, when the use of force against violence may be necessary and fully justified. In 1908 he stated, almost prophetically, that "of course, revolutions aiming at reforms have their justification; without revolutions no effective progress would be possible".[16]

Not until the First World War did the Czechs comprehend the full meaning of Thomas Masaryk's words. In the struggle, which he considered a conflict between democracy and theocratic autocracy, they placed themselves deliberately on the side of the Western democracies. But independent Czechoslovakia evolved primarily from the political and

---

[13] The Whitsuntide Prague revolution resulted from the efforts of representatives of the younger generation, composed mainly of students and workers and headed by Josef Václav Frič, Emanuel Arnold, and Karel Sladkovský. The insurrection, in which also the Slovak, L'udevít Štúr and, to a certain extent, Michael Bakunin, took part was suppressed by the Imperial forces under Prince Windischgrätz. – Relatively more successful, partly because of the conflict between Budapest and Vienna, was the revolutionary action organized by the Slovak National Council against the government of Kossuth, but even this action brought no tangible results.
[14] In his *Political Testament* of 1872, Palacký referred to the June 1848 uprising as follows: "I know of no other event of our times which could have more fatal and harmful consequences for the nation than this Whitsuntide insurrection..."
[15] T. G. Masaryk, *O naší nynější krisi* (Praha, Pokrok, 1908), p. 233.
[16] *Ibid.*, p. 241.

military action, undertaken at home and especially abroad, by a "spiritual élite" of the nation, headed by Masaryk. For a long time, the Czech official leadership in the Viennese *Reichsrat*, as well as a considerable part of the nation, refused, in keeping with their traditional tactics, to take any unnecessary risks which might lead to an all-out persecution of the Czechs. Believing in the ideal of progress and the ultimate effectiveness of non-violence, they preferred to await the general European developments which, they were convinced, would work in their favor. As a result, the Czech Declaration of Independence on October 28, 1918, came more than a month after Masaryk had secured recognition of the Czechoslovak state by the principal Allied Powers. Far from being a revolution in the usual sense of the word, the Czech action was an orderly transfer of power from Vienna to the authorities of the new state. Thus the "28th of October" represented a triumph of the democratic method; at the same time, it fully justified the many decades of essentially non-violent, evolutionary, and democratic political tactics pursued by the Czechs.

If, as is generally believed, rejection of violence is one of the prerequisites of democratic government, then the experiences in Austria prepared the Czechs well for the establishment of a parliamentary democracy. The non-violent nature of the October 28th, 1918, seizure of power became symbolic of later Czechoslovak democracy. It strengthened the belief of a large part of the nation in the effectiveness of evolutionary, legal, and constitutional methods, and reinforced its abhorrence of force and violence. Subsequent developments, however, proved that this outlook was to be not only an asset, but also a serious handicap to the new Republic.

Political Science in Czechoslovakia

EDWARD TÁBORSKÝ

The violent reversals in Czechoslovakia's political fortunes have inevitably affected Czechoslovak political science. More perhaps than any other field of knowledge the science of politics needs an atmosphere of genuine freedom to develop and to prosper; and it withers away or becomes corrupted whenever freedom is destroyed. It is by no means accidental that the science of politics has reached its highest stage of development in the Anglo-Saxon democracies, with their long-established and deep-rooted traditions of political freedom and tolerance, whereas it has been stifled and usually perverted to propaganda in dictatorships, such as Soviet Russia.

We may consider the developments of the Czechoslovak science of politics in five successive stages, corresponding to varying degrees of freedom in that country during the following periods:

1. the Hapsburg rule prior to 1918;
2. the "First Republic" from 1918 to 1938;
3. the Nazi occupation from 1938/39 to 1945;
4. the post-war period of the struggle between democracy and communism from 1945 to 1948; and
5. the era of Communist totalitarianism since the Communist coup of February 1948.

1. THE HAPSBURG ERA

As elsewhere in Central Europe, political science was not recognized as a distinctive discipline prior to World War I. When the Hapsburg régime finally permitted the restoration of a Czech university in Prague in 1882, no provision was made for an independent study of politics. Instead, the traditional pattern was followed of treating political science as an aspect of other studies such as public law, history, philosophy, and, later, sociology, when it was added to the roster of social sciences. Prompted by Western example, notably the French *École libre des sciences politiques* and the London School of Economics and Political Science, a number of Czech intellectuals, among them, Eduard Beneš, the young sociologist, who subsequently became the second President of Czechoslovakia, endeavored to establish a similar political study center under the auspices of the Czech National Council. However, their efforts failed to produce anything except a School of Politics, created in 1911 by the Young Czechs' Party as a party institution.

Under these circumstances, it is hardly surprising that no distinctive School of Political Science developed. Scholarly works that might qualify to some extent as political science literature were written predominantly by historians, jurists, and sociologists, from whose ranks also emerged the leading Czech political thinkers of the period. Among them, to mention only a few, were František Palacký, outstanding Czech historian, philosopher of history, and author of the monumental *History of the Czech Nation*; Josef Kalousek, the first professor of Czech history at the restored Czech section of Charles University and author of an important historico-political treatise on *Czech State Law*; Zdeněk Tobolka, a prominent politician of the Young Czechs' Party, keen student of Czech politics of the 19th century and author of several historico-political works in that field; Jiří Pražák, the founder of the Czech science, of public law; and most renowned, Thomas G. Masaryk, professor of philosophy and sociology, foremost Czechoslovak statesman, and author of such internationally recognized classics as *The Social Question: Philosophical and Political Foundations of Marxism* and *The Spirit of Russia*.

2. THE "FIRST REPUBLIC", 1919-1938

The emergence of an independent Republic of Czechoslovakia from the ruins of the Austro-Hungarian Empire ushered in an era of unprecedented political freedom and created an ideal atmosphere for unhindered inquiry into all issues and aspects of politics. Yet, the revolutionary break with the political past found no parallel in the realm of political theory. As before, political science continued to be treated as an adjunct of other social sciences. Public law and administration, Czechoslovak political institutions, and those aspects of political theory pertaining to the state and law were handled by schools of law. A good deal of political thought was also intermingled with the study of philosophy. International relations continued to be accommodated mainly in the field of modern history and, to a certain extent, in courses in international law offered as a constituent of law school curricula. The study of political parties, public opinion and other matters related to political behavior were claimed mostly by sociology. Comparative study of governmental systems was virtually non-existent.

A promising step toward elevating political science to a full-fledged subject of academic studies in its own right was the establishment of a Free School of Political Science in 1928. Thus the old dream of creating an institution of higher learning in the neglected field of political studies was finally realized. But the new school of politics was devised only as a junior two-year institution rather than a complete senior college. Unable to offer an equivalent to the university diploma, and laboring from the start against great odds, the school was no match for Czechoslovakia's flourishing universities and remained virtually a still-born child. Despite this continued Cinderella-like treatment of politics as an academic discipline, political science was not neglected in the "First Republic". A number of scholars, engaged professionally in other social sciences, especially law, showed a definite interest in the study of politics and produced literary works that may readily be included in the category of political science. Emil Sobota, a high-ranking civil servant in the Chancellery of the President of the Republic, worked and published in the field of politics. Emil Svoboda, professor of civil law at Charles University, wrote several books on philosophical-political topics, such as *Democracy as a Life and World Outlook*, *Man and Society*, and *Thoughts on Law, Ethics, and Religion*. Bohumil Baxa, professor of law at Masaryk University in Brno, concerned himself with modern parliamentarism and Central European public law, while his colleague, Jaroslav Krejčí, published studies on such problems of modern democracy as the position of the Head of the State and delegation of legislative powers. A pronounced interest in the political problems of modern parliamentarism was also manifested by Zdeněk Peška, professor of law of Komenský University at Bratislava, and František Vavřínek, professor of constitutional law at Charles University.

Indeed, many of the professors of international, constitutional and administrative law in Czechoslovak law school showed keen interest in related topics of political science, and occasionally published books, monographs and articles combining legal and political aspects. Among the works of sociologists crossing into the field of political science, we should mention Jan Mertl's *Political Parties, their Foundations and Types in Present-day World* and Emanuel Chalupný's studies of the Czech national character. Finally, some of Czechoslovakia's better newpapermen occasionally turned out monographs or books on politics, though few of them could qualify as truly scholarly works. The most noteworthy of such contributions to political science was Ferdinand Peroutka's *The Building of the State*, a massive and brilliantly written historico-political exposition of the early developments of Czechoslovak politics since 1918.

Politics also served frequently as the subject of periodic literature. Although pre-war Czechoslovakia had no review devoted exclusively to political science, a number of scholarly journals in related fields published articles dealing with various political science topics. Closest to the concept of a political science review was *Moderní stát* ("The Modern State") and *Parlament* ("The Parliament"), both edited by younger scholars concerned with questions of constitutional law and political institutions, domestic and foreign. Problems of public administration and administrative law were handled by the review, *Veřejná správa* ("Public Administration") and those pertaining to local government in *Československá samospráva* ("Czechoslovak Self-government"). Questions of foreign politics, international relations and international law were treated in the journal, *Zahraniční politika* ("Foreign Policy") and *Hlídka mezinárodního práva* ("Review of International Law"). The pages of the several law reviews published in pre-war Czechoslovakia were also open to contributions in the area of political science. That was particularly true of *Sborník věd právních a státních* ("Quarterly of Legal and State Sciences") published under the auspices of the Law School of Prague's Charles University. Furthermore, *Naše doba* ("Our Time"), a general review of public affairs founded by T. G. Masaryk, regularly published scholarly articles dealing with various aspects of politics.

Finally, three volumes of an encyclopaedic character should be mentioned. *Slovník veřejného práva československého* ("The Encyclopaedia of Czechoslovak Public Law"), though predominantly of a legal nature, contained much scholarly material touching on political science. So did *Slovník národohospodářský, sociální a politický* ("Encyclopaedia of Economic, Social and Political Affairs"). Volume V of *Československá vlastivěda*, a multivolume encyclopaedia of various facets of Czechoslovak life published under the auspices of the Masaryk Academy, gathered under the heading *Stát* ("The State") contributions dealing with the Czechoslovak State, its constitution, governmental system, parties and other related political topics.

3. THE NAZI OCCUPATION, 1938/39-1945

The Nazi occupation brought the hopeful growth of the Czechoslovak science of politics to an abrupt halt. The Czech universities were closed, and publication of the results of objective research in the field of political science became impossible. Some of those who had contributed most to the development of political science under the "First Republic" were jailed or sent to concentration camps, and the rest forced into silence. Thus, the only works in the field of political science that could be published during the Nazi occupation of Czechoslovakia were those written by Czechoslovak authors living abroad. These included Eduard Beneš's *Democracy Today and Tomorrow*, Josef Hanč's *Tornado Across Eastern Europe*, Frank Munk's *The Legacy of Nazism*, Hubert Ripka's *Munich: Before and After*, and Eduard Táborský's *Czechoslovak Cause* and *Czechoslovak Democracy at Work*.

4. THE POST-WAR STRUGGLE BETWEEN DEMOCRACY AND COMMUNISM, 1945-1948

The liberation of Czechoslovakia from the Nazi rule seemed to augur a new era of growth for political science. After the enforced silence of the Nazi occupation, interest in the study of politics surged back, especially among students returning to the re-opened Czechoslovak universities. Several younger scholars who had spent the war years in England and in the United States brought back a keen desire to see political science elevated to the status of an independent discipline as it is recognized in the Anglo-Saxon democracies. Most of the journals that used to carry articles in the political science field in prewar days resumed publication after the silence of the Nazi occupation. The heightened interest in the study of politics was perhaps best symbolized by the elevation of the former two-year Free School of Political Science to a full-fledged four-year University of Politics and Social Affairs. Despite the acute shortage of paper and other difficulties with which the publishing business was beset after the war, political science literature made a good start with the publication of such works as Zdeněk Neubauer's *Státověda a teorie politiky* ("State Science and the Theory of Politics"), Emil Sobota's posthumous *Glossy 1939-1945. Kniha české filosofie politické* ("Comments 1939-1945. A book of Czech Political Philosophy"), and Eduard Táborský's *Naše nová ústava* ("Our New Constitution").

5. THE COMMUNIST ERA

Unfortunately, this promising post-war beginning was nipped in the bud by the Communist seizure of power in February 1948. Since the Marxist-Leninist *Weltanschauung*, rather than an impartial search for the truth became the yardstick for the evaluation of all social factors, objective study of politics became impossible. While political literature published in Czechoslovakia increased in volume, it had become so distorted that none of it would qualify as genuine political science in the Western sense of the word.

Hence, as during the Nazi occupation of 1939-1945, truly objective investigation in the field of politics can once again be conducted only by those Czechoslovak scholars who have managed to escape from the stifling embrace of Communist totalitarianism. A number of them hold professorial positions in departments of political science in various American universities, such as Václav Beneš (Indiana University), Karl W. Deutsch (Yale University), Ivo Ducháček (City College of New York), Josef Korbel (Denver University), Frank Munk (Reed College of Oregon), Josef S. Rouček (University of Bridgeport), František Schwarzenberg (Loyola University), and Edward Táborský (University of Texas). They have since been joined by many younger Czechs and Slovaks who fled from Communist Czechoslovakia and obtained doctorates in political science at various America universites. Still others are active in political science fields outside the academic world, such as collaborators and researchers of the Free Europe Committee, the Czechoslovak Foreign Institute in Exile, and Eduard Beneš's Institute in London. Many Czechoslovak political scientists who teach and work in countries of the Free World are frequent contributors to scholarly journals, authors of papers read before political science conventions, and producers of a large number of books and monographs in the field of politics.

Thus the young tradition of Czechoslovak political science is being preserved and further developed in the free and hospitable atmosphere of the Western world until it is once again possible to conduct genuine research in politics in the old country.

Masaryk and Plato in the 20th Century

ERAZIM V. KOHÁK

Thomas Garrigue Masaryk, the first President of Czechoslovak Republic, died on a gloomy September day in the year 1937, and to the nation that mourned him it may well seem that an era died with him – the whole era of liberal strivings which culminated in that brief, often turbulent, yet joyous and productive interlude between world wars which we remember as our first Republic. Seldom has the world changed as completely in as short a time as in the years following Masaryk's death. A whole generation has grown up to whom that world and that era are less than a memory laced with an aura of gas-light, carriages, and stiff winged collars like the one President Masaryk wears in faded photographs from a distant time. The actors of the great drama of which Masaryk was a part, Franz Joseph, Hodža, Kramář, and a host of others lie dead and forgotten. Yet the present masters of the state which Masaryk founded, who have easily forgotten a legion of their violent enemies of yesteryear, continue to wage a tireless campaign, ranging from polemic to slander, against the one man who towers above that long forgotten time – Masaryk. The United States remembered him recently when it issued a postage stamp bearing his image, and Czechoslovak Communists showed that they had not forgotten him when they banned letters bearing that stamp from Czechoslovak mails. The dialectic, which the Communists would like to read as one of capitalism versus socialism has become a dialectic of Masaryk's idea of Czechoslovak democracy against the Communist state.

Thus the struggles of our era are forcing us to discover a Masaryk who does not belong to history: Masaryk, the philosopher of democracy. To be sure, this is not how we usually remember him. We remember Masaryk primarily as President-Liberator, and not without reason. It would be difficult to overestimate the importance of his role in the rebirth of Czechoslovakia and in the entire course of events during and after the first World War. Perhaps more than anyone else, he contributed to the change in Allied policy towards Austro-Hungary, and subsequently impressed his stamp on the reborn Czechoslovak republic. Yes, Masaryk was definitely a historical personage, whose place in the history of Central Europe in the early part of this century is assured, and it is not at all surprising that we tend to remember him in this role. Yet precisely to the extent to which we remember Masaryk in this, his most impressive role, his memory becomes only memory, something that belongs to the past. For such is the fate of historical figures. They belong to a fixed place in history, and recede into the past with it.

It is a different Masaryk who looms large in the present struggle for men's minds – Masaryk, the thinker and philosopher. Though it may have been his political importance which made Masaryk relevant to his contemporaries, it is the forgotten aspect of his life, as the philosopher, which is relevant to us today. Thus our concern today is with Masaryk as a philosopher, and with the significance of his philosophy. What is its significance? Or does it have any lasting significance at all? Is it possible that the Communist theoretician, Nejedlý, was right when he interpreted Masaryk as a practical politician, driven to philosophy by political exigency, and using philosophy as a practical tool, with little regard for consistency or method? Is it true that Masaryk's philosophy cannot be detached from the political problems and questions of his time, and loses significance as those problems recede into the past? It is true that Masaryk the philosopher is virtually unknown in the West. You would seek his name in vain in philosophy textbooks or in the standard histories of contemporary philosophy. His philosophy is not debated in learned journals, nor taught in colleges and universities, unless the professor is a Czechoslovak – and there are very few of those. The West may remember President Masaryk, but it never even discovered Masaryk the philosopher.

In this respect, of course, Masaryk is not alone. Even Kierkegaard, whose work had been translated into German as early as the mid-19th century, was not discovered in the Anglo-Saxon world until some eighty years later. And yet how much easier it would have been to study Kierkegaard! He had not been proscribed and censored as Masaryk. In fact, we have never really had a chance to study Masaryk's thought. Between the wars he was more of a symbol to us than a teacher. Then from 1939 on, his thought was suppressed or distorted by this or that censorship. But it is also true that even during the richest flowering of Czechoslovak thought under the Republic, Masaryk lacked philosophical pupils. To be sure, there are exceptions, but they are few. For instance Emanuel Rádl tried honestly to think through and complete Masaryk's philosophical work, but in the end he shared Masaryk's fate. We respected him more than we studied him. Hromádka also showed a thorough grasp of Masaryk's philosophy, and, in 1930, published one of the best books on the subject.[1] But Hromádka's first interest is, after all, theology, and even if it had not been for Hromádka's unfortunate flirtation with the Communists in the last decade, it would be difficult to consider him a philosophical pupil of Masaryk. There were, of course, other, such as Kozák or Krejčí, but their respective interpretations of Masaryk's philosophy are almost diametrically opposed. Here we encounter our greatest barrier to understanding Masaryk: we attempt to speak of the significance of his philosophy, but are not in the least clear about its meaning.

Most of Masaryk's contemporaries seem to have understood his philosophy as a version of positivism, and there is some justification for this. At a time when Czech philosophy was strongly influenced by German post-Kantian idealism, Masaryk sought to introduce us to the French positivism of Comte and the radical empiricism of Hume. We can trace the influence of both these thinkers, and of the English utilitarian, John Stuart Mill, in Masaryk's systematic works. Today, when the moral and intellectual barrenness of positivism has become so painfully obvious, we may hesitate to admit it, yet the fact remains that Masaryk does defend many essentially positivistic theses. Note for instance what he has to say about the relation of the sciences and philosophy. In *Rusko a Evropa* Masaryk denies both the right and the ability of philosophy to work or to know independently. Philosophy appears to him to be the logic of empirical sciences.

Modern philosophy is not the queen of the sciences, nor does it stand over and above special scientific disciplines. Rather, it is in them and with them, it is the *scientia generalis.*[2]

Similarly in his *Versuch einer konkreter Logic* he subordinates ethics to sociology and defines the former as a science of man's conduct as a social animal.[3]

Here we see Masaryk in his most clearly positivistic stance. But his views changed rapidly and radically. Already in *KL* we can note many

---

[1] Joseph L. Hromádka, *Masaryk* (Prague, Academic YMCA, 1930).
[2] T. G. Masaryk, *Rusko a Evropa*, 2d ed. (Prague, 1930), vol. I, p. 254. (*Rusko a Evropa* was also published in English, as *The Spirit of Russia*, tr. Jan Slavik, 2d ed., London, Allen & Unwin, 1955. Unless otherwise noted, my notes refer to Czech editions, in my own translation.) On the present topic, see also T. G. Masaryk, *Versuch einer konkreter Logik* (1887; hereafter *KL*), p. 303.
[3] *KL*, p. 149.

distinctly non-positivistic elements.[4] Unfortunately, at this point in Masaryk's philosophical development his political activity interfered, and Masaryk never systematised his objections to positivism. For this reason his systematic works, *Concrete Logic*, *Handbook of Sociology*, or *Social Question*, leave a positivistic impression with the reader. In that context then the many non-positivistic elements of his thought, whether in his systematic works or in works aimed directly at a particular question, such as the meaning of Czech history, appear to be accidental, inconsistent elements of a poorly developed philosophy. For this reason it is possible to understand Masaryk as a positivist, or simply as a politician using philosophy as an *ad hoc* idealogy of his political work.[5]

Yet philosophically both of these explanations are most superficial and esentially unsatisfactory. Both have to pick and choose their texts, and overlook much that is significant. The non-positivistic elements of Masaryk's philosophy go too deep, and appear even in his most posivistic works and periods. They cannot be accounted for by chance or expediency. Already Rádl pointed out that the very fact that Masaryk from the beginning sought an overall world-view, makes him essentially different from the positivists.[6] That is not an accident, but something quite basic. Similarly Masaryk's Prague lectures, later published under the title *Concerning the Study of Poetry*, are profoundly non-positivistic. In them, Masaryk speaks of artistic cognition as more direct and basic than the "positive" knowledge of the sciences.[7] Masaryk's explanation of the meaning of Czech history belongs in the same category. In both cases, Masaryk interprets his empiricism in a sense which is far closer to the phenomenology of Husserl, which Eugen Fink, with Husserl's approval, called "radical empiricism",[8] than to the empiricism of Hume or the positivism of Comte. And, ironically enough, in his reply to the Czech historian Pekař's critique Masaryk implicitly criticises his own positivistic tendencies.[9]

Yet in spite of these admitted inconsistencies Masaryk's philosophy is not merely a *unitas aggregationis*, but has an overall direction and meaning. Masaryk himself never considered himself a positivist. It is quite interesting that he reacted vigorously to the accusation of positi-

---

[4] For instance his remarks about metaphysics as *Prima philosophia*, KL, p. 274.
[5] Cf. Nejedlý in *Masarykův Sborník* (Prague, Čin; hereafter *MS*), vol. II (1928), p. 150ff.
[6] Emanuel Rádl, *Moderní Věda* (hereafter *MV*), p. 19.
[7] Masaryk, *O Studiu děl básnických*, 2d ed. (Prague, 1926), p. 11.
[8] Pierre Thévénaz, *What is Phenomenology?* (Chicago, 1962), p. 19.
[9] *Naše Doba* (Hereafter *ND*), XI, 71 f. Hromádka makes a similar point in *op. cit.*, p. 131.

vism. Thus, in his reply to von Soldern's review of the German edition of *Concrete Logic*, Masaryk insists that the book is not positivistic.[10] He refused to identify himself with positivism or with any other school of philosophy. Yet he does give us a few indications of how he regards his thought. In the *Talks* with Karel Čapek Masaryk calls himself a platonist.[11] And in fact, while Masaryk found much attractive in Comte, Hume, and J. S. Mill, he returned again and again to Plato. That in itself, of course, does not yet make him a platonist. But there are other suggestions as well. So again in Čapek's *Talks with TGM*, Masaryk tells us that Plato began to interest him already when he was a student in gymnasium.[12] And in fact we know that in the year 1876 he wrote to Leonard Čech that he was preparing for publication a book to be called *Das Wesen der Seele bei Platon*.[13] Unfortunately, the book was never published, but what was published testifies to Masaryk's continuing interest in Plato: "Theory and Practice" (1876), "Plato as a Patriot" (1877), and finally "Progress, evolution, and enlightenment" (1877). In *Blaise Pascal*[14] and later, in *Světová Revoluce*[15] Masaryk praises Plato, even though he criticised platonism sharply under the impact of Russian orthodoxy in *Rusko a Evropa*. In his speech of acceptance of his honorary doctorate in theology at the theological faculty in Prague in 1923 Masaryk ranked Plato along with Jesus and St. Paul.[16] Similarly, when in his interpretation of Czech history its meaning acquires a normative force,[17] we can sense the vestiges of Platonism and Plato's normative conception of the idea.

Thus we find many reasons for interpreting Masaryk's philosophy platonically rather than positivistically. But the grave weakness of the positivistic interpretation is precisely that it cannot account for the non-positivistic elements of Masaryk's thought. We must reverse the question now, and ask whether a platonic explanation of Masaryk's philosophy could account for its non-platonic, positivistic elements. Here we must start by asking what exactly we mean by "platonism". After all, even Plato's pupils could not agree about the meaning of his philosophy, and since that time it has acquired many, sometimes even contradictory, expla-

---

[10] Reprinted in *MS*, III (1929), pp. 261-272.
[11] Karel Čapek, *Hovory s TGM* (Prague, Čin, 1928), p. 98.
[12] *Ibid.*, p. 74ff.
[13] Hromádka, *op. cit.*, p. 81.
[14] T. G. Masaryk, *Blaise Pascal* (Prague, 1883).
[15] T. G. Masaryk, *Světová Revoluce* (Prague, 1925), p. 391, 562.
[16] *MS* II, 90-92, cited by Hromádka, *op. cit.*, p. 86.
[17] For instance, explanation of Czech history and struggle for the ideal in *Světová Revoluce*, p. 601. This is precisely the point attacked by Pekař, *Smysl českých dějin*, p. 19.

nations. Much of what we today consider platonism is a medieval deposit, and even in Plato's own writings it is necessary to distinguish basic elements from those which simply reflect the special conditions of ancient Greece. Usually we associate with Plato an idealism more characteristic of Plotinus and a philosophy of the state which Plato derives to a great extent from common Greek usages and revises in his *Laws*.[18] Here he understands man as a part of the *polis*: a conception radically revised by the Stoics and Christians, and of historic rather than philosophical importance today.

Less well remembered, but far more important, is Plato's defence of philosophy against the sophists, both Greek and later. Here Plato opposes specifically the relativism of the sophists, which would deny the self-identity of reality simply on the basis of the difference among individual things. Against them Plato defends the importance of the idea which in the last instance gives identity to the world and gives meaning and self-identity to the particulars. Plato is well aware that the idea is not a realisable ideal, nor does he so intend it. The reality of the ideal goes deeper than that: it is the essence of the actual, its norm, that which gives it direction and meaning. Here lies the crucial importance of Plato and platonism: in the realization that particulars, the individual entities and acts of which our life and world are made, are meaningless in themselves, that their meaning and the meaning of all human life lie in the fact that the particular objects and acts are bearers of the idea.

In this respect, it is not far from Plato to Masaryk. Compare, for instance, what Masaryk writes in *Naše Doba*:

Our object, our world, is not this particular instance, seen or heard at this moment. We know it as a whole, as a meaningful whole and not merely an aggregate of particulars. Yet this whole, of which we are a part, we do not perceive through the senses.[19]

Thus, at the decisive point, which mediaeval philosophy delineated clearly in the question of whether the first object of the intellect is being or *quidditas rei materialis*, Masaryk clearly chooses the platonic alternative. And this tendency becomes more pronounced in his explanation of Czech history. As against Pekař's positive reading, the Czech ideal for Masaryk is not merely an epiphenomenal product of historical accident, but a normative ideal, which hudges our present and gives it direction and meaning.

---

[18] Cf. Sabine, *History of Political Theory* (New York, 1958), p. 11-19; also Werner Jaeger, *Paideia*, passim, esp. Part I.
[19] *ND*, IV, 403.

Here we see Masaryk's basic platonism, the emphasis on the ideal not merely as a mystic idea in the sense of German idealism, but the real basis which gives unity and meaning to our life.[20]

Yet Masaryk's philosophy never becomes a blind platonism. He completes Plato precisely where such completion is most needed. He criticises him specifically when Plato, in his preoccupation with the ideal, tends to neglect the actual.[21] This in fact is the weakest point in Plato's thought, though even here Plato seems to yield to his time. A different interpretation of the problem is quite possible within his philosophical framework, and Plato suggests such interpretation already in the fact that his philosopher in the *Republic*, having seen the idea, returns to the cave. It is quite possible to formulate a philosophy which shares Plato's concern about the ideal, but follows an opposite view of the world. We can equally say that the world is not meaningless because it falsifies the idea, but is significant precisely to the extent to which it realises it. If the ideal is not a mere idea, but in fact the basis and norm of reality, such explanation is possible.[22]

At first sight such an explanation might appear more reminiscent of Aristotle than of Plato. It is for Aristotle that the forms do not exist except in the objects. Yet this is not Masaryk. Certainly, for Masaryk the ideal must be realised in thing and in act, but its reality does not depend on them or on its realizability. His ideal is truly an ideal: it has the validity of a norm rather than of an average. For when Aristotle places the forms in the world as the second substance, he is not adding to the world's significance. Quite the contrary, he is subtracting from it, because he is limiting the significance of the world to its own purely natural teleology. Platonic forms in Aristotle's interpretation became not norms, but simply descriptive, general terms. Thus, in Aristotle's departure from Plato we have the foundations of positivistic naturalism. This is not simply empiricism, which sees that our understanding must always proceed through the senses, even though in its insight into the meaning of the world it reaches radically beyond the senses. Plato knew this reality, though this aspect of his thought was developed by Aristotle, while Plato himself fell prey to Plotinus. No, we have here also the basis of the reductionism which rejects the very question of meaning and substitutes for it a descrip-

---

[20] Masaryk rejects, very much in the spirit of Plato, a romantic interpretation of his thought, in the first issue of *ND*, I, 1.
[21] *KL*, 291.
[22] Cf. my interpretation in "Road to Wisdom", *Classical Journal*, LVI, 3 (December 1960), p. 129 *et passim*.

tion of the actual. Thus, while it gains in accuracy of description, it loses all ability to understand the meaning of what it describes and make normative judgements about it.

Plato certainly realises that the actual is imperfect – but an imperfect ideal would cease to be an ideal, and would become an ideology. Truth for him must have an objective basis, beyond the approximations of the actual. Masaryk interprets Plato in this sense when the writes;

> Truth, according to Plato, comes from the outside, it is objective, absolutely objective, not subjective, and precisely because of its objectivity it is truth. Precisely because of his ideas Plato is an extreme objectivist.[23]

Masaryk sees his ideals in the same way. His conception of Czech history, his conceptions of justice, of democracy: these are not generalised descriptions of imperfect human aspirations: they are an objective standard whose validity is not diminished by human imperfection.

Masaryk rejects Plato's teaching about the ideas in the sense which it acquired in the late Middle Ages, that is, as an extra-empirical method of knowing empirical actuality. It seems rather likely that Plato would agree with this. In the *Statesman* he stresses that our world, as he says in his myth, is a world running backwards.[24] It is a twisted, perverted world, a caricature of its real being. Between empirical reality and essential reality lies a difference expressed by the terms "real" and "actual". Since the actual is a perverted form of the ideal (and not only the vague copy it seemed to be in the *Republic*), we cannot gain knowledge of the actual by deducduction from the ideal. Such deduction can show us the norm and meaning of the actual, but not the conditions of its existence *de facto*. This is the difference which later platonism (e.g. Anselm's), as well as later idealism (Hegel), tended to overlook. For this reason the astrologers and alchemists could see in Plato's teaching about the ideas a shortcut to empirical knowledge. But that then is not longer Plato: and Masaryk, in his positivistic moments which reject such teaching, returns to Plato's critical insight. Platonism of the 19th century retained from Plato only the last stage of knowledge, which Plato called *episteme* or *noesis*, that is, wisdom. Masaryk, like Plato, understands that this stage must be preceded by *eikasia*, *pistis*, and *dianoia*: empirical knowledge and reasoning. Hence he distinguishes between the knowledge of particulars, which must proceed empirically, and the quest for their meaning. Masaryk's platonism thus appears as a critical, socratic platonism. It attacks all spiritual laziness,

---

[23] *ND*, IV, 402, cited by Hromádka, *op. cit.*, p. 48.
[24] *Statesman*, pp. 269-270, Stephanus.

all attempts to get by without basic, exact and detailed observation and research. Note that that is exactly what Socrates did. As Masaryk, he attacked superstition and ideology, and, as Masaryk was accused of positivism, so Socrates was called a sophist. But they both criticize differently from either the positivists or the sophists. They criticise superstition and pseudo-ideals, not because they consider the ideal unreal, but because they understand the power and importance of a true ideal.

In this sense, I believe, we can understand Masaryk's struggle against the manuscripts forged to prove the existence of an ancient Czech culture. Masaryk was, at the time, accused of lack of patriotism and even treason. Today such accusations seem ridiculous, though there are people who repeat them, but at the time it seemed that Masaryk was attacking the national idea itself. Yet this is just what Masaryk was not doing. He questioned the authenticity of the manuscripts, not because he did not believe in or understand the idea of the national reawakening, but precisely because he grasped it best of us all, and so fought against any misuse of it. Thus it is possible to speak of his critical platonism: Masaryk uses critique always in the name of an ideal. Because he understood that our national ideal was not merely ethnic and descriptive, but an ethical and normative ideal, the understood that it could not be based on a lie.

Yet if Masaryk had as much in common with Plato as we have suggested in the foregoing lines, why did not he identify himself with platonism? Why does he turn so consistently and thoroughly in what seems to be just the other direction, to positivism? The question is basic, but it seems to me that it is not difficult to answer. Masaryk does not identify himself with the kind of platonism which we have described because in his age there simply was no such platonism. Ever since the time of Plotinus and especially in the nineteenth century, Plato was a captive of idealism and irresponsible metaphysical phantasy. Philosophers had forgotten that it was precisely Plato who had stressed that the road to wisdom leads through thorough, detailed, careful study – just think of the course of education he he required of the future philosopher-king! It was Plato who insisted on a careful analysis of reality and ever higher abstraction. But it was also Plato who realised that the highest abstraction is not yet insight, even though it may be its necessary condition. Plato does not reject empirical knowledge. Note that the second and third stages are indeed empirical knowledge, and in many cases serve us rather well. Plato does not deny its usefulness, indeed, he uses it himself, as in the *Laws*. But he warns us that just because we are able to manipulate something empirically, we do not yet understand its meaning. He warns us merely that if we wish to seek the meaning and the significance of man and his world, we cannot reach it by abstraction, which leads us only to descriptive, general terms. But Plato also realises that even in dealing with meaning, only empirical study of the world will trigger the eidetic insight we seek, and that the validation of the insight consists precisely in the fact that it is able to shed light on and interpret all actuality: that is, in the fact that the philosopher can return to the cave with it.

In its history from Plotinus down to Masaryk, platonism had lost sight of this. The Middle Ages created a climate of opinion which was sufficiently Aristotelean to be concerned with empirical description of the world – with what Husserl was later to call "natural standpoint" rather than "phenomenological attitude". Yet it was a climate of opinion sufficiently platonic, or better, plotinian, to seek to bypass Plato's laborious first three stages of cognition.

A platonist who recognises that Plato is concerned with meaning and not with constructing some trans-empirical reality, would inevitably criticize the idealised version of platonism current in the 19th century. In such a climate of opinion, the platonist would necessarily became a critic and that is precisely what Masaryk did. It seems to me that it was precisely what we have called his platonism, his sense of truth and of the depth of man, life, and the world, that led him to attack all that was distorted and false in contemporary platonism. In positivism Masaryk found an ideal weapon for his criticism. For though positivism may not be capable of achieving a unified world view or an insight into the meaning of experience, it is able to cut cleanly through all pretensions. But his positivism never becomes mere destructive, sceptical reductionism. It is true that Masaryk was too honest not to take scepsis seriously. He honestly comes to grips with the problems which arise from it. He takes it as seriously as all epistemological problems of the first three stages, because he is fully aware that on this level any irresponsibility or dishonesty distorts the insight of the fourth stage. To be sure, these are not the terms he uses. But the idea is the same: precisely because Masaryk understood the importance of immediate, direct insight into the meaning of reality, he was not willing to misuse it on the level of empirical inquiry, and severely criticised all pretensions in this direction. Yet this criticism is never destructive: it always serves to purify Plato's basic insight.

To be sure, in his struggle against the official church and philosophy which supported the rotting theocracies of the 19th century, Masaryk was forced into increasingly more radical positions. He was fighting for the very life of free thought, and was not squeamish in his choice of weapons.

Often he will say too much rather than not enough. Thus, at times he does allow positivism to mislead him, as, for instance, in the problem of myth, whose significance Masaryk fails to grasp – though he recognizes it implicitly in his *Study of Poetic Works*. It is true, that he completely misunderstands the term "revelation", which appears to him as an epistemological shortcut, and as such open to radical criticism. Similarly Masaryk never comprehends the significance of the church as a communion of redeemed sinners. To him the church remains an official imposition from above, advancing a heteronomous claim on a particularly dubious foundation. But it is also true that Masaryk did not understand these terms because they were also basically misunderstood in his time. Or, more accurately, Masaryk understood these terms as his time understood them, and therefore he rightly brought them under attack, even though he failed to distinguish between the fortuitous expression and the intention of the term. Yet even here his criticism was always criticism in the name of a half-felt understanding of the more profound significance which the institutions and philosophies he attacked failed to realize in spite of their nominal allegiance. Masaryk worked under the severe handicap of positivism, which made it imposible for him to formulate explicitly the phenomenological presuppositions of his own work. Yet even in his sharpest conflicts with tradition, he never lost his basic devotion to truth, and it was precisely during these struggles that he formulated and defended the most outspokenly platonic part of his philosophy, his philosophy of Czech history.

Masaryk was a platonist, but he was able to distinguish the essential insight of Plato from the sediment of centuries, and he did not hesitate to criticise that sediment. He was not afraid to use positivism, even though he could see where positivism led in Comte or de Maistre. He was not afraid of positivistic aimlessness and blindness, because he realised that positivism can clear away the sediment of history, but cannot deny the meaning and significance of man, history, and the world.

It is this rare combination of devotion to an ideal with a critical philosophical outlook which makes Masaryk important today. The disappointment which followed the uncritical idealism of the early part of the century – whether democratic or communist idealism – followed it necessarily because our idealism was often dishonest. We spoke of war to end wars, and pretended to believe that eternal peace can be built on a treaty. Our Communists, in spite of historical evidence, insisted on believing that social questions can be resolved by a revolution. Yet the reality we refused to face caught up to us and showed us the emptiness of our easy idealism. So now we criticise the Communists, democracy, past philosophy, ourselves – but again to no avail: we are afraid to believe. But as we can accomplish nothing without critical self-estimate, so we can accomplish nothing with empty criticism. We need to learn to believe critically. Where blind faith can lead us our recent history clearly shows. Masaryk shows us, however, that it is possible to trust, yet to trust critically.

And in this we find the meaning of Masaryk's philosophy, understood as a critical platonism. Philosophically speaking, Masaryk's thought purifies platonism of its plotinian, mediaeval, and even modern accretions. His platonism is socratic – and, I should say, truly platonic: a realistic, rather than idealistic, platonism, which with unshakeable faith in the ideal can be critical of ideologies. Thus it speaks directly to our fluctuations between militant anti-Communism and appeasement, as well as to our philosophical vacillation between an empty, formal, logical positivism and a formless existentialism. For philosophy today is badly in need of synthesis. On the one hand, it is positivistic, often competent and honest, but without any positive content, on the other hand, it is existential, relevant, courageous, but sorely lacking precisely Masaryk's critical elements. Nor are other disciplines in an essentially different situation: our time vacillates between cynicism and messianism. Thus in our time, more than ever we need to learn from Masaryk how to believe critically.

SOCIOLOGY

The Character of Czech Scholarship: A Contribution to the Sociology of Knowledge

OTAKAR MACHOTKA

People consider scientific knowledge as factual, objective, and everywhere the same, without regard to the nation which uses its fruits or adds new contributions. Yet sociologists know that scientific knowledge and scholarship are products of social life,[1] that they are deeply influenced by it, and that they share the characteristics of the surrounding social structure,[2] its values and attitudes. This is perhaps less true of the natural sciences than of the social sciences and, of course, the humanities. Thus, for example, every nation[3] has somewhat different interests and goals in the fields of scholarship. Its researchers have a different way of thinking, different working habits, and different emotional involvements in their work. The value of scholarly endeavor is lower in some nations than in others, and the content of this value varies considerably. Scholarly pursuit may be geared chiefly to the support of national political goals, as it is, for instance, in Soviet Russia, or it may be conceived as a service to humanity or as a goal in itself. It also may be chiefly an intellectual exercise glorifying the scholar and giving him personal satisfaction, or, possibly, high social status and prestige.

Some nations strive more for systematic organization of knowledge, others stress the empirical character of knowledge, and still others, its pragmatic value. Special interest in certain fields of knowledge, and almost

---

[1] M. Weber, *Gesammelte Aufsätze zur Wissenschaftslehre* (Tübingen, 1922); M. Scheler, *Die Wissensformen und die Gesellschaft* (Der Neue Geist Verlag, 1926); K. Mannheim, *Ideology and Utopia* (New York, Harcourt, Brace, 1936); K. Mannheim, *Essays on the Sociology of Knowledge* (New York, Oxford University Pres, 1952); R. K. Merton, *Social Theory and Social Structure* (Glencoe, Ill., The Free Press, 1957), pp. 456-508.

[2] E. Durkheim, *The Elementary Forms of the Religious Life* (Glencoe, Ill., The Free Press, 1947) (French original published in 1912), pp. 9-20, 439-447.

[3] R. Mueller-Freienfels, *Psychologie der Wissenschaft* (Leipzig, J. A. Barth, 1936), ch. 8; B. Russell, *Philosophy* (New York, W. W. Norton and Co., 1927), pp. 29-30; M. Scheler, *Genius des Krieges* (Leipzig, Verlag der Wissenbücher, 1915); R. K. Merton, *op. cit.*, pp. 460-461.

none in others may be found in many Western nations. In some national cultures, scholars generally engage in enthusiastic personal work; in others they stress cool, well-organized team work.

All these differences are only examples which, of course, are far from being exhaustive. But they do, I hope, convey the understanding that scholarship may, and generally does, have a particular character in different national cultures.

With this in mind we may try to present a sketchy picture of the character of Czech science and scholarship, especially during its era of free development between 1918 and 1938. Under the Communist rule, of course, many of its characteristics have changed under the pressure of the authoritarian regime. We are not in a position to discuss these changes, and we will briefly mention only a few of them. Yet we believe that most of the basic traits of Czech science and scholarship have not really disappeared, but would come to life again with the return of freedom. We do not intend to discuss the character of scholarly effort in Slovakia, either. It shares many of the characteristics of Czech scholarship, but it is characterized by some traits of its own.

The picture of Czech science and scholarship we will draw is only tentative, not meant to be accurate and complete, since this essay is written in exile, without access to necessary sources of information. Besides, the limited extent of a convention paper does not allow for more than a short, preliminary set of ideas which possibly later on may be worked out into a more solid and documented piece of knowledge.

In speaking of the characteristic traits of Czech sholarship we will try to comprise all the scholarly and scientific fields. Yet we are fully aware that some of our statements apply more to some and less to other fields. This again points to the tentative character of the picture we try to produce.

In our analysis of Czech scholarship we will use a number of descriptive terms. As in all descriptions of this kind, the adjectives often have an implicit comparative meaning. If we say that somebody is tall, we mean tall when compared with individuals of the same race and sex. Thus, qualifications of Czech scholarship mean that it has more of certain properties when compared with the scholarship of other nations, and less of other attributes.

Czech scholarship as a whole had very much the character of the well known "sacred cow". Scholarship was a vocation, a mission, and the scholar its dedicated and humble servant. As a profession it was considered superior to most others. Scholarly, scientific knowledge was greatly respected and kept on a very high pedestal. Scholarly work was undertaken with the utmost seriousness and with a strong feeling of responsibility. It was a supreme service to the nation and to humanity, but it also was a highly valued activity in itself.

Research was always conducted in the framework of international scholarship. There was a painstaking endeavor to be fully informed about the latest research achievements of other nations, and to gear one's own work accordingly. In this respect there was less insularity and provincialism than there often is in larger nations which are engrossed in their own scholarly problems. Another result of this effort to keep informed was a high degree of objectivity, discernible even in the works of historians who are often inclined to be influenced by patriotic attitudes.

Theoretical science was considered loftier than applied science. It was felt to have more intellectual merit. There was strong interest in the systematic presentation of the results of scientific work, interest sometimes too great for profit.

There was also an emphasis on logical succession and organization of ideas. On the other hand we find an inclination toward eclecticism (sometimes at the expense of creativity) and avoidance of extreme or radical theories. There were frequent efforts to find a safe place somewhere midway between two extremes.

The high place of theoretical science was complemented by a strong interest in facts. Yet a down-to-earth approach was linked with a strong liking for general ideas and philosophically grounded systems. This, of course, applies less to the natural sciences than to the social sciences or humanities. There was great respect for truth, stemming from a tradition established by the religious reformer John Hus, and, more recently, reasserted by humanists such as Havlíček and Masaryk.

Czech scholarly effort always had a strong element of interest in man and his life. There was no such detachment of ideas from life as was typical of certain German scientific fields. That is why Czech science kept a watchful eye on possible applications of scientific knowledge. There was a strong streak of practicality, yet we cannot label Czech science pragmatic. The applications were cautious and reasonable, without any wild innovations, and they took second place to the interest in knowledge for its own sake.

One of the most important aspects of Czech scholarship was its determination not to lag behind any other nation in the advancement of knowledge. As a matter of fact this has been almost fully achieved. Thus, Czech scholarship had a high academic standard and a solid grasp of the scientific achievements throughout the world. Much effort was given to this task. On the other hand there was not enough daring and originality. Czech academicians (with some exceptions) produced no revolutionary new ideas.

Let us now turn to the Czech scholar himself. In general, the Czech scholar mastered a rather broad field, broader than is usual, for instance, in the U. S. Only rarely was he a narrow specialist. His general education was also broad. He knew the fundamentals of most of the important fields of knowledge. His knowledge of foreign languages was usually impressive. He had to be able to read at least two or three of them. His library contained, as a rule, the important books of his field in English, French, German and, sometimes, Russian. Now, of course, he has more Russian books than any others. Many Czech scholars had studied for at least a year or two at foreign universities, and maintained personal contact with foreign fellow-scholars.

The production of the average Czech scholar was rather high. There were many opportunities to publish, because the manufacture of books was not expensive, and because there was an unusually good market for printed matter. A relatively large number of scientific journals was regularly published.

A Czech scholar's concept of himself was that of a servant of his specialty and his nation, rather than that of a man who indulged in his scholarly dreams and pursued them according to his heart's desire. It was not dissimilar to the role of a priest who serves God and is an intermediary between Him and his parishioners. He was dedicated to scholarship, and to his role of intermediary between world scholarship and his own people. His status as intermediary was supported by the large number of interested readers of scholarly books. He was characterized by strong, even passionate, interest in his scholarly field.

For these reasons, the Czech scholar was ready to accept a number of duties without financial recompense. He often served on a number of committees, wrote articles for the daily press, lectured to different groups, and advised different institutions without asking anything in return.

The social status of Czech scholars was high. They belonged to the national elite and enjoyed high prestige. At times, a scholar's opinions were accepted as fully authoritative even in matters quite unrelated to his field. Elderly scholars were revered for their achievements, even if no further contributions of note could be expected of them.

Thanks to his knowledge of world scholarly achievements, the Czech scholar had no inclination to overestimate his own or those of Czech scholarship in general. There was a minimum of intellectual ethnocentrism. Despite strong patriotism and interest in furthering national goals, Czech scholars had a sound factual attitude and Czech scholarship was more international in nature than that of most large nations.

Let us comment on several outstanding Czech scholars to illustrate what we have said of Czech science in general. The great Czech religious reformer, John Hus, is typical. In theology, he was not as original as his English predecessor, Wycliffe, but he grasped the importance of Wycliffe's teaching a hundred years before Luther and other reformers, and drew from it all practical conclusions. Hus spread the new ideas in his sermons and books, he worked hard to win followers for these ideas, and he did his best to improve the poor state of the church as well as the religious and moral standards of the Czech people.

John Comenius was another outstanding example of the same type. Though his ideas about education of children were original, they were rather more practical than theoretical. His interest in improving man's life and serving humanity led him to organize modern schools in a number of countries. He also cherished the idea of serving humanity by spreading all available scientific knowledge through his book of all knowledge, the *Pansophia*.

Among modern Czech scholars T. G. Masaryk bears similar characteristics. His very thorough knowledge of the world's philosophy led him toward practical rather than theoretical achievements. He worked hard to build the philosophical foundations of Czech national life, to lift the standards of Czech scholarship, to improve the moral standards of public life and, finally, to free his nation from political subservience to Austria-Hungary. These three great men of Czech history were scholars with a related practical interest in the improvement of human life on the basis of thorough knowledge of contemporary scholarship.

Although many similar examples could be cited, let us give only two more contemporary scientists. Dr. Heyrovský, a Nobel prize winner, discovered polarography. Although he is a theoretician, his scientific achievement has high practical value. Another man, the first president of our Society, Dr. Hlavatý, proved the validity of Einstein's new bold ideas, thus rendering them useful in practice. Heyrovský and Hlavatý thoroughly mastered the latest developments of world science in their respective fields before they were in a position to make their contribution.

There is no full explanation for the above-mentioned attributes of Czech scholarship. Some of them are part of the old cultural heritage, and it is hard to trace their origin; among them are the strong interest in the scientific achievements of other nations, and the interest in human betterment and in practical applications of knowledge. These interests had already been typical of the Czech theologians who preceded John Hus. More recently, there have been additional reasons for their reinforcement. The struggle for the revival of national existence in the 18th and 19th centuries employed chiefly scholarly weapons. Political and economic weapons were not available to begin with. Linguists, historians, and students of national folklore started the movement. Members of other academic disciplines followed suit. Probably the suppression of national life by Austrian authorities was another reason for the prevailing respect for scholarship. Austrian authorities were strongly resented and the nation unconsciously looked to another high authority for help against the oppressive power of the imperial government. There was only one such authority available – the authority of scholarship, to which was partly transferred the very high prestige of the antagonistic imperial family and its government. This transfer was supported by the prevailing cultural change – the shift from irrational feudal authority to a more rational one. Thus, on the one hand, scholars had a strong practical inspiration for their efforts, and on the other, they gained that national prestige and esteem so characteristic of Czech culture. This tradition has survived practically to the present. The influence of contiguous German culture, with its high esteem for scholarship and scholars, supported this tradition considerably.

The respect for the scholar was, I think, strengthened by still another factor. Czech people living in the Austro-Hungarian empire had little opportunity to rise to high political and administrative positions. Thus, for a long time the scholars as well as artists were the leading figures of national life. Only much later were they joined by political and business leaders.

The fact that the nobility was, with few exceptions, German and, as such, completely alien to the national life, contributed to the eminence of men of knowledge who stepped easily into the roles of national leadership, especially historians, jurists, philosophers and men in related fields. The prevalent importance of national life certainly stimulated scholars to work hard and prove themselves. It also explains the fact that scholarly disciplines attracted relatively more talented people than did other areas of national life.

Knowledge and education proved themselves powerful weapons in the struggle for national survival, and, later, in the fight for political independence. But as early as in the sixteenth century the Czech grade schools were among the best in Europe, and Charles University was a great international center of learning before any German university was in existence. This ancient tradition of emphasis on education was strengthened by the national revival movement; again, it contributed to the regard for science and scientists.

High educational standards, the almost total literacy which was achieved by the end of the 19th century, and the large proportion of people with higher education, resulted in a well-informed, general interest in books. People in all social brackets frequently had sizable libraries in their homes. The love of books probably was in part the heritage of the secret readers of the Bible in the 17th and 18th centuries, who were known as "písmáci". At that time the Counter-Reformation forbade the reading of the Bible, but the obstinate descendants of Protestants read it secretly and analyzed it thoroughly.

Thus, in Czechoslovakia before World War II, the number of books (titles) published yearly was very high, as a matter of fact as high as in the U.S.,[4] although the population of Czechoslovakia was about one tenth that of the U.S. It is understandable that the authors of these books were esteemed more than those in cultures less interested in the printed word.

People of a relatively small nation engaged in building its own culture are likely to be much interested in the achievements of large nations, and, therefore, make great efforts to keep abreast of scholarly achievements. Larger nations seldom have such a strong incentive. In this respect it is perhaps significant that our relatively small nation had a translation of Durkheim's *Rules of Sociological Method* about fifteen years before the U. S., despite the widespread knowledge of French among Czech scholars. The proportion of grade school and secondary school teachers, public servants, clerks, and, of course, lawyers and physicians who bought scholarly books was larger than in many other Western nations.

The solid polyhistoric outlook of Czech scholars derived from the broad and thorough education given in the secondary schools. It was easier for an adult to maintain this outlook by additional reading than to acquire it, if handicapped by the inadequate curriculum of the secondary schools in some modern educational systems. Furthermore, the public expectation that an outstanding scholar had well-founded opinions on many current

---

[4] The *Statistical Yearbook of the United Nations* (1956) indicates that in 1937, 10,994 books were published in Czechoslovakia. In the U.S.A. the average number of books published in 1937, 1938 and 1939 was 10,873. In France, 8,124 books were published in 1938. The figures cannot be compared without qualifications, because the definitions of a book in Czechoslovakia, U.S.A. and France are not identical.

problems, even those remote from his special field, stimulated him to be well-informed on many current problems. With increasing specialization, this was less and less possible, but in some scholarly fields, especially philosophy, this characteristic of Czech scholars has survived to the present day.

Since the number of scholars in any given field was rather limited, the Czech man of knowledge was more stimulated by the larger group of people who conducted national affairs, and by the whole of national life, than he would be in larger nations. There was less intellectual stimulation among small groups of scholars in a particular field than is generally true in large nations. This is not dissimilar to the difference in atmosphere of a small college department of two or three professors and that of fifteen or twenty members. Books, of course, stimulate, too, but they can not compare with the stimulation of personal contact. In addition, the larger group allows for more specialization and division of labor, which in themselves may lead to better scholarly work.

Thus, a Czech scholar felt more responsible for the fate of his own nation than may a scholar of a larger nation. That is why there was rather a large number of scholars among Czech political leaders. The historian, Palacký, was a political leader of long standing, as were Masaryk and Beneš. The first and second struggles for independence in World War I and World War II were led by university professors. In the Revolutionary National Council which led the uprising against Germans at the end of World War II, both the chairman and one of the vice-chairmen were scholars.

A strong sense of public responsibility required the man of knowledge to serve as a dependable intermediary between the world's scholarship and Czech students and readers, as well as to be advisor, consultant or, perhaps, a leader in public life. This undoubtedly diverted much of the creative energy of some outstanding scholars, and prevented them from producing a greater number of original concepts and new ideas.

In order to gain a sharper perspective on the Czech scholar, let us compare his dominant motives and interests with those of scholars of other nations. The French scholar, for example, is much interested in general and abstract ideas.[5] Like his Czech colleague, he is basically an individualist. But the Czech scholar was so chiefly because he had not had enough opportunity to work as a member of a team, while his French colleague is likely to be individualistic by conviction, by choice and by his very na-

---

[5] E. M. Earle, *Modern France* (Princeton University Press, 1951), p. 82.

ture.[6] The French scholar's usual motive for academic achievement is chiefly personal satisfaction in producing original ideas,[7] and in brilliant logical thought.

The principal motive of the American scholar is probably his deep belief in progress. His strong point is the rich application of results of scholarship,[8] American and others, to the betterment of humanity and to the improvement of business and industry. In this respect he is ahead[9] of his practical-minded Czech colleague, and far ahead of his French colleague, who often loses interest in a problem as soon as he has solved it theoretically.[10] The American scientist may be labeled a pragmatist.[11] He likes to organize teamwork[12] carefully and to be a disciplined member of the team. He has an especially strong interest in facts and empirical evidence, but distrusts general and abstract ideas. He proceeds rather by careful steps than by the daring insight which is so typical of the French.[13]

The German scholar is probably chiefly inspired by his concern with the incompleteness of knowledge in his field. Something must be done about it. He feels it as his duty and he always obeys the voice of duty with willingness and pleasure.[14] On the other hand, another aspect of scholarly motivation in Germany is the romantic dedication to a lofty goal.[15] Despite that, some German scholars are also very practical-minded.

We may say, with qualifications, that the Czech scholar is chiefly heir to his predecessors from the era of the national revival. The French scholar is chiefly the product of the Century of Enlightenment, with its rationalistic convictions. The German scholar is mostly heir to the German Romantic Movement combined with the thoroughness, orderliness, and practicality of the German national character. The American scholar draws his inspiration mainly from the pioneers' tradition of hard work, from their deep sense of reality, from a necessity to be practical and to pull together in order to survive. He assigns less value to daring

---

[6] Maurice Canellery, *French Science*, p. 210.
[7] *Ibid.*, p. 211.
[8] R. M. Williams, *American Society* (New York, A. A. Knopf, 1960), pp. 428-429; E. M. Earle, *op. cit.*, p. 82.
[9] R. M. Williams, *op. cit.*, p. 310; Max Lerner, *America as a Civilization* (New York, Simon and Schuster, 1957), p. 226.
[10] E. M. Earle, *op. cit.*, pp. 81-82.
[11] R. M. Williams, *op. cit.*, p. 310.
[12] Max Lerner, *op. cit.*, p. 219.
[13] E. M. Earle, *op. cit.*, p. 82.
[14] W. Wundt, *Die Nazionen und ihre Philosophie* (Leipzig, A. Kröner, 1915), p. 86.
[15] M. Ginsberg in *The German Mind and Outlook* (London, Chapman and Hall), p. 65.

new theories than do his European colleagues, who still have much of the monastic scholars' ascetic dedication to spiritual pursuits.

Also the character of scholarship in small nations may differ from one to the other because of each country's special national conditions. An excellent example is the Messianic streak in the inspiration of Polish scholarship which is common to Polish national consciousness, as well.

We may wonder which traits of Czech scholarship have changed under the impact of the present political regime. There is no doubt that there are changes. Certainly there is more planning and teamwork than there was before. In Communist states, scholarship does not depend as much on the dedication of the individual as on governmental planning, particularly with reference to scientific institutions. There is more money for scientific work than ever before, and the prestige of scientific work has been enhanced by strong governmental interest. Public recognition of scientific achievements (at least those which suit the government) is widespread, and the economic position of scientists is very good. All this conforms to the Soviet cultural pattern. But, without a doubt, Czech scholarship pays a high price for the advantages offered by the Communist regime. The humanities and social sciences suffer more than the natural sciences and mathematics. They must, at least on the surface, accept the Marxian philosophy of social life and distort their work accordingly. There is a serious danger that the younger generation will not easily recover from the distorted presentation of truth as they receive it from their teachers. The old tradition of deep respect for truth may be contaminated, perhaps irreparably, if the regime endures for several more decades. On the other hand, the prevailing opposition to Communism among students may help young Czechs to resist Soviet influence. A large proportion of scholars are not Communists, and the students are aware of it. The Communist professors at the universities are generally not real scholars. Some of them are propagandists and popularizers of Communist ideology under scientific guise, who were promoted into scholarly positions without having had to meet necessary scientific requirements, and the students accept their teaching with reservations.

On the other hand, the prestige of scholarly work, its strong public support, the improved remuneration of scientists, and the new habit of team work may survive the present regime and prove valuable to the future development of scholarship, if only the present regime does not last too long.

The Role of the Intelligentsia in the Development of the Czechoslovak Society

JAN HAJDA

It is a common characteristic of underprivileged groups that they are ruled, but not led, by individuals whose qualification stems from the sanctity of tradition, sheer expertise, proximity to the existing centers of power, or membership in a prominent institution within the established social order. In contrast to these rulers, the leaders of the underprivileged generally derive their legitimacy from an ideal, a concept of utopia, glorified collective virtues, or heroic achievements. This contrast between leaders and rulers reflects their differing position within the social order and the degree to which their collective identity – as leaders or rulers – is crystallized. Among the rulers, membership in and attachment to central institutions obligates them to perpetuate, refine, and praise the Establishment, to identify it with the "highest good". In return, the Establishment lends them not only power and prestige, but also an enduring collective identity. On the other hand, the spokesmen and prophets of the poor, the dispossessed, and the conquered generally stand on the fringes of the institutional order, or outside it altogether. Consequently, their relationship to the established civil and religious authority is characterized by ambivalence, estrangement, or hostility. Having little to fall back on but their vision of the future, they are engaged in a perpetual search for identity, the perplexing examination of "Who am I?" and "What do I stand for?" Their frequently doctrinaire answers to these questions are only an outward sign of an internal insecurity.[1]

In view of these facts, it is not surprising that the vaguely related Czech dialect groups were transformed into a national collectivity in the course of the 19th Century by the intelligentsia, rather than the church, the bureaucracy, or the military. Nevertheless, a deeper understanding of this

---

[1] For the discussion of the nature of charismatic authority see especially Max Weber, *Essays in Sociology* (New York, Oxford University Press, 1946), pp. 245-252; and his *The Theory of Social and Economic Organization* (Glencoe, Illinois, The Free Press, 1947), pp. 358-391.

transformation can be gained only by answering the following question: Why were the intelligentsia so readily accepted as leaders by the Czech people?

The spontaneous acceptance of intellectuals as leaders of the people was not due simply to the lack of any alternative. Rather, it had its roots in the peculiar position of the Bohemian and Moravian aristocracy, the composition and orientation of the Czech intelligentsia, and the lack of Czech institutions of more than local importance.

The Bohemian and Moravian nobility consisted mostly of a small number of high aristocrats (in 1848 they totaled about 2,300, including family members), separated from the lower estates by a considerable social gap as well as by national origin.[2] Most Czechs regarded the aristocracy as foreign rather than native, as a group of intruders or invaders. The nobility, therefore, was not acknowledged as a source of leadership, but was looked on as a group external to, even though at the top of, the stratified system. Given this general ambivalence, or even hostility, to the hereditary élite, successful opposition to the nobility became an easy way of winning popular favor. It is probably not accidental that the intelligentsia emerged as legitimate spokesmen and organizers of the lower estates first in the cities and only later in the villages, where the aristocracy was more dominant.[3]

From early times, the Czech intelligentsia was populist. They were predisposed to populism because of their social origins. If a survey of the status of parents of 94 outstanding 19th century Czechs is a reliable indicator, then we can conclude that about one-half of the intelligentsia came from the ranks of peasants, artisans, and tradesmen.[4] Kinship and childhood friendship ties to villagers and urban artisans made them aware of the problems of the underprivileged, and kept them in touch with public opinion.

However, a more profound cause of this populism was the intellectuals' fear of Germanization and fear of rootlessness. In order to counteract their fascination with the cultural achievements of Austrian Germans, which threatened to leave them rootless, the Czech intelligentsia

---

[2] Hans Raupach, *Der tschechische Frühnationalismus* (Essen, Essener Verlag, 1938), pp. 17-25; Robert H. Lowie, *Social Organization* (New York, Rinehart and Co., 1948), pp. 380-406.
[3] Otto Bauer, *Die Nationalitätenfrage und die Sozialdemokratie* (Vienna, Brand, 1907), pp. 216-233; Oscar Jászi, *The Dissolution of the Hapsburg Monarchy* (Chicago, The University of Chicago Press, 1929), ch. IV.
[4] Jindřich Matiegka, "Psychoanthropologie Československa", in *Československá vlastivěda* (Prague, Sfinx, 1933), vol. 2, pp. 243-346.

created a competitive ideal of their own: an intense belief in the creativity and superior moral worth of the ordinary people, of the uneducated and unintellectual. Similarly, in order to combat their feeling of inferiority about their ethnic origin, they felt it necessary to demonstrate to themselves and others a far more intense attachment to their own nationality and people. These are the reasons for the passion for the mother tongue – the language of the ordinary people; the passion for history and glorification of the past and forgotten national virtues; the passion for folk songs, dances, costumes and customs, the living evidence for belief in the creativity of the people.[5]

Populistic ideology was an ideology of mission, a kind of secular evangelism and revivalism which gave the people a feeling of dignity and self-respect. In return, the missionary intelligentsia gained not only an attentive audince, but also an enthusiastic following.

But equal weight should be given to the fact that the institutional system of Czech intellectuals emerged as the first autochthonous system of greater than local importance in modern Czech history. The network of university, gymnasia, theaters, newspapers, magazines, publishing houses, bookstores, museums, orchestras, choral groups, artistic, scientific, and professional clubs and associations – this network was the first institutional expression of wide-ranging, non-parochial cooperation among Czechs, the first element in their own, rather than the Hapsburg, Establishment. Many of the monuments of intellectual achievement became national monuments. Thus, the creation of the National Theater was not just a great event for theater-goers and art lovers, but also an event in the nation's history. To the non-intellectuals it symbolized the fact that their educated peers, and with them the whole national collectivity, had "arrived", that they had proved their intrinsic worth.

This was really the fundamental difference between the intelligentsia and other potential leadership groups. While village priests, small-town civil servants, and non-commissioned officers in the Austrian Army could and frequently did work on behalf of the emerging nation, their effectiveness was checked by the supra-national, dynastic character of the organizations within which they worked. Their influence was primarily personal and localized. It did not rub off on the institution itself, because the top

---

[5] Otto Bauer, *op. cit.*; Elizabeth Wiskemann, *Czechs and Germans* (New York, Oxford University Press, 1938). For a valuable parallel see a penetrating treatment of the same problem in Edward Shils, *The Intellectuals Between Tradition and Modernity: The Indian Situation* (The Hague, Mouton and Co., 1961), chs. V and VI.

hierarchy of such institutions was *Kaiser-treu* (loyal to the Emperor) and ignored the non-official activity of its subordinates, or disapproved of it. Thus non-intellectual institutions – even though managed by sympathetic Czechs – never lost their public image as pillars of the Empire, and consequently they never won the deep affection of the Czech people.[6] They could and did become rivals of universities, theaters, and publishing houses only after the establishment of independence.

The growth of Slovak national consciousness was much more belated and, up to the First World War, rather insignificant. In Slovakia, as well as in other Hungarian parts of the Empire, the aristocracy preserved most of its monopolies, privileges, and an extreme social exclusiveness throughout the first two decades of the twentieth century. Its power was due not so much to its ownership of enormous estates as to its firm hold on the administration of the country. Unlike the Czech lands, the Hungarian regions preserved feudal self-government. There was no centralized state bureaucracy directly responsible to the monarch or prime minister and independent of the feudal lords. The chief administrators of each region were elected by, and responsible to, the local nobility. This control over the bureaucracy gave the aristocrats an absolute veto power over any significant enterprise, including religious, educational, artistic, and scientific institutions.[7]

Coupled with this power was the acceptance of the nobles by the peasants as a God-given, undisputed elite. Achievement and intrinsic worth were generally measured by an aristocratic yardstick. It is characteristic that the villagers refused to treat any Slovak as a member of the intelligentsia unless he spoke Hungarian or had graduated from a Hungarian gymnasium. Under the pressure from above and a threat of non-recognition from below, the majority of the Slovak intelligentsia not only readily accepted Magyarization, but became in fact non-hereditary members of the gentry.[8] They accepted the glamorous style of life, the generally conservative and traditionalist orientation, the somewhat contemptuous attitude toward the uneducated, and an aristocratic self-conception. They thought of themselves as forming a society for and by itself, as a group of the "chosen ones", as a part standing for the whole, rather than

---

[6] In justice we should note that a few noble families such as the Schwarzenbergs provided valuable patronage for some of the activities of the intelligentsia.
[7] Otto Bauer, *op. cit.*; Oscar Jászi, *op. cit.*; C. A. Macartney, *Hungary and Her Successors* (London, Oxford University Press, 1937).
[8] Anton Štefánek, "Slovenská storočnica", *Sociologická revue*, vol. XIV, No. 2-3, pp. 107-119.

as "missionaries" or "awakeners", as the Czech intelligentsia came to conceive of itself during the nineteenth century.[9]

Thus, to speak of the role of the Slovak intelligentsia in the development of the Slovak society before 1918 is no more than to speak of the heroic effort at self-preservation by the nucleus of dedicated and educated patriots. How small a group this was is indicated by the fact that the maximum estimate puts the total number of non-assimilated Slovak intellectuals, together with their family members, at 1,000, around the year 1910.[10] A larger leadership role was assigned Slovak intellectuals only after 1918, particularly after the dispossession of the Magyar aristocracy.

The unification of Czechs and Slovaks was conceived and carried out, in the initial stages by intellectuals rather than conspirators, career politicians, administrators, or conquerors. It was a task for dreamers and idealists rather than pragmatists (an undertaking of people with pragmatic concerns). It is sufficient to consider the fact that before 1918 educated Czechs had fewer acquaintances among Slovaks than among Germans, Poles, Yugoslavs, or Frenchmen, and that in the spring of 1918 the Czech populace still generally mistook Slovaks for Yugoslavs.[11] Similarly, on the Slovak side: the Czechophiles among the intelligentsia were few in number and politically insignificant. The great majority of educated Slovaks felt at home in Budapest or Vienna. To the few Slovak villagers who came in contact with the Czechs, the latter were strangers compared to the Magyars.[12] There were no joint Czecho-Slovak institutions or associations on which Czechoslovak unity could be built. The establishment of Czechoslovak society was the embodiment of an idea rather than the outgrowth of gradual political or economic processes.

This mutual lack of awareness and sudden joining of national fortunes had a good deal to do with the relative failure of Czech intelligentsia in Slovakia after 1918. Czech intellectuals transferred their secular evangelism to Slovakia without taking into consideration the fact that the structure of the Slovak society, particularly its traditional system of authority, was not and could not be responsive to their appeal. On the whole they

---

[9] Anton Štefánek, "Novoslováci", *Sociologická revue*, vol. VI, No. 3-4, pp. 272-277; Ignác Gašparec, "Maďarizácia v sociologickom ašpekte", *Sociologická revue*, vol. XIII, No. 4, pp. 247-257.
[10] Anton Štefánek, "Novoslováci", *op. cit.*
[11] Jan Hajšman, *Mafie v rozmachu: vzpomínky na odboj doma* (Prague, Orbis, 1933).
[12] Anton Štefánek, *op. cit.*; "Anketa o československej vzájemnosti", *Prúdy*, vol. V (1919).

did not fit the model of leadership which their audiences were eager to follow. And they set themselves to a task for which their methods were inappropriate: to transform, rather than to form, a nation.[13]

In conclusion, the particular roles played by the Czech and Slovak intelligentsia during the emergence of a national collectivity were neither accidental nor predestined. They grew out of existing social situations. They responded to the structural changes the society experienced, as well as to the growth and differentiation within the ranks of the intelligentsia itself. But these past roles left an enduring heritage for future generations to follow in times of crisis and distress.

---

[13] Anton Štefánek, "Češi na Slovensku", *Sociologická revue*, vol. XII, No. 1, pp. 22-26; No. 2-3, pp. 36-41.

The Development of Sociology in Czechoslovakia before World War II

JOSEPH S. ROUČEK

Strictly speaking, Czechoslovak sociology, when conceived as a systematic and academically acceptable discipline, began with Thomas G. Masaryk – although some of its ideas and concepts, as we shall show, can be found in Czechoslovakia's intellectual history.

The roots can be found, in fact, in the ideas of John Hus (1369-1415), a follower of Wycliffe and precursor of Luther, known mainly as a religious reformer, whose influence is still felt among the Czechoslovak peoples and their spokesmen. He advocated, for instance, definite ideas on social reforms, defending the rights of the peasants against the landlords, and his followers carried on within his "frame of reference" (as the modern sociologist would say) in the Hussite movement.[1] Peter Chelčický (1390-1460) added to Hus' opposition to the church authorities his own to that of the temporal powers. His idea of not resisting evil and of non-cooperation with the state impressed Leo Tolstoy, but was on the whole refused by Masaryk.[2] Of more lasting importance and influence was John Amos Komenský (Comenius) (1592-1670), whose works on education foreshadowed modern educational sociology.[3] In his book *The Labyrinth of the World and the Paradise of the Heart*,[4] he anticipated some

---

[1] T. G. Masaryk, *Jan Hus, Our Renaissance and Our Reform* (Prague, 1908), in Czech. See also Jan Herben, *John Huss and His Followers* (London, 1926) and Matthew Spinka's *John Hus and the Czech Reform* (Chicago, University of Chicago Press, 1941); see further Count Francis Lützow, *Life and Times of Master John Hus* (London, J. M. Dent, 1921).
[2] Peter Cheltschitzki, *Das Netz des Glaubens* (Leipzig, Kurt Wolff, 1914); Carl Vogl, *Peter Cheltschizki* (Zürich, Rotapfel Verlag, 1926), in German.
[3] Matthew Spinka, *John Amos Comenius* (Chicago, University of Chicago Press, 1945); S. W. Monroe, *Comenius and the Beginnings of Educational Reform* (New York, Scribner, 1907); J. A. Komenský, *Selected Works on the Reform of Science* (Leipzig, 1924), in German; etc.
[4] Translated by Matthew Spinka (Chicago, National Union of Czechoslovak Protestants in America, 1942).

of the problems of the technological civilization and of modern propaganda and its abuses.

Among the generation of the "Awakeners" who started the Czech Renaissance in the 18th century, there were many who, working in various fields, were aware of the related social and sociological aspects. Josef Dobrovský (1753-1829), founder of comparative Slavonic philology, anticipated a sociologically directed theory of language. The Slovak Josef Šafařík (1795-1861), provided valuable sociographic material in his philological work. Another philologist, Josef Jungmann (1773-1837), analyzed nationalism from a sociological viewpoint.

All these writings, however, contained only sociological tendencies, since their authors specialized in other fields, and were, moreover, heavily influenced by speculative German romanticism, chiefly by Herder. This applies, also, to the Slovak poet and pan-Slavist, Jan Kollár (1793-1852). Hegel's influence shows itself in the work of the most important Czech historian, František Palacký. Karel Havlíček (1821-1856), the founder of modern Czech journalism, applied the sociological attitude to his observations on Russia and to his studies of political developments and traditions in Great Britain.[5] His sober descriptions were in deliberate opposition to the method of speculative romanticism. Czech philosophers like Augustin Smetana (1814-1851), Jan Hanuš (1812-1869), František Klácel (1808-1882), Karel Štorch (1812-1869), and others showed occasional interest in sociology. Under the influence of Herbart, and, partly, of Comte and Mill, were Gustav Adolf Lindner (1828-1887)[6] and Emanuel Makovička (1851-1890).

The turning point in Czechoslovak sociology came with Thomas G. Masaryk,[7] who took the decisive step from speculation to scientific

---

[5] T. G. Masaryk, *Karel Havlíček* (Prague, J. Laichter, 1896), in Czech.

[6] G. A. Lindner, *Ideas on the Psychology of Society as Basis of Social Science* (Prague, 1871), in Czech.

[7] Joseph S. Rouček, "Masaryk as Sociologist", *Sociology and Social Research*, XXII (May-June, 1938), 412-420; "President Masaryk of Czechoslovakia", *Current History*, XXXI (March, 1930), 1109-1112; "Internationally Minded State", *World Unity*, VI (April, 1930), 43-49; "Thomas Garrigue Masaryk as Politician and Statesman", *Social Science*, VI (May, 1932), 272-278; "Thomas Garrigue Masaryk – Advocate of International Justice", *World Order*, L (April, 1935), 12-14; "Eighty-fifth Birthday of President Masaryk", *Social Science*, X (April, 1935), 201-202; "A Great Teacher, Democrat and Statesman: Dr. Thomas Masaryk Reaches his Eighty-Fifth Birthday", *World Affairs Interpreter*, VI (April, 1935), 81-91; see also E. E. Eubank, "T. G. Masaryk: Sociologist", *Social Forces* (March, 1938), 455-462; Herben, Hartl, Bláha, *T. G. Masaryk, Sa vie, sa politique, sa philosophie* (Prague, Orbis, 1923), in French; Evžen Štern, *Le socialisme de Masaryk* (Brussels, L'Eglantine, 1926), in French; Emile Fournier-Fabre, *La vie et l'oeuvre politique et sociale de M. Thomas Garrigue Masaryk* (Paris,

research. While acknowledging his general indebtedness to Comte, he entirely disagreed with him in many respects. Quite unlike Comte, he stressed, throughout his life and writings, religion and its guiding relevance in morals. He firmly denied Comte's concept of religion as merely a preliminary historical stage in the development toward science. Furthermore, he rated psychology as a scientific discipline in its own right. His first larger work[8] was significantly based on research, field-work, facts and figures, brushing away the speculative tradition and turning to the study of environments. Even in later works he consistently applied the sociological attitude; his critique of Marxian socialism, especially, was based on the findings of contemporary sociology.[9] The same applies also to his standard work on Russia,[10] and to his writings on history and political questions.

Masaryk's influence on Czech sociology was overwhelming. His most outstanding follower was Edward Beneš (1884-1948), his successor in the office of President of Czechoslovakia. Beneš started his literary career with several works on the history of socialism, later took an active part in the political development of his country, in collaboration with Masaryk, and finally became the chief historiographer of Czechoslovakia's struggle for freedom. Next to Masaryk, Durkheim exerted some influence on Beneš, as, to a lesser degree, did Pareto. His studies on pan-Slavism follow Masaryk's ideas, on the whole. As a Westerner by education, he tried, even in his theoretical works, to reconcile East and West in the light of a progressive democracy implemented by social justice and completed by economic democracy.[11]

G. Ficker, 1927), in French; see also the valuable bibliography, Avrahm Yarmolinsky, ed., *Tomáš Garrigue Masaryk* (New York, New York Public Library, 1941), listing works by and about Masaryk.

[8] *Suicide as a Social Phenomenon in Modern Civilization* (Vienna, 1881), in German.
[9] *The Philosophical and Sociological Foundations of Marxism* (Vienna, C. Konegan, 1899), in German; *The Scientific and Philosophical Crisis within Contemporary Marxism* (Vienna, Die Zeit, 1898), in German, 117-119; 133-134 and 150-152.
[10] *The Spirit of Russia* (New York, Macmillan, 1919), 2 vols.
[11] Most of Beneš' earlier works are in Czech only. Among them are the following: *The Question of Nationalities* (Prague, 1909); *Our Political Education and the Necessity of a College of Social Sciences* (Prague, 1910); *Socialism in England* (Prague, 1911); *The Evolution of Modern Socialism*, 4 vols. (Prague, 1910-1912); *The Political Partisanship* (Prague, 1910-1912); *The Political Partisanship* (Prague, 1912); *The Problem of Alcohol Production and Abstinence* (Prague, 1915). An exception is *The Austrian Problem and the Czech Question* (Dijon, 1908), in French. Most of the later works were published also in translation. The most important of them are the following: *Destroy Austria-Hungary!* (Paris, 1916), in French; *The Slavs and Western Europe* (Prague, 1923), in Russian; *The Problem of the Small Nations after the World War* (London,

Outstanding among Czechoslovak sociologists is another follower of Masaryk, Inocenc A. Bláha (1879) who took an early interest in philosophy, especially in ethics,[12] but eventually turned to sociology under the influence of Durkheim and Lévy Bruhl. In his works much material is assembled and carefully analyzed.[13] While Bláha was a Professor of Sociology at the University of Brno, Josef Král (b. 1882) taught sociology at the Charles University, Prague, specializing in the history of sociology and philosophy.[14] One of the most original thinkers among Czechoslovak sociologists is Emanuel Chalupný (b. 1879), first a follower of Masaryk, later his opponent in many respects. He was also one of the most prolific writers in his field. He disagreed with Masaryk in the conception of Czech history and in the classification of the sciences, in which he placed sociology between biology and psychology. He carried his interest into the fields of journalism and history of literature, and dealt aggressively with current political and ideological problems.[15] Josef Fořt (1850-1929) specialized in the sociology of economics. J. L. Fisher (1894), a philosopher, discussed in several remarkable books current problems in politics and civilization in the light of sociological analysis.[16] Emanuel

---

1926); *The World War and Our Revolution*, 3 vols. (Prague, 1927); *France and New Europe* (Paris, 1932), in French; *Germany and Czechoslovakia* (Prague, 1937); *Democracy Today and Tomorrow* (New York, Macmillan, 1939). After World War II he published in Czech *Six Years in Exile* (Prague, Orbis, 1946) and the first volume of the *Memoirs* (Prague, Orbis, 1947); see also: F. Crabitès, *Beneš, Statesman of Central Europe* (London, Routledge, 1935) and Joseph S. Rouček, "Edward Beneš as a Sociologist", *Sociology and Social Research*, XXIII (September-October, 1938), 18-24; "Edward Beneš", *World Unity*, XIV (June, 1934), 136-146; "Fiftieth Birthday of Dr. Edward Beneš", *World Affairs Interpreter*, V (July, 1934), 154- 158. See also J. S. Rouček (ed.), *Twentieth Century Political Thought* (New York, Political Library, 1946), in which W. J. Ehrenpreis deals, in Chap. XXIV, 524-531, with Masaryk's and Beneš' work.

[12] *Philosophy of Morals* (Prague, 1922), in Czech.
[13] His more important works, all of them in Czech: *Sociology of the Worker and Peasant* (Prague, 1925); *Child Sociology* (Prague, 1927); *Sociology of the Intelligencia* (Prague, 1937). See also Joseph S. Rouček, "Trends in Educational Sociology Abroad", *The Educational Forum* (May, 1939), 491-493.
[14] His *Czechoslovak Philosophy* (Prague, 1937), in Czech is a valuable and comprehensive survey. Chap. IX, 183-220, deals with sociology.
[15] All his works are in Czech. His *Introduction into Sociology* (Prague, 1905) was one of the first systematic Czech books on this subject matter. Other important works: *The Character of the Czech People* (Prague, 1907); *Havlíček* (Prague, 1908); *The Mission of the Czech People* (1910). After 1916, he published 10 vols. of his monumental *Sociology*, projected in 15 vols. His last book, *The German Danger* (Prague, 1947), traced Nazism back to earlier forms of German nationalism.
[16] *The Future of European Culture* (Munich, 1929), in German; *The Crisis of Democracy* (Brno, 1935), in Czech; *The Third Reich* (Brna, 1932), in Czech; see also Ehrenweis, *loc. cit.*

Rádl (1873-1942), noted biologist and philosopher, showed occasional interest in sociology, as did the leading Czech literary critic, F. X. Šalda, (1867-1937). The subject matter of features in the Czech national character was treated by a host of writers, among whom were V. Dvorský, J. Matiegka, the anthropologist, F. Peroutka, brilliant Czech journalist and playwright, E. Rádl, J. Kallab, F. Žilka, K. Hoch, O. Vočadlo, F. V. Krejčí, V. Mathesius, J. Kohn, and many others. Analysis of the Czech national character seems to be, as a matter of fact, an obsession with sociologically inclined Czech intellectuals.

Otakar Machotka (1899) travelled extensively in the United States,[17] and considered problems of morals and of the family in the light of sociology,[18] and as already explored by Bláha. A. Boháč, C. Horáček and J. Auerhan were concerned with population problems, and Bláha, Matula and Galla with social stratification. Problems of economics were analyzed on the basis of the sociological method by Maiwald, Evžen Štern, J. Macek, Modráček, and others. The sociological foundations of theoretical politics were studied, chiefly under the influence of Masaryk and Beneš, by Kallab, Weyr, J. L. Fischer and A. Obrdlík. O. Butter analyzed the social function of the newspaper; Bláha, Chalupný, Fischer and J. Kohn specialized in regionalism. Lány was outstanding in the sociological evaluation of criminology, and the theory of social work was studied by the philosopher, Břetislav Foustka, Modráček, Galla and Fryček, J. B. Kozák, J. L. Hromádka and Vasil K. Škrach (Masaryk's bibliographer and able interpreter); Bláha studied the history of sociology as well.

The Slovaks also made definite contributions to sociology. Anton Štefánek was probably among the leaders. This group also published, for several years, the *Sociologický sborník* (Sociological Review).

Sociology was taught at the universities of Prague, Brno and Bratislava by Král, Bláha, Chalupný, Fischer, Galla and Machotka, as well as at various other schools. In 1920, the Social Institute was founded in Prague; it published the periodical *Sociální revue* (Social Review). In 1925, the Masaryk Sociological Society was founded, and elected a number of outstanding American sociologists to its membership; in 1930 the periodical *Sociological Review*,[19] and in 1932, the periodical *Social Problems*

[17] *Amerika* (Prague, 1946), in Czech.
[18] *Moral Problems in the Light of Sociology* (Prague, 1927), in Czech; *Contributions to the Sociology of the Family* (Prague, 1932), in Czech.
[19] *Sociologická Revue*, 13 volumes until 1947; Arnošt Bláha, Editor. See also: Joseph S. Rouček, "Sociological Periodicals of Czechoslovakia", *American Sociological Review*, I (February, 1936), 168-170.

began to appear. As Becker says in the conclusion of his chapter on Czechoslovakia, "There is no country anywhere of equal size that can display so impressive a list of contemporary sociologists or such a range and intensity of sociological activity".[20] It should be noted, also, at least in passing, that Czechoslovak sociologists showed an early and consistent interest in educational sociology.[21]

After the Communist coup d'état in 1948, the Czechoslovak sociologists tried to survive under the ever-growing Communist pressure. A short time thereafter, however, all true sociological literature disappeared, and whatever reappeared under the name of sociology was but a Marxian interpretation of what the Soviet authorities conceive as sociology, tainted with Pan-Slavic and anti-American tendencies. Some sociologists simply disappeared, and have not been heard of again; a few others, such as Machotka,[22] succeeded in escaping and are scattered in the United States, Egypt,[23] England and France.

---

[20] H. E. Barnes and Howard Becker, *Social Thought from Lore to Science* (Boston, D. C. Heath, 1938), II, 1067.

[21] See: G. Gurvitch & W. E. Moore (eds.), *Twentieth Century Sociology* (New York, Philosophical Library, 1945), Chapter XXV, V, "Czechoslovak Sociology", by Joseph S. Rouček. In Rouček's opinion, Lindner "can be considered a founder of Educational Sociology".

[22] Machotka was formerly Professor of Sociology at Charles University and the author of *American Sociology, Socially Needed Families in Prague*. He is now Professor of Sociology at Harpur College.

[23] Ullrich was Professor in Egypt until his untimely death in early 50's.

Anticipated Changes in Czechoslovakia

JIŘÍ NEHNĚVAJSA

1. No one can tell for certain what the future holds in store. But we know that tomorrow will follow today, and that there is going to be a day after tomorrow, a year after this year.... What tomorrow will be like depends on what men do today. The shape of the next year, the next decade, the next century, is slowly emerging out of all the actions of all men.

We may be unable to say what the future will be like. But images of the future have a direct bearing on what men do today.[1] Men have desires. They prefer some states of affairs. They would like to prevent other situations from arising. Men have expectations. They attach probabilities to alternative developments. Men also estimate what others want, particularly those whose behavior is significant as a major codeterminant of the future. Out of the fabric of desires and expectations, a choice is formulated regarding the present mode of conduct.[2]

2. The futures of Czechoslovakia are inextricably linked to the futures of the Cold War. In some ways, the Cold War as a whole subsumes Czechoslovakia's destiny. A nuclear war between the superpowers on one hand, or disarmament at the other end of the Cold War spectrum, are as much salient alternatives which Czechoslovakia must face as are numerous other prospects in the world picture.

But there are other potential, political futures of Czechoslovakia which significantly modify the nations's posture in the world without solving the Cold War as a whole. Thus, Czechoslovakia may experience an anti-

---

[1] Jiří Nehněvajsa, *Elements of Project Theory: From Concept to Design* (= Air Force Office of Scientific Research, TN-60-1361), October, 1960. – Albert S. Frances, *Anticipations and Behavior: Notes on an Intellectual Tradition* (A.F.O.S.R., AFOSR-1712), December, 1961.
[2] The underlying theoretical model of decision-making parallels the work of Franco Modigliani, for instance, Franco Modigliani and F. E. Balderston, "Economic Analysis and Forecasting", Chapter 20 in Eugene Burdick and Arthur J. Brodbeck, *American Voting Behavior* (Glencoe, Ill., The Free Press, 1961).

Communist revolution. Such a revolution may succeed in overthrowing the Communist dictatorship, or it may fail. Czechoslovakia's Communism might sever its ties of subordination to the Kremlin; a nationalistic version of Communism might emerge, much as in Yugoslavia, and perhaps like the recent Albanian model. The Communist leaders of Czechoslovakia, now or in the future, may also seek to reestablish genuine democracy; the nation might therefore "evolve" a Western-type regime.

Of course, there exist many significant interactions among the alternatives. A revolution in Czechoslovakia, successful or not, might lead to a limited engagement of Communist and Western powers, and this, in turn, might mushroom into a nuclear-spasm war. Efforts of Czechoslovakian Communists to nationalize the regime, and make it relatively independent of Moscow, might force the Soviets' hand and, in turn, lead to revolution within the USSR, with many other consequences.

Apart from all these intricate linkages of possible futures, it is still meaningful to ask: How likely is a revolution in Czechoslovakia? Its success or failure would be subordinate to the revolution itself, although not to the triggering of such a revolution. How likely is the emergence of nationalistic Communism? How likely is internal democratization?

3. As a small aspect of our total research program, parliamentarians and university students in a number of countries were asked, in 1960, 1961, and again in 1962:

How probable were anti-Communist revolutions in Communist nations by 1965-1966?
How probable was a revolution in the Soviet Union by 1965-1966?
How probable was a revolution in Communist China by 1965-1966?

They were similarly asked about the desirability of such revolutions. Furthermore, the respondents were provided with a listing of other Communist nations (the roster including Albania, East Germany, Czechoslovakia, Hungary, Bulgaria, Poland, Rumania, North Viet-Nam, and North Korea), and asked which of these might experience an anti-Communist revolution in the respective time frame.[3]

---

[3] The methodology on which this report is based has been developed in the parent Project Outcomes, sponsored by the Behavioral Science Division, Air Force Office of Scientific Research, Office of Aero-Space Research, under contact AF-49-(638)-743 at Columbia University (1959-1961) and AF-49-(638)-1116 at the University of Pittsburgh (1961-). Under contract AF 49-(638)-1011, the salient aspects of the methodology have been reported by Jiří Nehněvajsa, *An Application of Project Outcomes (Dilemma of Viet-Nam)*, January, 1962. The studies included parliamentarians and university

The probabilities of anti-Communist uprisings turned out to be relatively high and rather stable over a period of time. They were high in contrast with many of the alternative Cold War futures. They remained approximately the same from 1959 to 1962. For instance, Brazilian legislators (1960) assigned of a likelihood of 4.59, and Finnish parliamentarians (1960), 4.52 to revolutionary prospects. In 1961, Brazilian parliamentarians responded with 4.97; and Finish legislators, 3.30. (The latter average is lowered chiefly by an increased number of Communist legislators in the sample who, as might be anticipated, attached zero probabilities to anti-Communist revolutions.) French legislators (1961) yield an average likelihood of 4.39; in 1962, the average is 3.89. Yet, anti-Communist uprisings in either the Soviet Union or China were not expected. The probabilities are quite low and stable over time, regarding the Soviets; they are low and somewhat on the rise, regarding prospects for revolutionary activity within China. Communist respondents yielded zero probabilities in all countries named at all times.[4]

Asked about other Communist nations, the respondents singled out primarily (a) East Germany, (b) Hungary, and (c) Poland. For example, 51.0 percent of the 1960 Brazilian parliamentarians, and 50.0 percent of them in 1961, consider probable revolutionary prospects in East Germany; 30.0 per cent (1961) and 21.0 percent (1962), respectively, of Japanese legislators similarly cite East Germany. Hungary, as another example, is referred to by 49.0 percent of the 1960 Brazilian congressmen, and by 46.4 percent in 1961. Thirty-five per cent of the 1961 Japanese legislators

---

students in Brazil and Finland (1960-1961), Germany (1961), France, India, Japan and Spain (1961-1962). Samples of respondents from rural Arkansas and rural Ontario were also chosen (1962), as well as samples in Puerto Rico and St. Croix, Virgin Islands (1962). All in all, the respondents were evaluating the probabilities and desirabilities (along with other variables) of thirty-five alternative, future states of affairs of the Cold War.

[4] Revolutions in Communist nations are not viewed as particularly desirable. On the scale ranging from (+3) for maximally desirable to (−3) for maximally undesirable, Brazilian legislators (1960) yield + 0.38 and identically in 1961; Finnish Parliamentarians, + 0.22 (1960) and + 0.13 (1961). Indian Congressmen of 1962 actually consider such revolutions undesirable (−1.32), as do Japanese members of the Parliament of 1961 (−0.05). The Spanish legislators are most favorably disposed to such revolutions: + 2.22 in 1961 and + 2.37 in 1962. The student samples, if anything, are even less prone to view anti-Communist revolutions favorably. Brazilian, Indian and Japanese students actually evaluate such propensities negatively; and while other groups are more positive, the averages are quite low. The results are similar when the respondents were asked about the desirabilities of an anti-Communist revolution in the Soviet Union (which is, at the same time, believed to be highly improbable). All respondent samples, however, are somewhat more disposed to view a revolution in China as desirable.

mention it; only 8.4 percent in 1962. Although very few respondents in 1960 and 1961 discussed Albania, the percentages increases in 1962.[5]

Czechoslovakia's revolutionary prospects are mentioned far less frequently than those of East Germany, Hungary, and Poland. But revolutions are expected in Czechoslovakia by many more respondents – legislators and students alike – than are uprisings in Bulgaria, Rumania, Albania (except for 1962), North Viet-Nam, or North Korea. Furthermore, the percentages generally decline from 1960 through 1961 to 1962. For instance, 23.8 percent of all 1960 respondents mention Czechoslovakia; in 1961, 14.2 per cent; in 1962, 5.7 percent. As a result, Czechoslovakia is viewed as the most stable of the technologically advanced satellites, but less stable than Soviet-dominated nations of the Balkan region and of Asia.

4. Comparable information is available on tendencies toward the emergence of nationalistic Communism. If anything, the probabilities are higher than the corresponding chances for revolutions. Brazilian legislators (1960), 4.89; in 1961, 5.55; Indian legislators (1961), 3.39, and in 1962, 2.74, as compared with 2.82 and 1.95 for revolutionary changes. The respondents do, indeed, anticipate that China's Communism is increasingly becoming less Moscow-dominated and less Kremlin-oriented. Prospects for "nationalistic" Communism in China seem high to our interviewees.[6]

In 1960, nationalistic Communism is expected more frequently only for Poland (by 48.6 per cent of all respondents) than for Czechoslovakia (42.0 percent); in 1961, the percentages are lower, but they appear in the same order (Poland, 36.6 per cent; Czechoslovakia, 22.1; Hungary, 21.4;

---

[5] Further results have been reported in Jiří Nehněvajsa, *Anticipated Alignments of Nations in the Cold War* (= *A.F.O.S.R.*, *AFOSR*-92), January, 1961. – Stanley E. Shively and Martin Gannon, *Anticipated Changes in Communist Nations* (= *A.F.O.S.R.*, *AFOSR*-2317), March, 1962.

[6] Emergence of nationalistic Communism (in contrast with directly Moscow-controlled patterns of alignments) is much more desirable to all respondent groups than are anti-Communist revolutions. Still, while this future is positively valued, the students attach lower (positive) desirabilities to it than do the legislators, country by country, save for Finland (where the legislator samples include sizeable numbers of Communists, whereas the students are quite non-Communist, if not anti-Communist). Similarly, the growth of nationalistic Communism in China is believed quite desirable. It should be noted, of course, that despite the higher desirabilities of this outcome, other alternatives are far preferable to all respondent groups: particularly "complete or substantial disarmament" (which is not expected), and "reconciliation with agreements which all parties would honor" (which is also not expected).

East Germany, 18.0 and so on). In 1962, Albania is cited most frequently (43.2 per cent); Poland next (20.9 per cent); then Czechoslovakia and East Germany (12.5 and 12.3 per cent respectively). In simple terms this means that although Czechoslovakia is not particularly expected to evolve a nationalistic version of Communism independent of Moscow (although, perhaps, dependent on Peking), the respondents cite it much more often than they do in relation to revolutionary activity. Yet, from 1960 to 1962 the percentages have declined throughout, with the exception of Albania – a nation now in an open split with the Kremlin.

5. How about democratization? All in all, evolution of democratic governmental forms in the Communist nations is not expected. The probabilities are quite low. They are extremely low specifically for the Soviet Union and China.[7] The averages are uniformly lower than those concerning the possibilities for revolutions, and these, in turn, are substantially lower than those which consider the prospects for nationalistic Communism.

In 1960, only 17.1 per cent of Brazilians and Finns (legislators and students) mention Czechoslovakia in this context, far fewer than those who anticipate revolutions (23.8 of total) or nationalistic resurgence within the Communist party (42.0 per cent). East Germany (30.9), Poland (25.9), and Hungary (24.6) are mentioned more frequently; the remaining Communist nations with a much lower frequency.

All these percentages declined by 1961, although the order in which the nations are mentioned remains the same: East Germany (20.3); Poland (20.3); Hungary (14.1); Czechoslovakia (10.3). And again in 1962, the order is maintained, marked by a further decline in the percentages of respondents who anticipate eventual democratization of the Communist nations, or some of them: East Germany, 15.8 per cent; Poland 6.8 per cent; Hungary, 4.6 per cent; Czechoslovakia, 2.2 per cent.

6. The basic results can be readily summed up:[8]

---

[7] Democratization (i.e. evolution of Western-type governmental and social forms) is even more desirable than nationalistic Communism's emergence throughout the samples. This holds for democratization of the Communist nations in general, and of the Soviet Union and China in particular: but the basic frustrations of today's world are again reflected in the fact that these futures are believed quite improbable.
[8] Jiří Nehněvajsa, *Futures of the Cold War* (= *A. F. O. S. R., AFOSR*-2315), March, 1962, provides a quick summary of the results of the research in its first two years.– Jiří Nehněvajsa and Morris I. Berkowitz (et al.), *Cuban Crisis: Meaning and Impact* (University of Pittsburgh, October, 1962).

(a) The probabilities of anti-Communist revolutions in various Communist nations are generally fairly high – higher than, for instance, prospects for alternative forms of World War III, or chances for reconciliation or disarmament.

(b) These estimates of probabilities remain fairly stable between 1959 and 1962.

(c) The probability of a revolution within the Soviet Union is low and keeps being low over time.

(d) The probability of a revolution in China was low over time, but has been increasing into 1962 from 1961 and 1960.

(e) Emergence of nationalistic Communism in various Communist-dominated nations is anticipated as even more probable than anti-Communist uprisings.

(f) The probability of nationalistic Communism in China is fairly high, and it, too, has been on the rise over the years.

(g) Prospects for gradual evolution toward democratic social forms in the Communist nations are considered very unlikely.

(h) These probabilities are low both for the Soviet Union and for China, and neither rise nor decline between 1960 and 1962.

(i) In general, changes in Czechoslovakia are anticipated by fewer legislators and students, regardless of time, than changes in East Germany, Hungary and Poland, but more than are shifts in the regimes in Rumania, Bulgaria, North Viet-Nam and North Korea.

(j) Of the major alternative changes, emergence of nationalistic Communism in Czechoslovakia is postulated far more frequently than either democratization or anti-Communism rebellions.

(k) In terms of nationalistic Communism, the respondents refer to Czechoslovakia second only to Poland; whereas, otherwise, Czechoslovakia consistently ranks fourth (revolutions and democratization, in all countries studied, and at all times).

(l) The percentages of respondents who anticipate shifts in specific Communist satellites decline consistently over time. The percentages are lower in 1961 than in 1960; lower in 1962 than in 1961. This result holds for revolutionary changes and democratization, as well as for nationalistic upsurge.

Thus, the data indicate a degree of stabilization in the total Communist bloc, save for increased difficulties with China. This seems to reflect very well the actual unfolding of events in the past several months. The Soviet bloc is becoming less vulnerable – at least as far as our respondents see it – to internal drastic shifts. It is becoming more vulnerable to a Soviet-

Chinese schism, although the conflict is not expected to lead to a Soviet-Chinese war.

Among the smaller satellites, of which Czechoslovakia is one, least stability is associated with East Germany. By and large, the more technologically advanced satellites are viewed as least stable – of these, Czechoslovakia is considered, however, the safest from the Soviet standpoint.

The instability of the East German regime does not appear directly related to the Berlin issue either. Asked about alternative futures of Berlin, by far the greatest number of respondents in all countries expect that the present situation will continue essentially unchanged, at least for some time to come.

Above all, the data clearly indicate that influentials – such as parliamentarians and university students – in various parts of the world and at various points in time, do not expect the Czechoslovak question to be resolved in Czechoslovakia, or by Czechs and Slovaks. Rather, the information emphasizes that the future of Czechoslovakia, apart from resolution of the Cold War problem *as a whole*, will be but the continuation of the dreary existence in a totalitarian system which has characterized the nation's past decade and a half.

The destiny of Czechoslovakia appears never to have been less in the hands of Slovaks and Czechs. But this is a fate which Czechoslovakia is sharing with scores of small nations in a world of giants.

ECONOMICS

Teleological Construction of Economics
Professor Karel Engliš' Contribution to Economic Thought

JAROSLAV GEORGE POLACH*

Dr. Karel Engliš, who was born in Hrabyně, Silesia, in 1880 and died in the summer of 1961, started his teaching career before World War I as a professor of economics at Polytechnic Institute in Brno. During the period of the First Republic he taught economics and public finance at Masaryk University in Brno, whereof he was also elected the first Rector. After Czechoslovakia was liberated in 1945 and her universities reopened, Engliš was chosen by his peers to lead the academic community once more, this time as a Rector of Charles University in Prague. Moreover, during his lifetime, Engliš served successfully, at one time or the other, as Minister of Finance, and Governor of the Czechoslovak National Bank. It was he who deserved most credit for the successful monetary and fiscal reforms in Czechoslovakia.[1] In view of all these responsibilities, it is remarkable that Engliš still managed to find time for writing, and prolific writing, at that. He wrote competently on a wide range of subjects in theoretical and practical economics, and, sometimes, politics.[2]

It would, therefore, be difficult, if not outright impossible, to try to present Engliš' contribution here in its entirety. This would be a task too general and hardly meaningful. Therefore, I will restrict myself to discussing a few essential propositions which Engliš himself considered most significant in his teaching and which deal with, as he called it, the noetic foundation of economics. We may perhaps better refer to it as the methodology of economics.

---

* The author wishes to express his thanks for valuable comments he received during the final preparation of the text, particularly from Professor Emeritus Dr. Fritz Karl Mann and Professor Dr. Ernest Correll. Responsibility for the shortcomings of the paper and opinions expressed therein rests, obviously, solely with the author.
[1] The extent of the general esteem Engliš earned during his academic and public career was best manifested in the Munich days. At that time, according to Dr. Peter Zenkl, who was then a member of the Government and a prominent political leader, Engliš was considered a potential presidential candidate around whom the nation could rally.
[2] A selected bibliography of Engliš' publications is offered in the appendix.

In the first part, I will summarize Engliš' thoughts, following closely his own words and arguments and adding only what is necessary for fuller understanding. In the second part, I intend to comment on the significance of these ideas and their affinity with other economic models.

I

Meticulous as always, Engliš preceded his excursion into economic thinking with an inquiry into logic.[3] To know how we generally formulate the systematic connection in our thoughts about and among the things of the world was, for Engliš, a step preliminary to any real understanding of the particular processes of individual scientific systems. From there on he proceeded to delineate logical structure of economic thought so as to establish economics as a science in its own right. He saw the fundamental issue in this respect in the delineation of the subject of economics, that is, in defining the economic quality of our propositions and conclusions so that there would be a clear differentiation between economics and other social sciences. As he pointed out, none of the prevalent approaches could solve this problem because of the erroneous identification of the economic principle (that is, the particular rationality proper to economics) with economical characteristics, and, further, because only individual self-interest was considered to be this "economic-economical" rationality.[4]

Much like the German philosopher, H. Rickert, Engliš starts his inquiry with the proposition that it obviously cannot be the diversity of observed phenomena which makes for the diversity of sciences because the same phenomenon may be a subject of cognition and understanding of several logically ordered systems of thought, that is, of sciences.[5] In other words, one science does not appropriate the subject of its propositions and conclusions to the exclusion of another science; thus, for in-

[3] The following account is chiefly based, unless otherwise noted, on the following works of Engliš: *Teleologie jako forma vědeckého poznání* (Praha, F. Topič, 1930), hereinafter quoted as *Teleologie*; *Soustava národního hospodářství* (Praha, Melantrich, 1937), Vol. I, pp. 6-163, hereinafter quoted as *Soustava*; *Teorie hodnoty a hodnocení* (Praha, Melantrich, 1947), hereinafter quoted as *Hodnocení*. The principal Engliš theses subsequently expounded above may be traced, however, throughout all his principal writings quoted in the appended bibliography.
[4] See especially his *Základy hospodářského myšlení* (= *Sbírka spisů právních a národohospodářských*, Sv. 21) (Praha, 1922) pp. 38 ff.; *cf.* also Engliš' criticism of Liefmann's theories quoted here in the appended bibliography.
[5] Engliš acknowledges Rickert's influence in *Teleologie*, p. 11.

stance, an aspect of human conduct may be the subject of medical science as well as of law or economics. Ultimately, Engliš arrives at the conclusion that it is the mode of cognition and understanding which is the decisive criterion for constructing a separate body of scientific knowledge. This particular mode must be such as to assure a consistent logical procedure and also the sameness of the substantive content of the entire structure of propositions.[6] Consequently, he narrowed his task to finding the particular method by which we conceive and understand economic propositions.

Engliš' approach to this problem is essentially rooted in the Kantian dualism between the world which *is*, and the world which *ought to be*; i.e. the worlds of *Sein*, and *Sollen*.[7] That, however, does not mean Engliš believed there is another world in addition to that we assume we know exists. He accepted scientific *monismus* but what he did not accept is the assumption that to understand and explain phenomena in our world, we must conceive our propositions on only one level, namely that of existence. In other words, he rejected the idea that the only acceptable principle of scientific rationality is causality. Recognizing the validity of causal rationality in the area of existence Engliš argues that this method is not an appropriate mode of cognition and understanding for phenomena which involve human will, such as purposive acts of men. In such instances, a coherent and logically consistent conceptual framework may be constructed only if the principle of finality is employed. Accordingly, he then divides the entire scientific thought into two, respectively three, great categories.

One group includes all sciences whose logical structure of concepts is based on a descriptive explanation in terms of cause and effect. This is the world of ontological knowledge. In this cognitive process there is no true valuation since ontological qualities do not polarize and represent differences in degree only with respect to a conditionally accepted scale of measurement (e.g., temperature scale, etc.). The other group encompasses sciences which seek to understand and explain phenomena of the real world by conceiving them as "postulates", that is, as desirable for the realization of some purpose (*télos*).[8] This is the teleological rationality also

---

[6] *Ibid.*, pp. 12-14.
[7] *Ibid.*, pp. 22 ff.
[8] Engliš recognizes still another non-ontological scientific approach, that is, normology, used in the normative science of law. In effect, he acknowledges his great indebtedness to his colleague, Professor F. Weyr, and also to Professor Hans Kelsen, whose ideas about a normative theory of law provided Engliš with the necessary stimulus in his search for a method peculiar to economic analysis (*Cf., Soustava*, p.

called finality. Whereas in ontological cognition we look for cause and effect, teleological relationship is between purpose and instrument. Thus, one purpose may serve as an instrument, or a subordinated purpose to a higher, superordinated purpose. That means that the entire logical structure of thought in this group of sciences is teleologically ordered, since human conduct is interpreted with respect to an anticipated postulated goal. Engliš, however, emphatically warns against assuming that the concept of a desired purpose is a psycho-physical act, which obviously can be the object of medical observation, though not of economics. The concept of purpose, as it is used in Engliš' theory, is a purely logical construction which simply imputes to a subject a certain desire. In other words, teleological method uses hypothesis which should explain a typical behavior, by hierarchically ordered postulates. To illustrate the difference between this and the principle of causality, under which we conceive of phenomena merely that they are or are not, Engliš suggests looking at the purposive phenomena through the lens of human interest.[9] What appears then is the spectrum of desires which reflect these interests and explain the transitive order of purposes as successive levels of instruments serving to advance the attainment of still another and higher goal, up to the primary purpose. Though it may be evident from what I have said up to now, I think I should underline that the teleological method as conceived by Engliš must not be identified with the search for an ultimate superna-

---

XI). The relationship of normology to teleology is, however, beyond the scope of this paper. It may suffice to mention merely that Engliš believed that normative sciences are, in a way, a subgroup in the larger teleologically ordered systems and that a teleological stage precedes the normative explanation in law. Thus in *ibid.*, pp. 72-87. On the somewhat different attitude of the exponents of the normative theory of law, see František Weyr, *Teorie Práva* (Brno, Orbis, 1936); Hans Kelsen, *General Theory of Law and State* (Cambridge, Massachusetts, Harvard University Press, 1949); and Adolf Procházka, "Normativní teorie a tvorba práva", *Sborník Prací k Padesátým Narozeninám Karla Engliše*, ed. F. Weyr (Praha, Orbis, 1930), pp. 436-455. In the same publication is an article by Vladimír Vybral, a Professor of Public Finance at Masaryk University, giving an excellent review of the background to Engliš' theories; see "Problematika principů hospodárnosti v hospodářské teorii", *Sborník*, pp. 93-143.

[9] *Hodnocení*, pp. 29-44; *Teleologie*, pp. 29 ff. Of course, there are branches of economics as, e.g., economic history, economic statistics, etc., in which the "executed" purposes are the subject of analysis. Here the cause-effect principle is appropriately used. But for theoretical, anticipative cognition of economic behavior, only the teleological approach is practical. It should also be mentioned that Engliš strongly rejects any suggestion, as found in Kant and Wundt, that the *nexus finalis* is simply a reversed *nexus effectivus*. Engliš' arguments are involved and too lengthy to be examined here but may be found in *Soustava*, pp. 6-13, and namely in his *Apologia finalitatis*; *rozprava o Tardym* (Praha, Knihovna Sborníku věd Právních a Státních, 1947).

tural purpose and eternal truth.[10] For him, it is a method of cognition by which *human* behavior is understood and logically analyzed by means of a hierarchy of *human* purposes resulting from *human* volition. Engliš had no more use for the teleological approach as practiced in the Middle Ages than had Bacon.

Of course, the imputation process is not limited to the purpose desired by an individual. It is obvious, though, that a postulated purpose which explains human purposive behavior can be equally well imputed to a social organization, particularly a state. This does not mean we should start analyzing the decision process of different societal groups in whose power it is to formulate and impose – by some established procedure – an overall social (national) purpose. Such analysis would be as much out of place here as is the already rejected examination of an individual's psychophysical act of desiring. On the other hand, once it is granted that a purposive human process may and should be also logically conceived and understood in a way that permits imputing a purpose to a societal decision, then significant theoretical ramifications emerge. It leads Engliš directly to his delineation of economic quality and fundamental dichotomy in economic models.[11]

Engliš derives economic quality, that is, the subject of economics, from the formal construction and material content of the primary *economic* postulate. He then defines such an *economic postulate* in two ways. On the one hand, when constructed by individuals, it is a personal ideal of satisfaction, and, on the other, when constructed by a societal process, it is some kind of objective ideal of the optimal development of society. Thus human purposive conduct motivated by either of the primary economic postulates thus formulated represents economic phenomena and is the subject of practical economic sciences. The logical and understanding process by which we arrive at our proposition hierarchically derived, i.e., teleologically organized, from the one or the other primary economic postulate constitutes economic theory.

Collaterally to the two fundamentally different primary economic postulates, we have, on one side, an economic theory in which economic phenomena are explained by individually postulated purposes. This is what we call an atomistic individualistic model. On the other side is a solidaristic system in which economic behavior is to be understood and explained only in relation to an over-all societal purpose. A *caveat* is

[10] *Hodnocení*, pp. 64-67.
[11] Their best presentation can be found in Engliš' *Hospodářské soustavy* (Praha, Všehrd, 1946), p. 66b, hereinafter quoted as *Soustavy*, 1946.

advisable here, however, in order to avoid identifying this social purpose as a simple summation of individual purposes because these, being subjective, are neither comparable nor additive. The societal purpose, on the contrary, is objective, does not depend on a subjective evaluation, and is objectively communicable and comparable. It is obvious that between those two theoretical extremes, mixed systems, as, for instance, the national cooperative system are also possible.

Let me now turn briefly to concepts of utility, scarcity, and economic goods to see how they are affected by this methodological division. Generally speaking, as Engliš points out, utility or scarcity and the related concept of economic goods do not exist on the level of ontological knowledge. Utility or disutility, scarcity or abundance are economic qualities of acts and things (goods) which cannot be conceived without teleological thinking because they derive their conceptual validity only from a purpose for which they are demanded as instruments (intermediary purposes).[12] Evidently then, a notion of utility, etc., as seen in an individualistic model sharply differs from its synonym derived from the solidaristic economic primary purpose. Moreover, the transitive character of purposes *within each model* accounts for the similarly changing pattern of utilities, cost, scarcities, etc., although within one model they are all linked together by the hierarchy of superordinated purposes, and ultimately the primary postulate, so as to form an organic totality of purposes (*věcná solidarita účelů*).[13] The cost is, in effect, an amount of disutility incurred when procuring (producing) an instrument necessary to the realization of a desired purpose. The cost is a logical construction, not psycho-physical disutility, and must always be construed with respect to the same purpose as is utility evaluation, though in the opposite direction. This by itself excludes the validity of the notion of foregone opportunity as an alternative cost because (1) the foregone opportunity does not affect utility evaluation derived from a given purpose, i.e., it does not create any disutility; (2) it is a logically inconsistent intermingling of utility and cost considerations. The latter analyzes alternative disutilities created in the different ways by which an instrument for a *given postulate* can be produced (procured); the former considers alternative utilities resulting from the application of a *given instrument* to different postulates.

From the organic solidarity of purposes, which is contingent on maxi-

---

[12] *Soustava*, pp. 25-34.
[13] *Ibid.*, pp. 34, 52-53; compare with this "a personal solidarity of purposes" which characterizes a system in which all persons, i.e., a nation, are the object of care under the primary purpose set up by a state.

mization of the primary purpose, results a process of equilibrating relative marginal utilities of different intermediary purposes (instruments). The equilibrating factor, once more, is the purely logical concept based on the teleological structure of economic propositions rather than a derivation from a psychic act as envisaged in the Austrian School, which is based on the operation of Gossen's laws. Moreover, as Engliš points out, he is speaking about the *relative* marginal utilities of different purposes (instruments) and not about the absolute "Grenznutzenniveau" of the Austrian School.[14]

Needless to say, there are still other significant facets of Engliš' ideas, but the limited scope of this paper precludes their examination. Still, I hope that I have sufficiently elucidated what Engliš considered the paramount result of his analysis, that is, the apodictic relationship between economic theory and teleological method.

II

Of course, the teleological character of economic propositions has been recognized by many other economists, before and after Engliš, although explicitly by only a few. Among them was Thorstein Veblen, though in his case it was exactly the teleological quality of economic theory for which he banned economics from the category of (evolutionary) sciences. Science for him might have been based only on causality.[15] Schumpeter was similarly dissatisfied, at least in his early writings, with the inapplicability of causal reasoning to economics and tried to replace it with a functional relationship.[16] Later he also recognized that economic proposition may be a legitimate subject of a teleologically ordered system of thought but hesitated to embrace this concept because of the danger of a "teleological error" which he saw in an exaggeration of teleological rationality.[17] Schumpeter simply doubts that men really wish to realize their purposes in the most rational way.[18] In a sense, Schumpeter's interest in the entire

---

[14] *Ibid., pp.* 55-57.
[15] Thorstein Veblen, "Why is Economics Not an Evolutionary Science", *The Portable Veblen*, ed. Max Lerner (New York, The Viking Press, 1950), pp. 215-240, particularly pp. 234-235.
[16] Joseph A. Schumpeter, *Das Wesen und der Hauptinhalt der theoretischen Nationalekonomie* (Leipzig, Duncker und Humboldt, 1908), cf. pp. XVI, 47, 91-95.
[17] Idem, *History of Economic Analysis* (New York, Oxford University Press, 1954), p. 58, note 4.
[18] This, of course, is hardly an argument against teleological method since it attacks the principle of rationality in general and thus, in effect, makes any logical construction,

issue was an extension of a long debate about economic quality and method then in progress in Europe, particularly among German economists. Among the most prominent were A. E. Schäffle, Max Weber, H. Dietzel, R. Stammler, J. Liefmann, F. v. Wieser, A. Ammon, and O. Spahn.

Recently, it seems, Professor Stigler also has become dissatisfied with the prevalent concept of economics, since he has considered it necessary to remove the word "ends" (and that, we may say, is the same as "purposes") from his previous definition of economics. As he explains, he wishes to exclude from economics "... a vast area of which economists have no professional knowledge."[19] I doubt, however, that by this change the problem of a logical structure of economic propositions and conclusions is clarified or that we can hope to escape the fact that whenever we conceive of a choice, preference, selection, etc., our cognitive process, understanding and formation of concepts is, by force of logic, teleological.[20] Otherwise, however, I believe, Professor Engliš would have agreed with Professor Stigler's statement because this circumstance that economists do not know much about the logic which governs their economic conclusions, was the explicit reason why Engliš undertook his methodological inquiry.[21]

I am, however, inclined to believe that resistance to the teleological method is motivated by exactly what economists so strenuously claim to have excluded from their theory, that is, a value judgment, or in short, a preference for a certain concept of economics and with that underlying social order, excluding simply by definition all other conceptual frameworks of economics. In a teleologically constructed system of thought

---

even if based on causal rationality, a doubtful proposition. Moreover, it runs close to a confusing identification of economic rationality with economical characteristics.

[19] Cf. George J. Stigler, *The Theory of Price* (New York, Macmillan Co., 1950), p. 12, and the 1957 edition, p. 1, note 1. His new definition seems to run parallel to the one previously advocated by Heinrich Dietzel, *Theoretische Sozialökonomie* (Leipzig, C. F. Winter, 1895), I, p. 159.

[20] Cf. especially Morris Raphael Cohen, *A Preface to Logic* (New York, Meridian Books, 1956), particularly chapter VI; further, Stephen C. Pepper, *The Source of Value* (Berkeley-Los Angeles, University of California Press, 1958), chapters 1, 2, 3, and 9; also Ludwig von Mises, *Theory and History* (New Haven, Yale University Press, 1957), pp. 22-25, where he pointedly observes that no matter whether we utter it or not, a decision concerning selection is a value judgment (i.e., a teleological proposition). It may be of interest also to compare with that a Marxist refutation of teleological method in Georg Klaus, "Relationship of Causality and Teleology from the Cybernetic Viewpoint", *Deutsche Zeitschrift für Philosophie* (1960), No. 10, pp. 1266-1277, translated by U.S. Department of Commerce, Ref.: *JPRS*, 8374.

[21] *Teleologie*, pp. 9-14; *Soustava*, pp. 4-5, namely the last paragraph on p. 5.

there is, as I have shown above, no *a priori* logical ground on which to espouse and justify as the only permissible ordering principle one or the other purpose. And this seems to be the crux of contention against teleological method on both sides of the argument, as it may be gathered from references quoted above, in footnote 20.

Schumpeter, of course, unhesitatingly admitted that in addition to an economic theory based on methodological individualism, there is a legitimate alternative constructed with respect to a "soziale Betrachtungsweise" (which we may identify here with a societal purpose). Nevertheless, Schumpeter rejected this alternative on the ground that methodological individualism proved its value by practical results and, *eo ipso*, made the societal-purpose approach "überflüssig".[22] For my part, I fail to see the validity of arguments which bar scientific inquiry on such rather arbitrary grounds, even if supported by the authority of Schumpeter. In a way, I prefer Professor Knight's attitude, which indicates the ethical basis for our preference of methodological individualism when he says that what we mean by economics is the science as it has developed "with definite reference to the practical needs of *free* society" (my italics) ... of which the purpose is to "create conditions under which individuals will be able to realize their individual objectives".[23] By this procedure, if we disregard the definitional problems of some of the concepts, a societal purpose is more or less banned as a permissible methodological approach in our economics. This unfortunately, does not and can not remove the issue from the world of reality in which, as we know, the economic behavior of men is often governed by the hierarchy of societal purposes. Therefore, and with all deference to Professor Knight, I believe that Engliš' approach is superior, since it also permits us to understand and explain the allocation of resources in other systems than those we prefer.

It should not be assumed, however, that Engliš personally favored the societal-purpose economy over an individualistic model. On the contrary, when it came to political preferences, Engliš certainly shared those of Professor Knight. He was strongly attacked by the Communists for this attitude, particularly after 1945, when he warned against the introduction of solidaristic elements in the Czechoslovak economy, arguing, solely on the basis of his theoretical models, that it would lead to the loss of demo-

---

[22] Schumpeter, *Das Wesen*, p. 95.
[23] Frank H. Knight, *On the History and Method of Economics* (Chicago, University Press, 1956), pp. 144-145; cf. also Von Mises, *op. cit.*, p. 34. It seems that Professor Knight assumes that teleological method means analysis of the social processes by which societal purpose is formulated, a notion which has no place in the construction of Engliš' teleology as a formal logic. *Cf.* Knight, *op. cit.*, p. 150.

cratic freedom.[24] His political opinions notwithstanding, Engliš saw no reason, however, to deny validity to and exclude from scientific analysis a societal purpose. After all, in his inquiry into economic methodology, he was not seeking to impose and justify one or the other purpose in preference to another. His aim was to construct a *formal* science of teleologically oriented logic and nothing more, but also nothing less. Thus teleology to Engliš is a purely analytical tool for understanding and interpreting the economic behavior of men without reference to particular social philosophies.

This formal attitude differentiates Engliš also from those economists, non-Marxists, who, in contrast to Professor Knight, might see a societal purpose as the "natural" viewpoint for economics; this is the case, for instance, with Friedrich von Wieser.[25] Otherwise, however, there is considerable affinity between Engliš' models and Wieser's treatment of different economic calculations in different forms of society. And quite naturally, Engliš is very much akin, in spite of his criticism of its many ideas, to the Austrian School of economics in which he spent many of his formative years.[26] Another parallel exists between Engliš and some American economists (mostly his contemporaries), such as John Bates Clark, F. A. Fetter, R. A. Seligman, J. Maurice Clark, etc. But when it comes to a formal construction of a model, then, for my part, I see the strongest resemblance between Engliš and Pareto. The latter's "colline du plaisir", particularly when considered in connection with his residue and indexed ophelimities are not too far from similar hierarchically ordered utilities derived from correspondingly indexed intermediary purposes under a primary postulate. Engliš' selection of a purpose as an ordering principle in the model, however, is believed to be more objective and therefore preferable to pleasure in the teleological method.[27] The closeness of both models is even more clear from Professor Hicks' ex-

---

[24] See Vladimír Kadlec, *Kritika Engliše a jeho hospodářských soustav* (Praha, Práce, 1948). Though nominally disguised under the label of socialism, the whole criticism is typically Communist with all arguments of Marx, *Antidühring*, and Lenin thrown in. It is interesting to note in this connection that the Communists used Schumpeter's opinions about democratic socialism against Engliš; cf., *ibid.*, p. 7.

[25] See his *Natural Value* (Introductory analysis by W. Smart, editor. New York, Kelley and Millman, 1956), p. 55. Wieser's propositions are, of course, based on much deeper philosophical grounds than space permits me to examine here. However, the ideas of W. Windelband may cast more light on the notions described above.

[26] Lewis H. Haney, *History of Economic Thought* (New York, Macmillan Co., 1949), p. 819, places Engliš in the Austrian School among Schumpeter, von Mises, Wieser, Hayek, Philippovich, etc.

[27] On this point, see Pepper, *loc. cit.*

position of demand,[28] once we realize that the whole discussion of a weak or strong ordering of preferences and their transitive character is nothing other than a system of thought teleologically organized.[29]

In spite of all the affinity between Engliš and other economists, it seems to me that he was the only one who succeeded in establishing a method peculiar to economics, and who built on this foundation a logically coherent and complete system of economic rationality which permits us, as pure science should, to explain all aspects of economic propositions in any system. It seems to me also that his approach has now been fully vindicated by the development, for example, of linear programming, or the search and need for theoretical and practical criteria in the new areas of economic theory, as in the management of resources[30] and the development of underdeveloped countries. Our present approach cannot satisfactorily explain the allocation of resources in these cases without taking refuge in this somewhat nebulous zone of "welfare economics". And the Marxists can deal with these issues only under the old clichés of the class struggle and imperialist wars.

Thus, I might best summarize Engliš' contribution to economic thought as lying in two areas. First, Engliš, as a thinker, clarified the cognitive and understanding process behind economic theory, and consequently provided us with a more effective conceptual framework of economic analysis. The rather limited impact it had outside Czechoslovakia is attributable, I think, chiefly to the unfavorable combination of historical conditions in 1938 and 1948 which prevented the full exposition of Engliš' ideas in other languages exactly at the crucial moment of their ultimate formulation.[31] Therefore, the second area of his activity, that is, as a university professor, may seem to have a more immediate, recognizable impact. In fact, Engliš as a teacher stimulated great intellectual interest in economics, attracted more academic attention to this discipline, which,

[28] J. R. Hicks, *A Revision of Demand Theory* (Oxford, Clarendon Press, 1951), chapters III-V.
[29] *Cf.* Cohen, *loc. cit.*
[30] The central issue is that of public policy and "relative preferredness of alternatives", i.e. of goals. Cf. particularly, John V. Krutilla, *Welfare Aspects of Benefit-Cost Analysis.* Reprint No. 29 (Washington, D.C., Resources for the Future, Inc., 1961); further Irving K. Fox and Henry P. Caulfield, Jr., *Getting the Most out of Water Resources.* Reprint No. 28 (Washington, D.C., Resources for the Future, Inc., 1961). A review of prevalent theories in the field of resources expecially with respect to the issue of conservation may be found in Orris C. Herfindahl, "Goals and Standards of Performance for the Conservation of Minerals" (unpublished lecture delivered at the 1962 Western Resources Conference, Golden, Colorado, August 7, 1962).
[31] In addition to some of his publications in German, Engliš' *Finanční věda* was translated by Dr. Milič Kybal into Spanish (see the appended bibliography).

in Czechoslovakia, as elsewhere on the Continent, had suffered somewhat from having been placed in the legal curriculum. Moreover, his ideas gave rise to a vigorous school of thought which proved to be the leaven in the development of economic sciences in his country, an achievement which many teachers seek, but only a few attain.

APPENDIX

Selected Bibliography From Professor K. Engliš' Writings,[32]
compiled by Eva B. Polach[33]

Books:

Apologia Finalitatis; rozprava o Tardym ("Apologia Finalitatis; Discussion on Tardy") (Praha, Knihovna sborniku věd právních a státních, 1946). Engliš here denies the validity of Tardy's suggestion that finality is reversed causality.

Finanční věda. Nástin theorie hospodářství veřejných svazků ("Principles of Public Finance. Outline of Economic Theories of Public Corporations") (Praha, Borový, 1929). Also in German as *Finanzwissenschaft. Abriss einer Theorie der Wirtschaft der öffentlichen Verbände* (Brünn-Prag-Leipzig, R. H. Rohrer, 1931). Also translated into Spanish by Dr. Milič Kybal as *Karel Engliš' Introduccion a la ciencia financiera* (= Colección Labor, Sección X, Economía, no. 399-400) (Barcelona, 1937).

Grundlagen des wirtschaftlichen Denkens (Brünn, Rohrer-Verlag, 1925).

Handbuch der Nationalökonomie (Brünn-Leipzig, Rohrer Verlag, 1927).

Hospodářské soustavy ("Economic Systems") (Praha, Všehrd, 1946).

Národní hospodářství. Příručka ("Economics Manual"), 2. vydání (Brno-Praha, Borový, 1929).

O poznávání a hodnocení. Rozprava se Zd. Neubauerem ("About Cognition and Valuation Process. Discussion with Zd. Neubauer"). Vyd. 1 (Bratislava, Nákl. Právnickej fakulty slovenskej univerzity. V gen. komisi V. Linhart, 1947).

O řízeném hospodářství ("About Planned Economy") (= *Bráfova knižnice hospodářská*, sv. 1) (Praha, Melantrich, 1935). In German as *Regulierte Wirtschaft* (Praha, Orbis, 1936).

Peníze ("About Money") (Nákl. Úřednického peněžního ústavu v Brně, 1918).

Problémy hospodářské teleologie ("Problems of Teleology in Economics") (= *Sbírka spisů právn. a nár. hosp.*, sv. XLV) (Brno, 1930).

Teleologie jako forma vědeckého poznání ("Teleology as a particular form of epistemology") (Prague, F. Topič, 1930). German edition as *Begründung der Teleologie als Form des empirischen Erkennens* (Brno, Rohrer-Verlag, 1930).

Teorie hodnoty a hodnocení ("The Theory of Value and Valuation") (Praha, Melantrich, 1947).

Theorie státního hospodářství ("Theory of State Economy") (Praha, F. Topič, 1932).

Soustava národního hospodářství ("System of Economics"), sv. I & II (Praha, Melantrich, A. S., 1938).

---

[32] Only publications relevant to the subject under discussion in the preceding part of the paper were selected. Translation of Czech titles is provided and, where practical, an explanatory note was added.

[33] Library of Congress, Publishers' Liaison Section.

Vybrané kapitoly z národního hospodářství ("Selected Chapters from Economics") (= *Knihy pro každého*, roč. III, sv. 3) (Praha, Státní nakladatelství, 1925).

Základy hospodářského myšlení ("Fundamentals of Economic Analysis") (= *Sbírka spisů právnických a národohospodářských*, sv. XI) (Brno, 1922). Also in German, published by Rohrer-Verlag, Brno, 1927; reviewed, for instance, by Professor R. Streller in *Zeitschrift für die gesamte Staatswissenschaft*, Bd. 83 (1928), pp. 350 ff.

Articles:

"Bilimičovy námitky proti teleologické teorii hospodářské" (Bilimič's Objections Against the Teleological Construction of Economics), *Obzor Národohospodářský*, 1932, pp. 585 ff. The same is published in German as "Zum Problem der teleologischen Theorie der Wirtschaft", *Zeitschrift für Nationalökonomie*, 1933, pp. 220 ff.

"Erkenntnistheoretische Kritik der Grundlehren Liefmann's", *Zeitschrift für die gesamte Staatswissenschaft*, Bd. 88 (1930), pp. 240 ff.

"Erkenntnistheorie und Wirtschaftstheorie", *Jahrbücher für Nationalökonomie und Statistik*, III. Folge, Bd. 77 (1930).

"Hospodářská hodnota" (Economic Value), *Obzor Národohospodářský*, 1927, II.

"Hospodářství a hodnota v Schackově hospodářské morfologii" (Economics and Value in Schack's Economic Morphology), *Obzor Národohospodářský*, 1931, pp. 677 ff and 794 ff.

"Das Liefmann'sche Gesetz des Ausgleiches der Grenzertraege in der Konsumwirtschaft", *Jahrbücher für Nationalökonomie und Statistik*, N. F., Bd. 109 (1917), pp. 385 ff.

"Hospodářské zjevy jsou jednotné" (The Economic Phenomena Sameness), *Obzor Národohospodářský*, 1927, I.

"Probleme des wirtschaftlichen Denkens", *Zeitschrift für die gesamte Staatswissenschaft*, Bd. 84 (1928), pp. 578 ff.

"Psychický a teleologický subjektivismus v cenové teorii" (Psychical and Teleological Subjectivismus in the Theory of Prices), *Obzor Národohospodářský*, 1930, pp. 81 ff.

"Sociologický důkaz o nemožnosti teleologického výkladu směny" (Sociological Proof of the Impossibility of Teleological Interpretation of Barter), *Obzor Národohospodářský*, 1932, pp. 441 & 513 ff. This is somehow a misleading title of Engliš' answer to Maiwald's proposition that a teleological argument is not possible to apply to a barter.

"Die wirtschaftliche Theorie des Geldes", *Archiv für Sozialwissenschaft und Sozialpolitik*, Bd. 47 (1920), pp. 271 ff.

"Weddigenova sociologická teorie hospodářská" (Weddigen's Theory of Sociological Economics), *Obzor Národohospodářský*, 1929. See also "Weddigen's soziologische Wirtschaftstheorie", *Jahrbücher für Nationalökonomie und Statistik*, III. Folge, Bd. 76 (1929), pp. 161 ff.

"Užitek relativní a užitek mezní" (Relative and Marginal Utility), *Obzor Národohospodářský*, 1928, 405 ff. and 510 ff.

"Teleologická teorie hospodářská a normativní teorie právní" (Teleological Theory in Economics and a Normative Theory), *Obzor Národohospodářský*, 1929, I, II.

"Tschechoslowakei", in *Die Wirtschaftstheorie der Gegenwart*, eds. H. Mayer, F. A. Fetter and Rich. Reisch, 4 vols. Volume One: *Gesamtbild der Forschung in den einzelnen Ländern. Friedrich Wieser, in Memoriam* (Wien, J. Springer, 1927), pp. 193 ff.

Tomáš Baťa – Pioneer of Self-Government in Industry

The effect of self-administration of workshops and departments upon the world-wide growth of the Bata Organization

ANTHONY CEKOTA

Among the few men of Czech origin who have left a world-wide imprint upon the economy of many nations during this century, Tomáš Baťa occupies a unique position. He revolutionized the shoe industry in a way resembling Henry Ford's revolution of the automobile industry. At the time of his death in 1932, he was not only one of the greatest Czechoslovak industrialists; he was also one of the very few business leaders in the world who found an answer to the world-wide economic depression which was engulfing the United States and Europe.

The subject of this short paper is to outline his main ideas, born in the heat of his struggle with post-World War I crises and transplanted into the minds and hearts of thousands of men and women of Czechoslovak origin with whom he applied these ideas.

The effect of his basic ideas is visible even today, 30 years after his death, not only in the survival, but also in the expansion of the world-wide Bata Organization. Although its parent establishment was lost, first to the Nazis and then to the Communists, this Organization now consists of 73 companies, operating in 68 countries of the Free World. Actually it is in business with every one, with the exception of the Communist States and their satellites. If nothing else, this one single fact makes it worthwhile to investigate his basic ideas and their application in the modern economy of his, and of the present, generation.

Contrary to the views expressed by certain people during his life, Tomáš Baťa emerged from World War I with an enterprise engulfed in tremendous financial and economic difficulties. The Company, which had been under military command for four years producing army shoes, suffered heavy financial losses when the Austro-Hungarian Empire disintegrated. The disappearance of the Company's debtor turned its creditors, two great Czech banks, practically into its masters. The only reason they did not take over the business was that they knew they would never get even a fraction of what they carried against him in their books.

The large fire which destroyed the materials warehouse in 1919 brought this situation to the brink of catastrophe.

For several years Tomáš Baťa struggled to rebuild the factory for civilian business and to keep his creditors satisfied. However, in the fall of 1922 with the arrival of the first great post-World War I depression, the situation appeared hopeless. Czechoslovakia, a country with about 13 million people, had more than 400,000 workers unemployed. Inflation was raging all over Central Europe, as well as in Germany, making it very difficult to export to the neighboring countries whose currency was disintegrating.

Baťa, who in 1921 had exported shoes in the value of Kč. 64,400,000, within one year lost three-quarters of this business (the export in 1922 amounted to Kč. 15,400,000). On top of this, Dr. Rašin's financial policy, followed by the Czechoslovak Government at that time, drove the international value of Kč. up by 400% (4 x) compared to its average international quotations in 1921. This policy improved the position of heavy industry and creditors, but severely crippled the light and secondary industries. Many of them went into bankruptcy and the rest were forced to cut down production and reduce their staff.

After listening for two days to the various manufacturers speaking at the Conference of Czechoslovak Industrialists Association in Prague in 1922, Tomáš Baťa took the floor to outline his plan for dealing with the new situation. What he said was basically the following: "Gentlemen, for the past two days I have learned from all the speakers here what the Government should do to revive the industry. No one, however, mentioned what he would do, or what we should do. I am not the Government and politics is not my business. I am a shoemaker and our customers, the farmers, are coming to our stores saying: 'I received for my wheat only half of what I used to get last year and I am not going to buy your shoes until they cost half as much'. Gentlemen, we are going to cut the prices of our shoes in half, and from now on we are going to sell them for half the former price".

He was not a popular man with the industry when he left Prague, but he was a very serious man when he called all the company's employees together in Zlín and announced his plan: "The war must come to an end also in economy. From 1914 until today prices and wages have been rising continuously. Inflation is rampant and people in our country are crossing the border to shop in Germany or Austria. Factories are closing down and many manufacturers are saying 'Let's wait until the storm blows over and winter passes'.

There are two courses of action we can take, either to follow the trend and wait, or to cut all our figures in half and work. I am resolved to start selling shoes for half the present price, but the Company cannot do it alone. I am proposing to reduce wages and salaries by 40% and work. To those who will work with us, the Company will sell food and other commodities for half the present price. Our population needs shoes and I am confident that by working, we will find the ways and means to expand and not only restore wages to their present nominal level, but also increase them. If we stop working we are lost. Business is like a fish – you cannot expect to pull a fish out of the water, leave it on the bank and hope to find it still alive when you return several days later. What you will find instead is a smelly dead fish, beyond recovery".

His proposition was accepted by the workers without enthusiasm, but with dogged determination. The Czechoslovak public took the Baťa stores by storm. Within a few weeks inventories were turned into cash. However, the real problem remained in the factory, i.e. how to produce shoes for half the cost. Wages and salaries were only part of the production cost – perhaps 20 to 25%. Thus their reduction solved 10 to 12% of the problem. The remaining 38 to 40% represented the unknown factor.

Searching for the answer to this unknown factor, Tomáš Baťa discovered man – and the hidden potential of productive power within the mind and heart of man. It would take a book to describe how he discovered it – and what he did with it. Basically, however, he did the following:

He separated a small group of workers, about 40 or 50, and organized them into one small workshop. He then prepared a complete budget outlining the cost of everything which went into the production of shoes in this workshop. He allocated to this cost a manufacturing profit of about 10%. Then he called the group together, not once, but frequently, and what he said to these employees was basically the following: "This is your business. The figures in this estimate represent the true cost. I propose that you watch it daily and make an accounting of the cost and result at the end of each day. The foreman and those among you who influence this cost will receive in addition to your wages a share in the workshop's profit.

Those who are cutting leather or material shall account for it daily and everyone will share in the calculated profit.

By doing this we are changing the management of the business. It will begin where it should – in the minds and in the hearts of each one of you. Your hands we can buy – your hearts we want to win, and I want to win them by taking you into full confidence. We are fighting for the life of this business. You need it as much as our customers and our nation need it. Someone must find a way out of this vicious spiral created by the war and continuing in increasing costs and prices and unemployment".

I do not think that there was any factory in the country or for that matter anywhere else at that time, where individual workers knew the exact cost of everything they were doing. Certainly there was no other place in the world where they knew at the end of the day the precise financial result of their work, and at the end of the week, the Balance Sheet with the final figure for their workshop.

The "operational profit" was split 50/50 – half to the company and half to the employees (added to their regular piece-rate earnings). Within the employees' group the foreman received about 10% of the profit, while the keymen got 2% and participants 1%. No one was permitted to charge anything to such a workshop's account without the signature and approval of the foreman.

Not all the employees shared in such results. Those in junior positions or those engaged in operations which had no decisive influence upon the economy and quality of the work received only their regular weekly wage. Thus, a type of society was created within one small unit of the factory resembling society in a free democratic country, where a man's fortune depends upon his own efforts and the value of his service to the public.

After testing this experiment in one workshop for several months, Tomáš Baťa extended it to all the workshops. Then he started grouping these workshops into larger units of several workshops, and, ultimately, into manufacturing groups resembling independent business companies. Compared to a civil administration, his industrial system resembled communal, state (or provincial) and federal government. Compared to an army organization, it had the effect of the invention of the "division" which led towards the change in the whole army system by which eighteenth-century military thinkers and organizers, starting with Bourcet, Maréchal de Broglie and Guibert and ending with Napoleon, laid the foundations for modern army organization in the nineteenth and twentieth century. The impact of this "Bata System" of "self-administration of work", as Tomáš called it, upon the life of the Company was similar to the impact of democracy and the modern army upon the life of the last century.

During the 8 years of his life which were left to him to implement this system, its impact resulted in the figures given in Table I (from Eugen Erdely's *Bata – A Shoemaker Who Conquered the World*, Praha, Kahler-Orbis, 1935).

TABLE I

Year	Average Wage of Adult Skilled Workers	Average Profit Share	Average Price of Shoes, Kč.
1922	166	—	220
			119*
1923	180	—	
1924	205	50	99
1925	220	60	79
1926	240	80	69
1927	367**	90	53
1928	480	90	55
1929	469	90	53
1930	477	90	50
1931	514	98	46

* Price reduction on August 1, 1922.
** Introduction of conveyors into the manufacturing process.

In 1922 the Company produced a daily average of 7000 pairs of leather shoes. In 1931 this average expanded about 19 times to 133,000 pairs, of which about one-third were rubber shoes. The effect of Tomáš Baťa's organizational work is evident from the fact that during the deepest depression year, 1932, the daily average increased to 142,000 pairs.

By this basic change in the internal organization of private industry, Tomáš Baťa changed a proletarian into a business man. This change also represented a sort of technical liberation of the worker from the humdrum soulless daily work, and provided him with both the purpose and the opportunity to elevate himself to greater responsibility, status and property. Something similar to Napoleon's "every soldier carries the Marshal's baton in his knapsack" was created in the factory and within the economy of the industry.

Realizing the scarcity of well prepared men to staff the increasing number of workshops and retail stores, Baťa started a new type of school for the education of "young men for business" which, at the time of his death, had about 7000 graduates. The best of these were sent to various countries and, prepared by a knowledge of "the system", as well as in technology, languages and moral and physical fitness, they started to build and expand the Baťa companies all over the world.

The basic principle of this education was to prepare a man for self-management, first in his own private affairs, through mental, physical and economic self-discipline, and second in the art of managing a business independently within the framework of a large organization.

Although the great majority of such young men were Czech and Slovak, a number of men of other nationalities were educated and prepared for opportunities in their own countries. Thus, Bat'a was probably the only Czech whose efforts resulted in a number of Englishmen, Frenchmen, Egyptians, Pakistanis, Hindus and Malayans learning to speak Czech, as did the boys of German, Polish, Yugoslav and Dutch origin, while studying and working in Zlín.

As a technician and economist, Tomáš Bat'a advocated and practices strong centralized manufacturing combined with wide dispersion of sales, all under the same control to achieve maximum economy. The results of such economy he divided basically into three parts:

Decrease in consumers' prices

Increase in employees' earnings

Continuous re-investment into the technological and commercial expansion of the business

From the depression to expansion

Although he achieved excellent results, he was the first man in the country, and one of the very few men in the prosperous world between 1927 and 1929, who recognized the serious sociological and political problems which could drive great industrial nations into serious crises and depression. He felt that the idea of self-government would spread from the political area into the economy. Here, in short, are the thoughts which preceded his actual efforts to deal with these problems:

Every nation, ultimately, will build its own industry, especially those which produce the basic necessities of life. Our export of shoes, which is large, cannot grow forever. People will want to make shoes in their own country. However, the desire to have one's own industry does not mean that one can have a strong industry immediately. Before you start walking you have to crawl. No one can ever jump to the top of a tower; one has to climb up. The building of local and national shoe factories in the future is inevitable and we have to be in it. Thus, let's start now.

It was trains of thought like this which led Tomáš Bat'a towards the systematic development of shoe factories and shoe companies in many parts of the world, including countries living under colonial rule. He later reasoned:

We should not be afraid of losing our jobs at home. We will have more work than we now have. We will also have more exports than we now have. However, all that we will be doing and exporting will be different. We will export better types of shoes which the new factories cannot produce. We will sell them on the markets opened up by these new companies, who will teach people to wear shoes who have never worn them before. First of all, however, we are going to export to them the machinery for making shoes and many other things from which shoes are made. In addition to all this, we shall sell them education and our know-how. The world needs shoes – half of it runs around barefooted and only 5% of the people are really well shod. Unemployment? Nonsense! Look what a job is waiting for all shoemakers in the world!

Knowing deeply, as a Czech, the power of nationalism, and feeling still more deeply, as a man, that human progress in the twentieth century was possible only on an international basis, Tomáš Baťa combined both these powerful forces with his principles and method for self-government in industry, in many countries and among many nationas. Although he died in mid-career in an aeroplane crash, his work succeeded according to his expectations. His basic ideas were conceived and put into effect more than 35 years ago, but a careful observer in our time can discern in them the elements of survival and progress for all great and free industrial nations of the West. Their power and even their survival need the invention of unifying ideas which may rally all human forces within a factory and within an industry in one direction, towards a common goal.

Self-government in industry as invented and practiced by Tomáš Baťa during his lifetime has shown itself stronger than a house divided against itself as we see it in the free world today.

It was not by coincidence that Tomáš Baťa invented, applied and brought to full success his ideas of self-government in industry in the democratic republic of free Czechoslovakia. It may well be that such self-government adapted to present conditions could provide a basis for rallying the productive forces of free men with those who are not free.

REFERENCES

Bata Development Limited, *A World of Shoemaking* (London, Bata, 1961).
Cekota, A., *Baťa – Myšlenky – Činy – Život – Práce* ("Bata – Thoughts – Acts – Life and Work) (Zlín, T. & A. Bata, 1929). (In Czech.)
——, *Bata – neue Wege* (Brno, Internationale Verlags Anstalt Brno, 1928).
——, *The Battle of Home* (Toronto, MacMillan, 1944).
Dubreuil, R., *L'exemple du Bata* (Paris, Editions Bernard Grasset, 1937).
Devinat, P., *Die Arbeitsbedingungen in einem rationalisierten Betrieb*. International

Arbeits Amt in Genf (Berlin, 1930). Special reprint in *Internationale Rundschau der Arbeit*.

Erdely, E., *Baťa – Švec, který dobyl světa* ("Bata, a Shoemaker Who Conquered the World") (Praha, Kahler-Orbis, 1932).

——, *Pioneer Thomas Bata – Geist und Methoden eines erfolgreichen Unternehmen* Praha, Kahler-Orbis, 1932).

Hindus, Maurice, *The Bright Passage* (New York, Doubleday, 1945, 1946, 1947).

Czechoslovak Grain Monopoly System

LADISLAV K. FEIERABEND

The Czechoslovak grain monopoly system was the first economic experiment of its kind in the world. It guaranteed stable prices and markets to both producers and consumers, regulated prices of foodstuffs, and set production and marketing conditions in the milling industry. It represented an attempt to combine a state monopoly with private ownership, and central planning with individual initiative. After some initial difficulties, the monopoly system became successful and set an example for similar state intervention in other countries.

When tariff protection proved insufficient, and the disparity between prices of agricultural products and goods needed by farmers continued to widen,[1] the Czechoslovak government decided to introduce the grain monopoly system. In 1932, the purchasing power of products sold by farmers, in terms of the quantity of goods they needed, was only three-fifths what it had been before World War I. The country's economy had been heavily struck by the world economic crisis, it suffered greatly because of the drop in agricultural prices and the diminished purchasing power of a rural population comprising no less than one-third of the total population.

The Government vested the monopoly rights[2] with respect to all grain trading (i.e. internal, import and export trade), in the hands of a private joint stock corporation, the Czechoslovak Grain Company (Československá obilní společnost – ČOS).

The authorized share capital of 50 million crowns was subscribed by the top associations of those organizations or persons who had partici-

---

[1] Prices of goods needed by agriculture rose 7.85 times, but prices of agricultural products only 4.95 times compared with those before World War I. See Brdlík, Die *social-oekonomische Struktur der Landwirtschaft in der Tchechoslowakei* (Berlin, Verlag Franz Vahlen, 1938), p. 19.

[2] Government Decree of 13 July 1934, No. 134, Col., amended by Government Decrees of 13 July 1935, No. 152 Col., of 19 July 1936, No. 219 Col. and of 21 July 1937, No. 193 Col.

pated previously in trade in grain, foodstuffs, flour, and flour products. The Centrokooperatif – the center of agricultural cooperative unions –, representing agricultural producers, subscribed 40 percent, and 20 percent each of the share capital was subscribed by the Center of consumer cooperative unions, representing consumers by association representing the licensed trades in grain and fodder, and by societies representing commercial and grist-milling companies.

The highest organ of the Czechoslovak Grain Company was the general assembly. It elected the 20-member Board of Directors from among the four groups of shareholders described above, in proportion to their share capital, and four deputy chairmen, one for each of the four groups of shareholders; in addition, four members of the Supervisory Board, one for each of the shareholder groups, were elected. The Board transferred the administration of all matters, including those which had to be decided by the Board, to its Presidium. The Presidium consisted of the four elected deputy chairmen, and a Chairman appointed by the Government. The chairman had no vote in the Presidium or the Board, but his voice could become decisive in case of a tie in the Board. To be valid, the decisions of the Presidium had to be unanimous; otherwise, the decision was made by the Government. This rule also applied to the Presidium proposals decided upon by the Board.

The state reserved the right of supervision over the activities of the Czechoslovak Grain Company and the right to veto its decisions. These rights were exerted by government commissioners who took part in the deliberations of the company. The state had no financial participation in the company.

The company had to conduct its affairs according to business principles, which meant that current expenditures had to be covered by current income; it had to finance its own general activities. The state guaranteed that the income of the company from import trade would not be less than 60 million crowns, and also guaranteed losses the Company may have suffered in business transactions conducted by government order. The Company had to allocate profits from import trade into a special reserve fund; if this fund did not reach the annual amount of 60 million crowns, the state guaranteed, up to this amount, losses the company suffered from surplus grain trade. All other losses were born by the company either from current income or from a general reserve fund, into which the company had to pay annually, before distributing dividends, 5 percent of profits until the fund amounted to 30 percent of the share capital.

The company had an obligation to purchase, at fixed prices, all the grain from the year's harvest offered for sale by agricultural producers or other authorized sellers.[3] It had also to maintain a smooth-functioning supply system for grain consumers (flour mills, maltsters, brewers, bakers, etc.) and sell the required quantities of grain at fixed prices.

Producers of those foodstuffs under the control of the Grain Company[4] were able to market their produce only through the intermediary of the Grain Company and at fixed prices. Production and market conditions of the flour mills were regulated in a different way.[5]

The basic purchase prices of grain were fixed by the Government. They were applied at the beginning of the season for the standard quality of grain at the Prague Loading Station.[6] Actual purchase prices were set by the company by increasing or decreasing the basic price schedule according to varying qualities of grain and for different loading stations; monthly price increases were provided for deliveries later in the year. Grain offered by small producers selling less than 20 metric quintals had to be bought by the Company immediately; the Company could, however, acquire grain offered by larger producers in quarterly installments, but all grain had to be purchased no later than June 30 of the respective year. In order to persuade producers to sell their grain later in the year, the company set the monthly price increases, in operation from September to June, in such a way as to provide ample coverage for the risk and costs arising from grain storage and the loss of interest during the respective period of time.

The selling prices were fixed by the company. They were uniform throughout the year and included, in addition to the actual purchase price, an amount which covered all estimated costs of distribution incurred by the company, as well the monthly price increments. The difference between the purchase and sale price amounted to 8 to 9 crowns for one metric quintal of wheat in the early years of the grain monopoly system, and up to 12 crowns in later years. The Grain Company also fixed distribution compensations received by the Company's agents.

The Czechoslovak Grain Company operated through its commissioners

---

[3] Persons who acquired grain as rent, reserved portion, or in other similar ways.
[4] Except green foodstuffs, all other foodstuffs, including bran, dried broken grain, dried beet-cuttings, molasses, oil-cakes, etc.
[5] Government Decree of 20 July, 1935, No. 168 Col. introduced the quota system in commercial milling.
[6] In 1934 for a metric quintal of hard wheat 79 kg hectoliter weight, the price was 164 crowns, for rye 70 kg hectoliter weight, 125 crowns; for barley 67 kg hectoliter weight, 125 crowns, and for oats 50 kg hectoliter weight, 112 crowns. See Reich, *Die Tschechoslowakische Landwirtschaft* (Berlin, Verlags Buchhandlung Paul Parey, 1935), p. 145.

and general commissioners. Any dealers who, prior to the introduction of the monopoly system, traded in grain, fodder, flour, and flour-mill products, could become commissioners of the Company if they so requested. In every district, therefore, there were commissioners who belonged to all four categories of the Company's shareholders: agricultural cooperatives, consumers' cooperatives, licensed dealers in grain, foodstuffs, flour, and flour-mill products, and commercial and grist millers. All commissioners had equal rights and obligations. They had to buy all grain offered to them at the conditions set by the monopoly system. Every authorized person was entitled to sell to any commissioner in the district. The commissioner had to pay for the grain in full, and dispose of it within six weeks; he received a remuneration which took into consideration his work, the loss of interest for six weeks, adequate profit, and *delcredere*, i.e. guarantee for the buyer. Grain which the commissioner was unable to sell was turned over to the general commissioner to whom he was assigned, at the actual purchase price plus the amount of his remuneration. The general commissioners were all organizations – shareholders of the Company; they had the task of storing the grain received from the commissioners at their own risk, but at the expense of the Company. The general commissioners were likewise able to dispose of the surplus grain, with the agreement of, and at conditions set by, the Company.

The commissioners were subordinate to their general commissioners, to whom they had to report on their activities. General commissioners financed the transactions of the commissioners and were responsible for the activities of the latter; they received a special remuneration which covered all their expenses and provided for a small profit.

The Czechoslovak Grain Company acted in a financing and accounting relationship only with the general commissioners and needed only a small administrative apparatus: a general secretary, a small staff of administrative officers, and some accounting personnel. In addition, a control division supervised the commissioners and general commissioners and inspected their activities directly in the field.

The Grain Company imported only insignificant amounts of grain, since Czechoslovakia was self-sufficient and even had grain surpluses. By Government order, however, the Company was obliged to import annually certain amounts of wheat and corn from Yugoslavia and Rumania on the basis of agreements of the Economic Little Entente. Export of grain products, such as malt and beer, were an old tradition in the country, and the Czechoslovak Grain Company had to maintain the export trade in order not to lose old customers, although such trade resulted in considerable losses because of higher prices on the domestic market. The company paid equalization subsidies to exporters – the difference between domestic and world prices – and established a quota system according to the quantities exported by each exporter during the four years prior to the introduction of the monopoly system. The problem of allocation of trade on the basis of the past export trade of individual exporters was one of the most difficult points at issue in the monopoly system, since it posed the question of discrimination against newcomers in the field.

After the introduction of the monopoly system, the grain market revealed superficially no noticeable changes. Commissioners were selling grain, foodstuffs, flour, and flour products to their customers on grain exchanges as they had before. What was new was the stability of prices. Because of competition among commissioners, agricultural producers were assured of the chance to sell their products at prices and conditions set by the monopoly system. Some commissioners – mainly small millers – bought grain at prices even higher than that prescribed by the company, because they divided the difference between the fixed purchase and sale prices with the producers. If inspection disclosed that grain had been sold on the black market, both partners to the fraud declared that the grain had been brought to the grist mill for milling for the producer.

The financing of the monopoly system was very smooth, thanks to the method of grain warrants which had been introduced previously;[7] grain warrants assured that grain deliveries would be distributed evenly throughout the year and thus prevent the depression of prices by the dumping of grain on the market immediately after the harvest.

The grain warrants were a unique instrument existing only in Czechoslovakia. They made it possible for the producer to obtain a loan on grain stored in his own barn or in a warehouse, provided it was insured against fire or other natural calamities but not against the consequences of natural deterioration. It was thus a pledge without collateral, since it enabled the debtor to retain possession of his grain. The interest rate of the loans on grain warrants was low, and equivalent to the discount rate of commercial drafts. Sanctions against abuse of grain warrants were very severe and speedy. Under the monopoly system a producer was able to obtain a loan on grain warrants of up to 90 percent of the actual base value of his grain, and for a period of 6-9 months. Because of the system of monthly price increases, producers were in a better position

[7] Law of 28 June, 1933, No. 107 Col.

if they sold their grain later in the year after having taken out a loan on the basis of grain warrants at the beginning of the season. The general commissioners were likewise able to obtain loans on grain warrants, on the basis of grain stored in warehouses on account of the Grain Company, and in this way to acquire needed funds in order to finance surplus grain. In later years of the monopoly system, grain warrants were issued up to the amount of 2 billion crowns, and yet caused no inflation, as had been feared by some at the beginning.

In the very first year of its existence, the monopoly system encountered considerable difficulties from grain surpluses, competition among millers, and fraudulent grain transactions. The high wheat prices stimulated an expansion of sown acreage,[8] and it became clear that some measures had to be taken to stop such a development. It was also clear that the Company had to get rid of the excess stocks of surplus fodder grain, and that the unhealthy competition between millers, and the fraudulent grain transactions had to be brought to an end. This was achieved in the following way.

Agricultural producers who offered for sale to the Grain Company more than 20 metric quintals of grain from the 1935 harvest were compelled to take in return denatured barley, oats, and corn from the 1934 harvest up to the value of 10 percent of grain deliveries from the 1935 harvest.[9] In the same year, grain booklets were introduced, for future records, in which every farmer stated the acreage of his farm, sown areas, and actual grain yields; these data had to be confirmed by local authorities. The booklet also recorded all sales of grain to the Grain Company and the quantities the farmer brought to the grist mill to be milled for his own use. Producers with more than 5 hectares of cultivated land had to report by June 30, 1935, their total arable land and its distribution among individual crops: wheat, rye, barley, oats, and corn.[10] A further decree prohibited any enlargement of the arable land above the base year 1934-35, and ordered the sown wheat acreage restricted to 92 percent of its size in 1934-35. Those who did not obey the regulations were threatened with a reduction of up to 20 percent on the purchase price of grain.[11]

---

[8] The sown wheat area increased in 1935 to 965,829 hectares compared with a five-year average before the introduction of the monopoly system of 868,776 hectares. The wheat harvest in 1935 was exceptionally good and the yields of wheat per hectare were 17.5 metric quintals compared with 14.5 metric quintals in 1934. See *Statistical Yearbook of the Czechoslovak Republic*, 1938, p. 38.
[9] Government Decree of 13, July 1935, No. 152 Col.
[10] Government Decree of 25 June 1935, No. 135 Col.
[11] Government Decree of 20 July 1935, No. 173 Col.

In order to ascertain the stocks carried by flour mills, the latter were ordered to maintain an inventory of all the wheat, rye, and flour products that they stocked;[12] in addition, a quota system for commercial and grist mills was introduced on the basis of actual milled quantities of wheat and rye in the years 1931 to 1933.[13]

The results of these measures were very unsatisfactory. The sown acreage of wheat continued to increase, and good yields in 1935 contributed to higher surpluses.[14] The Czechoslovak Grain Company was aware that its considerable stocks would increase further in 1936 as a result of large deliveries from the 1935 harvest;[15] this would have constituted an unbearable financial burden for the Company, and the Company therefore called for a radical reduction in grain prices – a measure which would automatically result in a decline in sown acreage. The government, however, hesitated to take such a drastic step and consented only to a moderate price reduction; it was decided, moreover, to establish a state reserve stock of surplus grain of up to 10,000 carloads of wheat, 10,000 carloads of rye, and 5,000 carloads of oats (one carload equals 100 metric quintals); this measure greatly eased the financial position of the Company. In 1936 the regulation concerning arable land and total grain acreage remained the same as in the previous year, but wheat acreage was fixed for each community.[16]

The results were gratifying. In 1937 the sown wheat acreage declined to the same level as that prior to the introduction of the monopoly system,[17] and wheat surplus stocks held by the Czechoslovak Grain Company also decreased.[18] This was caused by the reduction in prices.

The functioning of the Czechoslovak Grain Company was very satisfactory. The unanimity of the Presidium which, at the beginning, had been considered by many as unpracticable, proved to be the key to the success of the monopoly system. Between 1934 and the time of the Munich Agreement in 1938, the Government was called upon only twice to

[12] Government Decree of June 25, 1935, No. 135 Col.
[13] Government Decree of 20 July 1935, No. 168 Col.
[14] The sown wheat acreage in 1935 was 965,829 hectares compared with 942,397 hectares in 1934; the average wheat yield per hectare was 17.5 metric quintals compared with 14.6 in 1934. For rye, the respect. magnitudes were: 1,017,366 hectares in 1935 against 1,000,899 in 1934, and 16.2 quintals in 1935 against 15.4 in 1934.
[15] Wheat stocks as of 31 March 1936 were 66,547 carloads, and as of 30 June 1936 were 78,523 carloads.
[16] Government Decree of 30 June, 1936, No. 157 Col.
[17] The sown wheat acreage was 852.892 hectares in 1937. See *Stat. Yearbook, op. cit.*, p. 38.
[18] In June 1937 wheat stocks amounted to 59,092 carloads. *Ibid.*, p. 42.

make a decision. All participants preferred to make concessions and come to an agreement rather than let the Government make the decision. I do not wish to imply that political influences played no part in such circumstances, since a democracy is unthinkable without them, but I wish to stress that this was an exception; the Czechoslovak Grain Company made its decisions on economic grounds and not on the basis of political pressures. The financial position of the Czechoslovak Grain Company was sound, and the company every year paid the highest dividend allowed by its statutes – 6 percent. The Government was satisfied with the performance of the Company, because it operated on business principles and without corruption. The state did not need to pay more to the Company than was agreed upon at its inception.

In view of the competition among commissioners, agricultural producers were never cheated with respect to the quality of their produce or otherwise; they found the domestic grain prices, which were much higher than world prices, quite satisfactory, but were dissatisfied with the regulation concerning sown acreages and the introduction of grain booklets.

Consumers were unhappy about the monopoly system because of the high grain prices they had to pay, and considered the system too expensive for the state to maintain. They resented especially the restriction of rice imports, which were found necessary since rice was a good substitute for wheat and much cheaper. Consumers had a great influence on public opinion and the entire press became opposed to the monopoly system, often misrepresenting the true situation.

Licensed dealers were opposed to the system because, from the very beginning, they lost much trade to the agricultural cooperatives.[19] It was estimated that the loss amounted to one-half the volume of their trade in grain. In subsequent years of the existence of the Czechoslovak Grain Company the dealers' trading position in grain did not deteriorate any further and they came to accept the monopoly. They were aware that speculation was out of question and that they had to base their activities on the principle of service.

Flour millers were among the most dissatisfied of the Company's shareholders. Large commercial millers resented the quota system because it put an end to the normal competition which they considered essential, thanks to greatly excess capacity in Czechoslovak flour milling. The quota system maintained in operation many enterprises which would

[19] Of the total quantity of grain bought by the monopoly from the 1934 harvest, agr. cooperatives bought 62.18 percent, consumer coops. 0.42 percent, grain dealers 25,83 percent and millers 11.57 percent. See Reich, *op. cit.*, p. 145.

have disappeared under free competition. In order to remedy this situation a plan was worked out according to which the Czechoslovak Grain Company would buy out small milling enterprises, if they were offered for sale. The change in the political situation after Munich, however, prevented the plan from being put into operation.

The economy of the country benefited considerably by the establishment of the grain monopoly system. The effects of increased purchasing power of the agricultural population was felt very soon in larger purchases of agricultural and other household supplies. This had a favorable influence on public opinion, which became reconciled to the monopoly system and began to appreciate its results, especially after 1937, when an end was put to the speculation by farmers. By 1938 all participants in the monopoly system had grown accustomed to it and supported its activities.

It is very difficult to pass a final judgment on the achievements of the Czechoslovak Grain Monopoly, since the experience covered too short a period of time, and events after Munich changed the entire economic and political order of the country. The Czechoslovak Monopoly system, however, was studied by experts of many countries, including those of the United States, and its experiences were used in similar attempts at state support of grain prices and markets.

Economic and Social Structure of Czechoslovak Society between the Two Wars

V. E. ANDIC

> "The Czechoslovak Nation will carry out far-reaching social and economic reforms." Declaration of Independence of the Czechoslovak Nation, Paris-London-Washington, October 18, 1918.

In our discussion of the economic and social structure of the Czechoslovak society between the two wars we will consider the following aspects:

1. High degree of industrial development;
2. Active foreign trade;
3. Stabilization of the Czechoslovak currency after World War I, at a time when neighboring countries were still suffering from inflation and economic instability;
4. Land reform necessitated by a) previous concentration of land ownership in the hands of the German and Hungarian landowners, b) restricted ownership by Czechoslovak nationals before 1918;
5. Development of the middle class by progressive social legislation and promotion of industrial expansion, especially in the eastern regions.

1. HIGH DEGREE OF INDUSTRIAL DEVELOPMENT

Czechoslovakia was industrially the most developed of the Slavic countries. Industrialization of any country presupposes and brings about better human relations and more democratic institutions. This was particularly so in the western half of Czechoslovakia, since the industries of Austria-Hungary were primarily located in Bohemia and Moravia-Silesia, while the eastern half of the Republic, specifically, Slovakia and Carpathian Ruthenia, were agricultural regions with very little manufacturing.

This industrial concentration of Austro-Hungarian industries in Czech lands in the year 1914 was as given in Table I.[1]

---

[1] Wanklyn, Harriet, *Czechoslovakia* (New York, Frederick A. Praeger, 1954), p. 232.

TABLE I

Product	Per Cent of Total Output	Product	Per cent of Total Output
Coal	86	Porcelain	100
Lignite	84	Sugar refineries	92
Metallurgical industry	60	Malting houses	92
Chemical industry	75	Breweries	57
Textiles	75	Leather	70
Glass	92	Paper	75

Approximately one third of the population of the Republic was supported by agriculture, as Table II shows.

TABLE II

Occupational distribution of population in Czechoslovakia, comparing the censuses of 1921 and 1930[2]

Occupation	1921 Numbers Absolute	Per 1000 Inhabitants	1930 Numbers Absolute	Per 1000 Inhabitants
Agriculture, forestry and fishing	5,384,787	395.6	5,101,614	346.4
Industry	4,552,398	334.4	5,146,937	349.4
Trade and finance	787,293	57.8	1,094,063	74.3
Transportation	658,683	48.4	814,468	55.3
Civil Service and the liberal professions	604,282	44.4	715,841	48.6
Army	159,870	11.8	193,463	13.1
Servants and domestics	132,253	9.7	183,814	12.5
Others, including non-professionals	1,107,602	81.4	1,272,171	86.3
No profession stated	225,256	16.5	207,165	14.1
Total	13,612,424	1000.0	14,729,536	1000.0

A breakdown of the occupational distribution by regions reveals why the per capita income in Slovakia in 1937 was little more than half (2,135

[2] Papánek, Ján, *Czechoslovakia, The World of Tomorrow*, ed. by George Gurevitch (New York, International Press, 1945), p. 132.

Czechoslovak crowns) that in Bohemia and Moravia-Silesia (4,202 Czechoslovak crowns).[3] (See Table III.)

TABLE III

Occupational distribution of the population of Czechoslovakia in 1930[4]

Occupation	Bohemia	Moravia-Silesia	Slovakia	Carpathian Ruthenia
Agriculture	1,636,976	976,089	1,822,114	424,048
Forestry and fishing	73,747	41,904	69,928	56,808
Industry and crafts	2,970,255	1,455,295	634,797	86,590
Trade and finance	633,327	237,908	181,278	41,550
Transportation	438,995	194,745	157,634	23,094
Civil Service and the liberal professions	364,534	165,252	155,983	30,072
Army	84,862	46,808	54,090	7,703
Servants and domestics	106,028	47,766	25,919	4,101
Other occupations	725,499	359,805	160,811	26,056
No profession stated	75,153	39,438	67,239	25,335
Total	7,109,376	3,565,010	3,329,793	725,357

2. ACTIVE FOREIGN TRADE

As already indicated, Czechoslovakia, as an industrial country with a rather high standard of living, was actively engaged in foreign trade. It had established markets, and a reputation for high-quality products and reliability in trading.

The extent of Czechoslovak foreign trade is attested by these official data (in Czechoslovak crowns)[5]:

[3] Bušek, Vratislav and Spulber, Nicolas, eds., *Czechoslovakia*, Mid-European Studies Center of the Free Europe Committee, Inc. (New York, Frederick A. Prager, 1957), p. 232.
[4] Based on the *Annual Statistical Report of the Republic of Czechoslovakia*, State Statistical Office (Prague, Orbis, 1936), pp. 12-13.
[5] *Annual Statistical Report of the Republic of Czechoslovakia*, State Statistical Office (Prague, Orbis, 1936).

Year	Export	Import	Balance
1929	19,987,858	20,498,869	—511.011
1934	6,391,566	7,287,549	895,983

The degree of production for the foreign market differed, as shown by the products listed below according to their dependence on foreign markets[6]:

Furniture	90 Per cent		Sugar	75 Per cent
Glass	90 ,, ,,		Textiles	70 ,, ,,
China	90 ,, ,,		Agricultural	
Beer	75 ,, ,,		machinery	70 ,, ,,

The list is, of course, far from complete. In fact, between 1918 and 1938, as much as 69 per cent of the total industrial output was sold on the foreign market.[7]

There was nothing unusual about the lively trade between Czechoslovakia and Germany,[8] although it is not hard to understand why Germany was particularly interested in this trade during the 30's, despite the drop in demand for consumer goods thanks to the depression and rearmament. (See Table IV.)

TABLE IV

	Czechoslovak Imports from Germany		Czechoslovak Exports to Germany	
	(Millions of Czechoslovak crowns)	Percentage of total import	(Millions of Czechoslovak crowns)	Percentage of total export
1920	5,603 Mil	24.0	3,331 Mil	35.1
1925	5,509	31.3	4,233	22.5
1930	3,966	25.4	2,970	17.7
1935	1,160	17.2	1,173	15.8
1936	1,383	17.5	1,150	14.3
1937	1,699	15.5	1,643	13.7

Dr. Basch[9] says of the decline in imports from Germany that "at best, one could speak of lively relations between the two neighboring states

---

[6] Wanklyn, Harriet, *Czechoslovakia*, p. 280.
[7] *Ibid.*, p. 280.
[8] Basch, Antonín, *Germany's Economic Conquest of Czechoslovakia*; published by the Czechoslovak National Council of America (Chicago, 1941), p. 9.
[9] University Professor, currently teaching at the University of Michigan.

which had traded together for centuries, but not of economic dependence which might lead to the conclusion that Czechoslovakia really formed part of the German Grossraumwirtschaft."[10]

It is interesting to discuss here the extent of the German share in import and export activities of Czechoslovakia and those of Hungary and Yugoslavia (in percentages):[11]

Country	Year	Export	Import
Czechoslovakia	1935	16.8	15.7
	1936	17.3	14.3
	1937	15.5	13.7
Hungary	1935	23.8	17.1
	1936	36.1	18.0
	1937	28.9	19.6
Yugoslavia	1935	16.2	18.6
	1936	26.7	23.7
	1937	32.4	31.7

Dr. Basch further reveals that the German share of all imports and exports from five countries – Czechoslovakia, Hungary, Rumania, Yugoslavia and Bulgaria – increased from 122 mil. $ in 1935 to 157 mil. in 1936, while exports to these five countries increased from 238 mil. $ in 1935 to 238 mil. in 1937.

The Sudeten German writers now emphasize the fact that more than half the Czechoslovak industries were run by Sudeten Germans: the porcelain and china industry, glass, coal and steel, wool, chemical, paper, sugar refineries and raw materials.[12]

3. STABILIZATION OF THE PURCHASING POWER OF CZECHOSLOVAK CURRENCY

> "Securing the stability of the state economy, a balanced budget, is the most important condition of the 'permanent' purchasing power of money."
> Dr. Josef Macek, *Práce, peníze a politika* ("Work, Money and Public Policy") (Prague, 1933), p. 114.

[10] Basch, Antonín, *Germany's Economic Conquest of Czechoslovakia*, p. 6.
[11] *Ibid*, p. 6.
[12] Polzer, Robert, *The Sudeten German Economy in Czechoslovakia* (Mainz, 1952). See also, *Renascence or Decline of Central Europe* by Dr. Wilhelm K. Turnwald, transl. by Gerda Johansen (Munich, University Press, 1954).

With the collapse of Austria-Hungary, the chief holder of the Czech national debt disappeared, and the peace treaties, in effect, wrote off most of the debt, leaving the succession (subsequently formed) states the job of helping themselves as best they could. Czechoslovakia took the following steps:

1. It deflated the much-inflated bank notes and exchanged them for a new Czechoslovak currency which became the legal tender;

2. It steadied (established) the purchasing power of the new currency; and

3. It collected property taxes in order to replace the unredeemable cheaper currency and strengthened the purchasing power of the Czechoslovak crown; by 1932 the sum of 8.75 billion Czechoslovak crowns had been collected, approximately enough to cover the internal debt.[13]

Thus, the most critical issues facing the Republic of Czechoslovakia, partly inherited from Austria-Hungary, partly arising from immediate post-war conditions, were: (1) The national debt; (2) elimination of dependence on Austria and Germany from foreign trade markets; (3) the danger of inflation and the need to establish a sound Czechoslovak currency.

As for point one, the national debt derived from three sources: (a) war debts, including that of Austria-Hungary (amounting to 10,084.3 million Czechoslovak crowns[14]) as held by its nationals in their own territory (within Austria-Hungary), as well as that of immediate post-war American aid (grain) to the population of war-plundered Czechoslovak territory; American and British aid to Czechoslovakia in fighting economic dislocation in Austria and Germany, and Bolshevism in Hungary (e.g. the invasion of Czechoslovakia by Bela Kun's Hungarian Communist forces), totalling 17,417.1 million Czechoslovak crowns[15]; (b) debts contracted by the Republic of Czechoslovakia for its own expenditures, including the repatriation of its own nationals, particularly its armies from Siberia and many other places, totalling 14,396.8 million Czechoslovak crowns; (c) Austrian and Hungarian pre-war debts and indemnification for state properties to be paid by the Republic, under the peace treaties, and totalling 34,413.9 million Czechoslovak crowns.[16]

---

[13] Macek, Josef, *Work, Money and Public Policy*, p. 123.
[14] Rašín, Alois, Minister of Finance for Czechoslovakia, *Financial Policy of Czechoslovakia during the First Year of Its History* (Oxford, Clarendon Press, 1923); publication of the Carnegie Endowment for International Peace, Division of Economics and History, John Bates Clark, Director, p. 115.
[15] *Ibid.*, p. 116.
[16] *Ibid.*, p. 118.

Regarding the second point, the new Republic had to establish its own direct contacts with foreign markets because exporting through Vienna and Berlin damaged the Czechoslovak currency, especially after the value of the German mark began to decrease and Germany suffered from inflation.

Fighting inflation in Czechoslovakia required firm measures for strengthening the Czechoslovak currency by payment of debts, increased direct and indirect taxation, and balancing the budget. "We must save – save and produce, otherwise our Czech krone (crown) will depreciate in the same way as the Austrian krone (crown) ... we can raise the value of our currency only if we all work and save", declared the Minister of Finance.[17]

Social Legislation Planned to Conform with Recommendations of the International Labor Office

Czechoslovakia complied with the principles and policies set up by the International Labor Organization, which was established by the Paris Peace Conference on January 31, 1919.[18] However, there were other influences shaping the nature of social legislation, specifically, the strongly organized labor organizations and the social orientation of the Czechoslovak people, who had suffered acutely from the lack of industrial and social protection under Austro-Hungarian rule.

In fact, much labor legislation existed in Czechoslovakia before the International Labor Organization had ever been established: the eight-hour law (July 19, 1918), unemployment compensation (December 10, 1918), workmen's compensation (law of 1887 of Austria-Hungary, supplemented and extended by laws of October 29, 1919 and December 20, 1921), health insurance (July 15, 1919), and retirement insurance (December 16, 1906).[19]

Other labor legislation followed, such as old-age and survivors' insurance. "The system of social insurance prior to Munich was administra-

---

[17] *Ibid.*, p. 75.
[18] Bloss, Esther, *Labor Legislation in Czechoslovakia* (New York, Columbia University Press, 1938), p. 210 states: "The attitude of the delegates to the International Labor Conference each year has been both sympathetic and helpful. This has been due to the experience of Czechoslovakia in its own legislation which in many cases antedated the discussion of questions at Geneva as a basis of Conventions and Recommendations, and to the pride which the Czechoslovaks have taken in the advanced position of their country in respect of social legislation".
[19] Masaryk Scientific Dictionary, *Masarykův Naučný Slovník* ("Dictionary of General Knowledge") (Prague, 1925), pp. 1094-1001.

tively divided into three separate branches: health (including maternity), insurance such as accident insurance, and pension insurance.[20]

A major step forward in the field of safety regulations and enforcement of wage and salary agreements was made by the establishment of works councils, first of all in the mining industries (February 25, 1920). "In regard to other undertakings beside mining, the Act of August 12, 1921 provided that a works committee be established for every independent undertaking carried on for profit, in which not less than thirty workers are employed regularly, and which has been in existence for not less than half a year".[21]

In 1938 there were registered about 103,860 unemployed. The index of unemployment in the years 1921-1938 is hereby given[22]:

1921	100
1924	134.9
1929	58.2
1934	1056.0
1935	1167.0
1938	358.0

During the ten years following 1931, the Czechoslovak Government spent a total of 5 billion 770 million Czechoslovak crowns to relieve the unemployment problem; some of this money went to specific industries, as, for instance, the 600 million crowns which were allocated to railways to maintain the level of employment. There were, of course, many imperfections in dealing with the enormous problems of unemployment:[23] 1) inadequacy of unemployment insurance funds, which were available to trade union members only; 2) lack of administrative uniformity, so that, for example, industrial workers' health insurance was administered by 295 insurance institutions, agricultural workers' health insurance by 69 separate insurance institutions, public employees' health insurance by these insurance institutions, miners' health insurance by four insurance institutions, etc.; 3) similar lack of uniformity in contribution rates, benefits and eligibility for benefits. Yet these deficiencies were relatively minor ones, hardly insoluble.

---

[20] "Public Health and Welfare", *Czechoslovakia*, ed. by Vratislav Bušek and Nicolas Spulber, Mid-European Studies Center of the Free Europe Committee Inc. (New York, Frederick A. Praeger, 1957).
[21] Bloss, Esther, *Labor Legislation in Czechoslovakia*, p. 137.
[22] *Czechoslovakia's Path to Socialism, The Labor and Social Policy of the People of Democratic Czechoslovakia* (Prague, Orbis, 1951), p. 41.
[23] Bušek and Spulber, *Czechoslovakia*, pp. 198-199.

4. LAND REFORM AN IMPORTANT STEP TOWARD DEMOCRATIZATION

> "The distribution of land in the old Hungary was proverbial. A full third of the land was owned by landowners with one thousand acres or more."
> Základy sociografie Slovenska ("Foundations of Sociography of Slovakia"), by Dr. Anton Štefánek (Bratislava, 1945), p. 244.

One of the crucial problems confronting the Republic of Czechoslovakia was land reform, primarily for two reasons: (1) agriculture remained an important source of livelihood; (2) landownership was distributed in such a way that most farmers, especially in Slovakia and Carpathian Ruthenia, were either landless or in possession of limited areas of arable land.

Professor Lucy E. Textor of Vassar College wrote, in "Agriculture and Agrarian Reform",[24] of the general desire of the people for land reform. "It was part of the wisdom to satisfy this expectation and thereby forestall agrarian disturbances which might, indeed, take the form of uprising in favor of bolshevism".[25]

A quick look at Table V on land distribution will reveal the seriousness of the situation:

TABLE V

Distribution of land[26] in Hungary, 1895, in acres	No of Farms	Land distribution in[27] Czechoslovakia, 1930, in acres	PC of Farms	PC of total land
0-1	562,949	up to 2½	28.1.	2.8
1-5	716,769	2½ to 12½	42.7	20.8
5-10	458,535	12½ to 25	15.7	19.9
10-20	385,381	25 to 75	11.4	31.1
20-50	205.181	75 to 250	1.5	10.4
50-100	36,032	over 250	.6	15.5
100-200	10,275			
200-500	6,448			
500-1000	3,144			
over 1000	3,768			

[24] In *Czechoslovakia*, Ed. Robert Kerner, p. 219.
[25] P. 220.
[26] Štefánek, *Foundations of Sociography of Slovakia*, p. 244.
[27] Young, Edgar P., *Czechoslovakia, Keystone of Peace and Democracy* (London, Golancz, 1939), p. 141. In the meantime landowners with over 1,000 acres owned 31.19 per cent of the total land even as late as 1945. *Foundations of Sociography of Slovakia*, p. 244.

Agriculture supported more than one third of the population (34.6 per cent)[28]; this percentage was of course still higher in Slovakia and even more so in Carpathian Ruthenia.[29] Pasvolsky reports for the whole country that agriculture gave employment to about 40 per cent of the total population.[30]

The United States Congress made this statement on land reform in Czechoslovakia: "Redistribution of land was an urgent problem facing the new government and a Land Reform Act therefore was one of the first measures passed by the Czechoslovak Parliament."[31]

This urgency is understandable from the economic as well as the social viewpoint. Overseas emigration, primarily to the United States from Slovakia (Hungary), just before World War I was increasing at an alarming rate. Hungarian emigrants totalled 91,762 in 1902; this number increased to 119,944 in 1903, to 170,430 in 1905, and to 209,169 in 1907.[32] The seriousness of the situation is illustrated by the fact that in 1905, the number of emigrants leaving Hungary exceeded by 40,000 the number of children born alive.

Emigration was not an altogether unmixed blessing. In Slovakia, for instance, "nothing is discussed with greater "expertise" and love by village people than America, the Eldorado of poor, working people. Children listen with bated breath to stories of Americans, and they know the geography of the United States better than of Slovakia".[33]

5. CZECHOSLOVAKIA – THE MIDDLE-CLASS COUNTRY

Compared to Hungary, or even to Yugoslavia and Rumania, one overwhelming fact seems evident: Czechoslovakia between the two wars was a middle-class country. As in the United States, no hereditary titles were recognized and everything possible was done to strengthen the democratic way of life.

---

[28] Papánek, *Czechoslovakia*, in Georges Gurevitch, *The World of Tomorrow*, p. 35.
[29] Jászi, Oscar, "The Problem of Sub-Carpathian Ruthenia", in *Czechoslovakia, Twenty Years of Independence* (Berkeley, University of California Press, p. 196), writes: "Looking back on the past history of the Hungarian Ruthenians, an English observer of considerable fairness, C. A. Macartney, declared in 1937: 'Ruthenia was really treated by the Magyars as a great deerforest.'"
[30] Pasvolsky, Leo, *Economic Nationalism of the Danubian States* (New York, McMillan, 1928), p. 231.
[31] *Special Report No. 8 of the Select Committee on Communist Aggression and Occupation of Czechoslovakia*, U. S. House of Representatives, 83 Congress, 2nd session, p. 6.
[32] Štefánek, Anton, *Foundations of Sociography of Slovakia*, p. 243.
[33] *Ibid.*, p. 342.

Expansion of industrial production into farming areas was accelerated by universal education, which wiped out illiteracy in the areas formerly under Hungary, by ending discrimination and by the promulgation of social legislation to strengthen the working classes.

The improved conditions of the population were reflected in wage distribution (see Table VI).

TABLE VI

Wage Categories in 1937[34]

Maximum income (in Czechoslovak crowns)	Per cent of total labor force
3,000	23.0
6.000	28.7
9,000	24.0
12,000	15.0
above 12,000	11.0

The Institute for Study of Economic Conditions at the National Bank of Slovakia reported the annual income from various sources as follows[35] (Table VII):

TABLE VII

Occupation	In millions of Slovak crowns	Per cent of the total
Primary production, including agriculture	2,567	32.6
Industry and crafts	1,969	25.0
Trade and transport	931	11.8
Services	1,800	22.8
Income from abroad	120	1.5
Income from housing (rent)	500	6.3

As seen here, industry and crafts employed 19 per cent fewer people than agriculture, but provided only 8 per cent less income. The income of 120 million Slovak crowns from abroad represents money sent by emigrants to their relatives in Slovakia for acquiring land and other savings in Slovakia.

[34] *Czechoslovakia's Path to Socialism*, p. 41.
[35] *Sociography of Slovakia* (quoting V. Krajčovič, "Die Structur der Slovakischen Wirtschaft"), p. 370.

Social legislation which was in accord with rising employment standards included legislation for the protection of women and children, health, old age and survivors' insurance, industrial accident compensation and umemployment insurance. Workers' committees, by encouraging workers' active participation on the job, led to improvement of working, health and safety standards.

An important factor in the expansion of the middle class, that backbone of democracy in any country, was of course, land reform. As many as 632,131 individual farmers received 4,022,131 acres of land.[36] As a result of this reform, over 60 per cent of those who had been employed in agriculture became independent farmers.

Professor Lucy Textor of Vassar College writes that "a homestead may come into existence in three ways. The Land Office may give a farm as a homestead; it may add a parcel to land already owned by the applicant on the condition that the whole become a homestead. A free hold may be transformed into a homestead at the wish of the owner.[37]

A homestead could be mortgaged only for one of the following purposes:

(1) to pay the price of an added parcel of land or to take over the obligation for a freehold which had not become part of the homestead;

(2) to build or enlarge the farmhouse;

(3) to provide for or add to equipment;

(4) to fulfill hereditary or testamentary arrangements, unpaid obligations on homesteads may be collected only through compulsory registration of the homesteads.

This determined effort on the part of the Government, coupled with other social and educational reforms, brought about the conditions which made Czechoslovak democracy flourish in the midst of nationalistic dictatorships all over Central and Eastern Europe.

The democratization of Czechoslovak society was further aided by the increase in the number of farm cooperatives, which claimed between 1,800,000 and 2,000,000 members in 11,673 organizations in 1937.[38] Altogether, 11.3 per cent of the total population of the Republic were members of cooperatives... In 1935 their business amounted to $ 591,985,000 including deposits in credit cooperatives and sales of producers' and consumers' societies.

Czechoslovakia obviously faced many social problems and economic

---

[36] Papánek, Ján, *Czechoslovakia*, p. 36.
[37] *Land Reform in Czechoslovakia* (London, 1923), p. 77.
[38] "Agriculture and Agrarian Reform", in *Czechoslovakia*, Ed. Robert Kerner, p. 230.

pressures. These were attributable to factors such as the separation of Czechs and Slovaks for almost one thousand years, Hungary's complete neglect and subordination of Ruthenia's economy, unfriendly or openly hostile neighboring countries (Nazi Germany and Horthy's Hungary), and the rising tides of international tensions beyond the control of any single nation.

Yet this brave country handled many of her economic difficulties in a surprisingly admirable democratic manner and would have been able, in a settled and peaceful world, to continue the program of industrialization of Slovakia and Carpathian Ruthenia, gradually solving her economic and social problems. This was already promised in the rising levels of education, in the strengthening of the democratic way of life by successful economic and social reforms, and in improving the standard of living of all citizens.

BIBLIOGRAPHY

Annual Statistical Report of the Republic of Czechoslovakia, State Statistical Office (Prague, Orbis, 1936).

Basch, Antonín, *Germany's Economic Conquest of Czechoslovakia* (Chicago, The Czechoslovak National Council of America, 1941).

Bloss, Esther, *Labor Legislation in Czechoslovakia* (New York, Columbia University Press, 1938).

Bušek, Vratislav, and Spulber, Nicolas, *Czechoslovakia*, Mid-European Studies Center of the Free Europe Committee Inc. (New York, Frederick A. Praeger, 1957).

Czechoslovakia's Path to Socialism, The Labor and Social Policy of the People's Democratic Czechoslovakia (Prague, Orbis, 1951).

Jászi, Oscar, "The Problem of Sub-Carpathian Ruthenia", *Czechoslovakia*, Ed. R. Kerner (1946).

Kerner, Robert, Editor, *Czechoslovakia, Twenty Years of Independence* (Berkeley-Los Angeles, University of California Press, 1946).

Krajčovič, V., "Die Struktur der Slovakischen Wirtschaft", in Štefánek's *Sociography of Slovakia* (1945).

Macek, Josef, *Práce, peníze a politika* ("Work, Money and Public Policy") (Prague, Jan Laichter, 1933).

Masarykův Naučný Slovník ("Masaryk's Scientific Dictionary") (Prague, Kompas, 1925).

Papánek, Ján, *Czechoslovakia, The World of Tomorrow*, Editor Professor Georges Gurevitch (New York, International Press, 1945).

Pasvolsky, Leo, *Economic Nationalism of the Danubian States* (New York, The Macmillan Company, 1928).

Polzer, Robert, *The Sudeten German Economy in Czechoslovakia* (Mainz, Kitzingen, 1952).

Rašín, Alois, *Financial Policy of Czechoslovakia during the First Year of Its History* (Oxford, Clarendon Press, 1923).

Štefánek, Anton, *Základy sociografie Slovenska* ("Foundations of Sociography of Slovakia") (Bratislava, Slovak Academy of Arts and Sciences, 1945).

extor, Lucy, *Land Reform in Czechoslovakia*, (London, George Allen and Unwin, 1923).
Turnwald, Wilhelm K., *Renascence or Decline of Central Europe* (Munich, University Press, Dr. C. Wolf und Sohn, 1954).
Wanklyn, Harriet, *Czechoslovakia* (New York, Frederick A. Praeger, 1954).
Young, Edgar P., *Czechoslovakia, Keystone of Peace and Democracy* (London, Victor Golancz, Ltd., 1939).

Problems of Measuring Industrial Output in Czechoslovakia

JAN MICHAL

Industrial production, as defined in Czechoslovak, American, or U.N. statistics, covers only output in mining, manufacturing, and some basic utilities such as electricity and gas. Industrial growth therefore is not an adequate measure of over-all economic growth, since it does not take into consideration the development in other important sectors, such as construction and building, agriculture, transportation, and output of various services. Nevertheless, there is some justification in limiting my discussion to industrial output, the most important reason being, of course, that I have been asked to do so, probably on the assumption that others will deal with the whole national income and product of Czechoslovakia. There are, however, some economic reasons for concentrating on the industrial sector alone.

Industrial output is obviously an extremely important determinant of potential economic growth. In fact, in economic isolation, without any foreign trade, it would be the only source of machinery and other fixed capital assets to maintain and enlarge productive capacities. And even if a country can obtain real capital from abroad by borrowing or in exchange for agricultural products, the important fact remains that the terms of trade tend to develop in favor of industrialized countries and against primary producing countries. Generally speaking, industrialization seems to be associated with increasing productivity, improving terms of trade, and faster economic growth, accompanied by an increasing standard of living.

Availability of statistical data over a long period is an additional reason for limiting my paper to industry only. In Czechoslovakia, as in most other countries, industrial output had been measured long before any attempts had been made to compute national income and product. Only educated guesses had been made about the latter before the second World War; the first genuine computation of national income was undertaken by Miloš Stádník and published only in 1946. This is nothing to be ashamed of; in many other European countries, e.g. Austria and the whole of Eastern Europe, national income computations were even less advanced than in pre-1948 Czechoslovakia. On the other hand, industrial output has been measured since the first years of Czechoslovak independence after the first World War. The first index of industrial output by Hotowetz was followed by another, produced and published cooperatively by the State Statistical Office and the economic review, *Obzor národohospodářský*; its construction has been described in some detail by Karel Maiwald in *Obzor národohospodářský*, 3 (1934).[1]

It is not the purpose of this paper to give a technical description of all the problems faced in establishing a reliable criterion to be applied in order to measure industrial growth. Yet it is essential to characterize the basic differences between the three methods I will refer to when discussing the prewar and postwar increase in industrial output.

In most Western countries the "physical volume" index is used. Selected statistical series in physical terms (in tons, yards, gallons, units etc.) are "weighted together" according to their relative importance. The statistical weights are usually based on the "net value" or "value added by manufacturing", i.e. relative prices of the products concerned minus material cost. Relative prices reflect, of course, value judgments, at least in a market economy without comprehensive price controls. Thus, the Czechs are big pork eaters, and pork relative to beef is more expensive than in America. If, for any reason, the output of commodities with a high statistical weight goes up faster than the average, this gives the index an upward bias. On the other hand, if the output of the high-weighted products rises more slowly than the output of other commodities covered by the index, a downward bias tends to develop. It would lead us too far afield to discuss the whole problem of index numbers; I may say (with extreme brevity) that the physical volume index reduces the impact of value judgments and is therefore internationally more comparable than the remaining two other methods of measuring industrial growth. The physical volume index has, however, the disadvantage of not covering all products within the industrial sector. In prewar Czechoslovakia, for example, the official index of industrial production covered only the 91 most important products; today this would be considered to be a rather narrow coverage, but in prewar times, it was certainly one of the

---

[1] Unless stated otherwise in footnotes, all statistical data have been taken from *Statistical Yearbooks of the Czechoslovak Republic* (since 1960; *Statistical Yearbooks of the Czechoslovak Socialist Republic*), 1957 to 1961, published annually by the State Statistical Office, Prague.

most reliable indexes of industrial output in Central Europe, especially in view of the fairly good quality of basic data, as collected by the well organized statistical service.

The second type of indexes is based on "net value", or "value added by mining and manufacturing", or "national income originating in industry". Such indexes reflect the changes in total price of industrial output minus material cost (of course, in terms of constant price tags attached to each product). Under competitive conditions and after correction for indirect taxes, this "net value" of industrial output would be identically equal to the sum of wages, salaries, interest on capital, rents and profits in the whole industrial sector. As I mentioned before, prices reflect value judgments, and this limits the international comparability of index numbers. But in periods of stable employment without severe inflation or deflation, a "net value" index usually shows a close correlation with a "physical volume" index.

The last type to be discussed, the "gross value" index, has been used mainly by the Communist countries to measure industrial output. It covers all final as well as intermediate products and material inputs at constant prices. Therefore it reflects, among other things, all changes in real cost of output. Since real cost tends to go up during periods of rapid industrialization, this tends to give the index an upward bias. (E.g. substitution of more expensive for less expensive materials, which may be induced by gross value indicator of plan fulfillment, blows up the index numbers.) Other possible sources of upward bias include: too much statistical weight given to fast-growing heavy industry; vertical disintegration (gross value for the industrial sector is obtained by adding up gross value of individual enterprises, so that increased specialization, or increased "roundaboutness of output", also blows up gross value index numbers), etc. For a more detailed discussion of this type of index, the reader is referred to the author's book, *Central Planning in Czechoslovakia*.[2]

There is a consensus between Western and most Communist economists and statisticians that the gross value index is not a satisfactory measure of industrial output. Therefore, the Hungarian Statistical Office has started to publish again a "physical volume" index together with the "gross value" index. In 1957, the gross value index stood at 276, while the physical volume index stood only at 232 (both indexes on 1949 = 100 basis).[3]

[2] *Central Planning in Czechoslovakia* (Stanford University Press, 1960; Oxford University Press, 1961), pp. 29 ff.
[3] *Hungarian Statistical Handbook for 1958* (Hungarian Statistical Office, Budapest, 1958), II, pp. 63-64.

In Czechoslovakia, however, the prewar physical volume index was published only until 1949; since then, only the gross value index is considered to be the official measure of industrial production.

In 1957, the Czechoslovak Statistical Office started also to publish index numbers on "national income originating in industry", retrospectively from 1948 on. This index is not quite comparable with a "value added" index, because the Marxist definition of national income differs from others, and because of the peculiarities of pricing under central planning in Czechoslovakia; the inclusion of varying amounts of turnover tax in national income may be especially distorting. Nevertheless, it is a more realistic measure of industrial output than the gross value index. It also seems to come fairly close to the "physical volume" index computed by Zauberman.[4] Over the 8 year period 1948-1956, it shows an 85% increase in industrial production, compared to a 72% increase according to Zauberman's index. Unfortunately, Zauberman's index was computed during the statistical black-out in Czechoslovakia and rests on a limited coverage of items; furthermore, it is available only up to 1956. In the absence of a reliable "physical volume" index,[5] I shall have to use the Marxist "income originating in industry" as the second-best measure of industrial growth.

The diagram on p. 377 shows, I hope, the varying rates of growth as produced by various types at various periods of time. The fastest rate of industrial growth is shown, of course, by the upward-biased gross value index for the twelve-year period 1948-1960 (the curve in the diagram is the steepest); it corresponds to a compound annual rate of increase of more than 11%, whereas the "income originating in industry" shows only an 8% average annual increase. But even this is substantially more than the $2\frac{1}{2}$% average annual increase over the 1923-1937 period as shown by the (possibly relatively downward-biased) physical volume index. The prewar rate of industrial growth was, of course, pulled down by the great depression in the thirties when industrial production dropped to 60% of the

---

[4] A. Zauberman, *Industrial Development in Czechoslovakia, East Germany and Poland* (London, Royal Institute of International Affairs, 1958).

[5] Recently, a detailed recomputation of the Czechoslovak index of industrial output has been published by G. J. Staller, "Czechoslovak Industrial Growth; 1948-1959", *American Economic Review*, Vol. LII, Number 3 (June 1962), pp. 383-407. Staller calls his index "value added", but it is basically a physical volume index with value added used only as statistical weights of physical volume series. Over the 1948-59 period, his index shows an increase in industrial output by 141% (index for 1959 is 241.8 on 1948 = 100 basis; *op. cit.*, p. 389), compared to a 138% increase shown by "income originating in industry" and 234% increase shown by the official gross value index.

INDUSTRIAL PRODUCTION IN CZECHOSLOVAKIA

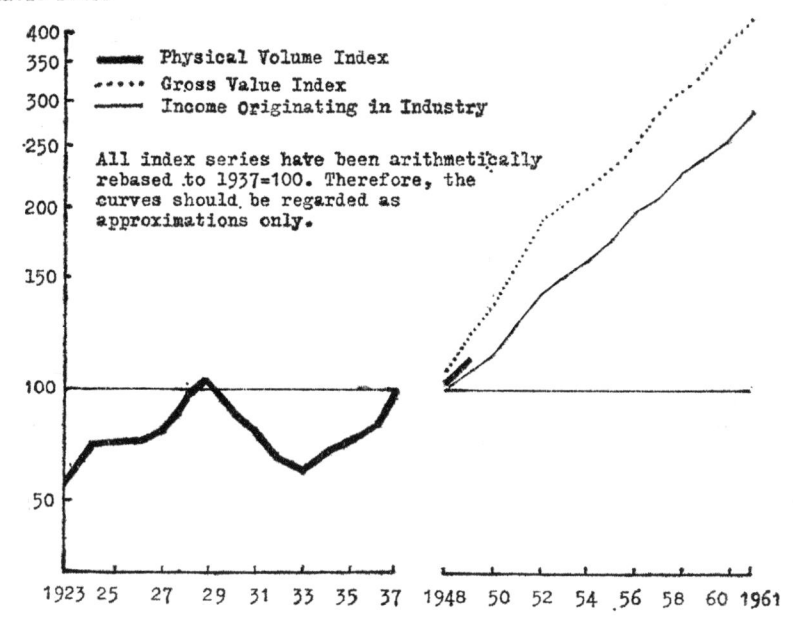

Ratio Scale

— Physical Volume Index
····· Gross Value Index
— Income Originating in Industry

All index series have been arithmetically rebased to 1937=100. Therefore, the curves should be regarded as approximations only.

1929 level. In times of prosperity, 1923-1929, and of recovery from depression, 1935-1937 (the latter period being characterized also by stepped-up armament production), the rate of industrial growth came close to the postwar rate according to the "income originating in industry" index.

It is noteworthy that the "gross value" curve has departed more and more from the "industrial income" curve since the industrialization drive in 1951, except for the years of economic détente 1945-1955. As I have mentioned, this widening gap denotes, i.a., increasing real cost. During the economic thaw in 1954 there is a slight kink in the gross value curve, while the industrial income curve continues to rise, so that the two curves come slightly closer together. If the "income originating in industry" index were corrected for the various distortions, this tendency would probably be even more pronounced; the industrial income index seems to show an upward bias up to 1953, and possibly no bias, or a slight downward bias in later years.[6]

It would be economically meaningless to study the rate of industrial growth without at least a very rudimentary input-output analysis. The

---

[6] This, too, seems to be corroborated by comparing, year by year, the index of income originating in industry with Staller's computations, *op. cit.*, p. 389.

most important factor contributing to the rapid postwar increases in industrial output has been the fast-increasing input of both labor and capital into industry. The number of persons working in industry went up from 1½ to well over 2 million, and the share of industry in total stock of fixed capital went up from 24% to approximately 30% over the 1948-1960 period. The increasing input of capital goods is connected with the fact that industrial output of capital goods went up much faster than industrial output of consumer goods,[7] except during the economic détente 1953-1956. During the first industrialization drive, output of some consumer goods decreased even in absolute terms (between 1948 and 1953, e.g., output of passenger cars dropped from 12.6 to 7.3 thousand and output of shoes from 36 to 23 millions of pairs annually). When industrial output was more balanced between capital and consumer goods during 1953-1956, the rate of industrial growth slowed down. If there is a new economic "thaw" with a greater emphasis on improving the standard of living, a certain slowing-down of industrial growth can be expected again. In any case, there are limits to further draining human and capital resources from other sectors of the national economy into industry. Czechoslovak planners seem now to realize that without more efficiency the high rates of industrial growth of the last 12 years cannot be maintained.

The purpose of this paper, however, is not to attempt to forecast future developments, but only to inquire into the past rate of industrial growth. Czechoslovakia's industrial growth, 1948-1960, has no doubt been impressive; but it has not been as fast as shown by the gross-value index, and it has been rather costly. Sooner or later, Czechoslovak planners will come to realize that they have been deluding themselves into undue optimism by having used the gross-value index for measuring industrial production.

---

[7] According to Staller, output of producer goods increased by 188.8% and output of consumer goods only by 92.7% over the 1948-1959 period. *Op. cit.*, p. 389.

LAW

The Origins and Development of the Study of History of Law in the Territory of Czechoslovakia (1775-1939)

JAROSLAV NĚMEC

The Western Provinces of present Czechoslovakia were the only Slavic territory which developed a voluminous legal literature during the Middle Ages. Apart from the *Statuta ducis Conradi* (an official codification dating from before 1189), this literature began in Bohemia in about 1320 with the *Kniha Rožmberská* ("Book of Rožmberk"), continued with *Řád práva zemského* ("Regulations of the Provincial Law", *Ordo iudicii terrae*, 1348), with the late 14th century work of the Supreme Judge of the Czech Kingdom, Ondřej of Dubá, *Výklad na právo zemské české* ("Interpretation of Bohemian Provincial Law") and culminated in the work of Viktorin Kornel of Všehrdy: *O práviech, súdiech i dskách země české knihy devatery* ("Nine Books on Laws, Courts and Land Registers of Bohemia") which was published in 1502 and revised in 1509. In Moravia, in about 1481, Governor (*zemský hejtman*) Ctibor Tovačovský of Cimburk wrote *Pamět obyčejů, řádů, zvyklostí starodávních a řízení práva v markrabství moravském* ("Recollections of the Old Customs, Regulations, Habits and Court Procedures in the Moravian Margraviate"), or the so-called *Kniha Tovačovská* ("Book of Tovačov"); Ctibor of Drnovice produced his *Kniha Drnovská* ("Book of Drnovice") in the first half of the 16th century.[1]

All these works provided the courts with valuable information, but had no authority because they were of a private character. Moreover, they described and commented only on the Provincial Law, which was applicable to the nobility, owners of independent estates and the rural population.[2]

There were many collections, official and unofficial, of laws applicable to the burghers, or city-dwellers. Mostly of German origin, they lost their special character in the process of adoption and were finally brought

---
[1] Němec, Jaroslav, *Documentation of Czechoslovak Law. With chapters on Czechoslovak history and history of law.* Dissertation (Washington, Catholic University of America, 1956), p. 28-31.
[2] The term "Provincial Law" in this essay is always equivalent of the Czech term *zemské právo* (*ius terrae*; *Landrecht*).

together in the work of Brikcí Kouřimský of Liczko, whose *Práva městská* ("The Town Laws") were published in 1536. Brikcí's collection was revised during the years from 1579 to 1590 by Kristián Pavel of Koldín. Koldín's *Práva městská* ("The Town Laws") acquired recognition in Bohemia and later in Moravia as well.

Koldín's book was the last in the long line of the Czech legal works. The White Mountain defeat (1620) with all its political and religious consequences, marked also the end of legal studies for a long time.[3]

Interest in Czechoslovakia in the theoretical aspects of law seems to have started in 1348, when Caroline University was founded in Prague, and Roman and Canon Law became better known. There was very little concern, however, with the origins and development of law. The time was not yet ripe for the study of the history of law; even the study of general history was still in its swaddling clothes. It was, therefore, up to the leaders of the Czech national revival at the end of the 18th century to introduce this important subject.

Before we begin our account we should mention briefly the conditions under which the study of history of law in Czechoslovakia originated.

The miracle of the Czech national revival used to be ascribed by the historians primarily to the influence of German philosopher J. G. Herder. Other influences, especially domestic, were underestimated. We know today, however, that the roots of the Czech renascence went much deeper. The seed of national sentiment that developed during the second half of the 17th century had been germinating for a hundred years. Among the Czech bourgeoisie the Latin works of the learned Jesuit, Bohuslav Balbín (1621-88), and canon Tomáš Pešina of Čechorod (1629-80) evoked at least a certain sympathy for the Czech cause.[4] Among the rural population, the history of Bohemia, by Václav Hájek of Libočany (d. 1538) written in the Czech language, was widely circulated and held in very high esteem.[5] There were many other Czech books, religious and non-religious, from before 1620, still circulating, especially among the non-Catholics. Furthermore, the Roman Catholic Church in its effort to convert the population published religious books for laymen in the Czech language. In these books reference was made often to the glorious Czech

---

[3] Němec, J., "Czechoslovakia, I: Historical evolution of laws in Czechoslovakia, and the law of inheritance valid prior to January 1,1951", in: Szirmai, Z., ed., *The law of inheritance in Eastern Europe and in the People's Republic of China* (Leyden, University of Leyden, 1961), p. 114-7.
[4] Balbín, Bohuslav, *Epitome rerum Bohemicarum* (Pragae, 1677); Pešina, Tomáš, *Prodromus Moravographiae* (1663); Pešina, Tomáš, *Mars Moravicus* (1667).
[5] z Libočan, Hájek Václav, *Kronyka česká* (Praha, 1541).

past in connection with the names of Saints such as Wenceslas, Ludmila and Adalbert. The new cult of Joannes Nepomucensis, canonized in 1729, spread quickly through all Europe and also appealed to national pride. Thus Czech national feeling, though very weak, was still alive!

Czech nationalism got an important new stimulus during the reign of Empress Maria Theresa and her son, Joseph II. Their radical reforms encroached, first of all, upon the nobility's constitutional privileges and its material interests. The noblemen of the Provinces of the Kingdom of Bohemia (Bohemia, Moravia, Silesia), in their fight against enlightened absolutism, looked for support to the population at large, and, therefore, whether directly or indirectly, helped Czech nationalism. By seeking historical precedent for legal arguments against absolute monarchy, they were also encouraging the study of Czech history.

Another factor was that the non-German clergy greatly resented the discarding by Emperor Joseph II of Latin as the official language in order to accelerate Germanization by force. In retaliation, the priests recommended the use of the Czech language and their advice was followed with enthusiasm by the laymen.

Moreover, from about 1750 on, the new ideas of nationalism penetrated the country. Enlightened opinion concerning personal freedom, Rousseau's ideas as expressed in his *Contrat social* (1762) – these were among the forces which set in motion the rising power.

In this situation, study of the history of domestic law became a very important factor in the national upheaval. It started in 1775, when Josef Vratislav Monse (1733-93), Rector of Legal Studies at the University of Olomouc, began his lectures on the Moravian Provincial Laws. He justified his decision by the opinion that "a student ignorant of the history of his country's laws could not be a good lawyer".[6]

Monse was no beginner in the field of the history of Moravian law. In 1771 he had already published the *Leitfaden zu den Vorlesungen über die Landgesetze des Markgrafthums Mähren*, and his publications multiplied steadily. The history of Moravian law was his first, but not his only, interest. He also studied political history and the history of Moravian literature. In 1776 his *Tabula iuris publici Marchionatus Moraviae* appeared, establishing him as an expert in the history of Moravian law.

Monse's example was followed in 1781 when the Benedictine monks of Rajhrad published the first collection of sources of ancient law under the title, *Jura primaeva Moraviae*. The book tries to give a critical evaluation

---

[6] Pekař, Josef, *Z duchovních dějin českých* (*Josef Vratislav Monse*) (Praha, Melantrich, 1941), p. 249-54.

of these sources and is the first publication containing explanations (though not always the best) of old legal terms and institutions.[7]

On July 2, 1785, in recognition of his scholarly activities, Monse was elected to membership in the *Böhmische Gesellschaft der Wissenschaften* in Prague. Apparently under his influence, this Society announced a contest for the best treatise under the Montesquieuan title: *Über den Geist der böhmischen Gesetze in den verschiedenen Zeitalten*. The prize was awarded to M. A. Voigt, whose treatise was published by the Society in 1788 in Dresden.[8] Influenced strongly by Montesquieu's *L'esprit des lois*, the work covered only the years to 1620 (the date of the Battle of the White Mountain), because the Austrian regime would permit no criticism of the Hapsburg dynasty subsequently in power. The book, however, did not fulfill general expectations, and its influence upon later Czech legal works was practically nil.

In 1786 the Society published in its *Abhandlungen* a text of the oldest Moravian Code of Laws, *Statuta ducis Conradi*, as confirmed in 1237 by Duke Oldřich of Břeclav. The text was apparently furnished from archives by Monse.

After the transfer of the university from Olomouc to Brno, Monse continued his lectures. When he died in 1793, the lectureship, however, was abolished.

If we are to gauge the significance of Monse's work, we must note that while he was the first to investigate the history of domestic law, he was also a pioneer whose work pointed the way to the study of all Slavic national law. His example was followed not only in his own country but also, although much later, in Russia, Poland and Serbia.

As to his originality, he was under the influence of the domestic trends mentioned above. He started his lectures three years before the publication of Herder's *Volkslieder* and nine years before the appearence of that author's *Ideen zur Philosophie der Geschichte der Menschheit*. In that respect, therefore, he preceded Herder.

The elimination of the courses at Brno was a damaging blow to the study of history of law. Monse, however, had prepared the ground very well, and thus his students and friends did not let his ideas die. The then fashionable romanticism, moreover, provided new students and investigators.

In 1804, Jan Luksche (1756-1824), a member of the Moravian Court of Appeals, published in Brno his first book *Über der Stellen und Ämter in*

---

[7] Habrich, Alexius, ed., *Iura primaeva Moraviae* (Brunnae, 1781).
[8] *Abhandlungen der königl. böhmischen Gesellschaft*, Prag, 1869, p. 1 ff.

Mähren seit 1628. His other works were concerned with the history of Moravian and Silesian law.

In Bohemia Josef Karl, Count of Auersperg from 1810 to 1816 published Balbin's *Liber curialis* (3 volumes) and worked on a history of the Bohemian Court of Appeals.

An old wish of Monse's was fulfilled in 1821 when a historical journal was established in Moravia, *Notizen-Blatt der Historisch-statistischen Section*, under the leadership of the able Christian Ritter d'Elvert (1803-1896). The journal provided space for writings not only on the history of Moravian, Silesian and Bohemian law, but also on the history of law of other provinces in the Hapsburg monarchy.

In 1775, when Monse started his lectures in Olomouc, the University of Prague, dominated by Germans, still ignored both domestic conditions and Czech history. The German language was still the language of all lectures and not until October 28, 1791, was a Chair of the Czech language established at the School of Philosophy.[9]

It is true that interest in the history of law in Bohemia was aroused by Monse, but its place was assured only with the work of František Palacký (1798-1876), a historiographer of the Bohemian Estates, and the founder of modern Czech history and historiography. It is well known that Palacký was charged by the Bohemian Estates with the preparation of a general history of Bohemia. To fulfill this task, he had to study many aspects of Czech cultural life. One result of this study was his series of articles on old Czech and old Slavic laws, published in 1831, 1835 and 1837 in the *Časopis Musejní*.[10] It is true, of course, that Palacký's work in our field was a little easier than that of Monse: he already had at his disposal Monse's pioneering work; he could consult Polish sources, especially J. S. Bandtkie's *Ius polonicum* (1831). The oldest Russian code, *Pravda Russkaia*, had been re-issued many times since its first printing in St. Petersburg in 1777, and was, therefore, readily available. *The Code of Tsar Štefan Dušan* (of Serbia) Palacký obtained from Pavel Josef Šafařík, who furnished him a copy from an old manuscript. Thus prepared, Palacký wrote the above-mentioned treatise, *Právo staroslovanské* ("The Old Slavonic Law") and, after some small

---

[9] Odložilík, Otakar, *Vzkříšení mateřštiny* (New York, ONRČ, 1941), p. 9.
[10] Palacký, F., "Pomůcka k poznání řádův zemských království Českého v druhé polovici 13. století", *Čas. mus.*, 1831. Palacký, F., "Pomůcky k poznání staročeského práva i řádu soudního", *Čas. mus.*, 1835. Palacký, F., "Právo staroslovanské aneb srovnání zákonův cara srbského Štefana Dušana s nejstaršími řády zemskými v Čechách", *Čas. mus.*, 1 (1837), 68-110.

corrections, published it as a supplement to books III-V of his *Dějiny národu českého v Čechách a v Moravě* ("History of the Czech nation in Bohemia and Moravia"), vol. I, published in 1836.[11] In this study Palacký first compares Czech law, as represented chiefly by the *Statuta ducis Conradi*, with the Serbian Code of Štefan Dušan. His conclusions about the similarity of all Slavic laws are also partly derived from *Pravda Russkaia*. He does not consider himself a legal expert, however, and says:

In so important and serious a question, it is enough for us laymen in the law to call it to the attention of experts in ancient law so that they can explain it in the proper manner.[12]

Despite this modest statement, Palacký was still the best in the field of Czech law. Only Jan Pravoslav Koubek in 1839 published in the *Časopis českého musea* an article on the legal language and legal techniques of the Slavs and, two years later, Václav Hanka (1791-1861), an expert in Slavistics, edited the *O práviech, súdiech i dskách země české knihy devatery* of Viktorin Kornel of Všehrdy.

As an expert in the history of Czech law, Palacký should also be named the founder of comparative studies of Slavic laws. It is true that the University of Warsaw in 1830 announced a competition for a comparative study on *successio ab intestato* in Roman, German and Slavic laws, but the comparison of Slavic laws in order to find a common denominator started only with Palacký. His publication was so successful that it was translated into Russian in 1846 by Josef Bodjansky and in 1849 into Serbian by Miloš Popovič.

In 1836 a publication began to appear in Moravia, entitled *Codex diplomaticus et epistolaris Moraviae*, edited by Antonín Boček (1802-1847), Archivist of the Moravian Estates. The *Codex* aimed to be a collection of important old documents; it also contained the ancient Moravian law code, *Statuta ducis Conradi*, sanctioned by the rulers in the years 1222, 1229 and 1237.[13] The value of the *Codex*, however, was greatly lessened by the later discovery that some texts had been forged by Boček. The suspicion that some of the documents were forged was first voiced in 1840 by the famous philologist, Bartoloměj Kopitar. One year later, Prof. Alois V. Šembera reached the same conclusion. The Czech historians thus faced the difficult task of separating the valid documents from the

---

[11] Palacký, František, *Dějiny národu českého v Čechách a v Moravě* (Praha, L. Mazáč, 1939), I, 395-427.
[12] Palacký, František, *op. cit.*, p. 397.
[13] Boczek, Anton, *Codex diplomaticus et epistolaris Moraviae*, II, (1836) 209-12, 325-8. Chytil, Josef, *Codex diplomaticus et epistolaris Moraviae*, V (1850), 224.

forgeries. This task was not completed until the beginning of this century.[14]

Distrust of the *Codex* also had regrettable effects upon the study of the history of old Moravian law. Historians failed to mention in their works the *Statuta ducis Conradi,* because they did not know if these were genuine or to what extent they had been "corrected" by Boček. Consequently, we still lack a proper evaluation of this old legal document.[15]

Boček's successor, Josef Chytil (1812-1861), continued the publication of the *Codex* (vol. 5 from Boček's material in 1850, vol. 6 in 1854 and vol. 7 in 1858), after a careful screening of the documents; in 1851 he published the old *Landes Ordnungen des Markgrafthumes Mähren* (Moravian Provincial Ordinances).

A solid basis for the study of the history of domestic law was first really established when independent publication of old legal sources started. In 1856 Chytil, with the cooperation of Peter Ritter Chlumecký, Karel Josef Demuth and A. R. Ritter Wolfskron, prepared a monumental work, *Landtafel des Markgrafenthumes Mähren* ("The Land Register of the Margraviate of Moravia"), printed at the expense of the Moravian Estates. The Land Register (*Zemské desky* = *Tabulae terrae*) was established at the end of the 13th century, probably during the reign of Wenceslas II as a record of the ownership of real estate. It introduced order into land ownership and was the first record of its kind in Europe.[16]

In 1858 Chlumecký and Demuth published *Kniha Tovačovská* ("Book of Tovačov") from old manuscripts.[17]

In Bohemia, there was very little interest in our subject during this period. Palacký was too busy to pay much attention to the field, and thus only Jan Erazim Wocel (1802-1871) made some small contributions. In Moravia, a new worker, Johann Adolf Tomaschek, Edler von Stadova (1822-1898), appeared and joined Chytil's group. His publications dealt

---

[14] The final word belonged to Lechner ("Beiträge zur Frage der Verlässlichkeit des Codex diplomaticus et epistolaris Moraviae", *Ztschr. Verein. Gesch. Mähr. Schles.,* 1898) and G. Friedrich ("Nová řadá moderních padělků v moravském diplomatáři", *Čes. čas. hist.,* 1901).

[15] The first critical article was written by Karel Jičínský in 1865, but the only good one is by V. Brandl in *Právník,* 1873.

[16] Chytil, Josef, and other, *Landtafel der Markgrafenthumes Mähren* (Brünn, 1856), 2 vols. Hrubý, V., "Jindřich Vlach z Isernie a počátky městských knih pražských i desk zemských", *Čas. Arch. školy,* 1 (1923), 142 ff.

[17] Chlumecký, Peter, and Demuth, Karel J., *Das Tobischauer Buch, eine Quelle zur Rechts-Geschichte des 14. Jahrhunderte in Mähren* (Brünn, 1858).

with the history of provincial law, mining law, and the influence of German laws on Czech territory.[18]

From Monse's time, all studies of the history of law were carried on privately, because the university forum was not accessible to them. The University of Prague, as mentioned above, did introduce lectures on Czech language and literature, but this was the only concession. In Moravia, the University declined and was transformed into a mediocre lyceum. At this school, lectures on Czech language and literature were first offered in 1815, but the history of domestic law was not taught. At the Lyceum at Bratislava, the Czech language was taught from 1803 on, but the school offered no legal studies at all. At *Právnická akademie* (Academy of Law), opened in 1776 at the Bratislava Castle, not even the Czech language was taught.[19]

Nevertheless, the study of the history of domestic law came into full bloom after 1860, led mostly by the students and friends of Palacký.

In 1861 there appeared in Prague a legal journal, *Právník*, which also became a forum for studies in the history of law. Two years later, *Právnická jednota* was founded, an organization for the fostering of political and legal sciences; it welcomed and supported studies in the history of law.

An important cornerstone of our discipline was laid by Jan Ferdinand Schmidt von Bergenhold (?-1873), who wrote the first work on the history of Czech civil law.[20]

In 1868, students at the School of Law in Prague formed an organization called *Všehrd*. One of its objectives was the publication of lectures delivered at the Law School. Among these publications there later appeared some in our field.

Around 1870, a new generation of historians of law stepped forward. Among the most famous in Bohemia were Jaromír Čelakovský (1846-1914), Jaromír Haněl (1847-?), Josef Kalousek (1838-1915), Bohuslav Rieger (1857-1907) and, finally, Emil Ott (1845-1924), an expert on the influence of Canon law in the Czech provinces.[21]

---

[18] Wocel, J. E., "O saudu zahájeném", *Čas. čes. mus.*, 1 (1845), 101 ff. Tomaschek Johann Adolf, Edler von Stadova, *Deutsches Recht in Oesterreich im 13. Jahrhunderte auf Grundlage des Stadtrechtes von Iglau* (Wien, 1859). id., *Recht und Verfassung der Markgrafschaft Mähren im 15. Jahrhunderte* (Brünn, A. Nitsch, 1863).

[19] Odložilík, Otakar, *op. cit.*, p. 15-16.

[20] Schmidt von Bergenhold, Johann Ferdinand, *Geschichte der Privatrechtsgesetzgebung im Königreiche Böhmen von den ältesten Zeiten bis zum 21. September 1865* (Prag, 1866).

[21] Their most important works: Čelakovský, Jaromír, *Povšechné české dějiny právní*

Special attention should be given to the activities of two brothers, Hermenegild Jireček (1827-1909) and Josef Jireček (1825-1888), who published either jointly or independently the old sources of domestic law. The most valuable was Hermenegild's work, the *Codex iuris Bohemici*, twelve volumes published between 1867 and 1898. Very important, too, was the brothers' joint compilation, *Sbírka zřízení zemských království Českého, markrabství Moravského a Slezských knížectví* ("The Collection of Provincial Ordinances of the Kingdom of Bohemia, Margraviate of Moravia and the Silesian Principalites") which appeared between 1879-1882.

In Moravia, Vincenc Brandl (1834-1901), Archivist of the Moravian Estates, published the first six Moravian court books dating from the years 1374-1493, under the title *Libri citationum seu Knihy půhonné a nálezové* (Brunae, 1872-1895). He reissued *Kniha Tovačovská* ("Book of Tovačov") in 1868 and, for the first time, *Kniha Drnovská* ("Book of Drnovice"). Brandl, an outstanding historian of his time, also compiled the *Glossarium illustrans bohemico-moravicae historiae fontes* (1876), a dictionary of old Czech terms which is still unique.

Vincenc Prasek (1843-1912) studied the history of law in Upper Silesia and in Moravian and Upper Silesian towns.[22] All of Lower Silesia and most of Upper Silesia were conquered in the 18th century by Frederick the Great. The law in this former part of the *Corona regni Bohemiae* was mostly of German origin and, therefore, studied by Prussian historians.

A great deal of rich source material, with comments thereon, was published in various journals concerned with general history.[23] Important

---

(Praha, 1882), Haněl, Jaromír: many articles. Kalousek, Josef, *České státní právo* (Praha, 1871). Rieger, Bohuslav, *Zřízení krajské v Čechách* (Praha, 1896 [?]). Ott, Emil, *Beiträge zur Rezeptionsgeschichte des Röhmisch-cannonischen Processes in den Böhmischen Ländern* (Leipzig, 1879); and *Das Eindringen des kannonischen Rechts, seine Lehre und wissenschaftliche Pflege in Böhmen und Mähren während des Mittelalters* (Weimar, 1913).

[22] Prasek, Vincenc, *Organisace práv magdeburských na severní Moravě a v rakouském Slezsku* (Olomouc, 1900).

[23] E.g. *Almanach České akademie císaře Františka Josefa* (Praha, 1890-1918); *Archiv český* (Praha, 1840-1935); *Časopis Matice Moravské* (Brno, 1876-); *Památky archeologické* (Praha, 1855-); *Věstník slovanských starožitností* (1898-1900); *Věstník slovanské filologie a starožitností* (Praha, 1900-1901), etc. – Articles on the history of Czech law were included also in German journals published in Bohemia, Moravia and Silesia. We might mention *Mittheilungen des Vereines für Geschichte der Deutschen in Böhmen*; *Quellen-Schriften zur Geschichte Mährens und österreichischen Schlesiens*; *Zeitschrift des Vereines für die Geschichte Mährens und Schlesiens*, etc. These journals, however, deal, as a rule, only with the influence of Germanic law in the Czech lands.

material was scattered also through journals of other provinces of the Austrian Monarchy and published not only in German, but also in Hungarian, Polish or Croatian. Outside the monarchy, Russia and Serbia were the countries most interested in our subject.

Under the pressure of the fully revived Czech nation, the Government of Vienna in 1882 divided the University of Prague (*Universitas Carolo-Ferdinandea*), governed thus far by Germans, into two schools: the Czech University and the German University. At the Law School of the Czech University in 1889, there was also established a Chair of the History of Czech Law. This was a great accomplishment, even if only as a re-establishment of the status instituted by Monse 114 years earlier. Thus the study of the history of domestic law finally acquired again a firm basis for its development.

In the field of general history a fight was raging at this time between the followers of Palacký and the supporters of Professor Jaroslav Goll. Palacký's opinion that Czech culture was original had been challenged by Goll, who maintained that Czech culture (with the exception of Byzantine influence in its earliest stages) evolved from West European influences and relationships.[24] This controversy was of little real concern to the historians of law. Every student of our discipline knew from his own investigation that there are some laws which may be considered typically Czech (or Slavic), and others which undoubtedly originated in foreign, non-Slavic countries. The historians of law, therefore, did not give unqualified support to either of these schools.

Up to the end of the 19th century, the history of Czech law was frequently studied in other Slavic countries, especially Russia, Poland and Serbia, mostly for comparative purposes. Some scholars, such as A. N. Iasinskii, even published special studies on the subject.[25]

We must, in all justice, also mention briefly the relevant contribution of German historians from the Czech Provinces. Originally, scholars of both nationalities cooperated closely. With the growing antagonism, a rift started in the second part of the 19th century. An early manifestation of this division was the work of Emil Franz Rössler, *Deutsche Rechtsdenk-*

---

[24] The program of Goll's school of history was laid down by the article "Dějiny a dějepis" ("History and historical science"), published by Goll in the journal *Atheneum* in 1888. In 1894 Goll, together with Antonín Rezek, founded a new journal, called *Český časopis historický*. This journal became the forum for Goll's followers and soon played a very important role in the country.

[25] Iasinskii, A. N., *Padenie zemskago stroiia v cheskom gosudarstve X-XII vekov* (Kiev, 1895).

mäler aus Böhmen und Mähren, two volumes published in Prague, 1845 and 1853, and followed by other works on the old Town Law. Among others working at least partly in our discipline, we should mention Julius Lippert, Alfred von Fischel and Johann Loserth. A very important role was played by Bertold Bretholz (1862-1936), who succeeded Vincenc Brandl as Director of the Moravian National Archives in Brno. Bretholz was a general historian, but he also made contributions to our subject and published the 7th volume of the Moravian *Libri citationum* in 1911. Among later scholars we should name, at least, A. Horcicka, E. Werunsky, O. Peterka and Adolf Zycha.[26] In the study of the development of law in the Czech provinces, these researchers concentrated mostly on the introduction of German law into the country, and the extent of its influence on Czech law and its institutions. They believed, with German historians (e.g. E.T. Gaupp, C. G. Homeyer, J. Weiske, L. Hildebrand, H. G. Gengler), that German law was superior to all non-German European legal systems. Because of this prejudice, they often ignored some important Czech sources and thus their objectivity was many times questionable. In all fairness, we must, however, admit that the situation on the Czech side wasn't much better.

In spite of its growing popularity, the history of domestic law had few followers. Therefore, no one even considered establishing an independent journal in this field. Articles and small studies on the history of law were published either in *Právník* (est. 1861) or in a new *Sborník věd právních a státních*, issued from 1901 by the Law School of the Czech University. Both journals survived World War I and continued publishing during the 1918-1939 period.

With the general decline of interest in history toward the end of the 19th century, there came also a lessening of interest in the history of law. Therefore, no important contribution to our field appeared up to the end of World War I.

When, on October 28, 1918, the Czechoslovak Republic emerged, composed of Bohemia, Moravia, Silesia, Slovakia and Ruthenia, there was

---

[26] Their most important works: Lippert, Julius, *Geschichte der Stadt Leitmeritz* (Prag, Verein für Geschichte der Deutschen in Böhmen, 1871). Fischel, Alfred, von, "Erbrecht und Heimfall auf den Grundherrschaften Böhmens und Mährens vom 13. bis 15. Jahrhunderte", Arch. öster. Gesch., Bd. 106, 1 Hälfte (1915). Loserth, Johann, *Die Krönungsordnung der Könige von Böhmen* (1876). Werunsky, Em., "Die Majestas Carolina", Ztschr. Savigny-St., Germ. Abt., IX, 94. Horcicka, A., *Das älteste Böhmisch-Kamnitzer Stadtbuch* (Prag, 1915). Peterka, O., *Rechtsgeschichte der böhmischen Länder* (Reichenberg, 1923). Zycha, Adolf, *Deutsche Rechtsgeschichte der Neuzeit*, 2.Aufl. (Marburg/Lahn, Simons, 1949).

renewed interest in the history of law. The new nation of Czechs and Slovaks had to revise its history and to fill in existing gaps.

The Law of January 19, 1920 (No. 135 Coll.) abolished the university's name, *Universitas Carolo-Ferdinandea*, and revived the old name of *Universitas Carolina*. This name, however, was assigned only to the former Czech part of the university and the German part was thenceforth called the *Deutsche Universität in Prag*.

One Czech and one German university no longer sufficed for the educational needs of 15 million people; therefore, *Masaryk University* in Brno (the second Czech institution) and *Komenský University* in Bratislava, for Slovaks, were established.

At all the Law Schools of those universities the history of domestic law was a part of the curriculum. But where the Czech universities assigned the greatest importance to the history of *zemská práva* (Provincial Laws), the German university stressed the importance of Town Laws and other laws of German origin.

Between 1930 and 1939, the history of domestic law was taught at all four Law Schools as a subject required for the so-called "First State Examination".[27] Every student had to have 10 credit hours during the first three semesters. Moreover, the "History of Law in Central Europe" was another required subject (8 credit hours in two semesters). It consisted of the history of German, Polish and Hungarian laws. At the State School for Archivists in Prague, the history of the law in the Czech Provinces and Slovakia, and its relations to the history of German laws was taught (4 credit hours in two semesters).[28]

Thus the universities became the centers of studies of the history of the Czechoslovak law. Every year about 8,000 students attended required lectures and, as a result, interest in our discipline grew steadily. Research in the history of law was conducted mostly at the Law Schools. At Caroline University, Prof. Karel Kadlec (1865-1928) soon became a world authority in the history of Slavic law; Prof. Jan Kapras (1880-) specialized in the history of domestic law; Prof. Miroslav Stieber (1865-1934), in the history of Central European law, and Prof. Theodor Saturník, in Slavic law. At the Law School of Masaryk University in Brno, Prof. Bohumil Baxa (1874-1942) and Prof. František Čáda (1895-)

---

[27] The "First State Examination" was called officially "Historico-Legal Examination" and covered also Roman Law, Canon Law and the Laws in Central European Countries.
[28] Turosienski, S. K., *Education in Czechoslovakia* (Washington, U.S. Govt. Print. Off., 1935), p. 118-20.

lectured on the history of domestic law and the laws of Central Europe.[29]

In Slovakia during the Hungarian rule, i.e. before 1918, there was very little interest in the history of domestic law. Only after the establishment of the Czechoslovak Republic did the first Slovak journal, *Právny obzor*, appear; interest slowly developed under the influence of the Komenský University Law School in Bratislava. The first publication in the Slovak language which deserves mention was the translation of Julius Osvath's book, *Stredoveké právne ustanovizne na Slovensku* ("Medieval legal institutions in Slovakia"), published in 1922 in Prešov. Then there appeared a number of pamphlets and journal articles written by Slovak lawyers.[30] Their purpose was to provide a firm basis for the establishment of the discipline in Slovakia. Professors of the new university in Bratislava also made contributions: Rudolf Rauscher (1896-) wrote some articles on general legal history, with special attention to the mining laws and published a textbook on history of law in Slovakia. Richard Horna was interested chiefly in early Moravian history and historical changes in the State frontiers, but also wrote some articles on the legal history of Slovakia.[31]

Experienced Czech historians of law could not participate properly in the development in Slovakia because of two basic obstacles: most of the important sources and nearly all reference books concerning the history of law were in the Hungarian language, which was unfamiliar to them. Furthermore, the legal order of Hungary, of which Slovakia was a part from the 10th century on, differed greatly from the legal order in force in Czech provinces. Studies in our field in Slovakia, therefore, were limited to those Slovaks who knew Hungarian and were familiar with the former Hungarian law. It was up to the Law School of Komenský University to awaken the proper interest in its students and prepare them for this work.

In 1937 a pioneering work appeared in Bratislava: Josef Karpat's *Corona regni Hungariae v dobe árpádovskej* ("Corona regni Hungariae

---

[29] Kadlec, Karel, *Dějiny veřejného práva ve střední Evropě*, 3. vyd. (Praha, 1923). Kapras, Jan, *Přehled právních dějin zemí koruny české* (Praha, 1922, 1926), 2 vols. Stieber, Miroslav, *Dějiny soukromého práva ve střední Evropě* (Praha, Všehrd, 1926 [?]). Saturník, Theodor, *O právu soukromém u Slovanů v dobách starších* (Praha, 1934). Baxa, Bohumil, *Dějiny veřejného práva ve střední Evropě od r. 1848* (Brno, Čs. A.S. Právník, 1926). Čáda, František, *Nejvyššího sudího království českého, Ondřeje z Dubé Práva zemská česká* (Praha, Hist. archiv ČSAVU, 1930).

[30] E.g. by Vladimír Fajnor, Antonín Hons, J. Karpat, E. Stodola, J. Hajný.

[31] Rauscher, Rudolf, *Slovenské právní dějiny v rámci dějin práva ve střední Evropě* (Bratislava, 1927). id., *Přehled vývoje horního práva na Slovensku*. Právny obzor VII, 1924. Horna, Richard, *Hranice republiky Československé ve světle historie* (Bratislava, Práv. fak. univ. Komenského, 1929). id., *O bratislavském vinařství* (Bratislava, 1935).

during the Arpad's Dynasty reign"). It showed that the history of law in Slovakia could not be studied apart from the history of Hungarian law. The disintegration of Czechoslovakia in 1938/39, and World War II, however, interrupted this promising development.

After the establishment of Czechoslovakia, new legal journals appeared: *Časopis pro právní a státní vědu* (Brno, 1918-), *Všehrd* (Prague, 1918-), and *Bulletin de droit tchècoslovaque* (Prague, 1924-). A serial, *Sbírka spisů právnických a národohospodářských*, was published in Brno between 1920 and 1938. There were still other legal journals, like *Právnické rozhledy, Právo a stát, Právní rádce, Právní praxe, Soudcovské listy*, etc., but their importance to the history of law was negligible.

After the student riots in Prague on November 17, 1939, the Czech universities in Prague and Brno were closed by the Nazis; only the German University in Prague continued its lectures. Thus the study of the history of law in the Czech Provinces again departed from the university and moved into the homes of law historians.

Slovakia, as an "independent state" under the protection of Adolf Hitler, retained its university, but very little work was carried on there in our field.

To summarize activities in the field in Czechoslovakia during the 1918-1939 period: leadership at this time was provided by the law schools of the four universities. They greatly expanded the study of the history of law and awakened interest in the subject. The number of articles and pamphlets which appeared is impressive. There are, however, very few major original publications from that period, with the exception of the textbooks. What is to be most regretted is the fact that very little was done to encourage the publication of old sources of the law. It is true that Prof. Čáda edited and annotated *Práva zemská česká* ("Provincial Laws of Bohemia") and the *Kniha Rožmberská* ("Book of Rožmberk"), but both these sources had already been published several times. In Bohemia G. Friedrich's publication of *Knihy dvorské* ("Books of the King's Court of Justice") continued, but in Moravia there was nothing comparable to the publication of the *Zemské desky* ("Land Register") and the *Libri citationum* after vol. 7. Thus the dreams of Vincenc Brandl and the Jireček brothers were not fulfilled even in our new and free Czechoslovakia.

After the closing of the Czech universities, the publication activities of the Czech scholars also stopped.[32] There remained only the publications

---

[32] Only one exception is known to the writer: *Miscellanea historico-juridica. Sborník prací o dějinách práva*, napsaných k oslavě šedesátin JUDra Jana Kaprase, řádného profesora Karlovy university, jeho přáteli a žáky. Uspořádal Václav Vaněček (Praha, nákl. vydavatelovým, 1940).

of the German University of Prague, strongly influenced by National Socialism and, from the professional point of view, hardly worth mentioning. In 1939 the status of the study of history of law in Czechoslovakia was, therefore, the same as it had been before Monse, that is, before 1775.

The Czechoslovak Constitutions of 1920, 1948, and 1960

VRATISLAV BUŠEK

Every constitution is only a framework. It is a fundamental law from which all other laws are supposed to derive their validity; constitutional amendments, statutes, interpretations, decisions, practices and procedures are added to it as expansions of the fundamental constitutional law by legislation, executive and administrative action, judicial interpretation, custom and usage.

The nation is a living organism and constitutional life is a legal rationalization of national life at a given historical moment, varying according to variable social forces and ideologies.

In discussing the Czechoslovak constitutions of 1920, 1948, and 1960, we must keep in mind that the word "constitution" had a completely different meaning, and represented different concepts, in these three periods, of Czechoslovak national life. Even the basic concept of the Czechoslovak national identity changed between 1920 and 1948, and again between 1948 and 1960.[1]

From 1920 to 1938 a single Czechoslovak nation was the originator and implementer of its constitution. The name of the (unhyphenated) Czechoslovak republic reflected that national unity, and the Czechoslovak national emblem was its symbol.

The constitution of February 29, 1920, No. 121 Collection of Statutes, reflected the spirit of liberal democracy and Western Christian civilization prevailing in 1918, when the Czechoslovak people emerged from World War I as a free nation and proclaimed themselves an independent state. Between 1920 and 1938 the Czechoslovak republic came close to being the model liberal democracy in Central Europe.[2]

[1] Vladimir Gsovski, Alois Böhmer, Jaroslav Jíra, Stephen Kočvara, Jindřich Nosek, *Legal Sources and Bibliography of Czechoslovakia*. Published for the Free Europe Committee, Inc., by Frederick A. Praeger (New York, 1959), 180 pp.
[2] *Československá vlastivěda* ("Czechoslovak Encyclopaedia"), vol. 5: *Stát* ("The State"), ed. Jan Kapras, published by Sfinx – B. Janda (Prague, 1931), 706 pp. (In

The Czechoslovak Constitutions of 1920, 1948, and 1960

Between 1938 and 1945 Czechoslovak national existence was shaken and pushed to the brink of annihilation by the Nazi occupation with its various projects for total Germanization of Bohemia and Moravia, and extermination of the Czech people.[3] The establishment of the "Protectorate of Bohemia and Moravia" and of the Slovak State, and the loss of Carpatho-Ruthenia, taken away from Czechoslovakia at the end of World War II, destroyed the geography of pre-war Czechoslovakia. Post-war expulsion of about 2,500,000 Germans fundamentally changed the internal social, economic, cultural and religious structure of the Czechoslovak republic. The constitutional continuity of Czechoslovakia was restored in 1945, but it was a new Czechoslovakia from many points of view.[4]

The most important normative fact reflected in the constitution of May 9, 1948, No. 150 Collection of Statutes, acknowledged the existence of two separate nations, the Czechs and the Slovaks, as a matter of law. Thus an evolutionary process was concluded which had started soon after 1938, accelerating after 1944.

The Czechoslovakia of 1948 no longer had any substantial national minorities, having emerged from World War II as a unified state of two nations of equal legal status.

Supported by Soviet influence and by the Soviet armed forces, the Czechoslovak Communists succeeded (though not yet quite completely) in substituting the concept of the so-called "people's democracy" for the liberal democracy which had been the fundamental concept of the Czechoslovak republic from 1920 to 1938. In 1945 the Communist forces won some very important beach-heads, but they still had to entrench themselves and spread to win the mainland in Czechoslovak economy and the social and cultural structure of Czechoslovakia. Perhaps the final

---

Czech language.) – *Czechoslovakia*, eds. V. Bušek and N. Spulber, published for the Mid-European Studies Center of the Free Europe Committee, Inc., by Frederick A. Praeger (New York, 1957), 520 pp. – *Czechoslovakia*, pp. 504, ed. Robert J. Kerner (Berkeley-Los Angeles, 1949), 504 pp. – *Statistical Handbook of the Czechoslovak Republic*, ed. Hubert Ripka, published by the Czechoslovak Department of Foreign Affairs, Department of Information (London, Williams, Lea and Co. [during World War II, sine dato]), 160 pp.

[3] *Zločiny nacistů za okupace a osvobozenecký boj našeho lidu* ("Nazi Crimes During the Occupation and the Struggle of Our People for Liberation") (Prague, 1961), documents Nos. 1-10. (In Czech language.)

[4] *Czechoslovakia*, eds. V. Bušek and N. Spulber, supra; *Government, Law and Courts in the Soviet Union and Eastern Europe*, pp. 2067, general editors V. Gsovski and K. Grzybovski, vol. 1-2, published by Mouton & Co., The Hague, and Praeger, New York (1959, 1960).

Communist victory was predictable almost as early as 1945, but then there still were some hopes for the liberal democratic forces. The Communist coup d'état in February, 1948, meant that the Communist take-over in Czechoslovakia was irreversible and final, at least for a long time.

The years from 1948 to 1960 were occupied with consolidation of the Communist regime. The constitution of 1948 is a document of the Communists' political victory; it is a program of the "way to socialism" or the "building of socialism" – that is, the way toward Communism. The victorious Communist party still found it expedient to hide behind the smoke-screen of the so-called "Revived National Front", a coalition of anti-Fascist political parties, but the only real force behind this front was the Communist Party of Czechoslovakia.

The significant difference between the constitutions of 1920 and 1948 was not in the wording of these constitutions, but in the new concept itself, of a Communist "constitution". The liberal democratic Czechoslovak constitution of 1920 was a true legal guarantee of individual human and civil rights against the powers of the state. The separation of legislative, judicial and administrative powers in the constitution of 1920 was a fundamental mechanism of this constitution and a basis of the liberal democratic program of the Czechoslovak republic from 1920 to 1938. This liberal democratic program of the Czechoslovak republic was generally proclaimed in the short but meaningful and well worded preamble to the constitution of 1920, even though the former was not deemed to have the binding force of law. This liberal democratic spirit was expressed in legally binding form in the usual list of rights, freedoms and duties of the citizen set forth in the constitution in Sections 106 to 127, and also in Sections 128 to 134, which deal with the protection of national, religious and racial minorities. The best guarantee of this liberal democracy, however, was the general consensus of the Czechoslovak people which supported these principles. The bulk of the constitution of 1920 consisted in a variety of technical legal provisions dealing with the system of the separation of powers and the functions of the several branches of government, to guarantee the supremacy of civil and minority rights against the state.

The constitution of 1948, and even more emphatically the constitution of July 11, 1960, No. 100 Collection of Statutes, guarantee nothing but the tyranny of the Communist Party of Czechoslovakia.[5]

[5] Vlastislav Chalupa, *Rise and Development of a Totalitarian State*, Part II: *The Case of Czechoslovakia*, pp. 75-294, published by H. E. Stenfert Kroese N.V. (Leyden, 1959) (= *Library of the Czechoslovak Institute in Exile*, vol. 2). – E. Táborský, *Communism*

Both of these constitutions are political programs in their entirety. There is no legal difference between the rather lengthy introductions to both constitutions and the texts of the constitutions proper. They are "legal documents" of the same standing in Communist semantics, merely political programs of the same importance as editorials in the Communist press and statements of various Communist leaders. Ever since 1948 the Communist party has been the only political force in Czechoslovakia which really counts.

The sole difference between the constitutions of 1948 and 1960 lies in their references to the Communist party: in the constitution of 1948 the leading role of the Communist Party of Czechoslovakia is still hidden behind the smoke-screen of the "National Front" and the various meanings of "people's republic", while in 1960 the leading role of the Communist Party of Czechoslovakia was openly admitted and legalized.

People who believed in the principles of the constitution of 1920 and who had lived under it, did not immediately realize the implications of the crypto-Communist constitution of 1948. In 1948 the Communist party still deemed it necessary to phrase the constitution with cautious ambiguity in order to confuse people during the period of transition needed to "build socialism". Many liberal democrats, both inside Czechoslovakia and elsewhere, therefore, relying upon the words of the constitution of 1948, considered many acts of the judiciary and of the administration of Czechoslovakia during the period from 1948 to 1960 as abuses and violations of the constitution of 1948. They did not realize that a new Communist legal philosophy and a new Communist moral standard had been introduced simultaneously, which made such abuses and violations absolutely "legal".

I should like to quote the excellent description of the Communist legal and constitutional philosophy from Vladimir Gsovski's *Government, Law and Courts in the Soviet Union and Eastern Europe*:[6]

The Soviet constitution is in no sense the supreme law of the land. It is rather a solemn declaration of general policies and a general approximate organizational and administrative scheme for government authorities. The procedures followed by these authorities, however, do not necessarily conform to constitutional provisions. Under the totalitarian concept of government power, the

---

in Czechoslovakia 1948-1960 (Princeton University Press, 1961), 628 pp. – J. Korbel, *The Communist Subversion of Czechoslovakia 1938-1948* (Princeton University Press, 1959), 242 pp.
[6] Supra, vol. 1 (1959), at 24.

relationships of the executive and legislative branches of the government which are common to free countries do not apply. Although the terms "constitution", "legislative act", and "administrative decree" are used in Soviet law, the authority attached to each of these sources of law in the Soviet Union is not the same as associated with these terms in democratic countries. A constitutional provision may be set aside by an administrative decree and the newly enacted rule incorporated into the constitution only at a later date.

How meaningless the enumeration of civil rights in a Communist constitution is, Gsovski makes very clear:[7]

The 1936 constitution contains a chapter on "Basic Rights and Duties of Citizens", but it is far from being a bill of rights. In the first place, right of ownership is not mentioned among the rights covered therein.

Secondly, statements of rights in the constitution are not phrased as limitations on the government... Instead a right is simply stated, and the statement is usually followed with a qualifying clause which frustrates the effect of the statement. For example, Section 127 begins with the liberal clause: "No person may be placed under arrest except by decision of a court", but the same sentence ends by permitting arrests based only on the "approval of the public prosecutor". Since approval by the public prosecutor is all that is needed for an arrest, the first part of the sentence could be omitted.

It is understandable that many Communists were themselves embarrassed by the words of their own constitution of 1948, because even they were still imbued with the principles of the constitution of 1920, which said what it meant without ambiguity.

The discrepancy between the words of the constitution of 1948 and many statements of Communist leaders after the Communist coup d'état in 1948, on one hand, and reality, on the other hand, was too often and too bluntly exposed between 1948 and 1960.

No fanatical Communist showed any reluctance to deprive former businessmen, industrialists or landowners of their properties without compensation. But they expressed real qualms when they saw that even 'little people' were expropriated and lost that freedom of enterprise supposedly guaranteed by the constitution of 1948.

Section 8 of the constitution of 1948 proclaimed that every citizen could acquire land and other property at any place in the Czechoslovak republic, limited only by the general provisions of law. A similar provision had appeared in Section 108 of the constitution of 1920. How, then, could it be explained that in 1930 there had been 919,970 small

[7] Supra, vol. 1 (1959), at 28.

artisans and independent tradesmen, and in 1960 there were only 56,000[8]? Where and why had some 850,000 of them disappeared in the twelve years during which the guarantees of Section 8 of the constitution of 1948 were in force? Something certainly had gone wrong, wrong enough to worry the small artisan or businessman or farmer, even those who were good Communists.

The constitution of 1948 does not acknowledge the institution of the collective farms, later known as "Uniform Agricultural Cooperatives" (*Jednotná zemědělská družstva*). They were disguised as voluntary cooperatives, until in 1949, the establishment of the "uniform agricultural cooperatives" (JZDs) was initiated. By the end of 1949 there were 28 JZDs. Ten years later there were 12,560 of them. Socialism was built too rapidly even for a Communist small landowner. Even today the landowners holding small agricultural lots (from ½ hectare to 2 hectares), who are Communist party members, are most reluctant to join the JZDs. At the end of 1959 there were about 897,000 small landowners in that category in Czechoslovakia, many of them Communists with a "capitalist soul", who refused to join the JZDs.[9]

Perhaps you remember the old joke about Ivan Ivanovich and Pjotr Pjotrovich? Ivan Ivanovich, a Communist, tries to explain the advantages of Communism to Pjotr Pjotrovich. "A Communist", says Ivan Ivanovich, "having two horses, does not hesitate to give one horse away and keeps only one!" "Fine!", exclaims Pjotr Pjotrovich. "What about cows?" "A good Communist", says Ivan Ivanovich, "keeps only one and gives away the other one." Pjotr Pjotrevich is delighted. "And what about goats?", he inquires. Well, Ivan Ivanovich is a little worried. No giving away of goats. "Why?", asks the amazed Pjotr Pjotrovich. "Because ... because", says Ivan Ivanovich, wavering, "I happen to have two goats." There are still about 897,000 Ivan Ivanoviches in present Czechoslovakia.

The constitutions of 1948 and 1960 are most confusing in their provisions about property ownership. Both recognize national (state or collective) ownership (Section 149/1948 and Art. 8/1960). Public, cooperative, and private enterprises are recognized in Section 151/1948; private ownership of small and middle-sized enterprises with no more than fifty em-

---

[8] *Czechoslovak Statistical Yearbook*, 1959, Prague, p. 61. – *Rudé Právo* (the principal political daily organ of the Communist Party of Czechoslovakia), Prague, issue of June 2, 1960.
[9] *Czechoslovak Statistical Yearbook*, 1959, Prague, p. 266. – B. Šedivý and M. Zubina, "Drobní držitelé půdy a jejich úloha v našem zemědělství" (Small Land-Owners and Their Role in Our Agriculture), *Nová Mysl* (The New Line), a monthly review, Prague, issue of January, 1960. (In Czech language.)

ployees is guaranteed (Section 158/1948). Such private enterprise, says Art. 9/1960, must be carried on personally and without exploiting the labor of others. There is a recognition of "personal" ownership, acquired by personal effort and without exploitation of other people's labor, which is guaranteed as "untouchable" and inheritable in Section 158/1948 and in Art. 10/1960.

But this "personal" ownership is quite different from the private ownership in real property, of landowners who hold less than 50 hectares of agricultural land and work it personally, without exploiting the labor of others (Section 159/1948). This private ownership in agricultural land is guaranteed, but it is *not* "untouchable" and *not* inheritable. A former individual owner of agricultural land who entered, and was admitted to, a JZD, "freely and voluntarily", to be sure, now toils on the land in company with the other members of the JZD; the land is only used, not owned, by the JZD. The land is still considered privately owned by the former independent farmer who is now a member of the JZD; this is similar to the empty title of the old Roman law. Private ownership of land is not guaranteed by the constitution of 1948 (Section 159), it is not "untouchable" nor is it inheritable. The constitution of 1960 no longer mentions private ownership of land at all.

The former independent farmer, upon entering the JZD, becomes *glebae adscriptus*. He cannot leave the JZD if and when he wants to; he may be expelled or dismissed, but only on condition that he finds someone else to perform his work for the JZD. I am not discussing here all the aspects of this modern slavery or serfdom introduced by the Communists, which is the main cause of the unsatisfactory agricultural economy in Czechoslovakia under the Communist regime. I am dealing only with the distinction between private ownership of land (sometimes reduced to the bare title) and "personal" ownership.

According to Viktor Knapp,[10] "it is a very doubtful and disputed question whether real property may also be the object of individual ('personal') ownership. This might involve small agricultural plots, building lots for one-family houses, small one-family gardens, etc. The question of the regulation of agricultural relations is presently in a stage of rather fermentative development in this country so that it is not ripe for any scientific determination of more than momentary validity".

Vladimir Procházka, member of the Czechoslovak Academy of Scien-

---

[10] Viktor Knapp, *Vlastnictví v lidové demokracii* ("Property Ownership in a People's Democracy"), chapter 13: "Vlastnictví k půdě" (Ownership in Real Property) (Prague, Orbis, 1952) (In Czech language.)

ces, author of the May constitution of 1948 and co-author of the constitution of 1960, confirms our observation concerning socialist, individual ("personal") ownership and ownership in real property in his article, "The New Constitution, A Testimonial to Our Progress". In it he points out the probability that private ownership of real property, no longer supported in the constitution of 1960, as distinguished from the May constitution of 1948, will be liquidated in the near future.[11] The question of private ownership of real property is at present dealt with in Czechoslovakia in ordinary statutes (i.e. the statutes concerning the uniform agricultural cooperatives, Nos. 69 of 1949 and 49 of 1959, respectively), rather than in the constitution.

A very practical question was seriously considered during the so-called "nation-wide discussion" of the draft of the constitution of 1960. Few questions were actually discussed, in fact, but one of these was very significant indeed: What about the ground on which a one-family house is built? Is it the subject of "personal" ownership like the house, or is the ground to be considered the subject of "private" ownership? Even loyal Communists were much interested, because the experience of the years 1948-1960 was still remembered vividly. No clear answer or reassurance was given to the bewildered citizens, prospective builders of one-family houses. No wonder, therefore, that the people of Czechoslovakia prefer to buy a motorcycle, a car, or a television set, unquestionably "guaranteed", "untouchable" and inheritable "personal" property, rather than to build a house on a ground of such dubious legal character! Even a good Communist is still anxious to preserve his "personal" property, like Ivan Ivanovich.

The constitution of 1948 was a crypto-Communist constitution of the "way toward socialism". In twelve years, socialism grew in Czechoslovakia at a very rapid pace. The constitution of 1960 is a document of victorious socialism and the "way toward Communism", when "everybody will work according to his abilities and everyone will get anything he needs" (Preamble to the constitution of 1960, third paragraph). Who will decide what a citizen needs? The Communist Party of Czechoslovakia, no doubt.

"Nothing", said the President of the Czechoslovak Socialist Republic, Antonín Novotný, "nothing happens in this country without the leadership of the Party and without its guiding directives."[12]

There is no separation of powers, but only a division of functions, and

[11] In the magazine *Czechoslovak Life*, July, 1960, pp. 8-9.
[12] *Rudé Právo*, Prague, issue of April 17, 1960.

the only will which counts is that of the Communist Party of Czechoslovakia. Constitutional laws are no longer relevant at all. Only the constitution and the structure of the Communist party are relevant; only sources and manifestations of the will of the Communist Party carry any weight in Czechoslovakia, as in all other Communist countries.

You can seldom win against a policeman who hands you a traffic ticket in the United States, but never could you invoke your constitutional rights against a Communist authority. Such a complaint would be an act in itself damning and would show that you are an "enemy of the people".

The Brno School of Jurisprudence

ADOLF PROCHÁZKA

INTRODUCTION[1]

This lecture deals with the philosophical concept of law which was cultivated principally at Masaryk University in Brno, and which was consequently often referred to as the "Brno School of Jurisprudence". We also describe it as a "normative" or "normological" theory, because, as will be indicated later, it takes its departure from the concept of a "norm". The term "Reine Rechtstheorie", by which Kelsen designated his own very closely related philosophy of law, has sometimes been translated as "pure theory of law". This translation appropriately recognizes the fact that this legal theory is deeply concerned with purity of method, and that it is sharply opposed to the syncretism of methods which has distinguished the traditional legal science.

The normative theory was taught chiefly at the University of Brno, but had a number of representatives in the Universities of Prague and of Bratislava. In addition, it penetrated deeply into Czechoslovak public opinion. Briefly, it became a cultural possession of Czechoslovakia, exercising a dominating influence not only on our legal science and our universities, but also on the practice of our courts and administration.

It is only fair to say that the Brno School of Jurisprudence developed under the powerful influence of Professor Hans Kelsen, a teacher at the University of Vienna. Nevertheless, it cannot be claimed that it represented merely a subordinate branch of Kelsen's teaching.

The founder of the Brno School of Jurisprudence, Professor František Weyr, devoted himself to the task of formulating the fundamental principles of his theory at the very time when Kelsen was working on the same subject[2] and when the latter published his *Hauptprobleme der Staatsrechts-*

---

[1] See my article "Czechoslovak Philosophy of Law", *Czechoslovak Yearbook of International Law*, London, 1942., pp. 89-103.
[2] See Weyr's writings of 1908: "Contributions to the Theory of Compulsory Corpora-

lehre (1911), Weyr had the satisfaction of discovering that he was not alone among the legal scientists with his philosophical-legal constructions, but that he could refer to, and find support in, the brilliantly designed system of the Viennese teacher. From that time on, the teachings of Weyr developed parallel to the philosophy of Kelsen, and the results of the research of both legal philosophers were often in agreement. Yet, in spite of great efforts to achieve conformity, dictated by the genuine desire of the two philosophers to provide a safe and unified foundation for legal science, each system, that of Vienna and that of Brno, preserved its individual character. Let me now draw attention to at least two of the fundamental traits of the Brno School of Jurisprudence as distinguished from that of Vienna.

Kelsen, in his *Hauptprobleme der Staatsrechtslehre*, plunged immediately *in medias res*, seeking support in neo-Kantian philosophy (Simmel, Wundt), and simply declared that he believed in the noetic dualism of nature and the norm, and then proceeded to concern himself more or less only with specifically legal problems. Weyr, on the other hand, using a typically Czech approach, strove to penetrate into the farthest noetic foundations of his teaching. He correlated his doctrine directly with that of Kant and Schopenhauer. In fact, he went further; in subjecting this theory to a thorough critical examination, he showed that these two philosophers, even though they are really the founders of noetic dualism, did not sufficiently adhere to it, or at least did not fully succeed in formulating it. Weyr particularly pointed out that *Kant actually created only an epistemology of natural sciences*, while he neglected the epistemology of valuating sciences (of norms and postulates), admitting, however, a dualism of nature and values (cf. *Kritik der reinen Vernunft* in conjunction with the *Kritik der praktischen Vernunft*). Thus Kant was certainly a dualist. But his normological and teleological epistemology is not developed. As far as Schopenhauer is concerned, Weyr demonstrated that this philosopher certainly made a correct distinction between causal and logical nexus, as indicated by his magnificent work *Satz vom Grunde*,[3] and that his work substantiated the distinction between two orders of cognition, etiological on the one hand, and normative-teleological on the other; but that in spite of all this he, Schopenhauer, remained a monist, or at least made a determined effort to overcome the dualism which was

---

tions", *Zum Problem eines einheitlichen Rechtssystem*, and "The Fundamentals of the Philosophy of Law" (1920).

[3] "On the Fourfold Root of the Principle of Sufficient Reason" (1813).

imposing itself upon him. As opposed to these two philosophers, Weyr openly declared his allegiance to epistemological dualism (in contradistinction to Schopenhauer), and also (in contradistinction to Kant) built it up on the methodological side (in normology). He was soon after supported and followed in this undertaking by Engliš, the Brno professor of economics, who worked out a methodology of aims (teleology).

Thus, the Brno School of Jurisprudence, Weyr, Engliš, Jaroslav Kallab, and their followers and pupils, during the happy twenty years of the Czechoslovak Republic (1918-1938) when science and art really flourished under the aegis of the democratic ideology of Masaryk and Beneš, made a rich contribution to the development of human thought.

Another characteristic trait of the Brno School of Jurisprudence – in relation to the Vienna School – is expressed by the personal attitudes of its representatives toward a number of fundamental legal concepts, as for instance, the primary and most important concept of the legal "norm".

While in the view of Kelsen a legal norm is a provision which stipulates certain behavior under the sanction of punishment or civil execution, the Brno School adheres to the thesis that a legal norm is simply an expression of "what ought to be", and that its legal character is provided by its place in a legal order. This characteristic is not affected by whether or not this norm is sanctioned.

Weyr and the Brno School did not accept Kelsen's definition of a legal norm as sanctioned norm for a wholly logical reason: the sequence of sanctions cannot extend indefinitely; at the end of the sequence there is always a custodian who himself is not supervised. Hence, even Kelsen cannot avoid legal norms without sanctions. Moreover there are certainly also typical *moral* norms which are sanctioned in a way very similar to the legal norms. In addition the result of this logical argument corresponds to the Czech ideological concept of law and the State. The Czech individual does not overlook the fact that the law, as opposed to morality, usually exhibits specific sanctions (punishment, civil execution). At the same time, however, he respects the social values of the legal order, and regards it as perfectly natural that even norms which are unsanctioned, and thus *leges imperfectae*, can be legal norms, and that the inhabitants of the State ought to respect this legal character by voluntary self-discipline and out of consideration for the general good.

It is appropriate to emphasize that the Brno School not only has its special *intellectual* character in relation to the Viennese School, but also has characteristics which are expressive of a Czech milieu. This, of course, is not to say that it has been deliberately influenced by Czech national ideology. Science must be universal, beyond the tenets of any particular ideology; its concepts must be evaluated entirely apart from the ideology and emotional content of the environment in which they have been formulated. Yet I still maintain that the *conclusions* reached by the Brno School by scientific argument are related to the Czech mentality and the Czech setting, and that the roots from which the school derives its creative strength thrive well in Czech soil.

Having introduced our subject with a few generalities, I now proceed to a more detailed study of the Brno concept of law. As stated above, this school was founded by Professor Weyr, who gave it its broad outline shortly before the First World War. He was, however, soon surrounded by coworkers and pupils, who not only developed his teaching, *but modified many of his concepts*. Thus, the Brno legal school developed as the collective work of a number of legal theoreticians. It is therefore comprehensible that among the exponents of Weyr's teaching there was no absolute unity of thought, and that even between the master and the pupils there were differences of opinion. Professor Weyr always encouraged discussion, rejected scientific authoritarianism, and rejoiced in the independent attitude of his followers. Interpreting some achievements of the teaching of the Brno School, I shall take the broader view of this theory as a whole, and give many formulations of my own. I wish to emphasize this particularly in order to avoid being reproached with inaccurate reproduction of Weyr's teaching.

A complete presentation of the teaching of the Brno School of Jurisprudence would comprise the following five chapters:
1) Legal science in the system of knowledge;
2) The definition of the legal norm;
3) The legal order and its scope;
4) Municipal and international law;
5) Conclusion.

I consider essential *especially* chapter No. 3, dealing with the clear distinction between the norm and its conditioning facts; we may also say between the norm and the process in which the norm is created. It is particularly in this area that I have supported (in my writings) a conception substantially different from that of Professor Weyr.

In short, adopting Merkl's[4] doctrine of the hierarchical structure of the legal order (the higher norm is the reason for the validity of the lower

---

[4] See Adolf Merkl, *Die Lehre von der Rechtskraft* (1923).

norm) and his dynamic theory (the lower norm – and every legal norm, except the "Grundnorm" or basic norm – is "created" in a process prescribed by a higher norm, thus the "creation of law", the legal "process", becomes the central concept of the legal theory), my writings have shown since 1924 that obligations too, based on quasicontracts, delicts and quasidelicts, should be conceived as concrete, individual legal norms, analogous to the contractual norms. In this way I think the full extent and scope of the hierarchically built legal order has been finally revealed. I earlier coined the term, *"automatic" creation of law*, for a process consisting of facts which are not delegated human acts. My writings also defended against Weyr[5] the distinction in Roman jurisprudence between contract and contractual obligation. The contract is a norm-creating fact, and thus belongs to the legal process, which conditions the emergence of the contractual obligation (a concrete legal norm). In this manner the strict distinction between norm-creating facts – to which belongs also the expressions of "Will" of norm-creating organs – and the norm itself has been stressed. My writings extended this division to all levels of the legal order, thus to constitutional norms, statutory norms, etc. and gave a new aspect to the noetic dualism of nature and the norm.[6]

Thus, the norm has been revealed as a *noumenon*, strictly distinguishable from any natural phenomenon, as an object of cognition which is not in space and time, and not subject to the law of causality, which is "eternal", in short, as *validity* or *value*, representing a world strictly separated from that of nature, and having its special methodology ("normology" as contrasted to "etiology"). The so-called "naive realism", apparent, for instance, in George Jellinek's theory of "two sides" of the State as the identical object of cognition (experience) for the legal science and the natural sciences[7] and its remnants in the theories of Kelsen and Weyr, and of other normative legal scientists, has been finally overcome.

On the other hand the concept of law which has been presented in my writings demonstrates how the legal norm, belonging to the world of *values*, is tied to the world of nature by its *factual* premise, by the conditioning facts (*Tatbestand*), which, formed by the higher norm, are phenomena in time and space, and subject to the law of causality. Also, the *content* of the legal norm (*a contrario* to its form) is determined by phe-

---

[5] See Weyr, *Teorie pravni* ("Theory of Law"), Orbis, 1936, p. 200.
[6] See Adolf Procházka, "Creation of law and its finding" (Praha-Brno, 1937), "Basis for Civil Actions" (Brno, 1932), "Normative Theory and Creation of Law" (1930).
[7] Georg Jellinek, *Allgemeine Staatslehre, Všeobecná Státověda*, Czech translation (1906), p. 184.

nomena of the world of nature, formed to satisfy the needs of the function of law, which is to regulate and motivate human behavior. Here in its practical function, the norm becomes a motive, thus a psychological phenomenon.

CONCLUSION

Finally, I wish to stress that what I have submitted here as the teaching of the Brno School of Jurisprudence is only a slight sketch of certain problems which have been worked out by Czech normative theory. But it may at least serve to make clear that our normative school seeks to develop a safe methodology for the cognition of law. It proceeds from the assumption that the law is a system of norms, and it adopts as its method of legal science, normology, i.e. the logic of the norm and of the relation between norms. The Brno school is convinced that this method makes it possible to solve all the traditional legal problems in a satisfactory manner.

Anyone who reads the studies of normative theoreticians on these conceptions and problems will frequently be surprised at the simplicity of the solutions which they provide. Thus, for instance, the concept of sovereignty is defined as the juridical underivability of the highest norm; the concept of retroactivity as the legal evaluation of past facts, and so on. We must realize that striving for a simple, uncomplicated solution is not necessarily detrimental to its quality. Quite the contrary: *simplex sigillum veri*.

In the writings of normative theoreticians, one can also detect these characteristics:

A striving for a purity of solution. The reader finds in them pure legal reasoning, rather than a rich mixture of legal, sociological, psychological and political conceptions. In so far as concepts from other sciences are introduced, it is made clear to what science they belong, in order to preclude any fatal confusion. For confusion is the beginning of all evil.

Finally, the reader may be struck by the reserved attitude of normative theory toward ideological trends of the past and the present. The reader ascertains that the normative theorists simply explain their scientific object, law, ensuring that they do not confuse this explanation with criticism of law, and in particular that they do not furnish ideological postulates under the cloak of legal statements. Here we must recall what was said at the beginning of this lecture. The object of science is to cognize, and science has only one ideal: to discover the truth, in other words, to find connections and to arrange in an intellectual unity the objects which are presented to it for systematic arrangement. Hence science is not dependent upon ideological currents. Anybody who wishes to place science at the mercy of an ideology is killing its very roots.

That has been done by the present régimes in Czechoslovakia and the other countries behind the Iron Curtain. These régimes have set up the Communist ideology as the directive for all social research, including legal science. Legal scientists in our captive countries are today under orders to teach Communist propaganda instead of the objective knowledge of truth.

The normative theory is just the antipode of such ideological Communist legal science. It is strictly non-ideological.

But being non-ideological, the normative theory is not anti-ideological. It must be non-ideological in order to serve the truth, to serve the cognition of law as opposed to the creation of law. Legislation is certainly ideological (in the sphere in which the legislator is free). But the cognition of what the legislator has created has to be non-ideological, that is, objective.

I know from prewar experience that the non-ideological character of the normative theory has often been considered a shortcoming, a desertion from the battlefield of ideologies on which the most vital issues of our epoch are fought out. Critics say for example: How can the normative theory be indifferent to the problems of democracy, of social justice, etc? Therefore many outstanding political personalities, from the left wing, the right wing and the center of political life as well, from among Socialists, Liberals, Christian Democrats, etc., have denounced the normative theory as being even destructive, because it has not been willing to serve their causes.

Such an attitude towards the normative theory is certainly incorrect, unjust and based on misunderstanding.

Moreover, a science which is faithful to its duties and seeks the truth, and only the truth, can never be an obstacle in the path of a good and honest ideology. This applies particularly to the reasoning of *de lege ferenda*. We must first know the structure and content of the legal order, and only then can we proceed to evaluate and improve it according to our ideological beliefs. In other words, reasoning and striving *de lege ferenda* presuppose reasoning *de lege lata*.

The Brno School not only desires and makes possible scientific considerations *de lege lata*, but by building up its methodology – normology – (and also teleology), it also contributes to the improvement of ideological considerations.

In every ideology there is involved the use of the norm, and of the postulate; and therefore normology, and the teleology which is akin to it, make it possible for us to think more clearly in terms of ideological conceptions. Thus, for instance, we are presented with the ideological task of working out the reform of law in accordance with the principles of justice. We perceive at once that if we are not to become entangled in hopeless disputes and confusions, we must begin by formulating the meaning of justice (for example, the substance of our social ideal), and deduce from it those aspects pertaining to the law. If we can reach agreement in the formulation of the substance of the social ideal, then the next two tasks are simple, provided that we proceed in a correct and methodical way. If we do not agree, then at least we shall realize clearly in what respects we differ. And by that something has been gained, too.

I am convinced that pure and lucid science and exact thought are particularly important means for the improvement of human (social) life. Obscurity and unintelligibility have done no less harm in human history than have weakness or lack of good will. The present era demands good will and the strength which should accompany it, but no less, of course, does it demand the search for truth, unbiased science.

GENERAL BIBLIOGRAPHY

The paper "The Brno School of Jurisprudence" is an abridged and revised version of the author's essay "Czechoslovak Philosophy of Law", published in *Czechoslovak Yearbook of International Law* (*Hlídka mezinárodního práva*), pp. 89-103. The *Yearbook* was edited by Václav Beneš, Alfred Drucker, and Edward Táborský, and published under the auspices of the Czechoslovak Branch of the International Law Association, by Czechoslovak, Domington House (London, 1942). (The chapters: "Legal Science in the System of Knowledge", "The Conception of a Legal Norm", "Legal Order and its Scope", "The State and International Law" were not included in the essay.)

The following works deal with the topics discussed in the paper:

Engliš, Karel, *Základy hospodářského myšlení* (Brno, Barvič a Novotný, 1922) (= *Sbírka spisů právnických a národohospodářských*, svazek 11).

Jellinek, Georg, *Allgemeine Staatsrechtlehre*. Dritte Auflage, unter Verwertung des handschriftlichen Nachlasses durchgesehen und ergänzt von Dr. Walter Jellinek (Berlin, J. Springer, 1929).

Kallab, Jaroslav, *Úvod ve studium metod právnických*, 2 svazky (Brno, Barvič & Novotný, 1920-21) (= *Sbírka spisů právnických a národohospodářských*, svazek 4).

Kant, Immanuel, *Werke*, sorgfältig revidierte Gesamtausgabe von G. Hartenstern, 10 vols. (Leipzig, 1838). Vol. II: *Kritik der reinen Vernunft*. Vol. IV: *Grundlegung zur Metaphysik der Sitten. – Kritik der praktischen Vernunft*.

——, *Critique of Pure Reason*. Translated into English by F. Max Mueller. Second, Revised Edition (Garden City, N.Y., Doubleday & Company, Inc., 1961).

——, *Critique of Practical Reason*. Translated, with an Introduction by Lewis White Beck (= *The Library of Liberal Arts*, Oskar Piest, General Editor, No. 52) (Indianapolis, New York, The Bobbs-Merrill Company Inc., 1900).
Kelsen, Hans, *Das Problem der Souveränität und die Theorie des Völkerrechts*; *Beitrag zu einer reinen Rechtslehre*. 2. photomechanisch gedruckte Auflage (Tübingen, Mohr, 1928).
——, *Allgemeine Staatslehre* (Berlin, 1925).
——, *Ryzí nauka právní. Metoda a základní pojmy* (Brno-Praha, 1933).
——, *General Theory of Law and State*. Translated by Anders Wedberg (= *20th Century Legal Philosophy Series*, vol. 1) (New York, Russel & Russell, 1961).
——, *Hauptprobleme der Staatsrechtslehre, entwickelt aus der Lehre vom Rechtssatze* (Tübingen, J. C. B. Mohr [P. Siebeck], 1923). Zweite, photomechanisch gedruckte, um eine Vorrede vermehrte Auflage.
——, *Reine Rechtslehre. Einleitung in die rechtswissenschaftliche Problematik* (Leipzig-Wien, 1934).
Merkl, Adolf, *Die Lehre von der Rechtskraft, entwickelt aus dem Rechtsbegriff* (Vienna, 1923).
Procházka, Adolf, *Žalobní důvod, studie k normativní konstrukci civilního sporného procesu* (Praha, 1932) (= *Sbírka spisů právnických a národohospodářských*, sv. 58).
——, Review of Jaromír Sedláček's book: *Právo obligační* ("Law of contracts"), in *Časopis pro právní a státní vědu*, VII (Brno, Barvič & Novotný, 1924).
——, "Normativní teorie a tvorba práva", *Sborník k poctě Karla Engliše* (Brno, Barvič a Novotný, 1930) (= *Sbírka spisů právnických a národohospodařských*, sv. 50).
——, "Normy a skutkové podstaty", *Sborník k poctě Jaroslava Kallaba* (Praha, 1939).
——, *Tvorba práva a jeho nalezání* (Praha-Brno, 1937) (= *Sbírka spisů pravnických a národohospodářských*, svazek 88).
——, "La théorie du Droit de Weyr", *Revue internationale de la théorie du droit*. Brno, R. M. Rohrer, année 1937.
——, *Základy práva intertemporálního se zvláštním zřetelem k par. 5 obč. zák* (Brno, Barvič & Novotný, 1928) (= *Sbirka spisů právnických a nárofohospodařských*, sv. 36).
——, "Normativní teorie a politika", *Časopis pro právni a státni vědu*, ročník 1948.
——, "Prakticke důsledky čisté nauky právní", *Sbírka k poctě Dra Ed. Beneše* (Londýn, 1944).
Schopenhauer, Arthur, *Sämtliche Werke in 12 Bänden*, mit Einleitung von Dr. Rudolf Steiner (Stuttgart, J. G. Cotta, 1900). Bd. 1: *Einleitung. Über die vierfache Wurzel des Satzes vom zureichenden Grunde*.
Simmel, Georg, *Einleitung in die Moralwissenschaft. Eine Kritik der ethischen Grundbegriffe* (Berlin, W. W. Hertz, 1892-93).
Weyr, František, *Teorie práva* (Brno-Praha, 1936) (= *Sbírka spisů právnických a národohospodařských*, svazek 83).
——, *Základy filosofie právní* (Brno, Barvič a Novotný, 1920).
——, *Příspěvky k teorii nucených svazků* (1908).
——, *Zum Problem eines einheitlichen Rechtssystems* (= *Archiv des öffentlichen Rechts*, 23) (1908).
——, "Über zwei Hauptpunkte der Kelsenschen Staatsrechtslehre", *Zeitschrift für das Privat- und öffentliche Recht der Gegenwart*, 40 (1914), 175-188.
——, *O metodě sociologické* (Brno, Barvič & Novotný, 1927) (= *Sbírka spisů pravnických a národohospodařských*, sv. 33).
Wundt, Wilhelm Max, *Ethik*; *eine Untersuchung der Tatsachen und Gesetze des sittlichen Lebens*. Vierte umgearbeitete Auflage (Stuttgart, F. Enke, 1912).

Election Laws and Democratic Government

JOHN G. LEXA

A discussion of Czechoslovak election laws – 24 years after Munich, and 14 years after the Communist coup d'état enslaved the Czechoslovak people a second time within one generation – must necessarily look both backward and forward, combining a historical outline of their main features during the twenty years of the first republic and the brief interlude of 1945-48 with suggestions for the future restoration of parliamentary democracy after Czechoslovakia's eventual return to a place among the nations of the Free World.

The first election laws for the Czechoslovak National Assembly, consisting of a 300-member Chamber of Deputies[1] and a 150-member Senate[2] were enacted by the Revolutionary National Assembly on February 29, 1920, immediately following its approval of the Czechoslovak Constitution on the same date;[3] they were followed, likewise on the same day, by the Electoral Court Act.[4] The two laws governing elections to the two chambers of the Czechoslovak National Assembly were based on identical principles of proportional representation[5] of almost mathematical exactness, creating two chambers whose partisan political divisions were exactly alike,[6] leading to some doubts regarding the necessity or desirability of such a two-chamber system.

They were based upon rigid party lists submitted by the political par-

---

[1] An Act concerning the Elections to the Chamber of Deputies, dated February 29, 1920, No. 123 Coll.
[2] An Act concerning the Composition and Jurisdiction of the Senate, dated February 29, 1920, No. 124 Coll.
[3] An Act concerning the Enactment of the Constitution of the Czechoslovak Republic, dated February 29, 1920, No. 121 Coll.
[4] An Act concerning the Electoral Court, dated February 29, 1920, No. 125 Coll.
[5] Act. No. 123/1920, supra, Secs. 46, 47, 51-53; Act No. 124/1920, Sec. 2
[6] Karl Braunias, *Das parlamentarische Wahlrecht*, I (1932), 567. The two-chamber system was abandoned after World War II: Constitutional Decree No. 47 of August 25, 1945, concerning the Provisional National Assembly, Art. 1 (2); Constitutional Act No. 65 of April 11, 1946 concerning the Constituent National Assembly, Art. 2.

ties;[7] the voters were forced to accept or reject these lists without any changes.[8] Seats were assigned to the parties in three stages: a first assignment of a fixed maximum number of seats set forth in the statute[9] was made within the district, based upon a simple quota.[10] Statewide remainders from all districts formed the basis of a second assignment to new statewide party lists compiled by the party central committees from among their unsuccessful candidates in any districts,[11] but splinter parties which had failed to poll a specified minimum at least in one district were excluded from this statewide assignment.[12] The election quota for this second assignment was the so-called Droop quota, i.e. the total of all remainders divided by the number of seats to be filled plus one;[13] this number was determined by dividing the total number of remainders by the average of the district quotas in the first assignment.[14] A third assignment picked up the (remainder) votes of the parties disregarded in the second assignment and assigned them to the successful parties of the same ethnic nationality.[15] Despite the provisions unfavorable to small parties,

---

[7] Sec. 21 of Act No. 123/1920, supra, calls for submission of the lists of candidates by "the parties" and requires for their validity the certified signatures of 100 registered voters.

[8] Sec. 40 of Act No. 123/1920, supra: "The voter may cast his ballot for the list of candidates of any party. Deletions, reservations, and other changes shall have no effect." Cp. Act of April 11, 1946, No. 65 Coll., Sec. 30 (2), and see Braunias, supra, I, 571.

[9] Act. No. 123/1920, supra, Art. I: 22 districts, electing from 6 to 24 deputies each; Act. No. 124/1920, supra, Sec. 9: 12 districts, electing from 4 to 24 senators each.

[10] Act No. 123/1920, supra, Sec. 46.

[11] Id., Sec. 49 (2).

[12] Id., Sec. 51 (1), in its original 1920 wording, required a minimum of 20,000 votes or the election quota at least in one district. By Act No. 58/1935 the minimum requirement was increased to 20,000 votes in at least one district *and* not less than a total statewide number of votes of 120,000.

[13] Id., Sec. 52 (3).

[14] Id., Sec. 52 (1).

[15] Id., Sec. 53. The past-war Constitutional Act No. 65 of April 11, 1946, concerning the Constituent National Assembly dispensed with any third assignment of seats, in view of the expulsion of the bulk of the German-speaking minority. Instead of providing in the statute for a fixed number of seats for each of the (now 28) districts, it called for a determination of seats per province by dividing the total number of registered voters by the total number of seats (300) and then dividing the provincial total of registered voters by this statewide quota (Sec. 2). After the election the total number of votes cast in each province was divided by the number of seats thus determined; the resulting provincial quota was used to ascertain the number of seats for each district by dividing the total number of votes cast in the district by the provincial quota (Sec. 34). The total number of votes cast in the district divided by the number of seats to be filled (election quota) was then used to assign seats to each party admitted to participation in the election, as a simple quota (Sec. 35). All unfilled seats were assigned in the second,

this system enabled a large number[16] of political parties to secure representation in the National Assembly. In the 1929 elections, only four parties[17] secured more than 10% (but less than 16%) each of the seats, while 19 parties obtained less than 9% each.[18] The influence of party committees upon the members of parliament secured by the rigid lists of candidates grew into outright party domination through a unique development of judicially enforceable party discipline based upon Section 13(b) of the Electoral Court Act.[19] Although the Constitution called for the free exercise of their mandates by the members of Parliament,[20] this section authorized their recall by the party enforced by the Electoral Court whenever a member of Parliament had, "for despicable or dishonorable reasons, ceased to be a member of the party from whose list of candidates he had been elected".[21] According to the interpretation by the Electoral Court, a breach of promise to the party in matters of discipline and party interests was held to constitute such "dishonorable" reasons.[22] Soon, however, it became unnecessary to look for specific "dishonorable" conduct as a basis for the recall of recalcitrant deputies: The parties resorted to blank (undated) resignations or resignation pledges, signed prior to

---

province-wide assignment, based upon provincial party lists, using a provincial Droop quota, as before on a statewide basis, to assign seats to the remainder votes (Sec. 36).

[16] From 16 to 23 parties, cp. Braunias, supra, I, 570, and P. Korbel, *Parliamentary Elections in Czechoslovakia*, 4, mimeographed (New York, National Committee for a Free Europe, Inc., Sept. 1952). After World War II, only the political parties "engaged in political activities" as of August 27, 1945 (Government Ordinance No. 48 dated August 25, 1945, concerning the election of the Provisional National Assembly, Sec. 4) or as of April 30, 1946 (Constitutional Act No. 65 of April 11, 1946, concerning the Constituent National Assembly, Sec. 14), respectively, were allowed to present lists of candidates, i.e. the (Czech) National Socialists, the (Catholic) People's Party, the Slovak Democrats, the Czech and the Slovak Communists, the Social Democrats, the Slovak Freedom Party and the Slovak Labor Party. All other parties of pre-war times were prohibited and excluded from participation in the elections, e.g. the Republican (Farmers') Party, the National Democrats, the Slovak People's Party, etc. See P. Korbel, supra, 7.

[17] The Republican (Farmers') Party, the Czech Social Democrats, the Czech National Socialists, and the Communists; cp. Braunias, supra, 1/570, 2/249.

[18] *Ibid.*

[19] Supra, note 6.

[20] Czechoslovak Constitution, 1920, supra, note 5, Sec. 13: "The members of the National Assembly shall exercise their mandate personally; they shall not accept any orders from anyone."

[21] By Act No. 145/1924 the wording was amended to read "... despicable *or* dishonorable..."

[22] Electoral Court Decision No. 186 dated December 17, 1921, Koschin reports (*Sbírka zásadních rozhodnutí volebního soudu*) No. 72. See Paul Hartmann, *Die politische Partei in der tschechoslowakischen Republik* (1931), 218.

nomination, in which the candidate promised to "act and vote in accordance with the decisions of the Central Executive Committee and the Parliamentary Club" and to "resign at any time upon demand by the Executive Committee in the event of a violation" of this promise. Resort to party recall based upon resignation pledges was not uncommon[23] and continued after the re-establishment of Czechoslovak parliamentarism in 1946.[24]

While this system of absolute domination of the party over its parliamentary representatives was defended as a logical consequence of proportional representation,[25] it transfers legislative power away from Parliament, into the hands of party bosses behind the scene. Parliamentary debates become meaningless and superfluous, because the result of the vote is known before the debate begins; the entire parliamentary procedure becomes an empty shell;[26] speeches in committees and on the floor merely announce the prior decisions of the party executive commitees. Few other countries would appear to have gone quite so far in enforcing party discipline;[27] even countries which assume that the seat belongs to the party may limit recall to cases of voluntary withdrawal from the party.[28] One post-war writer considered this matter so important that he

---

[23] See, e.g. Electoral Court Decision No. 383 dated June 22, 1923, Koschin reports No. 127 (Case Vrbenský); Decision No. 599 dated December 20, 1924, Koschin reports No. 131 (Case Kaderka); Decision No. 194 dated April 25, 1925, Koschin reports No. 132 (Case Prášek & Rychtera); Decision No. 767 dated December 29, 1926, Koschin reports No. 190 (Case Hirschl); Decision No. 47 dated January 8, 1928, Koschin reports No. 191 (Case Mayer-Hanreich); Decision No. 94 dated May 19, 1928, Koschin reports No. 192 (Case Stříbrný – Trnobranský); Decision No. 107 dated February 17, 1930, Koschin reports No. 252, etc. Cp. Eduard Táborský, *Naše nová ústava* ("Our New Constitution") (1948), 83-87; Paul Hartmann, supra, 227; Fritz Sander, *Verfassungsurkunde und Verfassungszustand der Tschechoslowakischen Republik* (1935), 110.

[24] Dr. Helena Koželuhová-Procházková, elected to the Constituent National Assembly on the ticket of the Catholic People's Party in 1946, was recalled on the basis of a pre-nomination pledge, even before taking the oath as a deputy. The stenographic report of the 3rd meeting of the Constituent National Assembly on July 8, 1946 (1 Stenographic Reports of the Meetings of the Constituent National Assembly, 3) set forth a curt announcement of the presidium that "Assembly woman Dr. Helena Koželuhová-Procházková has advised by letter dated June 12, 1946, that she has resigned her seat in the Assembly".

[25] Bohumil Baxa, *Parlament a parlamentarism* ("Parliament and Parliamentarism") 251 ff. Cp. Triepel, *Die Staatsverfassung und die politischen Parteien*, 33.

[26] Paul Hartmann, supra, 180

[27] As to Austrian municipal elections, see Decision of the Austrian Constitutional Court of January 22, 1930, No. 316, Z. W. II 4/29; Braunias, supra, II, 276.

[28] Wuerttemberg Landtag Election Law of April 4, 1924 (Reg. Bl. f. Wuerttemberg 1924, No. 26, p. 228), Art. 7, par. 1, No. 6, see 11 *Archiv d. oeff. Rechts*, 421, and Paul Hartmann, supra, 244.

proposed an express constitutional provision to the effect that loss of membership in the party on whose list the deputy had been elected should not entail loss of his seat.[29] There is no doubt that the opposite extreme – complete lack of any party discipline whatsoever, as shown in the French Third and Fourth Republics – is equally bad. A middle way may be desirable.

The above characterization of the Czechoslovak election system is not meant to convey a wholly negative impression. That Czechoslovak parliamentary democracy was basically successful, much more so than in some other European countries, was, however, due primarily to the personal leadership and the extra-legal, but enormously effective, influence of President Thomas G. Masaryk and other leaders, and less so to the election system itself. On the other hand, the party pledge system would appear to have been largely responsible for some of the negative aspects of party allegiance that may be felt to this very day by representatives of the Czechoslovak political parties in exile.

While Czechoslovakia remains under totalitarian rule, any proposals for a future new election system must be based upon a comparative study of the practical experience with a variety of election systems throughout the Free World. One hundred years ago the great debate began between proponents and opponents of proportional representation. The classic statements of the case for and against proportional representation are John Stuart Mill's *Representative Government*, published in 1861, and Walter Bagehot's *English Constitution*, in 1867. Despite a full 100 years of debate and practical experience, the arguments today are almost the same. When this debate began, parliamentary democracy was limited to a relatively small part of the world – it was going through its most serious crisis in this country just then, and it had temporarily disappeared in France – and where it was then in existence, it was still identified exclusively with the plurality system: in Britain, the United States, Switzerland, and elsewhere. The end of the First World War brought with it a wave of parliamentary democracy and proportional representation throughout Continental Europe, except only for Russia, Albania, and Portugal. It is perhaps the most outstanding fact of the following forty years that not merely the theoretical justification and practical feasibility of proportional representation were seriously challenged, but the whole conception of parliamentary democracy itself was under attack from totalitarian ideologies of the right and the left. Germany and Italy, which had both adopted proportional representation right after World War I, fell under the onslaught of

[29] Eduard Táborský, supra, 507, 521.

dictatorships, and opponents of proportional representation, under the leadership of Professor Hermens, now at Notre Dame University, blamed proportional representation for their collapse.[30] Even supporters of proportional representation realized how closely forms of government were controlled by the technicalities of election laws and systems.[31]

A survey of the election systems presently in force shows that most of the English-speaking countries[32] as well as France[33] use majority systems, at least for their lower chambers, with the exception of Ireland; the Scandinavian countries, Holland, Belgium, Switzerland, Italy and Israel retain proportional representation in one form or other, while West Germany uses a mixed system. A decision in favor of one or the other system necessitates, first of all, a reflection on the basic purposes to be achieved.[34] Government of the people, by the people and for the people can be striven for in many ways. There will be general agreement with the proposition that a legislature should bear some relation to the will of the people, but if it should turn out that there is no such thing as a uniform popular will, but only a complex mass with different aims and conflicting interests, a similarly composed legislature will be unlikely to warrant strong and stable government. Should "democratic" demands prevail by safeguarding government according to the wishes of the majority, or should it be limited by the "liberal" proposition of assuring representation for minority views?

The traditional Anglo-American plurality system has withstood attacks by proponents of proportional representation for 100 years. Its essence is the election of individual candidates in single-member constituencies by relative majority. It is often praised by opponents of proportional rep-

---

[30] F. A. Hermens, *Democracy or Anarchy. A Study of Proportional Representation* (Notre Dame Univ. Press, 1941); Id., *Europe between Democracy and Anarchy* (1951).
[31] Enid Lakeman & James D. Lambert, *Voting in Democracies, A Study of Majority and Proportional Electoral Systems* (London, Faber & Faber, 1955), 20.
[32] United States, United Kingdom, Canada, India, Australia (House of Representatives), South Africa (House of Assembly).
[33] Ordinance No. 58-945 of October 13, 1958 concerning the Election of Deputies to the National Assembly: Art. 1: Single-member constituencies; Art. 4: Absolute majority on first ballot, relative majority on run-off second ballot. For municipal elections in larger cities, however, proportional representation was retained for the 1959 elections (Ordinance of February 4, 1959). Since the start of the Third Republic in 1875, France has switched back and forth 9 times between single-member and multi-member constituencies, one and two ballots, but has used proportional representation systems for national elections only between 1945 and 1951; between 1951 and 1958 PR was used only for the City of Paris, otherwise only where no party or party alliance won an absolute majority.
[34] Lakeman-Lambert, supra, 19.

resentation as a guarantee of strong and stable government, a closer personal relation between voter and representative, a safeguard against bossism. Unfortunately experience shows that these claims will not stand up to close scrutiny. There have been examples of plurality elections which gave the winning party a very slim majority,[35] the close relation of voter and representative becomes a myth when voters vote for a party label regardless of the candidate – even in plurality elections the worst candidate of the largest party may defeat the best candidate of another party – and we hear as many complaints about boss rule from countries with plurality elections as elsewhere. Besides, plurality elections may, and sometimes do, lead to victory for a party polling a minority of votes,[36] or a very small majority of votes may result in a large majority in the legislature.[37] In a close district, a handful of votes may decide the outcome, while a considerable fluctuation makes no difference in a "safe" district.[38] Attempts to avoid some of these results by a second ballot,[39] sometimes restricted to the two candidates leading on the first ballot, or the alternative vote system (which basically combines the two ballots in one operation, asking the voter to indicate an alternative candidate if his first preference should be defeated[40]) have not been particularly successful. In all majority elections, however, there remains the serious problem of "election geometry" or "gerrymandering",[41] used to perpetuate the positions of parties in power, often of rural conservatives at the expense of growing municipal districts, unless there is a possibility of intervention by a court exercising constitutional review.[42]

[35] Id., 37; Braunias, supra, II, 184.
[36] Lakeman-Lambert, supra, 34.
[37] Id., 28.
[38] Id., 47.
[39] Id., 53.
[40] Id., 40.
[41] Id., 71; cp. Maurice Duverger, Introduction to Cotteret-Émeri-Lalumière, *Lois Electorales et Inégalités de Répresentation en France 1936-1960*, X (1960).
[42] Baker v. Carr, 368 U.S. 804, 30 U.S.L.W. 4203 (March 26, 1962), overruling a long line of decisions refusing to intervene in reapportionment cases – the earlier (Alabama) decision involving the redrafting of the municipal boundaries of the city of Tuskegee, Gomillion v. Lightfoot, 364 U.S. 339 (1960), involved racial discrimination rather than reapportionment as such (30 U.S.L.W. 4203, at 4216, 4220, 4233). Baker v. Carr dealt with Tennessee Assembly districts; it remains to be seen whether the Court will consider reapportionment of Congressional district less "justiciable" because the Constitution makes the House of Representatives judge of its members' qualifications (*The New York Times*, March 27, 1962, p. 20). For reports on the current reapportionment controversies in New York, see, e.g. *The New York Times*, 11/14/61, 11/16/61, 1/23/62, 1/30/62, 2/11/62, etc.; re British impartial Commissions for Parliamentary boundaries, see *The New York Times*, 4/8/62.

Despite such shortcomings of the plurality system, the use of proportional representation in the United States, for municipal elections only, has generally been shortlived,[43] but it is holding its own in some European countries and elsewhere. In English-speaking countries proportional representation has generally been propagated in the form of the single transferable vote, as distinguished from Continental list systems. In theory the voter casts his ballot for individuals rather than parties, though in practice the difference is often less pronounced. The main objections to this system are usually that it is too complicated and confuses the voters, the cost and delay in ascertaining the election results, or the desire to prevent representation for splinter groups or the election of Communists and fellow travellers.[44] On the European continent the debate over proportional representation has traditionally dealt with arguments for and against list systems. While proponents of proportional representation hoped it would cure all shortcomings of majority systems,[45] opponents attacked it as favoring an undue multiplication of parties, preventing any one from obtaining a working majority and necessitating coalition cabinets without clear authority or responsibility, leading to unstable government and eventual victory for enemies of democracy,[46] inducing a radicalization of parties by the rise of parties representing economic interest groups and classes subordinating national interest to class interests, destroying intra-party democracy, favoring boss rule, party oligarchy and political stagnation by stifling any election chances for younger party members relegated to hopeless positions on the party list.[47] While some of these charges should not be dismissed lightly, it has been shown that many cannot be blamed entirely on proportional representation. Countries with a multiplicity of parties often showed the same sit-

---

[43] New York City adopted PR by referendum on 11/3/36, effective 1/1/38 (City Charter, c. 43), but repealed it in 1947; Cincinnati defeated PR on Sept. 30, 1957, after 32 years. Both cities had used the single transferable vote, like Ireland, Australia (Commonwealth Senate), etc.

[44] Proportional Representation, What it is and how it works in New York City, Research Department of the Chamber of Commerce of the State of New York (1947); cp. Ralph A. Braetz, *PR Politics in Cincinnati* (1958).

[45] Braunias, supra, II, 191 ff., 257 ff.

[46] Lakeman-Lambert, supra, 149 ff.

[47] Braunias, supra, II, 221; F. A. Hermens, *Democracy or Anarchy?* (1941), 31 ff. Quaere whether Prof. Hermens' praise for parties under the majority system as "empty bottles with different labels" – while perhaps to some degree pertinent to the major American political parties – is really a desirable alternative to overradicalization of ideological parties. Cp. Russel Baker, "Growing Dilemma of the G.O.P.", in *The New York Times Magazine*, April 8, 1962.

uation under earlier majority systems,[48] while in other countries proportional representation brought no appreciable change in the number of parties[49] Obviously it would be foolish for any believer in democracy to advocate a system of election if its ultimate result would be to destroy the right to hold free elections at all;[50] in fact, however, this has rarely been the true reason for repeal of PR – while political scientists argue over the merits of election systems, politicians invariably prefer the system which they hope will favor their own parties.[51]

Countries using proportional representation with apparent success have tried to deal with some of the problems mentioned by measures against splinter parties[52] and efforts to limit the omnipotence of parties by giving the voter opportunity to influence the choice of representatives, replacing the rigid party list[53] by a loosely tied one[54] allowing the voter to cast preferential votes within the list or to delete some names,[55] or even to

---

[48] Lakeman-Lambert, supra, 149 ff. (Germany, France, Italy, Netherlands).
[49] Ibid., particularly as to Switzerland and the Scandinavian countries.
[50] Id., 21.
[51] Cotteret-Émeri-Lalumière, supra, 9: "... Au Parlement, le débat entre partisans d'un scrutin uninominal majoritaire et proportionalistes ne s'est jamais placé sur le seul plan des principes de justice, mais sur le terrain de la tactique politique. Les députés s'intéressent surtout à l'influence d'un mode de scrutin sur la répartition des forces politiques en présence. ... Les forces politiques qui sont avantagées par un mode de scrutin ont donc tendance à en assurer le maintien. Peu leur importent les inégalités de représentation que révèle le jeu de ce système électoral..."
[52] Supra, note 12, and cp. West Germany, Federal Election Law of May 7, 1956, BGBl. I, p. 383, as amended December 23, 1956, BGBl. I, p. 1011, republished August 1959 (BGBl. III, p. 126), Sec. 6 (4), which exempts national minority parties from the requirement of 5% of all "second" ballots or a minimum of 3 seats gained in the districts; Denmark Election Law of April 1, 1920, Sec. 43 (at least one seat in a district or statewide total equal to average number of votes per seat); Netherlands (entire country is one single election district): minimum: quota for first assignment, formerly 75% of quota, election law, art. 100); Austria National Council Election Law No. 129 of May 18, 1949, Sec. 97 (1) – one seat in the first assignment; Switzerland, Sweden and Norway limit PR to the district, without any national adjustments to utilize remainders. See 2 Braunias, supra, 247. Israel has a quorum requirement – 1% of the total vote (Knesseth Election Law 5715-1955, Sec. 43 (a)); cf. as to pre-war Rumanian election law and the Swiss cantons of Geneva, Fribourg and Neuchatel, Braunias, supra, II, 252.
[53] Israel still adheres to the rigid party list (Knesseth Election Law, supra, Sec. 45), cp. note 8, supra, and Lakeman-Lambert, Supra, 91.
[54] Braunias, supra, II, 217, 223.
[55] Austria National Council Election Law, supra, Secs. 78, 82, 90; Swiss National Council Election Law of February 14, 1919, Arts. 13, 15, 19; similar provisions allowing voters to cast preferential votes in Holland (Election Law, Sec. 75), Belgium (Election Law, Sec. 144) and in the French election laws of 1946 (No. 46-2151 of October 5, 1946) and 1951 (No. 51-519 of May 9, 1951), Arts. 15 and 16, are of lesser significance because they are disregarded unless a substantial number of ballots is so modified – $\frac{1}{2}$ of the quota (Holland), full quota (Belgium) or 50% of the ballots cast (France). Cp. Braunias, supra, II, 226.

split his vote among a number of lists or compile his own list freely.[56]

In Germany proposals had been made since the turn of the century to combine features of proportional representation with majority elections in the districts,[57] which led after World War II to the introduction in West Germany of a "personalized" PR characterized, since 1953, by the right of each voter to cast two ballots simultaneously, one for an individual candidate, elected by plurality in single-member districts, and an additional one for a party, which is assigned by PR to candidates listed on provincial lists. 50% of the seats in the Bundestag are reserved for this supplementary assignment on the basis of the 'second' ballots. Actually the decisive ballot is the second one, by PR; voting by plurality in the districts merely gives to voters an influence upon the choice of half of the party candidates.[58]

Despite the claims of the opponents of proportional representation, effective and stable government cannot be guaranteed by a switch to plurality elections. Even though some systems may well help or hinder the attainment of this important goal, it cannot be brought about by any voting system alone. It may be frustrated, even under the best-planned institutions, by human frailty, by the shortsightedness of politicians or by the circumstances of the hour,[59] particularly undue and overpowerful influences from abroad. Also, "the best institutions will fail, in any case, if the citizens are unwilling or unable to play their part".[60] A voting system which offers the voters a more direct share in the choice of representatives may tend to remove a widespread sense of frustration and make the citizen a responsible and conscious partner in government.[61] Even if statistics were to show that often only a small part of the politically

---

[56] "Panachage", see Swiss National Council Election Law, supra, Art. 13. Split votes were also admissible under the French election laws of July 12, 1919, and May 9, 1951 (in the latter subject to the 50% requirement, note 55, supra). When the split vote possibility enabled a party to defeat a leading candidate of another party by inducing its own members to cast split votes in favor of a mediocre candidate of the rival party, the Swiss law countered by authorizing the cumulation of one name twice on the same ballot (Art. 13 (3)).

[57] Braunias, supra, II, 240 ff.

[58] West German Federal Election Law, supra, Secs. 1, 4-6, 35, 41-42. The Danish election system differs despite certain similarities, because seats are assigned to the candidates on the basis of the total votes cast for the parties in multi-member constituencies; following the election of candidates lists in single-member districts, "additional seats" are assigned to the parties on the basis of their vote totals in the larger constituencies. Folketing Election Law, Secs. 42-46. Cp. Braunias, supra, I, 51, and 2 Id., 235 ("horizontal lists").

[59] Lakeman-Lambert, supra, 232.

[60] Id., 19.

[61] Id., 232.

conscious citizenry actually utilize such rights where they exist,[62] their psychological importance should not be underestimated – often the knowledge that a certain right is lacking may be felt strongly, while possession of the right is a cause for pride even if it is not used.[63]

---

[62] Braunias, supra, II, 246. According to a letter received by the author from the Austrian Federal Department of the Interior, Austrian voters avail themselves of their right to cast preferential votes within the list or to delete the names of some candidates (note 55, supra) only to a very small extent. In the National Council elections of 1949, 1953, 1956 and 1959, there were only very few incidents where preferential votes did cause a change in the order of the elected candidates; in all of these elections there was only one single occasion, in the National Council elections of 1953, when one candidate was elected because of preferential votes and the deletion by the voters of names of other candidates: a candidate of the Austrian Peoples Party, who had been listed in fifth place on that Party's list for the 22nd Election District (Oststeier), was moved up to third place by the voters, and thus elected, the party having obtained three seats in that District.
[63] Braunias, supra, II, 247.

Some Criminological and Socio-Political Aspects of Czechoslovak Pre-Communist and Communist* Legislation on Abortion

JAROSLAV JÍRA

I. INTRODUCTION

Many modern criminologists and social scientists have argued, not without justification, that the criminal law represents the basic minimum of the social morality of any nation at a given time. In fact, the culture, ethics, legal philosophy, and socio-economic policy of individual nations seem to be particularly well reflected in the choice of the basic social values and human relationships to which their criminal laws lend penal protection.

Among those basic social values which the criminal laws of all modern nations seek to protect, human life is paramount, and its protection by law often extends even to its embryonic stage. Historical sources show that artificial abortion has been practiced since ancient times, especially as a means of escaping the adverse consequences of an illegitimate childbirth. The Church denounced it as a sin, and secular rulers prosecuted it as a crime. In Czechoslovakia, as well as in all the Lands of the ancient Czech Kingdom, protection of the developing foetus by means of the penal prohibition and restriction of abortion has been a legal institution of long standing.[1]

As for contemporary criminal law, on the one hand, all related provisions on abortion show several common features with respect to legisla-

---

* This study covers, analyzes, and compares pre-Communist legislation and Communist legislation up to the issuance of the Proclamation of the Ministry of Health dated September 13, 1961, No. 104/1961 Coll. to Implement the Law No. 68/1957 Coll. on the Artificial Interruption of Pregnancy.

Some time after completing this study, the author learned, from a news article in *Rudé Právo* (Praha) for January 18, 1963, that Proclamation No. 104/1961 Coll. had been repealed, and that new regulations had taken force as of January 1963. He made inquiries at the Library of Congress and elsewhere, but as of early March 1963, neither the text of the new statute nor any other information about it had been received locally. See the Addendum at the end of this study.

[1] Cf. H. Jireček, *Svod zákonův slovanských* (Praha, 1880), pp. XXI, 482. – V. Vaněček, *Prameny k dějinám státu a práva v Československu*, I (Praha, 1957), p. 35.

tive motivation and intent. On the other hand, the extent of penal protection of the human foetus has characteristically differed under different political regimes, in accordance with their contrasting legal and social policies. This holds true for the criminal law of pre-Communist Czechoslovakia, as well as for the present Communist-dominated and Soviet-inspired Czechoslovak penal legislation.

II. ABORTION UNDER THE PRE-COMMUNIST CRIMINAL LAW (1918-1948)[2]

The pre-Communist Czechoslovak legal order consisted of two different systems, one of which applied to the Czech Lands[3] and the other to Slovakia and, until 1945, to Subcarpathian Ruthenia (since annexed by the Soviet Union).

A. Criminal law of the Czech Lands

Under the Criminal Code No. 117 of 1852, which was in force in the Czech Lands until 1950, abortion, whether accomplished or only attempted, constituted a major crime appearing in two forms.

1. *Abortion by the mother.* – This type of abortion was performed by the pregnant woman herself, or by another, her accessory, who acted with her consent and knowledge (Sec. 144).[4]

2. *Abortion by one other than the mother.* – The second basic form of abortion was the killing of the foetus by a person other than the pregnant woman. This crime was carried out, undertaken, or attempted by a third person as principal, against the will or without the knowledge of the pregnant woman (Sec. 147).

3. *Objective Elements of the Criminal Act.* – In both types of abortion (Secs. 144, 147), the offender's or the accomplice's activity consisted of

---

[2] I.e., the Criminal Code No. 117 of 1852, and the Legal Article No. V of 1878, as Amended. In 1950 the former criminal law was repealed and the new Communist Criminal Code for Courts No. 86/1950 Coll. was enacted. It applies to Slovakia as well as to the Czech Lands.

[3] I.e., Bohemia, Moravia, and Silesia. As to the pre-Communist criminal law of Slovakia, see II. B. below.

[4] The forms of guilt, the concepts of the accomplished crime and the attempt, the penalties for the principals, accessories, and those who aided and abetted were originally given extended treatment in this study, but limitations of publication space made it necessary to omit them from the final text.

the attempted or accomplished killing of the foetus. This included any act intended to cause or actually causing the artificial interruption of pregnancy, artificially induced childbirth, or any such childbirth whereby the child arrived into the world dead. Such an act would have to have been undertaken or accomplished at any stage of the pregnancy before the actual onset of labor. After the stage of actual childbirth or delivery had begun, even while the child was still in the mother's body, the killing would constitute the separate major crime of Murder of the Child by its Mother (acting with or without accomplices) during or soon after childbirth (Sec. 139).

4. *Permissible interruption of pregnancy (abortion).* – Under the pre-Communist criminal law of the Czech Lands, the interruption of pregnancy was permissible only exceptionally, under the specific conditions set forth in Sec. 2, clause (g) on the so-called "state of necessity" (duress, *stav nouze*).[5] Thus, abortion was permissible if, under existing circumstances, it was the only available means of averting the actual, serious, and immediate danger threatening the health or life of the pregnant woman. If these statutory requirements existed, the artificial interruption of pregnancy or abortion was not subject to punishment by virtue of Sec. 2 (g), regardless of whether it was performed by the pregnant woman herself or by a third person. The principle underlying the exculpation of acts committed in a state of necessity (duress) was the consideration that the criminal law cannot equitably require a person of average moral strength, under these circumstances, to endanger the mother's life or health rather than destroy the life of the foetus.[6]

In practice, the application of the doctrine of the state of necessity to factual situations which required a legitimate abortion did not always lead to satisfactory results. The legal requisite of imminent and serious danger to the life or health of the pregnant woman sometimes caused unduly prolonged postponement of the operation, and even *bona fide* physicians or midwives were often actually exposed to the possibility of criminal investigation and prosecution.

---

[5] Sec. 2 (g), like Art. 64 of the French Criminal Code of 1810, included the "state of necessity" or "duress" under the broader concept of "irresistible coercion". *Cf.* also G. Vidal, *Cours de Droit Criminel et de Science Pénitentiaire*, vol. 1 (Paris, 1949), p. 168, 337-383.

[6] *Cf.* Supreme Court Decisions, Off. Coll. "Vážný, Criminal Law", henceforth: (Sb.n.s.) Nos. 176, 181, 456, 2640, 2812; and Vl. Solnař, *Trestní právo hmotné, část obecná* ("Substantive Criminal Law, General Part") (Praha, 1947), p. 111-114. Similar principles on the state of necessity (duress) were also adopted by the Swiss Criminal Code of 1937 (Art. 34).

Therefore the leading pre-Communist Czechoslovak criminologists and the official drafters of the Bills of Criminal Law held that the future Criminal Code should not rely, in these instances, only on the general principle of "necessity", but should also contain a specific provision allowing for "impunity of abortion because of specified reasons, such as consideration of health...". In addition, certain other important reasons, such as considerations of social and eugenic order, should also be recognized as reasons for impunity, or even as the legal justification of abortion. It was also unanimously held that such operations should be performed under statutorily specified conditions and *lege artis*, only by qualified physicians and in medical institutions.[7]

B. Abortion under the criminal law of Slovakia

In Slovakia, before the introduction of the Communist Criminal Code of 1950, the offense of abortion was originally governed by the provisions of Secs. 285, 286, and 289 of the Criminal Code on major and minor crimes, Legal Article No. V of 1878. The original version was amended by Law No. 66/1941 Col. [of Slovak Laws] to Protect the Human Foetus and its Conception and to Change Secs. 285 and 286 of Criminal Law No. V of 1878. As in the Czech Lands, abortion in Slovakia constituted a major crime. Like the older criminal law of the Czech Lands, Secs. 285 and 286 of the Slovak Criminal Code also distinguished two basic forms of abortion. The first was carried out by the pregnant woman herself, or by some accessory with her consent; the second type was committed by someone other than the pregnant woman, and without her consent. Under Sec. 80 of the Slovak Criminal Code No. V of 1878, similarly as in the Czech Lands under Sec. 2 (g) of the Criminal Code of 1852, abortion was not subject to punishment if it was carried out in a state of "extreme necessity". Pre-Communist considerations *de lege ferenda* on abortion were common to Slovakia as well as to the Czech Lands.

III. ABORTION UNDER COMMUNIST CRIMINAL LAW

A. The Criminal Code of 1950 (Sec. 218)

1. *Origin.*

Protection of the developing foetus from illegal abortion was continued under Sec. 218 of the present Communist Criminal Code of 1950.[8] Com-

---

[7] *Cf.* Vl. Solnař, *Trestní právo hmotné, část zvláštní* ("Substantive Criminal Law, Special Part") (Praha, 1948), p. 54.

munist legislators followed, in respect to abortion, the basic legal principles of the former Czech criminal law, but they also adopted several concepts evolved *de lege ferenda* by pre-Communist Czechoslovak legal science and by the Bills of Criminal Law of the pre-Communist era.[9] This was true, in particular, for the principle of impunity regarding abortion dictated by important reasons of health of the pregnant woman, or by regard for the serious illness of the prospective parents. This impunity was thus based on the "medical reasons" or "eugenic indication" specified above.

However, this sound development was impeded by the politically motivated emulation of the then-existing Soviet criminal law by the Czechoslovak Communist regime. This tendency to follow the Soviet pattern whenever possible caused the Communist Criminal Code of 1950 to adopt only a few of the broader, more modern concepts of pre-Communist Czechoslovak legal science and the Bills of Criminal Law on abortion. Specifically, the 1950 Criminal Code did not excuse abortion dictated by important reasons of a social or legal character.

The 1950 Criminal Code (Sec. 218), in order to follow the pattern of the then Soviet criminal law, even abandoned some of the old politico-legal claims of the Czechoslovak Communist Party regarding abortion which the party had propagated for over two decades until it seized power in 1948 and began enactment of its new Codes of Law in 1950.[10]

2. *Statutory Framework*

The Criminal Code of 1950 provided as follows:

Sec. 218. *Killing the human foetus. Subsec. 1.* A pregnant woman who intentionally kills her foetus or asks someone else to kill it, or permits him to do so, shall be punished by confinement not to exceed one year.

Subsec. 2. Whoever, with the consent of a pregnant woman, intentionally kills her foetus, or whoever induces the pregnant woman to commit the act specified in Subsec. 1 or assists in the commission of such an act, shall be punished by confinement from one to five years.

---

[8] Law No. 86/1950 Coll., as amended by Law No. 63/1956 Coll. As to the text of the pertinent Sec. 218, and as to its later repeal by a separate Law on Abortion No. 68/1957 Coll., see below.

[9] Under the 1950 Criminal Code and other pertinent penal statutes, any violation of the penal law which is subject to the jurisdiction of the criminal courts constitutes an "offense". Thus Communist legislation has abandoned the trichotomy into major crimes (*zločiny*), minor crimes (*přečiny*), and petty offenses (*přestupky*), which obtained under the pre-Communist Czechoslovak criminal law.

[10] *Trestní právo, část zvláštní* ("Criminal Law, Special Part") (Praha, 1953), p. 343.

Subsec. 3. The offender shall be punished by confinement from three to ten years (a) if he commits the act specified in Subsec. 2 as a business, or (b) if such an act results in a serious injury to the health of the pregnant woman, or in her death.

Subsec. 4. A physician who kills a human foetus in a sanitary institution with the consent of the pregnant woman shall not be punished if it is established by another physician who is a medical officer that the act of bringing the baby to birth or the birth itself would seriously endanger the life of the pregnant woman or cause a serious and permanent impairment of her health, or that one of the parents suffers from a grave hereditary disease. Substitution for the consent of the pregnant woman may be made by the consent of her legal representative only in the event that the pregnant woman is under complete legal disability, or if she is not able to speak her mind.

Major injury to the health of the pregnant woman, as applied in Sec. 218, Subsec. 3, clause (b), was established by the following presumption:

Sec. 75, Subsec. 13 (h). A serious injury to health shall be understood as including one which interrupts pregnancy.

The above-quoted provisions of Sec. 218 governing abortion did not include the intentional interruption of pregnancy by a third person without the consent of the pregnant woman. Therefore this major interference with the health and physical freedom of the pregnant woman could be prosecuted only under the general provision of Sec. 220, concerning the intentional causing of a serious injury to the health of another. It reads:

Sec. 220, Subsec. 1. Whoever intentionally causes a serious injury to the health of another shall be punished by confinement from three to ten years.
Subsec. 2. The offender shall be punished by confinement from five to fifteen years if the act specified in Subsec. 1 results in death.

The reference of Sec. 220, Subsec. 2 to death related obviously to the pregnant woman only, not to the destruction of the life of the child in her womb. Thus the intentional killing of the foetus by an abortion performed in an utterly antisocial manner, that is, without the pregnant woman's consent, was not covered by any direct provision of the 1950 Criminal Code.

3. *Substance of the offense.*

Illegal abortion consisted of the intentional killing of a human foetus, whether one's own (by the pregnant woman) or that of another (by third persons as principals). The protection of the developing foetus extended from the moment when the foetus started its own life until the actual beginning of childbirth (Sec. 218).

4. *Extreme necessity.*

It must be noted that the severe penalty under Sec. 220 applied also to cases where the abortion was carried out without the pregnant woman's consent, but was actually dictated by "medical or eugenical reasons" which would fully justify the abortion if the consent of the prospective mother had been secured in advance.

The recent official university textbook on substantive criminal law stated:[11]

The act [the abortion] is liable to punishment even [in cases] where there otherwise existed medical or eugenic indications. Actions committed in the state of necessity [duress], of course, shall not be liable to punishment.

The pertinent provision reads:

Sec. 9. Extreme necessity. Subsec. 1. An act, otherwise liable for punishment, whereby a person averts a danger directly threatening the People's Democratic Republic, its socialist development, the interests of the working people or of an individual, shall not constitute a punishable offense if (a) the damage caused is less than that which threatened, and (b) the danger could not otherwise be averted.

Except for abortions allowed under the provision of Sec. 218, Subsec. 4, the 1950 Criminal Code extended impunity only to such abortions as were carried out under the rigid conditions of "extreme necessity" (Sec. 9, Subsec.1). Consequently, these provisions tended to cause postponement of abortion until the stage of "immediate danger" was reached, which might also constitute additional risk for the health or life of the pregnant woman. In this respect the 1950 Criminal Code represented no improvement over the provisions of the old Criminal Codes of 1852 and 1878, which were considered obsolete and inadequate by the democratic, pre-Communist Czechoslovak criminologists.

5. *Permissible abortion.*

On the other hand, it must be recognized that the 1950 Criminal Code (in Sec. 218, Subsec. 4) represents at least one substantial improve-

---

[11] *Trestní právo, část zvláštní, op. cit.,* p. 344.

ment by recognizing the excuse of an abortion[12] carried out under strictly specified conditions because of certain serious reasons established by medical science or by eugenics. However, if any of the requisites specified in Sec. 218 were not complied with in full, then all persons involved in the abortion, except the pregnant woman herself, were subject to punishment under Sec. 218, regardless of whether medical or eugenic reasons had existed.[13] In practice, the statutory concepts which were requisites for Sec. 218, Subsec. 4 and Sec. 9, Subsec. 1 proved to be so rigid that medical and legal science and judicial practice resorted to this extensive interpretation of Sec. 9, Subsec. 1:

Thus, if the danger can be averted or diminished by therapeutic care (*nefropathie*), one must first resort to this treatment. Only if it cannot be avoided may one interrupt the pregnancy. ... Of course, under certain circumstances, a danger to the life of the mother may already exist, such as tuberculosis. Therefore, for medical reasons it shall suffice if such a danger threatens only at the time of childbirth, that is, perhaps only after several months. ...[14]

6. *Principals.*

It was a characteristic feature of Sec. 218, Subsecs. 1 and 2 that they included as principals all participants in the abortion.

7. *Attempt.*

The Criminal Code of 1950 (Sec. 5, Subsec. 1) defines attempt as follows:

An action dangerous to society, which the offender committed with the intent of causing a result specified in the Law, shall constitute an attempted offense, if this result does not take place.

In general, under the present Communist law, the requisites of criminal attempt to commit an abortion are practically the same as those of the pre-Communist law (Sec. 8, Criminal Code of 1852). In addition, the present Communist criminal law has also received from the same source the concept of "an attempt incapable of succeeding" (*nezpůsobilý pokus*)

---

[12] Not the legality. Compare here the words of Sec. 218, Subsec. 4: "A physician ... shall not be punished if ..."
[13] Only the state of "extreme necessity" could exculpate them. *Cf. Trestní právo, část zvláštní, op. cit.*, p. 345.
[14] *Ibid.*, p. 345, 346.

as evolved by the so-called "subjective theory of attempt."[15] This carry-over from pre-Communist "bourgeois" law is evidenced especially in cases where the offender committed an overt act intended to perform an illegal abortion without knowing that a pregnancy actually did not exist. The recent university textbook stated:[16]

As a rule, liability for punishment of an attempt incapable of success follows from the reasoning ... that ... the social dangerousness of this type of attempt equals the social dangerousness of the normal attempt; that is, the attempt to kill a foetus which is already dead, etc.

The Communist criminologists clearly subscribe to the subjective concept of the "bourgeois" pre-Communist law, which was defined by Professor J. Kallab as follows:[17]

The adherents of the subjective theory ... hold that as soon as the criminal intent was manifested in any outward [overt] act which, according to the offender's belief, should have caused the criminal result, the offender cannot be excused by the mere fact that some external circumstance prevented the result from ensuing. The wickedness and culpability (guilt) consist in the clearness and firmness of the offender's criminal determination....

The Communist criminologists deny their adoption of the "bourgeois" subjective theory and claim that their concept of attempt is substantially different. However, their textbooks and commentaries have thus far failed to define such substantial differences or features. Instead, they have distorted the legal arguments of the pre-Communist Supreme Court and of criminologists by alleging that under the pre-Communist subjective theory the mere criminal intent of the offender constituted by itself sufficient basis for his conviction.[18] However, under pre-Communist law, conviction always required not only the criminal intent, but also the typical *overt act* which, at least in the offender's belief, led to the accomplishment of the criminal result and *started the actual execution* of the offense.

---

[15] After several decades of struggle between the "objective" and "subjective" theories of attempt, the subjective theory prevailed between 1940 and 1948 in legal theory as well as in legal decisions. The present author had the privilege of contributing directly to the reversal of the objective theory and the adoption of the subjective theory by the jurisprudence of the Czechoslovak Supreme Court during this period.

[16] *Trestní právo, část zvláštní, op. cit.*, p. 174.

[17] J. Kallab, *Trestní právo hmotné* (Praha, 1935), p. 66-68.

[18] In particular, the Communist university textbook undertook to distort in this way the legal arguments of the present author, which were published between 1943 and 1945. Cf. *Trestní právo, část obecná* (Praha, 1953), p. 181.

B. Law No. 68/1957 Coll. on the Artificial Interruption of Pregnancy

This new Law (Sec. 8, Subsec. 1) superseded Sec. 218 of Criminal Code No. 86/1950 Coll. It consists of five parts: Introductory Provisions (Sec. 1), Conditions for the Artificial Interruption of Pregnancy (Secs. 2 and 3), Illegal Interruption of Pregnancy (Secs. 4 and 5), Impunity of the Pregnant Woman (Sec. 6), and Concluding Provisions (Secs. 7-9).

1. *Illegal Abortion.*

a. *Substance of the Offense.* – The offense of illegal abortion (Secs. 4 and 5) can be committed only by a person other than the pregnant woman herself. The present law governs only such abortions as are committed with a direct intent to kill the live foetus of another and performed or attempted with the pregnant woman's consent. Consequently, intentional abortions committed without the consent of the pregnant woman are subject as before to the provisions of Sec. 220 of the Criminal Code of 1950 on the intentional infliction of a serious injury to the health of another.

The 1957 Law establishes two basic forms of abortion: first, inducing a pregnant woman and aiding and abetting her in an illegal abortion which is performed by her or by another person (Sec. 4); and, second, the performance of an illegal abortion carried out by another person with the consent of the pregnant woman (Sec. 5). The provisions of the 1957 Law are as follows:

Sec. 4. Illegal Interruption of Pregnancy. Subsec. 1. Whoever aids the pregnant woman or induces her to (a) artificially interrupt her pregnancy [or] (b) ask or permit another to interrupt her pregnancy in a manner other than that which is permissible under this law, shall be punished for the offense by confinement not to exceed two years.

Subsec. 2. The offender shall be punished [by confinement] from one to five years if the act described in Subsec. 1 caused serious injury to the health of the pregnant woman or her death.

Sec. 5. Subsec. 1. Whoever, with the consent of the pregnant woman, artificially interrupts her pregnancy in any manner other than that which is permissible under the present law, shall be punished for the offense by confinement from one to five years.

Subsec. 2. The offender shall be punished by confinement from three to ten years (a) if he commits the act described in Subsec. 1 for profit or (b) if such act has as its consequence a serious injury to the pregnant woman's health, or her death.

b. *Principals.* – The definitions of Secs. 4 and 5 show that Law No.

68/1957 Coll. follows the repealed Sec. 218 of the Criminal Code of 1950 in holding that all participants in an illegal abortion are principals.

2. *Legality of Certain Abortions.*

Similarly as did Sec. 218, Subsec. 4 of the 1950 Criminal Code, the 1957 Law has established that the abortion may be performed under certain conditions stipulated in Secs. 2 and 3 as follows: (1) The abortion may be performed only with the consent and at the request of the pregnant woman (Sec. 3, Subsec. 1) or, if she is fully incapacitated, with the consent and at the request of her legal representative. (2) The operation may be performed only in a health establishment which is equipped with beds (Sec. 2, Subsec. 2). (3) The abortion may be undertaken only after permission of the competent public authority has been obtained (Sec. 2, Subsec. 1). (4) The authority to grant such permissions is reserved to special commissions established under this Law (Sec. 3, Subsec. 1). (5) Official permission may be granted "only because of reasons of health or for other reasons deserving special consideration" (Sec. 3, Subsec. 3). (6) Under Sec. 7, the Ministries of Health and Justice have been entrusted to issue jointly such regulations as are necessary to implement the law.

It follows that if all the above-stated conditions are observed, the performance of the abortion is not only guiltless, as it was under the former provision of Sec. 218, Subsec. 4, Criminal Code of 1950, but under the 1957 Law it shall be deemed a lawful act. This is undoubtedly an improvement over the former law. The same conclusion holds true regarding the broader and more flexible definition of reasons for a permissible abortion, if it is compared with the unnecessary restrictiveness of Sec. 218, Subsec. 4.

3. *The Implementing Proclamations.*

Details were first determined by the Proclamation of Dec. 21, 1957, No. 249, U.L. (Official Gazette), issued by the Ministry of Health jointly with the Ministry of Justice, to Implement Law No. 68/1957 Coll. on the Artificial Interruption of Pregnancy. This 1957 Proclamation was later repealed by the Proclamation of Sept. 13, 1961, No. 104/1961 Coll. (see below), issued by the Ministry of Health. A brief comparative analysis of their provisions shows the following legal state of affairs:

Proclamation No. 249 of 1957 established two broad groups of reasons, medical and general, which justify permission to perform an abortion. Numerous medical reasons were listed exhaustively in the accompanying

Supplement to Proclamation No. 249 of 1957. The general reasons included personal, economic, social, and family considerations relating to the pregnant woman and her family. They were defined in Sec. 2, Subsec. 2, which read:

The following reasons shall be recognized as 'other reasons deserving special consideration,' which excuse an abortion: (a) the advanced age of the woman,[19] (b) several children, (c) loss or infirmity of the husband, (d) disruption of the family, (e) an overwhelming economic burden for maintenance of the family or the child resting upon the woman, (f) the difficult situation caused by the pregnancy of an unmarried woman, (g) a corroborating circumstance that the pregnancy resulted from rape or another offense ...

Sec. 3, Subsec. 3 listed various reasons of health for which permission to perform an abortion had to be denied.

Sec. 2, Subsec. 4 established for the Commissions on Abortions a very broad and flexible rule for evaluating the facts and deciding individual cases:

While deciding whether the artificial interruption of pregnancy shall be granted, one must take into consideration not only the main (statutory) reasons, but also the whole situation of the pregnant woman, including all conditions of her health, as well as her social and economic condition.

The rules of procedure were set forth in Secs. 3-6, which provided, in particular, that the pregnant woman might file her application for abortion, either directly or through her physician, with the District Health Bureau in whose area a suitable hospital or health institution was located. The competent District Commission on Abortions, consisting of the Chairman of the District Health Department as presiding officer, one or two physicians or specialists, and one laywoman "knowledgeable of life and enjoying public esteem and confidence", had the authority to grant or deny permission for abortions. The Commission was required to decide speedily upon an application, so that an abortion, if permitted, could be performed either within 14 days or before the completion of the first trimester of pregnancy, unless the abortion could be performed later (Sec. 4). In case permission was refused, the applicant could apply immediately for review to the Regional Commission on Abortions, which had

---

[19] The Supplement listed among the gynecological and obstetrical reasons for abortion: "If the woman became pregnant after 45 years of age (para. 13, clause (h)), or before 16 years of age, provided that the pregnancy was ascertained before its third month (para. 13, clause (g))."

a similar composition, jurisdiction, and duties (Secs. 3 and 4). All persons connected with these proceedings were bound to observe secrecy as to all facts learned therein (Sec. 6). The pregnant woman, under Proclamation No. 249/1957 U.L., was required to pay a fee covering the costs of the operation (Sec. 5).

This Proclamation and its Supplement seem to have included all medical reasons for the justification or exclusion of abortion in individual cases which were then known to medical science and eugenics in Czechoslovakia. The Proclamation also included several legal, economic, and social reasons which would justify abortion. In this respect, the Proclamation agreed with the demands of pre-Communist legal and medical science. However, the inclusion of some other, vaguely formulated socio-economic reasons, such as "the existence of several children," "the loss of the husband or his infirmity," or "the overwhelming economic burden on the woman for maintenance of the family or the child" (Sec. 2, Subsec. 1, clauses (b), (c), and (e)), opened the door to extreme liberality in granting abortions, and even to abuse of the privilege.

The Proclamation of the Ministry of Health dated September 13, 1961, No. 104/1961 Coll. to Implement the Law No. 68/1957 Coll. abrogated the entire Proclamation No. 249/1957 U.L. (as well as another related Proclamation, No. 129/1960 Coll.).[20] The 1961 Proclamation, in its demonstrative (not exhaustive) enumeration of "other reasons deserving special consideration which justify permission for abortion", stipulated that a woman applying for such permission must have at least three living children (Sec. 2, Subsec. 2, clause (b)). Sec. 5 of the 1961 Proclamation established that, henceforth, legally permitted abortions would be performed, in the appropriate medical institutions, free of charge.[21] In addition, Sec. 6 stipulated that the Commissions on Abortions may call to their hearings the "husband of the woman concerned, or the man who caused the pregnancy in question, and, in cases which involve a girl under 18 years of age, her parents as well". A special Supplement to the 1961 Proclamation enumerated the illnesses which constitute "medical indications" justifying permission for the artificial interruption of pregnancy.

The 1961 Proclamation upheld, with some qualifications, the substance of several important provisions of the 1957 Proclamation (cf. especially

---

[20] As to the reported recent abrogation of the Proclamation No. 104/1961 Coll., see footnote 1 above, and the Addendum at the end of this study.

[21] As to the recent partial repeal of this provision, see the Addendum at the end of this study.

Secs. 1-6, Proclamation No. 249/1957 U.L. and the corresponding Secs. 1-4, 6, and 7 of Proclamation No. 104/1961 Coll.). The 1961 Proclamation thereby retained some of the defects of the 1957 Proclamation, such as the vaguely formulated socio-economic reasons justifying abortion, mentioned above. Furthermore, by making abortions available entirely without cost, and by easing somewhat the conditions which must be met before permission for abortion can be granted (e.g., amending the requirement for several children to three children), the 1961 Proclamation opened the door to abuses even wider.

Moreover, official recognition (as reflected in this Proclamation) of socio-economic hardships as reasons justifying a pregnant woman's undergoing the hazard and anguish of abortion seems to throw a rather revealing light on conditions of life in Czechoslovakia under the present Communist regime. Such facts controvert Communist propaganda statements to the effect that under the people's democratic legal order of a socialist state on its way to achieving Communism, the justified needs of individuals, families, and particularly children are fully protected, or even provided for, by the local and central governments, and that any hardships caused by illness or by adverse social and economic conditions are alleviated by adequate social security and/or public assistance measures. In any event, a wide gap seems to exist between, on the one hand, the social and legal considerations apparent in the Proclamation No. 104/1961 Coll., which openly provides pregnant women with abortion as their only means of escaping dire social and economic hardship; and, on the other hand, the politically inflated provisions on the protection of the family and of youth in the former Czechoslovak Constitution of 1948 (Sec. 10) and in the present Constitution of the Czechoslovak Socialist Republic of July 11, 1960, No. 100/1960 Coll.

4. *The Commissions on Abortions.*

Decisions of the Commissions on Abortion are open to adverse criticism, particularly because of their inconsistency; some of them have shown undue harshness towards applicants, and others have granted abortions with excessive liberality. This situation arises from several factors.

First, the application of the Proclamation No. 104/1961 Coll., which is an integral part of Law No. 68/1957 Coll. on the Artificial Interruption of Pregnancy, is substantially a quasi-judicial function, and often a very difficult one. The composition of the Commissions enables them to decide medical questions with assurance; however, since their membership includes no trained lawyers, they are much less able to decide correctly and consistently on the many non-medical matters involved, in particular on the complicated legal, personal, economic, and social problems which beset many individual cases. Members who lack a proper legal training and experience can hardly be expected, in every case, to find adequate and reliable evidence, to evaluate impartially the highly emotional allegations which may be made, and to balance objectively the intricate, often contradictory considerations involved.

Second, the Commissions are affiliated with the organs of local government. Their members are often exposed, and sometimes susceptible, to personal pressures and/or undue political influence. Typical situations confronting the Commissions include the demands of pregnant young girls and their families for abortion as a means of escaping the hardships and embarrassments of childbirth out of wedlock; and the social needs of pregnant girls or women who must retain their employment in order to support themselves and, in many cases, dependent families as well. State-owned (socialized) enterprises (*Národní podniky*) contribute to this social hardship by their notorious reluctance to employ pregnant workers or to adjust their working conditions to the reduced state of their health and strength. The public press has several times severely castigated both the pregnant girls seeking abortion and their families for their "retrogressive petty-bourgeois points of view", as well as the managements of the national enterprises for personnel policies which lack the "proper socialistic conscientiousness".

In addition, the Commissions are exposed to political pressure from the government and the state industrial management. The government and all public media from time to time issue statements based on vital statistics which show that the birth rate is seriously and steadily declining, especially in the Czech Lands and in all industrial areas; since the issuance of Law No. 68/1957 Coll. this decline is more pronounced than ever. The authorities warn that the excessive number of legal and illegal abortions contributes to this decline, and, in the long run, will lead to a decrease in the labor force and hamper the growth of national production.[22] Such authoritative statements cannot but strongly influence at least some of the members of the Commissions on Abortion. Thus, their decisions swing

---

[22] Cf. *Rudé Právo* (official daily of the Czechoslovak Communist Party), Praha, November 22, 1962; broadcast statement of the radio station in Bratislava, June 26, 1962; and *News from Czechoslovakia* (New York, Free Europe Committee, Inc.) for July 16, 1962 (p. 6) and December 12, 1962 (p. 3, 4).

from extreme liberality to extreme strictness. This fluctuation, of course, does not obviate the fact that this legislation, and the abuses to which it is liable, remain among the major causes contributing to the unfavorable trend in the birth rate, to a potential decline in the level of public health resulting from the harmful effects of frequent or repeated abortions on individual women, and to the spread of immorality and crime, especially among youth, in Communist-dominated Czechoslovakia.

5. *Impunity of the Pregnant Woman in Matters of Abortion.*

Law No. 68/1957 Coll. constitutes a substantial departure from all previous legislation. While Secs. 4 and 5 severely penalize all third persons involved in any illegal abortion, Sec. 6 provides that the pregnant woman shall not be subject to any punishment for performing an abortion upon herself, or for asking or permitting another to do so. This provision, which removes all barriers to abortion by the mother, and to her solicitation of illegal abortion, is wrong in its substance as well as in the unwholesome consequences which must issue from it.

The framers of the present law went much too far in granting full impunity for any abortion that the pregnant woman chooses to solicit or to perform on herself for any reason and under any conditions whatsoever. The authorities, instead of deciding to give every pregnant woman this unrestricted license in abortion, might have better served the interests of public health if they had provided in the law that impunity for such abortion depends upon the conditions that the operation be performed by responsible physicians or in qualified health institutions, and that the abortion may be carried out upon the informal request of the pregnant woman, her legal representative, or her physician, without the necessity of any bureaucratic procedure.

The present alternative, either to disclose their private affairs by submitting to official proceedings of uncertain outcome, or to take a chance on self-inflicted abortion, may be found by some pregnant women to amount to a very hard choice. If the provisions suggested above were adopted, the pregnant woman's privacy and her health or life would be fully protected by the professional secrecy and the proficiency of the operating physicians. These important aims could be achieved easily and at little cost because medicine is fully socialized in present-day Czechoslovakia. In this respect, the present law has radically departed from the advanced and sound principles and legislative aims of the pre-Communist Czechoslovak Bills of Criminal Law and theories of *legis ferendae* and has, instead, perverted the domestic legal order with rather unsound Soviet-like[23] concepts.

The full impunity which the law now offers to any solicitation of abortion by the pregnant woman, together with the notorious hope of distressed women that their pregnancy will be terminated secretly and carefully, may rather increase illegal abortions and criminality. Thus the practical consequences of the provisions of Sec. 6 may indirectly contribute to an increase in the very dangers which are depicted in Sec. 1 and which the law seeks to prevent, remove, or decrease.

6. *Change in the Social Values to be Protected.*

One must also note a characteristic change in the social values to be protected by the new Law No. 68/1957 Coll. Its Sec. 1 seeks only the protection of the healthy development of families against injury to the lives and health of pregnant women. This Law does not even mention, as a legislator's motive or objective, the protection of the developing human life (foetus) in the mother's womb. This is another radical departure from the legislative motives of pre-Communist criminal legislation and even from the motives and aims of the Communist Criminal Code of 1950 (Sec. 218).[24] This novel disregard of human life in its most defenseless stage can only be strongly disapproved.

7. *Domestic Observations on the Application of the new Law.*

The underlying philosophy, the practical value, and, above all, the moral consequences to youth, of Law No. 68/1957 Coll., have caused considerable dissension among the Czechoslovak public. After the first year of its implementation, the law was discussed by a Communist Czech daily, *Mladá Fronta*, in an editorial entitled "Some Experiences with the Law on Artificial Interruption of Pregnancy."[25] As could be expected, the editorial upheld the law, on the whole, but it could not disregard some important objections raised against it. It reads:

The opponents of this law have been afraid that the law will not only bring about a serious decline of the birth rate, but that it will also exercise a fatal influence on public morals, while its adherents have pointed out, especially, that by

---

[23] *Cf.* Vl. Gsovski, "USSR – Penalty for Abortion Modified", *Highlights*, vol. 3, Nos. 5-6 (May-June 1955), p. 133.
[24] *Trestní právo, část zvláštní, op. cit.*, p. 343.
[25] *Mladá Fronta*, Praha, January 8, 1959, p. 4.

making available an artificial interruption of pregnancy in a hospital under the expert care of a physician, the considerable number of secret criminal abortions will decline and thus diminish the serious danger to women's lives....

During the first nine months of 1957, 192, 983 children were born alive, while [during the same period of] 1958, the total was 183,331 children. One cannot say, however, that this entire decline is attributable to the influence of this law.... The reasons for the decline are very complicated ... they include, especially, the trend to smaller families....

Although official statistics show that a preponderant number of applications for abortion were granted, this does not mean that all women who for some reason do not wish to have a child allow their pregnancy to be artificially interrupted.... The law fulfills its main task – the struggle against secret abortions, the number of which in the current year has undoubtedly declined....

In instances where the Commission *rejects* the application of a pregnant woman without convincing her in a humane manner of the correctness of its decision, *the woman seeks another way, the way to a secret abortion*... [author's italics].

A necessary complement of the law ... should be early education, especially of youth, in the right attitude regarding matters of sexual life ... Several hundreds of abortions carried out at the request of girls, the oldest of whom was 17 years of age, is more than convincing evidence of the need for this.

Insofar as some defects in the actual implementation [of the law] still exist, such as some inconsistencies in the decisions of the Commissions regarding individual cases, ... it may contribute to the removal of such defects if the People's Committees regularly occupy themselves with the activities of the Commissions in their respective areas....[26]

IV. SUMMARY AND CONCLUSIONS

Communist legislation on abortion follows the Czechoslovak penal statutes of the democratic era by penalizing as major crimes the solicitation to, aiding and abetting of, participation in, and perpetration of abortions. It has also gradually adopted several advanced legal concepts, evolved *de lege ferenda* during the democratic, pre-Communist period by criminologists and the official drafters of the Bills of Criminal Law; this holds true especially with regard to the penalization of the attempt to perpetrate an abortion, and to the impunity of abortions carried out in a safe, medically controlled manner, because of statutorily specified important legal, medical, eugenic, or social reasons.

The administration of the provisions for lawful abortion, however, has

---

[26] The same editorial indicates, as another necessary extra-legal complement to this law, the suitable instruction of the public concerning contraceptive means for preventing effectively any unwanted pregnancy.

not been altogether satisfactory. The Commissions which decide on applications for abortion, lacking suitably qualified members and being exposed to various pressures, have been subject to much criticism, even in the regimented domestic press, for the inconsistency of their decisions.

But the main defect of Law No. 68/1957 Coll. is to be found in the provisions of Sec. 6, which, abandoning sound criminological principles, establish the unrestricted impunity of abortions which the pregnant woman performs on herself, and the impunity of her solicitation of or her permission to third persons to bring about the interruption of her pregnancy. These provisions open the door to the perpetration of self-inflicted abortions, which are notoriously dangerous and often lethal, since they are carried out in unhygienic conditions by medically untrained pregnant women, often teenagers. By granting this impunity, the law contributes to the spread of criminality and to the undermining of public morals, especially among youth.

Moreover, by this provision the Communist legislators have utterly forsaken the basic social need of protecting the developing human life (the foetus), and the health and life of the pregnant woman.

Not only has this legislation failed to achieve its alleged main objective, i.e., a substantial decrease in the number of unnecessary or unjustified abortions; it has instead contributed to the significant decline in the birth rate, particularly in urban and industrialized areas, as evidenced in official statistics and in frequent complaints in the Czechoslovak press. Thus, on the whole, the present legislation on abortion has defeated, to a considerable extent, its own basic purpose.

ADDENDUM

A verbatim translation follows of the article referred to in footnote 1 above, which appeared in *Rudé Právo* on January 18, 1963:

New regulations [to implement the law] on the [artificial] interruption of pregnancy [of 1957].[27, 28]

Since January of this year [i.e., 1963] new regulations to implement Law No. 68 of 1957 on the Artificial Interruption of Pregnancy have taken force. Current experience has confirmed that the main objective of the law has been attained – that is, the reduction of the number of deaths suffered by pregnant

---

[27] Text in brackets supplied.
[28] These regulations were issued as the Government Decree of December 21, 1962, No. 126 Coll., to Establish the Interruption Commissions and to Implement the Law on the Artificial Interruption of Pregnancy (No. 68/1957 Coll.).

women in consequence of clandestine abortions.... The experience of the past five years has also shown that 85% of women applying for artificial interruption of pregnancy do so for reasons other than those of health. Thus, for example, in 1961, 45.1% of the applications referred to the fact that the applicants had more children. Unmarried women submitted 13.6% of the applications; 8.7% of the applicants gave lack of space in the home as their reason; and 7% referred to the disruption of their families, etc. During the last year [i.e., 1962] the total number of abortions performed by request was somewhat reduced; nevertheless, the relationship between the birth rate and the artificial interruption of pregnancy remains very unfavorable. Henceforth the causes of abortion as a social phenomenon will be examined more carefully. From now on, applications may be filed only with the Commission on Abortion in the district where the applicant permanently resides. ... The surcharge of from 200 to 500 Cz. crowns for partial coverage of the expenses of medical attendance has been reinstated. However, if the operative measure is necessary for reasons of health, it shall be free of charge....

Several points here deserve brief comment. The admission that in 1962 the number of abortions performed by request was only "somewhat reduced", and that the ratio between the birth rate and the number of abortions "remains very unfavorable" confirms our legal and sociological criticisms of this legislation and its application.

The high rate of abortions, and the fact that 85% of the women who applied did so for reasons other than those of health, not only demonstrate the widespread maladministration and abuse of this legislation, but also indicate the depressing conditions of life now prevailing in the Czechoslovak Socialistic Republic.

The reinstatement of a relatively high hospital charge on all abortions performed for other than health reasons shows that the Communist legislators themselves have now recognized the adverse effects of making all approved abortions available cost-free. However, the legislators should also have exempted from payment of this fee those women whose applications are approved for reasons of genuine hardship. At present, the exemption from the fee *"may be granted"* only "in exceptional cases". (Emphasis supplied.)

Still another example of the vacillation and short-sightedness of the Communist legislators is their new requirement that applicants file only with the Interruption Commission in the district of their permanent residence. This provision obviously seeks to prevent applicants from obtaining permission for abortion more easily in districts where they and their circumstances are less well known, and where their allegations might be less easily controverted. However, such circumventions can easily be rectified by any Commission which conducts its examinations with due care. Thus, there was no real need for this dubious innovation, which may seriously inconvenience some applicants and induce others to resort to clandestine or self-inflicted abortions rather than risk personal embarrassment and what may appear to them as a greater probability of having their applications refused. The Government Decree No. 126/1962 Coll. seems to have reinforced the self-defeating nature of the Communist legislation on abortion.

The Government Decree No. 126/1962 Coll., which took force on Jan. 1, 1963, abrogated the Proclamation No. 104/1961 Coll. and the pertinent procedural regulations issued by the Ministry of Health (No. 31/1961 Collection of Regulations for National Committees). The former provisions on "health" and "social" reasons for abortion have been retained. The present Decree has, to some extent, improved the composition and procedural rules of the Interruption Commissions (formerly Commissions on Abortion), but the politically minded lay elements still prevail over the medical experts in influence on the decisions. Moreover, the Commissions still lack any independent and judicially qualified experts. On the whole, the recent improvements constitute only half-measures.

SCIENCE AND TECHNOLOGY

The Purkinje Effect in the Evolution of Scientific Thought

KAREL HUJER

When Newton announced the principles of color vision in his classical work, *Opticks*, 1704,[1] and by means of a prism decomposed sunlight into seven rainbow colors, he only reaffirmed that the source of our knowledge rests exclusively outside the observer and his senses. The legend of the "falling apple" that was to guide the youthful natural philosopher to the discovery of the universal law of gravitation is epistemologically similar to Newton's observation of the prism decomposing sunlight. It indicates that the structure of light is an entirely external phenomenon which takes place outside of man's mind. Newton's views and his theory of knowledge, corroborated over the years by a series of triumphs, are epitomized in the scientific method which still guides much of our civilization. Certain phenomena in modern physics, however, ever more urgently indicate that Newton's world view no longer reigns without question. We shall investigate aspects of some new ideas as they now appear in optics through the Purkinje phenomenon.

According to Newton's theory of knowledge, there is the world external to our senses, and we learn about its reality by means of our perception. With the help of various tools such as telescopes, microscopes, spectroscopes, photometers, etc., it is possible to extend, amplify and increase the efficiency of our senses and thus augment the precision of our measurement. Therefore, according to Newtonian concepts, the complete externalization and objectification of color indicates that, as every physicist knows, each color from red to violet is associated either with a specific wavelength or a specific number of vibrations per second, called frequency. Thus, the yellow spectrum line D of sodium, for example, in the solar spectrum has a wavelength equivalent to 5896 angstrom units, i.e., 0.000,05896 cm, and appears yellow to anyone, anywhere in the universe. This is a reality whether or not such an organ as the human eye exists.

---

[1] Sir Isaac Newton, "A New Theory About Light and Colours", *Philosophical Transactions*, Vol. I (February, 1672). Also in *Treatise on Opticks* (London, 1704).

Because of Newton's long-unquestioned authority, this view has continued to dominate related thought to the present day.

In the realm of pure philosophy, as will be shown later, there were divergent opinions concerning the nature of reality, and experimental science, in its dominance, has relegated these ideas to the background. In 1819, however, a young physiologist, J. E. Purkyně, or Purkinje, published a paper in Prague entitled *Beiträge zur Kenntnis des Sehens in subjektiver Hinsicht*.[2] Purkinje's first paper was followed by a second on a similar subject, *Beobachtungen und Versuche zur Physiologie der Sinne. Neue Beiträge zur Kenntnis des Sehens in subjektiver Hinsicht* (Berlin, 1825).[3] The latter contained the idea of the Purkinje effect. These were the only works in which he happened to approach the field of physics. As often happens, the discoverer was little aware of the far-reaching significance of the phenomenon he described, particularly in relation to the theory of knowledge.

What is the Purkinje effect? By this phenomenon is usually meant the curious fact that blue and, especially, green colors look abnormally bright when illumination is diminished, and yellow and, especially, red colors look abnormally dull. When formulated in the language of mathematical physics, the Purkinje effect means that the change in the intensity of light is accompanied by a relative change in color or, according to the subjective experience, the perception of a definite color is not attached to the same numerically stated wavelength, but vacillates with the intensity of illumination. In the quantitative expression of a physicist, objective measurement shows that under the conditions of good illumination, the human retina is most sensitive to the radiant flux of wavelength 5550 angstroem units but when illumination is reduced, the highest sensitivity of the human eye is displaced toward shorter wavelengths. This shift in sensitivity of the retina toward a shorter wavelength, or a radiation of higher energy when illumination is dim, is the most characteristic feature of the Purkinje effect. Or, to state it differently, when the light is weak, the retina requires a higher energy impulse, i.e., shorter wavelengths, to register on our mind the perception of the same color. By 1891, Ladd-Franklin, followed by Ebbinghaus in 1892, the Purkinje effect was extended to color combinations which make colorless mixtures. Examined under various intensities of illumination, these reveal an even more startling aspect of the Purkinje phenomenon. The Purkinje effect evi-

---

[2] J. E. Purkyně, *Beiträge zur Kenntnis des Sehens in subjektiver Hinsicht* (Prague, 1819).
[3] J. E. Purkyně, *Beobachtungen und Versuche zur Physiologie der Sinne. Neue Beiträge zur Kenntnis des Sehens in subjektiver Hinsicht* (Berlin, 1825).

dently indicates that man's subjective experience in relation to the perception of colors does not accord with Newton's theory of colors. A given wavelength does not always produce an impression of the very same color.

It is particularly interesting to note that among those first to react most sympathetically to Purkinje's publication was Goethe, who wrote to his friend, J. P. Eckerman:[4] "I read the publication with great joy...", and further wrote that Purkinje's paper so well expounds his own theory of colors that he was suprised that the name, Goethe, is not quoted. It is little known that the Weimar poet dedicated the last forty years of his life to ardent study of the theory of colors and centered his philosophy and his Weltanschauung on the notion that, as with colors, all aspects of the external world have no reality outside man's sensory perception. Goethe set forth these ideas in such voluminous works as *Farbenlehre* and *Geschichte der Farbenlehre*, which, despite Goethe's literary fame, have remained relatively obscure.

It is indeed very startling to consider the obstinacy with which this literary giant, conceivably ill versed in mathematics, opposed Newton's scientific authority and his mechanistically based theory of colors which assign the production of colors outside of man's mind, i.e., into the behavior of light waves in the external world. Goethe, on the other hand, describes his method as empirical idealism, and maintains that the sense-perceptible world-picture, including color vision, is the sum total of constantly changing percepts *without any underlying matter*. This, of course, appears fantastic. Not even the fame of the great poet could uphold this radical view against the firmly established Newtonian tradition, and Goethe's concept is still considered a curious vagary of the prolific but occasionally erratic poet. Yet Goethe was so involved in these speculations that he valued his hard-won theory of colors above even his famous literary achievements. He was, therefore, eager to enlist any possible support for his ideas on optics; Purkinje's publication was the basis for the establishment of a continuing friendship between the two.

Goethe's interest in Purkinje's work apparently inspired the young physiologist's visit to the poet in Weimar on December 11-13, 1822; in 1823, Purkinje was appointed to this professorship at Breslau University, thanks partly to the influence of Goethe as well as Alexander von Humboldt. Purkinje dedicated his second paper,[5] previously mentioned, to

[4] O. V. Hykeš – D. E. Hykešová, "Goethe a Purkyně", *Goethův sborník. Památce 100. výročí básníkovy smrti vydali čeští germanisté* (Praha, Státní nakladatelství, 1932), p. 14.
[5] *Op. cit.*, pp. 26-29.

Goethe and expressed his appreciation for the inspiration he derived from the poet's theory of colors. This was rather precarious ground, because Goethe's scientific works were almost generally rejected by contemporary physicists, but his great literary fame outweighed the hostile opinions, and Purkinje did not hesitate to express his feelings openly in the "Habilitation" thesis for his Breslau University appointment.

In dealing with the problem of color vision, guided by Goethe's idea that color is inside, not outside, man's sensory perception, Purkinje turned toward the study of the structure of the human eye. That has since proved to be sound procedure. According to Goethe, the eye does not determine the color, but is the cause of its manifestation. Thus, any theory of color must start with the investigation of the eye. Goethe, in his procedure, thus places the physiological theory of color at the very beginning. Consequently, Purkinje followed the method called heautognosic, according to Gruithuisen's idea. Heautognosy is the preliminary conditioning of senses which are to be used for further scientific investigation. In other words, the researcher must first investigate himself, the value and the state of his senses of perception. The English astrophysicist, Sir James Jeans, gives an excellent example of heautognosy when he considers a physiologist examining the brain of a patient:[6]

Most people's opinion is that he sees the brain of the patient, but the philosopher insists that actually it is the brain of the physiologist himself.

For many years Jeans was the secretary of the Royal Society of London, and Goethe would surely have been pleased to hear such views from the twentieth-century successor to Isaac Newton in that learned society which bestowed its fellowship upon his friend, Purkinje.

The Purkinje phenomenon, however, points the way to iconoclastic consequences unforeseen either by Purkinje or almost any physicist, even to the present time. The Purkinje effect specifically indicates such subjective conditions of human cognition as were outlined by earlier philosophers, particularly in the Berkeleyan school, then by Schopenhauer and Kant, and most recently by Poincaré and Bergson, intuitive philosophy. The most important aspect of the Purkinje phenomenon is its empirical justification of this idea which extends from Berkeley to Bergson, challenging the questionable supremacy of quantity and space in scientific thought. Quantity and space dominate and motivate our interpretation of the nature of the world, reducing the quality and wealth of life to purposeless insignificance.

[6] Sir James Jeans, *Physics and Philosophy* (Cambridge, University Press, 1953), p. 87.

Most knowledge, both classical and contemporary, is based upon and ostensibly justified by the assumption that the world and everything we perceive in it has an existence independent of our cognizance, with all cosmic phenomena occurring in space and time quite apart from man, the only cosmic reality. It is misleading to take this erroneous assumption as the starting point in the investigation of cosmic phenomena. The fact that there is no absolute number associated with the sensation of a definite color consequently reveals evidence that each individual and his inner world are the only reality. In a similar trend Berkeley describes his ideas of space:[7]

I am disposed to think that whenever we speak of the extension as an idea common to visual and tactile senses, it is by tacit supposition that we can detach the extension from all other tangible and visual properties and create an abstract idea, an idea that would be common at the same time to both senses of touch and sight.

The French physicist, P. Chambadal, maintains:[8]

It is to Berkeley that belongs the merit of having demonstrated the independence of our visual and tactile sensations as far as concerns the property of space and geometry. It was reserved to Henri Poincaré to complete this doctrine and to demonstrate that the properties which we attribute to space and which are studied by geometry themselves depend upon our visual and tactile sensations.

Furthermore, Berkeley's eighteenth-century statement has a consequential relationship to that of the late astrophysicist, Sir Arthur Eddington, who remarks:[9]

The beautiful hues which flood our consciousness under the stimulation of the waves have no relevance to the objective reality.

In other words, whatever we observe as seemingly independent and self-contained in the physical world is actually a form of sense nature. Kant called it an a priori form of sensuousness. Consequently, the properties of the physical extension depend directly on the structure of our sense organs; the properties of mathematical space and all the phenomena it transmits,

---

[7] George Berkeley, *Essay Towards a New Theory of Vision* (London, 1707). Quoted from *La physique moderne et son interprétation* (Paris, Librairie Armand Colin, 1956), p. 46.
[8] P. Chambadal, *La physique moderne et son interprétation* (Paris, 1956), p. 47.
[9] Sir Arthur Eddington, *The Nature of the Physical World* (Cambridge, University Press, 1929), p. 94.

such as colors, are only an abstract and schematized expression produced by our senses. Whatever may be the individual divergences of the various philosphical concepts we have thus far considered, particularly those of Kant, Schopenhauer, Poincaré or Bergson, their researches on the genesis of geometry arrive at the same result – the physiological relativity and consequently the ideality of space.

As we observe the world about us on the macrophysical scale, it may appear absurd indeed to speak of its non-reality. Yet, the history of man's ideas about the structure of the universe records only a constant struggle between what man has called reality and what the evolution of ideas has always proved to be an illusion. At present, for example, the relativistic aspect of the physical world, which moved the concept of reality even farther away from our direct experience, is extremely elusive on the ordinary scale and at the customary velocities, and its proofs are only possible in the realm of most refined measuring technique. Likewise, in our affirmation of the unreality of an objective world, we must proceed to the very boundary of the physical world and consider the state of our knowledge of such ultimate particles of physics as electron or quantum, and only indirectly examine their reality through a series of intricate experiments.

Although the determination of the charge and mass of an electron secured Nobel prizes for both Millikan and J. J. Thomson, indicating official recognition of the "reality" of such a particle, Eddington, after speaking confidently about the electron existing in the objective world, nevertheless in the next breath tells us that the electron is "something unknown ... doing we don't know what". The electron is entirely invisible, yet what makes the word, electron, such a driving reality in our technology but our own thoughts? If the existence of electrons were established in a seemingly irrefutable manner, it would bring along grave problems: What is the dimension of an electron? Were the electron not dimensionless, its own existence would be self-inconsistent. Being thus utterly unstable, it would instantly explode, thanks to the fantastic forces of repulsion operating within the microcosmic region of its finite dimension. On the other hand, were the electron a dimensionless, geometrical point, we would have to attribute to it an infinite electrical energy which is inconceivable. Therefore, both the suggested and the merely feasible structures are mutually exclusive, because this particle is always associated with a definite electrical charge – the famous physical constant. Yet, our dilemma would not disappear were it possible to admit some finite extension of this corpuscle. We would still face another inscrutable mystery as to why this particle remains stable in its charge and mass during the frantic course of its fantastic activity. Were the electron strictly a geometrical point without dimensions, it could not enter into contact with another electron without being confounded with it. Were there no contact because of lack of dimension, how could electrons exert mutual interaction? Whatever form of answer or suggestion we may propose as to the mechanism of this ultimate particle, which evidently must represent some universal building material of our physical world, we always end in a blind alley. What then is the reality? Categorically, our question at this point is no different from that raised against an electromagnetic wave such as that which produced our sensation of color.

If the Purkinje phenomenon throws doubt on the reality of color or wavelength, our picture of the electron throws wide open to the fullest extent the mystery of the world about us. Does or does not the electron possess an extension? Why do we insist on one or the other affirmation? P. Chambadal maintains:[10]

The initial error that brought us to this impasse consisted precisely in the fact that we attributed to this ultimate particle an absolute existence which implies geometrical properties clearly defined. It is sufficient to renounce this "realistic" concept of the world and admit that it exists only in our representation and our antinomy, as many other inextricable problems produced by realistic illusion, and the initial error will reach its true solution. This solution can be expressed as follows: The ultimate particle, electron, is neither a dimensionless point, nor does it possess an extension, it simply does not have an objective existence.

So it appears that Purkinje's idea of tracing the origin of colors in the physiological field, in the study of the human eye, was sound. Evidently he was nearer the goal of the search for reality than Newton, who examined the sunlight with the prism. Nevertheless, not even Purkinje reached the goal; he only replaced Newton's tool – the prism – by another tool, the human eye. The actual distance between the prism and the human eye is not very great. The door of the human mind that receives the message of the physical, external world is somewhere much farther and deeper inside the mystery of being. Eddington says that in the realm of our physical plane we can trace the vestiges of these physical influences up to the door of the mind, where these influences ring the bell and vanish. In this respect, the behavior of the external world, its phenomena, may be described as not producing facts of some reality, but being merely symbols

---

[10] P. Chambadal, *op. cit.*, pp. 154-5.

of a picture of reality. Then, as H. Poincaré insisted, it is our arbitrary decision to create any convenient picture of reality. In this train of ideas, he maintained that since the earth's rotation is not a fact because we do not and cannot perceive the earth's motion, it is a matter of convenience to affirm that the earth rotates. Similarly, we can have direct experience of neither the atom nor the electron, but, as the physicist, C. F. von Weizsäcker, says, we force the atom or electron through experiment to tell us its properties in an inadequate language – and much to our hidden presumptions. And, Weizsäcker adds, the experiment is a violation of nature in which even more readily we force nature to play our game.

To sum up our subject, the Purkinje effect plays a most significant role in what one of the great scholars of Purkinje, A. Tschermak-Seysenegg, described as the foundation of exact subjectivism. It means even more. It adds another milestone to advancing man's understanding of the nature of the physical world in relation to which our present scientific method will have to make some revision in Galilean science. If such outstanding philosophers as J. Maritain, M. Buber, N. Berdyaev, and others, each in his own way, speak of the tragedy of "objectification", their voices, though little heard in the tumult of our triumphant dehumanized technology, are significant warnings that everything is not right with our objective scientific thought.

A last, though not least important fact, is that only recently Masaryk's University in Brno, Czechoslovakia, was renamed the J. E. Purkyně University. How strange that Masaryk, the realist philosopher, has been replaced by Purkinje, whose discovery, glorified as scientific, actually points the way toward an unfathomable change in the tide of ideas, from materialism of the objectified world and space and from dehumanized purposelessness, toward qualitative wealth of subjective life and the dignity of man.

LITERATURE

J. W. von Goethe, *Zur Farbenlehre* (1810).
Henri Poincaré, *La science et l'hypothèse* (Paris, 1906).
——, *Dernières Pensées* (Paris, 1913).
Henri Bergson, *L'évolution créatrice* (Paris, 1925).
Armin Tschermak-Seysenegg, *Goethe's Farbenlehre in ihrer Bedeutung für die physiologische Optik der Gegenwart* (Prague, 1932).
R. H. Kahn, *Goethe's Augen. Deren Beschaffenheit und Sehvermögen* (Prague, Physiological Institute, 1932).
Christine Ladd-Franklin, *Colour and Colour Theories* (London, 1932).
A. Tschermak-Seysenegg, *J. E. Purkyně als ein Begründer des exakten Subjektivismus* (Prague, 1937).

F. K. Studnička, "Kterak docházejí uznání objevy J. E. Purkyně", *Časopis lékařů českých*, č. 6 (Praha, 1947).
C. F. von Weizsäcker, *The World View of Physics* (Chicago, University of Chicago Press, 1952).
B. Němec – Otakar Matoušek, *Jan Evangelista Purkyně* (Praha, 1955).
M. H. Wilson and R. W. Brocklebank, "Complementary Hues of After Images", *Optical Journal of America*, Vol. 45 (1955).
Karel Hujer, "On the History and Philosophy of Purkinje Effect", *Actes du* VIII. *Congrès International d'Histoire des Sciences, Firenze, Italy, 1956*.
Herbert Dingle, *The Sources of Eddington's Philosophy* (Cambridge, 1954).
C. C. L. Gregory and Anita Kohsen, *Physical and Psychical Research* (Reigate, Surrey, The Omega Press, 1954).
Eva Rozsívalová, *Život a dílo J. E. Purkyně* (Praha, 1956).
C. W. Churchman and Ph. Ratoosh, *Measurement: Definitions and Theories* (New York, N.Y., 1959).
Milič Čapek, *Philosophical Impact of Contemporary Physics* (Princeton, N. J., Van Nostrand, 1961).

Jindřich Matiegka and the Anthropometric Approach to the Study of Body Composition

JOSEF BROŽEK

In the last two decades, the body composition of the living man has been an object of intensive study (cf. *Science*, 134, 1961, 920-930). As one of the focal points of human biology, it represents the methodological crossroads of physical anthropology, biophysics, and biochemistry. Quantitative anatomy (cf. *AIBS Bull.*, 11, No. 3, 1961, 10-11) and chemical analysis of whole cadavers and of individual organs provide crucial, fundamental data and the final criterion for the validation of all the *indirect* methods.

Among the indirect methods, the approximative analysis of body composition, based on body measurements, is of great practical significance on account of the speed and relative simplicity with which it can be carried out.

The basic principles were outlined in 1921 by the Czech anthropologist, Jindřich Matiegka (cf. *Am. J. Phys. Anthrop.*, 10, 1952, 515-519) in an article published under the cryptic title, "The Testing of Physical Efficiency". It represents the first systematic attempt to estimate the main components of body weight on the basis of body measurements, thus constituting an original and fruitful approach to the quantitative description of the human physique.

Forty-two years ago there appeared in the *American Journal of Physical Anthropology* (4, 1921, 223-230), an article by Jindřich Matiegka, professor of anthropology at Charles University. In it Matiegka presented a novel, indeed a revolutionary, approach to the quantitative characterization of human physique in terms of body composition.

As the title ("The Testing of Physical Efficiency") suggests, Matiegka's direct concern was to relate body measurements to the appraisal of man's "fitness", in the broad sense of this term.

He felt, with justification, that traditional anthropometry did not yield a satisfactory description of human physique. Clearly, it would be erroneous to assign too much importance to any single body dimension as an indicator of fitness. Thus tallness, as judged by stature, is not necessarily an indication of overall physical superiority, since it may be associated with a poorly developed musculature. Similarly, a large body weight may indicate an unhealthy obesity rather than a powerful physique. The traditional combinations of two or more anthropometric dimensions in the form of an "index" also do not yield the desired answer, the principal reason being that the initial measurements, such as body weight or chest circumference or bideltoid diameter, are anatomically complex data in which size and tissue composition are inseparably mixed.

Matiegka was interested in functionally oriented, "dynamic" anthropometry. His goal was to devise a system for an analytical, quantitative description of human physique, a system which would be adequate for the evaluation of the somatic facet of man's "fitness" – as we have seen, he spoke of "physical efficiency" – for such varied purposes as vocational guidance, choice of athletic pursuits or life insurance examinations.

Matiegka was anxious to place physical anthropology of the living man in a wider framework of human biology and visualized the somatometric evaluation of man's physique as a component of a broad, biomedical study of man's health and work capacity. Such a comprehensive evaluation was to include, in addition to body measurements, the physiological assessment of principal body functions, and the psychological (psychometric) evaluation of an individual. In fact, the term "somatotechnic" methods appealed to him as a parallel to the "psychotechnic" procedures of applied psychology. His goal was to enhance the biological significance of body measurements and to increase the utility of physical anthropology, measured in terms of medical and social criteria.

As far as we are aware, Matiegka's was the first systematic attempt to derive estimates of the main components of body weight on the basis of anthropometric data, chiefly the dimensions of the extremities.

In Matiegka's system the gross body weight (W) was divided, in fact, into four components:

$$W = O + D + M + R$$

where O = the weight of the skeleton ("ossa", bones)
  D = skin ("derma") plus the subcutaneous adipose tissue
  M = skeletal muscles, and
  R = remainder.

The estimate of the weight of the skeleton ("O"), was based on height and the lateral dimensions (thicknesses) of the bones of the extremities: humeral and femoral condyles, wrists and ankles.

The weight of skin plus subcutaneous adipose tissue ("D") was predicted from the body surface and skinfolds measured at 6 sites: upper arm, forearm, thigh, calf, thorax, and abdomen.

The equation for estimating the muscle mass ("M") included height and the measurements of the circumference (or the calculated value of the radius, minus skin and subcutaneous fat) of the upper arm, thigh, and calf.

The coefficients used in the estimation equations were derived on the basis of average values reported in the literature, theoretical considerations, and the author's personal experience.

Matiegka's pathbreaking, pioneering paper had a quadruple misfortune:

1) Its title ("The Testing of Physical Efficiency") was strange, indeed. It was cryptic, at best. The content of the article was concerned with physical anthropology but the title was couched in terms that would arrest the attention of a student of the physiology of human work or of physical education.

2) The ideas presented in the article were apparently too novel, both in regard to the specific procedures suggested for breaking down the body weight into more homogeneous tissue masses, and, more important, in regard to Matiegka's general emphasis on functionally oriented, "dynamic" applied physical anthropology.

3) The paper was published in a journal with a very limited circulation, at least as far as the number of published copies per issue was concerned (though not necessarily the international distribution). The paper was not familiar even to Matiegka's students at Charles University. This might be explained, at least in part, by the fact that it was never published, as far as I know, in Czech.

4) The paper, essentially programmatic in character, was not followed by systematic studies designed to validate the methodology and to explore the biological and medical significance of the new approach to a quantitative characterization of man's physique. Investigations on cadavers for the purposes of deriving empirically the coefficients used in the estimation equations were planned but were not carried out. In any case, they were not reported in the literature.

In summary, in 1921 Matiegka proposed an original and potentially useful approach to the estimation of tissue masses on the basis of body measurements, an approach that represents a significant contribution to physical anthropology. His first concern was to strengthen the practical usefulness of anthropological measurements made on the living man. At the same time, his ideas were of fundamental importance for quantitative human morphology in that he pointed to a new way for a meaningful synthesis of a multiplicity of individual body measurements. The soundness of Matiegka's emphasis on the fundamental role of body composition in describing man's physique was amply confirmed by the developments of the last 20 years, even though the current procedures for measuring body composition (cf. J. Brožek and A. Henschel, eds., *Techniques for Measuring Body Composition*, Washington, D. C., National Academy of Sciences-National Research Council, 1961) were developed largely on the basis of different principles than those proposed by Matiegka.

The Czechoslovak Contribution to the Change in Concept of Circulation of the Blood

WALTER REDISCH

"When I first applied my mind to observation from the many dessections of Living Creatures..., that by that means I might find out the use of the motion of the heart and things conducible...; I straighwayes found it a thing hard to be attained, and full of difficulty, so ... I did almost believe, that the motion of the heart was known to God alone..."

So wrote William Harvey in his *De Motu Cordis* in 1628. The quotation is from the first English text, printed in 1653 (1).[1]

The humbleness of that genius which emanates so impressively from these words of the discoverer of the circulation of the blood, is just as much in order today, after more than 300 years. As a matter of fact, until quite recently almost all advances in the field of circulation of the blood have been technical, elaborating in one way or the other on the principles discovered by Harvey. Some ingenious physiologists soon did realize that the key to the action of the heart and blood vessels had to be – in one way or the other – connected with the peculiarities of the cellular structure of these organs (2, 3). One of these outstanding early investigators was our famous fellow Czech Jan Evangelista Purkyně (4). Solomon Stricker (5) and Steinach and Kahn (6), whose names are intimately associated with the recognition of a non-mechanical autonomy of the peripheral circulation, happened to hail from the Czech lands. Hering (7), though not of Czech origin, accomplished most of his work concerning the neuroregulation of circulation in Prague.

By and large, however, the purely physico-mechanical approach to the problems of blood circulation continued to dominate. The well-known scheme depicting the heart as a central pump which pumped the blood through a system of elastic tubings, the blood vessels, has been widely taught in theory and in model experiments (8), leaving but a few kind sentences to the "metabolic exchange taking place in the capillaries".

---

[1] Numbers between parentheses refer to the Bibliography at the end of this paper.

Even very modern techniques such as angiography, angiocardiography and, to a great extent, also cardiac catheterization derive their parameters predominantly from physico-mechanical phenomena. Electrocardiography has of course been a big step in the other direction – and a very fruitful one indeed.

Recognition of the importance of hormonal regulation of blood flow has many of its roots in Prague. Prusík and his co-workers (9) have contributed much on the clinical level. William Raab (10), Professor emeritus of Experimental Medicine at the University of Vermont School of Medicine, though Viennese by birth and extraction, started much of his research work concerning neurohumoral regulation of blood flow in Prague.

By now we all know that one of the most easily demonstrated differences between the vascular tree and a system of elastic tubings is the response to the injection of one of the vasomimetic amines: this will cause profound changes in practically all physico-mechanical parameters within the circulatory apparatus, while it has no effect, of course, on a mechanical pump connected with a system of elastic tubes.

Recognition of the crucial role of biochemical, enzymatic tissue metabolism factors for the circulatory apparatus and its functioning as advocated by Raab for decades, is a recent development, but fortunately is spreading rapidly. The advances it has brought may be briefly summarized under 3 headings:

(1) Physiologic. The physical approach remains of course enormously valuable; much has been clarified by the work of Lyle Petersen, Donald McDonald and others (11, 12, 13).

Figures 1, 2, 3 describe pressure curves, velocity curves and volume curves. They are extremely helpful in our analysis of pulsatile flow and its conversion to steady flow, to mention just one of the important aspects. But they are not blood flow curves and their composition does not lead to the type of information we gather by measuring rate of blood flow, for example Figures 4, 5 and 6 are examples from our own work at New York University (14, 15, 16) which fits well with the classical experiments of Cannon and his co-workers (18,19) and the results of British workers (20, 21) (Barcroft, Edholm and co-workers). Figures 4 and 5 demonstrate the specificity of responses of various vascular beds to physiologic (Fig. 4) as well as pharmacologic (Fig. 5) stimuli. In response to the same stimulus, blood flow may increase in one bed and simultaneously decrease or remain unchanged in another. Fig. 6 shows the complete reversal of vascular response in a limb which has been deprived of its sympathetic

Fig. 1.

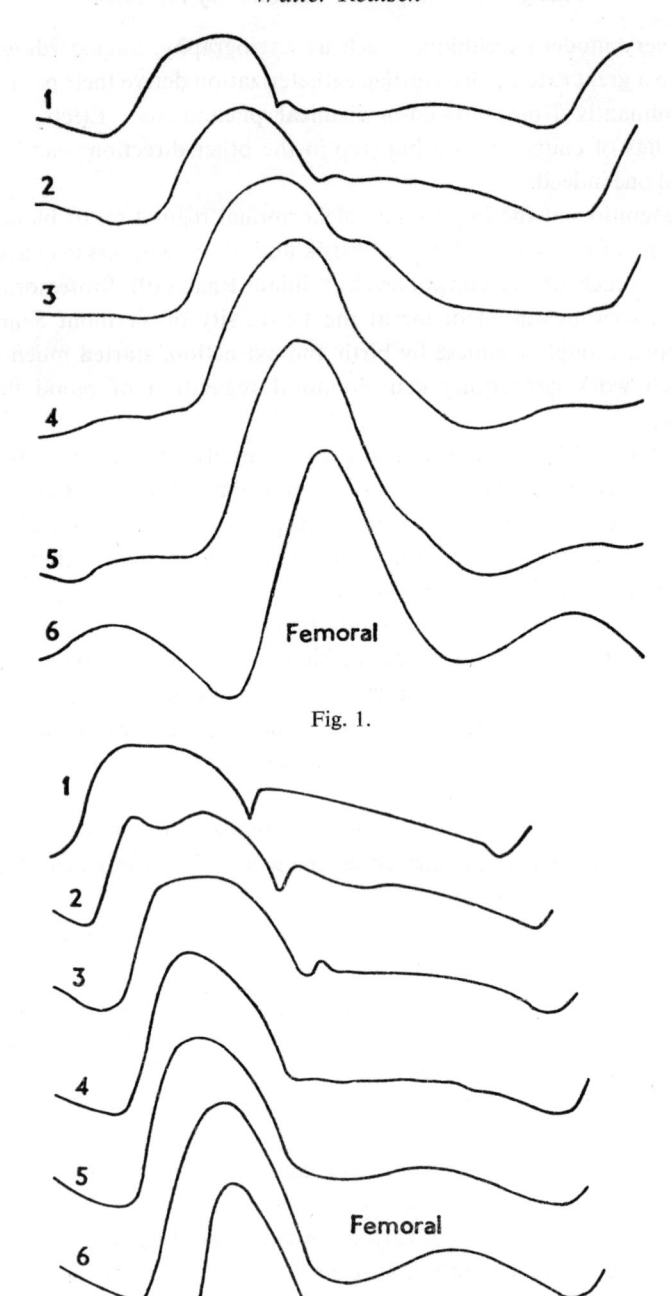

Fig. 2.

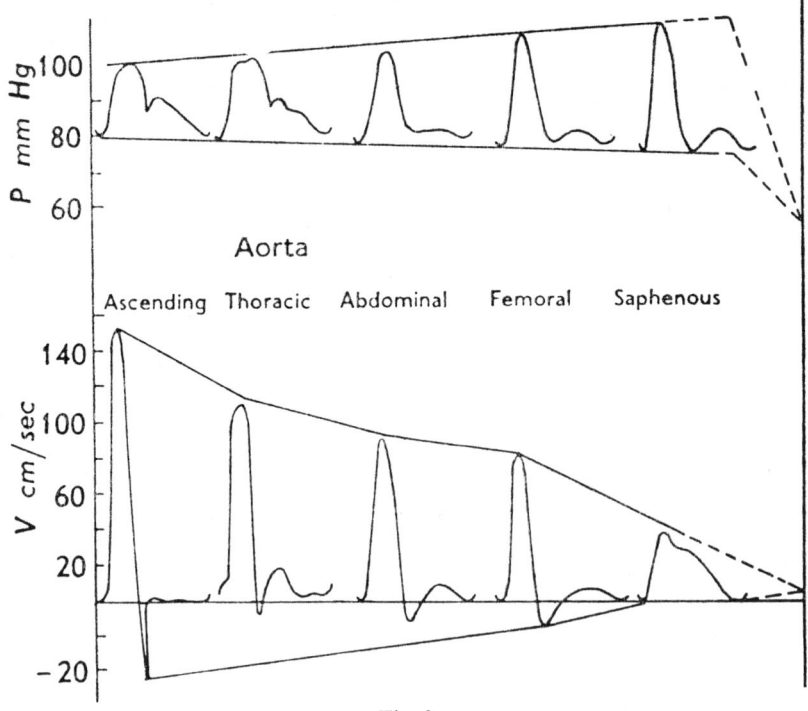

Fig. 3.

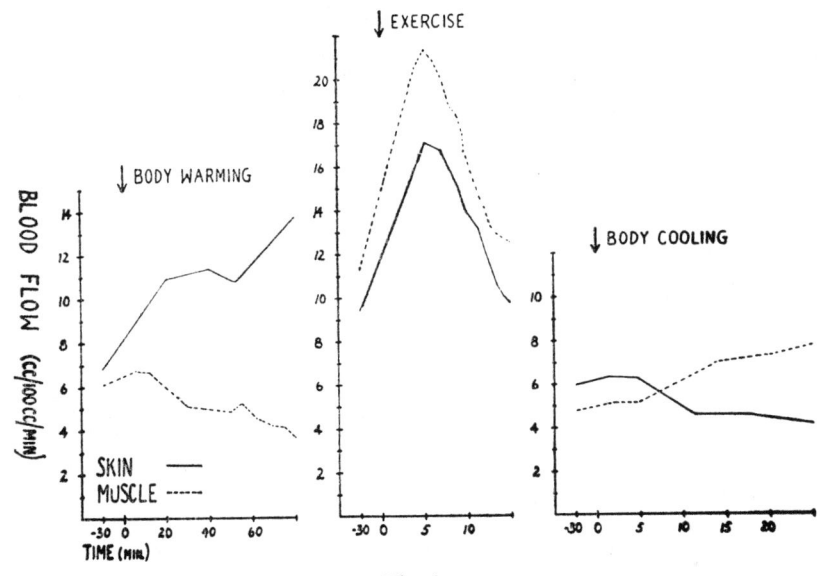

Fig. 4.

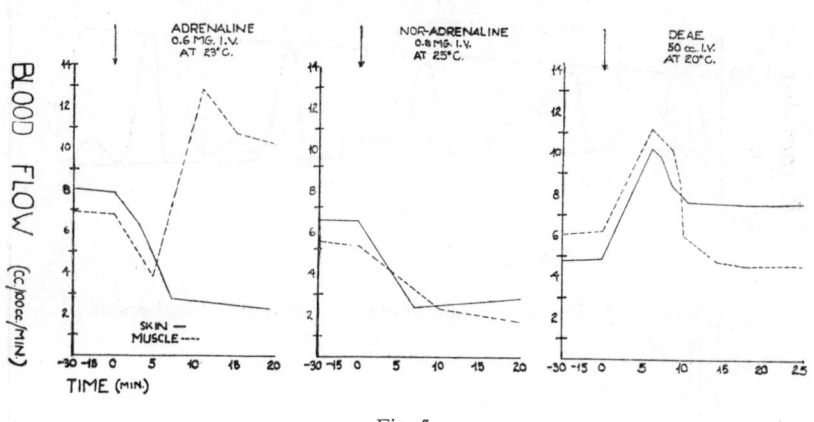

Fig. 5.

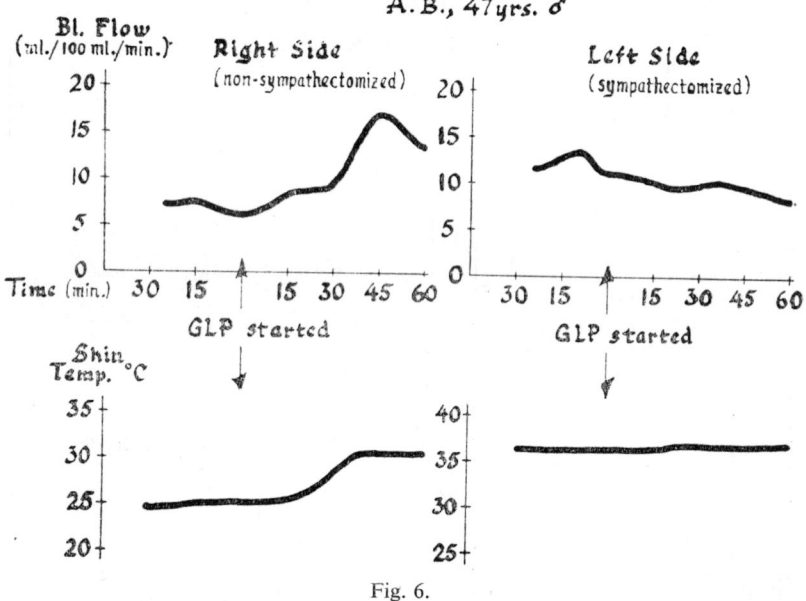

Response to G-L Procedure
A.B., 47 yrs. ♂

Fig. 6.

innervation. In these blood flow curves we originally glibly applied the equation,

increase in blood flow - - - vasodilation
decrease in blood flow - - - vasoconstriction.

We know now that even this is probably not quite accurate, but that changes in the vessel wall may take place, affecting blood flow, without appreciable changes in diameter or pressure. Likewise, the validity of the still dominant concept of "total peripheral resistance" becomes more and more questionable, as we advance in our knowledge of specificity of function of various vascular beds (17). In Prague, the workers at the Cardiovascular Research Institute (Brod, Linhart, Přerovský, Fejfar, Froněk, Froňková, Ehrlich and others (22-28)) have contributed greatly to this modification in our concept of the physiology of blood circulation.

(2) Morphologic. Capillary microscopy and x-ray microscopy have profoundly changed our ideas about the structure of minute blood vessels. Saunders and his co-workers (29) have demonstrated the existence of two different vasculatures in skeletal muscle, as previously advocated by

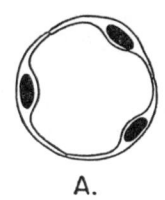

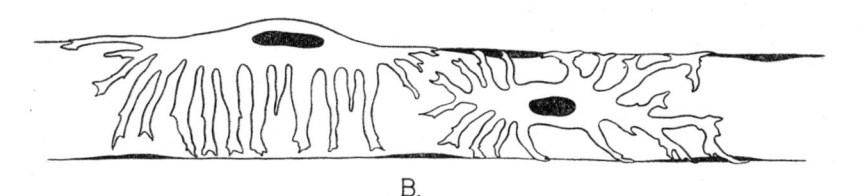

Fig. 7.

Barcroft (30) on the basis of comparative blood flow measurements in resting and working muscle. Our concept of the structure of the capillary as a simple endothelial tube has gone down the drain, and with it of course the plain filtration and osmosis theories of metabolic exchange. Bruno Kisch (31), a native of Prague and a co-worker of Hering's in Cologne, was one of the first to demonstrate the complex nature of the capillary wall as perceived through the electron microscope and to point at the implications of these findings. The differences between the old concept and the electron microscopic evidence are obvious from Figures 7 and 8.

(3) Biochemical and histochemical analysis of the heart and the vessel wall, its structural components and cellular elements. This phase of re-

search is the most recent, and in the opinion of many of us, the most important yet. It is difficult to give a bird's eye view of it at this time. It may be said, however, that again Czech workers in Czechoslovakia as well as in this country are contributing notably.

One of the major questions in the analysis of intrinsic disease of the blood vessels leading to disturbances in circulation is this: what changes are caused by the so-called ageing process per se, and what changes are caused by disease, or, let us say, are due to "the accidents of living"? R. J. Bouček (32), who is Director of Research of the Heart Institute of the University of Miami, and his co-workers have been studying the ageing vessel wall; on the other hand, Otokar J. Pollak (33) at the Dover Medical Research Center is a Czech who has been outstanding among those concerned with the biochemical and cellular aspects of atherosclerotic changes in the vessel wall.

This presentation has been designed to convey a smattering of the change in or perhaps rather the widening of, our approach to the study of blood circulation and its disturbances, and to point at the participating investigators of Czech origin in this field.

May I end as I started, with a quotation from the writings of the great William Harvey, this time from his *De Circulatione Sanguinis*, written as part of his controversy with Riolan, in 1649 (34):

But that this doubt may be more clear, that the pulsifick force does not flow through the tunicles of the arteries from the heart, I have a little piece of the artery descendant, together with two crural branches of it, taken out of the body of a very worthy Gentleman, which turn'd to be a bone like a pipe, by the hollow of which, whilst this worthy Gentleman was alive, the blood in its descent to the feet did agitate the arteries by its impulsion; ... wherefor it must needs follow, that in that worthy Gentleman, the inferiour arteries were dilated by the impulsion of the blood like baggs, and not like bellows, by the stretching of the tunicles...

Indeed, a most charming description of the puzzling, intricate and complicated relationship between structural changes in the arterial wall and blood flow. And this genius Harvey did not yet know about catecholamines and blood lipids.

BIBLIOGRAPHY

1. Harvey, W., *De Motu Cordis* (1682). First English Text 1653, reprinted Oxford, Blackwell, 1958.
2. Ringer, S., "A Further Contribution Regarding the Influence of the Different Constituents of the Blood on the Contraction of the Heart", *J. Physiol.*, 4 (1882), 29.
3. Evans, C. L. and Starling, E. H., "The Respiratory Exchanges of the Heart in Diabetic Animals", *J. Physiol.*, 49 (1914), 67.

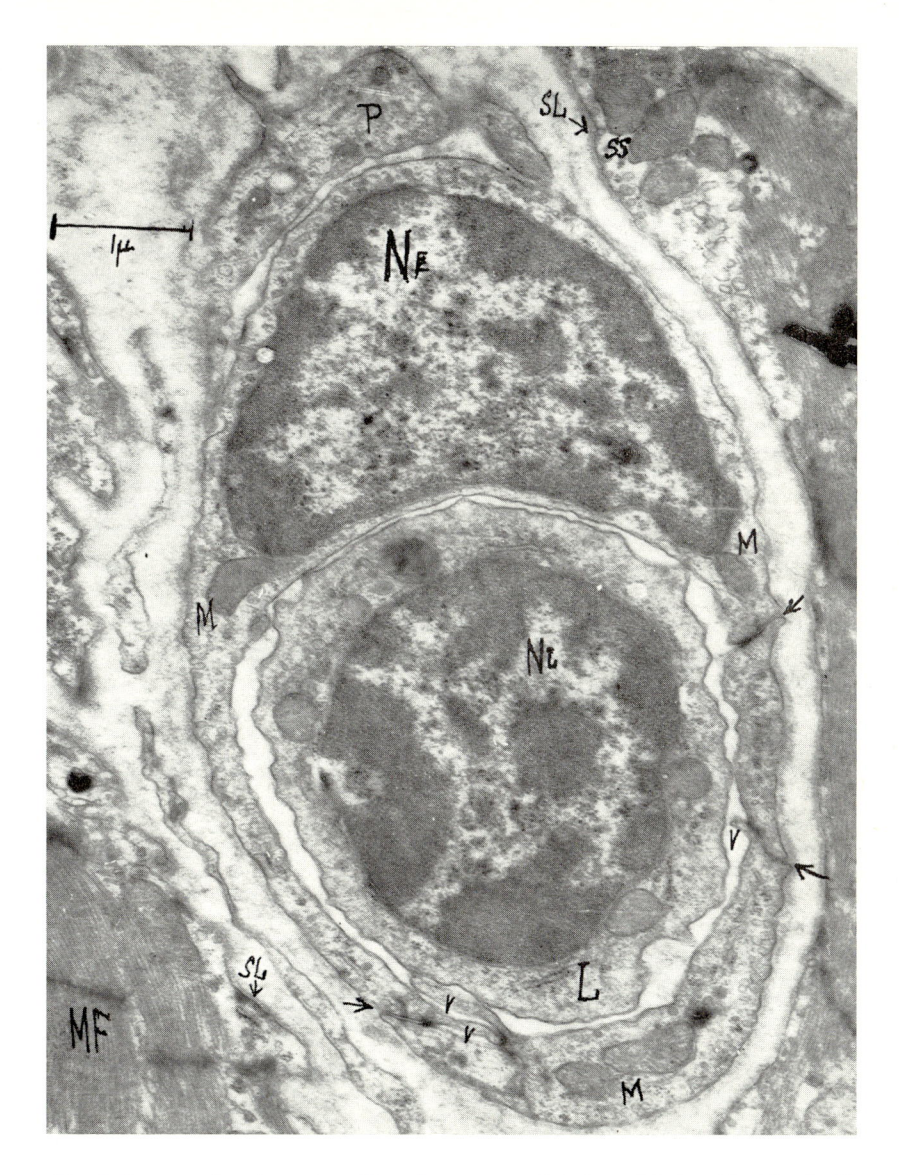

Fig. 8. Cross-section through capillary from myocard (guinea pig). L: white blood cell in capillary; NL: nucleus of white blood cell; NE: nucleus of endothelial cell; M: mitochondria; V: endothelial villi; P: pericyte; SL: sarcolem of surrounding muscle fibers; SS: sarcosomes; MF: myofibrils. Arrows point to slits in the capillary wall. Enlargement 25,000 X.

4. Purkyně, J. E., "Über die Struktur des Herzene der Säugetiere nach dem Grundtypus der Formation der Muskellfasern Desselben", *Opera Omnia*, 2 (1842), 95.
5. Sticker, S., "Untersuchungen Ueber die Contractilitaet der Capillaren", *Sitzgsber. der Ak. der Wissensch. in Wien, Math.-Naturwissensch. Klasse*, 74 (1876), 313.
6. Steinach, W. and Kahn, R., "Echte Contractilitaet und Motorische Innervation der Blutcapilaren", *Pfl. Arch. für die ges. Physiol.*, 97 (1903), 105.
7. Hering, E., *Die Karotissinusreflexe auf Herz und Gefässe* (Dresden, Steinkopf, 1927).
8. Best, C. H. and Taylor, N. B., *The Physiological Basis of Medical Practice* (Baltimore, Williams and Wilkins, 1950).
9. Prusík, B., "Klinische und experimentelle Untersuchungen über den Einfluss einiger Inkrete auf die periphereh Gefässe", *Zeitschr. für Kreislauffschg*, 24 (1932), 529.
10. Raab, W., *Hormonal and Neurogenic Cardiovascular Disorders* (Baltimore, Williams and Wilkins, 1953).
11. McDonald, D. A., *Blood Flow in Arteries* (Baltimore, Williams and Wilkins, 1960).
12. Petersen, L., "Certain Physical Characteristics of the Cardiovascular System and Their Significance for the Problem of Calculating Stroke Volume from the Arterial Tree", *Fed. Proc.*, 11 (1952), 762.
13. Petersen, L. and Shephard, R. B., "Some Relationship of Blood Pressure to the Cardiovascular System", *Surg. Clin. of N. America*, 35 (1955), 1613.
14. Redisch, W., Wertheimer, L., Delisle, C. and Steele, J. M., "Comparison of Various Vascular Beds in Man; Their Responses to a Simple Vasodilator Stimulus", *Circul.*, 9 (1954), 63.
15. Redisch, W., Tangco, F. F., Wertheimer, L., Lewis, A. J. and Steele, J. M., "Vasomotor Responses in the Extremities of Subjects with Various Neurologic Lesions", *Circul.*, 15 (1957), 518.
16. Redisch, W., de Crinis, K. and Steele, J. M., "Studies on Vasoactivity of Catecholamines in Man", *Am. J. Cardiol.*, 5 (1960), 660.
17. Folkow, B., Johansson, B. and Loefving, B., "Aspects of Functional Differentiation of the Sympatho-Adrenergic Control of the Cardiovascular System", *Medicina Experiment.*, 4 (1961), 321.
18. Cannon, W. B. and Rapport, D., "Studies on Condition of Activity in Endocrine Glands; Denervated Heart in Relation to Adrenal Secretion", *Am. J. Physiol.*, 53 (1921), 308.
19. Cannon, W. B. and Rosenblueth, A., "Sensitization of Denervated Structures", *Am. J. Physiol.*, 116 (1936), 25.
20. Barcroft, H. and Swan, H. J. C., *Sympathetic Control of Human Blood Vessels* (London, Edward and Co., 1953).
21. Edholm, O. G., Fox, R. H. and McPherson, R. K., "The Effect of Body Heating on the Forearm Blood Flow", *20th Intern. Congr. of Physiol., Brussels, Belgium, August 1st*, 1956.
22. Brod, J., "Essential Hypertension; Hemodynamic Observations with a Bearing on Its Pathogenesis", *Lancet*, 2 (1960), 773.
23. Linhart, J. and Přerovský, I., "Spotřeba kyslíku v nohou lidí a její změny po zahřátí těla", *Vnitř. Lék.*, 7 (1961), 5.
24. Švejcar, J., Přerovský, I. and Linhart, J., "Chemical Composition of the Venous Wall of the Lower Limbs", *Cor et Vasa*, 2 (1961), 90.
25. Brod, J. and Fejfar, Z., "The Origin of Edema in Heart Failure", *Quart. J. of Med.*, 19 (1950), 187.
26. Froněk, A. and Ganz, V., "The Effect of Papaverine on Coronary and Systemic Hemodynamics", *Cor et Vasa*, 3 (1961), 120.
27. Froňková, K. and Ehrlich, V., "Die Änderungen des Kreislaufs und der Atem-

frequenz beim Hunde während des unbedingten und bedingten Abwehrreflexes und dessen Hemmung", *Acta Neuroveget.*, 19 (1959), 207.
28. Ehrlich, V., *In the Pathogenesis of Essential Hypertension*, p. 163 ff. (Prague, State Medical Publishing House, 1960), p. 163 ff.
29. Saunders, R. L. de C., Lawrence, J., Maciver, D. A. and Nemethy, N., "The Anatomic Basis of the Peripheral Circulation in Man", in Redisch, W., Tangco, F. F. and Saunders, R. L. de C., *Peripheral Circulation in Health and Disease* (New York, Grune and Stratton, 1957).
30. Barcroft, H., "Problems of Sympathetic Innervation and Denervation", *Brit. Med. Bull.*, 8 (1952), 363.
31. Kisch, B., *Der ultramikroskopische Bau von Herz und Kapillaren* (Darmstadt, Steinkopf, 1957).
32. Bouček, R. J., Noble, N. L. and Woessner, J. F., Jr., "The Effects of Tissue Age and Sex upon Connective Tissue Metabolism", *Ann. N.Y. Ac. Sci.*, 72 (1959), 1016.
33. Pollak, O. J., "Mast Cells in the Circulatory System of Man", *Circul.*, 16 (1957), 1084.
34. Harvey, W., *De Circulacione Sanguinis* (1649). First English Text 1653, reprinted Oxford, Blackwell, 1958.

Prokop Waldfogel of Prague and the 15th Century Printers of the Kingdom of Bohemia

JAROSLAV NĚMEC

A student of the history of printing in the Kingdom of Bohemia may be surprised to learn that Czech historians, as early as the 16th century, were crediting Johann Gutenberg with the invention of printing. One's surprise however, is supplanted by confusion on reading that Gutenberg was born in Bohemia, that his real name was Johann Faust (Šťastný) and that he changed his name to "Kuttenberg" in Germany to show the place of his origin: Kutná Hora-Kuttenberg. This confusion of Gutenberg with Johann Fust (and sometimes also with Faust, the famous sorcerer of Prague) persisted in Czech historical writing until the 19th century.[1]

The early Czech historians, however, did not know about one of their countrymen who really was connected with the invention of printing – Prokop Waldfogel, a goldsmith of Prague.

The first traces of this interesting figure were uncovered in 1890, when Abbé Requin examined the 15th-century notarial records of the city of Avignon.[2] The search which followed Requin's discovery gives us the following picture:

Prokop Waldfogel belonged to a family of cutlers, originally German, but long settled in Prague. A certain Jiří Waldfogel (his father?) was resident, in the late 14th century in House No. 156 in the Old Town of Prague.[3] Prokop apparently left the country during the Hussite Wars (1420-1432). In 1439 we find him in Lucerne, Switzerland, where he made successful application for citizenship. Between 1440 and 1444, his name

---

[1] Zíbrt, Čeněk, *Z dějin českého knihtiskařství*. K novému vydání upravil Dr. Ant. Dolenský (Mladá Boleslav, Hajda & Zbroj, 1939), p. 15-20.
[2] Requin, Pierre Henri, *Origines de l'imprimerie en France (Avignon, 1444)*. (Paris, Cercle de la Librairie, de l'Imprimerie, de la Papeterie, etc., 1891). Teige, J., Review of Requin's book, *Čas. mus. král. čes.*, 66 (1892), 144-7.
[3] Tobolka, Zdeněk V., *Dějiny čs. knihtisku v době nejstarší* (Praha, Čs. společnost knihovědná, 1930), p. 8-9.

does not appear on the military register of Lucerne, which means that he could not have been living in the town.[4]

At the beginning of 1444, he appeared in Avignon and, on July 4 of that year, stated in a notarial document that he possessed 2 alphabets in steel, two iron forms, one steel screw, 48 forms of tin and various other forms pertaining to the *"ars scribendi artificialiter"*, or artificial writing.[5]

In Avignon, Waldfogel offered instruction in the new art to those who agreed to become his students as well as associates in his enterprise. His first apprentice-associate was Girard Ferrose of Trèves, a watchmaker. Ferrose, however, quit his apprenticeship on August 26, 1444, after promising under oath not to reveal the secrets of artificial writing to anyone. The secrecy which Waldfogel demanded of Ferrose and all other apprentices was very common at that time. Nearly every artisan who had developed some special technique or process in his craft protected himself against theft of his particular secret, and expected employees to observe the same secrecy. Ferrose apparently kept his oath, because we find him a little later again associated with Waldfogel.

Another apprentice-associate of Waldfogel who also joined him early in 1444, was a Jew, Davin Caderousse. Probably under his influence, Waldfogel made an alphabet of Hebrew letters, with the necessary instruments in wood, steel and iron. Davin invested some money in Waldfogel's enterprise, later pressing hard for reimbursement. In 1446, by court order, Prokop promised to hand over to him 27 Hebrew letters and related items.

There were two other apprentices, both students at the University of Avignon: Manaud Vitalis and Arnaud de Coselhac. They received from their master full equipment for printing: *"Omnia instrumenta sive artificia scribendi tam de ferro de calibe, de cupro, de lethone, de plumbo, de stagno et de fuste"*.

We have proof that Waldfogel was teaching printing with movable type. We do not know, however, whether he actually printed anything. So far, no book has been found which may be assigned to him. On the other hand, it seems logical to suppose that the man who offered instruction in a new

---

[4] O. H., "Vermischte Notizen", *Zentralblatt für Bibliothekswesen*, 17 (1900), 441-2 (Review of Theodor von Liebenau's book *Überblick über die Geschichte der Buchdruckerei der Stadt Luzern*, Luzern, H. Keller, 1900). Tobolka, Zdeněk V., *op. cit.*, p. 8-9.
[5] Requin, Pierre Henri, *op. cit.*, p. 6. Schottenloher, Karl, *Das alte Buch*. 2. Auflage (Berlin, R. C. Schmidt, 1921), p. 14. McMurtrie, Douglas C., *The Book; the Story of Printing and Book-Making* (London, Oxford University Press, 1943), p. 180-1.

craft had to have his "masterpiece", a specimen of his work to show prospective students.

Conditions for the establishment of a printing office in Avignon were not too favorable. Waldfogel probably left the town in 1446 because he could not earn enough even for mere subsistence. In August 1446, his associate, Girard Ferrose, is also mentioned as absent. There is no further trace of these two men.[6]

After this description, a question immediately arises: "Is Waldfogel Gutenberg's competitor for the honor of having invented printing?"

Czech historians answer this question mostly in the negative. Tobolka, for example, says: "Waldfogel was not the inventor of printing. He was only the first person from Bohemia who acquired a certain knowledge of printing from Gutenberg's first experiments".[7] Zíbrt, Teige and Truhlář agree that Waldfogel acquired his knowledge either from Gutenberg's associate, Dritzehn, or from Gutenberg himself, when he (Gutenberg) was in Strasburg between 1434 and 1439.

If we scrutinize this opinion, however, we find that there are no facts to support it. We have no proof that Waldfogel was in Strasburg or that he ever met Gutenberg. His connection with Dritzehn is also highly questionable. As mentioned previously, Waldfogel was in Lucerne in 1439, but after 1440 there are no more references to him in that city. A certain Jöry Drizechen is mentioned as being in Lucerne in 1443. We are not sure whether this was Gutenberg's former associate, but even if we could answer in the affirmative, this was three years after Waldfogel's departure!

Limitations of space do not permit us to go into further detail. We may state simply that Prokop Waldfogel's claim to the invention of printing is still not definitely settled. As Abbé Requin says: "This invention was in the air, and maybe it appeared simultaneously in Strasbourg and Avignon."[8]

Leaving the question open to further historical research then, we would like to turn our attention to the cultural conditions in Bohemia at that time.

During the directorship and subsequent reign of George of Poděbrady (1452-71), Prague again became a Mid-European business center, and renewed its cultural relations with other countries. The University of Prague, because of its anti-Catholic character, could not develop many

---

[6] Requin, Pierre Henri, *op. cit.*, p. 6-12. Claudin, A., *Histoire de l'imprimerie en France au XVe et au XVIe siècle*, Tome I (Paris, Imprimerie Nationale, 1900), p. 1-10.
[7] Tobolka, Zdeněk V., *op. cit.*, p. 8-9.
[8] Requin, Pierre Henri, *op. cit.*, p. 13-14.

contacts with the Catholic world, but this was partly compensated for by the fact that Catholic students from the Bohemian Kingdom went abroad to study, especially to Germany and Italy, where they served as mediators of cultural exchange.

The cultural level of the Czech population at that time is best described by the well-known statement of Aeneas Sylvius Piccolomini, later Pope Pius II: "In Bohemia every farmer knows the Bible better than a priest in Italy." There was a great thirst for knowledge and a great desire to read.

In Prague, Pilzen, Brno, Olomouc, Breslau and other large towns of the country, there flourished handicrafts related to printing; there were many gold- and silver-smiths, jewelers, painters and illuminators, scribes, sellers of paper, and so on. Papermills in Bohemia existed from 1370 on, and wood block prints were already very popular between 1430 and 1440. Both material and spiritual conditions were established for the introduction of printing with movable type.

Thus, we do not wonder that in 1468 there appeared the first Czech book "Chronicle of Troya" (*Kronika trojánská*), printed in black letters by an unknown printer. It was earlier believed that this book was published in Pilsen, but there is insufficient proof for it. Tobolka thinks that the printer was an apprentice of Ulrich Zell of Köln am Rhein, because of the similarity of some techniques.[9]

The first books known to have been printed in Pilsen were the *Statuta provincialia Arnesti* (1476) and the *Missale ecclesiae Pragensis* (1479), both probably printed by wandering printers.

The first known Czech printers in Pilsen were trained in Nuremberg, and were on very good terms with their colleagues in that city. Mikuláš Bakalář (Štětina), apparently of Slovak origin, started his printing business in Pilsen in 1488. Nearly all his books were in Czech, and of them we should mention: "the Almanac" (*Minucí*) 1489; "Equerry and the Student" (1498); "Treatise about the Holy Land" (1498); Life and teaching of Mohammed" (1498), etc.

Other printers of Pilzen who deserve mention include Jan Pekk Hazukův and his associate, Jan Mantuán Fencl.

The first works printed in Prague by unknown hands were a New Testament (1475), "The Psalter of David the Prophet" (1487) and the reprint in two colors, of the "Chronicle of Troya" (1487) – all of them in Czech. Jonata of Vysoké Mýto is mentioned as a printer in Prague in 1487.

J. Severyn established a large printing shop in the Old Town of Prague

---

[9] Zíbrt, Čeněk, *op. cit.*, p. 35-6.

in 1488. Jan Kamp is mentioned as a printer working for Severyn. The most important Czech publications of Severyn were the "Fables of Aesop" (1488), "Bible of Prague" (1488), "Roman Chronicle" (1488) – translated from the Latin by Beneš of Hořovice, "Almanac" (*Minucí*) for the years 1489, 1491, 1492 by Vavřinec of Rokycany, an astronomer at the University of Prague, "Illustrated Passional" (1495), "New Testament" (1498), etc. All Severyn's books had woodcut illustrations.

In the South Bohemian town of Vimperk, printing was started by Johann Alakraw, who learned the craft in Passau and brought the letters with him to Bohemia. In 1484 he published *Soliloquia* (Pseudo-Augustinus) and *Summa de eucharistiae sacramento*, of Albertus Magnus, both in Latin. In the same year, he also printed a Czech book, "Almanac (*Minucí*) for the year 1485", by Master Vavřinec of Rokycany. Then he returned to Passau.

In 1484 Konrad Stahel, a former associate of the printer Mayr in Passau, produced the *Breviarium Olomucense* in Venice and very soon after, apparently under the influence of the Bishop of Olomouc, Jan Filipec, established a printing shop in Brno together with Matthew Preinlein of Ulm. They published about 40 or 50 religious or scientific books, mostly in Latin, with some in German. Some of the most interesting are: *Agenda secundum chorum Olomucensem* (1468); Joannes Thuroczy's *Chronika Hungarorum* (1488), the most expensive book of that time, with many illustrations; Jacobus Canis' *De modo in iure studenti libellum* (1488), the first printed legal book in the country; *Missale Strigoniense* (1491), and *Psalterium Olomucense* (1499) with woodcuts.

Stahel and Preinlein probably left Brno in 1499, but were soon replaced by wandering printers.

Printing in Olomouc started with Preinlein in 1499. He published two books, but this work was much inferior to the publications he had earlier prepared with Stahel in Brno.

Another printer came to Olomouc between 1499 and 1500 from Gdansk. It was Konrad Baumgarten of Rotenburg. His first known work in Olomouc appeared in October, 1500, with the title *Tractatus de secta Waldensium*. The book is printed in two colors; it has many initials and woodcuts and the type faces are very good.

In Kutná Hora, the famous silver-mining center, we find Martin of Tišnov, a former apprentice of Anton Koberger in Nuremberg. In 1489, Martin published the Bible in Czech. He used two colors, black and red, and his colophon shows two miners in traditional costume holding the coat of arms of the city of Kutná Hora.

Toward the end of the 15th century, the Unitas Fratrum founded a printing shop in Mladá Boleslav where smaller publications were secretly printed starting in 1500.[10]

Czech printing reached full bloom in the 16th century. New printing shops were established in Bělá, Cheb, Hradec Králové, Kouřim, Litoměřice, Litomyšl and Prachatice in Bohemia, and in Ivančice, Kralice, Luleč, Mikulov, Náměšť, Prostějov, Velké Meziříčí and Znojmo in Moravia.

We might end this short account of the origins of printing in old Bohemia by a statement of the French historian, Ernest Denis, concerning this period: "The desire for knowledge was so great in the Kingdom of Bohemia that local printing facilities were inadequate".[11] Thus books in Czech were also printed abroad, especially in Nuremberg, Leipzig, Wittenberg, Bamberg, Vienna and even in Venice.

---

[10] Tobolka, Zdeněk V., *op. cit.*, p. 20-27 & ff. Zíbrt, Čeněk, *op. cit.*, p. 37-57.
[11] Denis, Arnošt, *Konec samostatnosti české*. Přeložil Dr. J. Vančura, 4. vyd. (Praha, Šolc a Šimáček, 1932), vol. I, p. 95.

Czechoslovak Engineering until the Second World War

JOSEPH Z. SCHNEIDER

Modern engineering, defined as "an art and science of the ingenious and competent organization of men and natural resources for the benefit of mankind", developed from the activities of military engineers of several hundred years ago. Those engineers designed, built and operated military equipment, chiefly artillery, and planned, built and maintained fortifications and roads.

In the territory of former Czechoslovakia, the process of development followed the normal pattern, although it started even before the emergence of army engineers as a recognized group.

The famous leader of the Hussite peasant army, John Žižka of Trocnov (1360 to 1424) was the first military man ever to use black powder artillery in tactical operations (stationary black powder artillery having been used previously for the defense of forts), and had constructed besieging rifles of up to 11" caliber which carried heavy balls as far as 1500 yards. He also designed field cannon mounted on wheels or on large battle-wagons used as mobile fortifications in military operations, and an original Hussite weapon, the "houfnice" (howitzer), up to almost 6.5" caliber, drawn by one or two horses.

Prior to World War I, Czech engineers of the Škoda Works at Plzeň designed and built the 30.5 cm motor-driven mortar, at the time an almost fantastic weapon, which has been credited for the speedy demolishment of the Belgian fortresses in 1914.

By the time of the Second World War, Czechoslovak engineers and workers of the Zbrojovka Works at Brno had designed, and were producing according to the most modern concepts of mass production, a light, reliable, accurate machine gun which the British Army found to be the world's best, introduced as the standard light machine gun for all British units. The British had it made under licence, as the Bren gun (BRno ENfield). Czech engineers and workmen assisted the British and were in charge of a Bren gun factory in India and elsewhere during and prior to the war.

There were several reasons for the extraordinary progress of Czechoslovak engineering of various types: the intensive utilization of agricultural and mineral resources, the inborn intelligence and skills of the citizens, and a spirit of progress, which naturally followed the Industrial Revolution in 18th- and 19th-century Western Europe. Other factors were the vision of intellectual and political leaders, the cooperation of foreign engineers, and later, in 1848, abolition of agricultural serfdom, necessitating the development of efficient agricultural machinery and large quantities of chemical fertilizers.

Technical education on various levels and in the various areas of technology replaced the slow master-apprenticeship method and the decaying guild system.

The Czech aristocracy started a school for military engineers in 1718, the first of its type in Europe. This was intended to replace with their own men the Italian fortification specialists on whom Central Europe had depended up to that time for their skills and knowledge. In 1806 to 1808 this school was enlarged in scope and equipment to form the Prague Polytechnicum, a university for civil (viz., non-military) engineers. The mission of this new school had already been defined in 1802 as "higher education in the exact sciences and those industrial arts required by large plants and for the promotion of small professions and crafts through scientific education".

The Prague Polytechnicum changed later into an Institute of Technology and gradually added courses in mechanical, electric, construction, chemical, agricultural and forestry engineering, and related architectural studies; in 1919 its divisions were enlarged to include business and administration. By that time another Institute of Technology came into existence at Brno, and there were many professional schools at college and high school level. (Eagerness for learning and, particularly, higher education, has long been characteristic of Czechs, for whom Charles IV founded a university in Prague in 1348!)

All the Government technical schools also engaged in research and development, testing of materials and constructions, and the solving of technical problems as they arose. Together with other scientific institutes and those operated by large industrial plants or companies, the schools kept abreast of technical progress elsewhere, and disseminated information about technological advances at home and abroad.

Societies of Czechoslovak engineers were soon formed for professional advancement and association, and these maintained active contacts with similar groups in other countries.

The relation of Czechoslovak engineers to their American colleagues was close. It was the Americans who suggested that the Czechoslovak engineers organize the first (and most successful) International Congress for Scientific Management in Prague in 1924. The Society of Czechoslovak Engineers and the Masaryk Academy of Work Management participated in 1930 in the 50th-anniversary celebrations of the American Society of Mechanical Engineers. Engineers of Czechoslovak nationality or origin formed the American Association of Czechoslovak Engineers in Chicago in 1922. During the 40 years of its activity, this enthusiastic group has been a clearing house for technical information and assistance to Czechoslovak educational and professional institutions, industries, engineers and industrialists, in the USA as well as in the old country.

Now let us look at some peacetime practical applications of engineering in that part of the world which became Czechoslovakia.

Alum schists were used originally in the production of sulphuric acid; one plant using this process employed 300 workers and five chemists in 1630! Czech sulphuric acid and oleum became famous throughout Europe. In 1836 there was introduced the use of pyrites instead of elemental sulphur. Superphosphates were made as early as 1865.

Raffination of imported raw (cane) sugar was successfully carried on as early as 1787, and industrial sugar mills were processing sugar beets from the beginning of the 19th century. Czech chemical and mechanical engineers are credited with many improvements and new methods used in sugar-processing, and entire sugar mills (both beet as well as cane) were exported to distant countries to be assembled, put into production and, often, operated or managed by Czech personnel. Washers and cutters of beets with constantly improved cutting knives, diffusion (1864), triple purification (saturation) of diffusion juice, filter presses and other techniques and equipment, later standard, were Czech contributions to the sugar industry. Czechoslovaks contributed greatly to the development and introduction of the chemical control of materials, semi-products and products to assure scientific and economic production of the highest-quality goods. Czechoslovak refined sugar was of world-renowned quality and was greatly in demand in many countries.

The excellence of the Czech metal-working industry was confirmed during the building of an enormous hydroelectric power station at Niagara Falls. There was no plant in America able to produce the necessary heavy forged shafts. They were, therefore, ordered from and delivered by Škoda at Plzeň.

Similarly when the American manufacturers of airplane motors needed crankshafts of certain very exact specifications and found it impossible to have them produced in the United States it was the Poldi Works of Bohemia that filled the gap to the complete satisfaction of US aviation. These same works contributed very substantially to the development and use of modern special steels.

Czech engineer V. Kaplan developed a water turbine which utilizes the full potential of the streams energy. At the time of this writing, Kaplan's turbines play an important role in the extensive electrification of Brasil.

Beer brewing, blessed by the famous Moravian malt and Žatec (Saatz) hops, was carried on in an empiric and sometimes secret fashion from early medieval days. In 1800 a Czech brewmaster, Fr. Ondřej Poupě, put this industry on a scientific basis and later established a school for master brewers, the first of its kind in Europe. He indoctrinated Czech brewmasters with the need for modern scientific techniques and chemical and mycological controls. Czech brewmasters were widely sought after. The present brewmaster of the Pilsen Brewery in Chicago is of Czech extraction (Spinka) and followed his father, who held the same position years ago.

Of the beers made in Czechoslovakia, those brewed at Plzeň (Pilsen) and České Budějovice (Budweis) became particularly famous and were exported to and imitated in many countries. Czech plant equipment was exported wherever first-quality beer was the brewery's objective.

Here is selected data which will further illustrate Czechoslovak technical progress:

calico printing, begun in 1746
the first English cotton spinning machine, installed in 1796
the first steam engine, installed in 1804
the first industrial paper mill, 1813
the first metal-processing and engineering plants, 1830 (equipment for textile, sugar, flour, alcohol plants, breweries, mines and building of steam boilers and engines, bridges, etc.)
the first modern blast furnace using Silesian coke, 1831
the first (horsedriven) railroad in Austria, 1840
the first gas street illumination, 1847
the first Portland cement plant, 1860
the first Bessemer steel plant, 1865
the first open-hearth steel mill, 1878
the first sulphite cellulose plant, 1881
the first electrotechnical plant, 1886

the first modern electric power plant for street and factory illumination, 1887; using the original Křižík electric arc lamps (1880)

the first (steam-driven) automobile, 1910

the first electric steel plant, 1914, and the first rayon plant at about the same time.

This admittedly incomplete history may partially explain how Czechoslovakia, which in 1918 covered only 20.7% of the area of the former Austro-Hungarian Empire with only 26.6% of its inhabitants, contained 100% of the porcelain, 92% of the sugar and glass, 90% of the glove-manufacturing, 87% of the malt, 75% of the chemical and shoe, and 70% of the leather industries of the former Empire.

It seems especially appropriate to close with a few words about the Bata Shoe Company, originally of Zlín.

Tomáš Baťa of Zlín (see Anthony Cekota, "Tomaš Baťa", p. 342 of this book), began to build his now famous Bata plants during World War I in a community of skilled, intelligent people, who had engaged in the home manufacture of shoes in Moravian Slovakia for centuries. By his organizational and business genius, by wise choice of collaborators from among the best, most experienced people in production and business administration, through the application and improvement of American mass production methods, by expert public relations and distribution techniques. Baťa succeeded in creating the first Baťa integrated industry at Zlín. The works was daily producing 350,000 pairs of shoes of every type before the beginning of World War II, and Baťa was instrumental in the development of Bata plants producing millions of pairs of shoes in numerous integrated factories all over the world. One may wonder what the relationship was between the "Miracle of Zlín" and the introduction of leather technology lectures and laboratory work some 60 years ago at the Prague Technical University, the first European continental university to offer this special and specific "skill and science" outside of England...

REFERENCES

František Palacký, *Dějiny Národu Českého w Čechách a w Morawě* (1877).
František Ladislav Rieger a Jakub Malý, *Slovník naučný, 1860-1890*.
Československá Vlastivěda. Technika (1929), *Práce* (1930).
Ottův Slovník Naučný, dodatky 1938.
František Kadeřávek a J. Pulkrábek, *250 let technických škol v Praze* (Nakladatelství Československé akademie věd, 1958).

Five Centuries of Czech Geography, Exploration, and Cartography
Comments on Major Trends and Present Status

MILOŠ ŠEBOR

In a paper so limited, it is impossible to treat fully all stages of a five-hundred-year-old field, closely connected with many aspects of Western civilization. The aim of this paper must be, simply, to recall the beginnings of Czech studies in the earth sciences, including geography, exploratory work, and map making and, secondly, to give the highlights of their historical development.

The Late Middle Ages

Where one starts depends largely upon one's concept of geography. Accepting at random a popular definition, for example, "geography is a description of the earth's surface", an integral part of our field would be toponymy, the science of geographic names. In this case, the oldest geographic source in Czech literature is the *Dalimil's Chronicle* of the early 14th century, which included some 150 place names of Bohemia, written possibly by a high-ranking clergyman.

A more elaborate definition of geography – for example, as "an evaluation of the spatial factor in the interrelationship of Nature and Man" – would place the origin of Czech earth's science at a later period, about five centuries ago. Our field of knowledge would then start with travel accounts, common in the last decades of the 15th century. This was descriptive geography, often of religious inspiration, or merely an accessory field, closely associated with religious trends and diplomacy; but it was a function of expanding European horizons.

The writings of a Czech brother, Martin Kabátník of Litomyšl, represent one of the first attempts at geographic study. Kabátník, a Christian of profound convictions, traveled widely in the Near East in search of the "original Christian church", the existence of which was postulated by non-Catholic scholars in the time. The Czech Catholics did not remain behind in the debate. One of them, Bohuslav Hasištejnský of Lobkovice, a humanist and intelligent observer, free from Utopian notions, studied distances, positions of stars and climatic phenomena when traveling from Venice to Palestine via Rhodes and Cyprus, as a visitor to the Holy Sepulchre.

As explorers, Czech diplomats and their retinues came next. Invested with official duties and feeling safer abroad than ordinary travelers, they could see more. Leo of Rožmitál, brother-in-law of King George of Poděbrady, set out from Prague on a journey which was to take him to all of the important countries of Western Europe. His squire, Václav Šašek of Biřkov, and Gabriel Tetzel, another in his suite, kept accounts of their adventures, observing nature, peoples and customs, and even attempting to probe the relationship of man to earth.

The Renaissance

The Renaissance witnessed the foundation of Czech cartography, our second phase. One product of a reaction against the medieval emphasis upon faith was the introduction of the *Cosmographiae*, a combination of text, atlas, and illustrated encyclopaedia of astronomy, geography, natural science and history. A *golden age of cartography*, the Renaissance, was represented by the Dutch school of Gerardus Mercator, Jodocus Hondius and Jan Janszoon. Their map making unfortunately often suffered from an indiscriminate use of dubious information. It appears, however, that the Czech cartographers of the time developed a good sense of reality.

In 1518, a Czech cosmographer of Mladá Boleslav, named Nicholas Claudianus, compiled the first relatively correct map of Bohemia. A universal scholar – he was physician, printer, humanist and follower of Desiderius Erasmus of Rotterdam, Bible student and member of the Czech Brethren's community – Claudianus drew a remarkable picture of the Kingdom of Bohemia. The map is oriented to the south, about 1:637,000 in scale on a sheet of about 25 × 47 inches, and shows water courses, forested areas, a cultural pattern including not less than 280 cities, towns, monasteries and castles, all classified by legal status, and the network of roads with indication of distances. The work was drawn with no projection, but symbols were well selected, both for topography and natural vegetation. The former is represented by hill-shaped pictures, reminiscent of the modern trachographic method, and East-illuminated from the left. For vegetation, symbols of trees and bushes were used. The map was published in a *Cosmographia* by Sebastian Münster of Basel, and translated into Czech by Zikmund of Puchov in 1553. Later maps of Bohemia were drawn by Jan Criginger in 1568 and Paulus Aretin of Ehrenfeld in 1619. In Moravia, the first map makers were Paulus Fabricius and Jan Amos Komenský (Comenius). A map of Silesia was drawn by Martin Helwig. All these maps were large-scale, providing a great many details, both physical and cultural, and showing political divisions very distinctly. Comenius' map was partly based upon the travels of its author.

The great spiritual changes brought about by the Renaissance in Central Europe were reflected everywhere by equally important transformations in attitudes of the wealthy and leisured middle class with its interest in arts and science. But it seems that it was rather the nobility, especially petty knights, who led in Bohemia. Václav Vratislav of Mitrovice, a Catholic, and Kryštof Harant of Polžice and Bezdružice, a Protestant, both traveled in the early 17th century in the Balkans and the Levant, later writing their observations. Almost forgotten, but unique, was Oldřich, Prefát of Vlkanov, geographer-mathematician, constructor of physics instruments and writer on the Near East, far ahead of his time in his approach to the natural environment, thanks to his instinct for objective description. Tadeáš of Hájek also deserves to be mentioned, among others, as a map maker and astronomer of the later 16th century.

The Age of Reason

This was the period of the reformation of geography and cartography, with an increasing emphasis on the accuracy of maps, their reliability, and discrimination between what was already known about the world and what was still unknown or doubtful; in brief, a sense of "geographic honesty". Cartography was gradually transformed from an area of a private endeavor into one under government control. Forerunners of this trend in Bohemia were private surveyors hired by the Royal Chamber under Rudolph II and Matthias in the early 17th century. About one hundred years later, a surveyor and cartographer, named Jan Kryštof Müller drew a set of sheets of Bohemia, Moravia, and Hungary, by order of the government. The scale was large for that time, about 1:150,000, so that Bohemia consisted of 25 sheets, showing both physical and political patterns. His series on Silesia remained unfinished. Müller was probably the last private cartographer in charge of a government mapping project.

Much as in other European countries, the Hapsburg Empire transferred the task of surveying state territory to the army. Stages of this new cartography were the so-called 1st, 2nd, and 3rd Military Mapping of 1780-90, 1810-69, and 1876-84, respectively.

Private cartography was less common. A rather exceptional career was that of František Kreybich, a Catholic priest and self-made geographer (1759-1833), who drew two maps of Bohemia and re-drew Claudinus' map for inclusion in a work on the history of the Church. Travels abroad were not frequent, because of the political situation and the "sit-at-home" conservatism of the population; so the earth sciences, on the whole, became a purely practical field of military and administrative endeavor, focused on state interests.

The Nineteenth Century

Modern Czech geography is largely a product of the fourth stage of our chronology, the 19th century, or more precisely, of its second half plus the first two decades of the 20th century (1850-1918).

Once they had moved out of the rather narrow frame of a "government-owned business", the earth sciences became a free field, separated from state-controlled cartography. The study of geography entered the graduate schools. With a reorganization of Charles University in Prague in 1882, and its division into two branches, the Czech and the German, a Chair of Geography was established under Professor Jan Palacký (1830-1908), the "offical founder" of modern Czech geography. He was succeeded by Václav Švambera (1866-1939), a methodologist, geomorphologist, and field-geographer specializing in limnology, a popular teacher and (as his students called him) "master of refined geographic language". Under Professor Švambera, the Chair grew into a Department of Geography, first in the School of Philosophy, later in the School of Natural Science.

Czech geography of the late 19th century developed as a combination of studies from Austrian, West European, and Slav sources. Our earth scientists took an active part in official projects of the Austro-Hungarian government, such as the work of the Military Geographic Institute in Vienna (the official mapping agency of the monarchy) and government-sponsored explorations. The crew of the frigate *Novara* and her scientific team, in 1872-74, included natives of Bohemia and Moravia. Private explorative journeys to remote and exotic countries obviously held a great attraction for the landlocked Czechs. Dr. Emil Holub, a physician, author of the *Seven Years in South Africa*, explored the remote regions between the Kalahari Desert and the Limpopo-Zambezi watershed. Other field-geographers of the tropics were E. St. Vráz, Josef Kořenský and Albert Frič. Czech travelers and explorers were also interested in the Balkans, the Crimea, and the Caucasus Mountains.

Czech geography, to be sure, did not create any "spirit of the age" comparable to Alexander von Humboldt, Sir Charles Lyell, Ferdinand von Richthofen, Albrecht and Walter Penck or William Morris Davis. Its strength lies elsewhere. First, the Czechs were no "unilateral scholars", since none of our geographers was strictly limited to a single field of knowledge. Each one was an expert in a science related to his own specialized branch of geography. For example, Karel Domin, Rector of Charles University, was a phyto-geographer and botanist. Stanislav Hanzlík, author of a once-revolutionary paper on anticyclones, was a climatologist-geographer and meteorologist. Cyril Purkyně was a geomorphologist, paleo-geographer, and glaciologist.

This period also produced a number of secondary-school teachers, professors of gymnasia, all university graduates, eminent in geography. Many were Ph.D.s. Since professorships at the universities were restricted in number, many gymnasium instructors engaged in higher research and writing, with no thought to a career at Charles University.

Third, special interest was accorded historical geography; it grew to a specifically Czech branch of geography, as a study of the past landscape, cultural rather than natural. However, it was the historians, not the geographers of the 19th century who were the first in this field. František Palacký is concerned with the past cultural landscape in his *History of the Czech Nation*, especially the first volume, which deals with political divisions prior to 1253 A. D., and shows a talent for geographic descriptions in his *Topography of the Kingdom of Bohemia* (1848). Palacký's most noted followers, more specialized in the geography of the past, included August Sedláček, author of a voluminous work on Bohemian castles, and two brothers, Hermenegild and Josef Jireček, to mention only a few.

Czechoslovakia, 1918-38

During the first Czechoslovak era geography became a well-established scientific field. Its main 19th-century characteristics remained, as delineated above, but the field as a whole widened and deepened. Human geography, a new subject, was introduced by Viktor Dvorský and Jiří Král, both influenced by the French and Yugoslav schools. Henceforth, the earth sciences grew harmoniously in their physical, human, and regional divisions. Exploration of national territory was promoted, with particular attention to the most remote province, Ruthenia, later lost to Soviet Russia. Geographic field work abroad was also frequent. Thus, Karel Domin and Jiří Daneš explored part of Indonesia; Daneš, a geomorphologist, after a brief period of service in Australia as general consul, made extensive studies in Oceania. He was killed in California in 1928 in a traffic accident. Dr. Jiří Baum, a popular traveller and zoögeographer, was interested mainly in India.

Among other leading figures were Václav Švambera, a senior of Czech geography, Karel Absolon (karst topography), František Machát (methodology and cartography), Julie Moschelesová (the Anglo-Saxon cultural world, with work in English, German, and French as well as Czech), J. Kunský and Quido Záruba-Pfefferman (geomorphology), Stanislav Nikolau (editor, political geographer, and author of secondary school textbooks), and František Vitásek (physical geographer, author of a three-volume manual of advanced geography, a standard work frequently quoted in foreign literature).

The advance of geography was closely connected with the Czechoslovak Geographic Society, founded in 1895 and firmly established during the Republic as a professional organization. Official centers were the institutes of geography at the universities – especially that of Charles University in Prague – the Military Geographic Institute as a core of scientific and applied military geography, and the main cartographic agency. In the first years of the Czechoslovak era, this Institute was rather conservative in its methods, as compared, for instance, with Poland, Yugoslavia, Austria, and Hungary. (For example, its preference was for hachuring instead of contour lines to represent relief outlines.) In the 1930's, its products began to improve. The leading military geographers were Col. Jiří Čermák, also a historical geographer and geomorphologist, who specialized in Alpine topography, and Col. Ubald Kolařík, professor of military geography.

Present Status

After the hiatus of the war, Czech geography was revived in 1945. Later, in 1948, its orientation was subject to the prevalent change, much like other phases of political, economic, and cultural life. Changes in geographic science were perhaps more striking than others, since geography is related to practically all aspects of nature and society. In this brief review, only conspicuous features can be cited and interpreted, with an attempt to distinguish between the positive and negative sides of the present situation in Czechoslovakia.

On the positive side, we must first mention an increase in the practical value of geography. Considering that a field of knowledge may pass through several stages, of which the most important are description, interpretation, and application, the present status of Czechoslovak geography may be classified as "applied geography". If we look to the past, the first two historical periods were "descriptive"; the Age of Reason developed a practical sense, although restricted to the surveying and cartography of the military; the 19th century and the Czechoslovak era of 1918-38 were, rather, "interpretative", concerned primarily with geographic causality of phenomena, but with a slowly rising emphasis upon possible practical applications. Under the present régime, however, geography is an applied field *par excellence*, widely used as a government-controlled tool of exploration of the national territory, exploitation of natural resources, and regional and city planning. The use of statistical methods is encouraged and it seems that the techniques of field work have improved considerably. National cooperation among geographers is now more intense than ever before. Attendance at regular meetings is compulsory. New chairs of geography have been created, and all the earth sciences are represented in the Academy of Science. A full geographic vocabulary has been compiled so that the Czech language today has its own terms for the most specialized items. Candidates for careers in geography have been steadily increasing. Professional publications on an advanced level are numerous, and there is no question of the originality of geographic thinking in many instances. Thus, a new system of orographic approach to the Czechoslovak territory was suggested by J. Hromádka (1956). It is a genetic classification based upon geologic structures and morphologic evolution. Another system, morphometric, devised by Karel Kuchař (1955), is suitable for cartographic purposes. Bio-geography, both geobotany and zoögeography, takes into consideration the evolutionary factor, and is at present strongly centered upon the conservation of natural resources. Economic geography was widely applied in re-shaping the internal administrative divisions.

However, there are darker aspects. Without mentioning the ideologic interference of the régime, which is obvious in the methodology of geography, the present Czechoslovak earth sciences appear to be confined strictly within the state boundaries. No serious geographic work done by Czechoslovak geographers abroad has ever been reported since 1948. Even contacts with other Eastern countries seem to be limited to an exchange of literature and occasional visits in large groups. Relations with Western geographers are limited, the only link, again, being literary sources. Reviews of American, British, and Spanish papers are frequent.

The most serious handicap of the present Czechoslovak geography as seen by Czechoslovak geographers themselves, is the lack of information needed for advanced research in specialized subjects, especially industrial geography and the analysis of the international economic relationships of the Czechoslovak Socialist Republic. Complaints, as read between the lines of the recent Czechoslovak geographic literature, are not uncommon.

BIBLIOGRAPHY

Häufler, Vlastislav et al., Zeměpis Československa ("Geography of Czechoslovakia") (Prague, Československá Akademie Věd, 1960).
Král, Jiří, "The West Slav Geographers. Part I: Czechoslovak Geography in the Twentieth Century", Geography in the Twentieth Century, Griffith Taylor, editor (New York, Philosophical Library, 1957), pp. 116-121.
Novák, Arne, Dějiny literatury české ("History of Czech Literature") (Prague and Olomouc, R. Promberger, 1946).
Palacký, František, Dějiny národu českého v Čechách a v Moravě ("History of the Czech Nation in Bohemia and Moravia"), 6 vols. (Prague, Kvasnička a Hampl, 1939).
Powers, Richard H. (ed.), Readings in European Civilization since 1500 (Boston, Houghton Mifflin, 1961).
Raisz, Erwin, General Cartography (New York, McGraw-Hill, 1948).
Sborník Československé společnosti zeměpisné ("Bulletin of the Czechoslovak Geographic Society"), Prague, 1946, 1954, 1960.
Vitásek, František, Fysický zeměpis ("Physical Geography"), 3 vols. (Prague, Melantrich, 1948).

CZECHS AND SLOVAKS ABROAD

The Present Day Significance of John A. Comenius

MATTHEW SPINKA

John Amos Comenius (1592-1670) is usually regarded primarily as the pioneer of modern educational theories and methods. But this by no means exhausts his astonishingly many-sided accomplishments. His works range over scientific, pedagogical, philosophical, political, and, above all, religious fields. His lifelong endeavor centered actually not so much in pedagogical realms as in pansophy – the principle of unification of all scientific, philosophical, political, and religious knowledge in an all-embracing, integrated system. This unified encyclopaedic system was to secure ultimately the unity of mankind and universal peace. This, then, became the dominant principle of everything he wrote and aimed for.

When he was forced to leave Fulnek in Moravia by the outbreak of the Thirty Years War, he eventually settled at Leszno in Poland. Being in charge of a school of the Unity of Brethren there, he turned his attention to pedagogic reform. In 1631 he published his *Janua linguarum reserata*, which made him internationally famous almost overnight. But even at this time he glimpsed a far larger goal, which he described, owing to the urging of his English admirer, Samuel Hartlib, in his *Pansophiae prodromus*. The system there outlined rests on three principles: the study of nature, the use of reason, and religion. He insisted that they are capable of being unified in one general system of all-knowledge. In this, Comenius differed from his contemporary, René Descartes who, although greatly impressed by the former's pansophy in principle, repudiated what he regarded as a confusion of science with religion. Nevertheless, Comenius persisted in his aim to instruct all men in what is necessary for a complete and worthy human existence.

Hartlib repeatedly invited Comenius to England and succeeded at last in 1641, when the already famous educator arrived in London, under the impression that he had been invited by Long Parliament. He was introduced to a circle of distinguished scholars and some members of Parliament, as well as to several private friends. But this group wanted him to engage primarily in the reform of the English schools, not in pansophy. Nevertheless, Comenius' interest in pansophy was uppermost. He explained his proposal in *Via lucis*, in which he proposed the establishment of a "pansophic college" in London. Parliament actually discussed the matter with him, and offered one of three existing institutions for the purpose. Unfortunately, however, the outbreak of the Irish rebellion interrupted the negotiations, and Comenius left England in disappointment. *Via lucis* suggests the establishment of a "pansophic college" which would reform all education in conformity with teaching the students "all things that are necessary for man in this and the future life to know, to believe, and to hope". This was to be done by means of establishing a universal, free public school system, and using universal textbooks which would not restrict the curriculum to "secular" subjects, but would train pupils for a life conscious of spiritual ends. Furthermore, he envisaged an international goal: hence, the textbooks must be written in an universal language in which every word would have a definite meaning. Thus he was something of a pioneer in semantics. Later he advocated English and French – and even Russian – for this purpose. Ultimately, his scheme was to attain not only a unified education, but also secure universal peace.

In 1645 he actually began to formulate his gigantic concept in a monumental work, *De rerum humanorum emendatione consultatio catholica*, which was to comprise seven volumes. Only the first two volumes and the Dedication were published during his lifetime (1656). The five remaining volumes were not completed by the time of his death, but were entrusted to his son, Daniel, and to his pupil, Christian Nigrin. Actually, the final work was done by Nigrin and Paul Hartmann. Unfortunately, they were never published, and in fact were lost, having been deposited in the library of the Orphanage at Halle. A few scholars consulted them there, but otherwise the greater cultural world knew nothing about them. Not until 1935 did Professor Dimitry Chyzhevsky find the first six volumes, and the seventh in 1940. Unfortunately, they have not yet been published. Only volumes IV and VI appeared in the Czech translation of the late Josef Hendrich.

The *Consultatio* is without a doubt Comenius' most important work, comprising his lifelong endeavor, and it is tragic that these volumes are not more generally known. For that reason I shall treat them more exhaustively than I have done in connection with his other works. The two volumes published during his lifetime were introductory: the first, *Panegersia* (Universal Awakening) suggests how human society may be improved. Education, Comenius asserts, is the chief means of accomplishing this task, and all men are capable of being educated. But again, education is not to be conceived in a narrow sense of the improvement of the mind: it includes, besides the intellect, also social and religious realism. The state of the world demands that it be begun at once. Specifically, the task comprises the conquest of nature by means of scientific research and application of its results; reorganization of society by introduction of educational methods which would result in universal harmony and peace; and the spiritual transformation of men's motivation, for men are generally selfish and their selfishness results in most of the evils afflicting humankind. This transformation is to be effected by means of religion.

The second volume, *Panaugia* (Universal Dawn), describes the educational process in greater detail. God has provided men with three books from which they can learn how to attain the goals described above: nature, reason, and revelation (Scripture). The first of these may be read by sense perception, observation, research, or what we call today the scientific method. In this he follows Bacon, and suggests a procedure not dissimilar from that of Descartes. The facts thus gathered must then be systematized into general principles by means of intelligence; in this aspect, too, Comenius does not essentially differ from Descartes. But to his educational system he adds faith, which to him is the perception of the spiritual realm not accessible to the scientific method or reason; only by acknowledging this realm and submitting to its categorical demands can the ethical and spiritual transformation be accomplished. Without good men and women there cannot be a good world, no matter how scientific or intelligent men may be. He acknowledged that many contradictions exist between these three means of attaining full knowledge, but he was wholly confident that they could be removed by the comparative method. For him, the totality of truth consists in the synthesis of all three, rather than in any single one.

The third volume, *Pantaxia* (Universal Correlation) corresponds to what Comenius formerly called pansophia, already discussed above. In the fourth volume, *Pampaedia* (Universal Education), Comenius reworked his previously publicized educational theories and methods; thus it should properly supersede all his previous works dealing with this subject, particularly his *Great Didactic*, which usually serves as the basis even of present-day discussions of the Comenian educational system. *Pampaedia* differs from the *Great Didactic* in that it extends the training from four to eight stages of human life – literally, from the cradle to the grave: it adds to the previous work a prekindergarten and three adult stages, a then novel emphasis on adult education. Comenius believed that man should never stop learning even in his old age. As has already been mentioned, this volume was translated by Josef Hendrich under the title of *Vševýchova*, but it should be made available in English to acquaint a wider public with the final educational theories of the Great Educator. His proposals concerning adult education are still only partially carried out, and since his own work is unavailable, such education is based on very different principles.

The fifth volume, *Panglottia* (Universal Language), deals not only with linguistics in general, but offers a sample of the new synthetic language, which is based on principles of absolute regularity of both grammatical construction and pronunciation. But since this volume has not been published as yet, no detailed discussion of it is possible. Moreover, the problem is in a sense being solved by the increasing use of certain languages such as English or French.

The sixth volume, *Panorthosia* (Universal Reform), is the most important of the entire series, for it offers practical suggestions as to how the theories and principles of pansophia may be applied to the actual social situation. Fortunately, it has been translated into Czech by Dr. Hendrich with the title of *Všenáprava* (although even in this form it is, of course, not accessible to English-speaking people). The work deals with the problem of inadequate or non-existent education, of poor and wrong conceptions of government, of the inequalities and injustices of the social order, and of wrong concepts of religion or lack of religion altogether. If Comenius faced the problems of the seventeenth century in these realms, we face all of them today in far more aggravated form, even though many improvements have been made in certain areas. Since Comenius regards all reforms under the aspects of culture, politics, and religion, his proposals may most conveniently be treated along these lines. He proposes as the practical means of reform three institutions: the Council of Light to deal with cultural reforms; the Court of Justice to govern political reorganization and serve as the supreme judicial tribunal; and the Ecumenical Consistory to assume responsibility of the religious concerns of mankind.

The Council of Light has the responsibility for the stupendous task of educating the human race along the lines long ago suggested by Comenius in his *Via lucis* and other works. It is to work out educational principles and methods applicable to the entire world. It must prepare and distribute suitable textbooks in a universal language, and must supervise schools and teachers, as well as exercise censorship of all publications. All published works must conform to pansophic principles.

The Present Day Significance of John A. Comenius

Once education were world-wide, every village would posses an elementary school (where instruction would be in the vernacular), every city would have not only elementary but also secondary schools, and every country one or more universities.

The Court of Justice would supervise the compilation of law codes, and the administration of justice; it would also supervise civil administration to ensure justice and the preservation of peace. That, for Comenius, was the chief aim of politics. Henceforth, all men would possess equal rights before law, equal opportunities in society; since all men would submit to the rule of law, universal peace would be preserved without the use of force. All men would thus become world citizens.

The Ecumenical Consistory would not only unite all Christians into one world Church (by means of spiritual unity, not necessarily uniformity of beliefs and rites), and would then supervise their priests and ministers, care for the establishment and support of churches and the ministry, and for the training of children in religion. Accordingly, it would be charged with the duty of preparing and supplying suitable literature which would eliminate everything non-essential and stress only the essentials, which he defined as containing everything that God has revealed, commanded, and promised.

These three organizations would be subject to one Universal Council consisting of three delegates from each nation representing education, politics, and religion.

The last volume, *Pannuthesia* (Universal Admonition), is addressed to the scientists, educators, statesmen, and religious leaders of the world. They are admonished to be faithful to their sacred trust for the good of all humanity. For although Comenius naturally thought first of the Western nations sharing a basically common culture deriving from Christian tradition, he envisaged the time when the hitherto relatively or almost wholly uneducated races would become participants in the common culture. It is the duty of the "men of light" to share their riches with the entire world!

Perhaps this oversimplified and greatly condensed statement of Comenius' aims may produce an impression of a visionary, impractical Utopia. What then remains as the solid achievement of his lifelong, devoted labors and aspirations? Has it all been merely a noble failure? Is anything left of his principles and practical proposals? It must be freely confessed that much of it is of relatively transient applicability or relevance, for undoubtedly Comenius was a child of his age, as we are of our own. His stupendous and grandiose ideas proved too "impractical" for his contemporaries as well as for the conditions of his time – the period following one of the most destructive of all world wars, the Thirty Years War (although its brutality has been exceeded by our own two World Wars). Moreover, as has already been mentioned, his ideas were not generally known even then, for his principal work, the *Consultatio*, remained practically unknown – in fact lost until recently, and has not even yet been published. Furthermore, some of his ideas have been rejected both by his contemporaries, such as Descartes, and by our modern age, which to a large extent is secularist, and consequently governed by concepts of the world which in many respects are directly contrary to those of Comenius.

Fortunately, however, many of his suggestions and contributions have proved either directly or indirectly acceptable and realizable. He is generally accorded grateful recognition as a pioneer in educational theory and method, even though his theories in their latest form have remained unknown because of the loss of his *Consultatio*. Nevertheless, some of them were realized under different auspices, although in a different form. Even Soviet pedagogy claims to have profited by his ideas! The ideal of universal education is fast becoming a reality, even though Comenius is generally not given credit for its early advocacy, and in many respects it diametrically opposes his principles, particularly those of integrating religious training into the general cultural system. His proposal of the Council of Light is partially realized in *Unesco*, although it must be admitted that the latter falls far short of Comenius' ideal. Nevertheless, it adumbrates it, although its creators may never have heard of Comenius! The United Nations and the Permanent International Court of Justice also bear a recognizable relationship to Comenius' idea of the Court of Justice, but he has not been given credit for his grandiose vision of a similar, although far more inclusive, world organization. As for religious unification, astonishing progress has been made even in this area: for much of Christendom is permeated today with the idea of spiritual unity. This has culminated in the organization, in 1948, of the World Council of Churches, the latest member to the membership of which is the Russian Orthodox Church along with other churches in the Soviet-dominated countries! Moreover, the missionary movements of the last and the present centuries have disseminated the knowledge of Christianity and gained new adherents throughout the world. In this so-called ecumenical movement the contribution and pioneering work of Comenius is acknowledged, although perhaps not generally known. All in all, what many have deemed as visionary and utopian in the grandiose thoughts and aspirations of the poor Moravian exile, who witnessed the ruin of his beloved nation and the Czech branch of the church of which he was the last bishop, has to a considerable degree been realized, albeit imperfectly, and without due credit to Comenius' pioneering and initiatory inception of those ideas. It is to be regretted that his contributions, so numerous and far-reaching, are not better known to educated men of our day. The blame for his being little known rests upon us who take pride in being the heirs of this great Czech "teacher of nations"! For Comenius was a pioneer of the new world, a world which would indeed be immeasurably better if his principles were more generally influential.

SELECTED BIBLIOGRAPHY

There is no complete modern edition of all his works, even in Czech, although this was once attempted, but never completed. This was published in Brno, between 1910-29; only seven volumes actually appeared. The present Czechoslovak regime promised to undertake the publication of the entire *corpus* in some thirty volumes; so far, it has not lived up to its promise. The volume on *Pampaedia* has just been published in Germany, in Latin and German: Dmitrij Tschiżewsky, ed., *Pampaedia* (Heidelberg, Quelle & Meyer, 1960). Among biographical treatments may be mentioned: Jan V. Novák, *Jan Amos Komenský; jeho život a spisy* (Praha, 1932); Anna Heyberger, *Jean Amos Comenius; sa vie et son oeuvre d'éducateur* (Paris, 1928); Matthew Spinka, *John Amos Comenius; that Incomparable Moravian* (Chicago, 1943); and G. H. Turnbull, *Hartlib, Dury, and Comenius* (Liverpool and London, 1947). Spinka also translated Comenius' *Labyrinth of the World* (Chicago, 1942), and *The Bequest of the Unity of Brethren* (Chicago, 1940). Josef Hendrich's translations of *Vševýchova* and *Všenáprava* were published in Prague in 1948 and 1950. A complete list of Comenius' writings are to be found in Novák's work.

Augustine Heřman of Bohemia Manor

M. NORMA SVEJDA

Since the start of American history, Czech and Slovak emigrés have played a minor but important role in the formation of this country. The life of one of these early pioneers is worthy of our close study not only because of his pre-eminent role in the establishment of New Amsterdam and the Maryland Free State, but also because of his positive belief in religious tolerance and the expression of individual freedom.

Augustine Heřman[1] was probably born in the city of Prague, Bohemia. The exact date is uncertain, but various indirect proofs place his birth in either 1605 or 1621. The latter date is inferred from the fact that he signed his will in 1684 with the notation, "Aetatis 63", meaning that he was sixty-three years old when he executed the document.[2] However, the earlier date, 1605, is more likely, since we know he acted as a witness to the Schuylkill River treaty. If Heřman had been born in 1621, he would have been only twelve years old – too young to witness so important a document.[3]

The exact origin and names of his parents are also in doubt. Thomas Čapek, in his life of Augustine Heřman, states that Heřman's father may have been Abraham Herman, the last Evangelical pastor at Mšeno, who had charge of the parish of St. John's Church.[4] After the Battle of White Mountain, Ferdinand the Second issued a proclamation that only Catholic worship would be tolerated, and in 1627 the Emperor finally

---

[1] Dutch chroniclers spell the name in many ways: Herman, Herrman, Harman, Heerman, Hermans, etc. The erratic spelling of proper names during the 17th century is truly astonishing. On his map of Virginia and Maryland, Heřman spells both his first name and last name differently; the name on the portrait is spelled, "Augustine Herrman Bohemian"; on the inscription plate, "Augustin Herrman Bohemiensis" and the southeast section of the map, "Aug. Herman".

[2] Gilbert Cope, "Copy of the Will of Augustine Herrman of Bohemia", *The Pennsylvania Magazine of History*, Vol. 15, pp. 321-326.

[3] Earl L. W. Heck, *Augustine Herrman* (Englewood, Ohio, 1941).

[4] Thomas Čapek, *Augustine Herrman of Bohemia Manor* (New York, 1928).

made it known that those refusing to conform with the state religion must leave the country. Many persons then emigrated, while others embraced the Catholic faith. Heřman emigrated to Saxony, and settled in the city of Zittau.

The German-American historian, H. A. Rattermann, in his article on Heřman, states (without citing his authority) that Heřman's father was a prominent citizen of Prague and a member of the City Council who kept a store in the old section of the city. His mother, Beatrix, was the daughter of Kasper Redel, of whom nothing is known except that he was affiliated with the rebel groups which met at Charles University in 1618. His father too, was an ardent partisan of the Sub-Utraque Church of the Hussites, and joined in the memorial protest to the Emperor.[5]

As insufficient data are available to relate either the pastor Heřman or the City Councilor Heřman conclusively to Augustine Heřman's father, neither inference can be corroborated without further research.

In any event, we know that Heřman's family left Bohemia and found their way to Amsterdam, Holland. In the earliest document signed by Heřman in 1633, the name is spelled Heerman, probably the Dutch form.[6] Augustine Heřman was a member of the Dutch West India Company in Holland. He probably met with little opposition when he first offered his services to that Company. Before visiting the North American mainland, he probably had made voyages to the Indies and Curaçao. In 1633 he was with Arendt Corssen on the present site of Philadelphia when the land in that vicinity was bought from the Indians. The document of conveyance was, among others, signed by "Augustin Heermans".[7]

For the years between 1634 and 1644, little documentary evidence is available. Čapek says of this period:

"Prior to settling in the Dutch metropolis of New Amsterdam Heřman probably resided in Virginia. It is of interest that traces of the Czech immigration in the first half of the 17th century lead to every section of the state. There is evidence that he did work as a public surveyor at Accomac, Va. The services of a surveyor in a new country must have been greatly in demand. In his spare time he traded with Indians and planted tobacco. 'I am the founder of the Virginia tobacco trade', he wrote to Governor Stuyvesant. The exact date of his removal to New Amsterdam is not known".[8]

[5] Heinrich A. Rattermann, "Augustin Herrman", in *Deutsch-Amerikanisches Magazin* (Cincinnati, Ohio), Vol. I (Jan-July, 1887), p. 202.
[6] Heck, *op. cit.*, p. 10.
[7] Samuel Hazard, *Annals of Pennsylvania*, 1850, p. 35.
[8] Čapek, *op. cit.*, p. 13.

In 1644 we have records of him as an agent for the New Amsterdam branch of Peter Gabry and Sons, the prominent merchant traders of Amsterdam.[9] One year later, Heřman was fully established in his own name. He shipped to Europe furs received from Fort Nassau, Fort Orange and Patuxent, Maryland; he also shipped cattle and horses to Virginia. From Amsterdam he imported pottery and glassware; he dealt in African slaves, and sent large numbers to Virginia in exchange for tobacco.

During the next fifteen years he was one of the important figures who shaped the political and commercial life of New Amsterdam. In 1647 the people of New Amsterdam selected the Council of Nine Men to assist the governor with every aspect of administration of the new Dutch colony. For the first two years. Heřman was President (or Chairman) and in 1649 he was replaced by Adrianen Van der Donck. Heřman continued to serve as Vice-Chairman. This Council was the forerunner of the Burgomasters and, eventually, of the municipal form of government of New York.

Heřman was elected to this post as the representative of the liberal "Country Party", which was opposed to Governor Peter Stuyvesant's dictatorial form of government. During Heřman's term, complaints about Stuyvesant were sent to the colonial authorities in Holland. The governor was severely rebuked, whereupon he set out to ruin Heřman and others who shared Heřman's views.

Stuyvesant, however, underwent a complete change of heart when he realized how much more he could achieve with the cooperation of the powerful leaders of his own people. However it was too late, because the Dutch had already suffered great loss of prestige in America, and this was one of the final acts that led to England's easy annexation of the whole of New Netherlands. Heřman's business was seriously damaged by the Acts of Navigation, and Governor Stuyvesant made a serious effort to ruin him financially by imprisoning him for non-payment of his debts. But it seems that Heřman, with the help of Anna Hack, his sister-in-law, met the demands of his creditors and was granted "liberty and freedom" by the city council. His commercial rise started again, to culminate in his most successful year in the tobacco trade, 1655. In 1651 Heřman married Janetje Verlett, daughter of Casper and Judith Verlett, whose son married Peter Stuyvesant's sister, Anna. These marriages smoothed out differences and helped to form an alliance between the two families. Heřman was

[9] *Calendar of Historical Manuscripts (1630-1664)*, Vol. I, p. 28.

sent on important diplomatic missions to Rhode Island, Massachusetts, Virginia and Maryland.

The trip to Maryland came as a turning point in Heřman's life. This mission was caused by the troubles concerning boundaries between the Dutch and English living in the Delaware district. In 1656 Stuyvesant determined to colonize more fully the west bank of the Delaware River. Permanent settlements were established at Horekill (Lewes), New Amstel (Newcastle), and on the west side of the river at Passaying (Philadelphia). In 1659 Governor Fendall of Maryland began to look on all these new Dutch settlements with an unenthusiastic eye, believing that the time was ripe to check further Dutch colonization on what he considered English territory. A dispute arose. Heřman, once again in high favor with Stuyvesant, saw the gravity of the situation and proposed a conference between representatives of the two provinces, whereupon he and Resolved Waldron were appointed special ambassadors to Maryland.

During the conference with Lord Baltimore's representative, Heřman wrote to Governor Stuyvesant of the need for an exact map of the area to settle anticipated differences. When Stuyvesant did not reply, Heřman wrote to Lord Baltimore that he, Heřman, would draw a map of the entire province if that dignitary would, in return, give him a tract of land. In a letter dated September 10, 1660, his lordship stated that he accepted the offer, and gave Heřman title to 5,000 acres of land.

Heřman named his land "Bohemia Manor" after his homeland. This grant figured in a plan of the powerful Calvert family to raise a new aristocracy in Maryland – an aristocracy based upon the ability and worth of the individual regardless of his religious affiliation. Seventy-four such manors were granted by the Calverts; they became a form of land tenure, but never resembled the feudal system of their English counterparts.

It took eight to ten years for Heřman to gather data for his map, "*Virginia and Maryland*". Until recently, we had no information on the preparation of this map, but a small ink sketch of the Bohemia Manor grant was found in the archives of Woodstock College, Maryland. This sketch may have been a preliminary drawing used in preparing the map of Maryland drawn by Heřman himself.

The original map drawing was sent to England and was engraved by William Faithorne, who resided with Wenceslaus Hollar, the distinguished Bohemian engraver. Heřman's map is not only notable for its geographic accuracy, but is also regarded as a masterpiece of 17th century cartography.

Heřman sought to bring many colonists to Maryland. One large group was that of the Labadists. Founded by Jean de Labadie, a former Jesuit priest, this community put much emphasis on the "inner light" and a strict and Spartan rule of conduct in everyday life. Because of their beliefs, they sought a free land in which to start their colony. Heřman gave a tract of 750 acres to the one hundred Labadists who came to Maryland. The group, similar to the Quakers in dress and customs, gradually died out, and their property was sold in 1727. Bohemia Manor's legal existence ended in 1787, one hundred and twenty-seven years after Augustine Heřman received the original grant.

Augustine Heřman died shortly after the Labadists came to Maryland. In his will he stipulated that a monument be erected, to bear an inscription stating that Heřman was the founder of Bohemia Manor. His five children were amply provided for with 20,000 acres of the finest farm lands.

Casparus Heřman, his eldest son, recently received belated recognition as builder, in 1685, of the first State House in Annapolis. Dr. Morris Radoff, in his recent book, *Buildings of the State of Maryland in Annapolis*,[10] devotes a full chapter to this early building.

Until seventy-five years ago little was known of Augustine Heřman's contribution to the early development of America. Mr. Thomas Čapek and Mr. Earl Heck's books on the life of Heřman have opened the door, but further research in many areas is needed, especially with respect to Heřman's achievements as artist and cartographer.[11]

---

[10] Morris Radoff, *Buildings of the State of Maryland in Annapolis* (Annapolis, Md., Hall of Records, 1959).

[11] An example of such research is that at present being conducted by Thurston Thatcher, Hyde Park, N.Y., on the oil painting "Embarkation of Rev. Borgadus", attributed to Augustine Heřman.

Aleš Hrdlička, Pioneer American Physical Anthropologist

T. D. STEWART

Physical anthropology, the study of man from the biological standpoint, is said to have gotten its start as an organized science when Broca founded the Société d'Anthropologie de Paris in 1859. Less than 40 years later, in 1896, Aleš Hrdlička, then a young medical graduate practicing in New York, went to Paris to study anthropology under Manouvrier, one of Broca's successors. Although Hrdlička intended to fit himself for a career in medical anthropology, it seems likely that the contact with French anthropology opened his eyes to the broader aspects of the science. Certain it is that when his expectations of continued employment in the Pathological Institute of the New York State Hospitals were disappointed, he turned to the main seat of anthropological learning in New York City, the American Museum of Natural History, and soon was engaged in a series of anthropological field trips to Mexico and the southwestern part of the United States. The results of these trips, presented at scientific meetings, so impressed W. H. Holmes, then Head Curator of Anthropology in the U. S. National Museum, that he induced Hrdlička to come to Washington in 1903 as the first curator of physical anthropology in that institution.

Hrdlička spent 40 years in and out of Washington pioneering in the young science which he had adopted. When he died in 1943 after a brief retirement, I had just succeeded him to the curatorship. That I received this honor was due largely to my apprenticeship under him of nearly 20 years duration. From this association I gained considerable insight into his ways of thinking and methods of working, as well as a high respect for his scientific accomplishments.

I will not dwell here on Hrdlička's accomplishments, for they have been gone into on at least three occasions: 1) on his 60th birthday by J. Matiegka(?),[1] 2) on his 70th birthday by myself, and 3) in his National

---

[1] I somehow got the impression – perhaps from something Dr. Hrdlička said – that this biography was mainly the work of Matiegka, but I find now that it is unsigned.

Academy obituary by A. H. Schultz. In the short space available it seems better to say something about the personal characteristics which he revealed to me.

I think of Hrdlička mostly as I saw him in his office and in the Divisional laboratory. Usually he was in his shirt sleeves or, if expecting a visitor, wearing a light-weight and light-colored jacket. His collar was always of the stiff, winged type. In the course of time the laundering of these collars became quite a problem and one of the museum employees was called upon regularly to take them to a Chinese laundryman across town, the only one who seemed able to do them to the Doctor's satisfaction. A preformed necktie, fastened by a hook to an elastic band around the neck, was worn with the collar. Both adorned a shirt the front of which often was made of a contrasting material, like a sewed-on dickey. Hrdlička never seemed the least concerned about the unfashionableness of this attire.

It was not the attire, of course, that you saw when you met him for the first time. Then your attention was held by his personality; by that combination of facial appearance, gestures, way of speaking, etc., which are difficult to sort out afterwards. This combination, everyone seems to agree, was impressive, even formidable. The first words, with their peculiar accent, revealed his foreign ancestry. This was emphasized by the bit of Mongoloid in his appearance: broad face, swarthy complexion, rather thin mustache, piercing dark eyes, and heavy main of hair combed straight back. He would have resented my mentioning the Mongoloid element, although others saw it too; he always insisted that the Hungarians had the Mongoloid strain, not the Czechs. He would explode when anyone asked, however innocently, whether he was Hungarian.

Hrdlička's attitude toward visitors was often quite obvious to the onlooker. I have seen him turn on the charm when disposed to be nice, and on the other hand I have seen him give visitors the cold stare. Once I recall being in his office when two girls from a local college came in to get information for a term paper. One girl, very ill at ease, began asking a question and was promptly interrupted by Hrdlička asking, "Why do you put that stuff on your lips?" I felt so sorry for the girls that I departed hastily and am not sure how the interview progressed.

As Hrdlička's question indicates, he disapproved of the modern fashions for women. Actually, he was of the opinion that women were not fitted for anything except housework and raising families. Thus women anthropologists often fared badly with him and when he visited anthropology departments in universities he did not hesitate to take issue with girl students on the subject of smoking or on their efforts to enter a field which he considered fit only for men.

This attitude is further illustrated by an episode which involved me. One morning I arrived in my office, having just become a father. Hrdlička had not been told of the impending event largely because he did not invite confidences or "small talk" of any kind. Of course other staff members knew, and so it happened that I was in my office receiving the congratulations of a colleague from across the hall when Hrdlička passed through on one of his regular inspection tours. Visiting among lowly staff members this early in the morning was so irregular by his standards that he exclaimed "What is this?" When told that my wife had just given birth to a daughter, he said, "That is good." Then on second thought he asked, "What did you say the sex is?" When told again that the baby was a girl, he said rather sadly, "Well, the first one is usually a weakling." It must be added, however, that later, when my daughter was old enough to be brought to the museum, Hrdlička delighted in picking her up and seemed pleased to be able to say "But she is strong!"

Hrdlička's characteristics as an individualist were already well established by the time I arrived at the National Museum in the early 1920's. Many staff members had learned by experience not to court his displeasure. Yet the one sure way of pleasing Hrdlička and getting a sympathetic reception was to go to him with a health problem. In addition to receiving a medical lecture, you would likely get a little round box of citrine ointment. Hrdlička kept citrine ointment on hand in bulk, it having been apparently a mainstay of his early medical practice. He dispensed it at the museum free of charge for everything from sore muscles to pyorrhea. The effectiveness of the remedy was widely accepted and I found myself repeatedly being asked by those out of favor with Hrdlička to replenish their supply without his knowledge. This I refused to do, even though it seemed likely that he would not have minded.

Hrdlička himself often used me in the role of intermediary. This was owing mainly to the fact that he never spoke to certain people, including the other curators in the anthropology department. Also, he delegated to me some chores for which he had little taste and could ill afford the time. These included taking specimens to the photographer and seeing that they were properly posed; taking manuscripts to the printer and seeing that inconsistencies were resolved. He never seemed concerned that I was able in this way to effect considerable editorial changes – changes which I felt were for the better. I see now that this freedom was what made my apprenticeship an effective way to learn.

I do not wish to imply that there was much need to change the text of Hrdlička's manuscripts. He wrote rather rapidly and quite clearly, if in a slightly foreign-sounding manner. Rarely, however, did he ask anyone to read a manuscript for the purpose of making suggestions. Although probably he sometimes wanted suggestions, it seemed to be beneath his dignity to ask for them. Rather, in my case, he would say that I might profit by reading the manuscript. On the occasions when I was given this opportunity and was bold enough to offer suggestions for improving the wording, I was listened to, but was given to understand that the wording had been carefully considered and that my suggestions would introduce undesirable changes in meaning. I doubt that anyone at the National Museum except Prof. Holmes succeeded in persuading Hrdlička to change the text of a manuscript. Prof. Holmes was a superior being in Hrdlička's opinion.

One of the things which impressed me deeply was Hrdlička's clarity of mind. Over and over I heard him demolish arguments by saying that there were 3 or 5 or some other number of reasons why they should not be accepted. And then he would proceed to list the stated number of reasons in a logical order. To one who in a debate rarely can tell in advance the number of points he is going to develop, such foresight seemed at times phenomenal. Yet it often appeared that Hrdlička's facility in this direction led him to become over-anxious to contribute to the discussion of papers in scientific meetings. His colleagues complained about this, but in retrospect few could deny that what he said was usually very much to the point.

Such clear thinking made it easy for Hrdlička to speedily prepare answers to letters. This was probably the secret of his voluminous correspondence. The remarkable thing is that, in view of the large amount of typing involved, he succeeded in keeping each secretary for a long period of time. Basically, I think they were awed by him and found it difficult to withdraw the help which meant so much in accomplishing his vast work-load.

The running of the office was only one aspect of Hrdlička's superior organizing ability. His collection of scientific data and specimens followed an orderly pattern determined early in his career. By the time I came along he was never at a loss for material for a paper, and the collections in his Division included close to 20,000 human skulls, mostly of his own gathering. When the *American Journal of Physical Anthropology*, which he founded in 1918 and edited until 1942, could not go to press for lack of copy, he would open a drawer, begin to organize the data accumulated therein, and soon the *Journal* pages would be filled. Those who complained about the *Journal* being Hrdlička's private publishing medium could not know that this was so largely because they were not submitting papers.

In addition to founding the *Journal*, Hrdlička founded the American Association of Physical Anthropologists (1929). By making the *Journal* the organ of the Association, he guaranteed the success of both. This was not fully appreciated at the time, because resentment developed, as I have indicated, over the dominant role he played. In this connection I know for a fact that he excluded papers from the programs of meetings and turned down others submitted for publication in the *Journal*, because their contents went contrary to his views. There is always some doubt as to the legitimacy of procedures of this sort, but I am inclined to think that Hrdlička generally exercised sound judgment in the interest of promoting higher standards.

Although his methods were sometimes questionable, there can be little doubt that Hrdlička always had the interest of physical anthropology fully at heart. If he felt that something was good for the science, the effort was never too great to obtain it. In the same way, if Hrdlička approved of a person, that person could count on his full support. Probably this was Hrdlička's motivation on one occasion when I was present for offering to finance the medical training of a physical anthropologist of my generation who had already been granted the Ph.D. Hrdlička felt strongly that only through a medical training was one properly fitted to be a physical anthropologist.

All things considered, it is understandable that a great change took place in American physical anthropology following Hrdlička's retirement and closely ensuing death. During a pioneering period progress is so rapid that almost inevitably it is followed by a less exciting period during which the gains must be consolidated. After 1943 young physical anthropologists had an opportunity for the first time to manage their science in America. Not surprisingly, therefore, the expression, "the new physical anthropology", soon began to find currency. However, the hard work had been done and the standards had been set by the pioneers, chief of whom was Aleš Hrdlička.

REFERENCES

Anonymous, "Dr. Aleš Hrdlička. A biographical sketch", *Anthropologie*, vol. 7, parts 1-2 (= *Dr. Aleš Hrdlička Anniversary Volume*) (Praha, 1929), pp. 6-49.
Schultz, Adoph H., "Biographical Memoir of Aleš Hrdlička, 1869-1943", *Biog. Mem. Nat. Acad. Sci.*, vol. 23, no. 12 (1945), pp. 305-338.
Stewart, T. D., "The life and writings of Dr. Aleš Hrdlička (1869-1939)", *Am. J. Phys. Anthrop.*, vol. 26 (= *Hrdlička volume*) (1940), pp. 3-40.

The Czechs in Texas

JOHN M. SKŘIVÁNEK

It was in the early eighteen fifties when the Czechs began coming to Texas in groups of from ten to fifteen families. It is true that Dr. Anthony Dignowity arrived in 1832, and a few came in the eighteen forties, but whole families began arriving in the eighteen fifties.

The population of the entire state was then less than a quarter of a million,[1] ten years later, it had almost trebled. It was during this period (1850-1860) that Texas was surpassed in rate of population growth by only California, Oregon, Iowa and Minnesota. There were still many unsettled and even wild regions in the state; these were being occupied by the Czechs and other immigrants and their families. Some of the larger towns were Galveston, with a population of only 4,177, San Antonio, with 3,488, Houston, with 2,396, Marshall, with 1,189, Victoria, with 806 and Austin, the present capitol city, with only 629 inhabitants.[2] Today, Houston, the largest city in the state, has a population of approximately a million, and of this number some 40,000[3] are of Czech extraction.

The first Czechs came to Texas to enjoy religious and political freedom, and to gain for themselves the right to "life, liberty, and the pursuit of happiness".

The earliest settlers crossed the Atlantic on the following boats: the Sava, Savanna, Victoria, Ammerland, and Elizabeth.[4] Many immigrants died en route because of overcrowded conditions and also because of poor food. Crossing the Atlantic took from seven to sixteen weeks. Most Texas colonists landed in Galveston and went from there to Houston by steamboat. Upon reaching Houston – a distance of about fifty miles – ox teams transported them to Dubina and Cat Springs. This is how an early

---

[1] *Texas State Census.*
[2] *Federal Census of 1850, Population by Counties, Ages, Color and Condition*, pp. 503-504.
[3] Figure arrived at by Dr. Henry R. Maresh, using telephone directory.
[4] Hudson, Estelle, and Dr. Henry Maresh, *Czech Pioneers of the Southwest*, pp. 28-31.

pioneer, Judge Haidušek, described his voyage to America, and the conditions which he found here upon his arrival in 1856. The sailing vessel, he stated, was about one hundred feet long and had only two masts. The very first night the ship ran into a storm which tossed it about like a small piece of wood. The suffering and sea-sickness of the passengers, especially the women and children, was something that no one ever forgot. After this initial experience, the sailing was fair, but it was fourteen weeks before Galveston Harbor was reached. From Galveston the immigrants were towed by a small steamboat up the Buffalo Bayou to Houston. Their belongings were loaded on wagons, and to each wagon were hitched five yoke of oxen. In six weeks, the immigrants reached their destination, Cat Springs in Austin County.[5] Here they built their first homes, called Loksáky or logsáky, meaning log houses, with dirt floors, and a roof of grass. The furniture consisted of a few items which they had brought from their homeland, and whatever could be hauled on wagons from Galveston. Usually, a few dishes, some clothes and a feather-bed were all that a family owned. The feather-bed was called "zlatá česká peřina" – a well-deserved name, for it saved many lives during the cold winter months. There were no beds in the "logsáky", but the pioneers drove wooden spikes into the ground in the corners of the log houses and covered these with tree branches and moss. These in turn were covered with the feather-beds. Wood blocks served as chairs.[6]

A story told by another old-timer will give a better picture of the conditions which existed in Texas over a century ago. Here is what he said of schoolhouses:

There were few school buildings; some classes were taught in the shade of trees during the summer months. Such school houses as did exist were built of logs with split-log floors. Puncheon seats were used. The roof was made of boards sawed from post-oak trees and attached to the rafters with rawhide strips; light was admitted by sawing out a log from each side of the building. The doors were cut above the first two or three logs, and small children had to be lifted over this high threshold. This was necessary in order to keep wild hogs from wandering into the buildings and endangering the lives of the students.[7]

Another early immigrant tells of frequent incidents in which wild cattle,

---

[5] Ibid., p. 84.

[6] Information given me by my father, J. J. Skřivánek, Sr., who in turn received it from his father and grandfather.

[7] Information passed down to author of this article by great grandfather who came to Texas in 1855 from Želechovice (Moravia) Czechoslovakia.

bullfights and stampedes disrupted school for as much as an entire day. During one of these episodes, he states, the teacher had to put the children on the top of the building and climb after them for protection from a stampeding herd of wild cattle.

Getting to school was sometimes a risky proposition. Children frequently had to remain on a rail fence for hours to avoid wild hogs before continuing on to school.

These incidents are mentioned in order to give some idea of what the immigrant faced upon his arrival in Texas over a hundred years ago. Now, let us turn to what has taken place during these years in Texas, and learn how the Czechs have fared in the New World, specifically in Texas, from 1850 to 1962.

Today, there is hardly a county or city in Texas which does not have a considerable number of citizens of Czech extraction.[8] From the original settlements in Fayette, Lavaca, Austin, Burleson, Williamson, and other counties, some 350,000 American-Czechs have scattered all over the state. They are represented in all walks of life. Motivated by the desire to form an all-Czech community where they would not be exploited or molested by groups of other nationalities, the Czechs invited fellow country men to move into areas which they themselves had already occupied. Within a few years, such areas were settled by large numbers of Czechs and a sort of Czech cultural island was created. A feeling of solidarity was thus established. Since they were culturally differentiated from people in surrounding areas, the Czechs founded community organizations in which their native language, customs, habits, traditions, and social values were perpetuated. Remaining virtually isolated from intimate contact with the surrounding population, such communities as Šebesta, Kovář, Praha and many others remained almost totally Czech in character until a few years ago. Certain modes of behavior traditional to these people have persisted for over a hundred years. Other modes of behavior, of course, have changed. First, the Czech has always been closely associated with farming, not only as a distinctive form of work, but as a distinct way of life. Because land was at such a premium in Czechoslovakia, it was and still is looked upon by the Czech-American as a symbol of status and security. So deeply is this idea embedded in the mind of these people that land ownership is characteristic not only of the farmer, but also of the city dweller who is also engaged in other occupations. Second, we may consider his adjustment to a new life.

[8] Preece, Harold, *Progressive Farmer*, March, 1938, p. 8.

Since the residents of each of these communities have their own organizations and agencies in which the Czech language is used, other ethnic groups play an insignificant role in these organizations. For a long time, both the Czech and Anglo-American groups attributed to themselves a certain superiority, which separated the two groups socially for many years. On the whole, however, the barriers which existed for so long have been broken down in most places. Third, the Czech family still functions as not only a social but also an economic unit, with strong family ties. This influence is so strong that one seldom reads or hears of a Czech youth running away from home; juvenile delinquency is relatively unknown. The children are usually well-mannered and, like their fathers and forefathers, are taught that hard work, thrift, politeness and honesty are virtues that every young Czech should possess or strive for. (Incidentally, only one Czech-American has received the death penalty in our state since the eighteen-fifties.)

Fourth, in religion, of the four communities from which I have gathered information two are Protestant and two Catholic. They are representative of most of the communities in our state. In the Šebesta community (now called Snook), for example, 80.3 percent of the community's population belongs to the Czech-Moravian Brethren Church (now called the Unity of the Brethren); 9.7 percent are Catholics; 5.3 percent are Pentecostal; 2.6 percent are Free Thinkers, and 2.1 percent belong to other denominations.[9]

The Unity of the Brethren Church exerts a strong influence in all community affairs. It sponsors several organizations, among them a Sunday School, a Ladies' Aid Missionary Society, a Vacation Bible School, a Young People's Union, a Sunday School teacher-training school known as the Hus School, and a Benevolent Society. It is difficult to overestimate the value of these organizations in the cultural and social life of the Czechs. In fact, one might go so far as to say that they are a Czech design for American living. The same can be said of Praha (that is, Praha, Texas), another small community, where the majority of the inhabitants are Catholics, and the Catholic church plays an important role in the affairs of that community. In all of these communities, the older people are making strenuous efforts to keep the Czech language alive as long as possible, especially in the churches, but English has, during the last ten years, gradually replaced Czech in most of the churches, even in rural areas. Czech, however is still used from time to time.

[9] Škrabánek, R. L., *Social Life in a Czech-American Rural Community* reprinted from *Rural Sociology*, Vol. 15 (Sept. 1950).

Our fifth consideration is education. Traditionally, the Czech is proud of the educational attainments of his people. The illiteracy rate among the Czech immigrants was among the lowest of all groups that entered the United States. In Texas, many have played important roles in various fields. Among those who have made lasting contributions to the Czech cause in Texas is Judge Augustine Haidušek, who was born in Czechoslovakia in 1846, came to Texas in 1856, fought in the Civil War, learned English by firelight, became a teacher, studied law and was admitted to the bar in 1870. In 1870, he was elected chairman of the Democratic Executive Committee of Fayette County, and mayor of La Grange in 1875. Later he was elected to the State Legislature, and in 1890, he became the owner of *Svoboda*, a Czech weekly newspaper.

Another notable Czech-American was Judge C. H. Chernoský, a prominent Houston attorney, member of the State Board of Education, and for many years president of the Slavonic Benevolent Order of the State of Texas. He was also a charter member of the University of Texas Czech Club, and paved the way for teaching the Czech language at the University. Since 1926, Czech language study has been offered under the tutelage of Dr. Eduard Míček, who had devoted his life to the teaching of the language of our forefathers.

A third figure is Dr. Joseph Kopecky, also a charter member of the University of Texas Czech Club. He graduated as valedictorian of his class from Sam Houston Normal College in 1915, received his M.D. from the University of Texas Medical School, taught there and was promoted to full professorship within a few years. He has also been president of the Texas Heart Association, the International Post-Graduate Assembly, the Texas Club of Internists and is now senior member of the medical firm of Kopecky and Kopecky of San Antonio, Texas.

Dr. Henry R. Maresh, prominent Houston physician and author of *The Czech Pioneers of the Southwest*, was also of pioneer Czech stock. Before his untimely death, Dr. Maresh was the president and a director of the Liberty Loan and Building Association. He was also the first officially to register for the Czech language course at the University of Texas. Dr. Maresh also served as first president of the All-State Folk Festival and was elected first president of the Czech Educational Foundation of Texas, established by the writer of this article in 1954.

The Honorable L. J. Šulák, former state Senator, editor of the *La Grange Record*, *Svoboda*, and other newspapers is a prominent Texan of Czech background. Senator Šulák was a member of the Texas delegation that nominated Franklin D. Roosevelt for the presidency in Chicago in

1932, and he later served as a member of the Board of Regents of the University of Texas.

In Texas, we have had, and still have many other outstanding Americans of Czech extraction. Among them are General Jerry Vrchlický Matějka, Colonel B. H. Pochyla, Senator Russek, the Honorable J. L. Duckett, the Honorable John R. Kuběna, the Honorable James Pavlica, Dr. Charles J. Holub, former Consul of the Czechoslovak Republic, the Honorable W. Matějowský, a State representative for many years, B. F. Matocha, former Secretary of the State of Texas, Josef V. Frnka, lawyer and member of the House of Representatives for many years, and Assistant Attorney General of Texas in 1945-46, Dr. Frank E. Lukša, professor and head of the Department of Sociology, Southwestern University, State Representative Charles D. Rutta, and many more.

In conclusion, it may be said that no immigrants brought more books to the New World than did the Czechs. True, they brought religious books, Bibles and prayer books, but these avid readers, once here, published newspapers and periodicals. Today we still have the *Věstník, Texaský Rolník, Nový Domov, Svoboda, Bratrské Listy, Našinec* and a newcomer, *Hospodář*, recently transferred from Nebraska to Texas.

With respect to religion, almost every Texas Czech is affiliated with some religious body. In our state, about 70 percent are Roman Catholics, 25 percent members of The Unity of the Brethren, or belong to some Protestant church, and the remainder are freethinkers. There are over 250 Czech communities and in these, over a hundred Catholic churches and some sixty churches of The Unity of the Brethren.[10] When Dr. Jan Masaryk visited Texas in 1942, he was not surprised at the progress made by the Czechs in our state. He was quite familiar with their inherent ability to make homes for themselves in a new land and he was both proud of and gratified by their progress and their contributions to our agricultural, industrial, professional and social life. The Czech easily orients himself in Texas because its freedom is the ideal of all true patriots. Texas has been good to the Czechs and the Czechs are a part of Texas' greatness!

---

[10] Maresh, Henry R. (M.D.), *The Czechs in Texas*, reprinted from the *Southwestern Historical Quarterly*, Vol. L, No. 2.

Czechs and Slovaks in Latin America

MILIČ KYBAL

Five hundred years ago the King of Bohemia, George of Poděbrady, conceived an utopian plan – a league of Christian rulers which would keep peace among them and provide for joint defense against the Turks. For this purpose he sent an embassy to persuade the courts of Western Europe but, unfortunately for our civilization, the scheme proved premature and it failed. Nevertheless, a knight who took part in the embassy in about 1460 left an account of his travels which has been made widely known by the Czech historical novelist, Alois Jirásek. It relates how the mission, after having visited the famous shrine of Santiago de Compostela in Spain, went to nearby Cape Finisterre, the end of the then-known world. They heard from Spanish and Portuguese mariners many legends and stories about mysterious lands beyond the sea, and the Czech envoys were fascinated by the inmensity of the ocean and seized by curiosity as to what truth these reports might hold. This spirit of inquiry must have been general among seafaring peoples, and some thirty years later Columbus set sail for the Indies.

Then, as for the past thousand years, the Czech lands were very much part of Western Europe, and the subsequent discovery of the Americas must have stirred the imagination of even this landlocked people. Proof of this is that Amerigo Vespucci's account of his discoveries, first printed in Florence in 1505, was promptly translated into Czech and published by Mikuláš Bakalář in Plzeň. (A new edition appeared in Prague in 1926.)

In the historical account I shall now give, most of the facts have been gathered and presented in a lecture delivered by my father, the late Vlastimil Kybal, a historian and diplomat, in 1935 at a plenary session of the Czech Academy of Sciences and Arts in Prague, of which he was a member. It was published as a monograph by the Academy that same year.[1] I hope that in a sense the Society under whose auspices we meet

---

[1] Vlastimil Kybal, *Po československých stopách v latinské Americe* (In Czechoslovak Footsteps in Latin America), Lecture delivered at plenary session on January 25, 1935 (Prague, Czech Academy of Sciences and Arts, 1935).

here might be considered as a successor, on a small scale, of the famous Czech Academy, and consequently that a topic worthy of the attention of the latter will not be out of place on this occasion. Furthermore, the fact that I am dealing with a historical subject while not being a historian but an economist, might be justified on the grounds of having specialized in Latin American affairs during most of my professional career, and also because of family ties with that area. Moreover, I do not believe that economics can be understood in a vacuum, and I have always tried to grasp the entire social process in Latin America as described by history and other social sciences.

Shortly after the discovery of America, two distant countries – namely, the Kingdom of Bohemia (Bohemia, Moravia and Silesia) and Spain (Castile and Aragon) – came to be ruled by monarchs of the same House of Habsburg. Actually, at the start, in the persons of Ferdinand I and Charles V, they were ruled by two brothers. After the Protestant defeat at the Battle of the White Mountain in 1620, Roman Catholicism again became the sole religion in the Bohemian Kingdom. These two facts – identity of religious affiliation and dynastic kinship – made possible a very interesting cultural relationship between the two realms.

These links led to a significant contribution, over a period of more than a century, by Jesuit priests, from the Kingdom of Bohemia, to the cultural and economic development of the Spanish and Portuguese colonies in the Americas. The Kingdom of Bohemia was one of the more important Provinces of the worldwide Society of Jesus; between 1664 and 1768, it sent some 124 priests to Latin America. Of these, over 40 were Czechs. It is a sad commentary on a nation torn by religious strife that at the time when Czech Jesuits were starting on their missions in Spanish America, some of their Protestant countrymen who had been forced to emigrate, and their descendants, were settling in the English and Dutch territories of what is now the United States.

The Czech Jesuits in Latin America served in the following countries: fifteen in Mexico, some nine in Paraguay, five in Peru and Bolivia, three in Chile, seven in New Granada (Colombia, Ecuador and Venezuela) and about six in Brazil. The impact of these highly educated and dedicated men was quite out of proportion to their small number. By the middle of the 17th century the Spanish conquest and exploration had been essentially completed, the administrative and ecclesiastical structure had been set up, and nearly all of the major cities that exist today had been founded. Yet there were still enormous areas which, because of geographic or climatic conditions, remained on the margin of economic and political life.

It is there – into the deserts and the jungles – that the Czech, German and Flemish Jesuits mainly went, as administrators, teachers and scientists. Their contribution to science and technology was particularly valuable since Central and Western Europe had already surpassed Spain in these fields. In this connection, we will note several of their works, written usually in Latin, in astronomy, botany and other natural sciences.

In Mexico, two Czech Jesuits acquired fame: Šimon Boruhradský, as an administrator, and Jiří (George) Hostinský, as a missionary and successful negotiator with the powerful Tarahumara Indians in the northern part of the country. Hostinský wrote four accounts dealing with the missions and a book entitled *Ophirium*. In 1724 Prague University published a history dealing with the uprisings of these same tribes by Josef Neumann, a German Jesuit from Bohemia, under the title *Historia Seditionum*.

In the vice-royalty of Peru, Czech priests were also in the frontier areas. This was chiefly the territory of the Mojos Indians in the Eastern lowlands of what is now Bolivia. Father František (Francis) Boryně, of the squires of Lhota, who was sent there from Bohemia with a group of eleven priests and eight monks, distinguished himself in the early 18th century. Together with Father Arlet of Silesia he founded the town of San Pedro. He christened the members of a large number of tribes, settled them in villages and taught them European agriculture and cattle raising. On two occasions Boryně was wounded by Indian arrows, and, to illustrate the remoteness of his station, he complained to a friend in Prague that during the 23 years he had been away he had received no news from Bohemia. Another Jesuit, Jan Eder from Kremnica in Slovakia, left an account of the Mojos territory which was printed in Buda, Hungary, under the title *Descriptio Provinciae Moxitorum in Regno Peruano*, in 1791, after his death. A Jesuit from Prague, Jan Roehr, drew the plans for the reconstruction of the famous cathedral in Lima, damaged by an earthquake in 1746, and wrote a meteorological treatise in Spanish entitled *El Conocimiento de los Tiempos*.

Father Supetius of Silesia, who was rector of the Jesuit college in Santiago, reported at the beginning of the 18th century that there were not enough novices from among young Chileans, since they preferred army service or commerce, and he clamored for reinforcements from his Bohemian province, adding that, together with the Flemish, they were preferred even to the natives from Spain. Among Czech Jesuits in Chile were Jan Josef Čermák and Václav (Wenceslas) Horský.

The greatest Jesuit enterprise at that time developed in Paraguay, but covered an area much larger than that of today's nation. The Society of Jesus had almost total power in that territory, which was inhabited mainly by numerous Guaraní Indians who had been Christianized and settled in so-called "reductions". This was a very successful endeavor, both from a cultural and economic standpoint, so much so that even Voltaire referred to it as a "triumph of humanity". Most of the priests from the Bohemian Province in Paraguay were German, but we might mention Václav Christman from Prague. In neighboring northern Argentina, Jindřich (Henry) Kordule distinguished himself as a missionary at the end of the 17th century.

A group of priests from Bohemia was sent to what was then called New Granada, of whom Vojtěch (Adalbert) Bukovský, of the Czech nobility, is noteworthy. In the Amazon watershed of this vice-royalty, part of which was disputed by the Portuguese from Brazil, two German Jesuits from Bohemia Province distinguished themselves; Henry Wenceslas Richter, who was killed by the Indians, and Samuel Fritz, who was more fortunate, having spent 42 years among them and thus having become known as the "Father of the Indians".

Among Jesuits in Brazil, an astronomer, Valentin Stansel, stands out. He was a professor at Prague University and in 1657 went to Bahia where he became dean of the Jesuit college. One of his studies, entitled *Observationes Americanae Cometae*, was published in Prague in 1683.

This is probably only a partial account of the Czech contribution in the 17th and 18th centuries, not only because the Jesuit Order was the most active one in Latin America, but also because of a greater availability of source materials. However, it is likely that additional contributions were made by members of other Catholic Orders, as well as by some laymen.

Since the end of the 18th century, an important aspect of the cultural contribution of the Czech lands to Latin America has been in the scientific field. This was initiated by Thaddeus Haenke, a naturalist educated in Prague University, who travelled throughout Latin America during the last period of Spanish rule and spent about 20 years in government service in Bolivia. His research was mainly in botany and geology; among his several studies, his publication, *Descripción del Perú*, printed in Lima, is outstanding. As a traveller and scientist in Spanish America he probably ranks with Alexander von Humboldt. Haenke's herbariums and family correspondence are at the National Museum in Prague which, together with the Náprstek Museum in the same city, houses the Latin American collections in the fields of natural history, archeology and ethnography of many scientists and travellers from the Czech lands.

Among travellers and explorers the most outstanding was E. Stanislav Vráz who in 1893 explored part of the river system between Venezuela and Brazil, formed by the Orinoco and Amazon rivers and their tributaries. Unfortunately, Vráz's two-volume description (*Napříč rovníkovou Amerikou*, published in Prague in 1900) has not been translated, not even in summary. It is a fascinating account of his trip over six rivers, in which he covered 2,000 kilometers and crossed 33 rapids. The hardships endured and determination required are shown by the fact that he had to change crews eleven times, including three times when they deserted him. In addition to his travels in other parts of the world, Vráz had a notable influence on the cultural life of the Czech settlers in the United States, where he married and lived many years. Among less pioneering travel description, we should not forget Josef Kořenský's journey to Mexico and other Latin American countries (*Amerika*, published in Prague in 1913).

In the natural sciences, perhaps the most significant contributions by Czechs were made in botany, while those in the social sciences were in anthropology and linguistics.

Benedikt Roezl, a botanist, spent twenty years (1854-1874) in Mexico and Central America, where he discovered a number of plants, some of which were named after him. He introduced several plants from these countries into Europe. Karel Domin, a distinguished professor of botany at Prague University, did research work in various Caribbean islands and published an account in three parts of his work and travel (*Dvacet tisíc mil po souši a po moři*, Prague, 1928-30).

Among anthropologists, Aleš Hrdlička (1869-1943) acquired world fame. A Czech from Bohemia, he made his career in the United States and his works are written in English. He was the distinguished curator of the Smithsonian Institution in Washington for most of his life. Hrdlička travelled widely in both North and South America, and his pioneering role in physical anthropology has been described in another lecture in this series. Suffice it to say that the results of Hrdlička's research in Spanish-speaking America are contained in his book, *Ancient Man in South America*, published in 1912.

In linguistics, A. V. Frič is noted for his research among the Bororo Indians in Mato Grosso, the results of which were published in England at the turn of the century. Another linguist, Čestmír Loukotka has studied Indian languages in Brazil and Argentina and since has published a number of studies since 1929 in Czech, Spanish, German and French.

Czech and Slovak emigration to Latin America began to be perceptible in the 1880's. It was interrupted during the first World War, and continued until the economic depression of the early 1930's. For climatic and economic reasons, it was concentrated mainly in the temperate zones of South America, especially Argentina and the States of São Paulo and Paraná in Brazil. By about 1930, Czech and Slovak settlers in Argentina were estimated to total some 40,000 and in Brazil, 7,000. In contrast with the emigrants who went to North America, it is probable that a higher proportion of the settlers in South America remained in the cities, mainly as industrial workers.

This emigration included its share, although a rather small one, of culturally active individuals. Some of them emigrated only temporarily, and their impact was felt much more in their home country than overseas. This was the case of Matěj Bencúr (1860-1928), a physician who practiced in Buenos Aires and in Punta Arenas, the southernmost town in Chile, and who is well known as a Slovak novelist under his pen-name, Martin Kukučin. A great Slovak patriot, Milan R. Štefánik, who was an astronomer in France, undertook observations in Brazil and an assignment in Ecuador, about which a book was subsequently published.[2] During the first World War, Štefánik became a general in the French Army and a close associate of Masaryk and Beneš in the founding of the Czechoslovak Republic.

Independent Czechoslovakia encouraged direct cultural and economic contrasts with Latin America, and in this effort several Czechoslovak diplomats took part. Among them Vlastimil Kybal, who was mentioned earlier, served as an envoy in Brazil, Argentina and Mexico. In addition to his works as a historian, he wrote six books in connection with his diplomatic assignments in Spain and Latin America, of which two were in Portuguese and four in Spanish.[3] For readers in Czechoslovakia, Kybal published three studies dealing with the political and economic conditions in Latin America.[4]

To some extent Czechoslovak businessmen, engineers and other tech-

---

[2] *Zápisník Dr. M. R. Stefánika z Equadoru z r. 1913*, edited by Vladimír Polívka (Bánská Bystrica, 1928).

[3] *Um Anno no Brasil* and *Segundo Anno no Brasil* (Rio de Janeiro, 1926 and 1927); *Tomáš G. Masaryk* (Madrid, 1930); *La República Checoslavaca* (Madrid, 1933 and Santiago, 1939); *La República checoslovaca y su formación como Estado democrático* (Mexico, 1938), and *La Defensa de Checoslovaquia* (Mexico, 1938). Also, *Los orígenes diplomáticos del Estado checoslovaco* (Madrid, 1930), a translation from its French original (Prague, 1929).

[4] *Jižní Amerika a Československo* (Prague, 1928); *Jižní Amerika ve světovém hospodářství* (Prague, 1934), and *Jižní Amerika: Přehled hospodářský, obchodní a politický* (Prague, 1935).

nicians have contributed to the economic development of Latin America since the turn of the century. This was the case, for instance, of Richard Lehký, a pioneer of the Argentine sugar industry. Several Czech engineering firms, particularly the world-renowned Škoda Company, designed and installed some manufacturing plants and delivered equipment for various major projects in Latin America. Mention should also be made of the factories established and operated by the world-wide Baťa enterprises in that region.

The Second World War and the Communist seizure of power in Czechoslovakia in 1948 have provoked a new wave of emigration to Latin America, but further departures were forcibly stopped shortly thereafter. This emigration included a high proportion of technically skilled and culturally active persons who would not have left their country were it not for political or racial persecution. In industry – particularly textiles, chemicals and engineering – as well as in commerce, their contribution was and still is notable. In the cultural sphere, it might be well to recall that among Czechs settled in other parts of the Free World, several renowned artists, such as Rafael Kubelík, Rudolf Firkušný and Jarmila Novotná, have repeatedly performed in Latin America.

Since 1948 a different type of relationship has been developing between Czechoslovakia and Latin America, one which does not quite fit into the topic of this lecture. It is limited mainly to countries which have diplomatic relations with the Prague government and is a relationship fully regulated by the latter, with political considerations dominating both cultural and economic contacts.

Taking a longer view of things, we have seen that the relationship between Latin America and Czechoslovakia (and her historical predecessor, the Kingdom of Bohemia) has been a surprisingly long one, covering a period of some three hundred years. Most of the time it was a tenuous contact, based often on the character and determination of a mere handful of men. It has varied considerably, mainly as the result of political factors. Quite likely it would have been very much different, had the Czechs and Slovaks had an independent state of their own during the whole period in question. Nevertheless, this relationship was a constructive one, because during nearly three centuries, and until 1948, the two areas were distinctly within the sphere of Western civilization, from both a political and cultural point of view. It can become fruitful again only if this basic condition is satisfied once more.

Trends in Czech and Slovak Economic Enterprise in the New World

V. E. ANDIC

In the absence of adequate and exhaustive studies on the industrial and business activities of Czechs and Slovaks in the United States and Canada, there seems to be a general misconception that most, if not all, Americans of Czech and Slovak descent are engaged in farm and factory occupations. There are, of course, other factors responsible for the lack of information concerning the extent of Czech and Slovak participation in American and Canadian economic enterprise. Among these are the following:

1. The industrialists and businessmen almost always operate in a neutral context that does not indicate the national origin of the owner.

2. Since most of these enterprising people are self-made individuals who have to work hard, with little capital during the early development of their business enterprises, their concentration often prevents their participation in time-consuming social activities.

3. Change of family name or isolation from their national communities often follows immigration.

Closer study, however, reveals evidence of the following main historical trends or stages:

I. The era of outstanding plantation owners and merchants of the XVII century;
II. The era of bankers, merchants and business leaders whose functions were important to their respective communities and who, in turn, became pioneering organizers of their respective local national groups;
III. The era of self-made men in industrial, agricultural and business pursuits;
IV. The period when founders of new industries and business ventures, forced out of their native countries where they already enjoyed excellent economic status, were forced by the Nazi and Communist totalitarian regimes to transfer their activities to free countries.
V. The era of professionals who became outstanding in their respective

fields thanks to new discoveries, inventions and other contributions to the economy.

In the first category we find two outstanding examples: Augustine Herrman (born in 1608), tobacco plantation owner and first tobacco trader in Virginia; and Frederick Philipse (born in 1626), "a Bohemian merchant prince", also known as the "founder of Yonkers". They both found opportunities for large-scale trading in the Netherlands. Herrman had the distinction of being "the first Czech in America", the founder of the Virginia trade who extended his export from Virginia and New Netherlands, and shipped tobacco, furs and salt to Europe. He made maps of Virginia and Maryland. Philipse was considered one of the wealthiest merchants of the pre-revolutionary era. In addition to his residence in Yonkers, the Manor Hall, he also had a palatial home in Philipsburg. Author Edgar Hagaman Hall, L. H. D., writes in *Philipse Manor Hall at Yonkers, N. Y.*, published by The American Scenic and Historic Society, New York, N.Y., 1926 (p. 45): "The career of the founder of Yonkers was one of the most remarkable of his time. ... The resources by which he became the foremost merchant and one of the foremost citizens of his generation were his craft as an architect and builder, his industry and shrewdness as a businessman and his substantial character."

Leaders in economic activities of the second category could never have had a chance to rise to their economic positions had there not been a distinct and considerable national community. For instance, a Czech bookbinder, August Geringer, arrived in the United States in 1869. Six years after his arrival, Geringer founded in Chicago the first Czech daily newpaper in America, *Svornost* (Harmony). At that time there were about 85,000 Czechs in America, and a quarter of those were concentrated in Chicago, the city which, to the present day, is the metropolis of American Czechoslovaks, the center of all important national and fraternal organizations. Geringer established a publishing company which printed other newspapers, yearbooks, dictionaries, etc. Similarly, among the Slovaks, Peter V. Rovnianek, formerly a clergyman, organized the first national Slovak society in America and assumed economic leadership among the Slovaks of America as publisher, shipping agent and banker. Michael Bosak organized a bank in Scranton, Pennsylvania; he also founded industrial and farmers' banks in Slovakia and the "American-Slovak Bank" in Bratislava, with a branch in Prague. Neither Rovnianek nor Bosak had special preparation for the economic role they were to play. Author Thomas Capek, called the historian of the American Czechs, served in various economic capacities and, as President of the Bank of Europe, his economic advice was sought by his countrymen.

There are innumerable examples of self-made men. One of them is Frank J. Vlchek, machine-tool industrialist in Cleveland, Ohio, born in Budin, Bohemia in 1871. Vlchek was known in Cleveland to be "to the tool industry what Ford is to the automobile trade." The Vlchek Tool Company in 1917 increased its capital to $ 900,000 with $ 600,000 in preferred stock and $ 300,000 in common stock. Another example is provided by the firm of B. Schwanda and Sons, which occupies the top-ranking position in the pearl button industry in the United States. In recent years the firm has normally employed 700 people. Below we list some other outstanding figures and firms:

James Triner, founder of Triner's Scale Company, makers of the finest scales in the United States which today appear in every U. S. Post Office;

Joseph Bulova, founder of the Bulova Watch Company;

John David Hertz, who established (in 1916) the Yellow Cab Corporation in Chicago and Omnibus Corporation of America;

John H. Shary, President of the Texas Fruit Growers Exchange, with $ 300,000 capital, developed the agricultural and citrus fruit industry in the Lower Rio Grande Valley, Texas; his irrigation plan proved so successful that thousands of people found a livelihood on the soil;

Andrew Duda, whose crop operations resulted (in 1943) in a net return running into seven figures, which probably sets the record for the success of any one family in Florida.

Many new industries have been established in the United States and Canada. In the initial stages, some of these industries were considered "refugee industries", having been started by industrialists many of whom were refugees from Nazism and hoped to return to liberated Czechoslovakia after the war, although this was prevented by the Communists. Outstanding examples include the following:

Henry Waldes (1884-1941) who died on his way to the United States from a concentration camp in Germany before the end of World War II, was a manufacturer of several zippers and fasteners. He had factories in Czechoslovakia; Dresden, Germany; Warsaw, Poland; Paris, France; Barcelona, Spain; and Long Island City, New York.

The Bata Shoe Company started operations during World War II in Belcamp, Maryland and in Batawa near Frankfort, Ontario.[1] The Canadian Bata Shoe

---

[1] While the Bata Shoe Company operated in many countries before the advent of Nazism the impetus for the expanded production in the United States was provided by the start of the Second World War.

Company gave impetus to several new enterprises. The Bata Shoe Company presents a case of a private enterprise operating on the basis of planning and facing the increasing complexities of government regulations of many different kinds.

The Alaska Pine Company, founded by Leon Koerner and his brothers, Otto and Walter, provided a startling lesson to all British Columbia industries in new methods, business structure and employer-employee relations.

Joseph F. Ruzicka is a well-known cultivator of roses. Hardly a florist shop in New York City does not have roses from Ruzicka, Inc. The firm's large gardens are located at Florham, New Jersey.

Examples of new industries may be found in many other fields, such as glove-making (Fischl in Canada), flax products (Hesky in Western Ontario), glass-making (Technical Glass, Ltd., a firm organized in Montreal in 1942 by Reiner; Kreuz Brothers, suppliers of glass products to major stores like Lord and Taylor, Wanamakers, Marshall Field, and so on;) leather goods and plastics (Hans Wyman) and wine production (Korbel in California).

There are hundreds of examples of outstanding achievements in many professions. For instance, Leopold Eidlitz, originally from Prague, the author of *The Nature and Function of Art, More Especially of Architecture* (1881) included among his buildings the Dry Dock Savings Bank and the State Capitol at Albany. Cyrus Lazelle Warner (1853-1921) built the New York Times building. Marc Eidlitz built the New York Hospitals (Presbyterian, St. Francis, St. Vincent), the Metropolitan Opera House and others. The New York Stock Exchange, the Riverside Church, The Cloisters Museum, Columbia University Library, and other renowned buildings were the work of Marc Eidlitz' sons Robert James Eidlitz and Otto Marc Eidlitz.

Hard work, inventiveness and thrift, we see in this brief article, have, together, been the miracle maker of ages, as today, benefiting both the present and future generations.

BIBLIOGRAPHY

Canadian House of Commons Record, January 31, 1941 (on Koerner's Saw Mills in British Columbia).
Thomas Čapek, *Ancestry of Frederick Philipse, First Lord and Founder of Philipse Manor of Yonkers* (New York, The Peabar Company, 1939).
Thomas Čapek and Thomas Čapek, Jr., *The Czechs and Slovaks in American Banking* (New York, Fleming H. Revell Co., 1920).
Daniel Droba (Editor), *Czech and Slovak Leaders in Metropolitan Chicago* (University of Chicago, Slavonic Club, 1934).

Fortune Magazine, "Hans Wyman Rushes Big Business – A Millionaire Czech Refugee's Comeback in the New World", April 1947.
L. W. Heck, *Augustine Herrman, Beginner of the Virginian Tobacco Trade of New Amsterdam and First Lord of Bohemia Manor* (Englewood, Ohio, 1941).
Estelle Hudson and Henry R. Maresh, *Czech Pioneers of the Southwest* (Dallas, Texas, South West Press, 1934).
Pavel Jamarík, on Peter V. Rovnianek's rise to economic power, *The Czechoslovak Review*, October, 1921.
Štefan Janšák, on American Slovak Bank, *Život Dr. Pavla Blahu* (Bratislava, 1946), Vol. II.
Guido Kisch, *The Search for Freedom* (London, Edw. Goldston and Son, Ltd., 1949).
Manufacturing and Industrial Engineering, Bata makes science of labor relations, (Toronto, Ontario, Consolidated Press, 1942).
E. P. Weber, "This is the Story of Slavia; on Duda's million dollar farming, University of Florida", in the *Lutheran Beacon Magazine*, August and September 1947.

Czech and Slovak Press Outside Czechoslovakia

VOJTĚCH N. DUBEN

CZECH AND SLOVAK MIGRATION

At the end of World War I – when the Czechoslovak Republic was established – there were over two million Czech and Slovak emigrants in foreign lands, almost one quarter the number of Czech and Slovak inhabitants of the new state.[1] More than 1,240,000 of them lived in the United States, about 25,000 in Canada, and 10,000 in South America. There were 850,000 expatriate Czechs and Slovaks in Europe, mostly in Austria, Yugoslavia, Hungary, Rumania, Germany, Poland and Russia, and small groups in Africa, Asia and Australia.

The flowering of the émigrés' cultural, social and political activities coincided with the height of the tide of Czech and Slovak emigration during the 1920's. The decline which followed was interrupted by a short spurt of activity in the United States during World War II and by the Communist overthrow of the Czechoslovak democratic regime in 1948, which set off an influx of 60,000 Czech and Slovak refugees to Western Europe. Most significantly strengthened by additions from this last group were the Czech and Slovak communities in Australia, which have grown to include over 15,000 people. Czech and Slovak groups in Canada and Western Europe were also considerably strengthened, and new Czech and Slovak blood began to pour into the United States.[2] Slovaks, followed by a smaller number of Czechs, renewed their immigration to South America, especially to Argentina.

The earliest Czech emigration was religiously inspired and dated back to the 17th century. The first group of exiles was composed of Czech (Moravian) Brethren under the leadership of John A. Comenius. They settled in Poland, Germany, the Netherlands, Sweden and England, and

---

[1] Czechoslovakia's 1921 census shows 8,760,957 Czechs and Slovaks.
[2] Over 30,000 newcomers in the period of 1948-1962.

some came later to America (Augustine Herrman 'Bohemian', in 1633).[3] The first Slovaks, who also emigrated for religious reasons, went in the 18th century to southern Hungary, an area that is now part of Yugoslavia. In the middle of the 19th century the Czechs began to emigrate for political reasons. Their goal was mostly Western Europe, but some also went to the United States. In the 1860's they began to leave their native country for the United States, Russia, etc., because of economic difficulties, and this wave lasted about 60 years. Slovaks began to emigrate for similar reasons in larger numbers in the 1880's – first mostly to the United States, then to South America, Canada and Western Europe. There were additional groups of Czech and Slovak political exiles in Western Europe, Russia and the United States during both World Wars. The newest political emigration began after the Communist coup d'état in Prague in 1948 and still continues.

Czechs and Slovaks living in foreign countries have played an important role in the history of their old country, especially by their effort to found the Czechoslovak Republic during World War I, and to liberate Czechoslovakia from the Nazi yoke during World War II. The Czech and Slovak press outside Czechoslovakia shared this role and even now it is an important element in the anti-Communist struggle.

The Czech and Slovak minorities in Austria, especially the Czech minority in Vienna, have a history of their own which began during the 300 years (1620-1918) when the Kingdom of Bohemia including Moravia was part of the Habsburg empire. Czech people who migrated to Vienna and other Austrian cities in those days did not consider themselves – at least up until 1918 – as "emigrants" or living abroad. When the Austro-Hungarian empire disintegrated and the Czechoslovak Republic was founded, over 500,000 Czechs and Slovaks remained in the Austrian Republic. Some of them later repatriated.[4] The role which Vienna and Austria played in the history of Czech migration was paralleled in the case of the Slovaks by Budapest and Hungary since Slovakia was for a thousand years a part of the Hungarian Kingdom.

The duality of Czech-Austrian and Slovak-Hungarian allegiance before 1918 explains why the first Czech newspapers appeared almost simultaneously in Prague and in Vienna, and why newspapers for readers in Slovakia were published not only in Slovakia but also in Budapest and Vienna.

---

[3] Thomas Čapek, *The Čechs (Bohemians) in America* (Boston and New York, 1920).
[4] Stanislav Klíma, *Čechové a Slováci za hranicemi* (Prague, 1925).

FIRST NEWSPAPERS

The forerunners of actual newspapers appeared in the Czech lands as early as 1515 but the very first Czech publication entitled "noviny" ("news" or "newspaper") had already appeared in Bohemia in 1495. The first regular Czech newspaper, a semiweekly called the *Sobotní a úterní pražské poštovské noviny*, was launched in Prague in 1719 by Karel František Rosenmueller (publisher) and František Kozuri (editor).[5] The first Czech newspaper outside the territory of present Czechoslovakia was published 200 years ago (April 1, 1761 – July 27, 1761) in Vienna, Austria by Leopold Kalivoda, a university and court printer. It was called the *Denník Wídeňský"*.[6]

In the modern sense of newspaper publishing, Czech journalism did not start until 1848. It was connected with the name of Karel Havlíček Borovský, editor of the famous *Národní Noviny*. Karel Havlíček Borovský was not only the founder of modern Czech journalism in the Czech lands, but to some extent he also inspired the founding of a Czech émigré press in the United States. In the 1850's, Czech immigrants in America were in direct contact with either Havlíček or his newspaper. Their first Czech-language newspaper, published in Racine, Wisconsin, on January 1, 1860, was named the *Slowan Amerikánský* after Havlíček's second periodical, the *Slovan*.[7]

The second Czech newspaper in America appeared three weeks later in St. Louis, Missouri and was named the *Národní Noviny* after Havlíček's first newspaper. It marked the beginning of a long line of Czech-American liberal papers, whose tradition is kept alive even today by several major newspapers.

On the conservative side there were fewer but no less important Czech Catholic newpapers. The first of these came out in October 1867 in Chicago, Ill. At the end of the 19th century there was established in Chicago the Czech Benedictine press which still carries the conservative banner.

The third category of Czech newspapers in America is the Socialist press founded in 1870. Its history has been marked by splinter movements and controversy. In the 1880's the Socialist movement and its press were split by anarchists. Shortly after World War I the Communists

---

[5] Josef Volf, *Dějiny novin v Čechách do r. 1848* (Prague, 1930).
[6] Karl Matal, "Streifzüge durch die Geschichte der Wiener Tschechen (I)", *Die österreichische Nation*, Vienna, July/August 1962.
[7] Tomáš Čapek, *Padesát let českého tisku v Americe* (New York, 1911).

Czechs and Slovaks outside Czechoslovakia and their periodicals (1925-1963*)

	1925			January 1963												
	Czechs and Slovaks	Number of Periodicals	Czechs and Slovaks	**Czech periodicals**							**Slovak periodicals**					Periodicals in Other Languages
				Total	Dailies	Semiweeklies and Weeklies	Semimonthlies and Monthlies	Quarterlies	Yearbooks	Circulation Per Year (in thousands)	Total	Dailies	Semiweeklies and Weeklies	Semimonthlies and Monthlies	Quarterlies	Yearbooks	Circulation Per Year (in thousands)	
Argentina	8,000	1	15-20,000	4	—	—	4	—	—	150	2	—	—	2	—	—	10	—
Australia	100	—	15,000	6	—	2	4	—	—	1	—	—	—	—	—	—	—	—
Austria	303,000	14	25-50,000	1	—	—	1	—	—	800	—	—	—	—	—	—	—	—
Belgium	1,000	—	10,000	2	—	—	—	2	—	5	—	—	—	—	—	—	—	2
Brazil	1,500	—	10,000	—	—	—	—	—	—	—	—	—	—	—	—	—	—	4
Bulgaria	3,000	2	2,000	—	—	—	—	—	—	—	—	—	—	—	—	—	—	1
Canada	24,800	—	75,000	7	—	2	5	—	—	500	7	—	2	2	—	3	500	—
France	22,000	—	20,000	3	—	—	3	—	1	10	3	—	—	3	—	—	130	—
Germany	70,400	1	5-10,000	10	—	—	4	5	—	155	1	—	1	—	—	—	200	1
Hungary	192,500	1	100,000	—	—	—	—	—	—	—	—	—	—	—	—	—	—	—
Holland	1,000	—	1,000	1	—	—	1	1	—	10	1	—	—	1	—	—	50	—
Italy	2,500	—	2,000	3	—	—	2	1	—	55	—	—	—	—	—	—	—	—
Poland	58,700	—	10-20,000	2	—	—	2	—	—	200	1	—	1	—	—	—	130	—
Rumania	47,000	—	20,000	—	—	—	—	—	—	—	—	—	—	—	—	—	—	1
Switzerland	2,000	2	2,000	1	—	1	1	2	—	4	—	—	—	—	—	—	—	—
United Kingdom	600	—	4,000	4	—	2	1	9	—	60	1	—	—	—	—	—	—	—
USA	1,242,000	123	918,000	47	2	12	21	—	3	24,420	34	—	8	18	3	5	6,160	9
USSR	16,300	—	?	—	—	—	—	—	—	—	—	—	—	—	—	—	—	—
Venezuela	?	—	2-5,000	—	—	1	—	—	1	300	1	—	1	1	1	—	5	—
Yugoslavia	138,200	5	100,000	2	—	—	—	—	—	—	2	—	—	—	—	—	400	—
Total	2,134,600	149	about 1,500,000	93	2	18	49	19	5	26,670	52	—	13	27	4	8	7,585	18

* All 1925 figures are quoted from: Stanislav Klíma, *Čechové a Slováci za hranicemi* (Prague, 1925). – The 1963 population figures are the author's estimates with the exception of the United States and Canada. The U.S. figure of 918,000 based on the 1960 U.S. Census represents first and second generation of immigrants from Czechoslovakia including Germans, Hungarians and Ruthenians – but excluding Czechs and Slovaks born elsewhere in Europe and all Czechs and Slovaks of third and fourth generations who in many cases (Texas) are still bilingual. The Canadian figure of 75,000 Czechs and Slovaks is based on the 1961 Canadian Census.

TABLE 2

Czechs and Slovaks in the United States and their periodicals* 1860-1963 (Population in thousands)

Year	Foreign-Born Czechs	Foreign-Born Slovaks	Native or Mixed Parentage Czechs	Native or mixed Parentage Slovaks	Total Foreign Stock Czechs	Total Foreign Stock Slovaks	Total Foreign Stock Czechs and Slovaks	Estimated Attribution to Czechoslovakia as Country of Origin	Periodicals Czech Total	Periodicals Czech Dailies	Periodicals Slovak Total	Periodicals Slovak Dailies
1860	25				25				2	—	—	—
1865	40				120				3	—	—	—
1870	85								8	—	—	—
1880	118				160				8	3	3	—
1890	157								24	4	?	—
1900	229	166	311	118	539	284	824		51	7	?	—
1910	235	275	388	345	623	620	1,243		103	8	44	1
1920	189	219							85	9	39	3
1925									84	?	?	?
1930	160	172	279	284	520	484	1,004	1,382 three generations	80	6	?	?
1940								1,877	?	5	31	2
1945	Born in Czechoslovakia: 278		Second gener. from Czechosl.: 706			Two generations from Czechosl. 984		2,212	57	5	?	?
1950	92	125				Two generations from Czechoslovakia: 918			?	5	?	1
1960									46	3	30	1
1963 January			All generations of Czechs and Slovaks: about 2,000						44	2	29	—

* Yearbooks are not included here... The 1860 and 1865 estimates of Czech population were made by contemporary Czech-American journalists. The 1870-1890 figures are taken from corresponding U.S. Censuses. First wave of Slovak immigrants reached the U.S. in 1880's but U.S. Census tabulates Slovaks for the first time in 1910. Starting with 1930 U.S. Census all immigrants from Czechoslovakia (including Germans, Hungarians and Carpatho-Russians) are usually combined into one figure. But the census sometimes divides the immigrants by their mother

detached themselves from the Socialist movement. Ironically, the Communist press survived and the newspapers of the democratic Socialists (with one minor exception) ceased to exist.

Club journals and religious periodicals comprise the fourth category. The first Czech daily outside Czechoslovakia was the Chicago *Svornost* whose first issue was published on October 25, 1875. It died on May 19, 1957 having established a record life span in the history of Czech and Slovak journalism.[8]

In the half-century after 1860, some 320-odd Czech nespapers were founded in the United States. The growth continued until the 1920's, when new immigration laws throttled the influx of fresh blood. In 1920, when the Czech press reached its circulation peak, there were 85 Czech newspapers in the United States, including four dailies in Chicago, two dailies in New York, two dailies in Cleveland and one daily in Omaha.[9] According to the 1920 census, there were then in the United States 620,000 first- and second-generation Czechs. In 1960, the corresponding census total was less than 450,00.

Today (in January 1963), American Czechs put out 47 publications with an annual total of 24,420,000 copies, including two dailies in Chicago and Cleveland, one semiweekly, 11 weeklies, 21 semimonthlies and monthlies, nine bimonthlies and quarterlies, and three yearbooks.[10]

SLOVAK JOURNALISM

The first regular newspaper published in Slovakia (mostly in the Czech language) appeared in Bratislava in 1783 (*Presspurské Noviny*). As early as 1848 the *Prjatel Ludu*, the first Slovak-oriented newspaper was published in Budapest by Hungarian government officials. Vienna followed the lead in 1849 with the semi-official *Slovenské Noviny*. Modern journalism in Slovakia started with the first issue of L'udovít Štúr's *Slovenskje Národňje Novini*, launched in Bratislava in 1845.[11]

---

[8] The Prague daily *Národní Listy* (1861-1941) is second and Brno *Moravské Noviny* third. Both dailies ceased to exist during W.W. II.
[9] Thomas Čapek, *The Čechs* (*Bohemians*) *in America* (Boston and New York, 1920).
[10] V. N. Duben, *Czech and Slovak Periodical Press Outside Czechoslovakia – Its History and Status as of January 1962* (Washington and New York, Czechoslovak Society of Arts and Sciences in America, Inc., 1962). The quoted figures are revised in this paper to show the situation in January 1963.
[11] Dr. Michal Potemra, *Bibliografia slovenských novín a časopisov do roku 1918* (Turčanský Sv. Martin, Czechoslovakia, 1958).

The first Slovak periodical outside Austria-Hungary was launched in 1885 in Pittsburgh under the name of *Bulletin*. It was a simple, mimeographed information sheet published by Jan Slovenský, an employee of the local Austro-Hungarian Consulate. The first printed Slovak newspaper, the *Amerikanszko-Szlovenszke Noviny* was published in 1886 also by Jan Slovenský.[12] The first newspaper printed in correct Slovak, however (the first two periodicals were written in a Slovak dialect) was the *Nová Vlast*, established by Edward Schwartz-Markovič in March 1888 in Streator, Ill. *Nová Vlast* lasted less than a year. In the meantime Peter V. Rovnianek became the co-owner and editor of the *Amerikanszko-Szlovenszke Noviny*.[13] He not only imbued it with the spirit of Slovak nationalism, but also increased the paper's popularity.[14] At the end of the 19th century its circulation reached 30,000. Before 1918, no other Slovak newspaper, not even in Slovakia, equaled this figure.

While the first Czech periodicals in the United States led their readers to think politically and chiefly advocated liberalism, the Slovak press had a more complicated task. In the first place it had to imbue the Slovak community with the desire to read a newspaper. Once this was accomplished, it tried to instill in them the Slovak national spirit. This was not easy considering the 1,000-year Hungarian rule over Slovakia.

The Slovak Catholic press in the United States began with the *Jednota*, the organ of the fraternalistic First Catholic Slovak Union of America. The *Jednota* originated in 1890 in Plymouth and Hazleton, Penna., as an independent newspaper and in May 1891 it became the official organ of the Union. In 1901, in Pittsburgh, Penna., Peter V. Rovnianek launched the first Slovak daily outside Slovakia and Hungary, the *Slovenský Denník*, which, unfortunately, lasted only about 10 years. P. V. Rovnianek introduced into the Slovak-American press not only the spirit of Slovak nationalism, but also its first liberal trend. In addition he helped organize American Slovaks on a nation-wide basis, stressing the idea of Czech-Slovak cooperation and friendly competition.

The Slovak Socialist press in America had its beginning very early in the century. After World War I it was almost completely taken over by the Communists.

Slovak journalism in America reached its peak in the early 1920's when,

---

[12] Konstantin Čulen, *J. Slovenský, Životopis zakladatela prvých slovenských novin Amerike* (Winnipeg, Man., Kanadský Slovák, 1954).
[13] P. V. Rovnianek-Rovinov, *Zápisky za živa pochovaného* (New York, 1924).
[14] P. V. Rovnianek changed the title of his newspaper from the original Hungarian spelling to the Slovak *Amerikánsko-Slovenské Noviny*.

according to the 1920 census, first- and second-generation American Slovaks totalled 620,000. They then had three dailies, and 41 weeklies and monthlies. By 1960 the number of Slovaks of the first and second generations dropped to about 470,000, and their periodicals to 35.[15]

In January 1963, there were in the United States eight Slovak weeklies, three semimonthlies, 15 monthlies, three quarterlies and five yearbooks and almanacs.[16]

American Czechs and Slovaks also publish nine English-language periodicals such as club journals, political reviews and general information bulletins.

CANADA AND SOUTH AMERICA

There were 9,000 Czechs and 16,000 Slovaks in Canada in 1920. Most of them were farmers and dock workers, but there was a sprinkling of artisans in the larger cities. The first sizeable immigration wave of Czechs and Slovaks hit Canada between the two World Wars. In 1945, the Czech and Slovak population there amounted to 50,000, and another influx of fresh blood was just imminent – the anti-Communists fleeing after the coup d'état in February, 1948. Today's Czech and Slovak population in Canada is about 75,000.

The first Canadian Slovak periodical, the *Slovenské Slovo*, was published in 1910 in Bellevue, B. C. Its editor and publisher was Juraj Kleskeň. The Slovak *Robotnické Slovo* came out in 1931 and a Czech sister publication, called the *Jiskra*, was founded later. In 1940, during the Hitler-Stalin rapprochement, Communist-type organizations in Canada, including Czech and Slovak, were outlawed and in June of that year, their press was shut down. When the situation changed under the impact of the Nazi-Soviet war, Slovak Communists resumed publication under the new name of *Ludové Zvesti*. The periodical is still being published.

Canadian Slovaks subscribing to the idea of Slovak autonomy or an independent Slovak state are represented by the Canadian Slovak League, founded in 1932. Since the early 1940's, they have been publishing a weekly, the *Kanadský Slovák*.

---

[15] According to the U. S. Census there were in the United States in 1960 918,000 people born in what is today's Czechoslovakia, and their children. Of this total, 92,000 spoke Czech and 125,000 Slovak as their mother tongue.
[16] V. N. Duben, *Czech and Slovak Periodical Press Outside Czechoslovakia*. The quoted figures are revised to show the situation in January 1963.

Democratic Czechs and Slovaks advocating the idea of a united Czechoslovakia have been organized for years in local benevolent and cultural societies. After the Nazi occupation of Czechoslovakia in March, 1939, these groups formed the Czechoslovak National Alliance of Canada in Toronto, which until 1948 supported a Czech and Slovak weekly, the *Nová Vlast*.

After the 1948 events in Prague, the ideals of democratic Czechoslovakia were propounded by an independent weekly, the *Čas*, edited and published by Jan Dočkálek. The periodical was followed in 1950 by a weekly, the *Nový Domov*, and others.

Canada has now seven Czech periodicals (two weeklies) and seven Slovak periodicals (including two weeklies and three yearbooks). The Canadian Czechoslovaks have two English-language publications.

Before World War I South America attracted only a scattering of Czechs and Slovaks, but in the early 1920's the situation changed. Just before World War II, a partial count showed that Argentina had become the home of more than 40,000 Czechs and Slovaks. Brazil had welcomed 10,000 of them, Uruguay more than 2,000 and Paraguay about 1,500. The oldest Czech-language periodical in the area was the *Jihoamerický Čechoslovák*, a Buenos Aires, Argentina weekly which first went to print in 1923.[17] The first Slovak language publication, entitled the *Slovenský Lud*, was launched in 1925, also in Buenos Aires. Both papers died in the 1940's. After 1948, Argentina, Brazil, Venezuela and other Latin American countries opened their doors to the Czechs and Slovaks who had fled their country after the Communist coup d'état. Most immigrant publications put out by Czechs and Slovaks in South America are mimeographed and come out irregularly; their publishers and places of publication change frequently. Their life-span is usually short, and most of them are written in Slovak. The author's attempt to compile their list for 1962 shows only two Czech periodicals in Brazil, one Slovak paper in Venezuela and two Slovak sheets in Argentina.

AUSTRALIA AND NEW ZEALAND

The Czech and Slovak community in Australia and New Zealand is of relatively recent origin. The first immigrant from Czech lands probably came in 1838. Others followed sporadically; until in the 1920's there were

[17] Stanislav Klíma, *Čechové a Slováci za hranicemi* (Prague, 1925).

only about 100 immigrants of our group, mostly Czech, in Australia. No periodicals were published, only occasional bulletins. By the end of 1961, however, some 10,000 Czech and Slovak anti-Communist refugees had already acquired Australian citizenship and had formed several Czech, Slovak and Czechoslovak organizations.[18] The history of their press reflects this combination.

The first publication was the Czechoslovak *Hlas Domova*, which appeared in January 15, 1950. In 1950 a Czech bi-monthly, the *Pacific*, was published in New Zealand. In 1952 it moved to Sydney, Australia. The Slovak group in Australia published between January, 1953 and 1960 a monthly, the *Štít*, first printed, then mimeographed. More Czech periodicals appeared and expired. Now there is only one regular periodical in Australia and New Zealand, the *Hlas Domova*, published twice a month in Czech in Melbourne. At least three other publications are club papers and bulletins.

EUROPE

As reflected in grave markers, house signs and old documents, Vienna, Austria was the temporary or permanent home of Czechs as early as the Middle Ages. Until 1918, when the empire disintegrated, Czechs and Slovaks moved freely to Austria in search of a better livelihood or political fortunes. After World War I, 141,000 Czechs and Slovaks returned to their homeland. Even this mass repatriation left behind about one-half million Czechs and several thousand Slovaks.

The earliest Czech publications in Vienna, dating back to 1761 (Kalivoda's *Denník Wídeňský*), were devoted primarily to the problems of culture, education, and general enlightenment. The Czech-language *Slovenské Noviny*, published in Vienna for readers in Slovakia, marked in 1849 the beginnings of Slovak journalism in Austria. The first newspaper truly designed for the Czech-Austrian minority was called the *Slovan* and made its bow in 1870.[19]

The mass repatriation which followed World War I weakened the minority in Austria, but the Socialist daily *Dělnické Listy*, and its middle-of-the road counterpart, the *Vídeňský Deník*, as well as about a dozen

---

[18] Available Australian statistics now support an estimate of 15,000 Czechs and Slovaks who came to Australia from Europe. Not included in the estimate are Australians of Czech and Slovak parentage.
[19] Stanislav Klíma, *Čechové a Slováci za hranicemi* (Prague, 1925).

other Czech and one Slovak periodical continued publication. The Nazi Anschluss in 1938 and World War II suppressed them all.

Between 1945 and 1948, the Czech and Slovak minorities in Austria shrank further, thanks to a new repatriation wave, but those who remained tried to return to their pre-war activities. A new weekly, called the *Vídeňské Menšinové Listy*, was published, but it was hampered by local Communists. The Communist coup in 1948 in Czechoslovakia helped to clarify the issues, and two new weeklies subsequently started their ideological competition. In addition to these two weeklies Viennese Czechs publish four political reviews and club papers.

Two centuries (1761-1962) have seen more than 200 Czech and Slovak periodicals published in Austria, mostly in Vienna.

Czech emigrant journalism in Europe, however, dates back to the arrival into exile of Josef Václav Frič, former leader of Czech students on the Prague barricades in the revolutionary year of 1848. Frič, the first known modern Czech political exile, started in Geneva in January, 1861 his monthly *Čech – La Voix libre de la Bohème* in the Czech language.[20] The revolutionary publication folded for lack of funds after the first twelve issues. J. V. Frič put out another Czech-language exile periodical, the *Blaník*, in Berlin. A monthly called the *Vlast* (the organ of Czech emigrant societies in non-Austrian Europe), was founded in 1876 in Stuttgart, following in the footsteps of Frič's democratic and liberal journalism. The periodical moved in 1886 to London, England and in 1890 to Berlin, where it ceased to exist during World War I.[21] The centers of Czech and Slovak emigrant activities in Europe then moved to France, Italy, England and Russia.

Czech groups in the Weimar Republic consisted primarily of communities which had once bordered on the Czech and Moravian language areas, or groups descended from 18th-century colonists, and, more recently, of workers and artisans who settled in German cities before Hitler's takeover. It is estimated that in 1933 there were 70,000 Czechs in Germany. Their semi-official organ was a semi-monthly called the *Zahraniční Čechoslovák*, which followed the democratic tradition of the *Vlast*. The *Zahraniční Čechoslovák* was published in Berlin from 1920 until 1933.[22]

The next period of Czech (and Slovak) journalism in Germany started

---

[20] J. V. Frič, *V dopisech a denících*, Karel Cvejn, edt. (Prague, Československý spisovatel, 1955).
[21] František Štědronský, *Zahraniční krajanské noviny, časopisy a kalendáře* (Prague, Národní knihovna, 1958).
[22] Ibid.

in the late 1940's when West German DP Camps became the haven for some 50,000 Czech and Slovak anti-communist exiles who produced dozens of periodicals, beginning with the *Svoboda, Československé Noviny* and *Integrál-Křižáci* on the Czech or Czechoslovak side and with the *Slobodné Slovensko, Informátor* and other periodicals published by various Slovak groups.

Now being published in the German Federal Republic are eight Czech, three Slovak and one German-language publication.

Czechoslovak journalistic history in Italy starts with a Slovak biweekly called *Vyst'ahovalecký Oznam*, published in Trieste for Slovak emigrants from 1903 to 1907.[23] The first Czech and Slovak political periodical, called the *V boj*, was published in Italy by the Czechoslovak Army-in-Exile from January 1917 to 1919. After the 1948 coup d'état in Prague several thousand Czech and Slovak political refugees were brought to Italy from West German DP camps. These exiles published several periodicals, but as their editors emigrated abroad, the publications died in short order. Remaining in Italy today are a few thousand - perhaps only hundreds - of Czechs and Slovaks, who publish three Czech, one Slovak and one English-language periodical.

Starting in the 19th century, France was the goal of Czech and Slovak intellectuals, students and artists as well as political émigrés. With J. V. Frič's assistance, the first European society or club of Czech emigrés was founded in Paris in 1862, just 12 years after the founding of the first Czech expatriate society in New York City. At the very beginning of World War I Paris became the base for various Czech or Czechoslovak organizations striving to liberate Czech and Slovak provinces from the Austro-Hungarian yoke. All of them published periodicals, every one of which was short-lived. As soon as T. G. Masaryk's movement secured a firm foothold, Dr. Lev Sychrava, a Czech exile journalist in Annemasse began publishing the *Československá Samostatnost* which became the official organ of the Czechoslovak political movement abroad.[24] In April, 1916 the periodical was transferred to Paris and at the end of the war to Prague.

Early in 1939 Paris was the birthplace of the weekly *Československý Odboj* (started by Dr. Štefan Osuský), a temporary organ of the second Czechoslovak independence movement led by Dr. Eduard Beneš.

The new wave of Czechoslovak refugees after the Communist victory

---

[23] Dr. Michal Potemra, *Bibliografia slovenských novín a časopisov do roku 1918* (Turč. Sv. Martin, 1958).
[24] Dr. Lev Sychrava, "Několik vzpomínek ze Švýcarska", *Sborník vzpomínek na T. G. Masaryka*, Prague, 1930.

in 1948 produced several exile periodicals, most of them short lived. The most important were *Svobodný Zítřek* (a Czech periodical) and *Slovenský Národ* (a Slovak publication).

At present, Czechs in France publish two Czech and three French-language periodicals.

The second European center of the first Czechoslovak independence movement during World War I was Russia. The Czech population in Russia are descendants of farmers who came to Wollin in the 19th century and artisans who settled during the same period in Ukrainian and Russian cities. During World War I, these emigrants or their sons provided the basis for the Czechoslovak Corps, an army of fifty to sixty thousand Czechs and Slovaks who fought against the Central Powers on the Eastern front. At the war's end, they made their way to the Pacific by crossing the vast expanse of Siberia on a single-track railroad in spite of massive ambuscade by the Bolsheviks.

The oldest Czech publication in Russia was the *Českoruské Listy*, launched in 1906 in Lodz.[25] The most successful early publication for Czechs in Russia was the Kiev bi-weekly *Čechoslovan*, edited by Věnceslav Švihovský. The latter was published from January 1911 until the end of 1914 and then from 1916 to 1918. At the outset of World War I, the *Čechoslovan* was the only Czech periodical in Europe to speak freely for the political aspirations of the Czech people everywhere. In 1915, the "Čechoslovák" was launched in Petrograd and, under the editorship of Bohdan Pavlů, continued as the organ of Masaryk's independence movement in Russia. In May 1917, the periodical was enlarged by a Slovak supplement, the *Slovenské Hlasy*. After the arrival of Thomas G. Masaryk in Russia and after the founding in 1917 of the Czechoslovak National Council, the semi-official Czechoslovak government in France, the Petrograd *Čechoslovák* was replaced (in December, 1917) by the daily *Československý Deník*, an official organ of the Russian-based organization of the independence movement.[26] Until March 2, 1918, the paper was published in Kiev; then its editorial offices were loaded on the Siberia-bound troop train, and the periodical was printed in various towns along the tracks. From April 28, 1920 until July 18 of the same year the *Československý Deník* was published in Vladivostok.

Other, smaller Czech and Slovak-language publications were put out by the Czechoslovak Corps or by individual military units during their

---

[25] Dr. Frant. Vl. Šteidler, *Československé hnutí na Rusi* (Prague, 1922).
[26] *Ibid.*

Siberian Odyssey either in occupied cities or on the Vladivostok-bound troop trains.

The third group of Czech periodicals in Russia was published first by left-wing Social Democrats and later by Czech Bolsheviks. In 1918 these periodicals merged and a new one, entitled the *Průkopník Svobody*, became the organ of the Czechoslovak Communist Party in Russia.[27] It did not last long. In 1921, when the Soviet Communist Party failed in an attempt to organize the remaining Czechs in Russia, the so called Wollin Czechs, into a pro-Communist ethnic group a temporary publishing venture called the *Volyňská Pravda*, also failed after six issues.[28]

The next and most recent Czech or Czechoslovak publishing period was during World War II, when a new Czechoslovak army was formed in the Soviet Union. At least one military paper was published from 1944 to 1945 by the Czechoslovak Army Corps and one political weekly was published and edited by Czechoslovak Communist refugees in Moscow... There is no Czech-language publication for the Czech minority in the USSR now.

Before 1918, when Slovakia ceased to be an integral part of the Hungarian Kingdom, the history of Slovak journalism was closely linked with Budapest, the publishing place of many periodicals for readers in Slovakia. These newspapers and journals fell roughly into two groups: those published privately – frequently critical of the government – and those sponsored by official Budapest in an effort to cultivate among the Slovaks the so-called "All-Hungarian patriotism". As early as 1848 Hungarian officials in Budapest published the first of their periodicals, the *Prjatel Ludu*. After the formation of the Czechoslovak Republic, Budapest became the propaganda headquarters for a group of Slovaks who sought Slovak autonomy under the auspices of another *Greater* Hungary. With the help of the Budapest government, the group for a short time published one or two publications. Later, Budapest launched the official journal for Slovaks in Hungary called the *Slovenské Noviny*. After the Munich agreement it was decided by arbitration in Vienna that Hungary would be given the Southern frontier regions of Slovakia. The Slovaks who made up part of the population of these regions increased the size of the Slovak minority in Hungary to 600,000. The Hungarian regime allowed them to have their own political party and a periodical, the *Slovenská Jednota*.[29]

[27] Jindřich Veselý, *Češi a Slováci v revolučním Rusku 1917-1920* (Prague, Státní nakladatelství politické literatury, 1954).
[28] Stanislav Klíma, *Čechové a Slováci za hranicemi* (Prague, 1925).
[29] R. T. Prst, "Slováci a Podkarpatorusi v Mad'arsku", *Nové Časy*, London, England, October 1943.

An officially sponsored weekly for the "Slovak working people in Hungary" is now put out by a quasi-Communist organization.

The history of Czech and Slovak minorities in Poland is tied up with the history of their counterparts in Russia. In the second half of the last century many Czech farmers set out for the then-Russian Wollin region and founded numerous communities. By the Treaty of Riga, however, the Wollin region was split between Poland and the Soviet Union, leaving about 37,000 Czechs in Poland and only about one-sixth of their total population in the Soviet Ukraine. The situation changed in 1939 and once more in 1945. During the two World Wars, Czechs in Wollin volunteered en masse for the Czechoslovak emigré army and at the conclusion of the hostilities many returned to Czechoslovakia. In addition to the Wollin population, the Czech and Slovak minority in Poland in the 1920's consisted of about 10,000 – 12,000 old immigrants and of another 8,000 Slovaks in the Polish areas of Spiš and Orava.

For a few years after World War I, a small group of Slovak political émigrés formed a Poland-based organization called the Slovak National Council. Purportedly an advocate of Slovak national autonomy, the group was primarily a launching pad for propaganda blasts against the Czechoslovak Republic. It published the periodical *Slovák* in the Slovak language and later the *Viadomosci Polsko-Slowackie* in Polish. The Wollin Czechs in Poland started their first periodical, the *Hlas Volyně*, in 1926, a second, called the *Buditel*, in 1928, and a third, the *Krajanské Listy* in 1938. Czech political refugees who came to Poland in 1939 published briefly a periodical called the *Přehled*.

There are now two periodicals published in Poland. A monthly picture magazine is published by the Social and Cultural Society of Czechs and Slovaks in Poland and an illustrated monthly is published by the Polonia State Publishing House primarily for readers in Czechoslovakia, rather than for Czechs and Slovaks in Poland.[30]

Between the two World Wars there were about 90,000 Slovaks and 50,000 Czechs in Yugoslavia, about 3,000 Czechs in Bulgaria and about 16,000 Czechs and 31,000 Slovaks in Rumania. The earliest Slovak émigré publishing venture in this area came out in 1883 in Békésczaba. There were five new Slovak and one Czech publication in Yugoslavia between the two Wars. A separate story is that of the press of the Czechoslovak brigade which during World War II fought side by side

---

[30] V. N. Duben, *Czech and Slovak Periodical Press Outside Czechoslovakia*. The quoted figures are revised here to show the situation in January 1963.

with the Yugoslav partisans against the Nazi invaders. The brigade and its units produced about six publications.

There are now two Slovak periodicals and two publications in Yugoslavia. Bulgaria had two Czech periodicals and now has none. Rumania had one Slovak periodical shortly before the outbreak of World War II and now has one again. Benelux and Scandinavia entered the history of Czech or Slovak journalism only after the arrival of political anti-Communist refugees in the 1950's. Spain saw some Czech publications put out by Czech volunteers during the Spanish Civil War and later some short-lived periodicals published by Slovak anti-Communist refugees who came to Spain in the 1950's.

The history of Czechs in England goes all the way back to 1636 when Václav Hollar, a famous engraver, settled there to escape religious persecution. From 1886 to 1890 London was the headquarters of the Czech *Vlast*, a monthly organ of the Czech emigrant societies in non-Austrian Europe, founded in 1876 in Stuttgart, Germany. During World War I at T. G. Masaryk's insistence, R. W. Seton-Watson, the prominent British political scientist and expert on Central European affairs, began publishing *The New Europe*, an important weekly which served as a guide for Czechoslovak political organs abroad. Among them were several Czechoslovak press bureaus which functioned from the end of 1916 in London, Paris, Rome, New York and other Allied capitals.

Refugee journalism in London reached a new high during World War II when the city played host to the Czechoslovak exile government headed by President Dr. Eduard Beneš. The first in a long list of publications of this era was the *Čechoslovák v Anglii*, introduced to the Czechoslovak community on October 16, 1939. In October 1942 the publication became the official organ of the exiled Czechoslovak Ministry of Foreign Affairs in London.

The influx into England of Czechoslovak anti-Communists who fled their country in the wake of the 1948 overthrow was reflected in numerous publications which sprouted – often for only brief periods – in the early 1950's. Most prominent among them were periodicals of the Information Service of Free Czechoslovakia (FCI), founded on April 25, 1948. Its weekly, the *Čechoslovák*, launched in 1951, is now a highly respected member of the free Czech and Slovak press in the West. The FCI puts out weekly English-language press releases compiled by local and foreign experts on the situation inside the Iron Curtain, especially in Czechoslovakia.

England now has four Czech and one English-language periodical, published by Czech or Czechoslovak residents.

There were 2,000 Czechs in Switzerland between the two World Wars. They were mostly artisans and small businessmen. Czech journalism in Switzerland dates back to the arrival into exile of Josef Václav Frič, whose monthly *Čech - La voix libre de la Bohème* was launched in Geneva in January, 1861 as the first Czech periodical of political exiles. Two Czech periodicals were published in Switzerland between the two World Wars. After the Prague coup d'état in 1948, Switzerland became a haven for a small group of Czechoslovak exiles, mainly students. The product of their journalistic endeavors was an independent critical revue called the *Skutečnost*, launched in Geneva in 1949. It died in 1953 two years after it had moved to London, England. There is one Czech publication originating in Switzerland now.

CONCLUSION

Czech and Slovak newspapers have been published on all continents including most recently, Australia and Africa. During World War I Czechoslovak soldiers published their newspapers as far East as Vladivostok, and their World War II counterparts had their own newspapers in Africa and the Middle East. One information bulletin called the *Africký Vlastenec*, was published in 1938 by a Czechoslovak emigrant society in Johannesburg, South Africa.

With the exception of Albania, Finland, Greece, Ireland and Portugal, there is no country in Europe in which a Czech or Slovak publication has not originated.

In the last two hundred years (1761-1962) émigré Czechs have published over 900 periodicals outside present-day Czechoslovakia, more then 500 of them in the United States. Slovak emigré publications reached a total of 500. Many of these periodicals, especially those published in this century, were written in both Czech and Slovak. Statistically, they are usually counted as Czech periodicals because their contents were predominantly Czech.

In January 1963, 137 publications in the Czech and Slovak language, including 12 yearbooks and almanacs, were being published west of the Iron Curtain. Of this total, 89 Czech publications have an estimated annual circulation of 26,200,000; the 48 Slovak periodicals have a circulation of 7,000,000 per year. The large difference between the two language groups is due not only to the larger number of Czech periodicals but also to the larger readership of Czech dailies in the United States, especially Chicago's *Denní Hlasatel* which is larger than any Czech or Slovak newspaper outside Czechoslovakia. There are four Czech and four Slovak periodicals in the Communist countries of Europe. Their estimated annual circulation is more than one million. All Czech and Slovak periodicals outside Czechoslovakia have an estimated circulation of 555,000 copies per issue.

In comparison Czechoslovakia in 1959 (population 13.5 million) had 1,447 newspapers and magazines with an annual circulation of more than 1,350,000,000.[31] The annual circulation (of less than 1,300 newspapers) should be over 1,600,000,000 in 1962, according to the regime's predictions.[32]

The world-wide journalistic activity of uprooted members of a small Central European nation is open to several interpretations. But one thing is certain: it reflects the intense cultural and social life of Czechs and Slovaks as well as their inclination toward political diversification which is the basis of their democratic tradition.

---

[31] *Statistická ročenka ČSSR* – 1960 (Prague, 1960).
[32] Jaroslav Veselý, "Vývoj československého tisku, jeho struktura a perspektiva", *Novinářský sborník*, No. 2 (Prague, 1961).

Early Czech Journalism in the United States

VLASTA VRÁZ

Early Czech journalism in the United States had its roots in the old country, in the ill-fated revolution of 1848 against Hapsburg oppression. A number of young Czech revolutionists had found it necessary to flee, and one of them, Vojta Náprstek of Prague, a law student at the University of Vienna, became the first Czech journalist in America.

In his homeland, Náprstek had been inspired by the example of Karel Havlíček Borovský, publisher and editor of *Národní Noviny* (National Gazette), a liberal and rebel who actively opposed the injustices perpetrated by the Austrian government against the Czech people. In the United States, Náprstek added two other men to his list of inspirational idealists: Thomas Paine and Thomas Jefferson.[1]

There were things about America that surprised Náprstek, especially slavery. He was shocked to see slaves sold in St. Louis, and he traveled south down the Mississippi to study the Negro problem. In 1856, he campaigned for John C. Fremont as president, because he believed in the emancipation of the slaves. Náprstek also sympathized with the Indians and, having studied the language of the Dakotas, served as guard on a peace expedition to the Dakota tribe.[2]

These American shortcomings did not, however, dim his faith in American democracy. Náprstek revelled in his own personal freedom, despite economic difficulties. From the start he recognized his countrymen's need of an educational, liberal newspaper and in 1852, three years after his arrival, founded the first journal for the Czechs in the United States: the *Flug-Blätter* of Milwaukee. It may seem strange that it was printed in German, but technical difficulties had proved insurmountable.

The Milwaukee *Flug-Blätter* (1852-1854) was sometimes a weekly, but always liberal, anti-clerical and anti-Austrian. Náprstek was a born champion of human rights; never losing sight of his Jeffersonian ideals,

---

[1] Stanislav Kodým, *Dům u Halánků* (Prague, Československý spisovatel, 1955).
[2] Ibid.

he fought with wisdom and restraint against injustice of any kind.

Náprstek spent almost 9 years in the United States; when granted amnesty by the Austrian government in 1857, he returned to Prague. He never lost contact, however, with his compatriots in the United States. When he went home, American ideals went with him; the old house on Bethlehem Square in Prague became "Little America" to a circle of influential and enlightened friends. He brought with him not only American newspapers, books and clippings on civic problems and politics, but also a Singer sewing machine.[3] His nation at long last was experiencing a great rebirth; his home became the headquarters for Czech patriots who under his hospitable roof planned a course of action in the old City Hall and in the Vienna Parliament.

Náprstek was active in practically everything of significance. Fortunately, as a man of means, he could support these causes liberally. He started a library, museum and the "American Club for Women", for he strongly believed in their emancipation.

In many respects, there was a close affinity between developments in Prague and the aspirations of the immigrants in America. Throughout the years, Náprstek kept in touch with the immigrants' heart beat as he continued to inspire them with his dream of a Czech liberal newspaper in America.

The first Czech paper, printed in Czech language but in German type, was the *Slowan Amerikánský* (The American Slav), which finally saw the light of day in Racine, Wis., in 1860.

Three weeks later, the Czechs of St. Louis, Mo., introduced another weekly, the *Národní Noviny* (National Gazette), an outspoken Unionist paper. Within a short time, however, both Czech weeklies found it impossible to keep afloat and therefore joined forces; *Slavie* was born of the merger.

Although *Slavie* was never to attain as large a circulation as other Czech newspapers – in its heyday it had only 4,000 subscribers[4] – nevertheless its voice of liberalism and Czech nationalism was to play an important part in the life of the immigrants.

These were very difficult years for the newcomers. The majority of them had come to escape both political oppression and economic depression. They hoped to find freedom from want and fear, but soon realized that here, they were "greenhorns", therefore inferior and very much on their own because of the language handicap.

[3] Stanislav Kodým, *Dům u Halánků* (Prague, Československý spisovatel, 1955).
[4] Thomas Čapek, *The Čechs in America* (Boston, Houghton Mifflin Company, 1920).

In the next decade, thirty other attempts were made to publish a weekly, but only one or two survived.

Despite these forbidding failures, August Geringer, a former school teacher from Březnice, Bohemia, had the courage to launch the first daily Czech newspaper in the United States, the *Svornost* (Concord). Its purpose was set forth in the first issue, which appeared in Chicago on October 8th, 1875: to bring world news to its readers who had not as yet mastered the English language and "to acquaint them with the advantages and duties of citizens in preserving political freedom and in fighting against any oppression, be it economical, political or religious".[5]

The *Svornost* had 210 subscribers to begin with and was kept alive only by the stubborn determination of its publisher, the self-sacrifice of his hard-working wife, Antonie Geringer, the dedication of his editor, František Zdrůbek, and the support of a handful of friends who felt the need for a fighting liberal, anti-clerical and anti-Austrian newspaper.

It is hard to say whose lot was harder, the publisher or the editor, who worked for $ 50 a month and had many other duties as teacher, orator, organizer of societies and movements, and fund-raiser. This was the common lot of all editors and publishers of that time.

The *Svornost* was addressed to the poor immigrant who had left his homeland to free himself from political, religious and economic oppression. In 1870, there were 40,289 immigrants born in Czech lands living in the United States,[6] and although there were comparatively few illiterates among them – on Ellis Island Czech immigrants had one of the highest literacy ratings – nevertheless, many had not acquired the habit of reading a daily newspaper. The women, especially, preoccupied with the struggle for bare existence and bringing up a family under very harsh circumstances, were satisfied to read a weekly installment of a novel. It became vitally important for the publisher to capture the reader's interest. Unfortunately, his choice of a novel was not always of the best. Although the publisher soon ventured boldly into publishing such works as the Czech translation of Thomas Paine's *The Age of Reason* and Karel Havlíček's *Křest sv. Vladimíra*, his selection of daily fare could not be so discriminating, unless he was willing to starve.

But by 1880, the number of Czechs in America had more than doubled, for a steady stream of immigration was flowing with ever-increasing force. It was then the peasants began to arrive from Bohemia and

---

[5] *Zlatá Kniha* (Golden Anniversary of *Svornost*) (Chicago, August Geringer, 1926).
[6] Josef Martinek, *Století Jednoty Č.S.A.* (One Hundred Years of the C.S.A.) (Cicero, 1955).

Moravia, from villages so small that they were often not on any map. For many, Chicago was but a stopping-place en route to their final destination somewhere in the virgin prairies and forests of the Middle West. The United States government had opened its vast territory and was offering homesteads to the pioneers. Here was a great opportunity for the land-hungry peasant to break soil, an opportunity for which they had to pay with years of hardship, back-breaking labor, loneliness and longing for old friends and the homeland with its cultivated fields and orchards.

To them the newspaper became an important link with civilization. With the pioneer's need in mind, August Geringer started a weekly, the *Amerikán*. It was necessary to send out a traveling salesman, which marked a turning point in the publisher's financial dilemma: the circulation of *Amerikán* soon reached 2,000 subscribers.[7]

The *Svornost* and *Amerikán*, very often the immigrant's only source of information, carried important government news, advice to homesteaders, and, of course, world news. Special attention was given to developments in the old Autro-Hungarian Empire: Austria's annexation of Bosnia-Herzegovina, Serbia's brave stand, the struggle of the Slavs against the Turks, etc.

Amerikán, the bearer of this news, found its way to the Náprstek library in Prague and to other Czech patriots in Bohemia. No wonder the Austrian government thought the newspaper dangerous and the Czechs in America mere heretics and rebels. Geringer publications were banned, and the publisher found it necessary every so often to change the name on the front page of copies going to Bohemia, to fool the Austrian censor.

In many respects, the *Svornost* office had to take the place of the Austrian consulate, an office avoided by immigrants. "Lost" relatives were located through the paper, mail from Bohemia was delivered and money was advanced to stake the westward-bound pioneer.

Every issue of the *Svornost* and *Amerikán* carried advertisements of steamship companies, for the chief need driving the immigrant to toil 60 hours a week and set aside one penny after another from his low wages was the desire to save money for passage for other members of his family.

Many young men who had come alone and started homesteading needed a wife and often advertised for a bride. Young girls serving as domestic help answered the call and left the city for the sod hovel or log cabin. Their moving life-stories are to be found in the early issues of the Almanac

[7] *Zlatá Kniha* (Golden Anniversary of *Svornost*) (Chicago, August Geringer, 1926).

Amerikán, published by August Geringer. For anyone who wishes to understand the hardships and heartaches of the early settlers, these Almanacs are an unsurpassed source of first-hand information.[8]

In the cities, having once thrown off old-world shackles, the Czechs began to develop their individuality as well as their communities. The moving force was the young rebels to whom the pen was a weapon. It all began with Náprstek, but there were others who took up his war against the church as a political institution and partner of the Hapsburgs. In the old country, they had been taught obedience to both the church and the master, and therefore, to the immigrant, the church and the Hapsburgs were indivisible: to free their homeland, they had to fight both at the same time. In America, their long-suppressed national qualities, which Masaryk called latent Hussitism, finally broke forth.[9] A powerful freethinkers' movement grew rapidly; over 60 percent of the Czechs abandoned their faith on coming to America.[10] The first rebels came from the intelligentsia, later ones, from the working class.

There was Charles Jonáš, another student and political exile, who became editor of *Slavie* and married the daughter of the publisher, Frank Kořízek. Charles Jonáš became active in political life, unusual among the Czechs at that time, and rose to the office of Lt. Governor of Wisconsin.

František Zdrůbek was also a young rebel. As editor of the *Svornost* he was for many years the spokesman for the Czech rationalist movement. In Bohemia, he had studied for the priesthood, but left the Catholic Church and in the United States was at first pastor of the Czech-Moravian Brethren in Caledonia, Wis., until he finally broke away entirely.

Another influential journalist was young Václav Šnajdr, editor of the *Dennice Novověku* (Modern Times) of Cleveland for 35 years, from 1877 to 1911. Like Zdrůbek, Šnajdr had pledged himself to uphold the cause of free religious discussion, and adhered to this faithfully.

Lev Palda, sometimes called the father of Czech socialism in the United States, advocated socialism by evolution. He was one of the co-founders of *Dělnické Listy* (Workingmen's Journal) in Cleveland in 1875. A self-made man, he was an eloquent speaker and an able organizer in the labor movement. There were, however, editors of other Socialist papers who were not as restrained as Palda; some even were radicals and anarchists.

---

[8] Unfortunately, when the Geringer publishing house changed hands in 1947, after having been in the family for 72 years, the new owners destroyed the vast collection of Almanacs and newspapers. Perhaps the only place one can find a complete set of Almanac *Amerikán* is the Náprstek Museum in Prague.

[9] Thomas Masaryk, "Čech Liberals in America", *Naše Doba*, Prague, Oct. 1902.

[10] Thomas Čapek, *The Čechs in America* (Boston, Houghton Mifflin Company, 1920).

The only rebellious individual who was not young, but old, when he arrived in the United States in 1869 was Ladimír Klácel, a well-known pedagogue and friend of prominent Czech patriots in Bohemia. Klácel had been educated for the priesthood, but at the age of 61 finally broke away from the Catholic Church and came to America. As a social reformer, he was a dreamer with Utopian ideas, and died broken in spirit. Nevertheless, he was a remarkable man who left his imprint on the evolution of thought of the Czechs in America.

One of the most pugnacious editors was Josef Pastora, a firebrand, who edited *Pokrok* (Progress) in Chicago in 1867. His anti-clerical belligerence forced the Catholics to rally and, in self-defense, start publishing their first newspaper, *Katolické Noviny* (Catholic News) edited by Father Joseph Molitor. There was sustained hostility between the two camps, Catholic and Rationalist; neutrality was practically impossible. However, the life of the first Czech Catholic weekly was brief and the paper soon passed out of existence. A few years later, in 1872, another Catholic paper, *Hlas* (Voice), came into being in St. Louis with Father Hesoun as the defender of the faith, but its voice was drowned out by the battlecry of the dissenters. It was not until the peasants began to arrive in great numbers from Bohemia and especially from Moravia in the eighties that the Benedictines began to publish *Katolík* (The Catholic) and *Národ* (Nation) in Chicago in 1893 and 1894 respectively.[11]

Remaining true to its past, the Catholic press more or less ignored the Czech national struggle for independence until the final stage of World War I. Thus, the liberation movement was left almost entirely to the liberals who had broken away from the church and from everything that had to do with the Hapsburgs. "A free spirit in a free land" was their motto.

With every passing year they gained strength and when the shot was fired at Sarajevo, they went immediately into action. In his *Světová revoluce*, Thomas Masaryk acknowledges their part in the war for independence for Czechoslovakia.[12]

The torch of the revolution had been passed on from Havlíček to Náprstek, and by him to lesser but nonetheless dedicated men. With the downfall of the Hapsburgs, the main political goal of the revolutionists had finally been achieved. There began a mellowing process toward religious tolerance and every-day life in the United States.

---

[11] Tomáš Čapek, *Padesát let českého tisku v Americe* (New York, Bank of Europe, private edition, 1911).
[12] Tomáš Masaryk, *Světová revoluce* (Prague, Čin a Orbis, 1925).

BIBLIOGRAPHY

Czechoslovakia and its Arts and Sciences: A Selective Bibliography in the Western European Languages

MILOSLAV RECHCIGL, JR.*

INTRODUCTION

The purpose of this survey is to provide a student of Slavic studies with a comprehensive and up-to-date bibliography on the territory of present Czechoslovakia and its cultural accomplishments and influences throughout history.

The last comprehensive bibliography concerning Czechoslovakia and its people was published in French over forty years ago by Prof. Eugène Bestaux, entitled *Bibliographie tchèque* (Prague, 1920). The latest English bibliographies appeared two years earlier, one with the title *Slavic Europe* (Cambridge, Mass., 1918), compiled by Prof. Robert Joseph Kerner and the second, *Bohemian (Čech) Bibliography* (Chicago, Ill., 1918), compiled by Thomas and Anna V. Čapek. All these works are, of course, out of date now although they can still be very useful to those who are interested in the older literature.

Most of the recently published bibliographies cover only the field of social sciences, e.g., Jiřina Sztachová's *Mid-Europe* (New York, 1953), and furthermore they are usually limited to the postwar literature, e.g., Robert F. Byrnes's *Bibliography of American Publications on East Central Europe, 1945-1957* (Bloomington, Ind., 1958). In most bibliographies which have so far been published, very little space is devoted to the Czechoslovak arts and humanities, while fields like natural sciences and tech-

---

* The advice and assistance of Prof. Antonín Basch, Prof. Josef Čada, Prof. Milič Čapek, Dr. Paul J. Edwards, Dr. Mojmír S. Frinta, Prof. Jan Hajda, Prof. Karel Hujer, Prof. Karel B. Jirák, Prof. Jiří Kolaja, Prof. Henry Kučera, Prof. Jiří Nehněvajsa, Dr. Jaroslav Němec, Prof. Edward Táborský and Prof. René Wellek are gratefully acknowledged. – It would be greatly appreciated if the readers would inform the author of this bibliography of any omissions or errors in the text. Although special care was taken to select the most representative references in a given area, a number of important books undoubtedly escaped his attention.

nology have been completely ignored. These reasons should be sufficient justification for the appearance of this bibliography.

Because of the enormous volume of literature available, the coverage of this bibliography is necessarily limited to books and a few general review articles published in the Western European languages (primarily English, French and German). In fields like history, there is such abundant literature that only the most important works could be cited. In other fields, like sociology and philosophy, on the other hand, there are very few books published in the Western European languages, although considerable literature exists in both Czech and Slovak. In these instances, general review articles and the most important essays published in various journals are given.

Those who want further references to the older literature should consult the publications cited above, by R. J. Kerner and E. Bestaux. For older references on Slovaks, particularly prior to the establishment of the Czechoslovak Republic in 1918, one should consult the extensive bibliography by Jozef Kuzmík, published under the Slovak title *Bibliografia kníh v západných rečiach týkajúcich sa slovenských vecí vydaných od XVI. stor. do r. 1955* (Martin, 1959). On the historiography of Czechoslovakia, L. I. Strakhovsky's *A Handbook of Slavic Studies* (Cambridge, Mass., 1949), S. H. Thomson's *Czechoslovakia in European History* (Princeton, 1953), and, particularly Francis Dvornik's *The Slavs in European History and Civilization* (New Brunswick, N.J., 1962) are recommended.

Information concerning the books on Czechoslovakia published during the period of the First Czechoslovak Republic and during the early stages of the Second World War can best be found in the Orbis' *Publikace o Československu v cizích jazycích* (Publications on Czechoslovakia in Foreign Languages) (Prague, 1928), and Janko Šuhaj's *Books on Czechoslovakia. Selected List of English Books on Czechoslovakia* (London, 1944).

To keep abreast of the current literature, especially in the field of social sciences and humanities, one should consult the recent volumes of *The American Bibliography of Russian and East European Studies* (published annually by Indiana University) and follow such specialized journals as the *Journal of Central European Affairs, Slavic Review, Slavonic and East European Review, Revue des études slaves, Publications of Modern Language Association* (*PMLA*), etc. None of these publications, however, contains any bibliographies on Czechoslovak science. The most comprehensive bibliography on current studies in the field of the history of Czechoslovak science and technology is published in Czech as a yearly

A Selective Bibliography 557

supplement to *Sborník pro dějiny přírodních věd a techniky* (Prague). A bibliography on Czechoslovak agricultural history is similarly published once a year in *Sborník Československé akademie zemědělských věd. Historie a musejnictví* (Prague). A bibliography of the current Czechoslovak medical literature is published once a year by Státní lékařská knihovna under the title *The Annual of Czechoslovak Medical Literature* (Prague).

Information regarding the books currently published in Czechoslovakia, including those in the Western European languages, can be best obtained from bulletins published periodically by Artia or by the Publishing House of the Czechoslovak Academy of Sciences, e.g., *New Czechoslovak Books, Bulletin, New Books, Review of Publications*, etc.

BIBLIOGRAPHY

CONTENTS

I. Bibliographies	557
II. General References	561
III. Humanities	564
A. Literature	564
B. Linguistics	567
C. Philosophy	571
D. History	575
VI. Arts	581
A. Music and Drama	581
B. Fine Arts	584
V. Social Sciences	589
A. Sociology	589
B. Economics	592
C. Political Science	597
D. Law	603
E. Education	606
VI. Natural Sciences	609
A. General	609
B. Biological Sciences	611
C. Physical Sciences	615
VII. Technology	618
VIII. Czechs and Slovaks Abroad	620
A. U.S.A.	620
B. Other Countries	623
IX. Addendum	625

I. BIBLIOGRAPHIES

1. *The American Bibliography of Slavic (Russian) and East European Studies* (Bloomington, Indiana University Press, 1958-63).

2. Besteaux, Eugène, *Bibliographie tchèque, contenant un certain nombre d'ouvrages sur la Tchécoslovaquie, en langues diverses* (à *l'exclusion des langues slaves*) (Prague, 1920).
3. Besterman, Theodore, *A World Bibliography of Bibliographies*, 2nd ed. (London, T. Besterman, 1947), pp. 380-1, 711-5.
4. *Die Bibliografie in den europäischen Ländern der Volksdemokratien. Entwicklung und gegenwärtiger Stand.* Von Todor Borov, M. Dembowska, M. Tomescu, J. Drtina, J. Kuzmík and P. Bélley (Leipzig, VEB Verlag für Buch- und Bibliothekswesen, 1960); see "Tschechoslowakei", pp. 89-131.
5. *A Bibliography of the Publications of Dmitry Čiževsky in the Fields of Literature, Language, Philosophy and Culture* (Cambridge, 1952).
6. Borovský, F. A. and Wirth, Zd., *Kunstgewerbliches Museum der Handels- und Gewerbekammer in Prag. Bibliothek, Bücher-Katalog* (*Prag*, 1907).
7. Byrnes, Robert F., *Bibliography of American Publications on East Central Europe, 1945-57* (Bloomington, Indiana University Press, 1958).
8. Čapek, Thomas and Čapek, Anna Vostrovský, *Bohemian* (*Čech*) *Bibliography. A Finding List of Writings in English Relating to Bohemia and the Čechs* (Chicago, New York ..., Fleming H. Revell Co., 1918).
9. Čejchan, V. and Černá, M. L., "Tchécoslovaquie", in *Les sources du travail bibliographique.* Ed. L. N. Malclès (Genève, Librairie E. Droz, 1950), Vol. II, pp. 770-5.
10. Československá akademie věd, *Bulletin* (*of the*) *Publishing House of the Czechoslovak Academy of Sciences in Prague* (*and of the*) *Publishing House of the Slovak Academy of Sciences in Bratislava* (Prague, Czechoslovak Academy of Sciences; a monthly).
11. ——, *New Books. Publishing House of the Czechoslovak Academy of Sciences – Prague. Publishing House of the Slovak Academy of Sciences – Bratislava* (Prague, Czechoslovak Academy of Sciences; a yearly).
12. ——, *Review of Publications* (Prague, Publishing House of the Czechoslovak Academy of Sciences, 1955 and ff.).
13. Československá akademie věd; Sekce historická, *25 ans de l'historiographie tchécoslovaque, 1935-1960* (Prague, Publishing House of the Czechoslovak Academy of Sciences, 1960).
14. Chevalier, Ulysse, *Répertoire des sources historiques du moyen âge*

(Montbéliard, Société anonyme d'imprimerie montbéliardaise, 1894-9), pp. 426-31 ("Bohême"), 249-51 ("Prague").
15. Crous, Ernest, "Die böhmischen Wiegendrucke", *Zentralblatt für Bibliothekswesen*, 45 (1928), pp. 7-11.
16. Frels, Wilhelm, *Deutsche Dichterhandschriften von 1400 bis 1900. Gesamtkatalog der eigenhändigen Handschriften deutscher Dichter in den Bibliotheken und Archiven Deutschlands, Österreichs, der Schweiz und der ČSR* (= Modern Language Association of America, Bibliographical Publications, vol. ii) (Leipzig, 1934).
17. Grolig, Moriz, *Die Klosterdruckerei im Prämonstratenserstifte Bruck a.d. Thaya (Mähren), 1595-1608* (Wien, 1908).
18. Hanslik, Joseph A., *Geschichte und Beschreibung der Prager Universitätsbibliothek* (Prag, 1851).
19. Hanusch, G., "Osteuropa-Dissertationen", *Jahrbücher für Geschichte Osteuropeas*, Breslau, N.F., 3 (1955), 4 (1956), 6 (1958).
20. Horna, Dagmar, *Current Research on Central and Eastern Europe* (New York, Mid-European Studies Center, Free Europe Committee, 1956).
21. Jakovenko, Boris, *La bibliographie de T. G. Masaryk* (= International Philosophical Library, Vol. 1, fasc. 9-10) (Prague, 1935).
22. Kerner, Robert Joseph, *Slavic Europe, a Selected Bibliography in the Western Languages* (Cambridge, Mass., Harvard University Press, 1918).
23. Kleinschnitzová, Flora, "Seltene Bohemica des XVI. Jahrhunderts in schwedischen Bibliotheken", *Nordisk tidskrift*, 18 (1931), pp. 1-32.
24. Kolaja, Jiří and others, "The Bibliography", *Tribuna* (Czechoslovak Foreign Institute in Exile, 1954 and ff.).
25. Kotcka, Jozef, *Short Slovakian Bibliography* (Pittsburgh, National News Print, 1935).
26. Krasnopolski, Paul, "Tschechische Inkunabeln", *Zeitschrift für Bücherfreunde*, 17 (1925), pp. 95-102.
27. ——, "Prager Drucke bis 1620", *Gutenberg Jahrbuch* (1927), pp. 72-84.
28. Kuzmík, Jozef, *Slovak Bibliography in the Past and Present* (Martin, Matica slovenská, 1955).
29. ——, *Bibliografia kníh v západných rečiach týkajúcich sa slovenských vecí vydaných od XVI. stor. do r. 1955* (Martin, Matica slovenská, 1959).
30. *New Czechoslovak Books* (Prague, Artia, 1961 and ff.) (A monthly).

31. New York Public Library, *Dictionary Catalog of the Slavonic Collection of the New York Public Library*, 26 vols. (Boston, G. K. Hall, 1959).
32. ——, Slavonic Division, *A Bibliography of Slavonic Bibliography in English* (New York, New York Public Library, 1947).
33. New York Public Library, Slavonic Division, *Tomáš Garrigue Masaryk. A List of Works by and about the First President of Czechoslovakia in the New York Public Library*. Ed. Avrahm Yarmolinsky (New York, The New York Public Library, 1941).
34. Orbis, firm, *Publikace o Československu v cizích jazycích* (Prague, Orbis, 1928).
35. Philip, W., Smolitsch, I. and Valjavec, F., "Verzeichnis des deutschsprachigen Schriftums 1939-1952 zur Geschichte Osteuropas und Südosteuropas", *Forschungen zur osteuropäischen Geschichte*, Berlin, Vol. 1 (1954), pp. 251-316.
36. Podlaha, Anton, *Catalogus incunabulorum quae in bibliotheca capituli metropolitani Pragensis asservantur* (= *Editiones archivii et bibliotheca s.f. metropolitani capituli Pragensis*, vol. xx) (Pragae, 1926).
37. Rouček, Joseph, S., *Recent Literature on Central-Eastern Europe* (New York, ..., J. S. Rouček, 1945).
38. Ruggles, Melville J. and Mostecký, Václav, *Russian and East European Publications in the Libraries of the United States* (New York, Columbia University Press, 1960).
39. Schubert, Anton, "Die beiden ältesten vollständigen Biblio-bohemica-Inkunabeln", *Zentralblatt für Bibliothekswesen*, 14 (1897), pp. 104-9.
40. ——, "Die sicher nachweisbaren Inkunabeln Böhmens und Mährens vor 1501", *Zentralblatt für Bibliothekswesen*, 16 (1899), pp. 126-36, 176-85, 217-30.
41. *Slavica-Auswahl Katalog der Universitäts-bibliothek Jena*. Von e. Slawist. Arbeitsgruppe in d. Universitätsbibliothek Jena unter verantwortl. Leitung von Othmar Feyl. Vol. I, *Allgemeine Literatur, Tschechoslowakei und Polen* (Weimar, Böhlau, 1956).
42. Spolek československých knihovníků a jejich přátel, *L'Hommage fait par l'Association des bibliothécaires tchécoslovaques et de leurs amis au 1er Congrès mondiale des bibliothèques et de bibliographie tenu le 15-30 juin 1929 à Rome et Venise*. Redigé par Adolf Lad. Krejčík (Prague, Association des bibliothécaires tchécoslovaques, 1929).

43. Šuhaj, Janko, *Books on Czechoslovakia. Selected List of English Books on Czechoslovakia* (London, The New Europe Publishing Co., 1944).
44. Sztachová, Jiřina, *Mid-Europe, a Selective Bibliography* (New York, Mid-European Center of the National Committee for a Free Europe, 1953).
45. Thomson, S. Harrison, "Eastern Europe", in *The American Historical Association's Guide to Historical Literature*. Ed. G. F. Howe and others (New York, Macmillan Co., 1961), pp. 567-620.
46. Tobolka, Z. V., *Die Einblattdrucke des 15 Jhdts. auf dem Gebiete der Tschechoslovakei* (Prag, 1928).
47. Truhlář, Joseph, *Catalogus codicum manuscriptorum latinorum qui in c.r. bibliotheca publica atque universitatis Pragensis asservantur* (Pragae, 1905-6).
48. Ungar, Karl, *Neue Beyträge zur alten Geschichte der Buchdruckerkunst in Böhmen, mit einer vollständigen Vibersicht (sic) aller einer dazu gehörigen Daten aus dem fünfzehnten Jahrhundert* (Prag, 1795).
49. U.S. Library of Congress, *East and East Central Europe. Periodicals in English and Other West European Languages*. Compiled by Paul L. Horecký (Washington, D.C., U.S. Library of Congress, 1958).
50. ——, *East European Accession Index*. Vols. 1-10 (Washington, D.C., U.S. Government Printing Office, 1951-61).
51. ——, *Introduction to Europe. A Selective Guide to Background Reading*. Compiled by Helen F. Conover (Washington, D.C., U.S. Library of Congress, 1950).

Addendum: 1225, 1234, 1273, 1275, 1180-3.

Crossreferences: 82, 83, 103, 106, 110, 167, 212, 255, 311, 319, 362, 400, 573, 648, 676, 817, 839, 857, 863, 972, 977, 1006, 1110, 1111

II. GENERAL REFERENCES

52. American Institute in Czechoslovakia, *Czechoslovak Literature and Science – 1935* (Prague, The American Institute in Czechoslovakia, 1935).
53. Beuer, Gustav, *New Czechoslovakia and Her Historical Background* (London, Lawrence and Wishart, 1947).
54. Buday, T. and others, *Tectonic Development of Czechoslovakia* (Prague, Československá akademie věd, 1960).

55. Bušek, Vratislav and Spulber, Nicolas (ed.), *Czechoslovakia* (New York, F. A. Praeger, 1957).
56. Butter, O. and Ruml, B., *La République tchécoslovaque. Aperçu de la vie intellectuelle, politique, économique et sociale* (Prague, Orbis, 1920).
57. *La Cecoslovacchia: organizzazione politica, economica, organizzazione culturale, grandi personalità...* (Roma, Istituto per l'Europa orientale, 1925).
58. Císař, Jaroslav and Pokorný, F., *The Czechoslovak Republic. A Survey of Its History and Geography, Its Political and Cultural Organization, and Its Economic Resources* (London, Fisher Unwin, 1922).
59. Czechoslovak Republic, Ministry of Foreign Affairs, *Czechoslovakia Fights Back* (Washington, D. C., American Council on Public Affairs, 1943).
60. *Czechoslovakia – Old Culture and New Life at Crossroads of Europe* (Prague, Orbis, 1947).
61. Dědeček, V., *La Tchécoslovaquie et les Tchécoslovaques* (Paris, Bossard, 1919).
62. Druce, Gerald, *Czechoslovakia. Past and Present* (Prague, Orbis, 1948).
63. Eisenmann, Louis, *La Tchécoslovaquie* (Paris, F. Rieder 1921).
64. *Encyclopédie tchécoslovaque*. Rédigé par Jaroslav Veselý, Jan Smetana and Vladislav Brdlík (Paris, Editions Bossard, 1923).
65. Hajda, Jan (ed.), *A Study of Contemporary Czechoslovakia* (Chicago, The University of Chicago, for the Human Relations Area Files, 1955).
66. Heisler, J. B. and Mellon, J. E., *Czechoslovakia. Land of Dream and Enterprise* (London, L. Drummond, 1945).
67. Hindus, Maurice, *We Shall Live Again* (New York, Doubleday, Doran, 1939).
68. ——, *The Bright Passage* (New York, Doubleday & Co., 1947).
69. Kerner, Robert J., *Czechoslovakia* (Berkeley and Los Angeles, University of California Press, 1945).
70. Konček, Mikuláš and Luknis, Michael, *Geographica Slovaca* (Bratislava, 1949).
71. *The Lands of the Bohemian Crown. Their History and Glory*. Ed. M. Hipmanová (Prague, Česká grafická unie, 1947).
72. McBride, Robert M., *Romantic Czechoslovakia* (New York, R. M. McBride, 1930).

A Selective Bibliography

73. Martel, René, *La Ruthénie Subcarpathique* (Paris, Paul Hartmann, 1935).
74. Monroe, W. S., *Bohemia and the Czechs. The History, People, Institutions, and the Geography of the Kingdom* (London, G. Bell and Sons, 1910).
75. Mothersole, Jessie, *Czechoslovakia, the Land of an Unconquerable Ideal* (New York, Dodd, Mead, 1926).
76. Nikolau, Stanislav, *Géographie de la Tchécoslovaquie* (Prague, Librairie des professeurs tchécoslovaques, 1926).
77. Nosek, Vladimír, *The Spirit of Bohemia. A Survey of Czechoslovak History, Music, and Literature* (London, George Allen and Unwin, 1926).
78. Rouček, Joseph S. (ed.), *Slavonic Encyclopedia* (New York, Philosophical Library, 1949).
79. Seton-Watson, R. W. (ed.), *Slovakia Then and Now. A Political Survey by Many Slovak Authors* (London, G. Allen and Unwin, 1931).
80. ——, *The New Slovakia* (Prague, Fr. Borový, 1924).
81. ——, *Twenty Five Years of Czechoslovakia* (London, New Europe Publishing Co., 1945).
82. Stanoyevitch, Milivoy S. (ed.), *Slavonic Nations of Yesterday and Today*. Select Readings and References on Russia, Poland, Czechoslovakia, Yugoslavia and Bulgaria (New York, H. W. Wilson, 1925), Chapter IV, Czechoslovakia, pp. 267-322.
83. Strakhovsky, Leonid I. (ed.), *Handbook of Slavic Studies* (Cambridge, Mass., Harvard University Press, 1949).
84. Street, C. J. C., *Slovakia, Past and Present* (London, 1928).
85. Urzidil, Johannes, "Die Tschechen und Slovaken", in *Die Welt der Slawen*. Hrsg. von Hans Kohn. Vol. I (Frankfurt a. M. und Hamburg, Fischer Bücherei, 1960).
86. Wanklyn, Harriet, *Czechoslovakia* (London, G. Philip, 1954).
87. Weiss, Loise, *La République Tchécoslovaque* (Paris, Payot 1919).
88. *The Yearbook of the Czechoslovak Republic*. Ed. Bohuslav Horák (Prague, 1929).
89. Young, E. P., *Czechoslovakia, Keystone of Peace and Democracy* (London, Gollancz, 1938).

Addendum: 1163, 1164, 1168, 1187, 1195, 1211, 1234, 1236, 1265, 1266, 1294, 1298, 1312

Crossreferences: 343, 605, 663.

III. HUMANITIES

A. Literature

90. Brabec, Ad., *Čechische Literaturgeschichte* (Wien, 1906).
91. Brod, Max, *Franz Kafka. Eine Biographie, Erinnerungen und Dokumente* (Prag, 1937).
92. ——, *Franz Kafka's Glauben und Lehre, Kafka und Tolstoi. Eine Studie* (München, K. Desch, 1948).
93. ——, *Franz Kafka. A Biography* (New York, Schocken Books, 1960).
94. Brückner, A., "Böhmische Studien, Abhandlungen und Texte", *Archiv für slavische Philologie*, Berlin, 2 (1888), pp. 81-104, 189-217, 421-522; 12 (1890), pp. 321-58; 13 (1891), pp. 1-25; 14 (1892), pp. 1-45.
95. Chudoba, František, *A Short Survey of Czech Literature* (London, K. Paul, Trench, Trubner Co., 1924).
96. Čyzevskyj, D., *Outline of Comparative Slavic Literature* (Boston, American Academy of Arts and Sciences, 1952).
97. ——, *Aus zwei Welten. Beiträge zur Geschichte der slavisch-westlichen literarischen Beziehungen* ('s-Gravenhage, Mouton and Co., 1956).
98. Demetz, Peter, *René Rilkes Prager Jahre* (Düsseldorf, Eugen Diederichs, 1953).
99. Eisner, Pavel, *Franz Kafka and Prague* (New York, Griffin Books, 1950).
100. ——, *Die Tschechen. Eine Anthologie aus fünf Jahrhunderten* (München, R. Piper and Co., 1928).
101. Fejfalík, J., "Alttschechische Leiche, Lieder und Sprüche des 14. und 15. Jhr.", *Sitzungsberichte der Akademie der Wissenschaften, philosophisch-historische Klasse*, Wien, 39 (1862), pp. 627-745.
102. Foltin, Lore Barbora, *Franz Werfel, 1892-1945* (Pittsburgh, University of Pittsburgh Press, 1961).
103. Hanuš, Ignác J., *Quellenkunde und Bibliographie der böhmisch-slovenischen Literaturgeschichte von 1348-1868* (Prag, Böhm. Gesellschaft d. Wissenschaften, 1868).
104. Harkins, William Edward, *The Russian Folk Epos in Czech Literature 1800-1900* (New York, King's Crown Press, 1951).
105. ——, *Karel Čapek* (New York, Columbia University Press, 1962).
106. ——, and Šimončič, Klement, *Czech and Slovak Literature* (New York, Columbia University Press, 1950).

107. Jakobson, Roman, "The Kernel of Comparative Slavic Literature", *Harvard Slavic Studies*, 1 (Cambridge, 1953), pp. 1-81.
108. ——, "Medieval Mock Mystery (The Old Czech Unguentarius)", in *Studia Philologica et Litteraria in honorem Leo Spitzer* (Bern, 1958).
109. Jakubec, Jan and Novák, Arne, *Geschichte der čechischen Literatur* (Leipzig, C. F. Amelang, 1913).
110. Janeček, Blanche, "Bibliography of Czech Literature in English Translation", *Bulletin of Bibliography*, Boston, 16 (1937-39), pp. 47-9, 70-1, 98, 111.
111. Jelínek, Hanuš, *La littérature tchèque contemporaine* (Paris, Mercure de France, 1902).
112. ——, *Études tchécoslovaques* (Paris, Bossard, 1927).
113. ——, *Histoire de la littérature tchèque des origines à 1850*, 3 vols. (Paris, Éditions du sagittaire (anciennes Éditions Kra), 1930-35).
114. Karásek, J., *Slavische Literaturgeschichte*, 2 vols. (= *Sammlung Göschen*, No. 277 and 278) (Leipzig, 1906).
115. Kramoris, Ivan J., *A Chronological Outline of Slovak Literature and History* (Passaic, N. J., The Slovak Catholic Sokol Press, 1946).
116. Kučera, Henry and Kovtun, Emil, "Literature", *Czechoslovakia*, eds. V. Bušek and N. Spulber (New York, F. A. Praeger, 1957), pp. 173-97.
117. Lützow, Francis, Count von, *A History of Bohemian Literature* (London, 1899 and 1907).
118. ——, *Bohemian Literature* (London, J. M. Dent and Sons, 1911).
119. Marchant, Francis P., *An Outline of Bohemian Literature* (London, 1911).
120. Meriggi, Bruno, *Storia della letteratura ceca e slovacca* (Milano, Nova accademia, 1958).
121. Mráz, Andrej, *Die Literatur der Slowaken* (Berlin, Volk und Reich Verlag, 1943).
122. Novák, Arne, *Die tschechiche Literatur aus der Vogelperspektive* (Prag, J. Flesch, 1923).
123. ——, *Die tschechische Literatur* (*Handbuch der Literaturwissenschaft*, ed. O. Walzel) (Potsdam, 1931-2).
124. Rádl, Otto, "Czech and Slovak Literature", *A Handbook of Slavic Studies*, ed. L. I. Strakhovsky (Cambridge, Mass., Harvard University Press, 1949), pp. 484-511.
125. Reiman, Pavel, *Von Herder bis Kisch*. Studien zur Geschichte

der deutsch-österreichisch-tschechischen Literatur-Beziehungen (Berlin, Dietz Verlag, 1961).
126. Ripellino, Angelo Maria, *Storia della poesia ceca contemporanea* (Rome, 1950).
127. Seifert, Josef L., *Literaturgeschichte der Čechoslowaken, Südslawen und Bulgaren* (Kempten, J. Kösel and F. Pustet, 1923).
128. Selver, Paul, *Otokar Březina, a Study in Czech Literature* (Oxford, London, B. Blackwell, 1921).
129. ——, *Czechoslovak Literature, an Outline* (London, G. Allen and Unwin, 1942).
130. Součková, Milada, *A Literature in Crisis: Czech Literature, 1938-1950* (New York, Mid-European Studies Center, National Committee for a Free Europe, 1954).
131. ——, *The Czech Romantics* ('s-Gravenhage, Mouton, 1958).
132. Wellek, René, "Czech Literature" and "Slovak Literature" and forty articles on the major figures in Czechoslovak literature since 1870, in *Columbia Dictionary of Modern European Literatures*, ed. Horatio Smith (New York, Columbia University Press, 1947), pp. 185-9, 757-9, etc. (By far the fullest account in English).
133. ——, "Letteratura ceca, Teatro, Letteratura slovacca", *Il Milione, Enciclopedia di Geografia*, Vol. 4 (Novara, Istituto Geografico de Agostini, 1960), pp. 76-90.
134. ——, *Essays on Czech Literature* (The Hague, Mouton and Co., 1963).

Anthologies:

135. Albert, Eduard, *Poesie aus Böhmen* (Wien, Hölder, 1893).
136. ——, *Neuere Poesie aus Böhmen* (Wien, Hölder, 1895).
137. ——, *Neueste Poesie aus Böhmen*, 2 vols. (Wien, A. Hölder, 1895).
138. *Lyrisches und Verwandtes aus der böhmischen Literatur* (Wien, Hölder, 1900).
139. Eisner, Paul, *Slovakische Anthologie* (= *Insel-Bücherei* No. 103) (Leipzig, Insel-Verlag, 192).
140. ——, *Tschechische Anthologie* (Vrchlický-Sova-Březina) (= *Insel-Bücherei* No. 106) (Leipzig, Insel-Verlag, 1922).
141. French, Alfred, *A Book of Czech Verse* (London, Macmillan, 1958).
142. Ginsburg, Roderick Aldrich, *The Soul of a Century* (Chicago, Czechoslovak National Council of America, 1942).

143. Harkins, William E., *Anthology of Czech Literature* (New York, King's Crown Press, 1953).
144. Jelínek, Hanuš, *Anthologie de la poésie tchèque* (Paris, 1930).
145. Kramoris, Ivan J., *An Anthology of Slovak Poetry* (Cleveland, Benedictine High School, 1947).
146. Kunstmann, Heinrich H., *Denkmäler der alttschechischen Literatur von ihren Anfängen bis zur Hussitenbewegung* (Berlin, Deutscher Verlag der Wissenschaften, 1955).
147. Manning, Clarence A., *An Anthology of Czechoslovak Poetry* (New York, Columbia University Press, 1929).
148. Munzer, Zdenka and Munzer, Jan, *We Were and We Shall Be. The Czechoslovak Spirit through the Centuries* (New York, F. Ungar, 1941).
149. Osers, Ewald and Montgomery, J. K., *Modern Czech Poetry. An Anthology* (London, G. Allen and Unwin, 1945).
150. *Selected Czech Tales*. Translated by Marie Busch and Otto Pick (= *The World's Classics*) (Oxford University Press, 1925).
151. Selver, Paul, *An Anthology of Czechoslovak Literature* (London, Kegan Paul, Trench, Trubner and Co., 1929).
152. ——, *A Century of Czech and Slovak Poetry* (London, New Europe Publishing Co., 1946).
153. Weisskopf, F. C., *Hundred Towers. A Czechoslovak Anthology of Creative Writing* (New York, L. B. Fischer, 1945).

Addendum: 1170, 1171, 1191, 1200, 1205-8, 1220, 1221, 1227, 1228, 1231, 1250, 1256, 1270, 1281, 1287, 1289

Crossreferences: 5, 52, 77, 166, 224

B. Linguistics

154. Bauernöppel, Josef and Fritsch, H., *Grammatik der tschechischen Sprache* (Berlin, Volk and Wissen, 1957).
155. de Bray, R. G. A., *Guide to the Slavonic Languages* (London, J. M. Dent and Sons, 1951).
156. Broch, Olaf, *Slavische Phonetik* (= *Sammlung slavischer Lehr- und Handbücher*, Reihe 1, Bd. 2) (Heidelberg, 1911).
157. Cronia, A., *Gramatica della lingua Cèca* (Florence, Ed. "Le lingue estere", 1949)
158. Dobrovský, Josef, *Geschichte der böhmischen Sprache und ältere Literatur* (Prag, G. Haase, 1818).

159. ——, *Lehrgebäude der böhmischen Sprache* (Prag, G. Haase, 1819).
160. ——, *Geschichte der böhmischen Sprache und Literatur*. Hrsg. und mit einem Vorwort versehen von Herbert Rössel (Halle/Saale, M. Niemeyer, 1955).
161. Entwistle, W. J. and Morison, W. A., *Russian and the Slavonic Languages* (London, Faber and Faber, 1949).
162. Fischer, Rudolf, *Tschechische Grammatik*, 2 vols. (Halle/Saale, M. Niemeyer, 1954).
163. Frinta, Antonín, *A Czech Phonetic Reader* (London, University of London Press, 1925).
164. Fritsch, Hermann and others, *Čeština. Lehrbuch der tschechischen Sprache*, 2 vols. (Berlin, Verl. Volk und Wissen, 1960).
165. Garvin, P. L., *A Prague School Reader* (Prague, 1955).
166. Halle, Morris and others (comp.), *For Roman Jakobson*, Essays on the Occasion of his Sixtieth Birthday (The Hague, Mouton and Co., 1956).
167. Harkins, William E., *Bibliography of Slavic Philology* (New York, King's Crown Press, 1951).
168. ——, with Hnyková, Marie, *Modern Czech Grammar* (New York, King's Crown Press, 1953).
169. Hattala, Martin, *Grammatica linguae Slovenicae collatae cum proxime cognata Bohemica* (Schemnicii, Typis Francisci Lorber, 1850).
170. Jakobson, Roman, *Slavic Languages* (New York, King's Crown Press, 1955).
171. ——, *Selected Writings*. Vol. I, *Phonological Studies* (The Hague, Mouton and Co., 1962).
172. Kučera, Henry, *The Phonology of Czech* (The Hague, Mouton and Co., 1961).
173. ——, "Entropy, Redundancy and Functional Load in Russian and Czech", in *American Contributions to the Fifth International Congress of Slavists, Sofia, September 1963*, Vol. I: *Linguistic Contributions* (The Hague, Mouton and Co., 1963).
174. Lee, William Rowland, *Teach Yourself Czech* (London, English Universities Press, 1959).
175. Liewehr, Fr., *Einführung in die historische Grammatik der tschechichen Sprache* (Brünn, Rohrer, 1933).
176. Macht, A., *Praktisches Lehr- und Übungsbuch der slovakischen Sprache*, 2 vols. (Vienna – Leipzig, Hartlebens, 1931).

177. Mann, Stuart E., *Czech Historical Grammar* (London, University of London, 1957).
178. Mazon, A., *Grammaire de la langue tchèque*, 3rd ed. (Paris, Institut d'études slaves, 1952).
179. Meillet, A., *Le slave commun*, 2nd ed. Rev. by A. Vaillant (Paris, H. Champion, 1934).
180. Meriggi, B., *Grammatica Slovacca* (Florencia, 1955).
181. Mikkola, J. J., *Urslavische Grammatik*, 3 vols. (Heidelberg, C. Winter, 1913-50).
182. Miklosich, Fr., *Vergleichende Grammatik der slavischen Sprachen*, 4 vols; 2nd ed. (Wien, Braumüller, 1875-83).
183. Mikula, Bohumil E., *Progressive Czech (Bohemian)* (Chicago, Ill., Czechoslovak National Council of America, 1948).
184. Palacký, František, *Jos. Dobrowský's Leben und gelehrtes Wirken* (Prag, 1833).
185. Rubenstein, Herbert, *A Comparative Study of Morphophonemic Alterations in Standard Serbo-Croatian, Czech, and Russian* (Ann Arbor, 1950).
186. Šafařík, Pavel Josef, *Die ältesten Denkmäler der böhmischen Sprache* (Prag, In Commission bei Kronberger und Riwnac, 1840).
187. ——, *Geschichte der slawischen Sprache und Literatur nach allen Mundarten*, 2. Abdruck (Prag, F. Tempsky, 1869).
188. Schwarz, J., *Colloquial Czech* (London, K. Paul, 1951).
189. Sova, Miloš, *A Modern Czech Grammar* (New York, Stechert-Hafner, 1944).
190. ——, *A Practical Czech Course for English Speaking Students* (Prague, Státní pedagogické nakladatelství, 1962).
191. Štěpánek, O., *Czech (Bohemian) Grammar* (Omaha, The Czech Historical Society, 1933).
192. Trautmann, R., *Die slavischen Völker und Sprachen* (Göttingen, Vandenhoeck and Ruprecht, 1947).
193. ——, *Die alttschechische Alexandreis* (= *Sammlung Slavischer Lehr- und Handbücher*, 3. Reihe: *Texte und Untersuchungen*) (Heidelberg, 1916).
194. Trávníček, František, *Phonetik der tschechischen Schriftsprache* (Halle/Saale, M. Niemeyer, 1954).
195. Vaillant, A., *Grammaire comparée des langues slaves*, 2 vols. (Paris IAC, 1950, 1954).
196. Vey, M., *Morphologie du tchèque parlé* (Paris, C. Klincksieck, 1948).

197. Viktorin, J. K., *Grammatik der slovakischen Sprache*, 3 Ausg. (Pest, Druck von M. Bagó, 1865).
198. Vondrák, V., *Vergleichende slavische Grammatik*, 2 vols., 2nd ed. (Göttingen, 1924-8).

Dictionaries:

199. Caha, Jan and Krámský, Jiří, *English-Czech Dictionary* (Prague, State Pedagogical Publishing House, 1960).
200. Čermák, A., *English-Czech, Czech-English Dictionary* (Třebíč, J. Lorenz, 1922).
201. Cheshire, H. T., Jung, V., Klozner, K., Procházka, J., Ryan, R. E., Šrámek, Ant., *Czech-English Dictionary*, 2 vols. (Prague, J. Otto, 1933, 1935).
202. Filo, Adolf and Detrich, Julius, *Slovakian-English Dictionary* (Ružomberok, Koruna, 1946).
203. Jung, V. A., *A Dictionary of the English and Bohemian Languages* (Prague, J. Otto, 1920).
204. Kabesch, F., *Czech-German, German-Czech Dictionary* (Berlin, Langenscheidt, 1929).
205. Konuš, J. J., *Slovak-English and English-Slovak Dictionary* (Pittsburgh, 1941).
206. Osička, Antonín and Poldauf, Ivan, *Anglicko-český slovník*, 3rd ed. (Prague, Československá akademie věd, 1957).
207. Poldauf, Ivan, *Czech-English Dictionary* (Prague, State Publishing House of Instructional Literature, 1959).
208. Procházka, J., *English-Czech and Czech-English Dictionary*, 16th ed. (Prague, Orbis, 1959).
209. Schultz, Johann, *Wörterbuch der deutschen und slowakischen Sprache*, 2 vols. (Bratislava, Verlags- und literarische Gesellschaft "Komenský", 1941).
210. Schwartz, Michael, *Slowakisch-deutsches und deutsch-slowakisches Wörterbuch* (Berlin, Alex. Junker, 1943).
211. Šedivý, V., *Small Differential Czech-Slovak Dictionary* (Prague, 1937).
212. Vedral, Dalibor, *Czech and Slovak Lexicographic Materials and Dictionaries* (Washington, D.C., Department of the Army, 1959).
213. Vilikovská, Julia and others, *Slovak-English Dictionary* (Bratislava Slovenské pedagogické nakladatelstvo, 1959).

Addendum: 1234, 1311, 1316

Crossreferences: 5, 276

C. Philosophy

214. Bergmann, H., *Das philosophische Werk B. Bolzano's* (Halle, 1909).
215. Betts, R. R., "The Influence of Realist Philosophy on John Hus and Predecessors in Bohemia", *Slavonic and East European Review*, 29 (1951), pp. 402-19.
216. Bittner, Karl, *Herders Geschichtsphilosophie und die Slawen* (Reichenberg, Gebrüder Stiepel, 1929).
217. Caldwell, William, "Masaryk as Philosopher", *The Central European Observer*, 8 (1930), p. 133.
218. Čapek, Karel, "T. G. Masaryk, a Modern Type of Universalism", *The Central European Observer*, 8 (1930), p. 129.
219. Čapek, Milič, *The Philosophical Impact of Contemporary Physics* (Princeton, D. Van Nostrand, 1961).
220. Charvát, O., "J. Kratochvíl e la neoscolastica in Cecoslovacchia", *Rivista di filosofia neoscolastica* (1934).
221. Chopin, Jules, "Un philosophe de la démocratie, T. G. Masaryk", *Mercure de France*, Paris, 286 (1938), pp. 558-75.
222. Čyževskyj, D. (ed.), *Hegel bei den Slaven* (Reichenberg, Gebrüder Stiepel, 1934).
223. David, Madeleine, "La philosophie de Masaryk", *La Revue française de Prague*, 5 (1926), pp. 213-77, 293-315.
224. *Dichter, Denker, Helfer. M. Brod zum 50. Geburtstag*. Ed. F. Weltsch (Mähr. Ostrau, Julius Kittls Nachfolger Keller und Co., 1934).
225. Drtina, Fr., "L'idée humanitaire dans la vie et l'œuvre de Jean Amos Comenius", *Revue internationale de l'Enseignement*, 60 (1913).
226. Durdík, Josef, "Über die Verbreitung der Herbartschen Philosophie in Böhmen", *Zeitschrift für exakte Philosophie* (1883).
227. Essertier, Daniel, "Philosophie de Masaryk et J. J. Rousseau", *La Revue française de Prague*, 7 (1928), pp. 193-4.
228. Eucken, R., *Beiträge zur Geschichte der neueren Philosophie vornehm. der Deutschen* (Leipzig, Dür, 1886; 2nd ed. 1906), pp. 38-53.
229. Fels, H., *B. Bolzano, sein Leben und sein Werk* (Leipzig, F. Meiner, 1929).
230. *Festschrift Th. G. Masaryk zum 80. Geburtstage*, 2 vols. (Bonn, Friedrich Cohen, 1930).

231. Fischer, J. L., "Ein skeptischer Gnostiker", *Slavische Rundschau* (1929).
232. ——, Čechische philosophische Übersetzungsliteratur nach dem Kriege", *Slavische Rundschau*, 2 (1930), pp. 443-7.
233. Giusti, Wolfango, *Studi sulla ceca contemporanea* (1932), pp. 37-47.
234. Gumposch, V. Ph., *Die philosophische Literatur der Deutschen von 1400 bis auf unsere Tage* (Regensburg, G. J. Manz, 1851).
235. Herben, Hartl, Bláha, *T. G. Masaryk. Sa vie, sa politique, sa philosophie* (Prague, Orbis, 1923).
236. Hromádka, Josef Lukl, *Masaryk as European* (= *International Philosophical Library*, Vol. 2, No, 1) (Prague, 1936).
237. ——, "Emanuel Rádl und die Philosophie", in *La philosophie tchécoslovaque contemporaine*, 2nd ed. (1935).
238. —— (ed.), *Von der Reformation zum Morgen* (Leipzig, Koehler und Amelang, 1959).
239. Jakowenko, Boris, *Eduard Beneš als Denker* (1935).
240. Kozák, J. B., "Masaryk as Philosopher", *Slavonic Review*, 8 (1930), pp. 478-95.
241. Král, Josef, *La philosophie en Tchécoslovaquie. Aperçu historique* ... (Prague, Státní tiskárna, 1934).
242. ——, "Les tendances principales du développement des recherches philosophiques tchécoslovaques", *Revue des travaux scientifiques tchécoslovaques*, section première, 1, 1919 (1924), pp. 3-8.
243. Krause, Fr., *Weg und Welt des Goetheanisten Joh. Ev. Purkyně* (1936).
244. Krejčí, František, *Kritische Blicke auf den gegenwärtigen Stand des philosophischen Denkens in Böhmen* (Věstník Královské české společnosti nauk) (Prag, 1924).
245. Lapschin, I. "Über die Philosophie Karel Vorovkas", *Der russische Gedanke*, 2 (1930).
246. Loewe, H., *Der Kampf zwischen dem Realismus und Nominalismus im Mittelalter* (1876).
247. Loserth, Jos., *Huss und Wiclif. Zur Genesis der hussitischen Lehre* (München und Berlin, R. Oldenbourg, 1884; 2nd ed., 1925).
248. Lossky, N., "Contemporary Czech Thinkers", *The Slavonic Review*, 9, No. 25 (1930).
249. Mahnke, D., "Der Barockuniversalismus des Comenius", *Zeitschrift fur Geschichte der Erziehung und des Unterrichts* (1931-32).
250. Moysset, Henry, "Un philosophe dans la cité. Le président Masaryk", *Le Monde Slave*, Paris, 13 (1936), pp. 194-228.

251. Ott, Em., *Beiträge zur Receptionsgeschichte des römisch-kanonischen Processes in den böhmischen Ländern* (Leipzig, Breitkopf und Härtel, 1879), pp. 250-2.
252. Patočka, Jan, "Die tschechische Philosophie seit 1918", *Prager Rundschau* (1932).
253. ——, "Bericht über die tschechische Literatur zur gesamten Geschichte der Philosophie (von 1922 bis 1931)", *Archiv für die Geschichte der Philosophie* (1932).
254. ——, "La philosophie tchécoslovaque et son orientation actuelle", *Etudes philosophiques*, Nouvelle serie, 3e année, No. 1 (1948), pp. 63-74.
255. Pawlov, Andrej, and Jakowenko, Boris, *Kurze Bibliographie der neuen tschechoslovakischen Philosophie* (= Internationale Bibliothek für Philosophie, Vol. 1, No. 3) (Prag, 1935).
256. Pelikán, Ferd., "Die neueste tschechoslowakische Philosophie", *Kantstudien*, 26 (1924), pp. 472-81.
257. ——, "Die tschechische Philosophie", in *Fr. Überwegs Grundriss der Geschichte der Philosophie*, Vol. 5, 12th ed. (Berlin, E. S. Mittler und Sohn, 1928), pp. 289-98.
258. ——, *Karel Vorovka, l'uomo e l'opera* (= Biblioteca internazionale di filosofia, Vol. 2, fasc. 5/6) (Praga, 1936).
259. Pelzel, F. M., *Abbildungen böhmischer und mährischer Gelehrten*. Vol. I (1773), pp. 80-85.
260. *La pensée de T. G. Masaryk. Recueil* (= International Philosophical Library, vol. 3, fasc. 3-9). By B. V. Jakovenko (Prague, 1937).
261. *La philosophie tchécoslovaque contemporaine*. Ed. Boris Jakowenko. 2nd ed. (Prague, Russische Gedanke, 1935).
262. Prager Presse, *Masaryk, Staatsmann und Denker* (Prag, Orbis, 1930).
263. Rádl, Emanuel, *History of Biological Theories* (London, Oxford University Press, 1930).
264. ——, *La philosophie de T. G. Masaryk* (= Bibliothèque internationale de philosophie, Vol. 4, No. 1-2) (Prague, 1938).
265. Shaw, Nellie, *A Czech Philosopher on the Cotswolds, Being an Account of the Life and Work of Francis Sedlak* (London, The C. W. Daniel Co., 1940).
266. Silberstein, L., "Le travail philosophique et sociologique en Tchécoslovaquie", *Le Monde Slave* (1935), pp. 286-315.
267. ——, "L. N. Tolstoj und T. G. Masaryk", *Slavische Rundschau* (1935).

268. Škrach, V. K., "Masaryk et la pensée française", *La Revue française de Prague* (1923-24).
269. Staedke, Hildegard, *Die Entwicklung des encyklopädischen Bildungsgedankens und die Pansophie von Comenius* (Leipzig, Julius Klinkhardt, 1930).
270. Svoboda, Karel, "Neuere Richtungen in der tschechischen Ästhetik und Kunstwissenschaft", in *M. Dessoir's Zeitschrift für Ästhetik und allgemeine Kunstwissenschaft*, 29 (1935), pp. 217-27.
271. Tijan, Pablo, *Crisis del liberalismo en la Europa Centrali; el mito Masaryk* (Madrid, Editora Nacional, 1958).
272. Tvrdý, Josef, "Masaryk als Philosoph", *Philosophia Belgradi*, 3 (1938), pp. 98-115.
273. Vogl, Carl, *Peter Cheltschizki* (Zürich, Rotapfel-Verlag, 1926).
274. Walschmidt, L., *Bolzano's Begründung des Objektivismus in der theoretischen und praktischen Philosophie* (Würzburg, 1937).
275. Warren, William Preston, *Masaryk's Democracy: A Philosophy of Scientific and Moral Culture* (Chapel Hill, N. C., University of North Carolina Press, 1941).
276. Weingart, Miloš, "Joseph Dobrovsky, the Patriarch of Slavonic Studies", *Slavonic and East European Review*, 8 (1929), pp. 663-75.
277. Wellek, René, "The Philosophical Basis of Masaryk's Political Ideas", *Ethics*, 55 (1945), pp. 289-304.
278. Winter, Eduard, "Die Persönlichkeit und geistige Entwickelung B. Bolzano's", *Philos. Jahrbuch der Görresgesellschaft* (1932).
279. ——, *Religion und Offenbarung in der Religionsphilosophie B. Bolzano's* (= *Breslauer Studien zur historischen Theologie*, XX) (Breslau, Müller und Seiffert, 1932).
280. ——, *B. Bolzano und sein Kreis* (Leipzig, J. Hegner, 1933).
281. Zába, G., "Slavische Philosophie in Böhmen", in *Fr. Überwegs Grundriss der Geschichte der Philosophie*. 11th ed. (Berlin, E. S. Mittler und Sohn, 1916), pp. 726-34.
282. Zimmermann, R., *Ueber den wissenschaftlichen Charakter und die philosophische Bedeutung Bernhard Bolzano's* (1849).

Addendum: 1213, 1214, 1243, 1271, 1293, 1308, 1309.

Crossreferences: 5, 315, 320, 363, 391, 392, 401, 559, 709, 754, 878, 883, 903, 968, 978, 1002, 1005, 1026, 1154, 1155, 1156, 1157.

A Selective Bibliography 575

D. History

283. Bachmann, Adolf, *Geschichte Böhmens*, 2 vols. (Gotha, F. A. Perthes 1899 and 1905).
284. Benadík, B., Vlček, E. and Ambros, C., *Keltische Gräberfelder in der Südwestslowakei* (Bratislava, 1957).
285. Beninger, Edu., *Die germanischen Bodenfunde in der Slowakei* (Reichenberg, Sudetendt. Verl. F. Kraus, 1937).
286. Beninger, Edu., and Freising, Hans, *Die germanischen Bodenfunde in Mähren* (Reichenberg, Sudetendt. Verl., 1933).
287. Berger, W., *Johannes Hus und König Sigmund* (Augsburg, 1871).
288. Bittner, Konrad, *Deutsche und Tschechen* (Brünn und Leipzig, 1936).
289. Boczek, A., *Codex diplomaticus et epistolaris Moraviae*, 10 vols. (Brünn and Olmütz, 1835-78).
290. Böhm, Jaroslav and others, *La Grande-Moravie. The Great Moravian Empire* (Prague, Publishing House of the Czechoslovak Academy of Sciences, 1963).
291. Bouillon, Georges, *L'information française et la question tchèque de 1800 à 1867*. Diplôme d'Etudes supérieures (Paris, Fac. des Lettres, 1947).
292. Bretholz, Bertold, *Geschichte Böhmens und Mährens bis zum Aussterben der Přemysliden 1306* (München-Leipzig, Duncker und Humblot, 1912).
293. ——, *Neuere Geschichte Böhmens (1526-1576)* (Gotha, 1920).
294. ——, *Geschichte Böhmens und Mährens*, 4 vols. (Reichenberg, P. Sollors' Nachf.G.m.b.H., 1921-24).
295. Brock, Peter, *The Political and Social Doctrines of the Unity of Czech Brethren in the 15th and Early 16th Centuries* (The Hague, Mouton & Co., 1957).
296. Čapek, Thomas, *The Slovaks of Hungary. Slavs and Panslavism* (New York, The Knickerbocker Press, 1906).
297. Czerwenka, B., *Geschichte der Evangelischen Kirche in Böhmen* (Bielefeld-Leipzig, 1860, 1870).
298. Daum, H., *Die Verfolgung der Evangelischen in Böhmen* (Darmstadt, 1860).
299. Delaisement, Gérard, *L'information française et la question tchèque et slovaque de 1867 à 1914*. Diplôme d'Etudes supérieures (Paris Fac. des Lettres, 1950).
300. Denis, Ernest, *La fin de l'indépendance bohême*, 2 vols. (Paris, A. Colin, 1890).

301. ——, *Huss et la guerre des Hussites* (Paris, Leroux, 1878).
302. ——, *La Bohême depuis la Montagne Blanche*, 2 vols. (Paris, E. Leroux, 1902-03).
303. ——, *La Question d'Autriche. Les Slovaques* (Paris, Delagrave, 1917).
304. Dittrich, Zdeněk R., *Christianity in Great-Moravia* (= *Bijdragen van het Instituut voor Middeleeuwse Geschiedenis der Rijksuniversiteit te Utrecht*, Vol. XXXIII) (Groningen, J. B. Wolters, 1962).
305. Dobiáš, Josef, *Il Limes romano nelle terre della Republicca Cecoslovacca ed i tentativi di portare le frontiere dell'Impero sui monti Sudeti e Carpati* (= *Quaderni dell'Impero. Il limes romano*, No. 8) (Roma, 1938).
306. ——, *Le Strade romane nel territorio cecoslovacco* (= *Quaderni dell'Impero. Le grandi strade del mondo romano*, No. 5) (Roma, 1937).
307. Dvorník, Francis, *Les légendes de Constantin et de Méthode, vues de Byzance* (Prague, Orbis, 1933).
308. ——, *Les Slaves, Byzance et Rome au IXe siecle* (Paris, 1926).
309. ——, *The Making of Central and Eastern Europe* (London, The Polish Research Centre, 1949).
310. ——, *The Slavs, their Early History and Civilization* (Boston, Mass., American Academy of Arts and Sciences, 1956).
311. ——, *The Slavs in European History and Civilization* (New Brunswick, N.J., Rutgers University Press, 1962).
312. Eberlein, H. L., *Schlesische Kirchengeschichte: Das evangelische Schlesien*, Vol. 1 (Düsseldorf, 1952).
313. Emler, J., *Regesta diplomatica necnon epistolaria regni Bohemiae et Moraviae*. Ed. C. J. Erben, J. Emler. 4 vols. (Prague, 1855 ff.).
314. Friedrich, G., *Codex diplomaticus et epistolaris regni Bohemiae*, 3 vols. (Prague, 1904-42).
315. Friedrich, O., *Helden des Geistes: Jan Hus, Chelčický, Komenský* (Zürich, 1935).
316. Frind, A., *Der heilige Johannes von Nepomuk* (Eger, Prag, 1879; rev. by W. A. Frind, 1929).
317. Gindely, A., *Geschichte der Böhmischen Brüder*, 2 vols. (Prague, 1857-58).
318. ——, *Geschichte des dreissigjährigen Krieges*, 4 vols. (Prague, 1869-80). English translation by A. Ten Broek, *History of the Thirty Years War*, 2 vols. (New York, 1884).

A Selective Bibliography 577

319. Goll. J., *Quellen und Untersuchungen der Böhmischen Brüder*, 2 vols. (Prag, 1878 and 1882).
320. Heyberger, Anna, *Jean Amos Comenius (Komenský)* (Paris, 1928).
321. Heymann, Frederick G., *John Žižka and the Hussite Revolution* (Princeton, Princeton University Press, 1955).
322. *Historica*, Prague, 1959 and ff.
323. Höffler, K., *Kaiser Karl IV and Kaiser Karl V. Eine Parallele* (Prag, 1891).
324. Hrejsa, F., *Kirchengeschichte Böhmens* (= *Ekklesien*, Vol. 5) (Leipzig, 1937).
325. Hutton, J. E., *A History of the Moravian Church*, 2nd ed. (London, 1909).
326. Jelínek, Jan, *Anthropologie der Bronzezeit in Mähren* (= *Anthropos*, Vol. II) (Brno, Grafia, 1959).
327. Kapras, Jan, Jr., *Évolution historique de l'état tchécoslovaque* (Prague, 1919).
328. Kazbunda, Karel, "Deux mémoranda de Rieger", *Le Monde Slave* (Paris, 1925), pt. III, pp. 102-38.
329. Kerner, Robert J., *Bohemia in the Eighteenth Century. A Study in Political, Economic, and Social History, with Special Reference to the Reign of Leopold II, 1790-1792* (New York, Macmillan, 1932).
330. Kohn, Hans, *Pan-Slavism. Its History and Ideology* (Notre Dame, Ill., 1953).
331. Krajcar, J., *Bohuslav Balbín S. J. als Geschichtschreiber* (Rome, 1956).
332. Kroess, A., *Geschichte der böhmischen Provinz der Gesellschaft Jesu*, 2 vols. (Wien, 1910-27).
333. Krofta, Kamil, *Das Deutschtum in der tchechoslowakischen Geschichte* (Prag, Orbis, 1934).
334. ——, *A Short History of Czechoslovakia* (New York, R. M. McBride, 1934).
335. ——, "Bohemia to the Extinction of the Přemyslids", in *The Cambridge Medieval History*, Vol. 6. Ed. John B. Bury (New York, Macmillan Co., 1936), pp. 422-47.
336. ——, "Bohemia in the Fourteenth Century", in *The Cambridge Medieval History*, vol. 7, pp. 155-82.
337. ——, "John Hus", in *The Cambridge Medieval History*, vol. 8, pp. 45-64.
338. ——, "Bohemia in the Fifteenth Century", in *The Cambridge*

Medieval History, vol. 8, pp. 65-115.
339. Krummel, L., *Utraquisten und Taboriten. Ein Beitrag zur Geschichte der böhmischen Reformation im 15. Jahrhundert* (Gotha, 1871).
340. Léger, Louis, *La renaissance tchèque au XIXe siècle* (Paris, Alcan, 1911).
341. Léger, Louis, *La renaissance tchèque au dix-neuvième siècle* (Paris, Librairie Felix Alcan, 1911).
342. ——, *Les anciennes civilisations slaves* (Paris, 1921).
343. Lettrich, Jozef, *History of Modern Slovakia* (New York, F. A. Praeger, 1953).
344. Locher, T. J. G., *Die nationale Differenzierung und Integrierung der Slovaken und Tschechen in ihrem Geschichtlichen Verlauf bis 1848* (Haarlem, 1931).
345. Lützow, Franz Count, *Bohemia: An Historical Sketch* (London, J. M. Dent, 1939).
346. ——, *Lectures on the Historians of Bohemia* (London, H. Frowdie, 1905).
347. ——, *The Life and Times of Master John Hus* (London, Dent and Co., 1909).
348. Macartney, C. A., *Hungary and Her Successors* (London, Oxford University Press, 1937).
349. Macek, J., *The Hussite Movement in Bohemia*, 2nd ed. (Prague, 1958).
350. Martinů, J., *Die Waldesier und die husitische Reformation in Böhmen* (Vienna-Leipzig, 1910).
351. Masaryk, Tomáš G., *Palacký's Idee des böhmischen Volkes* (Prag, 1898).
352. Matiegka, Jindřich, *The Origin and Beginnings of the Czechoslovak People*. From the Smithsonian Report for 1919, pp. 471-86 (Washington, D.C., 1921).
353. Matouš, Lubor, *Bedřich Hrozný. The Life and Work of a Czech Oriental Scholar* (Prague, Orbis, 1949).
354. Maurice, Charles Edmund, *Bohemia from the Earliest Times to the Fall of National Independence in 1620, with a Short Summary of Later Events* (London, Fischer and Unwin, 1896).
355. Müller, J. T., *Geschichte der Böhmischen Brüder*, 3 vols. (Herrnhut, 1922-31).
356. Naegle, A., *Kirchengeschichte Böhmens. I. Einführung des Christentums in Böhmen* (Vienna and Leipzig, 1915-18).
357. Němeček, O., *Das Reich des Slawenfürsten Samo* (Mährisch-Ostrau, 1906).

358. Neustupný, E. and Neustupný, J., *Czechoslovakia before the Slavs* (New York, F. A. Praeger, 1961).
359. Niederle, Lubor, *Manuel de l'antiquité slave*, 2 vols. (Paris, Champion, 1923-26).
360. ——, *La race slave. Statistique, démographie, anthropologie* (Paris, 1911).
361. Novotný, B., *Die Slowakei in der jüngeren Steinzeit* (Bratislava, 1958).
362. Novotný, V., *Zur böhmischen Quellenkunde* (Prag, 1907).
363. Odložilík, Otakar, *Wiclif and Bohemia* (Prague, 1937).
364. ——, "Modern Czechoslovak Historiography", *The Slavonic and East European Review*, 30 (1952), pp. 376-92.
365. ——, "Russia and Czech National Aspirations", *Journal of Central European Affairs*, 22 (1963), pp. 407-39.
366. Oman, Lenanton, C., *Elizabeth of Bohemia* (London, 1938).
367. Palacký, František, *Geschichte von Böhmen*, 5 vols. (Prague, 1864-1896).
368. ——, *Die Vorläufer des Hussitentums* (Leipzig, 1869).
369. ——, *Würdigung der alten böhmischen Geschichtsschreiber* (Prag, 1830; 2nd ed. 1869).
370. Pech, Stanley Zdeněk, " F. L. Rieger: The Road from Liberalism to Conservatism", *Journal of Central European Affairs*, 17 (1957), pp. 3-23.
371. Pekař, J., *Wallenstein, 1630-1634: Tragödie einer Verschwörung* (Berlin, 1937).
372. Peschke, E., *Die Theologie der Böhmischen Brüder in ihrer Frühzeit*, 2 vols. (Stuttgart, W. Kohlhammer, 1935-40).
373. Pfeifer, W., *Städtewappen und Städtesiegel in Böhmen und Mähren* (München, 1952).
374. Pfitzner, Josef, *Sudetendeutsche Geschichte*, 2nd ed. (Reichenberg, Sudeten-deutscher Verlag, F. K. Kraus, 1937).
375. Píč, Josef Ladislav, *Die Urnengräber Böhmens* (Leipzig, Hiersemann, 1907).
376. ——, *Le Hradischt de Stradonitz en Bohême* (Leipzig, Hiersemann, 1906).
377. Plaschka, Richard G., *Von Palacký bis Pekař. Geschichtswissenschaft und Nationalbewusstsein bei den Tschechen* (Graz, H. Böhlaus Nachf., 1955).
378. Polišenský, J. V., *History of Czechoslovakia in Outline* (Prague, Sphinx, Bohumil Janda, 1947).

379. ——, "Archives in Czechoslovakia and the Study of World History", *Historica*, 1 (1959), pp. 267-77.
380. Preidel, Helmut, *Die vor- und frühgeschichtlichen Siedlungsräume in Böhmen und Mähren* (Munich, Oldenbourg, 1953).
381. Prokeš, Jaroslav, *Histoire tchécoslovaque* (Prague, Éditions Orbis, 1927).
382. Rezek, A., *Geschichte der Regierung Ferdinands I in Böhmen* (Prag, 1878).
383. Šafařík, P. J., *Slawische Altertümer* (Leipzig, 1843).
384. Schmidtmayer, Alfred, *Geschichte der Sudetendeutschen: Ein Volksbuch* (Leipzig, Adam Kraft Verlag, 1938).
385. Schránil, Josef, *Die Vorgeschichte Böhmens und Mährens* (Leipzig, W. de Gruyter und Co., 1928).
386. Seton-Watson, Robert W., *Racial Problems in Hungary* (London, Archibald Constable, 1908).
387. ——, *German, Slav and Magyar: A Study in the Origins of the Great War* (London, Williams and Norgate, 1916).
388. ——, *History of the Czechs and Slovaks* (London, Hutchinson, 1943).
389. —— (ed.), *Prague Essays. Presented by a Group of British Historians to the Caroline University of Prague on the Occasion of its Sixhundredth Anniversary* (Oxford, Clarendon Press, 1949).
390. Šimák, Josef Vitězslav and Pežek, Josef, *La nation tchécoslovaque à travers l'histoire* (Prague, Orbis, 1925).
391. Spinka, Matthew, *John Hus and the Czech Reform* (Chicago, The University of Chicago Press, 1941).
392. ——, *John Amos Comenius, that incomparable Moravian* (Chicago, The University of Chicago Press, 1943).
393. Stocký, A., *La Bohême à l'âge de la pierre* (Prague, 1924).
394. ——, *La Bohême à l'âge du bronze* (Prague, 1928).
395. ——, *La Bohême à l'âge du fer* (Prague, 1933).
396. ——, *La Bohême préhistorique. I, Le néolithique* (Prague, 1926).
397. Tapié, Victor L., *La politique étrangère de la France et le début de la guerre de Trente ans (1616-1621)* (Paris, P.U.F., 1934).
398. Thomson, S. Harrison, *Czechoslovakia in European History* (Princeton, Princeton University Press, 1953).
399. Uhlirz, K. and Uhlirz, M., *Handbuch der Geschichte Österreichs und seiner Nachbarländer Böhmen und Ungarn*, 3 vols. (Graz, Wien, Leipzig, 1927-39).
400. Weizsäcker, Wilhelm, *Quellenbuch zur Geschichte der Sudeten-*

A Selective Bibliography 581

länder (München, Verlag Robert Lerche, 1960).
401. Werstadt, Jaroslav, "The Philosophy of Czech History", *The Slavonic Review*, 3 (1925), pp. 533-46.
402. Werunsky, E., *Geschichte Kaiser IV und seiner Zeit* (Innsbruck, 1888-92).
403. Winter, Eduard, *Der Josefinismus und seine Geschichte* (Brünn, 1943).
404. Wiskeman, Elizabeth, *Czechs and Germans: A Study of the Struggle in the Historic Provinces of Bohemia and Moravia* (London, Oxford University Press, 1938).
405. Yurchak, Peter P., *The Slovaks, their History and Traditions* (Whiting, Ind., J. J. Lach, 1947).
406. Zeithammer, Antonín O., *Zur Geschichte der böhmischen Ausgleichversuche (1865-71)* (Prag, Selbstverlag, 1912-13).
407. Zycha, A., *Ueber den Ursprung der Städte in Böhmen und die Stadtpolitik der Přemysliden* (Prag, 1914).

Addendum: 1173, 1190, 1209, 1213, 1214, 1218, 1235, 1237, 1238, 1260-3, 1276, 1278-81, 1292, 1301, 1302, 1306, 1307.

Crossreferences: 13, 14, 45, 69, 71, 74, 77, 79, 83, 84, 85, 238, 247, 273, 766, 866, 878, 884, 899.

IV. ARTS

A. Music and Drama

408. Bartoš, František, *Bedřich Smetana, Letters and Reminiscences* (Prague, Artia, 1955).
409. Batka, Richard, *Geschichte der Musik in Böhmen* (Prag, Dürerverlag, 1906).
410. Benyovszky, Karl, *Das alte Theater. Kulturgeschichtl. Studie aus Pressburgs Vergangenheit* (Bratislava, Karl Augermayer, 1926).
411. ——, *J. N. Hummel, der Mensch und Künstler* (Bratislava, Eos-Verlag, 1934).
412. Blass, Leo, *Das Theater und Drama in Böhmen bis zum Anfange des XIX. Jahrhunderts* (Prag, 1877).
413. Boese, Helmut, *Zwei Urmusikanten: Smetana, Dvořák* (Zürich, Amalthea Verlag, 1955).
414. Branberger, Johann, *Musikgeschichtliches aus Böhmen* (Prag, I. Taussig, 1906).

415. ——, *Das Konservatorium für Musik in Prag* (Prag, Verein zur Beförderung der Tonkunst in Böhmen, 1911).
416. Burney, Charles, 1726-1815. *Dr. Burney's Musical Tours in Europe*. Ed. Percy A. Scholes, 2 vols. (London-New York, Oxford University Press, 1959).
417. Chvála, Emanuel, *Ein Vierteljahrhundert böhmischer Musik* (Prag, F. A. Urbánek, 1887).
418. *Czechoslovak Music*. Collection of articles by various authors (Prague, Orbis, 1946).
419. *Czechoslovak Music* (Prague, Orbis, 1948).
420. Dlabač, Jan Bohumír, *Allgemeines historisches Künstlerlexikon für Böhmen und zum Theil auch für Mähren und Schlesien*, 3 vols. (Prag, Gedruckt bei G. Haase, 1815).
421. Elvert, C. d', *Geschichte der Musik in Mähren und Österr.-Schlesien* (Brünn, Verlag der Hist.-stat. Sektion, 1873).
422. ——, *Geschichte des Theaters in Mähren und Österreichisch Schlesien* (= *Schriften der k. mährisch-schlesischen Gesellschaft*, IV) (Brünn, 1852).
423. Fles, Barthold, *Slavonic Rhapsody: The Life of Antonín Dvořák* (New York, Allen, Towne and Health, 1948).
424. Hantich, H., *La musique tchèque* (Paris, Nilsson, 1910).
425. Helfert, Vladimír and Steinhard, Erich, *Geschichte der Musik in der Tschechoslovakischen Republik* (Prag, Orbis Verlag, 1936).
426. ——, *Die Musik in der Tschechoslovakischen Republik. Mit einer Bibliographie* (Prag, Orbis, 1938).
427. ——, *Die schöpferische Entwicklung Friedrich Smetana's: Präludium zum Lebenswerk* (Leipzig, Breitkopf und Härtel, 1956).
428. Honzl, Jindřich (ed.), *The Czechoslovak Theatre* (Prague, Orbis, 1948).
429. Jirák, Karel B., *Antonín Dvořák, 1841-1961* (New York, Czechoslovak Society of Arts and Sciences in America, 1961).
430. Komma, Karl Michael, *Johann Zach und die tschechischen Musiker im Umbruch des 18. Jahrhunderts* (Kassel, Bärenreiter-Verlag, 1938).
431. Lang, Miroslav, *Die Laienspielbühne in der Tschechoslowakei* (Prag, Orbis, 1956).
432. Lindlar, Heinrich (ed.), *Tschechische Komponisten: Janáček, Martinů, Hába, Weinberger* (Bonn-London, Boosey and Hawkes, 1954).
433. Lowenbach, Jan, *Czechoslovak Music: The Voice of a People* (New

York, Czechoslovak Information Service, 1943).
434. Mackenzie, A. C., *The Bohemian School of Music* (1905-06).
435. Matějček, Jan, *Tschechische Komponisten von Heute* (Prag, "Hudební rozhledy", 1957).
436. *Musik-Almanach für die Tschechoslowakische Republik* (Prag, J. Hoffman's Wwe, 1922).
437. *Music Lives in Prague* (Prague, Orbis, 1949).
438. Nejedlý, Zdeněk, *Smetana, the Great Master* (London, Čechoslovák, 1945).
439. Nettl, Paul, *Musik-Barock in Böhmen und Mähren – Beiträge zur böhmischen und mährischen Musikgeschichte* (Brünn, R. M. Rohrer, 1927).
440. ——, *Mozart in Böhmen. Hrsg. als 2., vollständig neubearb. und erweiterte Ausg. von Rudoph Freiherrn von Procházka's Mozart in Prag* (Prag, Neumann, 1938).
441. ——, *Forgotten Musicians* (New York, Philosophical Library, 1951).
442. Newmarch, Rosa, *The Music of Czechoslovakia* (London, Oxford University Press, 1942).
443. *Orchestral Music in Czechoslovakia* (Prague, Artia, 195?).
444. Prick van Wely, Max Arthur, *Dvořák* (Haarlem, Gottmer, 1956).
445. Procházka, Rudolph F., *Das romantische Musik-Prag* (Saaz, H. Erben, 1914).
446. ——, *Alt-Wien und Alt-Prag* (Regensburg, Almanach der Deutschen Musikbücherei, 1926).
447. Purdy, Clair Lee, *Antonín Dvořák, Composer from Bohemia* (New York, J. Messner, 1950).
448. Richter, Carl Ludwig, *Zdenko Fibich. Eine musikalische Silhouette* (Prag, F. A. Urbánek, 1900).
449. Ritter, William, *Smetana* (Paris, F. Alcan, 1907).
450. ——, "Les tendances de la musique en Tchécoslovaquie depuis la mort de Smetana", in *Encyclopedia de la musique et dictionnaire du Conservatoire* (Paris, 1913-31).
451. Rychnovsky, Ernst, *Smetana* (Stuttgart, Deutsche Verlags anstalt, 1924).
452. Šafránek, Miloš, *Bohuslav Martinů. The Man and his Music* (New York, Knopf, 1944).
453. Schmid, Otto, *Musik und Weltanschauung. Die böhmische Altmeisterschule Czernohorsky's und ihr Einfluss auf den Wiener Classicismus* (Leipzig, H. Seemann Nachfolger, 1901).

454. Schürer, Oskar, *Prag, Kultur, Kunst, Geschichte*, 2nd ed. (München, G. D. Callwey, 1939).
455. Šíp, Ladislav, *Opera in Czechoslovakia* (Prague, Orbis, 1955).
456. ——, *An Outline of Czech and Slovak Music*, 2 vols. (Prague, Orbis, 1960).
457. Soubies, Albert, *Histoire de la musique Bohême* (Paris, Libraire des bibliophiles, E. Flammarión successeur, 1898).
458. Šourek, Otakar, *Antonín Dvořák, his Life and Works* (New York, Philosophical Library, 1954).
459. ——, *Antonín Dvořák, Werkanalysen* (Prague, Artia, 1954).
460. Štědron, Bohumír, *The Work of Leoš Janáček* (Prague, Czechoslovak Composers Association, 1959).
461. ——, *Leoš Janáček in Briefen und Erinnerungen* (Prague, Artia, 1955).
462. Suermondt, R., *Smetana and Dvořák* (Stockholm, Continental Book Co., 194?).
463. Wellek, Bronislav, *Friedrich Smetana* (Prag, H. Dominicus (T. Gruss), 1895).

Addendum: 1162, 1197, 1249, 1254.

Crossreferences: 77, 903

B. Fine Arts

464. Angyal, Andreas, *Die slavische Barockwelt* (Leipzig, VEB E. A. Seemann, 1961).
465. *L'art ancien à Prague et en Tchécoslovaquie*. Catalogue de l'exposition au Musée des arts décoratifs à Paris (Paris, 1957).
466. *L'art décoratif tchécoslovaque* (À l'occasion de l'Exposition internationale des Arts décoratifs de Mons, 1923) (1923).
467. *L'art vivant en Tchécoslovaquie*. Numéro spécial de la revue *L'Art Vivant*, quatrième année, No. 78, 15 Mars 1928 (Paris, Librairie Larousse, 1928).
468. Bartušek, A. and others, *Gothic Mural Painting in Bohemia and Moravia* (Prague, 1959).
469. Blažíček, J., *L'Italia e la scultura in Bohemia nei secoli XVII° e XVIII°* (= *Quaderoni dell' Istituto di Cultura Italiana di Praga*, No. 8).
470. Bouzek, Jan and others, "Czechoslovakia", in *Encyclopedia of*

World Art, Vol. IV (New York-Toronto-London, McGraw Hill Book Co., 1961), pp. 197-223.
471. Braunne, Heinz and Wiese, Erich, *Schlesische Malerei und Plastik des Mittelalters* (Leipzig, 1929).
472. Bretholz, B., *Brünn, Geschichte und Kultur* (Brünn, Rohrer, 1938).
473. Bučina, Ferdinand, *A Book of Madonnas* (Prague, Artia, 1958).
474. Chytil, K., *Die Kunst in Prag zur Zeit Rudolf's II* (Prag, 1904).
475. Denkstein, V. and Matouš, F., *Gothic Art of Southern Bohemia* (Prague, Artia, 1955).
476. Deschamps, L., *A. Mucha et son oeuvre* (Paris, 1897).
477. Dostál, E. and Šíma, J., *L'architecture baroque à Prague* (Paris, 1926).
478. Drobná, Z., *Les trésors de la broderie religieuse en Tchécoslovaquie* (Prague, 1950).
479. ——, *Gothic Drawing* (Prague, Artia, 195?).
480. Dvořák, František, *Kupecký, the Great Baroque Portrait Painter* (Prague, Artia, 195?).
481. Dvořák, M., *Von Mánes zu Švabinský* (Graph, Künste, 1904).
482. Ernst, R., *Beiträge zur Kenntnis der Tafelmalerei Böhmens im XIV und am Anfang des XV Jahrhunderts* (Prag, 1912).
483. Fodor, Pavol M., *The Contemporary Art of Slovakia* (Bratislava, Tatrat, 1949).
484. *Folk Art in Czechoslovakia*. 2 vols. (Prague, Artia, 1955).
485. Foltyn, Ladislav, *Volksbaukunst in der Slowakei* (Prag, Artia, 1960).
486. Forman, Werner and Forman, Bedřich, *Kunst der Vorzeit in der Tschechoslowakei* (Text von Josef Paulik) (Prag, Artia, 1956).
487. Friedl, A. *Magister Theodoricus. Das Problem seiner malerischen Form* (Prag, Artia, 1956).
488. Hantich, H., *L'art tchèque au XIXe siècle (Peinture, sculpture, architecture)* (Paris, Nilson, 1910).
489. Hegemann, H. W., *Die deutsche Barockbaukunst Böhmens* (Munich, F. Bruckmann, 1943).
490. Hlávka, J. (ed.), *Topographie der historischen und Kunst-denkmale im Königreiche Böhmen von der Urzeit bis zum Anfange des XIX Jahrhunderts*, 30 vol. (Prag, 1898-1911).
491. Kletzl, O., "Studien zur böhmischen Buchmalerei", *Marburger Jahrbuch für Kunstwissenschaft* (1933), pp. 1-76.
492. Kloss, E., *Die schlesische Buchmalerei des Mittelalters* (Berlin, 1942).

493. Knox, Brian, *Bohemia and Moravia: an Architectural Companion* (London, Faber, 1962).
494. Krejcar, J. (ed.), *L'architecture contemp. en Tchécoslovaquie* (Prague, Orbis, 1928).
495. Kubíček, A., *The Palaces of Prague* (1946).
496. Květ, J., *Max Švabinský, der grosse tschechische Maler und Graphiker* (Prag, Artia, 1960).
497. Květ, J. and Swarzenski, H., *Czechoslovakia. Romanesque and Gothic Illuminated Manuscripts* (UNESCO World Art Series, 1959).
498. Lamač, M., *Contemporary Art in Czechoslovakia* (Prague, Orbis, 1958).
499. Lapaire, H. and Chopin, J., *Prague et la Tchécoslovaquie* (Grenoble, 1932).
500. Lehner, F. J., *Die böhmische Malerschule des XI. Jahrhunderts*, I (Leipzig, 1902).
501. Loriš, J., *Czech Baroque Drawing* (Prague, 1948).
502. Mašin, J., *Romanesque Mural Paintings in Bohemia and Moravia* (Prague, 1954).
503. Matějček, A., *Die böhmische Malerei des 14. Jahrhunderts* (Leipzig, E. A. Seemann, 1921).
504. —— (ed.), *Gotische Malerei in Böhmen, Tafelmalerei 1350-1450* (Prag, Kunsthistorisches Institut der Karls-Universität, 1939).
505. Matějček, Antonín and Pěšina, Jaroslav, *Gothic Painting in Bohemia, 1350-1450* (Prague, Artia, 1955).
506. Matějček, Antonín and Wirth, Zdeněk, *Modern and Contemporary Czech Art* (London, G. Routledge, 1924).
507. ——, *L'art tchèque contemporain* (Prague, 1920).
508. Mencl, Václav, *Czech Architecture of the Luxemburg Period* (Prague, Artia, 1955).
509. ——, *Elf Jahrhunderte tschechischer Architektur* (Prag, Staatliche Denkmalverwaltung, 1957).
510. Míčko, Miroslav, *Mikuláš Aleš* (Prague, Orbis, 1952).
511. Mikowec, Ferd. B., *Alterthümer und Denkwürdigkeiten Bohm* (Prag, 1860).
512. Morper, J. J., *Der Prager Architekt Jean Baptiste Mathey (Mattheus Burgundus)* (München, Callway, 1927).
513. Nebeský, V. M., *L'art moderne tchécoslovaque* (Paris, 1937).
514. Neumann, Jaromír, *Czech Classic Painting of the 19th Century* (Prague, Artia, 1955-58).

515. ——, *Die neue tschechische Malerei und ihre klassische Tradition* (Prag, Artia, 1958).
516. Neuwirth, Josef, *Zur Geschichte der Miniaturmalerei in Böhmen* (= *Mitteilungen der k.k. Central-Commission*, Vol. II) (Vienna, 1885).
517. ——, *Geschichte der christlichen Kunst in Böhmen bis zum Aussterben der Přemysliden* (Prag, 1888).
518. ——, *Geschichte der bildenden Kunst in Böhmen*, I (Prag, 1893).
519. Novotný, K. and Poche, E., *The Charles Bridge of Prague* (Prague, 1947).
520. Opitz, J., *Die Plastik in Böhmen zur Zeit der Luxemburger* (Prague, Jan Stenc, 1936).
521. Ortay, T., *Geschichte der Stadt Pressburg* (Bratislava, 1892).
522. Öttinger, K., *Altdeutsche Bildschnitzer der Ostmark* (Vienna, A. Schroll und Co., 1939).
523. Pangerl, M. (ed.), *Das Buch der Malerzeche in Prag* (= *Quellenschriften für Kunstgeschichte und Kunsttechnik des Mittelalters und der Renaissance*, Vol. XIII) (Vienna, 1878).
524. *La peinture moderne tchécoslovaque.*
525. Pěšina, J., *Tafelmalerei der Spätgotik und der Renaissance in Böhmen* (Prag, 1958).
526. ——, *Painting of the Gothic and Renaissance Periods, 1450-1550* (Prague, Artia, 1958).
527. Petas, F. and Paul, A., *Das jüngste Gericht. Mittelalterliche Mosaik vom Prager St. Veits Dom* (Prague, 1954).
528. Petrová, E., *František Tkadlík* (Prag, Verlag der Tschechoslowakischen Akademie der Wissenschaften, 1960?).
529. Philpotts, Adelaide Eden, *Tomek, the Sculptor* (London, Th. Butterworth, 1927).
530. Plichta, D., *The Modern Symbolist. The Painter Jan Zrzavý* (Prague, Artia, 1958?).
531. Plicka, K., *Die Slowakei* (Prague, Artia, 1955).
532. Pollak, O., *Studien zur Geschichte der Architektur Prags 1520-1600* (Wien, 1910).
533. Prokop, A., *Die Markgrafschaft Mähren in Kunstgeschichte, Beziehung I-IV* (Vienna, 1904).
534. Šafařík, Eduard, *Joannes Kupezky, 1667-1740* (Prag, Orbis, 1928).
535. Schlosser, Julius von, "Die Bilderhandschriften Königs Wenzel I", *Jahrbuch der Kunsthistorischen Sammlungen ...*, XIV (1893), pp. 214-313.

536. Schmerber, H., *Prager Baukunst um 1780* (Strassburg, 1913).
537. Schürer, Oskar and Wiese, Erich, *Deutsche Kunst in der Zips* (Leipzig, R. M. Rohrer, 1938).
538. *Slovak Folk Art*. Ed. R. Mrlian, 2 vols. (Prague, Artia, 1955).
539. *La sculpture moderne tchécoslovaque*.
540. Šourek, Karel (ed.), *Die Kunst in der Slowakei. Eine Sammlung von Dokumenten* (Prag, Melantrich,1939).
541. Štech, Václav Vilém, *Baroque Sculpture* (London, Spring Books, 1959).
542. ——, *Josef Václav Myslbek* (Prague, Artia, 1954).
543. Štech, Václav Vilém and Hnízdo, V., *Wandmalereien des Biedermeiers. Ein Werk Josef Navrátil's* (Prague, Artia, 1958).
544. Strettiová, Olga, *Das Barockporträt in Böhmen* (Prague, Artia, 1957).
545. Swoboda, K. M., *Peter Parler: Der Baukünstler und Bildhauer* (Wien, A. Schroll, 1940; 2nd ed. 1942).
546. —— (ed.), *Beiträge zur Geschichte der Kunst im Sudeten- und Karpathenraum*, 4 vols. (Brünn, Leipzig, Dt. Ges. d. Wiss. u. Künste in Prag, 1938-43).
547. Trenkler, E., *Das Evangeliar des Johannes von Troppau* (Klagenfurt, 1948).
548. *Tschechoslowakische Illustrationskunst*. Hrs. Ausstellungs-Abt. d. Dt. Akademie d. Künste (Berlin, 1955).
549. Urzidil, Johannes, *Wenceslaus Hollar, der Kupferstecher des Barock*, unter Mitarbeit von Franz Sprinzels (Wien-Leipzig, R. Passer, 1936).
550. Vaculík, K., *Die slowakische Kunst des 19. Jahrhunderts* (Prag, 1954).
551. Vermeiren, Louise, "La bible de Wenceslas du Musée Plantin-Moretus à Anvers", *De Gulden Passer* (Antwerp, 1953), pp. 191-229.
552. Volavka, Vojtěch, *French Paintings and Engravings of the XIXth Century in Czechoslovakia* (Prague, Artia, 1954).
553. Wagner, V., *Czech Baroque* (Prague, 1940).
554. Wirth, Zdeněk, *Czechoslovak Art from Ancient Times until the Present Day* (Prague, Orbis, 1926).
555. ——, *Kutná Hora: La ville et son art* (Prague, 1931).
556. Žákovec, František, *Les arts graphiques en Tchécoslovaquie* (Prague, Orbis, 1921).
557. Zaloziecky, W. R., *Gotische und barocke Holzkirchen in den Karpathenländern* (Wien, 1926).

Addendum: 1244, 1272, 1283

Crossreferences: 6, 420, 903

V. SOCIAL SCIENCES

A. Sociology

558. Adamec, Čeněk, Pospíšil, Bohuš and Tesař, Míla, *What's Your Opinion? A Year's Survey of Public Opinion in Czechoslovakia* (Prague, Orbis, 1947).
559. Bláha, Innocenc Arnošt, "Les théories philosophiques et sociologiques de Masaryk", *Revue internationale de sociologie*, 18 (1910), pp. 313-21.
560. ——, "La sociologie tchèque contemporaine", *Revue internationale de sociologie*, 29 (1921), pp. 224-48.
561. ——, "La sociologia ceca contemporanea", in *La Cecoslovacchia* (Roma, 1925), pp. 318-36.
562. ——, "Die zeitgenössische tschechische Soziologie", *Jahrbuch für Soziologie*, Karlsruhe, 2 (1926), pp. 441-61.
563. ——, "Contemporary Sociology in Czechoslovakia", *Social Forces*, 9 (1930), pp. 167-79.
564. ——, "Der gegenwärtige Stand der čechischen Soziologie", *Slavische Rundschau* (1936), pp. 77-86.
565. Böher, H. and Bülow, F. W. von, *The Rural Exodus in Czechoslovakia* (Geneva, International Labor Office, 1935).
566. Bregha, František, *La deshumanisation du travailleur dans l'univers communiste* (Montreal-Québec, Société canadienne d'éducation des adultes, 1953).
567. Chalupný, E., "La sociologie tchécoslovaque pendant les dernières dix années", *Revue internationale de sociologie*, 38 (1930), pp. 411-9.
568. Chalupný, E., *Précis d'un système de sociologie* (Paris, Marcel Riviere, 1930).
569. Deutsch, Karl Wolfgang, *Nationalism and Social Communication* (Cambridge, The Technology Press of the M.I.T., 1953).
570. Foustka, Břetislav, "Der Soziologe des Lebens", in *Masaryk, Staatsmann und Denker* (Prag, Orbis, 1930), pp. 103-19.
571. Galla, Karel, *Sociology of the Cooperative Movement in the Czechoslovak Village* (Prague, Spolek péče o blaho venkova, 1936).

572. Hajda, Jan, "Sociological Aspects", in *A Study of Contemporary Czechoslovakia*, ed. Jan Hajda (Chicago, The University of Chicago, for the Human Relations Area Files, 1955), pp. 56-256.
573. Halpern, Joel, with John A. McKinstry and Dalip Saund, *Bibliography of Anthropological and Sociological Publications on Eastern Europe and the U.S.S.R.* (*English Language Sources* (= *Russian and East European Studies Center Series*, Vol. 1, No. 2) (Los Angeles, University of California, 1961).
574. Kolaja, Jiří, "Arnošt Bláha and Czechoslovak Sociology", *American Sociological Review*, 25 (1960), pp. 741-2.
575. Kubát, Daniel, "Social Mobility in Czechoslovakia", *American Sociological Review*, 28 (1963), pp. 203-12.
576. ——, "Writers in a Totalitarian State: Czechoslovakia 1945-1956", *American Journal of Sociology*, 67 (1962), pp. 439-41.
577. ——, "Patterns of Leadership in a Communist State: Czechoslovakia 1946-58", *Journal of Central European Affairs*, 21 (1961), pp. 305-18.
578. Masaryk, Tomáš Garrigue, "Skizze einer sociologischen Analyse der sogenannten Grüneberger und Königinhofer Handschrift", *Archiv für slavische Philologie*, 10 (1887), pp. 54-101.
579. Mertl, Jan, "Neuerscheinungen aus der tschechischen soziologischen Literatur", *Kölner Vierteljahrshefte für Soziologie*, 10 (1931).
580. Mukherjee, R., *The New Czechoslovakia: An Indian Sociologist Looks at Czechoslovakia Today* (Bombay, Current Book House, 1951).
581. Nahodil, Otakar, *Zehn Jahre tschechoslowakischer Ethnographie (1945-1955)* (München, Lerche, 1958).
582. Nehněvajsa, Jiří, Articles on Czech and Slovak Sociologists. In Bernsdorf, Wilhelm, *Internationales Soziologen-Lexikon* (Stuttgart, Ferdinand Enke, 1959).
583. ——, *T. G. Masaryk. Soziologische Skizze der modernen Gesellschaft* (St. Margrethen, 1953).
584. Obrdlík, Antonín, "Sociological Activities in Czechoslovakia", *American Sociological Review*, 1 (1936), pp. 653-6.
585. ——, "Gallows Humor – A Sociological Phenomenon", *The American Journal of Sociology*, 47 (1942), pp. 709-16.
586. ——, and Zwicker, B., "Survey of Recent Sociological Production in Czechoslovakia", *American Sociological Review*, 2 (1937), pp. 424-7.

587. Obrdlík, Juliana, "Social Distance in the Village", *Proceedings of the Fourteenth International Congress of Sociology* (Rome, International Institute of Sociology, 1950), pp. 69-83.
588. Odstrčil, B., "Masaryk's Economical and Sociological Writings", *Czechoslovak Review*, Chicago, 4 (1920), pp. 119-22.
589. Rouček, Joseph S., "Sociological Periodicals of Czechoslovakia", *American Sociological Review*, 1 (1936), pp. 168-70.
590. ——, "Masaryk as Sociologist", *Sociology and Social Research*, 22 (1938), pp. 412-20.
591. ——, "Eduard Beneš as a Sociologist", *Sociology and Social Research*, 23 (1938), pp. 18-24.
592. ——, "Czechoslovak Sociology", in *Twentieth Century Sociology*, ed. by Georges Gurvitch and Wilbert E. Moore (New York, The Philosophical Library, 1945), pp. 717-31.
593. ——, "The Development of Czech and Slovak Sociological Thought", *Etudes slaves et esteuropéennes – Slavic and East European Studies*, 2 (1957), pp. 101-6.
594. ——, "Soviet Russia's Satellite Europe", in *Contemporary Sociology*, ed. J. S. Rouček (New York, Philosophical Library, 1958), pp. 932-78.
595. Schapowal, Mykyta J., "Masaryk als Soziologe", in *Festschrift Th. G. Masaryk zum 80. Geburtstage*, Vol. II (Bonn, Friedrich Cohen, 1930), pp. 337-64.
596. Škola, J., "Czech Sociology", *American Journal of Sociology*, 28 (1922), pp. 76-8.
597. Škrach, Vasil K., "Glossen über die tschechische Soziologie", *Kölner Vierteljahrshefte für Soziologie*, 5 (1925), pp. 329-37.
598. Smakalová, Iva, *An Integral Village. Study of a Slovak Rural Community* (Prague, Czechoslovak Social Institute, 1936).
599. de Sola Pool, Ithiel, *Satellite Generals: A Study of Military Elites in the Soviet Sphere* (Stanford, Calif., Stanford University Press, 1955), pp. 28-54.
600. Štefánek, Anton, *Zur Sociografie der geistigen Kultur in der Slowakei* (Bratislava, Slovenska akademia vied a umení, 1944).
601. Ullrich, Zdeněk, *La doctrine et l'enseignement de la sociologie à l'étranger* (1930).
602. ——, *Soziologische Studien zur Verstädterung der Prager Umgebung* (Prag, Revue Soziologie und soziale Probleme, 1938).
603. Walzel, V., *History of Czechoslovak Trade Unionism* (New York, Mid-European Studies Center, 1952).

604. Wit, Kurt, *Wirtschaftskräfte und Wirtschaftspolitik der Tschechoslowakei* (Leipzig, Weiner, 1936).
605. Wynne, W., Jr., *The Population of Czechoslovakia* (Washington, D.C., U.S. Government Printing Office, 1953).
606. Ziegler, H. O., *Die berufliche und sociale Gliederung der Bevölkerung in der Tschechoslowakei* (Brünn, Rohrer, 1936).

Crossreferences: 266, 727

B. Economics

607. Adams, A., *Report on the Industrial and Economic Situation in Czechoslovakia* (London, 1925).
608. Adolf, Bernhard, *Die Wirtschaft der Slowakei* (Prag, Volk und Reich Verlag, 1941).
609. Alton, T. P. et al., *Czechoslovak National Income and Product, 1947-1948 and 1955-1956* (New York, Columbia University Press, 1962).
610. *Annuaire statistique de la République Tchécoslovaque* (1937).
611. Banker, Theo, *Czechoslovakia: An Economic and Financial Survey* (London, 1938).
612. Basch, Antonín, *Germany's Economic Conquest of Czechoslovakia* (Chicago, The Czechoslovak National Council of America, 1941).
613. ——, *The New Economic Warfare* (New York, 1941).
614. ——, *The Danube Basin and the German Economic Sphere* (New York, 1943).
615. ——, "Land Reform in Czechoslovakia", in *Family Farm Policy* (Chicago, Ill., University of Chicago Press, 1947).
616. Blažek, Miroslav, *Wirtschafts-Geographie der Tschechoslowakei* (Marburg/Lahn, Johann Gottfried Herder-Institut, 1959).
617. Braibant, Guy, *La planification en Tchécoslovaquie* (*Le plan biennal*) (Paris, Colin, 1948).
618. Brdlík, Vladislav, *A Short Survey of Agriculture in Czechoslovakia* (Prague, 1938).
619. ——, with Franc Kubec and Jaroslav Prokeš, *Die Sozialökonomische Struktur der Landwirtschaft in der Tschechoslowakei* (Berlin, F. Vahlen, 1938).
620. Brzorád, Vilém J., *Economy of Czechoslovakia* (Washington, D.C., Council for Economic and Industry Research, 1955).

A Selective Bibliography

621. Cekota, Anton, *Baťa. Neue Wege. Vom Schusterschemel zur Weltfirma* (Brünn-Prag, Iva, International Verlags-Anstalt, 1928).
622. Československá akademie věd, *Czechoslovak Economic Papers* (Prague, Publishing House of the Czechoslovak Academy of Sciences, 1959 and ff.).
623. Chanel, E., *Monnaie et économie nationale en Tchécoslovaquie 1918-1928* (Paris, 1929).
624. Chmela, Leopold, *The Economic Aspects of the German Occupation of Czechoslovakia* (Prague, Orbis, 1948).
625. Czechoslovak Republic, Ministry of Information, *First Czechoslovak Five-Year Plan* (New York, Universal Distributors, 1948).
626. ——, Ministry of Foreign Trade, *Czechoslovak Economy and Foreign Trade: Facts and Figures, 1955*. Ed. Miroslav Vondra (Prague, Chamber of Commerce of Czechoslovakia, 1956).
627. ——, Ministry of Social Welfare, *Twenty Years of Social Welfare in the Czechoslovak Republic* (Prague, 1938).
628. Demel, Jaroslav, *Geschichte des Fiskalamtes in den böhmischen Ländern bis 1620* (= *Forsch. z. inn. Gesch. Österreichs*, V) (Innsbruck, 1909).
629. Douglas, Dorothy W., *Transitional Economic System: the Polish-Czech Example* (London, Routledge and Kegan Paul, 1953).
630. Dubský, S., *The Economic Development of Czechoslovakia* (Prague, Orbis, 1958).
631. Dvořák, L. F., *Das tschechoslovakische Genossenschaftswesen* (Prag, Ústřední jednota hospodářských družstev, 1922).
632. Elvert, C. d', *Zur österreichischen Finanz-Geschichte mit besonderer Rücksicht auf die böhmischen Länder* (= *Schriften der mährisch-schlesischen Gesellschaft*, XXV) (Brünn, 1881).
633. Engliš, Karel, "Tschechoslowakei", in *Die Wirtschaftstheorie der Gegenwart*. Eds. H. Mayer, F. A. Fetter and Rich. Reisett, 4 vols., volume one, *Gesamtbild der Forschung in den einzelnen Ländern*. Friedrich Wieser, in Memoriam, pp. 193 ff.
634. Federer, Kurt, *Obst-Erzeugung, Handel und Verwertung in der Tschechoslowakischen Republik* (Prag, Im Selbstverlag, 1931).
635. Feierabend, Ladislav, *Agricultural Cooperatives in Czechoslovakia* (New York, Mid-European Studies Center, 1952).
636. *Genossenschaftswesen und soziale Fürsorge in der Tschechoslovakei*. Ed. A. Klimt (Prag, Orbis, 1924).
637. George, Pierre, *L'Economie de l'Europe Centrale Slave et Danubienne* (Paris, Presses Universitaires, 1949).

638. Gindely, A., *Geschichte der böhmischen Finanzen von 1526 bis 1618* (= *Denksch. d. k. Akad. d. Wissensch. phil.-hist. cl.*, XVIII) (Wien, 1869), pp. 89-167.
639. ——, *Das Zunftwesen in Böhmen von XVI. bis XVIII. Jahrhundert* (Prag, 1884).
640. Goldman, Josef and Flek, Josef and others, *Planned Economy in Czechoslovakia* (Prague, Orbis, 1948).
641. Gruber, Josef (ed.), *Czechoslovakia. A Survey of Economic and Social Conditions* (New York, Macmillan, 1924).
642. Hallwich, H., *Böhmens Industrie und Handel* (= *Die österreichisch-ungarische Monarchie in Wort und Bild*, XIV) (Wien, 1896), pp. 600-66.
643. *Handbuch der tschechoslovakischen Wirtschaft*. Herausgeber Dr. Jar Arthur Katz-Foerstner (Berlin-Hallensee, Internationale Verlags-Gesellschaft, 1926).
644. Hermann, Vladimír, *Die tschechoslovakische Handelspolitik seit ihren Anfängen bis zur Gegenwart* (Prag, Verlag Heinr. Mercy Sohn, 1927).
645. Hertz, Friedrich Otto, *The Economic Problem of the Danubian States: A Study in Economic Nationalism* (London, Gollancz, 1947).
646. Herz, Erich, *Die Konsumgenossenschaften in der Tschechoslowakei* (Prag, Orbis, 1932).
647. Hexner, Ervin, *The International Steel Cartel* (Oxford, 1943).
648. Hieke, Wenzel (ed.), *Literatur zur Geschichte der Industrie in Böhmen bis zum Jahre 1850* (= *Beiträge z. Gesch. d. deut. Indust. in Böhmen*, I) (Prag, 1893).
649. Hodža, Milan, *Federation in Central Europe, Reflections and Reminiscences* (London-New York, Jarrolds Ltd., 1942).
650. Hoetzel, G., *Die nationale Steuerleistung und der Landeshaushalt im Königreiche Böhmen* (Prag, 1905).
651. Horbaly, William, *Agricultural Conditions in Czechoslovakia, 1950* (Chicago, Ill., University of Chicago, 1951).
652. Horna, Miloš and Blažej, Zdenko, *La Tchécoslovaquie économique et financière* (Geneva, 1948).
653. Hübsch, F. L., *Versuch einer Geschichte des böhmischen Handels* (Prag, 1849).
654. Hudler, Emil, *Die wirtschaftliche Tschechoslowakei* (Reichenberg, Allgemeiner deutscher Textilverband, 1928).
655. Juritsch, G., *Handel und Handelsrecht in Böhmen bis zur hussitischen*

A Selective Bibliography 595

Revolution (Wien, 1907).
656. Kiesewetter, Bruno, *Die Wirtschaft der Tschechoslovakei seit 1945* (Berlin, Duncker and Humblot, 1953).
657. Krajčovič, Vojtěch, *Die Struktur der slovakischen Wirtschaft* (Bratislava, Čas, 1941).
658. Krblich, J., *Survey of Czechoslovak Agriculture* (Prague, Institute of International Collaboration in Agriculture and Forestry, 1947).
659. Krejčí, Dobroslav, *La statistique agricole en Tchécoslovaquie* (Rome, L'Institut international d'agriculture, 1926).
660. Kříž, A. and Mareš, V., *The Iron and Steel Industry in Czechoslovakia* (Prague, 1930).
661. Lazarčik, Gregor, *The Performance of Socialist Agriculture, a Case Study of Production and Productivity in Czechoslovakia, 1934-38 and 1946-1961* (New York, L. W. International Financial Research, 1963).
662. Lockhart, R. H. Bruce, *Report on the Industrial and Economic Situation in Czechoslovakia* (London, 1925).
663. Machatschek, F., *Landeskunde der Sudeten- und West-Karpatenländer* (Stuttgart, J. Engelhorns Nachf., 1927).
664. Meisner, A., *Agrarische Handelspolitik 1921-1924* (Prag, 1925).
665. Michal, J. M., *Central Planning in Czechoslovakia* (Stanford, Calif., Stanford University Press, 1960).
666. Moscheles, J., *Wirtschaftsgeographie der Tschechoslowakischen Republik* (Leipzig, A. Haase, 1921).
667. Müller, Alois, *Geschichte des Grundsteuerwesens des Königreichs Böhmens seit der Urzeit bis zur Gegenwart* (Prag, 1880).
668. Müller, B. R., *Wirtschafts-Geologie d. Tschechoslovakischen Republik* (Reichenberg, P. Sollors Nachf., 1921).
669. Niederle, Miloslav, *L'évolution et l'état actuel de la collaboration économique dans le bassin du Danube* (Prague, Orbis, 1938).
670. Nistor, J., *Die auswärtigen Handelsbeziehungen der Moldau im XIV, XV und XVI Jahrhundert* (Gotha, 1911).
671. *Oxford Regional Economic Atlas: the U.S.S.R. and Eastern Europe* (1956).
672. Pasvolsky, Leo, *Economic Nationalism of the Danubian States* (Washington, D.C., Brookings Institution, 1928).
673. Pavel, A., *Land Reform in Czechoslovakia* (New York, 1925).
674. Pešek, Boris P. and others, "Economic Aspects", in *A Study of Contemporary Czechoslovakia*. Ed. Jan Hajda (Chicago, Ill., The University of Chicago, 1955), pp. 402-626.

675. Peterka, O., *Das Gewerberecht Böhmen in XIV Jahrhundert* (Wien, 1909).
676. Petermann, Karl Hermann, *Beiträge zur Bibliographie der Wirtschaft der Tschechoslowakischen Republik, unter besonderer Berücksichtigung des Sudetendeutschtums und der Beziehungen zum Deutschen Reiche* (Berlin, Verlag Grenze und Ausland, 1936).
677. Petschek and Co., *Economic Review of the Years 1932-1936 in Czechoslovakia*, 5 vols. (Prague, 1933-37).
678. Piot, A., *La couronne tchécoslovaque jusqu' à la mort de Rašín, 1918-1923* (Paris, Edition de la Vie Universitaire, 1923).
679. Plamínková, F., *Economic-Social Position of Women in the Czechoslovak Republic* (Prague, 1920).
680. Polin, Raymond and Charon, J. G., *Les coopératives rurales et l'Etat en Tchécoslovaquie et en Roumanie* (Paris, Alcan, 1934).
681. Pribram, A. F. *Das böhmische Commerzcollegium und seine Tätigkeit: ein Beitrag zur Geschichte des böhmischen Handels im Jahrhundert nach dem westfälischen Frieden* (= *Beiträge z. Gesch. d. deutsch. Industrie in Böhmen*, VI) (Prag, 1898).
682. Rašín, Alois, *Die Finanz- und Wirtschaftspolitik der Tschechoslowakei*. Einzig autorisierte Übersetzung von Dr. Paul J. Eisner (München-Leipzig, Duncker und Humblot, 1923).
683. Reich, Edvard, *Die tschechoslowakische Landwirtschaft, ihre Grundlagen und ihre Organization* (Berlin, P. Parey, 1935).
684. Rist, Charles, *La déflation en pratique* (Paris, M. Giard, 1924).
685. Salz, Arthur, *Geschichte der böhmischen Industrie in der Neuzeit* (München-Leipzig, 1913).
686. Šimáček, Radovan, *Czechoslovak Economy in a Nutshell, 1948* (Prague, Czechoslovak Ministry of Foreign Trade, 1948).
687. *Social Policy in the Czechoslovak Republic*. Ed. the Social Institute of the Czechoslovak Republic (Prague, Orbis, 1924).
688. Spulber, Nicolas and others, "The Economy", in *Czechoslovakia*. Eds. Vratislav Bušek and Nicolas Spulber (New York, F. A. Praeger, 1957), pp. 220-416.
689. *Statistical Digest of the Czechoslovak Republic* (Prague, 1937).
690. Temperley, H. W. V., *Ten Years of the National Bank in Czechoslovakia* (Prague, 1936).
691. Textor, Lucy E., *Land Reform in Czechoslovakia* (London, Allen and Unwin, 1923).
692. Tibal, André, *La Tchécoslovaquie. Etude économique* (Paris, Colin, 1935).

693. Vondruška, Ed., *Czechoslovak Reform* (Prague, 1924).
694. Voženílek, J., *La réforme agraire en Tchécoslovaquie* (Paris, 1931).
695. Výškovský, Eduard, *Czechoslovakia's First Five-Year Plan* (Prague, Orbis, 1955).
696. Zauberman, A., *Industrial Development in Czechoslovakia, East Germany and Poland* (London, Royal Institute of International Affairs, 1958).

Addendum: 1165, 1166, 1186, 1196, 1202, 1203, 1253, 1257, 1258, 1285, 1290
Crossreferences: 604

C. Political Science

697. *At the Cross-Roads of Europe. A Historical Outline of the Democratic Idea in Czechoslovakia*. By Karel Čapek, Václav Chaloupecký, J. L. Hromádka, František Hrubý, Albert Pražák, and Ferdinand Peroutka (Prague, P.E.N. Club, 1938).
698. Baernreither, J. M., *Zur böhmischen Frage, eine politische Studie* (Vienna, 1910).
699. Barton, Paul, *Prague à l'heure de Moscou: Analyse d'une démocratie populaire* (Paris, 1954).
700. Beck, Curt and others, "The Government and the Party", in *Czechoslovakia*. Eds. Vratislav Bušek and Nicolas Spulber (New York, F. A. Praeger, 1957), pp. 40-127.
701. Beneš, Edvard, *My War Memoirs* (London, G. Allen and Unwin, 1928).
702. ———, *Memoirs. From Munich to New War and New Victory* (London, 1954).
703. *Biographisches Handbuch der Tschechoslowakei*. Compiled by Heinrich Kuhn, Otto Boss, et al. (Munich, Robert Lerche, 1961).
704. Bolton, Glorney, *Czech Tragedy* (London, 1955).
705. Borovička, J., *Ten Years of Czechoslovak Politics* (Prague, Orbis, 1929).
706. Borsody, S., *Triumph of Tyranny* (New York, Macmillan, 1960).
707. Braun, Madeleine, *Tchécoslovaquie, carrefour de l'Europe* (Paris, Chambeiron, 1950)
708. Brown, John, *Who's Next? The Lesson of Czechoslovakia* (London, Hutchinson, 1951).
709. Čapek, Karel, *President Masaryk Tells his Story* (London, G. Allen and Unwin, 1934).

710. Čelovský, Boris, *Das Münchener Abkommen* (Stuttgart, Deutsche Verlags-Anstalt, 1958).
711. Chalupa, Vlastislav, *Rise and Development of a Totalitarian State* (Leiden, H. E. Stenfert Kroese, 1959).
712. Chmelař, Josef, *Political Parties in Czechoslovakia* (Prague, Orbis, 1926).
713. ——, *The German Problem in Czechoslovakia* (Prague, Orbis, 1936).
714. ——, *National Minorities in Central Europe* (Prague, Orbis, 1937).
715. Cobban, Alfred, *National Self-Determination* (London, 1945).
716. Cohen, Victor, *Life and Times of Masaryk, the President-Liberator* (London, J. Murray, 1941).
717. Crabites, Pierre, *Beneš: Statesman of Central Europe* (London, 1935).
718. Crane, John O., *The Little Entente* (New York, 1931).
719. Czechoslovak Republic, *Declaration of Independence of the Czechoslovak Nation by the Provisional Government* (New York, 1918).
720. ——, Ministry of Information, *Czechoslovakia on the Road to Socialism* (Prague, Orbis, 1949).
721. ——, Ministry of Foreign Affairs, *Czechoslovak Sources and Documents* (Prague, 1931-38; London, 1940-44).
722. Dérer, Ivan, *The Unity of the Czechs and Slovaks* (Prague, Orbis, 1938).
723. Diamond, William, *Czechoslovakia Between East and West* (London, Stevens, 1947).
724. Ducháček, Ivo, *The Strategy of Communist Infiltration: The Case of Czechoslovakia* (New Haven, Conn., Yale Institute of International Studies, 1949).
725. Eubank, Keith, *Munich* (Norman, University of Oklahoma Press, 1963).
726. Friedman, Otto, *The Break-up of the Czech Democracy* (London, Gollancz, 1950).
727. Gaďourek, I., *The Political Control of Czechoslovakia. A Study in Social Control of a Soviet Satellite State* (Leiden, Stenfert Kroese, 1953).
728. Gasiorowski, Z. J., "Polish-Czechoslovak Relations 1918-1922", and "Polish-Czechoslovak Relations 1922-1926", *Slavonic and East European Review* (1956-57).
729. Gedye, George E. R., *Betrayal in Central Europe: Austria and Czechoslovakia, the Fallen Bastions* (New York, 1939).

730. Grant-Duff, Sheila, *Europe and the Czechs* (New York, Penguin Books, 1938).
731. ——, *A German Protectorate: The Czechs under Nazi Rule* (New York, Macmillan, 1942).
732. ——, *Czechoslovakia: Six Studies in Reconstruction* (London, Fabian Society, 1947).
733. Hanč, Josef, *Tornado Across Eastern Europe* (New York, 1942).
734. Hartmann, Paul, *Die politische Partei in der Tschechoslowakischen Republik, eine juristische Studie* (Brünn, 1931).
735. Hadley, William W., *Munich: Before and After* (London, 1944).
736. Hitchcock, E. B., *Beneš: The Man and the Statesman* (London, 1940).
737. Hoch, Karel, *The Political Parties in Czechoslovakia* (Prague, Orbis, 1936).
738. Hoch, K. and others, *World Peace and Czechoslovakia* (London, A. A. M. Stols, 1936).
739. Jacoby, G., *Racial State: The German Nationalities Policy in the Protectorate of Bohemia-Moravia* (New York, Inst. of Jewish Affairs of the American Jewish Congress and the World Jewish Congress, 1944).
740. Jászi, Oscar, *The Dissolution of the Habsburg Monarchy* (Chicago, 1929).
741. Josten, Josef, *Oh, My Country* (New York, MacDonald, 1949).
742. Kaplan, Morton A., *The Communist Coup in Czechoslovakia* (Princeton, N. J., Center of International Studies, Princeton University, 1960).
743. Klepetář, Harry, *Seit 1918 ... Eine Geschichte der tschechoslowakischen Republik* (M. Ostrau, Verlag Julius Kittls Nachfolger, 1937).
744. Korbel, J., *Communist Subversion of Czechoslovakia 1938-1948* (Princeton, Princeton University Press, 1959).
745. Kramář, Karel, *Anmerkungen zur böhmischen Politik* (Vienna, 1906).
746. Krofta, Kamil, *La Tchécoslovaquie et la Petite Entente dans la politique actuelle de l'Europe* (Prague, Orbis, 1937),
747. ——, *The Germans in the Czechoslovak Republic* (Prague, Orbis, 1937).
748. Kunoši, Alexander, *The Basis of Czechoslovak Unity* (London, Dakers 1944).
749. Kybal, Vlastimil, *Origines diplomatiques de l'état Tchécoslovaque* (Prague, 1929).

750. Lavergne, Bernard, *Munich, défaite des démocraties* (Paris, 1939).
751. Lemberg, Eugen, *Die Grundlagen des nationalen Erwachens in Böhmen* (Reichenberg, Gebrüder Stiepel, 1932).
752. Lewis, Brackett, *Facts about Democracy in Czechoslovakia* (Prague, American Institute in Czechoslovakia, 1937).
753. Lias, Godfrey, *Beneš of Czechoslovakia* (London, 1941).
754. Lobkowicz, N., *Marxismus-Leninismus in der ČSR: Die tschechoslowakische Philosophie seit 1945* (Dordrecht, D. Reidel, 1961).
755. Lockhart, Sir Robert Hamilton Bruce, *Jan Masaryk* (New York, Philosophical Library, 1951).
756. ——, *Retreat from Glory* (New York, G. P. Putnam's Sons, 1934).
757. ——, *What Happened to the Czechs*? (London, Batchworth P., 1953).
758. Lowrie, Donald A., *Masaryk of Czechoslovakia* (London, Oxford University Press, 1937).
759. Ludwig, Emil, *Defender of Democracy, Masaryk of Czechoslovakia* (New York, R. M. McBride and Co., 1936)
760. Lyon, Samuel P., "Political Aspects", in *A Study of Contemporary Czechoslovakia*. Ed. Jan Hajda (Chicago, Ill., The University of Chicago, 1955), pp. 257-401.
761. Machray, Robert, *The Little Entente* (New York, 1929)
762 Mackenzie, Compton, *Dr. Beneš* (London, Harrap, 1946).
763. Mamatey, Victor S., *The United States and East Central Europe: A Study of Wilsonian Diplomacy and Propaganda* (Princeton, Princeton University, 1957).
764. Masaryk, Thomas G., *The New Europe* (New York, 1918).
765. ——, *The Making of a State: Memories and Observations, 1914-1918* (London, Allen and Unwin, 1927).
766. "T. G. Masaryk, 1850-1950", by O. Jászi and others, *J. Central European Affairs*, 10 (April 1950), pp. 1-52.
767. Molisch, Paul, *Vom Kampf der Tschechen um ihren Staat* (Vienna-Leipzig, Braumüller, 1929).
768. Münch, H., *Böhmische Tragödie: das Schicksal Mitteleuropas im Lichte der tschechischen Frage* (Braunschweig, 1949).
769. Munk, Frank, *The Legacy of Nazism* (New York, Macmillan, 1944).
770. Němec, František and Moudrý, Vladimír, *Soviet Seizure of Subcarpathian Ruthenia* (Toronto, W. B. Anderson, 1955).
771. Němec, Ludvík, *Church and State in Czechoslovakia* (New York, 1955).

772. Newman, Edward Polson, *Masaryk* (London, Campion Press, 1961).
773. Odložilík, O., *Masaryk's Idea of Democracy* (New York, Masaryk Institute, Inc., 1952).
774. Opočenský, Jan, *The Collapse of the Austro-Hungarian Monarchy and the Rise of the Czechoslovak State* (Prague, Orbis, 1928).
775. Paleček, Anthony, "Antonín Švehla: Czech Peasant Statesman", *Slavic Review*, 21 (1962), pp. 699-708.
776. Papoušek, Jaroslav, *The Czechoslovak Nation's Struggle for Independence* (Prague, Orbis, 1928).
777. ——, *Czechoslovakia, Soviet Russia and Germany* (Prague, Orbis, 1936).
778. Pechány, Adolph, *Les voies de la politique slovaque* (Budapest, 1929).
779. Perman, D., *The Shaping of the Czechoslovak State: Diplomatic History of the Boundaries of Czechoslovakia, 1914-1920* (Leiden, E. J. Brill, 1962).
780. Picek, W. T., *Politische Fragmente über Böhmen; ein Beitrag zur Würdigung der nationalen und politischen Bestrebungen der Čechoslaven* (Prag, 1850).
781. Polakovič, Štefan, *L'évolution des idées fondamentales de la politique slovaque* (Bratislava, Slovenská akademia vied a umení, 1944).
782. Rádl, Emanuel, *Der Kampf zwischen Deutschen und Tschechen* (Reichenberg, Gebrüder Stiepel, 1928).
783. Reisky de Dubnic, Vladimír, *Communist Propaganda Methods* (New York, F. A. Praeger, 1961).
784. Ripka, Hubert, *Munich Before and After* (London, 1939).
785. ——, *Czechoslovakia Enslaved: The Story of the Communist Coup d'Etat* (London, Gollancz, 1950).
786. ——, *Eastern Europe in the Postwar World* (New York, F. A. Praeger, 1961).
787. Roessler, Fritz, *Die Slowakei zwischen Gestern und Heute* (Dresden, Krueger und Horn, 1943).
788. Schmidt, Dana Adams, *Anatomy of a Satellite* (Boston, Little, Brown, 1952).
789. Selver, Paul, *Masaryk, a Biography* (London, M. Joseph, 1940).
790. Seton-Watson, Robert William, *Munich and the Dictators* (London, 1939).
791. ——, *Masaryk in England* (New York, Macmillan, 1943).
792. Seton-Watson, Hugh, *Eastern Europe between the Wars: 1918-1941*

(London, Cambridge University Press, 1945).
793. ——, *The East European Revolution* (New York, F. A. Praeger, 1951).
794. Skilling, Harold Gordon, *Soviet Impact on Czech Politics*. A dissertation (Dartmouth, 1954).
795. Spinka, Matthew, *Church in Communist Society, a Study in J. L. Hromádka's Theological Politics* (Hartford, Hartford Seminary Press, 1954).
796. Stránský, Jaroslav, *East Wind over Prague* (New York, Random House, 1951).
797. Strauss, Emil, *Tschechoslovakische Aussenpolitik* (Prague, 1936).
798. Street, C. J., *President Masaryk of Czechoslovakia* (London, Bles, 1930).
799. *Survey of International Affairs*. Ed. Arnold J. Toynbee (New York, Oxford University Press, 1925-). See especially Vol. II, 1938, *The Crisis over Czechoslovakia*. By R. G. D. Laffain, rev. by V. M. Toynbee, P. E. Baker, with introduction by Arnold J. Toynbee (1951).
800. Táborský, Edward, *Czech Democracy at Work* (London, Allen and Unwin, 1945).
801. ——, *Conformity under Communism. A Study of Indoctrination Techniques* (Washington, 1958).
802. ——, *Communism in Czechoslovakia, 1948-1960* (Princeton, Princeton University Press, 1961).
803. ——, "The Triumph and Disaster of Eduard Beneš", *Foreign Affairs*, 36 (1957-58).
804. Vondráček, Felix John, *Foreign Policy of Czechoslovakia* (New York, Columbia University Press, 1937).
805. Wandycz, Piotr S., *France and her Eastern Allies 1919-1925* (Minneapolis, University of Minnesota Press, 1962).
806. ——, *Czechoslovak-Polish Confederation and the Great Powers 1940-43* (Bloomington, Indiana University Press, 1956).
807. Wheeler-Bennet, J. W., *Munich: Prologue to Tragedy* (New York, Duell, Sloan and Pearce, 1948; 2nd ed. 1962).
808. Wiskemann, E., *Germany's Eastern Neighbors* (London, 1956).
809. Zeman, Z. A. B., *The Break-up of the Habsburg Empire 1914-1918: A Study in National and Social Revolution* (New York, Oxford University Press, 1961).
810. Zimmern, A., *Czechoslovakia To-day* (London, Royal Institute of International Affairs, 1938).

811. Zinner, Paul, *Communist Tactics and Strategy in Czechoslovakia, 1918-48* (New York, F. A. Praeger, 1963).
812. ——, "Czechoslovakia", in *The Fate of East Central Europe: Hopes and Failures of American Foreign Policy*. Ed. S. D. Kertesz (Notre Dame, Ind., University of Notre Dame Press, 1956).
813. Zürcher, A. J., *The Experiment with Democracy in Central Europe* (New York, 1933).

Addendum: 1159, 1167, 1173-5, 1178-86, 1188, 1194-5, 1198-9, 1201, 1204, 1212, 1217-8, 1222-3, 1226-7, 1232-3, 1236, 1239-41, 1243, 1245-8, 1251, 1253, 1255, 1259, 1264-5, 1267, 1269, 1282, 1285-6, 1310, 1313-5, 1317-8

Crossreferences: 1, 7, 19, 20, 33, 35, 37, 55, 59, 69, 79, 89, 230, 235, 262, 271, 275, 599, 649, 820, 821, 822, 853

D. Law

814. Bazovský, Ján, *La codification du droit civil en Tchéco-Slovaquie* (Paris, Les Presses Universitaires de France, 1927).
815. Bloss, Esther, *Labor Legislation in Czechoslovakia* (New York, 1938).
816. Čelakovský, Jaromír, *Das Heimfallsrecht auf das freivererbliche Vermögen in Böhmen* (Prag, 1882).
817. Československá akademie věd, Ústav práva, *Bibliography of Czechoslovak Legal Literature, 1945-1958* (Prague, Pub. House of the Czechoslovak Academy of Sciences, 1959).
818. Chytil, Josef, *Die Landes-Ordnungen des Markgrafthumes Mähren von der ältesten Zeit bis zum Jahre 1894* (Brünn, 1851).
819. *Codex iuris municipalis Regni Bohemiae*. Vols. 1 and 2, ed. J. Čelakovský (Prague, 1886-95), from 1225 to 1419; vols. 3, ed. G. Friedrich (Prague, 1948), from 1420 to 1526.
820. *The Constitution of the Czechoslovak Republic*. With introduction by Jiří Hoetzl and V. Joachim (Prague, 1920).
821. Czechoslovak Republic, Ministry of Information and Public Culture, *The Constitution of the Czechoslovak Republic. Promulgated on June 9th, 1948 ...*, 2nd ed. (Prague, Orbis, 1948).
822. ——, *The Constitution of the Czechoslovak Republic*, 2nd ed. (Prague, Orbis, 1961).
823. *Czechoslovak Yearbook of International Law*. Eds. V. Beneš, A.

Drucker and E. Táborský (London, Czechoslovak Branch of the International Law Association, 1942).
824. Deml, Josef, *Tschechoslowakische Rechtsgeschichte* (Prag, 1929).
825. Demuth, Karl Josef, *Geschichte der Landtafel im Markgrafthume Mähren* (Brünn, 1857).
826. Elvert, C. d', *Die Vereinigung von Böhmen, Mähren und Schlesien zum gemeinschaftlichen Landtag und einer Central-Verwaltung*, 2nd ed. (Brünn, 1868).
827. ——, *Die Verfassung und Verwaltung von österreichisch Schlesien in ihrer historischen Ausbildung, dann die Rechtsverhältnisse zwischen Mähren, Troppau und Jägerndorf, sowie der mährischen Enklaven zu Schlesien* (= *Mährisch-schlesische Gesellschaft ... Schriften*, VII) (Brünn, 1854).
828. ——, *Zur österreichischen Verwaltungs-Geschichte mit besonderer Rücksicht auf die böhmischen Länder* (= *Mährisch-schlesische Gesellschaft ... Schriften*, XXIV) (Brünn, 1880).
829. Engelmayr, Anton, *Die Unterthans-Verfassung des Königreichs Böhmen*, 2 vols. (Vienna, 1830-31).
830. Falk, Vincenz, *Die landverfassungsmässigen Verhältnisse der königlichen Städte als vierten Standes im Königreich Böhmen* (Prag, 1847).
831. Gsovski, Vladimir, *New Codes in the New Slavic Countries* (*Poland, Czechoslovakia, Yugoslavia*) (Washington, 1934).
832. Herbst, J., *Das juristische Doktorenkollegium in Prag* (Prag, 1861).
833. Jireček, Hermenegild, *Das Recht in Böhmen und Mähren geschichtlich dargestellt* (Prag, C. Bellmann, 1865-6).
834. ——, *Codex iuris Bohemici*, 12 vols. (1867-98).
835. Jolly, E., *Le pouvoir législatif dans la République tchécoslovaque* (Paris, 1924).
836. Kadlec, K., *Introduction à l'étude comparative de l'histoire du droit public des peuples slaves* (Paris, 1933), pp. 226 ff.
837. Kalousek, Josef, *Einige Grundlagen des böhmischen Staatsrechts*, 2nd. ed. (Prag, 1871).
838. Kapras, Jan, Jr., *Das Pfandrecht im böhmisch-mährischen Stadt- und Bergrechte*, etc. (= *Untersuchungen zur deutschen Staats- und Rechtsgeschichte*, Hft. 83) (1906).
839. Mid-European Law Project, *Legal Sources and Bibliography of Czechoslovakia*, By A. Böhmer, J. Jíra, S. Kočvara and J. Nosek (New York, F. A. Praeger, 1959).
840. Ott, Emil, *Beiträge zur Receptions-Geschichte des römisch-cano-*

nischen Processes in den böhmischen Ländern (Leipzig, 1879).
841. ——, Das Eindringen des kanonischen Rechts, seine Lehre und wissenschaftliche Pflege in Böhmen und Mähren während des Mittelalters (Weimar, 1913).
842. Peterka, Otto, Rechtsgeschichte der böhmischen Länder. Vol. I, Geschichte des öffentlichen Rechtes und die Rechtsquellen in vorhussitischer Zeit (Reichenberg, 1923).
843. ——, Rechtsgeschichte der böhmischen Länder in ihren Grundzügen dargestellt, 2 vols. (Prag, 1928 and 1933).
844. Procházka, Adolf, Changes in the Philosophy of Czechoslovak Law since the Prague coup d'etat of February, 1948. Unpublished manuscript, U.S. Library of Congress microfilm, 1953.
845. Sander, Fritz, Grundriss des tschechoslovakischen Verfassungsrechtes (Reichenberg, 1938).
846. Schmidt von Bergenhold, J. F., Geschichte der Privatrechts-Gesetzgebung und Gerichtsverfassung im Königreich Böhmen von den ältesten Zeiten bis zum 21. September 1865 (Prag, 1865).
847. Schnabel, G. N., Geschichte der juristichen Fakultät an der vereinigten Carl-Ferdinandeischen Hochschule zu Prag, 3 vols. (Prag, 1827).
848. Schopf, F. J., Die organische Verwaltung der Provinz Böhmen und die landesverfassungsmässigen Verhältnisse der Bewohner als Einleitung zur politischen Gesetzkunde (Prag, 1847).
849. Siegel, F., Lectures on Slavonic Law (London, New York, 1902), Bohemia, pp. 63-99.
850. Singer, Josef, Das in der Slowakei geltende Recht, 2 vols. (Prag, Heinrich Mercy Sohn, 1923-24).
851. Sobota, Emil, Das Tschechoslovakische Nationalitätenrecht (Prag, Orbis, 1931).
852. Stieber, M., Das österreichische Landrecht und die böhmische Einwirkung auf die Reformen König Ottokars in Österreich (= Forschungen zur inneren Geschichte Österreichs, II) (Innsbruck, 1905).
853. Táborský, Edward, The Czechoslovak Cause. An Account of the Problem of International Law in Relation to Czechoslovakia (London, H. F. and G. Witherby, 1944).
854. Toman, Hugo, Das böhmische Staatsrecht und die Entwicklung der österreichischen Reichsidee vom Jahre 1827 bis 1848 (Prag, 1872).
855. ——, Schicksale des böhmischen Staatsrechtes in den Jahren 1620 bis 1627, nach urkundlichen Quellen skizziert (Prag, 1872).

856. Tůma, Anton, *Rechtsgrundlagen der sozialen Fürsorge in der Tschechoslovakischen Republik* (Reichenberg, 1926).
857. U.S. Library of Congress, Law Library, *Czechoslovakia: Catalogue of Sources of Legal Information* (Washington, D.C., The Library of Congress, 1952).
858. Weiss, Egon, *Die Zivilprozessgebung d. Tschechoslovak. Republik* (Brünn, Rohrer, 1921).
859. Wellner, Max, *Beiträge zur Geschichte des böhmischen Staatsrechtes* (Vienna, 1863).
860. Weyr, F. and Dominik, R., *Grundriss des čechoslovakischen Verwaltungsrechtes* (Prag, R. M. Rohrer, 1922).
861. Zycha, A., *Das böhmische Bergrecht des Mittelalters auf Grundlage des Bergrechts von Iglau* (Vienna-Berlin, 1900).

Addendum: 1159-61, 1169, 1172, 1176-7, 1193, 1215-6, 1284, 1288, 1294-5, 1299-1300, 1304-5

Crossreferences: 734, 771

E. Education

862. *Act Relating to the School System and Training of Teachers in Czechoslovakia, Education Act, 1953* (Prague, Orbis, 1953).
863. Apanasewicz, Nellie, in collaboration with Rosen, Seymour M., *Selected Bibliography of Materials on Education in Czechoslovakia* (Washington, D.C., U.S. Department of Health, Education, and Welfare, 1960).
864. Bach, Teresa, *Education in Czechoslovakia* (Washington, D.C., U.S. Government Printing Office, 1923).
865. Bloch, Franz, *Das Schulwesen der Tschechoslovakei* (Reichenberg, Verlag von Gebrüder Stiepel, 1923).
866. Chaloupecký, Václav, *The Caroline University of Prague – Its Foundation, Character and Development in the Fourteenth Century* (Prague, Orbis, 1948).
867. Czechoslovak Republic, Ministerstvo školství a osvěty, *Die gewerblichen Fortbildungs-(Lehrlings-)schulen in der Čechoslovakischen Republik; eine Zusammenstellung der wichtigsten Vorschriften* (Prag, Staatliche Verlagsanstalt, 1934).
868. Ducháček, Ivo, "Education", in *Czechoslovakia*, eds. V. Bušek and N. Spulber (New York, F. A. Praeger, 1957), pp. 154-72.

869. *Education in Czechoslovakia* (London, The Czechoslovak Ministry of the Interior, Dept. for Educational Reconstruction, 1943).
870. Elvert, C. d', *Geschichte der Studien-, Schul- und Erziehungsanstalten in Mähren und österreichisch-Schlesien* (Brünn, 1857).
871. Free Europe Committee, *Sovietization of the Czechoslovak School System*. Res. ed. Pavel Korbel (New York, 1954).
872. Hammer, W., *Geschichte der Volkschule Böhmens von den ältesten Zeiten bis zum Jahre 1870* (Warnsdorf, 1904).
873. Hendrich, Josef and Šmok, Mikuláš, *L'enseignement secondaire dans la République tchécoslovaque* (Prague, Ústřední spolek československých profesorů, 1923).
874. Kasková, Alena (ed.), *Education in Czechoslovakia* (Prague, Státní pedagogické nakladatelství, 1958).
875. Kisch, Guido, *Die Prager Universität und die Juden, 1348-1848* (Mährisch-Ostrau, Verlag Julius Kittls, Nachfolger, 1935).
876. Krčmář, Jan, *The Prague Universities* (Prague, Orbis, 1934).
877. Kvačala, Jan, *Die pädagogische Reform des Comenius in Deutschland bis zum Ausgange des XVII Jahrhunderts* (Berlin, 1903).
878. ——, *Johann Amos Comenius, sein Leben und seine Schriften* (Berlin, 1914).
879. Matula, Antonín and Bous, František, *L'éducation populaire dans la République tchécoslovaque* (Prague, Édition de l'Association des Professeurs Tchécoslovaques, 1928).
880. ——, and Praus, František, *Adult Education in Czechoslovakia. A Survey of Five Years' Public Work* (Prague, State Publishing Office, 1925).
881. Mauer, Jean (ed.), *L'enseignement dans la République tchécoslovaque* (Prague, Société d'Edition "L'Effort de la Tchécoslovaquie", 1920).
882. Monroe, W. S., *Comenius and the Beginnings of Educational Reform* (New York, Charles Scribner's Sons, 1907).
883. Needham, J. (ed.), *The Teacher of Nations. Addresses and Essays in Commemoration of the Visit to England of the Great Czech Educationalist Jan Amos Komenský – Comenius – 1641, 1941* (Cambridge, University Press, 1942).
884. Odložilík, Otakar, *The Caroline University, 1348-1948* (Prague, The Caroline University, 1948).
885. Palkovič, J., *Die Schicksale des slovakischen Schulwesens und Kulturlebens in Vorkriegs-Ungarn* (Prag, Orbis, 1937).
886. Paur, Jaroslav, *Education in Czechoslovakia* (Prague, Orbis, 1947).

887. Pick, Friedel, *Denkschrift des Rektors Johannes Jessenius von Gross-Jessen über Erneuerung der Prager Universität* (1920).
888. Rabecq, Marie-Madeleine, "Comenius, Apostle of Modern Education and of World Understanding", *UNESCO Courier*, November 1957, pp. 4-15.
889. Reich. Edvard and Škoda, Václav (eds.), *Agricultural Education in Czechoslovakia* (Prague and Brno, Ministry of Education, 1931).
890. Rouček, Joseph S., "Education in Czechoslovakia", *Comparative Education*, eds. A. H. Moehlman and J. S. Rouček (New York, The Dryden Press, 1952), pp. 358-83.
891. *School Reform in Czechoslovakia* (Prague, Orbis, 1948).
892. Sitenský, František, *Agricutural School in Czechoslovakia* (Prague, Czechoslovak Foreigners' Office, 1919).
893. Šmok, Mikuláš, *Organisation de l'enseignement en Tchécoslovaquie* (Prague, Orbis, 1924).
894. Štefánek, Anton, *Das Schulwesen der Slowakei* (Bratislava, 1921).
985. Štěpánek, B., "The Spirit of Jan Amos Comenius in the Education of the Czechoslovak Republic", *School and Society*, 13 (1921), pp. 651-4.
896. Stránský, R., *The Educational and Cultural System of the Czechoslovak Republic* (Prague, Vladimír Žikeš, 1938).
897. Stuerm, Francis H., *Training in Democracy: The New Schools of Czechoslovakia* (New York, Inor Publishing Co., 1938).
898. Swift, Fletcher Harper, *European Policies of Financing Public Educational Institutions. II, Czechoslovakia* (London, Cambridge University Press, 1934).
899. Tomek, W. W., *Geschichte der Prager Universität* (Prag, 1849).
900. Turosienski, Severin K., *Education in Czechoslovakia* (Washington, D.C., U.S. Government Printing Office, 1936).
901. Veleminský, Karel, *Czechoslovak Secondary Schools* (Prague, Czechoslovak Foreigner's Office, 1919).
902. *The Way of Light. The Glory and Martyrdom of Czechoslovak Schools.* By O. Odložilík, S. H. Thomson, V. A. Andic, J. L. Hromádka (Chicago, The Czechoslovak National Council of America, 1942).

Addendum: 1189, 1274, 1276

Crossreferences: 18, 320, 392, 916, 924, 968

A Selective Bibliography 609

VI. NATURAL SCIENCES

A. General

903. *Abbildungen böhmischer und mährischer Gelehrter und Künstler ...,* I-IV (Prag, 1773-82).
904. *Abhandlungen einer Privatgesellschaft in Böhmen zur Aufnahme der Mathematik, vaterländischen Geschichte und der Naturgeschichte* (Prag, 1775-84).
905. *Abhandlungen der böhmischen Gesellschaft der Wissenschaften* (Prag, 1785-87).
906. *Abhandlungen der königlichen böhmischen Gesellschaft der Wissenschaften vom Jahre 1802-23.* Dritte Folge, 1824-36. Neue Folge, 1837-66. Fünfte Folge, 1867-83. Sechste Folge.
907. Anonym., "Science: Czechoslovakia", *Slavonic Encyclopedia*, ed. J. S. Rouček (New York, Philosophical Library, 1949), pp. 1116-9.
908. Balbin, Bohuslav, *Bohemica docta* (Prague, Raphael Ungar, 1776-80).
909. Brauner, Bohuslav, "Science in Bohemia", *Nature*, 109 (1922), pp. 625-7.
910. Československá akademie věd, *The Czechoslovak Academy of Sciences Handbook.* Arranged by Ladislav Javůrek (Prague, Publishing House of the Czechoslovak Academy of Sciences, 1959).
911. Československá akademie věd, Komise pro Mezinárodní geofysikální rok, *International Geophysical Year and Cooperation in Czechoslovakia, 1957-1959* (Prague, Československá akademie věd, 1960).
912. *Die Deutsche Karl-Ferdinands-Universität in Prag, unter der Regierung seiner Majestät des Kaisers Franz Josef I* (Prag, J. G. Calve'- sche Universitätsbuchhandlung, 1899).
913. Druce, Gerald, "Czechoslovakia's Contribution to Science", in *Czechoslovakia*, ed. Robert Joseph Kerner (Berkeley and Los Angeles, University of California, 1945), pp. 316-26.
914. Hanuš, J., *Systematisch und chronologisch geordnetes Verzeichnis sämtlicher Werke und Abhandlungen der Königlichen böhmischen Gesellschaft der Wissenschaften* (Prag, 1854).
915. Herz, H., "Die Dokumentation in der Tschechoslowakei", *Nachrichten für Dokumentation*, 9 (1958), pp. 63-70.

916. Jelinek, Carl, *Das ständisch-polytechnische Institut zu Prag* (Prag, J. G. Calve, 1856).
917. Kalousek, Joseph, *Geschichte der kön. böhmischen Gesellschaft der Wissenschaften sammt einer kritischen Uebersicht ihrer Publikationen aus den Bereichen der Philosophie, Geschichte und Philologie* (Prag, Kön. böhm. Gesellschaft der Wissenschaften, 1885).
918. *Neuere Abhandlungen der königlichen böhmischen Gesellschaft der Wissenschaften*, Prag, 1791-98.
919. Pelzel, Franz Martin, *Boehmische, maehrische und schlesische Gelehrten und Schriftsteller aus dem Order der Jesuiten von Anfang der Gesellschaft bis auf die gegenwaertige Zeit* (Prag, 1786).
920. Sandberg, Karl von, *Versuch einer Beantwortung der von der Böhmischen gelehrten Privatgesellschaft auf das Jahre 1784 aufgegebenen die Naturgeschichte Böhmens betreffenden Preisaufgabe* (Prag, 1785).
921. *Sitzungsberichte der k. böhmischen Gesellschaft der Wissenschaften*, Prag, 1859 and ff.
922. Slamecka, Vladimír, *Science in Czechoslovakia* (New York, London, Columbia University Press, 1963).
923. Společnost Národního musea, Prague, *Das Vaterländische Museum in Böhmen im Jahre 1842*. Vom Verwaltungsausschusse der Gesellschaft (Prag, Im Selbstverlag des Museums, 1842).
924. Stark, Franz, Wilhelm Gintl and Anton Grünwald, *Die k. k. deutsche technische Hochschule in Prag 1806-1906. Festschrift zur Hundertjahrfeier* (Prag, 1906).
925. Sternberg, Kaspar, Graf von, and Krombholz, J. V. Edler von, *Bericht über die Versammlung deutscher Naturforscher und Ärzte in Prag im Sept. 1837* (Prag, 1838).
926. Studnička, F. J., *Bericht über die mathematischen und naturwissenschaftlichen Publikationen der Königlichen böhmischen Gesellschaft der Wissenschaften während ihres hundertjährigen Bestandes* (Prag, K. böhm. Gesellschaft der Wiss., 1885).
927. Teich, Mikuláš, "The Royal Bohemian Society of Sciences and the First Phase of Organized Scientific Advance in Bohemia", *Historica*, 2 (1960), pp. 161-81.
928. Tibenský, Ján, "Die deutsche Aufklärung im 17. und 18. Jahrhundert und ihre Bedeutung für die Entwicklung des wissenschaftlichen Denkens in der Slowakei", *Tschirnhaus und die Frühaufklärung in Mittel- und Osteuropa*, 7 (Berlin, 1960), pp.

193-204.
929. Urban, R., *Die Organisation der Wissenschaft in der Tschechoslowakei* (Marburg/Lahn, Johann Gottfried Herder Institut, 1957).
930. Vetter, Q., "Czech Science during the War", *Scripta Math.*, 12 (1946), pp. 141-6.

Addendum: 1192

Crossreferences: 52, 899

B. Biological Sciences

931. Bateson, W., *Mendel's Principles of Heredity*. With translation of Mendel's original papers on hybridization (Cambridge University Press, 1902).
932. Československá akademie věd, *Advances in Biological Sciences – The Czechoslovak Academy of Science* (Prague, The Czechoslovak Academy of Sciences, 1962).
933. ——, Sekce biologicko-lékařská, *Biological Institutes of Czechoslovak Academy of Sciences 1950-1960. Anniversary Volume and Bibliography* (Prague, Publishing House of the Czechoslovak Academy of Sciences, 1961).
934. ——, Sekce biologicko-lékařská, *Philipp Maxmilian Opiz und seine Bedeutung für die Pflanzentaxonomie*. By B. Němec, I. Klášterský, M. Deyl, M. Svrček, J. Holub, E. Hadač and F. Weber (Prag, Verlag der tschechoslowakischen Akademie der Wissenschaften, 1958).
935. Československá akademie zemědělská, Prague, *The Czechoslovak Academy of Agriculture, its Foundation, Programme, Organization and Activities*. Ed. E. Reich and B. Vláčil (Prague, Czechoslovak Academy of Agriculture, 1931).
936. Československá botanická společnost, *Studies in Plant Physiology. Dedicated to the 85th Anniversary of the Birth of Bohumil Němec* (Prague, Československá akademie věd, 1958).
937. Českoslovenká eugenická společnost, Prague, *Memorial-Volume in Honor of the 100th Birthday of J. G. Mendel* (Prague, F. Borový, 1925).
938. Dokládal, Milan and Brožek, Josef, "Physical Anthropology in Czechoslovakia: Recent Developments", *Current Anthropology*, 2 (1961), pp. 455-78.

939. Ernest, A., "Julius Stoklasa, chimiste agricole (1858-1936)", *Archeion*, 23 (1941), pp. 206-10.
940. *Festschrift anlässlich des siebzigsten Geburtstage von Julius Stoklasa*. In Verbindung mit zahlreichen Mitarbeiten hrsg. von Ernst Gustav Dorell, Eduard Reich, Jaroslav Kříženecký und Bohuš Vláčil (Berlin, Paul Parey, 1928).
941. *Festschrift zur Feier des 100 jährigen Gründungs-Jubiläums des K.k. allgemeinen Krankenhauses in Prag*. Hrsg. von den Vorständen der deutschen Kliniken und des Deutschen pathologisch-anatomischen Institutes (Berlin, Fischer, 1890).
942. Fundárek, Radoslav, "Taxa Pharmaceutica Pessoniensis, bedeutsames Werk der tschechoslowakischen pharmaceutischen Literatur", in *Die Vorträge während des Internationalen Pharmaziegeschichtlichen Kongresses in Luzern, October 4-8, 1956* (Wien, 1957), pp. 87-95.
943. Hanzlik, P. J., "Purkinje's Pioneer Self-Experiments in Psychopharmacology", *California and Western Medicine*, 49 (1938), pp. 52-5, 140-2.
944. Hasner, Josef, "Die älteste Medicin in Böhmen. Eine literarhistorische Ferienstudie", *Vierteljahrschrift für die praktische Heilkunde, herausgegeben von der medicinischen Fakultät in Prag*, 90 (1866), pp. 1-35.
945. ——, "Zur Geschichte der Medicin in Böhmen. Zweiter Beitrag: das fünfzehnte und sechzehnte Jahrhundert", *Ibid.*, 109 (1871), pp. 134-48.
946. ——, "Zur Geschichte der Medicin in Böhmen. Dritter Beitrag: des siebzehnten Jahrhunderts erste Periode (1600-1621)", *Ibid.*, 110 (1871), pp. 1-18.
947. ——, "Das medicinische Wien und Prag. Eine historische Skizze", *Prager med. Wschr.*, 9 (1884), pp. 174-6.
948. Hinztische, Erich, *G. G. Valentin* (Basel, 1952).
949. *Dr. Aleš Hrdlička Anniversary Volume*, in *Anthropologie*, Prague, 7, No. 1-2 (1929).
950. Hrubý, Karel, "Genetics in Czechoslovakia", in *Czechoslovak Literature and Science 1935* (Prague, The American Institute in Czechoslovakia, 1935), pp. 83-93.
951. *Hundert Jahre Zellforschung* (= *Protoplasma-Monographien*, Band 17). Von L. Aschoff, E. Küstler und W. J. Schmidt (Berlin, Verlag von Gebrüder Borntraeger, 1938).
952. Hyrtl, J. J., *Geschichte der Anatomie an der Carl-Ferdinands Univer-*

sität in Prag (Prag, 1841).
953. Iltis, Hugo, *Life of Mendel* (New York, W. W. Norton and Co., 1932).
954. *In Memoriam Joh. Ev. Purkyně, 1787-1937* (Prague, Purkyňova společnost, 1937).
955. John, Henry J., *Jan Evangelista Purkyně. Czech Scientist and Patriot (1787-1869)* (Philadelphia, The American Philosophical Society, 1959).
956. John, Jon.-Dion, *Arzneiwissenschaftliche Aufsätze böhmischer Gelehrter, nebst einem Verzeichnisse der böhmischen lebenden medicinischen Schriftsteller mit Anzeige ihrer Schriften* (Dresden, 1798).
957. Jungmann, A., *Skizzierte Geschichte der medicinischen Anstalten an der Universität zu Prag* (= *Medicinische Jahrbücher des k.k. österreichischen Staates*, Vol. 31) (Vienna, 1840).
958. Kisch, Bruno, "Forgotten Leaders in Modern Medicine. Valentin, Gruby, Remak, Auerbach", *Trans. Amer. Soc.*, Series 44, Pt. 2 (Philadelphia, American Philosophical Society, 1954), pp. 137-317.
959. Klinkosch, J. T., *Dissertationes medicae chirurgae et anatomicae selectiores Pragenses*, Vol. I (Dresdae, 1775), Vol. II. Collegit et edidit J. D. John (Pragae et Dresdae, 1792).
960. Krombholz, Julius Vincenc Edler von, *Fragmente einer Geschichte der medicinisch-praktischen Schule an der Carl-Ferdinands-Universität zu Prag. Programm zum feierl. Rectoratswechsel* (Prag, 1831).
961. Kruta, Vladislav, "Georgius Prochaska. A Pioneer in Modern Physiology 1794-1820)", *Bull. Czechoslov. Med. Assoc.*, II/I (1943), pp. 30-9.
962. ——, 'Purkyně's Contributions to the Physiology of Digestion", *Physiologica Bohemoslovenica*, 7 (1958), pp. 1-8.
963. Maiwald, V., *Geschichte der Botanik in Böhmen* (Wien-Leipzig, 1904).
964. Matoušková, B., "The Beginnings of Darwinism in Bohemia", *Folia Biologica*, 5 (1959), pp. 169-85.
965. Neilreich, August, *Geschichtlicher Ueberblick. Aufzählung der in Ungarn und Slavonien bisher beobachteten Gefässpflanzen* (Wien, 1866).
966. Němec, B., "Julius Sachs in Prague", *Science, Medicine and History*, 2 (1953), pp. 211-6.

967. *Neue Technik und neue Technologie in der Landwirtschaft der ČSSR und der DDR* (Berlin, VEB Deutscher Landwirtschaftsverlag, 1961).
968. Pick, Friedel, *Joh. Jessenius de Magna Jessen, Arzt und Rektor in Wittenberg und Prag, hingerichtet am 21. Juni 1621* (Leipzig, J. A. Barth, 1926).
969. Pleischl, A., *Bemerkungen zu dem Werke Kilian's in Beziehung auf die Universität Prag* (1829).
970. Prát, Silvestr, "Progress of Plant Physiological Investigations in Czechoslovakia", *Plant Physiology*, 13 (1938), pp. 1-3.
971. *Georgius Prochaska (1749-1820), Professor of Anatomy, Physiology, and Ophthalmology at the Universities of Prague and Vienna* (Brno, Masaryk University, 1949).
972. Procházková, Marta, *Bibliographia Bohemoslovenica gynaecologico-obstetricia atque oncologica, annorum 1945-1955*) (Publicatio Instituti Documentationis Medicae) (Prague, 1955).
973. Rosický, B., "Young in Years, but Important and Vital in its Results and Plans", *Folia Biologica*, 6 (1960), pp. 397-402.
974. Sebald, Ant., *Geschichte der medicinisch-praktischen Schule an der k.k. Karl-Ferdinand. Universität in Prag* (Prag und Leipzig, 1796).
975. Sommer, J. L., "Hutterite Medicine and Physicians in Moravia in the Sixteenth Century and After", *Mennonite Quarterly Review*, (1953), pp. 111-27.
976. Sootin, Harry, *Gregor Mendel: Father of the Science of Genetics* (New York, Vanguard Press, 1959).
977. Státní lékařská knihovna, Prague, *The Annual of Czechoslovak Medical Literature, 1956 and ff.* (Prague, Státní zdravotnické nakladatelství, 1958 and ff.).
978. Studnička, Fr. J., *Joannes Marcus Marci a Cronland, sein Leben und Gelehrtes Wirken* (1891).
979. Sternberg, Kaspar Graf, *Abhandlung über die Pflanzenkunde in Böhmen* (= Abh. der k. böhm. Ges. der Wiss., Neue Folge, 6 Band) (Prag, 1817 and 1818).
980. Studnička, F. K., *Joh. Ev. Purkinjes und seiner Schule Verdienste um die Entdeckung tierischer Zellen und um die Aufstellung der "Zellen"-Theorie* (= Práce Moravské přírodovědecké společnosti, Vol. 4, No. 4) (Brünn, 1927).
981. Stur, Johann, "Die Leistungen von Georg Prochaska (1749-1820) für die Gynäkologie", *Archiv f. Gynäkol.*, No. 149 (1932), pp. 757-78.

982. Thurzo, V., Winkler, A., and Šándor, L., "The Development of Experimental Oncology in Czechoslovakia", *Neoplasma*, 9 (1962), pp. 239-52.
983. Vámossy, Stephan, *Beiträge zur Geschichte der Medizin in Pressburg* (Pressburg, Stampfel, 1902).
984. Volf, M. B., *George Holik, inventeur du greffage moderne* (Prague, 1937).
985. Weitenweber, Wilh. Rud., *Die medicinischen Anstalten Prag's nach ihrem gegenwärtigen Zustande* (Prag, 1845).
986. ——, *Denkschrift über die Gebrüder J. Sw. und C. B. Presl* (Prag, 1854).

Addendum: 1219, 1277, 1291, 1308

Crossreferences: 243, 263

C. Physical Sciences

987. Agricola, Georg, 1494-1555, *Ausgewählte Werke* (Berlin, VEB Deutscher Verlag der Wissenschaften, 1955-196?).
988. Alter, Georg, *Kepler und die moderne Naturwissenschaft* (= *Publ. d. Sternw. d. Deutschen Univ. in Prag*, Neue Folge, No. 14) (Prag, 1931).
989. ——, *Two Renaissance Astronomers. David Gand and Joseph Delmedigo* (= *Rozpravy Československé akademie věd*, Series MPV, Vol. 68, No. 11) (Prague, 1958).
990. *Ball Memoir of the Life and Work of Ferd. Stoliczka* (London, 1886).
991. Born, Ignaz, Edler von, 1742-1791, *Travels through the Banat of Temeswar, Transylvania, and Hungary, in the Year 1770. Described in a Series of Letters to Prof. Ferber, on the Mines, and Mountains of these Different Countries, by Baron Inigo Born ... To which is Added, John James Ferber's Mineralogical History of Bohemia*. Translated from the German, with some explanatory notes ... by R. E. Raspe... (London, Printed by J. Miller, for G. Kearsley, 1777).
992. ——, *Baron Inigo Born's New Process of Amalgamation of Gold and Silver Ores, and Other Metallic Mixtures, as, by His Late Imperial Majesty's Commands, Introduced in Hungary and Bohemia*, from the Baron's account in German, translated into

English by R. E. Raspe (London, T. Cadell, 1791).
993. Brahe, Tyge, 1546-1601, *Tychonis Brahe Dani Opera Omnia*, edidit I. L. E. Dreyer (Hauniae, Libraria Gyldendaliana, 1913-19).
994. Caspar, Max, *Bibliographia Kepleriana* (München, Beck, 1936).
995. Doppler, Christian, 1803-1853, *Abhandlungen, von Christian Doppler*. Hrsg. von H. A. Lorentz (Leipzig, W. Engelmann, 1907).
996. Doppler, Christian, "Über das farbige Licht der Doppelsterne und einiger anderer Gestirne des Himmels", *Abhandlungen der königlichen Böhmischen Gesellschaft der Wissenschaften*, 2 (Prague, 1843), p. 467.
997. Dreyer, J. L. E., *Tycho Brahe, a Picture of Scientific Life and Work in the Sixteenth Century* (Edinburgh, A. and C. Black, 1890).
998. Druce, Gerald, *Two Czech Chemists. Bohuslav Brauner (1855-1935). František Wald (1861-1930)* (London, The New Europe Publishing Co., 1944).
999. ——, "The Mendeléeff-Brauner Tradition in Czech Chemistry", *Nature*, 150 (1942), pp. 623-4.
1000. ——, "Chemical Science in Czechoslovakia", *The Central European Observer*, 24 (1947), p. 349.
1001. Ferber, J. J., *Beytraege zu der Mineral-Geschichte von Boehmen* (Berlin, 1774).
1002. Gade, John Allyne, *The Life and Times of Tycho Brahe* (New York, Princeton University Press, 1947).
1003. Halaschka, Cassian, *Versuch einer geschichtlichen Darstellung dessen, was an der Karl-Ferdinandischen Universität zu Prag in der Experimentalphysik bearbeitet wurde...* (Prag, 1818).
1004. Hasner, J., *Tycho Brahe und Johann Kepler in Prag* (Prag, 1872).
1005. Henning, Hans, *Ernst Mach als Philosoph, Physiker und Psycholog* (Leipzig, J. A. Barth, 1915).
1006. Heyrovská, M., "Scientific Publications of Professor Heyrovský", *Collection of Czechoslovak Chemical Communications*, 25 (1960), pp. 2949-57.
1007. Hoppe, E., "Marcus Marci de Kronland. Ein vergessener Physiker des 17. Jahrhunderts", *Archiv für Geschichte der Mathematik und Physik*, 10 (1927).
1008. Hujer, Karel, "Father Procopius Diviš – the European Franklin", *Isis*, 43 (Summer 1952).
1009. ——, "Christian Doppler in Prague", *Royal Astronomical Society of Canada* (August 1963).
1010. Loewenfield, C., *Ernst Florens Friedrich Chladni. Skizze von Leben*

und Werk (= *Abhandlungen des Naturwissenschaftlichen Vereins zu Hamburg*) (Hamburg, 1929).
1011. Lukeš, R., "Die Lage und Perspektiven der Chemie in der ČSR", *Journal für praktische Chemie*, 4 Reihe, Band 10 (1960), pp. 67-70.
1012. Obenrauch, Ferd. J., *Geschichte der darstellenden und projectiven Geometrie mit besonderer Berücksichtigung ihrer Begründung in Frankreich und Deutschland und ihrer wissenschaftlichen Pflege in Österreich* (Brünn, 1897).
1013. Peithner, J. Th. A., *Beytraege zur Wassergeschichte von Boehmen*, I-II (Leipzig, Prag, 1770 and 1772).
1014. Purkyně, C., *Le rôle de D. Štur dans l'étude de la stratigraphie des bassins houillers de Tchécoslovaquie* (Heerlen, 1929).
1015. Reuss, F. A., *Mineralogische Geographie von Böhmen* (Dresden, 1793-7).
1016. Rychlík, Karel, *Theorie der reelen Zahlen in Bolzano's Handschriftlichem Nachlass* (Prag, Czechoslovak Academy of Sciences, 1962).
1017. Small, Robert, *An Account of the Astronomical Discoveries of Kepler* (Madison, Wisc., The University of Wisconsin Press, 1963).
1018. Sternberg, Kaspar Graf, *Umrisse einer Geschichte der böhm. Bergwerke* (Prag, 1836).
1019. ——, *Umrisse der Geschichte des Bergbaues und der Berggesetzgebung des Königreiches Böhmen* (Prag, 1838).
1020. Strunz, Franz, "Chemie und Mineralogie bei Joh. Amos Comenius", *Chemiker-Zeitung*, No. 62 (1908), pp. 731-4.
1021. Vydra, Stanislav, *Historia matheseos in Bohemia et Moravia cultae* (Pragae, 1778).
1022. Wolf, R., *Johannes Kepler und Joost Bürgi* (Zürich, 1892).
1023. Wrany, Adalbert, *Die Pflege der Mineralogie in Böhmen* (Prag, Verlag von H. Dominicus-Th. Gruss, 1896).
1024. ——, *Geschichte der Chemie und der auf chemischer Grundlage beruhenden Betriebe in Böhmen bis zur Mitte des 19. Jahrhunderts* (Prag, Verlag von Fr. Řivnáč, 1902).
1025. Zellweker, E., *Das Urbild des Sarastro Ignaz v. Born* (Wien, 1953).
1026. Zinner, Ernst, *Johannis Kepler, der grosse Führer und Mensch* (Lübeck, 1934).
1027. ——, *Deutsche und niederländische astronomische Instrumente des 11.-18. Jahrhunderts* (Munchen, Beck, 1956).

1028. Zuman, Petr and Elving, Philip J., "Jaroslav Heyrovský: Nobel Laureate", *Journal of Chemical Education*, 37 (1960) pp. 562-7.

Addendum: 1230, 1271

Crossreferences: 229, 282

VII. TECHNOLOGY

1029. Balling, Carl J., *Die Eisenindustrie Böhmens* (Wien, 1868).
1030. Beer, A., *Studien zur Geschichte der österreichischen Volkswirtschaft unter Maria Theresia. Teil I, Die österreichische Industriepolitik* (Wien, 1894).
1031. *Bericht der Beurtheilungscommission über die 1829 und 1936 ausgestellten Industrie-Erzeugnisse Böhmens* (Wien).
1032. *Bericht des Verbandes mährischer Industrieller in Brünn* (Brünn, 1920 and ff.).
1033. *Bericht des Vereines der Wollindustriellen Mährens* (Brünn, 1903 and ff.).
1034. Brodhuber, L., Holdhaus, C., and Martin, A., *Industrie und Handel im Kaiserthume Oesterreich nach ihrem gegenwärtigen Standpunkte dargestellt* (Wien, 1861).
1035. Demuth, A., *Das Manufacturhaus in Weiswasser* (= Mitteil. Vereines für die Geschichte der Deutschen in Böhmen, Vol. 28) (Prag, 1890).
1036. Elvert, C. d', *Die Culturgeschichte Mährens und österr. Schlesiens besonders im Landbau und in der Industrie wärhend der letzten 100 Jahre* (Brünn, 1854).
1037. ——, *Zur Geschichte des Bergbaues and Hüttenwesen in Mähren und österr. Schlesien* (Brünn, 1866).
1038. *Encyclopédie Tchécoslovaque*. Vol. I, *Industrie et commerce* (Prague, 1923).
1039. *Die Gömörer Eisenindustrie* (Rosenau, 1885).
1040. *Die Gross-Industrie Oestereichs. Festgabe zum 50-Jährigen Jubileum des Kaisers Franz Josefs I*, Vols. I-VI (Wien, 1898).
1041. Hallmich, *Die erste Fabrik in Reichenberg* (1869).
1042. Horský, František, *Mein Streben, Wirken, meine Resultate* (Kolin, F. Sudek, 1873).
1043. *Die hundertjährige Geschichte der ersten Brünner Maschinenfabrik von 1821-1921* (Leipzig, 1921).

A Selective Bibliography 619

1044. *Jahrbuch für Fabrikanten und Gewerbetreibende* (Prag, 1838 and ff.).
1045. Karpe, L., *Böhmen in der Geschichte der Technik* (Prag, 1936).
1046. Kees, St. von, *Darstellung des Fabriks- und Gewerbewesens in seinem gegenwärtigen Zustande* (Wien, 1824).
1047. Kreutzberg, *Übersicht des Standes und der Leistungen von Böhmens Gewerbes- und Fabriks-Industrie* (Wien, 1836).
1048. Mayer, F. M., *Die Anfänge des Handels und der Industrie in Oesterreich* (Innsbruck, 1882).
1049. Milosevics, M., *Die Entwicklung der Roheisen-Erzeugung im Gömörer Komitate* (Budapest, 1896).
1050. *Mitteilungen für Gewerbe und Handel* (Prag, 1835-42).
1051. *Mitteilungen der mährisch-schlesischen Gesellschaft zur Beförderung des Ackerbaues, der Natur- und Landeskunde*, Brünn, 1821-91.
1052. Peithner, J., *Versuch über die natürliche und politische Geschichte der böhmischen und mährischen Bergwerke* (Wien, 1780).
1053. Ressel, Josef, *Denkschrift herausgegeben vom Comité für die Centralfeier Jos. Ressels* (Wien, 1893).
1054. Rieger, *Materialien zur alten und neuen Statistik von Böhmen* (Prag, Leipzig, 1787-94).
1055. Schebeck, E., *Böhmens Glasindustrie und Glashandel. Quellen zu ihrer Geschichte* (Prag, 1878).
1056. Schram, W., *Ein Buch für jeden Brünner*, Vols. I-V (1901-05).
1057. Schreyer, J., *Commerz, Fabriken und Manufacturen des Königreichs Böhmen* (Prag-Leipzig, 1770).
1058. *Schriften der historisch-statistischen Section der k.k. mährisch-schlesischen Gesellschaft des Ackerbaues*, Brünn, 1851-95.
1059. Schwoy, *Topographie von Mähren*, 2. vols. (1793-94).
1060. *Skizzierte Übersicht des gegenwärtigen Standes und der Leistungen von Böhmens Gewerbs- und Fabriksindustrie in ihren vorzüglichsten Zweigen* (Prag, 1936).
1061. Slokar, Johann, *Geschichte der österreichischen Industrie und ihrer Förderung unter Kaiser Franz I* (Wien, F. Tempsky, 1914).
1062. Sugar, O., *Die Industrialisierung Ungarns unter Beihilfe des Staates und der Kommunen* (Leipzig, 1908).
1063. Vlček, Bohumil, *Handbuch der Weberei* (Berlin, Springer, 1933).
1064. Weber, O., *Die Enstehung der Porzellan- und Steingut-Industrie in Böhmen* (Prag, 1894).
1065. Woat, Th., *Umriss der Entstehung- und Entwicklungsgeschichte des fürstl. Auersperg'schen Mineralwerkes zu Gross-Lukavic in Böhmen* (Gross-Lukavic, 1873).

1066. Wolny, G., *Die Markgrafschaft Mähren, topografisch, statistisch und historisch geschildert*, 6 vols. (Brünn, 1835-42).
1067. *Zeitschrift des Vereines für die Geschichte Mährens und Schlesiens* (Brünn, 1896).
1068. Zimmermann, A., *Blüte und Zerfall des Leinengewerbes in Schlesien* (Breslau, 1885).

Crossreferences: 653, 660

VIII. CZECHS AND SLOVAKS ABROAD

A. U.S.A.

1069. American Czechoslovak Engineers Society, *These Twenty-Five Years. 1922-1947*. Ed. John H. Hruska (Chicago, Ill., American Czechoslovak Engineers Society, 1947).
1070. Balch, Emily Green, *Our Slavic Fellow Citizens* (New York, Charities Publications Committee, 1920).
1071. Battershell, C. F., and Svarc, Ven., *The Moravians and the Czech Contribution to the Early History of Ohio* (Cleveland, American Alliance of Czechoslovaks, 1932).
1072. Burgess, Ernest W. and Newcomb, Charles, *Statistical Data of the City of Chicago* (Chicago, 1920).
1073. Čada, Joseph, *The Catholic Central Union* (Chicago, Cash Central Union, 1952).
1074. Čapek, Thomas, *The Czechs (Bohemians) in America, a Study of their National, Cultural, Political, Social, Economic and Religious Life* (Boston and New York, Houghton Mifflin Co., 1920).
1075. ———, *The Čech (Bohemian) Community of New York, with Introductory Remarks on the Czechoslovaks in the United States* (New York, The Czechoslovak Section of America's Making Inc., 1921).
1076. ———, *Augustine Herrman of Bohemian Manor* (Prague, State Printing Office, 1930).
1077. ———, *Ancestry of Frederick Philipse. First Lord and Founder of Phillipse Manor at Yonkers, N.Y.* (New York, The Paebar Co., 1939).
1078. ———, *Czechs and Slovaks in the United States Census, with Reference to all Slavs* (New York, The Paebar Co., 1939).

1079. ——, *American Czechs in Public Office* (Omaha, Czech Historical Society of Nebraska, 1940).
1080. ——, *Slavs in the United States Census 1850-1940, with Special Reference to Czechoslovakia* (Chicago, The Czechoslovak National Council of America, 1943).
1081. ——, "Sociological Factors in Czech Immigration", *Slavonic Review*, 22 (1944), pp. 93-8.
1082. Čapek, Thomas and Čapek, Thomas, Jr., *The Czechs and Slovaks in American Banking* (New York and Chicago, Fleming H. Revell Co., 1920).
1083. Droba, Daniel D., *Czech and Slovak Leaders in Metropolitan Chicago* (Chicago, Slavonic Club, 1934).
1084. Dvornik, Francis, *Czech Contribution to the Growth of the United States* (Chicago, Bohemian Benedictine Press, 1961).
1085. Foreign Language Information Service, *Slovaks under the Stars and Stripes* (New York, 1900).
1086. Fries, Adelaide L., *Road to Salem* (Chapel Hill, N.C., University of North Carolina Press, 1944.)
1087. Gottfried, Alex., *Boss Cermak of Chicago. A Study of Political Leadership* (Seattle, University of Washington Press, 1962).
1088. Heck, E. L. W., *Augustine Herrman* (Englewood, Ohio, 1941).
1089. Hrbková, Sarka, The Bohemians in Nebraska (Lincoln, Nebraska State Historical Society, a manuscript).
1090. Hudson, Estelle and Maresh, Henry R., *Czech Pioneers of the Southwest* (Dallas, Tex., Southwest Press, 1934).
1091. *Index of Czechoslovak Organisations in the United States* (Chicago, 1933).
1092. James, B. B., *Labadist Colony in Maryland, 1899* (Baltimore, The Johns Hopkins University Press, 196?).
1093. Kisch, G., *In Search of Freedom. A History of American Jews from Czechoslovakia* (London, Goldstone and Son, 1949).
1094. Koger, Marvin V., *Index to the Names of 30,000 Immigrants into Pennsylvania* (Pannington Gap., Va., 1931).
1095. Kohlbeck, V., "Bohemians in the United States", *The Champlain's Educator*, 25 (Jan.-March 1906), pp. 36-54.
1096. Kraus, Adolf, *Reminiscences and Comments* (Chicago, 1935).
1097. Kutak, Robert T., *Story of Bohemian-American Village. A Study of Social Persistence and Change* (Louisville, Ky., Stanford Printing Co., 1933).
1098. Ledbetter, Eleanor E., *The Slovaks of Cleveland, with some General*

Information on the Race (Cleveland, Americanization Committee, 1918).
1099. ——, *The Czechs of Cleveland* (Cleveland, Americanization Committee, 1919).
1100. Lynch, Russell W., "Czech Farmers in Oklahoma", *Econ. Geogr.*, 20 (1944), pp. 9-13.
1101. Mallory, Charles Payson, *Ancient Families of Bohemia Manor, their Homes and their Graves* (Wilmington, Del., Historical Society of Delaware, 1888).
1102. Miller, Kenneth D., *The Czecho-Slovaks in America* (New York, G. H. Doran Co., 1922).
1103. ——, *Peasant Pioneers* (New York, 1925).
1104. Pergler, Charles, *America in the Struggle for Czechoslovak Independence* (Philadelphia, Dorrance and Co., 1926).
1105. Prantner, E. F., *Those Who Help to Build America* (Chicago, Czechoslovak Review, 1923).
1106. Reichman, John J., *Czechoslovaks of Chicago* (Chicago, The Czechoslovak Historical Society of Illinois, 1937).
1107. Riis, Jacob A., *How the Other Half Lives* (New York, 1890).
1108. Rosicky, Rose, *A History of Czechs (Bohemians) in Nebraska* (Omaha, Czech Historical Society of Nebraska, 1929).
1109. Rouček, Joseph S., *Die Tschechen und Slowaken in den Vereinigten Staaten* (Stuttgart, Publikationsstelle, 1943).
1110. ——, *American Slavs, A Bibliography* (New York, Bureau for Intercultural Education, 1944).
1111. ——, *The Immigrant in Fiction and Biography* (New York, Bureau for Intercultural Education, 1944).
1112. ——, "Czechoslovak Americans", in *One America. The History, Contributions, and Present Problems of our Racial and National Minorities*, eds. Francis J. Brown and J. S. Rouček, 3rd ed. (New York, Prentice Hall, 1952), pp. 157-68.
1113. Sears, Charles Hatch, *The Czechoslovaks in America* (New York, 1922).
1114. Škrabánek, R. L., "The Influence of Cultural Backgrounds on Farming Practices in a Czech-American Rural Community", *South-West Social Science Quarterly*, 31 (1951), pp. 258-66.
1115. Škrabánek, R. L. and Parenton, Vernon, J., "Social Life in a Czech-American Rural Community", *Rural Sociology*, 12 (1950), pp. 221-31.
1116. Smetanka, Jaroslav, "Bohemians and Slovaks", *Annals Amer.*

Academy of Political and Social Sciences, XCIII (1921), pp. 149-53.
1117. Steiner, Edward, *From Alien to Citizen* (New York, 1914).
1118. Stump, H. Arthur, Jr., *Augustine Herrman, 1606-1686, Founder of Bohemia Manor, 1661* (Baltimore, Abrams Printing Co., 1929).
1119. Wilson, J. G., "A Maryland Manor", *Publications Baltimore, Maryland Historical Society Fund*, No. 30 Part 2 (1890).
1120. Writers' program Minnesota, *The Bohemian Flats* (Minneapolis, 1941).
1121. Zeman, Josefa H., "The Bohemian People in Chicago", *Hull House Papers*, Chapter VI (Boston, 1893).
1122. Žižka, Ernest, *Czech Cultural Contributions* (Chicago, Bohemian Benedictine Press, 1941).

Addendum: 1259, 1268, 1291, 1297, 1303

Crossreferences: 949, 1132

B. Other Countries

1123. Baerlein, Henry, *March of Seventy Thousands* (London, Leonard Parsons, 1926).
1124. Beaumont, A., *Heroic Story of the Czech Legions* (Prague, 1926).
1125. Becvar, Gustav, *Lost Legion* (London, P. Stanley, 1939).
1126. Beneš, Bohuš (ed.), *Wings in Exile. Life and Work of the Czechoslovak Airmen in France and Great Britain* (London, Čechoslovák, 1942).
1127. Bolton, J. R. G., "Anglo-Czech", *Speculum*, 174 (1945), pp. 239 and ff.
1128. Brož, Josef A., *Czechoslovakia and Great Britain. Their Contacts in the Past*. Historical and Bibliographical Research (London, the London "Sokol", 1944).
1129. *Die Čechen in Preussisch-Oberschlesien. Stimme eines Rufenden aus Preussisch-Oberschlesien*, von einem Slaven (Prag, 1875).
1130. Cekota, A., *A Battle of Home. Some Problems of Industrial Community* (Toronto, Macmillan Co. of Canada, 1944).
1131. Drzardzynski, *Die slavischen Ortsnamen des Kreises Leobschütz* (Leobschütz, 1896).
1132. Duben, V. N., *Czech and Slovak Periodical Press outside Czechoslovakia. History and Status as of January 1962* (Washington, D.C., Czechoslovak Society of Arts and Sciences, 1962).

1133. Feyl, O., *Beiträge zur Geschichte der slawischen Verbindungen und internationalen Kontakte der Universität Jena* (Jena, 1960).
1134. Hind, Arthur M., *Wenceslaus Hollar and his Views of London and Windsor in the Seventeenth Century* (London, John Lane, 1922).
1135. Jelínek, Břetislav, *Die Böhmen im Kampfe um ihre Selbständigkeit 1618-1648* (Prag, 1916).
1136. Kruta, V., "Czech Doctors in Great Britain," *Notes of the Czechoslovak Med. Assoc. in Great Britain*, No. 2 (1945), pp. 58-69.
1137. Ledderhose, Karl Friedrich, 1806-1890, *Johann Jänicke, der evangelish-lutherische Prediger an der böhmischer – oder Bethlehems-Kirche zu Berlin*, nach seinem Leben und Wirken dargestellt. Hrsg. von G. Knak (Berlin, Selbstverlag des Herausgebers, In Commission bei E. Beck, 1863).
1138. Letts, Malcolm H. I., ed., *Travels of Leo of Rožmitál through Germany, Flanders, England, France, Spain, Portugal, and Italy, 1465-1467* (= *Publications of the Hakluyt Society*, Second Series) (Cambridge, Cambridge University Press, 1957).
1139. Loesche, G., *Die böhmischen Exulanten in Sachsen* (1923).
1140. Lowrie, Donald Alexander, *The Hunted Children* (New York, Norton, 1963).
1141. Maetschke, E., *Geschichte des Glatzer Landes vom Beginne der deutschen Besiedelung bis zu den Hussitenkriegen* (Breslau, 1888).
1142. Medek, R., *The Czechoslovak Anabasis* (London, 1925).
1143. Mellon, J., *Czechoslovak Industrial Effort in Great Britian* (London and New York, Hutchinson, 1943).
1144. Odložilík, Otakar, "Czech Missionaries in New Spain", *Hispan. His. R.*, 25 (1945), pp. 428-54.
1145. Peukert, H., *Die Slaven der Donaumonarchie und die Universität Jena* (Berlin, 1958).
1146. Rösel, Hubert, *Die tschechischen Drucke der Hallenser Pietisten* (Würzburg, Holzner-Verlag, 1961).
1147. Rössler, Hubert, "Der Slowake Mathias Bel – ein bedeutender Mitarbeiter an den Tschechischen Halleschen Drucken", *Zeitschrift der M. Luther Universität, Halle*. Ges-Sprach. w. Jahrg. 3, Heft 1, pp. 91-8.
1148. Sommer, Ernest, *Into Exile. The History of the Counter-Reformation in Bohemia (1620-1650)* (London, The New Europe Publishing Co., 1943).
1149. Sousek, Charles J., *Czechs in South Africa* (Johannesburg, The Author, 1942).

1150. Sveton, Ján, *Die Slowaken in Ungarn* (Bratislava, Slowakische Rundschau, 1943).
1151. Urzidil, J., *Hollar, a Czech Emigré in England* (London, Čechoslovák, 1943).
1152. Welzl, Jan, *Thirty Years in the Golden North* (New York, Macmillan, 1932).
1153. Winter, E., *Die tschechische und slowakische Emigration in Deutschland im 17. und 18. Jahrhundert. Beiträge zur Geschichte der husitischen Tradition* (Berlin, Deutsche Akademie der Wissenschaften zu Berlin, 1955).
1154. Young, Robert Fitzgibbon, "Bohemian Scholars and Students at English Universities from 1347 to 1750", *English Historical Review* (1923).
1155. ——, *A Bohemian Philosopher at Oxford in the 17th Century, George Ritschel of Deutschkahn (1616-1683)* (London, 1925).
1156. ——, *A Czech Humanist in London in the 17th Century, Jan Sictor Rokycanský (1593-1652)* (London, 1926).
1157. ——, *Comenius in England* (London, Oxford University Press, 1932).
1158. Zeschau, W. von, "Die Germanisierung des vormals tschechischen Glatzer Landes im 13. und 14. Jahrhunderte", *Vierteljahrschrift f. Gesch. und Heimatkunde der Grafschaft Glatz* (Habelschwerdt, 1887-88).

Addendum: 1242

Crossreferences: 265, 392, 549, 791, 877, 878, 883

IX. ADDENDUM

1159. Adamovich, Ludwig, *Grundriss des tschechoslowakischen Staatsrechtes* (Wien, Oesterreichische Staatsdruckerei, 1929).
1160. Adler, Franz, *Die Grundgedanken der tschechoslowakischen Verfassungskunde in der Entwicklungsgeschichte des Verfassungsrechtes* (Berlin-Breslau, H. Sack, 1927).
1161. ——, *Grundriss des tschechoslowakischen Verfassungsrechtes* (Reichenberg, Gebrüder Stiepel, 1930).
1162. Atcherson, Thomas, *Ein Musikwissenschaftler in zwei Welten* (Wien, Verlag Schönborn, 1962).
1163. *Atlas de la République Tchécoslovaquie* (Prague, Orbis, 1935).

1164. Baerlein, Henri Philip Bernard, *In Czechoslovakia's Hinterland* (London, Hutchinson, 1938).
1165. Balthasar, Else, *Die Staatsfinanzen der Tschechoslowakei, 1918-1928*... (Dux, C. Weigend, 1929).
1166. Behaghel, George, *Kohle und Eisen in der Tschechoslowakei* (Breslau, Priebatsch, 1939).
1167. Bílek, Bohumil, *Fifth Column at Work* (London, Drummond, 1945).
1168. Blau, Josef, *Landes- und Volkskunde der tschechoslovakischen Republik*, 2nd ed. (Reichenberg, Paul Sollor, 1927).
1169. Böhmer, Alois, Kočvara, Stephen and Nosek, Jindřich, "Church and State in Czechoslovakia", *Church and State Behind the Iron Curtain*, Ed. Vladimir Gsovski (New York, F. A. Praeger, 1955), pp. 1-67.
1170. Bradbrook, Bohuslava, "Karel Čapek and the Western World" (Unpublished master's essay) (Oxford University, 1958).
1171. Buber-Neumann, Margareta, *Kafka's Freundin Milena* (München, Gotthold Müller, 1963).
1172. Buk, Pierre, *La Tragédie Tchécoslovaque de Septembre 1938 à Mars 1939* (Paris, Sagittaire, 1939).
1173. Čapek, Milič, *A Key to Czechoslovakia. The Territory of Kladsko (Gratz): A Study of a Frontier Problem in Middle Europe* (New York, Richard Vogel, 1946).
1174. Čapek, Thomas (ed.), *Bohemia under Hapsburg Misrule* (New York-Chicago ..., Fleming H. Revell Co., 1915).
1175. Čapek, Thomas, Jr., *Origins of the Czechoslovak State* (New York, The Revell Press, 1926).
1176. Chlumecky, Peter and Demuth, Karel J., *Das Tobitschauer Buch, eine Quelle zur Rechtsgeschichte des 15. Jahrhunderts in Mähren* (Brünn, 1858).
1177. Chytil, Josef, and others, *Landtafel des Markgrafensthums Mähren* (Brünn, 1856).
1178. Clementis, Vlado, *The Czechoslovak Magyar Relationship* (London, Central European Observer, 1943).
1179. ——, *Panslavism, Past and Present* (London, Czechoslovak Committee for Slav Reciprocity, 1943).
1180. Council on Foreign Relations, *Foreign Affairs Bibliography, 1919-1932*. Ed. W. L. Langer and H. F. Armstrong (New York-London, Harper and Brothers, 1933).
1181. ——, *Foreign Affairs Bibliography, 1932-1942*. Ed. R. G. Woolbert

(New York-London, Harper and Brothers, 1945).
1182. ——, *Foreign Affairs Bibliography*, 1942-1952. Ed. H. L. Roberts with J. Gunther and J. A. Kreslins (New York, Harper and Brothers, 1955).
1183. ——, *Foreign Affairs Bibliography*, 1952-1962. Ed. H. L. Roberts (New York, R. R. Bowker Co., 1964).
1184. Czechoslovak National Council of America, *Thomas G. Masaryk and his Country* (Chicago, 195–).
1185. ——, *Ten Years, the Czechoslovak Question in the United Nations*. With a foreword by Ján Papánek (Chicago, 1958).
1186. Czechoslovak Republic. Laws, statutes, etc., *Czechoslovak National Insurance, a Contribution to the Pattern of Social Security, the Czechoslovak National Insurance Act*. With an introduction by Evžen Erban (Prague, Orbis, 1949).
1187. Descotes, Maurice, *Aspects de la Tchécoslovaquie* (Paris, Editions du Temps Présent, 1948).
1188. Diekroeger, Emma, *Political History of Czechoslovakia, October 1918-May 1938. A Bibliography of References in English* (Madison, Library School, University of Wisconsin, 1938).
1189. Dittrich, Anton and Spirk, Anton, *Monumentes historica universitatis Carlo-Ferdinandeae Pragensis*, Vol. I-III (Prague, 1830-1845).
1190. Dittrich, Z. R., *Het verleden van Oosteuropa* (Zeist and Arnhem, W. de Haan and Van Loghum Slaterus, 1962).
1191. Dvořáček, Jaroslav, *The Museum of Czech Literature* (Prague, Orbis, 1955).
1192. *The Eastern European Academies of Sciences: A Directory*. Prepared by the Office of the Foreign Secretary, National Academy of Sciences (Washington, D. C., National Academy of Sciences, National Research Council, 1963).
1193. Edwards, Paul J., "Trend of Law in Czechoslovakia", *Wisconsin Law Review* (1947), pp. 654-80.
1194. Eisenmann, Louis, *Un grand Européen: Edouard Beneš* (Paris, Hartmann, 1934).
1195. Eisner, Karel, *The "Unknown" Little Democracy* (Toronto, Karel Eisner, 1945).
1196. Elias, Andrew, *The Labor Force of Czechoslovakia: Scope and Concepts* (= *Industrial Populations Reports*, Series P-95, No. 61) (Washington, D. C., U. S. Department of Commerce, Bureau of the Census, 1963).

1197. Emmanuel, Maurice, *Antonin Reicha* (Paris, H. Laurens, 1937).
1198. Erdely, Eugene V., *Prague Braves the Hangman* (London, "The Czechoslovak" Independent Weekly, 1942).
1199. Fischel, Alfred, *Das tschechische Volk* (Breslau, Priebatsch, 1928).
1200. Flores, Angel (ed.), *The Kafka Problem* (New York, New Directions, 1946).
1201. Fournier-Fable, Emile, *La vie et l'oeuvre politique et sociale de M. Thomas Garrigue Masaryk* (Paris, Ficker, 1931).
1202. Freudenberger, Herman, *The Waldstein Woolen Mill: Noble Entrepreneurship in Eighteenth-Century Bohemia* (Boston, Harvard Graduate School of Business Administration, 1963).
1203. Georges-Picot, Georges M. E., *La politique de déflation en Tchécoslovaquie* (Paris, Presses Universitaires, 1925).
1204. *Germany and Czechoslovakia*, 2 vols. (Prague, Orbis, 1937).
1205. Ginsburg, Roderick A., *Jan Kollar, a Poet of Pan-Slavism* (Chicago, Czech Literary Press, 1942).
1206. Giusti, Wolfango, *Un contributo allo studio dell' ideologia panslava – la figura di Svatopluk Čech* (Trieste, Editrice Università, 1950).
1207. ——, *Vrchlický e Carducci* (Trieste, Università degli studi di Trieste, 1957).
1208. Granjard, Henri, *Mácha et la renaissance nationale en Bohême* (Paris, Institut d'études slaves de l'Université de Paris, 1957).
1209. Grivec, Franz, *Konstantin und Method, Lehrer der Slaven* (Wiesbaden, Otto Harrassowitz Verlag, 1960).
1210. Hanak, Harry, *Great Britain and Austria-Hungary during the First World War: A Study in the Formation of Public Opinion* (London, New York-Toronto, Oxford University Press, 1962).
1211. Hanč, Josef, "Czechoslovakia", *A Handbook of Slavic Studies*, ed. L. I. Strakhovsky (Cambridge, Mass., Harvard University Press, 1949), pp. 582-603.
1212. Hartmann, Paul, *Die politische Partei in der Tschechoslowakischen Republik* (Brno, Rohrer, 1931).
1213. Herben, Jan, *Huss and his Followers* (London, G. Bles, 1926).
1214. Heymann, F. G., "John Rokycana: Church Reformer between Hus and Luther", *Church History*, 28 (1959), pp. 240-80.
1215. Horcicka, A., *Das älteste Böhmisch-Kamnitzer Stadtbuch* (Prag, 1915).
1216. Horna, Miloš and Blažej, Zdenko, *La Tchécoslovaquie économique et financière* (Geneva, 1948).
1217. Hromádka, Josef Lukl, *The Church and Theology in Today's*

Troubled Times, a Czechoslovak Contribution to Ecumenical Discussions (Prague, Ecumenical Council of Churches in Czechoslovakia, 1956).

1218. ——, *Theology between Yesterday and Tomorrow* (Philadelphia, Westminster Press, 1957).
1219. Hykeš, Oldřich Vilém, *J. E. Purkyně et la médicine moderne* (Prague, 1937).
1220. Järv, Harry, *Die Kafka-Literatur. Eine Bibliographie* (Malmö und Lund, Bo Cave fors Verlag, 1961).
1221. Jensen, Alfred, *Jaroslav Vrchlický, en literär studie* (Stockholm, 1904).
1222. Kaind, Raimond Friedrich, *Der Voelkerkampf und Sprachenstreit in Böhmen* (Wien, Braumüller, 1928).
1223. Kann, Robert A., *The Multinational Empire. Nationalism and National Reform in the Habsburg Monarchy 1848-1918* (New York, Columbia University Press, 1950).
1224. Karch, John J., "Czechoslovakia", in *The Worldmark Encyclopedia of the Nations* (New York, Worldmark Press, 1960).
1225. Kerner, Robert J., *The Foundations of Slavic Bibliography* (Chicago, The University of Chicago Press, 1916).
1226. Kirschbaum, Joseph M., *Slovakia: Nation at the Crossroads of Central Europe* (New York, R. Speller, 1960).
1227. ——, *Ludevit Štúr and his Place in the Slavic World* (Winnipeg, The Slovak Institute, 1958).
1228. ——, *Pavel Jozef Šafárik and His Contribution to Slavic Studies* (Cleveland and Winnipeg, The Slovak Institute, 1962).
1229. Kozák, Jan, *How Parliament Can Play a Revolutionary Part in the Transition to Socialism and the Role of the Popular Masses* (London, Independent Information Centre, 1961).
1230. Král, Jiří, "The West Slav Geography. I.: Czechoslovak Geography in the Twentieth Century", in *Geography in the Twentieth Century*. Ed. Griffith Taylor (New York, Philosophical Library, 1957), pp. 116-21.
1231. Krčméry, Štefan, "A Survey of Modern Slovak Literature", *Slavonic and East European Review*, 6 (1928), pp. 160-70.
1232. Lederer, Julius, *Tschechoslowakisches Steuerrecht*, 2 vols. (Berlin, Carl Heymann, 1927-1929).
1233. Leveé, Madeleine, *Les Précurseurs de l'indépendance Tchèque et Slovaque à Paris* (Paris, Payet, 1936).
1234. Lewanski, Richard C., *Bibliography of Slavic Dictionaries*, Vol. II

(New York, New York Public Library, 1963).
1235. Lippert, Julius, *Social-geschichte Böhmens in Vorhussitischer Zeit*, 2 vols. (Wien, F. Tempsky, 1896-98).
1236. Liscova, Mila, *Religious Situation in Czechoslovakia* (Prague, Orbis, 1925).
1237. Lützow, Count Francis, *The Hussite Wars* (London, J. M. Dent and Sons, 1914).
1238. ——, *The Story of Prague* (London, J. M. Dent and Co., 1902).
1239. Macek, Josef, *An Essay on the Impact of Marxism* (Pittsburgh, University of Pittsburgh, Press, 1955).
1240. Masaryk, Tomáš Garrigue, *The Slavs Among the Nations* (London, The Czech National Alliance in Great Britain, 1916).
1241. ——, *Les Slaves après la guerre* (Prague, Orbis, 1923).
1242. Masaryk Memorial Institute, Toronto, *A Gem for the Canadian Mosaic, Pictures of the Life and the Work of Canadians of Czechoslovak Origin*. Ed. Rudolf Nekola and Edna Ash (Toronto, 1957).
1243. *Masaryk on Thought and Life. Conversations with Karel Čapek* (New York, Macmillan, 1938).
1244. Matějček, Antonín, *Art and Architecture in Europe* (London, Batchworth Press, 1960).
1245. Mikuš, Joseph A., *Slovakia in the Drama of Europe: A Political History 1918-1950* (Milwaukee, The Marquette University Press, 1963).
1246. Mirkin-Getsevich, Boris and Tibal, André, *La Tchécoslovaquie* (Paris, Delagrave, 1929).
1247. Moravec, Emanuel, *The Strategic Importance of Czechoslovakia for Western Europe* (Prague, Orbis, 1936).
1248. Mousset, Jean, *Les villes de la Russie Subcarpathique (1918-1938): L'effort Tchécoslovaque* (Paris, Droz, 1938).
1249. Muller, Daniel, *Leoš Janáček* (Paris, Rieder, 1930).
1250. Murko, Matthias, *Deutsche Einflüsse auf die Anfänge der Böhmischen Romantik* (Graz, 1897).
1251. Nani, Umberto, *T. G. Masaryk e l'Unità Cecoslovacca* (Milan, Treves, 1931).
1252. Nejedlý, Zdeněk, *Alois Jirásek* (Prague, Orbis, 1952).
1253. Němec, František, *Social Security in Czechoslovakia* (London, Czechoslovak Ministry of Foreign Affairs, 1943).
1254. Nettl, Paul, *Der kleine Prophet von Böhmisch-Brod: Mozart und Grimm* (Esslingen, Bechtle Verlag, 1953).

1255. Nosek, Vladimír, *Independent Bohemia. An Account of the Czecho-Slovak Struggle for Liberty* (London-Toronto, J. M. Dent and Sons, 1918).
1256. Novák, Arne, "Czech Literature In and After the War", *Slavonic and East European Review*, 2 (1923), pp. 114-32.
1257. Novotný, Jan Maria, *Fiscal Science* (Montreal, McGill University Book Store, 1952). See especially Chapter XXIV, "Czech Fiscal Science", pp. 775-829.
1258. Novotný, Jan Maria, Hanuš, O., and Beneš, J. F., *Steuerhandbuch* (Reichenberg, Stiepel, 1937).
1259. Oddo, G. L., *Slovakia and its People* (New York, R. Speller, 1960).
1260. Odložilík, Otakar, "George of Poděbrady and Bohemia to the Pacification of Silesia", *University of Colorado Studies*, I (1941), pp. 265-88.
1261. ——, "Problems of the Reign of George of Poděbrady", *Slavonic and East European Review*, 20 (1941), pp. 206-22.
1262. ——, "Comenius and Christian Unity", *Slavonic and East European Review*, 9 (1930-31), pp. 79-93.
1263. ——, "Karel of Žerotín and the English Court (1564-1636)", *Slavonic and East European Review* (1936-37), pp. 413-25.
1264. Opočenský, Jan (ed.), *Edward Beneš* (London, Allen and Unwin, 1945).
1265. Paličkar, Stephen Joseph, *Slovakian Culture in the Light of History, Ancient and Modern* (Cambridge, Hampshire Press, 1954).
1266. Papánek, Ján, *Czechoslovakia* (New York, International Universities Press, 1945).
1267. ——, *La Tchécoslovaquie* (Prague, Orbis, 1923).
1268. Paučo, Jozef, *Flight to Wonderland* (New York, Robert Speller and Sons, 1963).
1269. Peroutka, Ferdinand, *Democratic Manifesto* (New York, Voyages Press, 1959).
1270. Pistorius, Jiří, *Destin de la culture française dans une démocratie populaire; la présence française en Tchécoslovaquie, 1948-1956. Études et documents* (Paris, Les Iles d'or, 1957).
1271. Prague, Brentano-Gesellschaft, *Naturwissenschaft und Metaphysik. Abhandlungen zum Gedächtnis des 100. Geburtstages von Franz Brentano* (Brünn-Leipzig, 1938).
1272. Prague, Národní galerie, *Treasures of the Prague National Gallery*. By Vladimír Novotný (London, Batchworth Press, 1960).
1273. Prague, Novinářský studijní ústav, *Selective Bibliography of Publi-*

cations on Journalism Published in Czechoslovakia since 1945 (Prague, 1957).
1274. Prague Universita Karlova, Burschenschaft "Arminia", *Alma Mater Pragensis, ein Dank an Prag und seine hohen Schulen* (Erlangen, K. Müller, 1959).
1275. Prague, Universita Karlova, Knihovna, *Librarianship in Czechoslovakia, Almanac of Materials on the State and Activities of the Basic Nets of the Unified System of Czechoslovak Libraries* (Prague, 1958).
1276. Prague, Universita Karlova, *L'Université Charles IV dans le passé et dans le présent*. By V. Novotný and J. Čech (Prague, Pražská akciová tiskárna, 1923).
1277. Prague, Výzkumný ústav pro farmacii a biochemii, *Pharmacotherapeutica 1950-1959* (Prague, Státní zdravotnické nakladatelství, 1961).
1278. Pražák, Albert, "Czechs and Slovaks in the Revolution of 1948", *Slavonic and East European Review*, 5 (1926), pp. 565-79.
1279. ——, "Czechs and Slovaks after the Revolution of 1848", *Slavonic and East European Review*, 6 (1927), pp. 119-29.
1280. ——, "The Slavonic Congress of 1848 and the Slovaks", *Slavonic and East European Review*, 7 (1928), pp. 141-59.
1281. ——, "The Slovak Sources of Kollar's Pan-Slavism", *Slavonic Review*, 6 (1928), pp. 579-92.
1282. Raupach, Hans, *Der tschechische Frühnationalismus* (Essen, Essner Verlag, 1938).
1283. Reade, Brian, *Art nouveau and Alphonse Mucha* (London, H. M. S. O., 1963).
1284. Rössler, Emil Franz, *Deutsche Rechtsdenkmaler aus Böhmen und Mähren*, 2 vols. (Prag, 1845 and 1853).
1285. Rozehnal, Alois, *Unfulfilled Promises. Social Insurance in Czechoslovakia* (Roma, Accademia cristiana cecoslovacca, 1961).
1286. Rychnovsky, Ernst, *Masaryk* (Prag, Staatliche Verlagsanstalt, 1931).
1287. Salzmann, Zdeněk, *Czech Literature before Hus* (Sedona, Arizona, 1961).
1288. Sander, Fritz, *Das Staatsverteidigungsgesetz und die Verfassungsurkunde der Tschechoslowakischen Republik* (Brünn, Rohrer, 1936).
1289. Santen, Aime van, *Over Karel Čapek* (Amsterdam, J. van Campen, 1949).

1290. Schoenbaum, Emil, *A Programme of Social Insurance Reform for Czechoslovakia* (Montreal, 1945).
1291. Schultz, Adolph H., "Biographical Memoir of Aleš Hrdlička, 1869-1943", *Biog. Mem. Nat. Acad. Sci.*, 23 (1945), pp. 305-38.
1292. Schwarz, Henry F., "Bohemia under the Habsburgs", *A Handbook of Slavic Studies*, ed. L. I. Strakhovsky (Cambridge, Harvard University Press, 1949), pp. 243-70.
1293. Siebenschein, Hugo, *Goethe und Masaryk* (Bern, A. Francke, 1948).
1294. *Statistisches Gemeinde Lexikon der Čechoslovakischen Republik* (Prag, Orbis, 1935).
1295. *Stiepels Gesetz-Sammlung ab Tschechoslowakischen Staates*. Kommentierte Ausgaben, 80 vols. (Reichenberg, Gebrüder Stiepel, 1920-1938).
1296. Strauss, Emil, *Die Entstehung der Tschechoslowakischen Republik* (Prag, Orbis, 1934).
1297. Swehla, Francis, J., *Bohemians in Central Kansas* (Topeka, Kansas State Historical Society, 1915?).
1298. *La Tchécoslovaquie* (Paris, Crès, 1921).
1299. *Tchécoslovaquie*. By Kallab, Jaroslav, Kizlink, Karel and others (Paris, Librairie Delagrave, 1932).
1300. *Textausgaben der Tschechoslowakischen Gesetze*, 17 vols. (Reichenberg, Gebrüder Stiepel).
1301. Thomson, S. Harrison, "Medieval Bohemia", *A Handbook of Slavic Studies*, ed. L. I. Strakhovsky (Cambridge, Harvard University Press, 1949), pp. 97-121.
1302. ——, "Learning at the Court of Charles IV", *Speculum*, 25 (1950), pp. 1-20.
1303. *Three Score Years of Church Activity. An Historical Sketch of St. Procopius Parish. Its Contribution to Chicago's Social and Religious Life* (Chicago, 1935).
1304. Tomaschek, Johann Adolf, Edler von Stadova, *Deutsches Recht in Oesterreich im 13. Jahrhunderte auf Grundlage des Stadtrechtes von Iglau* (Wien, 1859).
1305. ——, *Recht und Verfassung der Markgrafschaft Mähren im 15. Jahrhunderte* (Brünn, A. Nitsch, 1863).
1306. Tomek, Václav Vladivoj, *Geschichte Böhmens in übersichtlicher Darstellung* (Prag, F. Řivnáč Verlag, 1875).
1307. Tourtzer, Helene, *Louis Štúr et l'idée de l'indépendance Slovaque, 1815-1856* (Cahors-Alencon, A. Coeurant, 1913).

1308. Tschermak-Seysenegg, A., *J. E. Purkyně als ein Begründer des exakten Subjektivismus* (Prag, 1937).
1309. Turnbull, G. H., *Hartlib, Dury, and Comenius* (Liverpool-London, 1947).
1310. Uhlíř, František, *Prague and Berlin, 1918-1938* (London-New-York, Hutchinson and Co., 1944).
1311. Vachek, Josef, in collaboration with Josef Dubský, *Dictionnaire de linguistique de l'École de Prague* (Utrecht, Spectrum éditeurs, 1960).
1312. Weil, Friedrich, *Tschechoslowakei* (Gotha, Perthes, 1924).
1313. Weil, Fritz, *Das Werden eines Volkes und der Weg eines Mannes* (Dresden, Reissner, 1930).
1314. Winter, Eduard (ed.), *Die Deutschen in der Slowakei und Karpatho-Russland* (Münster, Aschendorff, 1926).
1315. ——, *Tausend Jahre Geisteskampf im Sudetenraum* (Salzburg-Leipzig, Otto Müller, 1938).
1316. Wolný, Jan, *Česko-německý slovnik*. Zpracoval dr. František Widimský, 2 vols. (Prag, Státní pedagogické nakladatelství, 1963).
1317. Zenkl, Petr, *T. G. Masaryk and the Idea of European and World Federation* (Chicago, Czechoslovak National Council of America, 1955).
1318. Zinner, Paul E., *National Communism and Popular Revolt in Eastern Europe* (New York, Columbia University Press, 1956).

Contributors to this Volume

ANDIC, VOJTĚCH ERVIN, was born in 1910 in Dobronivá, Czechoslovakia. He graduated from Teachers College in Banska Štiavnica (1930) and the School of Commerce Prague (1934). He entered the U.S. in 1935, became editor of Czechoslovak newspapers in New York, worked for the Czechoslovak Information Service, New York (1940–48), and the U.S. Dept. of State, International Broadcasting (1948–54), meanwhile pursuing his studies at the Graduate School of Economics, Columbia University (M.A. 1950) and New York University (Ph. D. 1954). He was Associate Professor at Willamette University (1954–57), Assistant Professor of Economics at the University of Pittsburgh (1957–1963), and is now Associate Professor of Economics at the Union University (Albany College) and Visiting Professor at the New School for Social Research in New York City. At the University of Pittsburgh Prof. Andic initiated a Czechoslovak Forum of Arts and Sciences. He published articles in the *Slavonic Encyclopaedia* (New York, 1949), *Slavic and East European Review*, and *Journal of Central European Affairs*. He was President of the Centenary Sokol Festival in Pittsburgh in 1962. He holds memberships in the American Economic Association, Pennsylvania Economic Association, American Association of University Professors, and American Association of Teachers of Slavic Studies.

Present Address: Academy Station, P.O. Box 8552, Albany 8, N.Y., 12208.

BENEŠ, VÁCLAV, born in Brandýs n/L, Czechoslovakia, 1910, and attended Charles University in Prague, where he received the degree of Doctor of Law in 1934, and McGill University, Montreal, Canada where he received a degree of Master of Civil Law (1950). He was an official of the Czechoslovak Ministry of Foreign Affairs in Prague (1936–39) and spent the war years in London, where he was an official of the Ministry of Foreign Affairs and the Ministry of Justice of the Czechoslovak Government in Exile. After the war he became Head of the U.N. Division to the Czechoslovak Ministry of Foreign Affairs (1946–48), and Counsellor of the Czechoslovak Embassy in Paris (Feb., 1948). He then left for Canada and was the Lady Davis Foundation Fellow at Montreal (1949–50). He entered the United States in 1950, where he became Associate Professor of Government at Indiana University, Bloomington, Indiana, a position he still holds. Dr. Beneš was Delegate of Czechoslovakia to the U.N. Conference in San Francisco in 1945, Vice President of the Indiana Academy of Social Science, 1952–53, and has been a member of the Executive Committee of the Russian and East European Institute of Indiana University since 1960.

He co-edited and contributed to the *Czechoslovak Yearbook of International Law* (London 1942), and *The Second Soviet-Yugoslav Dispute* (Bloomington, Indiana, 1959). In addition he is a frequent contributor of articles and reviews to the *Journal of Central European Affairs, American Bar Association Journal, Indiana Law Review* and other scholarly publications in his field. He holds membership in the Political Science

Association, American Society for International Law, and the American Association for the Advancement of Slavic Studies.

Address: Dept. of Government, Indiana University, Bloomington, Indiana.

BROŽEK, JOSEF, was born in Mělník, Czechoslovakia in 1913. He attended Charles University, Prague, where he received the degree of Ph. D. in psychology in 1937. He was a psychologist at the Laboratory of Physiological Hygiene, School of Public Health, University of Minnesota, 1941–43, Associate Scientist, 1944–49, Associate Professor 1949–56 and Professor 1956–59. In 1959 he took his present position as Professor and Chairman, Dept. of Psychology, Lehigh University, Bethlehem, Pa. He was Secretary of the Committee on Nutritional Anthropometry, Food and Nutrition Board, National Research Council 1950–55, and holds membership in the American Psychological Association, American Association of Physical Anthropologists, American Physiological Society and American Association of Public Health. He was editor of *Symposium on Nutrition and Behavior* (1957); *Body Measurements and Human Nutrition* (1956); *Performance Capacity–A Symposium* (1961); *Techniques for Measuring Body Composition* (1961); *Soviet Studies on Nutrition and Higher Nervous Activity* (1962). He is the co-author of *The Biology of Human Starvation* (1950), and a frequent contributor to numerous scientific periodicals. His areas of research are nutrition and behavior, effect of physiological stresses, aging, evaluation of nutritional status, including body composition, fatigue, and history of science with special reference to Slavic Countries and the U.S.S.R.

Address: Lehigh University, Bethlehem, Pa.

BUŠEK, VRATISLAV, was born in 1897 in Prague, Czechoslovakia. He graduated from Charles University, Prague with the degree of Doctor of Law (1920), became an Instructor of Canonic Law at that University (1921–22), Assistant Professor (1922–24), Associate Professor (1924–29). He was a Professor of Canonic Law at Komenský University Law School, Bratislava, Czechoslovakia (1929–38). He was Dean of that University (1931–32) and (1938–39) and Chancellor (1936–37). He taught Canonic Law as Professor at Masaryk University Law School, Brno, Czechoslovakia (1939–40). Dr. Bušek spent the war years as political prisoner in a German concentration camp. After the war he taught Canonic and Roman Law as Professor at Charles University Law School, Prague, Czechoslovakia (1945–48). He fled Czechoslovakia in April, 1948, was research assistant to M. Pierre Caron, Paris, France and did research work at various institutions in Paris until 1950 when he entered the U.S. He taught at Seton Hall College, South Orange, N.J. (1950) and worked for Radio Free Europe (1950–61). He has since been a free lance writer. He was editor of legal periodicals in Czechoslovakia, wrote chapters on Church Law in Czech legal publications and contributed frequently to scholarly journals in his field. He also wrote a *Manual of the History of Canon Law* (Prague, 1946–47), and was co-editor of *Czechoslovakia* (New York, 1956).

Address: 85-10 34th Ave., Jackson Heights 72, N.Y.

ČAPEK, MILIČ, was born in 1909 in Třebechovice, Czechoslovakia. He attended Charles University, Prague, where he obtained the degree of Doctor of Philosophy (1935). He was an assistant librarian in the Dept. of Philosophy of Charles University, Prague (1935–36), taught at various schools in Czechoslovakia (1937–39), left Czechoslovakia in 1939 and studied at the Sorbonne, Paris (1939–40). He entered the U.S. in 1941, attended the University of Chicago (1941), was Instructor in ASTP (Univ. of Iowa, 1943–44), Instructor of Physics, (Univ. of Nebraska, 1944–46), Lecturer in Physics (Palacky University of Olomouc, Czechoslovakia, 1946–47). He rose from Assistant Professor of Philosophy at Carleton College (1948–51) to Associate Professor, 1951–57, Professor, 1957–62, and is now Professor of Philosophy, Boston University.

Dr. Čapek is a member of the American Philosophical Association, American Association for the Advancement of Science, Peirce Society, and the History of Science Society. He has published the following books: *Bergson and the Trends in Contemporary Physics* (Prague, 1938), *Henry Bergson* (Prague, 1939), *Key to Czechoslovakia: the Territory of Kladsko* (New York, 1946), *The Philosophical Impact of Contemporary Physics* (Princeton, N.J., 1961). He has contributed many articles to Czech and American scholarly periodicals.

Address: Dept. of Philosophy, Boston University, Boston, Mass.

CARDEW, ANGELIKA KRULIŠ-RANDA, was born in 1931 in Prague, Czechoslovakia. She left Czechoslovakia in 1950 and came to the U.S., where she attended the University of Michigan and obtained the degrees of B.A. and M.A. She is presently finishing her studies for a Ph.D. degree in Medieval German. Miss Cardew is a member of Phi Beta Kappa, German Honorary Society, Modern Language Association, and American Association of Teachers of German. She has been a teaching fellow at the University of Michigan and instructor at Eastern Michigan University.

Address: 819 Murray Ct., Ann Arbor, Mich.

CEKOTA, ANTONÍN, was born in Napajedla, Moravia, in 1899. He attended the Academy of Industry in Pardubice, Czechoslovakia, and worked for the Czechoslovak Bata Enterprises as publicity director and publisher of several newspapers and magazines published by Bata interests from 1926-39. He entered Canada in 1939, became Research Director of the Bata Organization operating in the Free World and is the author of several books dealing with the work and life of Tomáš Baťa, the founder of the Bata Enterprises. In addition, he has written technical papers on the manufacturing of shoes and industrial relations. He also translated John Masefield's poetry into Czech.

Address: Bata Limited, 100 University Avenue, Toronto 1, Ontario, Canada.

DEMETZ, PETER, was born in 1922 in Prague, Czechoslovakia. He studied German and English at Charles University, Prague (Dr. phil., 1948), German at Columbia University, New York (M.A., 1954) and comparative literature at Yale University. After receiving his Ph.D. (1956) he stayed at Yale University, where he rose to the rank of full Professor of German and Comparative Literature (1962) and a Chairman, Department of Germanic Languages and Literatures (1963). Prof. Demetz is the author of *Goethe's "Die Aufgeregten": Zur Frage der politischen Dichtung in Deutschland* (Hann. Münden, 1952), *René Rilkes Prager Jahre* (Düsseldorf, 1953), *Marx, Engels und die Dichter* (Stuttgart, 1959), and a number of scholarly essays and reviews in various periodicals published here as well as abroad. Together with his wife, Hana Demetz, he translated from Czech into German the novel by Božena Němcová, *Die Grossmutter* (Zürich, 1959) and short stories by Jan Čep, *Zeit und Wiederkehr* (Wien, 1962). He also edited *Twentieth Century Views: Bertolt Brecht* (Englewood Cliffs, 1962) and a volume of Czechoslovak poetry in exile, *Neviditelný domov: Verše exulantů 1948–1953* (Paris, 1953).

Address: Department of Germanic Languages and Literatures, Yale University, New Haven, Conn.

DRESLER, JAROSLAV, was born in 1925 in Brno, Czechoslovakia. He studied philosophy and the history of art at Masaryk University, Brno (1946-49) serving at the same time as one of the editors of cultural affairs of *Lidové Noviny*, Brno. He had to leave Czechoslovakia in 1949, studied modern art for two years in Paris and since 1951 has been one of the editors of Radio Free Europe, Munich. His articles on developments

in the field of arts, sculpture, etc., on both sides of the Iron Curtain appear regularly in European periodicals.
Address: Englischer Garten 1, München 22, Germany.

DUBEN, VOJTĚCH N., is the pen name of an information specialist, born in 1920, in Fryčovice, Czechoslovakia, and educated in Czechoslovakia, where he was both a reporter and a member of the editorial staff of various dailies specializing in labor relations. He escaped in 1948 to West Germany where he edited a Czech weekly for political refugees, and directed a press service for the free Czech press in France, England, and the U.S. He entered the U.S. in 1950 and became editor of a Czech daily in New York. He is now holding a position as a foreign language information specialist in an international broadcasting service where he specializes in Czechoslovak political and economic affairs, labor relations and the history and present status of Czech and Slovak journalism.
Address: 3675 Camden Street, S. E., Washington 20, D.C.

FEIERABEND, LADISLAV K., was born in 1891 in Kostelec n/O, Czechoslovakia. He attended the University of Neuchatel, Switzerland, Jesus Christ College at Oxford, England, and the Charles University of Prague, where he received the degree of Doctor of Law. He specialized in the field of cooperatives in Czechoslovakia, a subject in which he is the leading authority. He was general manager of the Kooperativa, a trade organization of agricultural cooperative societies, Vice Chairman of the Czechoslovak export board and, since 1930, Chairman of the Prague Produce Exchange. In 1934 he organized and became chairman of the State Grain Monopoly. In 1938 Dr. Feierabend became active in politics and served as Minister of Agriculture in the governments of Premier Syrový and Beran (1938) and Gen. Eliáš (1939). He escaped in 1940 to England and was Minister of Finance of Dr. Beneš' government in exile until Feb. 1945, when he resigned in protest against cooperation with the Soviets. He returned to Czechoslovakia in June 1945, but had to leave in Feb. 1948; he remained until 1950 in England, then entered the U.S. where he works with the Voice of America. He wrote a number of books on Czechoslovak cooperatives in Czech, French and English and is the author of two books describing his experience as member of the governments of Czechoslovakia. He is also the author of numerous contributions to periodicals in his chosen field.
Address: 38–21 Newark St., N.W., Washington 16, D.C.

FRINTA, MOJMÍR SVATOPLUK, was born in Prague, Czechoslovakia, in 1932. He studied painting at the Prague School of Graphic Arts and the School of Decorative Arts, and history of art at the Charles University, Prague. He also attended the Académie André Lhote and École des Beaux-Arts and the École du Louvre in Paris. His paintings and lithographs were exhibited in Paris where he specialized as a restorer of old paintings. He entered the U.S. in 1951, graduated from the University of Michigan, Ann Arbor (M.A. 1953, Ph.D. in History of Art, 1960). Since 1955 he has been on the staff of the Metropolitan Museum of Art as Senior Restorer at the Cloisters. In 1963 he became Assistant Professor, Fine Arts Dept., State University of New York at Albany. He is the author of two studies to be published in the *Studies in Conservation* (on the frescoes from Berlanga) and in *Gesta* (on a technique of plastic brocade on medieval statues). He is also a contributor to *The Art Quarterly* and *Speculum*. He is a member of the College Art Association of America, The Mediaeval Academy of America, and the International Institute for Conservation of Artistic and Historic Monuments, London.
Address: 134 Maple Avenue, Altamont, N.Y.

HAJDA, JAN was born in 1927 in Policky, Czechoslovakia. He attended the University of Political and Social Sciences, Prague, Willamette University, Salem, Oregon (B.A., 1952), University of Chicago, Chicago, Ill. (M.A. 1957, Ph. D. 1963). He was first affiliated with the National Opinion Research Center at the University of Chicago, then became Assistant Professor at the Johns Hopkins University and since 1963 is Assistant Professor of Sociology at the University of California at Riverside. He is the editor of a monograph, *A Study of Contemporary Czechoslovakia* (Chicago, 1955). He contributed a chapter on "Alienation and Integration of Student Intellectuals," *American Sociological Review*, Vol. 26 (1961), pp. 758-777. He is a member of the American Sociological Association.

Address: Dept. of Sociology, University of California, Riverside, Cal.

HARKINS, WILLIAM EDWARD, was born in 1921 in State College, Pa. He studied at Pennsylvania, State University (B.A. 1942), Columbia University (M.A. 1946 and Ph.D. 1950). He was an Instructor in Slavic Languages at the University of Pennsylvania (1948–49) and then at Columbia University, where he rose to the position of Full Professor of Slavic Languages, achieved in 1963. He is a member of Phi Beta Kappa and Modern Languages Association and was a Guggenheim Fellow (1958–59). Prof. Harkins is the author of several books: *The Russian Folk Epos in Czech Literature* (New York, 1951), *A Modern Czech Grammar* (New York, 1953), *An Anthology of Czech Literature* (New York, 1953), *Dictionary of Russian Literature* (New York, 1956), *An American Reader* (New York, 1958), *Karel Čapek* (New York, 1962). He is also a frequent contributor to scholarly publications.

Address: 601 Philosophy Hall, Columbia University, New York 27, N.Y.

HEYMANN, FREDERICK G., was born in 1900 in Berlin, Germany. He studied sociology, history, philosophy and economics at the Universities of Berlin, Goettingen, Heidelberg, and earned his doctorate at the Joh. W. Goethe University at Frankfurt a/M. From 1926 to 1932 he was a member of the editorial board of the Frankfurter Zeitung. From 1935 to 1939 he acted as foreign editor and diplomatic correspondent of German newspapers in Prague. In 1939 he went to England where he taught German and German history. In 1944 he was employed by the U.S. Office of War Information for political and historical work, and at the end of the war was sent to Germany as one of the editors of publications of the U.S. military government. Dr. Heymann immigrated to the U.S. in 1946, taught European history at the Ethical Culture School in Fieldston, N.Y., and from 1952 to 1955 taught Eastern European and Recent European History at the New School for Social Research. During 1956/58 he was a member of the Institute for Advanced Studies, Princeton, N.J. and 1958/59 Visiting Professor, University of Iowa. In 1959 he became Associate Professor and since 1961 has been Professor of History and Chairman, Dept. of History, University of Alberta, Calgary, Canada. Prof. Heymann wrote several books, i.e., *Der Young-Plan* (Frankfurt, 1929), *Gold aus Glas* (Prague, 1938), Chapters on "Germany and her Satellites", *Illustrated History of the Second Great War* (London, 1945), *John Žižka and the Hussite Revolution* (Princeton, N.J., 1955), *George of Bohemia, King of Heretics* (Princeton, 1964, in print). In addition, he frequently contributes articles to scholarly periodicals.

Address: Dept. of History, University of Alberta, Calgary, Canada.

HUJER, KAREL, was born in 1902 in Železný Brod, Czechoslovakia, attended Charles University, Prague where he earned the degree of D. Sc. (1932). He continued his studies at the Imperial College of Science, University of London, and at Yerkes Observatory, University of Chicago. Dr. Hujer taught physics at Iowa Wesleyan College (1942–43), was Assistant Professor of Physics and Astronomy, Michigan State College (1943–46), and is Associate Professor of Astronomy and Physics and Head of Jones

Observatory, University of Chattanooga since 1946. Besides modern astronomy, Dr. Hujer has studied the history of astronomy of ancient civilizations and this, together with solar eclipse expeditions, has taken him to many parts of the world, to India (including Tibet), China, Japan, Peru, Mexico, and three journeys across all of Siberia, etc. In India, he stayed as a guest of Mahatma Gandhi at Wardha in 1935, lecturing at his evening meetings. He was also a guest of the poet, Tagore, and delivered a course of lectures at Tagore's University in Shantiniketan. Dr. Hujer has participated in International Science Congresses including the Congress of the International Union of the History of Science, with papers published in Florence, Italy, and by the International Archives of the History and Philosophy of Science in Paris in 1960, etc. He is a Fellow of the American Association of the Advancement of Science and the Royal Astronomical Society of London and a member of many scientific societies, and is a frequent contributor of articles to scientific journals.

Address: University of Chattanooga, Chattanooga 3, Tenn.

JÍRA, JAROSLAV, was born in 1906 in Chvalkovice, Czechoslovakia. He attended Charles University, Prague (Dr. of Laws and Political Science, 1932), George Washington University (Master of Comparative Law, 1953), Catholic University of America (M.S. in Library Science, 1956). In Czechoslovakia he was Military Judge (1936–39) and District Judge (1939–48). In the U.S. he was Legal Analyst, Library of Congress (1951–61), Librarian, National Press Club, Washington, D.C. (1961–62) and in the D.C. Dept. of Health, Glenn Dale Hospital (1962 to date). Dr. Jíra published in Czechoslovakia a book on *Perjury Committed by an Accessory to the Crime* (Prague, 1939) and numerous extensive legal studies on criminal law and procedure in Czechoslovak Law Reviews. In the U.S. he contributed to the U.S. Library of Congress *Serial Highlights* and to *Government Law and Courts in the Soviet Union and Eastern Europe* (New York, 1959) and is co-author of *Legal Sources and Bibliography of Czechoslovakia* (New York, 1959).

Address: 2129 Suitland Terrace, S.E., Washington 20, D.C.

JIRÁK, KAREL BOLESLAV, was born in 1891 in Prague, Czechoslovakia. He studied music and musicology at Charles University, Prague. Mr. Jirák was an opera conductor, 1915–1919, in Prague, Hamburg, Brno and Ostrava, assistant conductor of the Czech Philharmonic Orchestra, Prague, (1920–21), Director of *Hlahol Choral Society*, Prague (1920–21), Professor of Composition at The State Music Conservatory, Prague (1920–30), and Director of Music Programs and Conductor, Czechoslovak Broadcasting Corp. (1930–45). Since 1947 he has been Professor of Composition at the Roosevelt University, Chicago Musical College, Chicago, Ill. From 1924 to 45 he appeared as guest conductor in almost every country in Europe and in Russia. He is the author of a textbook on *Musical Forms* (in Czech, five editions, 1924–45), and a Serbian translation (Belgrad, 1948), Czech biographies of *Zdeněk Fibich*, pianist *Jan Heřman* and *W. A. Mozart* (Prague, 1946–47) and an English biography of *Ant. Dvořák* (New York, 1961).

In addition to an opera, *Apollonius of Thyane*, Mr. Jirák is the author of a great many symphonies, serenades, sonatas, sonatinas and other compositions and songs. He is a Chevalier of the Légion d'Honneur (France), officer of the Order of the Roumanian Star (Roumania), officer of the Yugoslav Order of St. Sava (Yugoslavia). He has won many prizes including the Czechoslovak State Prize for Composition (three times), Smetana Prize, prizes of the Czech Academy of Sciences and Arts, and the International Prize in Edinburgh (1951) for his 5th symphony.

Address: 1050 N. Paulina St., Chicago 26, Ill.

KAMINSKY, HOWARD, was born in 1924 in New York City. He attended Cornell University, New York University, and the University of Chicago (M.A. 1949, Ph.D. 1952). He also studied at Charles University, Prague (1949–50). He rose from Instructor in history at Stanford University to Assistant Professor at the University of Wisconsin (1956–57), Assistant Professor at the University of Washington (1957–62), and is presently Associate Professor at the University of Washington. He is a member of American Historical Association and Medieval Academy of America. His interests lie in the Hussite movement and in the late medieval intellectual history. Among his articles are "Hussite Radicalism and the Origins of Tabor, 1415–1418", *Medievalia et Humanistica;* and "Chiliasm and the Hussite Revolution", *Church Hist.*

Address: Dept. of History, University of Washington, Seattle 5, Washington.

KOHÁK, ERAZIM VÁCLAV, was born in 1933 in Prague, Czechoslovakia. He left Czechoslovakia in 1948, studied philosophy at Colgate University (B.A. 1954), Yale University (M.A. 1957, Ph.D. 1958), and theology at Yale Divinity School. He taught philosophy at Gustavus Adolphus College, 1958–60, and is now Assistant Professor of Philosophy at Boston University. His special interest in philosophy is Plato and Platonism, and in history it is recent Central European history. He is a Danforth Teaching Fellow, Fellow of the Society for Religion in Higher Education, member of Phi Beta Kappa, American Philosophical Association, Metaphysical Society of America, Society for Existential Philosophy & Phenomenological Research, and Society for Ancient Greek Philosophy.

Address: 218 Gardner Street, Hingham, Mass.

KUČERA, HENRY, was born in Třebarov, Czechoslovakia in 1925. He studied at Charles University, Prague (1945–48), and at Harvard University (1949–52), where he was a Graduate Research Fellow and Research Associate of the Russian Research Center. He obtained the degree of Ph.D. from Harvard University in 1952, and then became Assistant Professor of Foreign Languages at the University of Florida (1952–54). He then went to Brown University where he became Assistant Professor (1955–58), Associate Professor (1958–63), and since 1963 is Professor of Slavic Languages and of Linguistics. He was also a Guggenheim Foundation Fellow and Howard Foundation Fellow (1960–61). His research interests have been chiefly in the analysis of the phonological structure of Slavic languages and in the field of mathematical linguistics, regarding, in particular, the relevance of information theory techniques and other quantitative methods in the study of languages. He is also particularly interested in the application of digital computers in linguistic research. Prof. Kučera wrote *The Phonology of Czech* (The Hague, 1961), and is a contributor of articles, essays and reviews to scholarly periodicals in his field.

Address: Box E, Brown University, Providence 12, R.I.

KYBAL, MILIČ, was born in 1914 in Prague, Czechoslovakia. He attended Toulouse University (B.L., 1932), Prague University (Doctor of Laws and Economics, 1937) and did graduate work in economics at the University of California (1940–42). He lectured in Economics at Whittier College, Cal. (1940–43) and Iowa University (1943–44), then served the Federal Government (1944–46) in the Office of War Information, New York, and the U.S. Military Government in Germany. Dr. Kybal was an economist with the Federal Reserve Bank (1947–48) and the United Nations (1948–60). In the latter capacity he was stationed with the Economic Commission for Latin America (ECLA) in Santiago, Chile (1948–50) and in New York (1950–56). From 1956 to 1960 he was Head of the ECLA office in Washington, D.C. Since 1960 Mr. Kybal has been employed with the Inter-American Development Bank in Washington, D.C., and since

1962 has been on loan to the Economic Development Institute of the World Bank. He has contributed to a number of United Nations reports, including several *Economic Surveys of Latin America*. He is co-author of *Foreign Capital in Latin America*, published by the United Nations in 1955. He is a member of the American Economic Association, and Chairman of the Washington (D.C.) Chapter of the Czechoslovak Society of Arts and Sciences in America.

Address: 1 Buttonwood Lane, Tulip Hill, Washington 16, D.C.

LEXA, JOHN GEORGE, was born in Ústí n/L, Czechoslovakia, in 1914. He attended the Charles University School of Law in Prague where he obtained the degree of Dr. jur. in 1937. He entered the U.S. in 1946 and attended New York University School of Law where he received the degree of LL.B. in 1949. He has been a member of the New York Bar since 1952. He has been Lecturer on Comparative Constitutional Law at N.Y.U. School of Law Graduate Division since 1953 and Head of the Legal Dept. of Waldes Kohinoor, Inc., Long Island City, New York. Mr. Lexa is co-editor of *International Seminar on Constitutional Review* (New York, 1963), Secretary, Conference of Americans of Central and Eastern European Descent, New York City, Chairman, New York Chapter, Czechoslovak Society of Arts and Sciences in America.

Address: 47–16 Austel Place, Long Island City, 1, N.Y.

MACHOTKA, OTAKAR, was born in Prague, Czechoslovakia, in 1899. He studied at Charles University, Prague, where he received the degree of Ph.D. in sociology in 1926. He then taught sociology at that university, rising from Instructor to full Professor in 1939. During the war he worked in the National Statistical Office and after the war resumed this teaching position until 1948, when he left Czechoslovakia. Having entered the U.S., he lectured at the University of Chicago (1948), Syracuse University (1949) and lectured as Visiting Professor of Sociology at Cornell University. Since 1951 he has been Professor of Sociology and Head of the Dept. of Sociology and Anthropology at Harpur College (State University of New York). Prof. Machotka published eight books on sociological subjects in Czechoslovakia and in addition wrote numerous articles in newspapers, magazines and in scientific journals. He also contributed fifty sociological items to the Czech *Masaryk Encyclopedia* and for the Czech *Otto Encyclopedia*, and is the author of *The Unconscious in Social Relations* (New York, 1964). He was decorated in 1946 by Pres. Beneš with the Military Cross (1939) and the Medal for Bravery.

Address: Harpur College, Binghamton, N.Y.

MATĚJKA, LADISLAV, was born in 1919 in Suché Vrbné, Czechoslovakia. He attended Charles University, Prague (Ph.D., 1948) and Harvard University (Ph.D., 1961). In Czechoslovakia he was editor of the cultural section of Lidové Noviny (1945–48). After leaving Czechoslovakia he worked in Sweden as Lecturer in the Slavic Dept. of Lund University (1949–54); having entered the U.S., he became cultural reviewer, Radio Free Europe, N.Y. (1954–55), Research Assistant in the Russian project of Prof. Roman Jakobson, Harvard University (1956–57), Research Assistant at Harvard University Computation Laboratory (Russian-English Automatic Dictionary) and since 1959 had been in the Dept. of Slavic Languages and Literature, University of Michigan, where he is now Associate Professor. He is the author of reviews and editorials published in Czechoslovak and Swedish periodicals, and contributed to the *American Slavic and East European Review* ("Rilke and the Czech Language"), *Design and Operation of Digital Calculating Machinery* ("Grammatical Specifications in the Russian-English Dictionary"), *Mathematical Linguistics and Automatic Translation*

NSF-2 ("The Automatic Interpretation of Russian Verbal Endings") and to other scholarly publications in his field.

Address: Dept. of Slavic Languages and Literatures, University of Michigan, Ann Arbor, Michigan.

MICHAL, JAN M., was born in 1920 in Czechoslovakia. He attended Charles University, Prague, where he obtained the degree of Doctor of Law (1946). He also studied economics at the Universities of Grenoble, France, Louvain, Belgium and at the London School of Economics. He was an economist, employed by the Economic Council of the Czechoslovak Government (1946–48) and later a Reader in Economics for the Workers Educational Association. In 1960 he became Associate Professor of Economics at Western Maryland College and since 1964 is Associate Professor of Economics at Harpur College. He is a member of the American Economic Association, Royal Economic Society (London) and Pi Gamma Mu. He has published two major studies in economics: *Postwar Economic Systems* (Prague, 1946) and *Central Planning in Czechoslovakia-Organization for Growth in a Mature Economy* (Stanford, Calif., 1960).

Address: State University of New York – Harpur College, Binghampton, N.Y.

NEHNĚVAJSA, JIŘÍ, was born in Dyjakovice, Czechoslovakia in 1925. He escaped from Czechoslovakia in 1944 and served in the Czechoslovak Army in England, in the Royal Air Force. In March, 1949, following the Communist coup he fled again and entered the U.S. in 1951. He studied at Masaryk University (1945–48), Université de Lausanne (1948–49), and the University of Zürich (Ph.D. 1950). He was Instructor (1951–52) and Assistant Professor of Sociology at the University of Colorado (1952–56), Columbia University (1956–61) and has been Professor of Sociology since 1961 and Chairman of the Dept. at the University of Pittsburgh (1962–). He was associated as consultant with research organizations including the Social Affairs Dept. of the Pan American Union, The American Institution of Research, The System Development Corp., Dunlap Associates and others. In addition to articles in scientific journals he has contributed to *Automation Society* (1961), *Contemporary Sociology* (1961), *Sociometry: Science of Man* (1957), *Soziologen-Lexikon* (1960), *Handbuch der empirischen Sozialforschung* (1961), *Reader in Sociometry* (1961). He co-authored with J. B. Pearson, *Message Diffusion* (1956). At the present time he is directing a number of research projects with special emphasis on futures of the Cold War. He is a member of the American Rocket Society, member of Space Law and Sociology Committee, American Association for Public Opinion Research, Pi Gamma Mu, and Fellow of the American Sociological Assn.

Address: Dept. of Sociology, University of Pittsburgh, Pittsburgh 13, Pa.

NĚMEC, JAROSLAV, was born in 1910 Ořechov, Czechoslovakia. He attended the Masaryk University School of Law at Brno, where he received the degree of Doctor of Law (1937). He served in the Czechoslovak Army Abroad as General Field Prosecutor. He entered the U.S. in 1952 and attended Catholic University, Washington, D.C., where he obtained the degree of M.S. in Library Science (1956). He was a Legal Research Librarian with the A.M.A., Washington, D.C. (1956–59) and has since 1959 been Reference Librarian (Medical Jurisprudence), National Library of Medicine, Bethesda, Md. He is the author of the chapter "Czechoslovakia", in: Szirmai, Z., ed., *The Law of Inheritance in Eastern Europe and in the People's Republic of China* (Leyden, 1961). His article, "Documentation of Czechoslovak Law" (*American Documentation*, 1957), is an account of efforts to bring order into the complicated Czechoslovak legal system. While in Czechoslovakia he contributed about fifteen articles on history and history of law to various Czech historical journals (1945–48). Dr. Němec is Past Secretary General of the Czechoslovak Society of Arts & Sciences in America.

Address: 2067 Park Rd., N.W., Washington, D.C.

NĚMEC, LUDVÍK, was born in Staré Město-Velehrad, Czechoslovakia in 1913. He attended the Theological Faculty of Charles University, Prague (S.T.B., 1939), was ordained a Catholic priest in Prague (1940), studied at International Papal University of Angelicum, Rome (S.T.L. 1949), Catholic University of America, Washington, D.C. (S.T.D., 1953), was chaplain of New Castle Hospital and is now Professor of Church History at Rosemont College. He published and is about to publish a total of ten books, including *Church and State in Czechoslovakia* (New York, 1955), *The Great and Little One of Prague* (Philadelphia, 1959), and *The Infant of Prague* (New York, 1958). He also contributed thirty major studies in Byzantine and Slavic history to various learned journals. Mr. Němec is an elected member of the Medieval Academy of America, the Historical Association, the Catholic Historical Association, the Catholic Theological Society of America, the American Association for the Advancement of Slavic Studies, etc.

Address: 3813 Spring Garden St., Philadelphia 4, Pa.

PISTORIUS, GEORGE, was born in Prague in 1922. He studied at Charles University, Prague, University of Paris, University of Strasbourg and finally at the University of Pennsylvania (Ph.D. in Romance Languages, 1963). He taught German at the National Conservatory of Music and Dramatic Art in Prague, 1943–45, and for the following three years was Assistant in the Dept. of Comparative Literature at Charles University. From 1948 to 1950, he carried on research at the Institute of Comparative Literature at the Sorbonne, and then was associated with the French Broadcasting Corporation on cultural and educational programs. He entered the U.S. in 1958, was Assistant Professor of French at Lafayette College and since 1963 is Associate Professor of Romanic Languages at Williams College. Since 1959 he has also been associated with Colby College Summer School of Languages. Dr. Pistorius, in addition to articles published in Prague and Paris, is the author of two books of literary cirticism: *Bibliography of the Works of F. X. Šalda* (Prague, 1948) and *Destin de la culture française dans une démocratie populaire* (Paris, 1957). He is a member of the Modern Language Association of America, International Comparative Literature Assoc., American Association of Teachers of French.

Address: Dept. of Romanic Languages, Williams College, Williamstown, Mass.

POLACH, JAROSLAV G., was born in 1914 in Ostrava, Czechoslovakia. He studied at Masaryk University, Brno (Doctor of Law, 1938), George Washington University (M.C.L., 1959), American University, (M.A. 1958 and Ph.D. in Economics 1962). In Czechoslovakia he worked for the Czechoslovak Steel Industry. After entering the U.S. he was an economist with the U.S. Government (1948–60). Since 1961 he has been with the Resources for the Future, Inc. Washington, D.C. as an economist. He specializes in economic and legal questions of international economic and atomic integration; European communities; atomic and other energy questions, particularly in Western Europe. Among his articles are: "Beginnings of Trade Unionism among the Slavs of the Austrian Empire", *Am. Slavic & East European Rev.*; "German Atomic Energy Legislation" and "Harmonization of Laws in Western Europe", *Am. J. Comp. Law*. In addition to articles he is the author of *Euratom. Background, Issues and Economic Implications* (New York, 1964).

Address: 186 Chesapeake St. S.W., Washington, D.C.

PROCHÁZKA, ADOLF, was born in Napajedla, Czechoslovakia in 1900, and attended Masaryk University, Faculty of Law, Brno, where he graduated with the degree of Doctor of Law in 1924. Member of the Bar of Czechoslovakia 1929–1938. Appointed Private Docent of Civil Law of Masaryk University, 1929–34, Associate Professor of

Civil Procedure, 1934–45, and Professor, 1945. He was active in the Czechoslovak Underground Movement (P.U.) 1939–40. He then spent the war years in Paris and London, where he served as Legal Advisor to the Prime Minister of the Czechoslovak Government in Exile, and Chairman of the Legal Council. He returned to Czechoslovakia with President Beneš and was a member at the Czech National Assembly, Prague, and Minister of Public Health, 1945–48. He left Czechoslovakia in Feb. 1948 and after staying in Germany, France and England, entered the U.S. He is Chairman of the Executive Committee of the Christian Democratic Union of Central Europe, and is an active member of the Council of Free Czechoslovakia and the General Committee of Assembly of Captive European Nations. Dr. Procházka was appointed a member of the Prague Academy of Science and Arts (1948). He developed his theory of law and published the following books: *Fundamentals of Intertemporal law* (1928), *Cause of Action* (1932), *The Making of Law and its Finding* (1937) *The Legal Case of Dr. Charles Pergler* (1931). He also contributed a number of essays and articles on legal and political subjects to Czech, French, and English periodicals.

Address: 251 East 51 Street, New York 22, N.Y.

PROCHÁZKA, THEODORE, was born in 1904 in Prague, Czechoslovakia. He attended Charles University in Prague where he obtained a Ph.D. degree in 1937, and the University of Paris, where he received a doctorate (1954). While in Czechoslovakia he was a member of the editorial staff of the Czech Press Agency (ČTK), and also a correspondent for American and English newspapers. After leaving Czechoslovakia he worked in Paris as a research fellow of the Centre National de la Recherche Scientifique. He has been active since 1955 as a radio script writer of the Voice of America, Washington, D.C. Among his publications are a chapter on "English Constitutional History in the 19th Century" (in Czech, in *Slovník politický, hospodářský a sociální*, Prague 1929), and *On the Eve of the War. A selection of documents* (Prague, 1945) and translated *Ciano's Diaries* (Prague, 1947).

Address: 3530–39th St. N.W., Washington 16, D.C.

RECHCIGL, MILOSLAV, JR., the editor of this volume and one of the organizers of the First Congress of the Czechoslovak Society of Arts and Sciences in America, was born in 1930 in Mladá Boleslav, Czechoslovakia. After entering the U.S. in 1950, he studied biochemistry, nutrition and physiology at Cornell University, Ithaca, N.Y. (B.S., 1954; M.N.S., 1955; Ph.D., 1958). While at Cornell, he was a Teaching Assistant at the Division of Modern Languages and Graduate Research Assistant at the Graduate School of Nutrition. After obtaining his Ph.D., he was a Research Associate at the Department of Biochemistry at that University and then accepted a U.S. Public Health Service Research Fellowship under the late Dr. Jessie P. Greenstein at the National Cancer Institute, N.I.H., Bethesda, Md. (1958–1960). In 1960 he was appointed to the staff of the Laboratory of Biochemistry at that Institute. He is a member of a number of national professional and honorary organizations, including the A.A.A.S., American Chemical Society, American Association for Cancer Research, Society for Experimental Biology and Medicine, New York Academy of Sciences, American Institute of Nutrition, American Institute of Biological Sciences, the History of Science Society, the American Association for the Advancement of Slavic Studies, the Honorary Society of Phi Kappa Phi, Sigma Xi, etc., and is a Fellow of the American Association for the Advancement of Science. His interests lie in the biochemistry of cancer, tumor-host relationships, protein and amino acid metabolism and nutrition, biochemistry of starvation and cachexia, protein-vitamin relationship and in the *in vivo* turnover of enzymes (particularly of catalase). In addition he is actively interested in the history of science, with special emphasis on Czechoslovakia. He wrote a chapter, "The Rates and the Kinetics of Enzyme Formation and Destruction in the Living Animal", for

Newer Methods of Nutritional Biochemistry (New York, 1963), and contributed numerous articles to scientific journals. He is also an abstractor of *Chemical Abstracts*.
Address: 1703 Mark Lane, Rockville, Md., 20852.

REDISCH, WALTER, was born in Prague, Czechoslovakia in 1898. He attended the German University Medical School in Prague, where he obtained an M.D. degree in 1922. He was at the German University in Prague as Demonstrator, Dept. of Physiology (1921–28) and University Assistant, Dept. of Clinical Propedeutics (1928–38), at the same time holding fellowships in various Austrian and German university hospitals. Dr. Redisch entered the U.S. in 1938, and was a research fellow of the N.Y.U. College of Medicine (1938–40). During the war he was a Major, U.S.A. Medical Corps, first in New Guinea, and then Chief of Medical Service, Regional Hospital, Camp Shelby, Miss. (1943–46). He is now Associate Professor of Medicine at New York University School of Medicine, and Research Associate, New York University Research Service, Goldwater Memorial Hospital, where he is also a visiting physician. He is an Associate Visiting Physician, Bellevue and University Hospitals and a consultant in peripheral vascular diseases, St. Michael's Hospital, Newark, N.J. Dr. Redisch has published close to a hundred articles in medical scientific publications, and is a co-author of *Peripheral Circulation in Health and Disease* (New York, 1957). He is a member of Am. Bd. Int. Med.; Am. Fed. Clin. Res.; Am. Gerontol. Soc.; Am. Heart Assoc.; Am. Med. Assoc.; Am. Physiol. Soc.; Assoc. Am. Med. Colleges; Assoc. Military Surgeons of U.S.; Fellow Am. Col. Phys.; Harvey Soc.; N.Y. Acad. Med.; N.Y. Acad. Sci.; N.Y. Heart Assoc.
Address: NYU Research Service, Goldwater Memorial Hospital, Welfare Island, New York 17, N.Y.

ROUČEK, JOSEPH S., was born, 1902, in Slaný, Czechoslovakia, entered the United States 1921, and attended Occidental College, Los Angeles (B.A., 1925), and New York University (Ph.D., Political Science, 1927, M.A., Sociology and Education, 1937). He taught at Centenary Junior College, Hackettstown, N. J. (1929–1933), Pennsylvania State University (1933–1935), New York University (1935–1939), Hofstra College (1939–1948) and University of Bridgeport (1948–) where he is Professor and Chairman of the Departments of Sociology and Political Science. Dr. Rouček was Visiting Professor in numerous American, Canadian and European Colleges and Universities. Dr. Rouček is the author, co-author, editor and co-editor of about 90 books and has written articles and book reviews for leading American and foreign periodicals in the field of political sciences, sociology and education. He was awarded the Order of Knighthood of Romania and Yugoslavia (pre-Communist), and served as President, Delta Tau Kappa, International Social Science Honor Society. He is American editor of *Il Politico*, University of Pavia, Italy; *Indian Journal of Social Research*, J. V. College, Baraut, India; *V. O. C. Journal of Education*, Teachers College, Tuticoria, India.
Address: Dept. of Sociology, University of Bridgeport, Bridgeport, Conn.

SCHNEIDER, JOSEPH Z., was born in 1897 in Prague, Czechoslovakia. He attended the Institute of Technology, Prague (M.S., 1920). He worked as a chemist in Manila, P. I., meanwhile studying bacteriology at the Bureau of Science, Manila (1920–22). He studied at the Institute of Technology, Prague (Dr. Sc. 1923) and lectured on the technology of commodities at the Institute of Technology, Prague, where he rose to full Professor and Dean (1923–38). In 1927–28 he lectured as Visiting Professor at Chicago University. He entered the U.S. in 1938 and taught chemistry at the Madison College, Harrisburg, Va. (1939–42), joined the Board of Economic Warfare as Analyst, later becoming Deputy Division Chief (1942–45). He was an economic advisor with the U.S. Forces in Austria (1945–49), senior staff member at the Brookings Institution,

Washington, D.C. (1950), expert consultant and general economist, Dept. of the Army (1950–53), technical advisor, Pakistani Planning Board at Karachi (1954–55), industrial engineer and economist (1956), and industrial economist, U.S. Operation Mission in Ecuador (1957–62) when he retired. He was awarded the Order of Merit, First Class of Czechoslovakia (1948), Order of the Gorgeous Jade, Nationalist China (1939) and the U.S. Medal of Freedom, 1952. He is a member of the Virginia Academy of Science, American Association for the Advancement of Science, National Society of Professional Engineers, American Association of Czechoslovak Engineers, American Chemical Society, Delta Sigma Pi.

Address: 127 Hesketh St., Chevy Chase, Md.

ŠEBOR, MILOŠ MARIE, was born in 1911 in Zbiroh, Czechoslovakia. He attended Charles University, Prague (Doctor of Law and Political Science, 1936). He served in the Ministry of the Interior, Prague where he was in charge of the research division of the Criminal Investigation Department. He was Permanent Delegate from Czechoslovakia to the International Criminal Police Commission, Paris, 1946–48. He left Czechoslovakia in 1948, and studied geography and planning in France and at McGill University, Montreal (M.A., 1955). He was Instructor in Geography at the University of Ottawa (1946), Project Planner, Baton Rouge, La. (1958), and since then has been Associate Professor of Geography, Tennessee Polytechnic Institute at Cookeville and Senior Project Planner in the Tennessee State Planning Commission. Dr. Šebor holds membership in the Association of American Geographers, American Institute of Planners, Tennessee Academy of Science. He specializes in historical geography, cartography, and regional planning. Among his articles are "Centralizing or Decentralizing in Industrial Relations", "Problem of Nature of Cartography", *Rev. Can. Geogr.;* and "Historiographic Aspects of Piracy", *Ann. Asn. Am. Geog.*

Address: Dept. of Geography, Tennessee Polytechnic Institute, Cookeville, Tenn.

ŠEJNOHA, JAROSLAV, was born in 1889 in Sebranice, Czechoslovakia, and studied history of art at the Institutes of Fine Arts in Prague and Paris. During the First World War he served as Captain in the Czechoslovak Legion. He then entered the Czechoslovak Diplomatic Service, where he rose to the rank of Ambassador Extraordinary and Plenipotentiary in India. Mr. Šejnoha is an expert in paintings, and an artist himself.

Address: 559 St. Clements Ave, Toronto, Ont., Canada.

SKŘIVÁNEK, JOHN MARION, was born in Caldwell, Texas in 1913. He is a fourth generation Czech-American whose great-grandfather settled in Texas in 1885. He attended the University of Texas (B.A., 1938, M.A., 1946), and Charles University, Prague (Ph.D., 1948). He was an instructor in Slavic languages at the University of Texas (1941–46), Head, Dept. of Slavonic Languages, University of Houston (1948–51), Head, Dept. of Modern Languages, South Texas College (1951–52), and since 1952 has been Professor of Modern Languages (Russian, Czech, Spanish) at Texas A.& M. College, College Station, Texas. Dr. Skřivánek is the author of *Education of Czechs in Texas*, co-author of *Russian Conservation and Reading* (College Station, Texas, 1962), founder of the Czech Educational Foundation of Texas, a member of Phi Delta Kappa and Phi Eta Sigma, and a Fellow of Institute of International Education.

Address: Dept. of Modern Languages, Texas A & M University, College Station, Texas.

ŠKVOR, JIŘÍ, was born in 1916 in Martinice, Czechoslovakia. He attended Charles University of Prague where he earned the degree of Doctor of Law (1945), and the Université de Montréal ,(M.A.1956, Ph.D., 1960). He was Secretary of the Masaryk Educational Institute, Prague (1939–42), Deputy Member of the Czechoslovak Parliament (1946-1948) and is now Assistant Professor at the Université de Montréal, Faculté des Lettres. He is also attached to the International Service of the Canadian Broadcasting Corporation. He is known, under the pen name of Pavel Javor, as a Czech poet who has been awarded many prizes, including the annual award of the Foundation of the Czechoslovak Academy of Arts and Sciences, Prague; first prize of the Czech Cultural Council Abroad, of the Czechoslovak Christian Academy in Rome, etc. He has published twelve books of poems, some of which were translated into English, French, German and Ukrainian. He is a member of the International PEN Club in London, honorary member of the University of Bridgeport, International Social Science Honor Society "Delta Tau Kappa" and serves as the Secretary of the L'Institut de Recherches sur l'Europe Centrale et Orientale at the Université de Montréal.

Address: Université de Montréal, Slavic Dept., Box 6128, Montréal, P.Q., Canada.

SLÁVIK, JURAJ, was born in Dobrá Niva, Slovakia, in 1890, and attended the University of Budapest, University of Berlin, École de Droit and École Libre Des Sciences Politiques, Paris. He received the degree of Doctor of Law from Budapest University. After practicing law he went into politics and became Secretary of the Slovak National Council at Bratislava, and, later, a member of the Czechoslovak National Assembly in Prague. He was Head of the County of Zvolen (1922-1924), Head of the County of Košice (1925), Minister of Agriculture and of the Unification of Laws (1929-1932), Minister Plenipotentiary and Envoy Extraordinary to Poland (1935-1939), Minister of the Interior and of Education of the Czechoslovak Government in London (1940-1945), Czechoslovak Ambassador to the United States (1945), Member of the Czechoslovak U. N. Delegation (1946-1947). He is now Chairman of the Central Committee on the Council of Free Czechoslovakia.

Address: 2733 36th St., N.W., Washington, D.C.

SPINKA, MATTHEW, born 1890 in Štítary, Czechoslovakia, entered the U.S. in 1905, and was educated at Coe College, Cedar Rapids, Iowa (B.A. 1918), The Chicago Theological Seminary (B.D., 1916), The University of Chicago (M.A. 1919, Ph.D. Magna cum laude, 1923). He was Professor of Church History, Central Theological Seminary (1919-1926), Librarian and Associate Professor of the History of Eastern Christianity in The Chicago Theological Seminary (1926-1938), and Associate Professor of Church History of Chicago Seminary and Divinity School of the University of Chicago (1936-1943). He is Waldo Professor of Church History, Emeritus, The Hartford Seminary Foundation, Hartford, Conn. and Professor of Historical Theology in the University College at Claremont, Calif.

He holds the following honorary degrees: Th. D., John Hus Ev. Theological Faculty, Prague (1946); D.D., Coe College (1948); Th. D., University of St. Andrews, Scotland (1954) and D.D., Chicago Theological Seminary (1962).

He is the author of the following books: *The Church and the Russian Revolution* (New York, 1927); *A History of Christianity in the Balkans* (Chicago, 1933); *Christianity Confronts Communism* (New York, 1936); *Chronicle of John Malalas* (Chicago, 1940); *John Hus and the Czech Reform* (Chicago, 1941); *A History of Illinois Congregational and Christian Churches* (1944); *John Amos Comenius* (Chicago, 1943); *Nicholas Berdyaev, Captive of Freedom* (Philadelphia, 1950); *Advocates of Reform* (editor and contributor) (= *Library of Christian Classics*, XIV) (Philadelphia, 1953); *Church in Communist Society* (Hartford, Conn., 1954); *The Church in Soviet Russia* (New York, 1956); *The Quest for Church Unity* (New York, 1960); *Christian Thought from Erasmus to Berdyaev* (Englewood Cliffs, N.J., 1962); *John Hus before the Council of Constance* (New York, 1964).

Prof. Spinka, an Ordained Minister of the Reformed Church in the U.S. 1915-26 and of the Congregational Christian Churches, 1926 to date, was President of the

American Society of Church History and editor of its *Church History, 1932–48.* He translated Comenius' *Labyrinth of the World* (Chicago, 1942) and Comenius' *Bequest of the Unity of Brethren* (Chicago, 1940). He was Assistant Secretary, American Society of Church History, 1932–37, Secretary, 1938–41, Vice President, 1945, and President, 1946. He is a member of Phi Beta Kappa. He also is a frequent contributor of essays and articles to scholarly publications in his chosen field.
Address: 588 W. 8th St., Claremont, Calif.

STEWART, THOMAS DALE, was born in Delta, Pa., in 1901. He attended George Washington University, where he obtained the degree of A.B. in 1927, and Johns Hopkins Medical School (M.D., 1931). After graduation, he was made Assistant Curator under Aleš Hrdlička in the Division of Physical Anthropology, U.S. National Museum, Smithsonian Institution. He arose through the Associate Curatorship to Curatorship in the same Division and was then made Head Curator of the Department of Anthropology. Since November, 1962, he has been Director of the U.S. National Museum (Natural History). He has traveled extensively, particularly in the Americas, Europe, Near East, and Japan. Dr. Stewart visited Czechoslovakia in 1959 in connection with the 90th anniversary of the birth of Aleš Hrdlička. He served as editor of the *American Journal of Physical Anthropology* (founded by Aleš Hrdlička) from 1942 to 1948. Dr. Stewart is the author of about 150 technical papers and monographs on anthropometry, skeletal identification, paleopathology, and ancient man. His most recent research interest is in Neanderthals from Shanidar Cave in northern Iraq. He holds an honorary degree of D. Sc. from the University of Cuzco, Peru, and was elected a member of the National Academy of Sciences. He is also a member of the American Association for the Advancement of Science, American Anthropological Association, American Association of Physical Anthropologists, American Institute of Human Paleontology, Anthropology Society, Wash., D.C., Washington Academy of Science, and Sigma Xi.
Address: U.S. National Museum, Washington 25, D.C.

STURM, RUDOLF, was born in Doubravice, Czechoslovakia in 1912. He graduated from Charles University, Prague, Faculty of Law and Political Science, in 1937, and attended Harvard University, where he obtained a degree of Ph.D. in Slavic languages and literatures in 1956. During the War he served with the Criminal Investigation Committee of the U.S. Army. Having returned to Czechoslovakia, he was appointed Head of the American Division, Ministry of Information, Prague, directing cultural relations between the U.S. and Czechoslovakia, 1946–48. He re-entered the U.S. in 1948, taught at Boston College, Hershey Junior College, City College of N.Y., Union College (N.Y.), served as research associate at Yale University and the Mid-European Studies Center. He is now Associate Professor of Modern Languages and Literatures at Skidmore College, Saratoga Springs, N.Y. He wrote a number of articles and studies on literary, linguistic, and related studies which were published in the *Slavonic Encyclopedia, Harvard Slavic Studies, Books Abroad, The Central European Federalist,* and other periodicals in America and Europe. Prof. Sturm holds membership in the American Association of University Professors, Modern Language Association, American Association of Teachers of Slavic and East European Languages, Czechoslovak Society of Arts and Sciences in America (Sec'y General, 1959–60 and 1962– to date).
Address: 107 Regent Street, Saratoga Springs, N.Y.

SVEJDA, MARIE NORMA, was born in 1924 in Baltimore, Md. She studied at The Art Institute, Chicago (1948), Institute Pius XII, Florence, Italy (1950) on a Fulbright Scholarship to study fresco mural painting, and at Maryland Institute of Art, where she received a M.F.A. (1961). Her works have been exhibited at Chicago, Baltimore, Florence, Italy and St. Augustine, Fla. She painted murals for the Kenwood High School, Kernan Hospital, and All Nations Festival, all in Baltimore, Md. Her portrait bust of Augustine Herman is in the State Office Building, Baltimore, Md. She is one of the organizers of the Augustine Herman Czech American Historical Society and the Charles Carroll American Heritage Society, of which she is also President.

Address: 700 N. Collington Ave., Baltimore, Md.

TÁBORSKÝ, EDWARD J., was born in Prague, Czechoslovakia, in 1910 and educated at Charles University, Prague, where he received a doctor's degree in law and political science in 1934. He served in the Czechoslovak Army (1934–1936). In 1936 he became an official of the provincial administration in Bohemia and in 1937 joined the Czechoslovak Ministry for Foreign Affairs, where he became Personal Secretary to the Foreign Minister.

After the Nazi conquest of Czechoslovakia in 1939 he escaped to England, where he served from 1939 to 1945 as Personal Aide to Czechoslovakia's President-in-Exile, Eduard Beneš.

In 1945 he was sent to Sweden as Czechoslovakia's Envoy Extraordinary and Minister Plenipotentiary. He resigned from this position after the Communist seizure of Czechoslovakia in 1948, and was appointed Lecturer in Political Science at the University of Stockholm. In 1949 he came to the United States, where he taught at the Universities of Ohio State, Tennessee, Southern Illinois and Texas, and presently serves as Professor of Government at the University of Texas.

He has written eight books, three of them in English, and numerous articles in the American and British scholarly journals.

Address: Dept. of Government, University of Texas, Austin, Tex.

TUMLÍŘ, JAN, was born in 1926 in Prague, Czechoslovakia. He studied at Charles University, Prague, and was active as poet, translator, and journalist. In 1949 he went to West Germany where he worked first for the World Council of Churches as a resettlement officer and later for Radio Free Europe as an editor and writer. During that time he published numerous poems and short stories in various exile publications. Having entered the U.S., he studied at Yale University where he attained the degrees of B.A., M.A., and Ph.D. in economics. He is now Assistant Professor of Economics at Yale.

Address: Dept. of Economics, Yale University, New Haven, Conn.

VOGL, EDITH GARRETT, was born in 1914 in Nyrsko, Czechoslovakia, and studied musicology and classical archeology at Charles University, Prague, where she obtained a Ph.D. degree. She also studied piano at the Academy of Music, Prague, and subsequently wrote a column on music for Prague newspapers. She entered the U.S. in 1938 and taught musicology and piano at Keuka College (1939–1942), German and Italian at the Northeast Conservatory of Music, Boston, Mass. (1942–1945), musicology at Boston University (1950–1962) and Wheaton College (1962–1963). Presently Dr. Vogl is Lecturer on Musicology, Harvard University, Cambridge, Mass. She is preparing a book on 18th century Czech music. She is a member of the American Musicological Society and the Gesellschaft für Musikforschung.

Address: 96 Ivy Street, Brookline 46, Mass.

VRÁZ, VLASTA, born in Chicago in 1902, began to write in Czech at an early age to the *Svornost*, a Czech daily founded and published by her grandfather August Geringer. During Masaryk's Republic, Miss Vráz spent some years in Prague as secretary to her father, E. St. Vráz, Czech explorer and writer, and contributed articles to Czech-

American and Prague journals. She was a member of the Svaz českých spisovatelů. She also supervised the revised edition of her father's works on exploration and wrote his biography *Život a cesty E. St. Vráze* (Unie, Praha, 1937). Returning to Chicago after the Nazi occupation of Czechoslovakia, she was active on the managerial and editorial staff of the *Svornost* and in war work. In 1945, Miss Vráz came to Czechoslovakia with American Relief for Czechoslovakia and later served as its Field Director until her expulsion by the Communists in 1949. At present, she is president of the Czechoslovak National Council of America, a national organization representing Americans of Czechoslovak descent, and editor of its publications, the *Věstník* and the *American Bulletin*.

WASKOVICH, GEORGE, was born in 1896 in Greenwich, Conn. He attended Tufts University (B.S. 1923), University of London, Harvard University and Charles University, Prague (Ph.D. 1927). Subsequently he taught history at the College of St. Teresa, Winona, Minn. (1928-32), St. John's University, Brooklyn N.Y. (1933-37), and since 1934 he has been associated with Hunter College, New York where he is Professor of History. He is a member of the American Historical Assoc., the Catholic Historical Assoc., and the American Assoc. for Advancement of Slavic Studies. He contributed to *Origins and Consequences of World War II* (New York, 1948), *The Slavonic Encyclopaedia* (New York, 1949), *The Development of Historiography* (Harrisburg, 1954) and is the author of a large number of articles and book reviews in scholarly periodicals.

Address: Dept. of History, Hunter College, New York, N.Y.

WELLEK, RENÉ, was born in 1903 in Vienna, Austria, studied English and Germanic philology at the Charles University, Prague, Czechoslovakia (Ph.D., 1926) and became Procter Fellow in English at the Graduate School of Princeton University (1927-1928); Instructor, Smith College, Northampton, Mass. (1928-1929); Instructor in Modern Languages, Princeton University (1929-1930); Lecturer, University of London (1935-1939); Assistant Professor (Docent), Charles University, Prague (1930-1935).

He entered the United States in 1939 and taught at the University of Iowa, Iowa City, where he rose to full Professor in the English Department (1939-1946). He then was Professor of Slavic and Comparative Literature at Yale University (1946-1952) and was appointed Sterling Professor of Comparative Literature (1952 to date). He was Chairman of the Slavic Department (1947-1959), and is Chairman of the Department of Comparative Literature. He is also Director of Graduate Studies in Comparative Literature.

Professor Wellek has received many awards and honors, including M. A. (Hon.) Yale University; D. Lit., Oxford and Harvard Universities; a prize for distinguished scholarship in the humanities from the American Council of Learned Societies; and he was a Fulbright Research Professor in Italy, etc.

Professor Wellek is now serving as President of the Czechoslovak Society of Arts and Sciences in America and President of the International Association of Comparative Literature and the American Association of Comparative Literature.

In addition to teaching at Yale University, he taught at Columbia University (1948); Kenyon College, Gambier, Ohio (1940); Harvard University (1950, 1953-1954); Princeton University (1950); and the University of Hawaii (1961).

Professor Wellek is the author of *Immanuel Kant in England, 1793-1838* (Princeton, N.J., 1931), *The Rise of English Literary History* (Chapel Hill, N.C., 1941), *Theory of Literature* (New York, 1956), *A History of Modern Criticism: 1750-1950* (New Haven, Conn., 1955-), *Concepts of Criticism* (New Haven, Conn., 1963), and *Essays on Czech Literature* (The Hague, 1963). In addition he contributed numerous articles to scholarly periodicals.

Address: Department of Comparative Literature, Yale University, New Haven, Conn.

ZABORSKI, JERZY, born in 1931 in Kraków, Poland, attended McGill University, Montréal (B.A., 1953), and the Université d'Ottawa (M.A. in Geography, magna cum laude, 1959), and presently plans to obtain his Ph.D. degree from that university. He was active as research geographer and research planner for Canadian government agencies, federal, provincial and municipal, and as a Director, Research Programming and Reports Division, General Planning and Resource Consultants, St. Louis, and is now Assistant Professor of Geography at Arizona State University, Tempe, Arizona.

Two of his major works concerned with typology and geographical distribution of dwellings on the Eurasian continent are about to be published, in English and Italian; he has also prepared for publication two books, in English and Polish, dealing with the geography of religion. He is a member of the Gamma Theta Upsilon National Professional Geographic Fraternity, Association of American Geographers, Canadian Association of Geographers, National Council for Geographic Education, Society for American Archaeology, Archeological Institute of America, American Anthropological Association, American Association for the Advancement of Science, l'Association Canadienne-Française pour l'Avancement des Sciences, American Association of University Professors, and recently was elected member of the Polish Institute of Arts and Sciences in America, and Fellow of the American Geographical Society.

Address: Dept. of Geography, Arizona State University, Tempe, Arizona 85281.

ZACH, JAN, was born in Slaný, Czechoslovakia in 1914. He graduated from the Superior School of Industrial Arts and the Academy of Fine Arts in Prague. He is presently Associate Professor of Arts and Head of the Sculpture Department, University of Oregon, Eugene, Oregon. Professor Zach is Honorary Professor of Fine Arts, Institute of Architecture and Fine Arts, Belo-Horizonte, Minas, Brazil. He was President of the Northwest Institute of Sculpture (Oregon Chapter) in 1959–1960. His work is represented in private collections and in galleries in Czechoslovakia. In 1939 he decorated the Czechoslovak Pavilion at the World Fair in New York. From 1940 to 1951, he lived in Brazil where he was Art Director of the Magazine, *Cocktail*, founded the Museum of Modern Art in Resende, Estado do Rio, and the school of painting connected with the museum. He has executed public and private commissions for portraits in sculpture and paintings and his works were shown in many exhibitions. From 1951 to 1958 he lived in Canada, taught at the Banff School of Fine Arts, and participated in many exhibitions. He entered the United States in 1958, received a Research Award from the University of Oregon Scientific Research Office (1959–1960), and is working on sculpture and reliefs for the new City Hall of Eugene and teaching art at the University of Oregon.

Address: School of Architecture, University of Oregon, Eugene, Oregon.

Index

Aachen, Hans von, 147
Abortion, 425-45; and birth rate, 439-45; and public health, 440-3; and public morals, 440-1, 443; and youth, 436 n., 437, 440-3; applications for (*see* Abortion, Commissions on); as means of avoiding illegitimate childbirth, 425, 436, 439; attitude of Church to, 425; commissions on, 436-9, 442-5; compositions and procedure of, 436, 445; criticisms of, 438-40, 442-3, 445; committed by pregnant woman, 426, 428-30, 440, 443-5; committed by third persons, 426-30, 432-5, 441-3; Communist Czechoslovak legislation on, 428-45; abuses of, 437-8, 444; critical evaluation of, 441-5; consent of pregnant woman or her representatives to, 426, 428-30, 434-5; fees for, 437-8, 445; illegal, 425-35, 439-42; penalties for, 426 n., 429-30, 434; in ancient Czech law, 425; local government concerned with (*see* Abortion, Commissions on); performed by physicians or other qualified persons, in medical institutions, 427-8, 430, 432, 435, 437, 440; permissible, 427-32, 435-45; because of rape, 436; for economic, social, and criminological reasons, 436-9, 442, 444-5; for medical and eugenic reasons, 427-32, 435-8, 442, 445; pre-Communist Czechoslovak legislation on, 426-8
Absolon, Karel, 487
Abstract art, 169, 170, 171, 172
Ackermann aus Boehmen, 112, 114
Agriculture, in Czechoslovakia, 360, 361, 367; land distribution, 367; land owners, 367; land reform, 359, 367, 368, 370; grain monopoly system, 350-8
Akhmatova, Anna, 23

Alakraw, Johann, 474
Albania, probability of anti-Communist revolution, 322; probability of nationalistic Communism, 322-3
Aleš, Mikuláš, 149, 177
Alexandreis, Czech, 30
Alexy, Janko, 153
Alpine region, 203, 204
Alps, 185, 187, 193, 196
Altaian nation, 202
Ammann, E., 263
Ambrose, 214
American Association of Czechoslovak Engineers, 479
American Association of Physical Anthropologists, 509
American economic enterprise, contribution of Czechs and Slovaks to, 523; American Slovak Bank, 524; Bank of Europe, 525; Bata Shoe Company, 526
American Journal of Physical Anthropology, 508
American Museum of Natural History, 505
Amerikán, almanac, 550
Amerikán, newspaper, 549
Amerikanszko-Szlovenszke Noviny, 534
Ammon, A., 336
Andic, V. E., 359, 523; biography of, 635
Angiocardiography, 462
Angiography, 462
Anjou, Dynasty of French origin, 225
Anne, daughter of Charles IV, 145
Anselm, 290
Antes, 202
Anthropologists, Czech; Jindřich Matiegka, 458-61; Aleš Hrdlička, 505-9
Anthropology, physical, 505-9
Anthropometry, 458
Anti-Communist revolution, 319, 321;

desirability of, 320, 321 n.; desirability of in China, 321 n.; desirability of in Soviet Union, 321 n.; probabilities of, 321, 323, 324; probability of in Albania, 322; probability of in China, 321, 324; probability of in Czechoslovakia, 322, 323, 324; probability of in East Germany, 321-2; probability of in Hungary, 321-2; probability of in Poland, 321-2; probability of in Soviet Union, 321, 324; probabilities of vs. nationalistic Communism and Democratization, 323

Antwerp Bible, 159, 161
Apollinaire, 169
Aragon, Kingdom of, 234
Aretin of Ehrenfeld, Paulus, 484
Aristotle, 289
Arno, Bishop, 199, 200
Arnold, Emmanuel, 275 n.
Arnulf, King, 192
Ars nova, 121
Art, abstract (*see* Abstract art)
Art, Czech, in 14th century, international recognition of, 156 n., 157 n.
Art, in Czechoslovakia (*see* Fine arts, in Czechoslovakia); bibliography on, 581 ff.
Attempt, criminal, 432; incapable of succeeding, 432-3; objective theory of, 433 n.; overt act of, 433; subjective theory of, 433; to commit abortion, 432-3, 442; penalties for, 442
Auden, Wystan Hugh, 23
Auerbach, Berthold, 76
Auerhan, J., 317
Auersperg, Josef Karl, Count of, 385
Augustine, 214
Ausgleich of 1867, 270 n., 271
Austria, 193, 198, 204 (*see also* Lower Austria, Upper Austria); attitude of Czech Deputies toward, 271, 276; constitutionalism of, 274; Czech political tactics in, 271, 272, 274, 276; democratization and federalization of, 271; nature of Habsburg rule in, 274; Masaryk and, 271, 275; Palacký and, 271, 275; Slovak political tactics in, 271
Austroslavism, developed by František Palacký, 271; Karel Havlíček as spokesman of, 272; Masaryk and, 271
Avars, 189, 202, 203, 204, 205; Avar Confederacy, 203, 204; Avar domination, 203; Avar rule, 204; Avar-Slavic symbiotic relationship, 204; Avar state, 203; Avar tributaries, 203; Avar yoke, 204

Bab, Julius, 72
Bach, Joh. Seb., 123, 135
Bachmann, Adolf, 232 n., 247
Bacon, Francis, 333, 495
Bagehot, Walter, 418
Bakalář, Mikuláš (Štětina), 474, 516
Baker, Russel, 421 n.
Bakunin, Michael, 257, 275 n.
Balbín, Bohuslav, 34, 382
Balkan Peninsula, 203
Baltimore, Lord, 503
Balts, 207
Balzac, Honoré de, 24
Bandtkie, J. S., 385
Barcroft, H., 463, 467
Baronius, Cardinal Caesar, 262
Baroque, 21, 22, 142, 176; Baroque painting in Bohemia, 147
Bartoš, F. M., 229 n., 233 n., 239 n., 243
Barvitius, Karel, 150
Basch, Antonín, 362, 363
Basel, Council of, 219, 224, 225, 230, 237, 240, 250
Baťa, Tomáš, 481; pioneer of self-government in industry, 342-9
Bata Organization, 342 ff.
Bata Shoe Company, 481, 525, 526
Batawa, 525
Bauch, Jan, 151
Bauer, Otto, 308 n., 309 n., 310 n.
Baum, Dr. Jiří, 487
Baumgarten, Konrad, 475
Baumgarter, 86
Bavaria, 186, 187, 188, 192, 193, 195, 197, 199
Bavaria, Duchy of, 232
Bavarians, 191
Baxa, Bohumil, 279, 392, 417 n.
Becker, Henrik, 96
Becker, Howard, 318
Beer-brewing, 480
Beethoven, influence of Czech composers on, 138, 139
Belgium, 183, 185, 186, 195, 199
Bencúr, Matěj (Martin Kukučin), 46, 521
Benda family, 134, 137; Benda Jiří Antonín (Georg), 123, 127, 137, 138
Benedictine Press, Czech, in Chicago, 530

Index

Benedictines, 551
Beneš, Eduard, 209, 304, 407, 413, 539, 543; as a political scientist, 278, 281; as a sociologist, 315, 317; his sociological works, 315 n., 316 n., writings on, 316 n.; Institute, in London, 282
Beneš of Hořovice, 474
Beneš, Václav, 267, 282; biography of, 635
Beneš, Vincenc, 152, 153
Benka, Martin, 153
Béranger, Pierre Jean de, 18, 22, 28
Berdyaev, N., 456
Bergson, Henri, 452, 454
Berkeley, George, 452, 453
Bernini, 176
Bernolák, Antonín, 34
Bertram of Minden, Master, 144
Bezold, Friedrich von, 210
Bezruč, Petr, 36
Bible Kralická, 33
Bibliography, on Czechoslovakia and its arts and sciences, 555 ff.; bibliographies, 557-61; general references, 561-3; humanities, 564 ff.; literature, 564-7; linguistics, 567-70; philosophy, 571-4; history, 575-81; modern history (*see* Bibliography, social sciences, political science); religion (*see* Bibliography, humanities, history *and* Bibliography, social sciences, political science); arts, 581 ff.; music and drama, 581-4; fine arts, 584-9; social sciences, 589 ff.; sociology, 589-92; economics, 592-7; political science, 597-603; law, 603-6; education, 606-8; natural sciences, 609 ff.; general references, 609-11; biological sciences, 611-5; physical sciences, 615-8; technology, 618-20; Czechs and Slovaks abroad, 620 ff.; U.S.A., 620-3; other countries, 623-5; addendum, 625-34
Bidlo, Jaroslav, 260
Biochemical factors, role in circulation, 463
Biological sciences, in Czechoslovakia; bibliography on, 611-5
Biondo, Flavio, 229 n.
Bláha, Inocenc A., 316, 317
Blahoslav, Jan Bishop, 21, 33
Blažíček, 150
Blood capillaries, structure of, 467
Blood circulation, change in concept,

Czechoslovak contribution to, 462-70; physiologic advances, 463; morphologic advances, 467; biochemical and histochemical advances, 467-9
Blood circulation, peripheral autonomy of, 462; physico-mechanical approach to, 462; physico-mechanical parameters of, 463; disturbances in, 469
Blood flow, curves, 463; hormonal regulation of, 463; neuro-humoral regulation of, 463; peripheral, 462; pulsatile, analysis of, 463; reversal of, 463;
Blood-and-soil literature, 77
Boček, Antonín, 386, 387
Body composition, 458
Boemus Teutobrodensis, 135
Boháč, A., 317
Bohemia, 193, 196; Bohemia and Moravia, 187, 201
Bohemia Manor, 500, 503, 504
Bohemian Brethren, 20, 27, 121
Bohemian Forest, 187, 188, 190, 191, 192, 193, 198, 199, 201
Bohemian medieval book illumination, 156-66
Böhm, J., 201 n.
Bohmer, Alois, 396 n.
Böhmische Gesellschaft der Wissenschaften, 384
Bolland, J., 195, 196
Bologna, University of, 233
Book illumination, Bohemian, medieval, 156-66
Books, number published in Czechoslovakia and in the U.S., 303
Boruhradský, Šimon, 518
Boryně, František (Francis), 518
Bosak, Michael, 524
Boskovice Bible, 162
Bosnia, Kingdom of, 227
Bossism, 420, 421
Bossjak, 80
Botto, Ján, 45
Botto, Ján (Krasko, Ivan), 46
Bouček, R. J., 469
Bouillon, Godfrey of, 231
Bourdelle, 170
Bourgeoisie, 20, 26, 27
Bourges, Pragmatic Sanction of, 225, 231
Braetz, Ralph A., 421 n.
Branberger, Dr. Jan, 133
Brandes, Johann Christian, 138
Brandl, Peter, 148

Brandl, Vincenc, 389
Bratislava, University of, 318, 405
Bratrské Listy, Czech newspaper in Texas, 515
Braun, M., sculptor, 176
Braunias, Karl, 414-24, 414 n. -424 n.
Brdlík, Vladislav, 350 n.
Bregenz, 187, 197
Bren gun, 477
Breslau, University of, 451
Bretholz, Bertold, 391
Březina, O., 82
Brikcí Kouřimský of Liczko, 382
Brixi, Fr. X., 124
Brixi family, 137
Brno, 477, 478
Brno School of Jurisprudence, 405-13
Brno, University of, 316, 317, 384, (*see also* Masaryk University)
Broca, 505
Brod, J., 467
Brokoff, J., 176
Bronze Age, 205
Brožek, Josef, 458, 461; biography of, 636
Brožík, Václav, 150
Bruhl, Lévy, 316
Brussels, Capital City of Burgundy, 232
Bubák, Alois, 150
Buber, M., 456
Bukovský, Vojtěch (Adalbert), 519
Bulgaria, probability of anti-Communist revolution of, 322
Bulova, Joseph, 525
Burgundy, Duchy of, 197, 231, 232, 234
Burian, Karel, 131,
Burke, Kenneth, 62
Burney, Dr. Charles, 119, 123, 140
Bury, J. B., 262
Bušek, Vratislav, 14, 396, 397 n.; biography of, 636
Butter, O., 317
Byron, George Gordon, 39, 40
Byzantine studies, at Charles University, 260; studies of F. Dvorník, 262-3
Byzantium, 105, 204

Čáda, František, 392, 394
Caderousse, Davin, 472
Caldara, Antonio, 139
Calvert family, 503
Camus, Albert, 23, 90
Canadian economic enterprise, contribution of Czechs and Slovaks to, 523;
Alaska Pine Company, 526; flax, glass and glove products, 526; refugee industries, 525
Canis, Jacobus, 475
Cannon, W. B., 463
Čapek, Josef, 36; as a painter, 151, 152
Čapek, Karel, 36, 60-7, 68-75, 85, 267; legacy of, 60-7; author of scientific fantasies, 60-3, 64; on politics and political thought, 63, 64; author of trilogy, *Hordubal, Meteor*, and *An Ordinary Life*, 63, 65-7; author of the *First Rescue Party*, 67; his contribution to philosophy, 65 ff.; and Communism, 68-75; on proletarian art, 71, 72, 73; "Why I am not a Communist", 68, 69; author of *Hovory s TGM* ("Conversations with T. G. Masaryk"), 53 n., 68; author of *Mother, The White Plague*, 70; author of *Pragmatism or the Philosophy of Practical Life*, 68; author of *On Matters of Universal Interest*; *or, Zoon Politicon*, 69
Čapek, Milič, 183; biography of, 636
Čapek, Thomas, 524; his research on Augustine Herman, 500, 501, 502
Carvaggio, 148
Cardew, Angelika K., 112; biography of, 637
Carinthia, 184, 185, 186, 187, 196
Carlerius, Aegidus, 219
Caroline University (*see* Charles University *or* Prague, University of)
Carpatho-Ruthenia, 397
Carpathians, 202
Carracci, 148
Carreto, Otto de, 231 n.
Cartography, Czech, 482-9, (*see also* Geography, Czech)
Casimir IV, King of Poland, 225, 227, 243
Časopis Českého Musea, 54, 56
Časopis Musejní, 385
Cassou, Jean, 172
Castile, Kingdom of, 234
Catholic church, 382
Catholic press, of Czechs, in the U.S., 551
Catholicism, 257
Čech, Leonard, 287
Čech, Svatopluk, 35, 54, 177
Čechoslovák, periodical, 543
Čechoslovan, periodical, 540

Index 657

Cekota, Anthony, 342; biography of, 637
Čelakovský, František Ladislav, 21, 35
Čelakovský, Jaromír, 388
Čep, Jan, 36; art of, 76-82; author of *Zeměžluč*, 77; *Polní tráva*, 78, 81; *Domek*, 78; *Husopas*, 78; *Samomluva*, 79; *Děravý plášť*; *Člověk na silnici*, 79; *Oldřich Babor*; *Elegie*, 79; *Rozárka Lukášová*, 79; *Dvojí domov*, 81; *Svatojánská pouť*, 81; *Zápisky Jiljího Klena*, 82
Čermák, Jan Josef, 518
Čermák, Jaroslav, 149
Čermák, Col. Jiří, 487
Černohorský, Bohuslav, 123
Černý, Karel, 151, 152
Černý, Václav, 18, 21, 22, 27, 62, 64
Cervantes (Miguel de Cervantes Saavedra), 42
Česká Matice, 273 n.
České Budějovice (Budweis), 480
Československá obilní společnost, 350-8
Československá Samostatnost, periodical, 539
Československá vlastivěda, 103, 280
Československý Denník, periodical, 540
Československý Odboj, periodical, 539
Cézanne, 168, 169
Chalcedon, 214
Chalupa Vlastislav, 398 n.
Chalupka, Ján, 45
Chalupka, Samo, 45
Chalupný, Emanuel, 280, 316, 317
Cham, 192, 199
Chambadal, P., 453
Charlemagne, 189, 193, 194, 252
Charles IV, Holy Roman Emporer and King of Bohemia, 33, 113, 114, 144, 156, 175, 176, 252, 478
Charles VI, 134
Charles Bridge, in Prague, 176
Charles University, 250, 251, 253, 254, 260, 303, 316, 485, 487, 501; founding of, 382, 478; (*see also*, Prague, University of)
Chateaubriand, François René, 43, 43 n.
Chatterton, 255
Chelčický, Peter, 20, 21, 31, 32, 212, 222, 258, 313
Chernoský, C. H., 514
Cherubini, 138
Chiaroscuro effect, 158, 160, 163
Chittussi, Antonín, 150

Chlumecký, Peter Ritter, 251, 387
Christian I, King of Denmark, 234
Christianity, on the territory of Czechoslovakia, before the ninth century, 183 ff.
Church Slavonic, 94
Chytil, Josef, 387
Chytil, Karel, 157
Chyzhevsky, Dimitry, 494
Cibulka, Josef, 108
Clark, Bates John, 338
Clark, Maurice J., 338
Claudianus, Nocholas, 483
Clement, writer of the Moravian school, 106
Clementis, Vladimir, 47
Cluny, 201
Code of Tsar Štefan Dušan, The 385
Codex Caroli, 112
Codex diplomaticus et epistolaris Moraviae, 386
Color, theory of, 451, 452; Newton's theory, 449, 451; Goethe's concept, 451, 452; Purkinje effect, 449-57
Comenius, Daniel, 494
Comenius, John Amos, 12, 21, 31, 33, 85, 122, 301, 313, 484, 528; map maker, 484; pansophy, 493; *Janua linguarum reserata*, 493; *Pansophiae prodromus*, 493; invited to England in 1641, 493; *Via lucis*, 494; pansophic college in London, 494; *De rerum humanorum emendatione consultatio catholica*, 494; his educational theories in *Panegersia*, 494-5, *Panaugia*, 495; *Pantaxia*, 495, *Pampaedia*, 495 (translated as *Vševýchova*, 496), *Panglottia*, 496 *Panorthosia*, 496 (translated as *Všenáprava*, 496), *Pannuthesia*, 497, *Great Didactic*, 495; proposes the organization of the Council of Light, the Court of Justice, and the Ecumenical Consistory, 496-8, the achievement of his life-work, 497-9; (*see also* Komenský, Jan Amos)
Commune, Paris, 22
Communism, and Czech literary criticism, 21, 23, 27; effect on scholarship, 298, 306; "People's Democracy", 397, 399; "Way toward Socialism", 398, 403
Communist China, desirability of anti-Communist revolution, 321 n.; desirability of democratization, 323 n.; desirability of nationalistic Communism, 322

n.; difficulties with, 324; probability of anti-Communist revolution, 321, 324; probability of democratization, 323-4; probability of nationalistic Communism, 322, 324; Soviet-Chinese schism, 324
Communist concept of constitution, 398-400
Communist legal philosophy, 399
Communist legal science, 405
Communist moral standard, 399
Communist semantics, 399
Compacts, of Basel, 225
Composers, Czech, in Berlin; Benda family, 137
Composers, Czech, in Mannheim; Jan Václav Stamic, 135-6; František Xaver Richter, 136; Antonín Fils, 136
Composers, Czech, in Italy; Josef Mysliveček, 139
Composers, Czech, in Paris; Antonín Rejcha, 138; Jan Václav Stich, 138
Composers, Czech in Vienna; František Tůma, 139; Florian L. Gassman, 139; Leopold Koželuh, 139; František Krommer-Kramář, 139
Composers (see also Music)
Compte, Auguste, 246, 285, 286, 287, 293, 314, 315
Conrad, Archbishop, 218
Conrad of Vechta, Bible of, 145, 157
Constance, Council of, 229 n., 230, 233
Constantine, 94, 105 ff., 220; (see also Cyril and Methodius)
Constantinople, 206, 214, 233
Constitutional Court; Austria, 417
Constitutions, Communist Czechoslovak, on family welfare, 438
Constitutions, qualifying clauses, 400; preambles, 398
Constructivist movement, 178
Consultatio, 494, 498; consists of Panegersia, 494-5; Panaugia, 495; Pantaxia, 495; Pampaedia, 495; Panglottia, 496; Panorthosia, 496; and Pannuthesia, 497
Consumer goods, output of, in Czechoslovakia, 378
Contemporary Czech and Slovak painting, 152
Contraceptive means, use of, 442 n.
Contract and contractual obligation, 409
Cooper, James F., 54
Čordák, Ludovít, 150

Corssen, Arendt, 501
Coselhac, Arnaud de, 472
Cosmas Chronicle, 30
Cosmographiae, 483
Cotteret-Émeri-Lalumière, 420 n., 422 n.
Counter-Reformation, 34
Courtenay, Baudouin de, 98
Cranach, Lucas, 146
Criginger, Jan, 484
Criminologists, pre-Communist Czechoslovak, 428-9, 431-3, 437, 440-2
Croats, 204
Croce, Benedetto, 23
Ctibor of Drnovice, 381
Ctibor Tovačovský of Cimburk, 381
Cubism, 152, 168, 170, 172
Currency, in Czechoslovakia, 363-5
Cyril (see Constantine)
Cyril and Methodius, 29, 120, 183, 206, 207
Cyrillic (alphabet), 207
Czech Academy of Sciences and Arts, 516
Czech, language, 93, 94, 100, 102, 103; continuous development of, 86; evolution of, 41; first lectures on, 388; use of, during the reign of Josef II, 382; Chair of, established at the School of Philosophy, 385
Czech literary language, 40
Czech literary tradition, 40
Czech Massif, 203
Czech settlements, on the Danube, 200
Czechoslovak Foreign Institute in Exile, 282
Czechoslovak Geographic Society, 487
Czechoslovak Grain Monopoly, 350-8
Czechoslovak independence, declaration of, 276
Czechoslovak nation, 396-7
Czechoslovak national emblem, 396
Czechoslovak-Polish Confederation, 209
Czechoslovak Society of Arts and Sciences in America, Inc., the, 11-14, 27, 126; aims and objectives of, 11-12; the First Congress of, 13-14
Czechoslovak Statistical Office, 376
Czechoslovakia, agriculture; agricultural cooperatives (JZD), 401; grain monopoly system, 350-8; (see also Agriculture, in Czechoslovakia)
Czechoslovakia, artisans and tradesmen, 401
Czechoslovakia, bibliography on (see

Bibliography on Czechoslovakia)
Czechoslovakia, Bill of Rights, 398, 400
Czechoslovakia, changes in, 324
Czechoslovakia, collective farms, 401; Communist coup d'etat, 1948, 398; Constituent National Assembly, 414-7
Czechoslovakia, Constitution: 1920, 396, 414, 416; Constitution: 1948, 397-403; Constitution: 1960, 398, 401-3; constitutional continuity, 397
Czechoslovakia, Constitutions, preambles, 398
Czechoslovakia, election laws, 414-6; elections, 1929, 416; Electoral Court Act, 414
Czechoslovakia, expulsion of Germans, 397
Czechoslovakia, landowners 401
Czechoslovakia, name, 396
Czechoslovakia, one-family houses, 402-3
Czechoslovakia, political futures of, 319-20, 325; probability of anti-Communist revolution, 322, 324; probability of democratization, 123-4; probability of nationalistic Communism, 322-3, 324; probability of nationalistic Communism vs. revolution, 323
Czechoslovakia, political parties; Communist Party, 398-9, 403-4, 416; Czech National Socialist Party, 416; National Democrats, 416; National Front, 398-9; People's Party, 416, 417; Republican (Farmer's) Party, 416; Slovak Democrats, 416; Slovak Freedom Party, 416; Slovak Labor Party, 416; Slovak People's Party, 416; Social Democrats, 416
Czechoslovakia, private enterprise, 402; property ownership: "national ownership", 401; property ownership: "personal ownership", 402-3; property ownership: "private ownership", 401-3; property ownership: real property, 402-3; property ownership: "socialist ownership", 403
Czechoslovakia, Provisional National Assembly, 414 n., 416 n.; Revolutionary National Assembly, 414
Czechoslovakia, separation of power, 398
Czechoslovakia, stability of, 322, 325
Czechs, 200, 397; first contact with Western civilization, 183-201; Czechs in Texas, 510-5; religion, 515; in the U.S., their part in the war for independence for Czechoslovakia, 551; in the U.S., free thinkers' movement, 550; in the U.S., Catholic Church, 551; (*see also* Czechs and Slovaks abroad)
Czechs and Slovaks abroad, 491 ff.; bibliography on, 620 ff.; present day significance of John A. Comenius, 493-9; Augustine Heřman, 500-4; Aleš Hrdlička, 505-9; Czechs in the U.S. (*see also* Czechs, in the U.S.); Czechs and Slovaks in Latin America, 516-22; Jesuit priests from the Kingdom of Bohemia, 517-8; Thaddeus Haenke, 519; E. S. Vráz, and Josef Kořenský, 520; Benedikt Roezl and Karel Domin, 520; Aleš Hrdlička, 520; A. V. Frič and Čestmír Loukotka, 520; Matěj Bencúr, 521; Milan R. Štefánik, 521; Vlastimil Kybal, 521; Richard Lehký, 522; contribution to economic enterprise in the New World, 523-7; Czech and Slovak Press abroad, 528-45; early Czech journalism in the U.S., 546-51; Comenius, in England, 493, 494; (*see also* Literature, Czech, on America; Emigrants, Czech and Slovak)
Czechs and Slovaks, unification of, 311
Czekanowski, Jan, 202 n., 206 n.

Dacia, 202
Dada, 90
Dagobert, King, 186, 190, 191, 195, 197
Dalimil's Chronicle, 30, 482
Daneš, Jiří, 487
Daniel of Veleslavín, Adam, 33
Dante, 25
Danube, river, 184, 185, 187, 188, 189, 190, 191, 192, 194, 195, 196, 197, 200, 201, 203
Danubian basin, 202
Darwin, Charles, 81
Davists, 47
Dějiny národu českého v Čechách a v Moravě, 386
Delaunay, Robert, and Sonia, 169
Dělnické Listy, 550
Demetz, Peter, 76; biography of, 637
Democracy, Czech, and Karel Čapek, 65-7
Democracy, Czechoslovak, background of, 267-76; causes of, 267 ff., 273; and Czech Reformation, 268, 269; demo-

cratic ideology, 268-9; and political experience in Austria, 271-6; Palacký and, 268, 269, 270; Masaryk and, 269, 270, 275, 276
Democracy, liberal, 396-7
Democracy, "people's", 397, 399
Democracy, philosophy of Masaryk, 283
Democratization, 320, 323; desirabllity of, 323 n.; desirability of in China, 323 n.; desirability of in Soviet Union, 323 n.; probability of evolution of, 323, 324; probability of in China, 323, 324; probability of in Czechoslovakia, 323-4; probability of in East Germany, 323; probability of in Hungary, 323; probability of in Poland, 323; probability of in Soviet Union, 323, 324; probability of vs. anti-Communist revolutions and nationalistic Communism, 323
Demuth, Karel Josef, 387
Denis, Ernest, 475
Dennice Novověku, 550
Denník Wídeňský, 537
Derwan, 205, 206
Descartes, Rene, 493, 495
Destinn, Emmy, 127
Deutsch, Karl W., 282
Deutsche Universität in Prag, 392, 395; (*see also* Prague, University of)
Devětsil, 71, 151
Děvín (Theben), 191, 206
Dialectical materialism, 19
Dictionaries, Czech and Slovak, bibliography on, 570
Dietzel, H., 336
Dignowity, Anthony, 510
Dissertatio apologetica pro linqua slavonica, praecipue bohemica, 34
Dobrovský, Josef, 21, 34, 94, 245, 255, 314; and B. Kopitar, 274
Dočkálek, Jan, 536
Doležil, Hubert, 128
Domin, Karel, 487, 520, 486
Dostál, Jiří, 133
Dostoevsky, Fedor Mikhailovich, 24, 257
Doucha, František, 55
Drama, in Czechoslovakia, bibliography on, 581-4
Drava, river, 204
Dresler, Jaroslav, 68; biography of, 637
Dritzehn, German printer, 473
Droop, H. R., 415

Dualism, noetic, 406, 409
Dualism of nature and values, 406
Duben, Vojtěch N., 528, 533 n.; biography of, 638
Dubois, Pierre, 230
Ducháček, Ivo, 282
Duda, Andrew, 525
Dukla, 203
Duckett, J. L., 515
Durchánek, Louis, 178
Durkheim, E., 303, 315, 316
Durych, Jaroslav, 36
Durych, Václav Fortunát, 245
Dusík, Czech composer, 139
Dutch West India Company, 501
Duverger, Maurice, 420 n.
Dvořák, Antonín, 117, 122, 177; Dvořák School, 122, 124 ff., 129
Dvořák, Karel, 21, 177
Dvorník, František (Francis), 20, 105, 202 n.; success of his research in the vindication of the Patriarch Photius, 262-4; author of *Les Slaves, Byzance et Rome au IXe Siècle*, 262, *Les Légendes de Constantin et de Méthode vues de Byzance*, 262, *The Photian Schism, History and Legend*, 263, *The Idea of Apostolicity in Byzantium and the Legend of the Apostle Andrew*, 263, *The Patriarch Photius in the Light of Recent Research*, 263
Dvorský, Bohumír, 153
Dvorský, Viktor, 487
Dvůr Králové, Manuscript of, 124, 149, 253, 270

Earle, E. M., 304 n., 305 n.
Earth sciences, 482
East Germany, changes in, 324; probability of anti-Communist revolution, 321, 322; probability of democratization, 323; probability of nationalistic Communism, 322-3; stability of, 325
Eastern Church, 257
Eastern Orthodox Church, 256, 257
Ebbinghaus, 450
Eckerman, J. P., 451
Eclecticism, 299
Ecole des Chartres, 250
Economic and social structure, of Czechoslovak Society, 359-72; industrial development, 359-61; foreign trade, 361-3; stabilization of currency, 363-6;

land reform, 367-8; development of the middle class, 368-71
Economic models, individualistic, 333; mixed, 334; solidaristic, 333-4
Economic principles, rationality of, 330-1, 339; causality, 331; finality, 331-3, 335-6
Economic principles, quality of propositions, 330, 333
Economic theory and methodology, 329-32; Austrian School, 335, 338; methodological individualism (Schumpeter), 333, 337; social-purpose method, 333-4, 337-8; teleological method, 331-3, 335-6; error of (Schumpeter), 335; Marxist attitude to, 336 n.
Economic theory with respect to, Kantian dualism, 331, 332 n.; ontological knowledge, 331-2; normative systems, 331 n.; scientific nomismus, 331; scientific systems, 330-3, 338; teleological knowledge, 331-3, 334-6; transitive (logical) orders, 338-9
Economics, in Czechoslovakia, 327 ff.; bibliography on, 592-7; Czechoslovak Grain Monopoly System, 350-8; economic and social structure of Czechoslovak society between the two wars, 359-72; problems of measuring industrial output in Czechoslovakia, 373-8; teleological construction of economics – Karel Engliš' contribution to economic thought, 329-41; Tomáš Baťa – pioneer of self-government in industry, 342-9
Economics, definition of, 300 335-7
Economics, teleological model, cost 334; differentiated from one causally organized, 331-3, 335; purposes, hierarchy of, 332-3; compared with Paretian ophelimities, 338; organic totality of, 334; personal solaridity of, 334 n.; postulates (see purposes, above); scarcity, 334; utility-disutility, 334
Eddington, Arthur, 453
Eder, Jan, 518
Edholm, O. G., 463
Education, 302
Education, in Czechoslovakia; bibliography on, 606-8; (see also Comenius)
Ehrlich, V., 467
Eidlitz, Leopold, 526
Einstein, A., 178, 301
Election geometry, 420

Election laws, Albania, 418; Australia, 419, 421; Austria, 422, 424; Belgium, 419, 422; Canada, 419,; Czechoslovakia, 414-6; Denmark, 422, 423; France, 419, 422, 423, Fribourg, 422; Geneva, 422; Germany, 419, 422, 423; Great Britain, 418; Holland, 419, 422; India, 419; Ireland, 419, 421; Israel, 419, 422; Italy, 419, 422, Neuchatel, 422; Norway, 422; Portugal, 418; reapportionment, 420; Rumania, 422; Scandinavian countries, 419, 422; South Africa, 419, 422; Sweden, 422; Switzerland, 418, 419, 422, 423; Tennessee Assembly District apportionment, 420; United Kingdom, 419; United States, 418, 419; USSR, 418; West Germany, 419, 422, 423; Wuertemberg, 417
Election quotas, 415
Election systems, alternative vote, 420; cumulative vote, 423; horizontal lists, 423; list systems, 421, loosely-tied lists, 422; majority systems, 419, 421, 422; national adjustments, 415, 422; "personalized" proportional representation, 423; plurality system, 418-21, 423; preferential votes, 422, 424; remainder votes, 415; resignation pledges, 416, 417; rigid lists, 414, 416, 422; second ballot, 420, 422, 423; single transferable vote, 421; split vote, 423
Elections, municipal, Austria, 417; Cincinnati (Ohio), 421; New York City, 421
Electrocardiography, 463
Eliot, Thomas Stearns, 23, 88
Elizabeth of Habsburg, Queen of Poland, 226
Elizabeth Rejčka, Queen, 143
Elnon, 183, 199
Elvert, C. d', 385
Embryo, human, statutory protection of, 425-6, 428-31, 441, 443
Emigrants, Czech and Slovak; Augustine Heřman, 500-4; in Canada, 535; in Australia and New Zealand, 536, in France, 539; in South America, 536; in Germany, 538; in Italy, 539; in Russia, 540; in Hungary, 541; in Poland, 542; in Yugoslavia, Bulgaria and Rumania, 542; in England, 543; in Switzerland, 544; in Virginia, 501; in Austria, 529, 537; number of, at the end of World

War, 528; the earliest (17th century), 528; the first Slovak (18th century), 529; participation in the foundation of the Czechoslovak Republic, 529; (*see also* Czechs and Slovaks abroad; Migration)
Emigration, 368
Emmeram's glosses, 109
Empiricism, 285, 286, 289
Engels, Friedrich, 22, 24, 72
Engineering, in Czechoslovakia, 477-81; process of development, 477; Hussite weapons, 477; modern military weapons, 477; reasons for progress of, 478; technical schools, 478; societies, 478-9; Czech sulphuric acid production, 479; metal working industry, 479-80; beer brewing, 480; examples of progress of, 480-1; bibliography on, 618-20
Engineers, Czechoslovak, societies of, 478-9; relation to American engineers, 479
England, 234, 493
Enlightenment, 305
Engliš, Karel, Czech economist, 329-41, 407, 412-3; career, 329; Communist attitude to, 337; criticism of Liefmann, 330 n.
Engliš' economic system (*see* Economic theory and models; Economics)
Enns, river, 186, 188, 191, 194, 195
Ephesus, 214
Epistemology, 406-7
Epištoly kutnohorské, 53
Erasmus of Rotterdam, Desidericus, 483
Erben, Karel Jaromír, 21, 35
Ericinio, Ranconis de, 31
Ernst, Max, 160
Eugene IV, Pope, 229 n.
"Execrabilis", Bull issued by Pope Pius II, 230
Exiled writers, Czech; Jan Čep, 76-82; Egon Hostovský, 76
Exploration, Czech, 482-9; (*see also* Geography)
Expressionism, 151, 153

Faithorne, William, 504
Falstaff, 24
Faust, Johann, 471
Fauvism, 153, 168, 169
FCI (Information Service of Free Czechoslovakia), 543

Feierabend, Ladislav K., 350; biography of, 638
Fejfar, Z., 467
Fencl, Jan Mantuán, 474
Feudalism, 20
Fendall, Governor of Maryland, 503
Ferdinand I, of Hapsburg, 119, 253, 517
Ferdinand II, Emperor, 500
Ferrante of Aragon, King of Naples, 225
Ferrose, Girard, 472
Fetter, F. A., 338
Fibich, Zdeněk, 127, 129 n.
Filip, Jan, 203 n.
Filipec, Jan, Bishop of Olomouc, 474
Filla, Emil, 152
Fillmore, Millard, 52
Fils, Antonín, 136
Fine arts, in Czechoslovakia, painting, 141-55; sculpture, 175-9; the Gerona Master, 156-66; Frank Kupka, 167-74; bibliography on, 584-9
Fink, Eugen, 286
Firkušný, Rudolf, 132, 522
Fischel, Alfred von, 391
Fischer, Jan Otokar, 18, 22, 28
Fischer, Otokar, 17
Fischl, glove-maker in Canada, 526
Fisher, J. L., 316, 317
Fitzgerald, Scott, 84
Flaubert, 82
Florence, Republic of, 233 n.
Flug-Blätter, of Milwaukee, 546
Foerster, Jos. B., 127
Fogg Art Museum, in Cambridge, Mass., 163
Folklore, 19, 21, 22
Ford, Henry, 342
Foreign trade, of Czechoslovakia, 359, 361-3; between Czechoslovakia and Germany, 362; dependence on foreign markets, 362; dependence on Germany, 364
Formalism, 17, 26
Fořt, Josef, 316
Four Articles of Prague (*Čtyři artikule pražské*), 31
Foustka, Břetislav, 317
France, 226, 231, 232, 237, 239
Francesco Sforza, Duke of Milan, 231 n.
Franco-Flemish foyer, 162
Franklin, Benjamin, 51, 52, 54
Franks, 183, 197, 198; confederacy of the, 205

Franz Josef, 283
Fredegar's Chronicle, 190 n., 195, 204
Frederick the Great, 389
Frederick III of Hapsburg, Holy Roman Emperor, 228 n., 238, 239
Free Europe Committee, Inc. (New York), 282, 439 n.
Freisingen, 199, 200
Fremont, John C., 546
French Criminal Code of 1810, 427 n.
Frič, A. V., 520
Frič, Albert, 486
Frič, Josef Václav, 275 n., 538, 539, 544; on America, 57, 58
Friedrich, G., 394
Frinta, Mojmír S., 141, 156; biography of, 638
Fritz, Samuel, 519
Frnka, Josef V., 515
Froněk, A., 467
Froňková, K., 467
Frýček, 317
Fulla, Ľudo, 153
Fulnek, in Moravia, 493
Fux, Joh. Josef, 139

Galla, 317
Gallneukirchen, 198
Gallus (Handel), Jacobus, 122
Gandhi, Mahatma, 52
Garlandia, Johannes de, 113
Gassmann, Florian Leopold, 139
Gaupp, E. T., 391
Gebauer, 256
Gengler, H. G., 391
Geography, Czech, in the Late Middle Ages, 482; the renaissance, 483; the Age of Reason, 484; the nineteenth century, 485; Czechoslovakia, 1918-38, 486; present status, 487
George of Poděbrady, King of Bohemia, 122, 223, 473, 483, 516; his plan for an International Peace League, 224-44
George, Stefan, 23
Geringer, August, 524, 548, 549
Germanization, 273, 308
Germany, 195, 234, 237, 238
Gerona Martyrology, 145, 165
Gerona Master, the, 156-66; Bible of Conrad of Vechta, in the Museum Plantin Moretus in Antwerp, 157; Martyrology in the Diocesan Museum in Gerona, 159; the Sedlec Antiphonary of 1414, 161; gradual in the Cantonal Library in Lucerne, 161; the *Korczek Bible* in Vienna, 162; two drawings of the Virgin and the angel, in the Fogg Art Museum in Cambridge, Mass., 163; Panici-Junkers, 163; and the Třeboň Master, 163
Gerrymandering, 420
Geschichte der böhmischen Sprache und Literatur, 34
Gibbon, 246
Gide, 88
Giengon, Battle of, 238
Gindely, Antonín, 248, 250-3, 258
Glagolita Clozianus, 108
Glagolitic alphabet, 105, 207
Glogau, meeting of, 226, 227, 228, 229, 231
Gluck, influence of Czech composers on, 138, 139
Goethe, Johann Wolfgang von, 43 n.; and J. E. Purkyně, 451, 452
Goll, Jaroslav, historian, 254, 255, 258-9, 390; and his historical school, 258-61
Gontcharova, 169
Gooch, George P., 258
Gorki, Maxim, 71, 80
Gospodi pomilui ny, 29, 111
Gothic, 175, 176; Gothic murals, 143; Gothic manuscript illumination, 143; Gothic painted panels, 144
Government, totalitarian concept of, 399
Governments, coalitian cabinets, 421; limitation of powers, 400
Goya, 148
Grande Record, Svoboda, La, newspaper, 514
Gray, Thomas, 43 n.
Great Didactic, of Comenius, 495
Great Moravia, 29, 93, 105 ff., 116, 190, 191, 198, 206, 207
Great Schism, 256
Greece, 233
Greeks, alliance of Greater Moravia with, 206
Gregor-Tajovský, Jozef, 46, 47
Gregory, 214
Grégr, 256
Grillinger Bible, 165
Grivec, 108
Group of Six, 130
Gross, F., 152

Gruithuisen, 452
Grumel, Venance, 263
Grund, Norbert, 148
Grundnorm, 409
Grzybowski, K., 397 n.
Gsovski, Vladimir, 396 n. – 7 n., 441 n.
Günther, German hermit, 193
Gutenberg, Johann, 471-3
Gutfround, 177

Hába, Al., 129 ff.
Hack, Anna, 502
Haenke, Thaddeus, 516
Haidušek, Augustine, 511, 514
Hainburg, Heinrich, 113
Hajda, Jan, 307; biography of, 639
Hájek of Libočany, Václav, 382
Hajšman, Jan, 311 n.
Hálek, Vítězslav, 35
Halle, Morris, 101
Haller, Jiří, 102
Hanč, Josef, 281
Hancke, M., 262
Handel (Gallus), 122, 135
Haněl, Jaromír, 388
Hanka, Václav, 253, 255, 386
Hanreich, 417 n.
Hanuš, Jan, 314
Hanzlík, Stanislav, 486
Hapsburgs, the, 57-8
Harant of Polžice and Bezdružice, Christoph, 33, 122, 484
Harkins, William E., 60; biography of, 639
Hartlib, Samuel, 493
Hartmann, Paul, 416 n., 417 n., 494
Harvey, William, 462, 469
Hasenhöhrl, V., 194
Hasištejnský of Lobkovice, Bohuslav, 483
Haupt, Hermann, 210
Hauptmann, Gerhart, 80
Havlíček Borovský, Karel, 21, 35, 272, 299, 314, 530, 546, 548; his criticism of J. K. Tyl's, *The Last Czech*, 53; his views on America, 51-4, 56-8; Masaryk on, 248
Havránek, Bedřich, 150
Havránek, Bohuslav, 103
Haydn, influence of Czech composers on, 136, 139
Hayek, F. v., 338 n.
Heart, central pump, 462; catheterisation of, 462

Heck, Earl, 500 n., 501 n., 504
Hegel, 246, 248, 291, 314; Hegelian dialectic, 246
Heidler, Jan, 246
Helfert, Baron von, 251
Helfert, Vladimír, 132, 133
Helwig, Martin, 484
Hemingway, 84
Hendrich, Josef, 494, 496
Herbart, 314
Herben, Jan, 35
Herder, J. G., 34, 35, 125, 247, 268, 314, 382, 383
Hergenroether, J. Cardinal, 262
Hering, Ewald, 462, 467 524, 529
Heřman, Augustine, 500-4; his parents, 500-1; in Holland, 502; activities in America, 502-4; in Virginia, 502; in New Amsterdam, 502; marriage, 502; founding of Bohemia Manor, 503; making of the map, 503; Labadists' settlement, 504; death, 504
Herman, Casparus, 504
Hermens, F. A., 419 n., 421 n.
Hertz, John David, 525
Hesky, 526
Heyduk, 35
Heymann, Frederick G., 224; biography of, 639
Heyrovský, Jaroslav, 301
Hicks, J. R., 338
Hildebrand, L., 391
Hiller, 138
Hilsner, L., 270
Hirschl, 417 n.
Historical relativism, 19, 25
Historiography, Czech, development of, 245-57; František Palacký, 245-9; Václav Vladivoj Tomek, 249-50; Antonín Gindely, 250-1; Josef Kalousek, 252-3; Antonín Rezek, 253-4; Jaroslav Goll and his school, 258-61; Tomáš G. Masaryk, 254-7
Historiography, positivist, 259
History, of Czechoslovakia, 183 ff.; the first contact of Czechs with Western civilization, 183-201; dynamics of the spatial concept of Czechoslovakia, 202-9; the religion of Hussite Tabor, 210-23; George of Poděbrady's plan for an international peace league, 224-49; the development of Czechoslovak historical writing, 245-57; Jaroslav Goll and his

school, 258-61; the success of Professor Dvorník's research in the vindication of the Patriarch Photius, 262-3; bibliography on, 575-81, 597-603
History of law, in Czechoslovakia, study of, 381-95
History of science, in Czechoslovakia, bibliography on, 609 ff.; (see also Science)
Hlahol, in Prague, choral society, 273 n.
Hlas, 551
Hlas Domova, periodical, 537
Hlasists, 271 n.
Hlavatý, Václav, 11, 301
Hnilička, Alois, 133
Hoch, K., 317
Hodža, Michal Miloslav, 44, 45, 283
Hoffstädter, Bedřich, 153
Hofler, 251
Hohenzollern, dynasty, 238
Holeček, 35
Hollar, Václav (Wenceslaus), 142, 504, 543
Hollar, association of graphic artists, 152
Hollý, Ján, 44
Holmes, W. H., 505, 508
Holstein, Duchy of, 234
Holub, Charles J., 515
Holub, Emil, 486
Homeyer, C. G., 391
Hondius, Jodocus, 483
Horáček, C., 317
Horálek, Karel, 107
Horcicka, A., 391
Horna, Richard, 393
Horský, Vaclav (Wenceslaus), 518
Horvath, Ivan, 47
Hospodář, Czech newspaper in Texas, 515
Hospodine pomiluj ny, 29, 111
Hostinský, Jiří (George), 518
Hostovský, Egon, 54, 76
Howitzer, 477
Hrabák, Josef, 18
Hrdlička, Aleš, 505-9, 520
Hrejsa, Ferdinand, 183
Hromádka, Josef L., 285, 317, 488
Huber, Alois, 192, 199
Hudeček, F., 150, 152
Hujer, Karel, 449; biography of, 639
Humboldt, Alexander von, 451
Humanists, German, 112
Humanitarianism, Czech, 268, 269, 270
Humanities, in Czechoslovakia, bibliography on, 564 ff.
Hume, David, 246, 285, 286, 287,
Hungarians, 207
Hungary, 231, 234, 239; changes in, 324; probability of anti-Communist revolution, 321-2; probability of democratization; probability of nationalistic Communism, 322
Hurban, Jozef Miloslav, 44, 45
Hurban-Vajanský, Svetozár, 46
Hus, Jan (John), 12, 20, 21, 31, 114, 121, 210, 216, 247, 259, 269, 299, 301; created a new orthography for the Czech language, 94; writings on, 313 n.
Husa, Karel, 132
Husserl, 286, 292
Hussite movement, 146, 210, 224, 225, 259, 268; Hussite reformation, 31; Hussite religious songs, 121; Hussite weapons, 477
Hussite Tabor, religion of, 210-23
Hussites (*see* Hussite movement)
Huxley, Aldous, 23
Hynais, Vojtěch, 150

Iasinskii, A. N., 390
Idealism, 288
Ideology, Czech national, 408, 411, 412
Illyricus, Flacius, 211
Industrial development, in Czechoslovakia, 359; industries run by Sudeten Germans, 363; industrialization of Slovakia and Carpathian Ruthenia, 371; occupational distribution, 359-60, 369
Industrial production, in Czechoslovakia, 373-8; gross value, index of, 375-8; net value, index of, 373-7; physical volume, index of, 374-7
Industry, Czechoslovak, relation to Austro-Hungarian Empire industry, 481
Industry, persons working in, in Czechoslovakia, 377
Insularity, 299
Intellectuals, Czech, the institutional system of, 309
Intelligentsia, the role of, in the development of Czechoslovak society, 307-12; Czech, 307, 308, 309, 311, 312; Slovak, 310, 311, 312
International Congress for Scientific Management, the First, in Prague, 479
International Peace League, plan for, by George of Poděbrady, 224-44

Iro-Scottish origins of Christianity, in Czechoslovakia, 200
Irving, Washington, 55
Isačenko, A., 107
Isernia, Henricus de, 113
Italy, 234, 237, 240
Iura primaeva Moraviae, 383
Iuvavum, Roman, 199

Jagiellonians, 207
Jakobson, Roman, 20, 96, 97, 98, 100, 101, 102, 103, 109
Jakoubek of Stříbro, 211, 217
Janáček, Leoš, 128, 133, 177
Jánošík, Juro, the Slovak Robin Hood, 45, 50
Janszoon, Jan, 483
Janua linguarum reserata of Comenius, 493
Jaroměřice castle, 124, 133
Jászi, Oscar, 308 n., 310 n.
Jażdżewski, Konrad, 202 n., 203 n., 205 n.
Jeans, Sir James, 452
Jednota, Slovak Catholic newspaper, 534
Jefferson, Thomas, 456
Jelen, Alois, 125
Jellinek, George, 409, 412
Jerome, 214
Jesenský, Janko, 46, 47, 48
Jesuits, Czech, in Latin America, 517
Jesus, 287
Jihoamerický Čechoslovák, periodical 536
Jíra, Jaroslav, art critic, 175
Jíra, Jaroslav, 396 n., 425, 433 n.; biography of, 640
Jirák, Karel Boleslav, 14, 119, 129, 133; biography of, 640
Jirásek, Alois, 34, 54, 177, 516
Jiránek, Miloš, 150
Jireček, Hermenegild, 250, 252, 389, 425 n., 486
Jireček, Josef, 389, 486
Joannes Nepomucensis, 383
Johannes Noviforensis (*see* John of Neumarkt)
Johannes of Opava, 156 n., 145
John VIII, Pope, 109
John Mandeville, Book of, 164
John of Humpolec, 122
John of Jenštein, 112 ff.
John of Neumarkt, the influence of, 112-5, 145, 156
John of Středa (Neumarkt), Bishop (*see* John of Neumarkt)
John of Teplá, 114, 115
Jonáš, Charles, 550
Jonata of Vysoké Mýto, 474
Josef II, Emporer, 148, 383
Journalism, Czech, 530; Karel Havlíček Borovský, the founder of modern, 530; (*see also* Newspapers, of Czechs...)
Journalism, Czech, in the U.S., early, 546-51; Vojta Náprstek and founding of the *Flug-Blätter* of Milwaukee, 546; *Slowan Amerikánský*, 547; *Národní Noviny*, 547; August Geringer and founding of the *Svornost*, 548; *Amerikán*, 549, 550; *Slavie*, 550; *Dennice Novověku*, 550; *Dělnické Listy*, 550; *Pokrok*, 551; *Katolické Noviny*, 551; *Hlas*, 551; *Katolík*, 551; *Národ*, 551; (*see also* Newspapers of Czechs and Slovaks abroad)
Journalism, Slovak, 533; (*see also* Newspapers, of Czechs and Slovaks abroad)
Jungmann, Josef, 34, 43, 94, 177, 245, 314
Jurisprudence, 405-13

Kabátník of Litomyšl, Martin, 482
Kabeláč, Miloslav, 130
Kaderka, 417 n.
Kadlec, Karel, 392
Kahn, Richard, 462
Kallab, Jaroslav, 317, 407, 412-3, 433
Kolařík, Col. Ubald, 487
Kolinčiak, Janko, 45
Kalivoda, Leopold, 530
Kalousek, Josef, 248, 252-3, 278, 388
Kalvoda, 150
Kamb, river, 193
Kaminsky, Howard, 210, 217 n., 223 n.; biography of, 641
Kämmel, O., 193
Kamp, Jan, 474
Kandinsky, 169
Kanon st. Vjačeslava, 111
Kant, Immanuel, 34, 246, 257, 331, 332 n. 406-7, 412-3, 452, 453, 454
Kaplan, V., 480
Kapras, Jan, 392, 394, 396 n.
Karpat, Josef, 393
Katolické Noviny, 551
Katolík, 551
Kaván, 150
Kejř, Jiří, 243
Kelsen, Hans, 331 n., 405-7, 413

Index

Kerner, Robert J., 397 n.
Kierkegaard, 284
Kiev Leaflets, 110
Kisch, Bruno, 467
Klácel, František Matouš, 55, 314, 551
Klácel, Ladimír, (*see*, Klácel, František Matouš)
Kleinmeisters, 123
Kleskeň, Juraj, 535
Kliment, J., 228 n., 233 n., 243
Klimkovič, Fr., 150
Klostermann, Karel, 54
Knapp, Viktor, 402 n.
Kniha Drnovská, 381, 389
Kniha Rožmberská, 30, 381, 394
Kniha Tovačovská, 381, 387, 389
Knight, Frank, H., 337, 338
Knüpfer, Beneš, 150
Kočvara, Stephen, 396 n.
Koerner, Leon, 526
Kohák, Erazim V., 283; biography of, 641
Kohn, J., 317
Kojan, Jan, 153
Kokoschka, Oskar, 142
Kolár, Josef Jiří, 55
Kollár, Jan. 34, 45, 268, 314
Komenský, Jan Amos (*see* Comenius, John Amos)
Komenský University, Bratislava, 392, 393
Kopecký, Joseph, 514
Kopecký, Václav, 74
Kopitar, Bartoloměj, 386
Korbel, Josef, 282, 399 n.
Korbel, Mario, 178
Korbel, Pavel, 416 n.
Korczek Bible, the, 162
Kořenský, Josef, 486, 520
Kořízek, Frank, 550
Kornel of Všehrdy, Viktorin, 32, 381, 386
Korowicz, Marek, 206 n.
Kosárek, Adolf, 150
Koschin reports, 416 n., 417 n.
Kosciusko, Thaddeusz, 57
Kosmas, 20
Kossuth, Louis, 57
Kostka, 177
Kostka of Postupice, Lord Albert, 239, 240
Kostrzewski, Jozef, 203 n.
Kotík, Pravoslav and Jan, 152
Koubek, Jan Pravoslav, 386
Kozák, J. B., 285, 317

Koželuh, Leopold, 139
Koželuhová, Helena, 64, 417 n.
Kozuri, František, 530
Kráľ, Janko, 45
Král, Jiří, 487
Král Josef, 316, 317
Králík, Oldřich, 67
Královédvorský rukopis (*see Dvůr Králové, Manuscript of*)
Královská česká společnost nauk, 34
Kramář, 207, 283
Kramoris, Ivan I., 50
Krasko, Ivan, 46
Kratochvíl, Jar., 179
Krčméry, Štefan, 50
Krejčí, F. V., 285, 317
Krejčí, Iša, 130
Krejčí, Jaroslav, 279
Kremlička, Rudolf, 151, 152
Kreuz Brothers, 526
Kreybich, František, 485
Křička, Jaroslav, 130
Křička, Petr, 36
Křižík, Czech inventor, 481
Křížkovský, Pavel, 125
Krofta, Kamil, 260, 261
Krok, periodical, 35
Krommer-Kramář, František, 139
Kronika trojánská, the first Czech printed book, 473-4
Krumlov Madonnas, 176
Krusch, B., 190
Kuba, 150
Kubelík, Jan, 131
Kubelík, Rafael, 132, 522
Kuběna, John R., 515
Kubíček, 177
Kubín (Coubine), Otakar, 152
Kubišta, Bohumil, 152
Kučera, Henry, 93; biography of, 641
Kuchař, Karel, 488
Kukučin, Martin (*see* Bencúr, Matěj)
Kun, Bela, 364
Kundera, Milan, 18, 23, 27
Kunský, J., 487
Kupecký, Jan, 142, 148
Kupka, František (Frank, Franz), 152, 167-74
Kutná Hora, 260, 471, 475
Kuznetsov, Anatoli, 23
Kybal, Milič, 516; biography of, 641
Kybal, Vlastimil, 259, 261, 516, 521

Labadie, Jean de, 504
Labadists, 504
Labor legislation, in Czechoslovakia, 365-6
Labuda, Professor, 203 n., 204, 205 n., 206 n.
Labyrinth of the World and the Paradise of the Heart, The, by Comenius, 313
Lada, Josef, 153
Ladd-Franklin, Christine, 450
Ladislav Posthumus, King of Bohemia, 226
Lakeman, Enid, 419 n., 421 n., 422 n., 423 n.
Lambert, James D., 421 n., 422 n., 423 n.
Land reform, in Czechoslovakia, 359, 367, 368, 370
Languages, Czech (*see* Czech, language)
Languages, Slovak, Western dialect, 44; Central dialect, 44; (*see also* Literature, Slovak; Slovak, language)
Lány, 317
Lapôtre, A., French Jesuit, 262
Larionov, 169
Latin America, Czechs and Slovaks in, 516-22
Lauda, 177
Law, automatic creation of, 409
Law, Brno School of, 405-13
Law, Chair of history of Czech law established, 390
Law, concept of, 408-9
Law, in Czechoslovakia, 379 ff.; origin and development of the study of history of law, 381-95; the Czechoslovak constitutions of 1920, 1948 and 1960, 396-404; the Brno School of Jurisprudence, 405-13; election laws and democratic government, 414-24; criminological and socio-political aspects of legislation on abortion, 425-45; bibliography on, 603-6
Law, dynamic theory of, 409
Law, German, 391
Law, history of, in Czechoslovakia, 381-95; first lectures on the history of Moravian law, 383; Chair of history of Czech law established, 390; history of law studied in Slovakia, 393-4
Law, of towns, 382
Law, old literature, in Bohemia, 381-2; in Moravia, 381-2
Law, provincial, in Bohemia, 381 ff.; in Moravia, 381 ff.
Law, pure theory of, 405-13
Law, theory of, 405-13
Law, Vienna School of, 405-7, 413
Law of causality, 409
Lebeda, 150
Lebedev, A. P., 262
Legal norm, 407-9
Legal order, its hierarchical structure, 408-9
Legal science, Communist, 411
Legend of St. Catharine, 21
Legend of St. Procopius, 21
Legislatures, two chamber system, 414
Lehký, Richard, 522
Leisner, George, 178
Lelli (Laelius), Theodore, Bishop of Feltre, 232
Leo of Rožmitál, 483
Leopold, II, 34
Lerner, Max, 305 n.
Leszno, in Poland, 493
Lettenbauer, Wilhelm, 109
Lex imperfecta, 407
Lex lata et ferenda, 411
Lexa, John G., 414; biography of, 642
Lhoták, Kamil, 153
Libice, of the Slavniks, 207
Liběchov castle, 149
Liefmann, J., 330 n., 336
Liesler, Josef, 153
Limbourg brothers, 159
Linda, J., 255
Lindner, Gustav Adolf, 314
Linguistics, Czech contribution to, 93-104; contribution of Great Moravia to, 105-11; influence of John of Neumarkt, 112-5
Linguistics, in Czechoslovakia, bibliography on, 567-70
Linhart, J., 467
Lippert, Julius, 391
Literacy, 303
Literary criticism, Czech, 17-27; and the Communists, 21, 23, 27; between the two World Wars, 17; recent, 17-28; Communist, of Čapek, 74
Literary history, Czech, 17-27; and the Communists, 21, 23, 27
Literátská bratrstva, 122
Literature, American, in Czech translation, 54, 55, 56
Literature, Czech, humanistic and demo-

cratic thought in, 29-38; two paradoxes of, 39-43; traditions of, in exile, 83-90; recent history and criticism of, 17-28; legacy of Karel Čapek, 60-7; Karel Čapek and Communism, 68-75; art of Jan Čep, 76-82; 19th century, on America, 51-9; bibliography on, 564-7
Literature, Czech, humanistic and democratic thought in, activities of Cyril and Methodius, 29; oldest religious songs, 29; The *Cosmas Chronicle* of Bohemia, 30; the *Czech Alexandreis*, 30; *Dalimil's Chronicle*, 30; *Rožmberk's Book*, 30; *An Exposition of Bohemian Law*, 30; Hussite reformation, 31; John Hus, 31; Unitas Fratrum, 32; Peter Chelčický, 32; Renaissance era, 32; Czech Reformation, 33; John Amos Comenius, 33; Golden Era of Czech literature, 33; Counter-reformation, 34; National revival, 34
Literature, Czech, in exile, 83-90; Egon Hostovský, 76; Jan Čep, 76-82
Literature, Czech, on America, 51-9; Karel Havlíček Borovský, 51-3; Josef Kajetán Tyl, 53-4; Josef Jiří Kolár, 55; *Slovník naučný*, 56; Božena Němcová, 57-8; Josef Václav Frič, 57, 58
Literature, Czech, originality of, 42
Literature, in Czechoslovakia, anthologies of, 566-7
Literature, Slovak, 44-50; Slovak literary language, development of, 44; Ľudovít Štúr and his School, 44-5; Romanticism, 45; Realism, 45-6; Symbolism, 46; Surrealism, 46; "Davists", 46; post World War I era, 47; era of the so called Slovak State, 47; three exiles, 47-9; under the Communists, 49
Literature, Soviet, 23, 24
Literature and literary criticism, in Czechoslovakia, 15 ff.; bibliography on, 564-7
Litoměřice-Třeboň Bible, the, 165
Locke, 34
Lolek, 150
Long Parliament, 493
Longfellow, Henry W., 55-6
Lorch (Laureacum), 191, 194, 199
Lorch-Passau, 199
Lorenz, O., 252
Loserth, Johann, 210, 252, 391
Louis XI, King of France, 225, 230, 232 n., 238, 239, 241
Louis the German, 190, 191
Louis the Rich, Duke of Bavaria, 229 n.
Loukotka, Čestmír, 520
Lowenbach, Jan, 130
Lower Austria, 190, 193, 198
Lucretius, 22
Luden, 246
Ludmila (*see* St. Ludmila)
Lukács, George, 19
Lukša, Frank E., 515
Luksche, Jan, 384
Lulby, composer, 134
Lumír, 56
Lusatia, 203, 205, 206; Lusatian culture, 203; Lusatian monarch, 205;
Luther, M., 301, 313
Lützow, Count Francis, 43 n.
Luxeil, 197
Luxemburg, Rosa, 88
Luyton, Charles, 122
Lydius, Balthasar, 212

Maastricht, 183
Macaulay, 253
McDonald, Donald A., 463
Macek, Josef, 317, 363
Mácha, Karel Hynek, 20, 21, 35, 39, 40, 41, 43 n.
Machal, J., 256
Machát, František, 487
Machek, Antonín, 149
Machotka, Otakar, 297, 317, 318; biography of, 642
Macpherson, 255
Maeterlinck, Maurice, 62
Magyarization, 310
Mahomet (Mohammed), 233
Main, river, 186, 191
Mair, Dr. Martin, 229, 230, 232, 239, 241, 243
Maistre de, 293
Maiwald, Karel, 317, 374
Majerník, Cyprián, 153
Makovička, Emanuel, 314
Makovský, 177
Malevitch, 169
Malouel, Jean, 165
Malý, Jakub, 55, 56
Mánes, Antonín, 149, 177
Mánes, association of artists, 151
Manouvrier, 505
Mantua, Congress of, 230, 240

Mannheim Orchestra, 135
Manuscripts of *Dvůr Králové* and *Zelená Hora*, 270; (*see also Dvůr Králové, Manuscript of*)
Mařák, Julius, 150
Mareš, V. F., 107
Maresh, Henry R., 510 n., 514
Marie Theresa, Empress, 383
Marini, Antoine, 226, 228, 229 n., 230, 231, 232, 239, 241, 243, 244
Maritain, J., 456
Marold, Luděk, 150
Maróthy-Šoltésová, Elena, 46
Marr's language theory, 104
Martin of Tišnov, 475
Martinů, Bohuslav, 130, 131, 133
Marx, Karl, 17-22, 24-7, 72, 74, 257
Maryland, 502, 503, 504; settling of, 503; map of, by Augustine Heřman, 503
Masaryk, Jan, 515
Masaryk, Tomáš Garrigue, 12, 35, 64, 201, 207, 259, 299, 301, 304, 407, 418, 456, 539, 540, 543, 550, 551; and Austria, 271, 273; and Czech democratic ideology, 269, 270; and Palacký, 269, 270; and platonism, 287, 288, 289, 290; and positivism, 285, 286, 291, 292; and revolution, 275; as historian, 248, 254-7; as philosopher, 283, 284; as political scientist, 278; as sociologist, 314, 315, 316, 317; Čapek's conversations with, 68; conception of Czech history, 287, 290, 293; critical platonist, 289, 290, 291, 293, 294; founder of *Naše Doba*, 280; humanitarian philosophy of, 269, 270; idea of Czechoslovak democracy, 283; opinion about "American materialism", 53 n.; writings on, 254 n., 314 n.
Masaryk, Tomáš Garrigue, author of, *Jan Hus*, 248; *Světová Revoluce*, 248, 279; *Rusko a Evropa*, 285, 287; *Versuch einer konkreten Logic*, 285; *Concrete Logic*, 286, 287; *Handbook of Sociology*, 286; *Social Question*, 286; *Concerning the Study of Poetry*, 286, 293; *Talks with Karel Čapek*, 287; *Blaise Pascal*, 287; *Karel Havlíček*, 248;
Masaryk Academy, 280
Masaryk Academy of Work Management, 479
Masaryk Sociological Society, 317
Masaryk University, in Brno, 392, 405, 456

Massachusetts, 223
Matěj of Janov (*see* Matthew of Janov)
Matějček, Antonín, 157, 175
Matějka, Jerry Vrchlický, General, 515
Matějka, Ladislav, 105; biography of, 642
Matějowský, W., 515
Mathesius, Vilém, 14, 96, 97, 101, 102, 103, 317
Matiegka, Jindřich, 317, 458-61, 505
Matocha, B. F., 515
Matthew of Arras, 175
Matthew of Cracow, 112
Matthew of Janov, 31, 211
Matthias, Corvinus, King of Hungary, 231 n., 232, 239
Matthias, Emperor, 484
Matula, 317
Maugham, Somerset, 23, 94
Maulbertsch, F. A., 148
Maxmilian II of Hapsburg, 122
Mayr-Hanreich, 417 n.
Medicine, in Czechoslovakia, bibliography on, 611-5
Medieval painting, in Bohemia, 156-66; in Slovakia, 146
Medňanský, Ladislav, 150
Melantrich, Jiří, 33
Melka, Čeněk, 149
Melodramas, 127
Mercatov, Gerardus, 483
Mercereau, Alexandre, 170
Merkl, Adolf, 408, 413
Merovingian dynasty, 199
Mertl, Jan, 280
Merton, R. K., 297 n.
Meshchaninov, Ivan Ivanovich, 104
Messer, Richard, 28
Methodius, 94, 105 ff.; *A Life of Methodius*, 106; (*see also* Cyril and Methodius)
Meung, Jean de, 22
Míča, František Adam, 139
Míča, František (Francis) Václav, 124, 139
Míček, Eduard, 514
Michal, Jan M., 372, 373, 375; biography of, 643
Microscopy, capillary, 467; X-ray, 467; electron, 467
Migration, of Czechs and Slovaks, 528, 529; to Latin America, 520-1, 522; (*see also* Emigration; Czechs and Slovaks abroad)

Milan, Duchy of, 239
Milíč of Kroměříž, 31, 112, 113, 114
Miliduch, 206
Milikan, 454
Mill, John Stuart, 285, 314, 418
Milo, monk, 188, 189, 190, 191, 194, 198
Milton, John, 43 n.
Mináč, Vladimír, 24
Minorities, 379-8
Minority representation, 419
Mises, L. v., 338 n.
Mladá Boleslav, 475, 483
Mladá Fronta, 441
Moderní Stát, political revue, 280
Modráček, 317
Mojmír, 206; Mojmír Confederacy of Great Moravia, 206
Moldavia-Wallachia lowland, 202
Molière, 402
Molitor, Joseph, 551
Monse, Josef Vratislav, 383, 384, 385
Monte, Philip de, 122
Montesquieu, 34
Moore, Henry, 178
Moravia, 183, 198, 201, 203, 204, 206, 207; (*see also* Great Moravia)
Moravian Gate, 203
Moravian Brethern, 121
Morawetz, Oskar, 132
Moreau, Edouard de, 183, 190, 195 n.
Moro, Cristoforo, Doge of Venice, 231, 233, 238
Morphology, 102
Moschelesová, Julie, 487
Mozart, W. A., 123, 124; similarity of his music to that of František Xaver Richter, 136; his visits to Mannheim, 137; Josef Mysliveček's influence on, 139
Mráz, Andrej, 50
Mrkvička, O., 149
Mrštík, Alois, 35
Mucha, Alfons, 150, 151
Mukařovský, Jan, 18, 19, 20, 24, 25, 27, 40, 43 n., 102, 103
Müller, Jan Kryštov, 484
Munch, Charles, 131
Munch, Edvard, 151
Munk, Frank, 281, 282
Münster of Basel, Sebastian, 484
Mural painting and manuscript illumination of the Romanesque period, 142
Museum Království českého, 273
Museum of Modern Art, New York, 178

Music, Czech, in 18th century, influence on classical music, 134-40; influence on Gluck, Haydn and Mozart, 136, 137, 138, 139; influence on Beethoven, 139; Jan Václav Stamic, 135, 136; other Czech composers at Mannheim, 136; Benda family, 137; Jiří Anton (Georg) Benda, 137-8; Czech composers in Paris, 138; Josef Mysliveček, 139; Czech composers in Vienna, 139; František Václav Míča, 139
Music, Czech, universality of, 39
Music, in Czechoslovakia, 119-33; origins of, 120; religious songs, 120; Hussite hymns, 121; during the reign of Rudolf II, 122; after the Battle of White Moutain, 122; "Kleinmeisters", 123; in 18th century, 123-4, 134-40; Czech renascence, 125; Antonín Dvořák, 126; Zdeněk Fibich, 127; Jos. Bohuslav Foerster, 127; Dvořák's School, 128 ff.; Vítězslav Novák and Slovak music, 129; Bohuslav Martinů, 130, 131; contemporary composers, 130; performing artists, 131; musicians abroad, 130, 131; bibliography on, 581-4
Music and fine arts, in Czechoslovakia, 117 ff.; bibliography on, 581 ff.
Mussorgsky, M. P., 128
Myslbek, Josef Václav, 175, 177
Myslbek, association of artists, 152
Mysliveček, Josef, 123, 139
Mysliveček-Venatorini, Joseph (*see* Mysliveček, Josef)
Myth, in literature, 21

Nachtigal, Rajko, 107
Naples, Kingdom of, 225
Náprstek, Vojta, 546
Národ, Benedictine Press, 551
Národní Noviny, 51, 530, 547
Naše Doba, 280
Našinec, 515
National emancipation, 40
National enterprises (národní podniky), attitude of, toward pregnant employees, 439
National income and product, in Czechoslovakia, 373-4
National revival, Czech, 21, 27, 34, 35, 94, 302, 305, 382
Nationalism, 259, 383
Naturalism, 77, 78

Nationalistic Communism, 320, 322; desirability of, 322 n., desirability of in China, 322 n.; probability of, 322, 324; probability of in Albania, 322-3; probability of in China, 322, 324; probability of in Czechoslovakia, 322, 323, 324; probability of in East Germany, 322-4; probability of in Hungary, 322; probability of in Poland, 322-3; probability of vs. revolution, 322, 323, 324;
Natural sciences, in Czechoslovakia, bibliography on, 609 ff.
Nature of reality, 450
Navrátil, Josef, 149
Necessity, state of (see State of necessity)
Nechleba, Vratislav, 151
Negro spirituals, 126
Nehněvajsa, Jiří, 319; biography of, 643
Nejedlý, Zdeněk, 21, 132, 133; on Masaryk, 284
Nejedlý, Otakar, 151
Němcová, Božena, 18, 21, 35, 55, 57-8, 76, 81, 85, 90, 177
Němec, Jaroslav, 14, 381, 382, 471; biography of, 643
Němec, Ludvík, 262; biography of, 644
Němeček, Zdeněk, 54
Neo-Kantian philosophy, 406
Neruda, Jan, 35
Netherlands, 183, 184
Netherlands Schools in music, 121
Neubauer, Zdeněk, 281
Neumann, Josef, 518
Neumann, Stanislav Kostka, 64
New Amsterdam, settling of and Augustine Heřman, 501-2
New Europe, The, periodical, 543
New York State Hospitals, 505
News from Czechoslovakia, 439 n.
Newspapers, Czech, Karel Havlíček Borovský, 530
Newspapers, of Czechs and Slovaks abroad, first Czech newspapers, 530, 533; first Slovak newspapers, 533-5; in Africa, 544; in Australia and New Zealand, 536, 537; in Canada and South America, 535, 536; in Europe, 537-44; tables, 531, 532; (see also Journalism)
Newton, Isaac, 449, 450, 451, 452, 455; Newton's theory of knowledge, 449; Newton's theory of colors, 451
Nexus causal and logical, 406
Nezval, Vítězslav, 61

Neveux Georges, 131
Nicaea, 214
Nicholas of Brno, 146, 165
Nicholas of Kroměříž, 112
Nicholas of Pelhřimov, Bishop, 211-4, 217-21
Nieder Altaich, 199
Niederle, Lubor, 188, 192, 193, 194, 200, 209 n.
Nigrin, Christian, 494
Nikolau, Stanislav, 487
Nitra, 183, 206
Nobility, Bohemian and Moravian, 308; in Slovakia, 310
Nomokanon, 180, 109
Noricum, Roman province of, 189
Norm, basic, 409; higher and lower, 408-9; legal, 407-9; sanctioned, 407
Normative theory, 405-13; Czech, 405-6, 410
Normological theory (see Normative theory)
Normology, 405-7, 410
Norms, hierarchy of, 408-9; moral, 407
North Korea, changes in, 324; probability of anti-Communist revolution, 322;
North Viet-Nam, changes in, 324; probability of anti-Communist revolution, 322
Nosek, Jindřich, 396 n.
Nová Říše, monastery at, 161
Novák, Arne, 17
Novák, Vítězslav, 127, 129
Novák, V. V., 153
Nováková, Tereza, 35
Novomeský, Ladislav, 47
Novotná, Jarmila, 522
Novotný, Antonín, 403
Novotný, Václav, 259, 261
Nový Domov, periodical, 516
Nowak, Willy, 142

Obrdlík, 317
Očadlík, Mirko, 13
Occupational distribution, in Czechoslovakia, 360-1; agricultural employment, 368; middle class character, 370; social legislation, 361; unemployment, 366; wage categories, 369
Očko of Vlašim, John, 112, 144
Okáli, Daniel, 47
Old Church Slavonic, 105 ff.
Old Slavic language, 29

Oldřich of Břeclav, Duke, 384
Olomouc Bible, 162
Olomouc, University of, 383, 385
Ondřej of Dubá, 31, 381
Orel, Dobroslav, 132
Orphism, 169
Országh-Hviezdoslav, Pavel, 45, 46
Orwell, George, 20, 23
Osma, 151, 152
Ostrčil, Otakar, 127
Osuský, Štefan, 539
Osváth, Julius, 393
Oswiecim (Auschwitz), City and Duchy in Upper Silesia, 226
Ott, Emil, expert on Canon law, 388
Ottův slovník naučný, 98
Ovid, 22

Pächt, Otto, 159
Paderlík, Arnošt, 153
Paine, Thomas, 546, 548
Painters, Czech, Frank Kupka, 167-74
Painting, in Czechoslovakia, 141-55; mural painting and manuscript illumination of the Romanesque period, 142; Gothic murals, 143; Gothic manuscript illumination, 143; Gothic painted panels, 144; medieval paintings in Slovakia, 146; Renaisance painting in Bohemia, 147; Baroque painting in Bohemia, 147; Rococo painting in Bohemia, 148; Josef Mánes, 149; modern landscape painting, 149; contemporary Czech and Slovak painting, 152
Painting, in Czechoslovakia, bibliography on, 548-9
Palacký, František, 34, 183, 205 n., 245 ff., 258, 259, 278, 304, 314, 486; and Czech political ideology, 268, 269, 270; and Hussite revolution, 268; and Jaroslav Goll, 259, 390; and Karel Havlíček, 272; policy of Austroslavism of, 271; studies on history of Czech and Slavic laws, 385, 386; *Brief View of Czech History*, 247
Palacký, Jan, 485
Palda, Lev, 550
Palko, Francis Xaver, 148
Palkovič, Jiří, 34
Pampaedia, by Comenius, 495, 496
Panachage, 423
Panaugia, by Comenius, 495
Panegersia, by Comenius, 494-5

Panlottia, 496
Panici brothers, illuminators, 163
Panici-Yunkers, 163
Pannonia, 197; Pannonian plain, 203
Pannuthesia, by Comenius, 497
Panorthosia, by Comenius, 496
Panslavic Congress, 207
Panslavism, 35
Pansophiae prodromus, by Comenius, 493
Pansophic college in London, 494
Pansophy, 493, 495
Pantaxia, by Comenius, 495
Panuška, 150
Papermills, in Bohemia, 473
Pareto, Vilfredo, 315, 338
Paris, City of, 232
Paris, University of, 233
Parisian Six, 89
Parler, Peter, 175
Parliamentary debates, 417
Pasternak, Boris, 23, 89, 90
Pastora, Josef, 551
Paul II, Pope, 228
Paul of Jenštein, 112
Pavlica, James, 515
Pavlů, Bohdan, 540
Pečírka, Josef, 43 n.
Pekař, Josef, 248, 249, 253, 259-60, 261, 286, 288; and Masaryk, 259
Pekk, Jan Hazukův, 474
Pelcl, 34
People's democracy, 397, 399
Periodicals, Czech and Slovak abroad, type and number published in 1925 and 1963, by countries and compared with population figures, 531; type and number published in the U.S., from 1860-1963, compared with population figures, 532; (*see also* Newspapers, of Czechs and Slovaks abroad)
Permanent International Court of Justice, 498
Peroutka, Ferdinand, 280, 317
Persians, 204
Pertz, 250
Pešánek, 178
Pěšina of Čechorod, Tomáš, Cannon, 382
Peška, Zdeněk, 279
Peterka, O., 391
Petersen, L., 463
Phenomenology, 286, 292
Philip the Good, Duke of Burgundy, 232 n., 231

Philippovich, 338 n.
Philipse, Frederick, founder of Yonkers, 524
Philipse Manor Hall, 524
Philosophy, Czech, 285, 287; (*see also* Comenius, John Amos; Masaryk, Tomáš Garrigue; Purkyně, Jan Evangelista)
Philosophy, of democracy, and Karel Čapek, 65 ff.
Philosophy, in Czechoslovakia, 285, 287; Masaryk and Plato in the 20th century, 283-94; bibliography on, 571-4
Philosophy, neo-Kantian, 406
Philosophy, political, Palacký, 269; Masaryk, 269, 270
Phonology, 97, 99, 100, 101
Photian schism, 263
Photius, Patriarch, vindication of, 262-3
Physical anthropology (*see* Anthropology, physical)
Physical sciences, in Czechoslovakia, bibliography on, 615-8
Piabia, 169
Piasts, 207
Picasso, 170
Piepenhagen, August, 149
Pinkas, Soběslav, 150
Pirandello, Luigi, 62, 63
Pirenne, Henri, 22
Písecký, Václav, 33
Pistorius, Jiří (George), 39, 85, 86; biography of, 644
Pišút, Milan, 50
Pius II, Pope, 224, 228 n., 229 n., 230, 231, 232, 239, 240, 243, 473
Plato, 287, 288, 289, 290, 291; Masaryk and, 283-94
Platonism, 287, 288, 289, 290, 291, 293, 294
Plotinus, 289
Plavec, Jos., 133
Plzeň (Pilsen), 477, 480
Pochyla, B. H., Colonel, 515
Poe, Edgar Allan, 56
Poetism, 87, 88
Poetry, Czech, 39; European, 41
Poincaré, Henri, 452, 453
Poitiers, 199
Pokrok, 551
Polach, Jaroslav G., 329; biography of, 644
Poland, 225, 234, 243; changes in, 324; probability of anti-Communist revolution, 321-2; probability of democratization, 323; probability of nationalistic Communism, 322-3;
Polášek, Albin, 178
Poldi Works, 480
Political futures, 319; anti-Communist revolution (*see this topic for specific reference*); democratization (*see this topic for specific seference*); nationalistic Communism (*see this topic for specific reference*)
Political parties, 414-6, 418; bosses, 417; Central Executive Committee, 417; discipline, 416-8; "empty bottles with different labels", 421; in exile, 418; parliamentary club, 417; party domination, 417; recall (of members of parliament), 416, 417; splinter parties, 415, 421, 422
Political science, in Czechoslovakia, 277-82; the Hapsburg era, 277; the First Republic, 1918-1938, 278; the Nazi occupation, 1938-1945, 281; the post-war struggle between democracy and Communism, 1945-1948, 281; the Communist era, 282; scholarly journals, 280; (*see also* Democracy, Czechoslovak)
Political science, in Czechoslovakia, bibliography on, 597-603
Pollak, O. J., 469
Polná trial, 270
Poničan, Ján, 47
Popularity ("lidovost"), in literary criticism, 19
Population of Czechoslovakia, occupation distribution in 1921 and 1930, 360; occupational distribution in different provinces in 1930, 361
Populism, 308, 309
Positivism, 285, 286, 291, 292
Postl, Karel, 149
Postilla, by John Hus, 31
Poupě, Fr. Ondřej, Czech brewmaster, 480
Pragmatism, 299, 305
Pragmatism, American, influence on Karel Čapek, 68, 69
Prague, 176, 192, 201, 214, 215, 218, 220, 221; Prague of the Přemyslides, 207; Praguers, 212
Prague Linguistic Circle, 17, 93, 95-9, 101-4

Prague masters, 210, 211, 222
Prague Polytechnicum, 478
Prague, University of, 233, 251, 259, 317, 385, 388, 405; Czech, restoration of, 272, 277; division into the Czech University and German University in 1882, 390; naming of "Universitas Carolina", and of "Deutsche Universität in Prag", in 1920, 392; closing of Czech University in 1939, 395 (*see also* Charles University)
Praha, Texas, 513
Prasek, Vincenc, 389
Prášek, 417 n.
Práva městská, codification of the Town Laws, 382
Pravda Russkaia, the oldest Russian code, 385
Právnická jednota, organization of Czech lawyers, 388
Právník, first Czech legal journal, 388, 391
Právny Obzor, Slovak periodical, 393
Pražák, Jiří, 278
Pražské zlomky hlaholské, 29
Prefát of Vlkanov, Oldřich, 484
Pregnancy, artificial interruption of (*see* Abortion)
Preinlein, Matthew, 473-5
Preisler, Jan, 151
Přemysl Otakar II, 30, 113, 252, 260
Přemyslides, 207
Přerovský, I., 467
Prescott, William H., 55
Presl, 35
Press, Czech and Slovak (*see* Newspapers; Journalism)
Příbram, John, 211, 213, 215, 216
Printing, in Avignon, 471-2; in the Kingdom of Bohemia, 471
Printing, with movable type taught by Waldfogel, 472
Printing shop, of Unitas Fratrum, Mladá Boleslav, 475
Printing shops, in Bohemia, 473-5; in Moravia, 474-5
Přítomnost, weekly, 68
Prjatel Ludu, periodical, 541
Procházka, Adolf, 405, 409, 413; biography of, 644
Procházka, Antonín, 152
Procházka, Theodore, 258; biography of, 645

Procházka, Vladimír, 402
Professional Painters Brotherhood, 176
Progress, "Progressiveness", in literature, 20, 26
Proletarian art, 71-3
Prologue, 110
Proměny, a quarterly, 11
Proportional representation, 414, 417-8, 421-2
Prose, Czech, evaluation of, 43
Protectorate Bohemia and Moravia, 397
Provincialism, 299
Průcha, Jindřich, 150
Prusík, B., 463
Prussia, 225
Przerwa-Tetmajer, Kazimierz, 45
Puchner alterpiece, Master of, 146
Puchmajer, 34
Pujman, Ferd., 133
Punto, Giovanni (*see* Stich, Jan Václav)
Puritans, 223
Purkinje effect, in the evolution of scientific thought, 449-57
Purkinje phenomenon, 449, 450, 452; (*see also*, Purkyně, Jan Evangelista)
Purkyně, Cyril, 486
Purkyně, Jan Evangelista, 449-57, 462
Purkyně, Karel, 150
Purkyně University, 456

Raab, William, 463
Rabas, Václav, 153
Racek, Jan, 133
Rada, Vlastimil, 153
Radimský, L., 150
Rádl, Emanuel, 284, 286, 317
Radnitz, river, 186, 191
Radoff, Morris, 504
Räffelstatlen, the charter of, 193
Rainer, Václav Vavřinec, 148
Rais, Karel Václav, 54
Rajhrad altarpiece, Master of, 146, 164
Ramsden, E. H., 173
Ranke, Leopold v., 250
Rašín, A., 343
Rattermann, H. A., 501
Rauscher, Rudolf, 393
Rázus, Martin, 46, 49
Realism, 77
Realism, naive, 409
Reality, nature of, 449, 450, 455
Rechcigl, Miloslav Jr., 4, 14, 555; biography of, 645

Redisch, Walter, 462; biography of, 646
References, general, on Czechoslovakia, 608-10; (see also Bibliography on Czechoslovakia)
Reformation, 268, 269; Czech, 31, 33
Refugee industries, 525
Regensburg, 183, 186, 191-5, 199
Regnard, Jacques, 122
Reich, Edvard, 352 n.
Reine Rechtstheorie, 405 ff.
Reiner, 526
Religion, in Czechoslovakia, bibliography on (see Philosophy, in Czechoslovakia, bibliography on; History, in Czechoslovakia, bibliography on)
Religion, of Hussite Tabor, 210-23
Religious hymns, Czech, "Hospodine pomiluj ny", 120; "Svatý Václave, etc.", 121
Religious songs, Czech, 29
Renaissance, 32, 176, 177; painting in Bohemia, 147; sculpture, 177
Requin, Pierre Henri, Abbé, 471, 473
Retroactivity of laws, 410
Revolution of 1848, Czech, 250
Rezek, Antonín, 248, 253-4, 390
Rhine, 185, 187
Richard II, 25
Richter, Fr. X., 124, 136
Richter, Henry Wenceslaus, 519
Rickert, H., German philosopher, 330
Rieger, Bohuslav, 388
Rieger, František Ladislav, 35, 55, 56, 253, 254, 256
Riezler, Sigismund, 195
Rimbaud, 168, 172
Rinchnach, the monastery of, 193
Riolan, 469
Ripka, Hubert, 281, 397 n.
Robertson, Alec, 133
Robertson, 246
Rococo painting in Bohemia, 148
Rodin, sculptor, 168, 177
Roehr, Jan, 518
Roezl, Benedikt, 520
Rokycana, John, 32, 211-3, 215
Roman champêtre, 76
Roman Christians, 187, 198
Roman curia, 227, 231, 237
Roman Empire, 203
Romanesque mural paintings, 143
Romans, 187
Romantic movement, 305

Romanticism, European, 40
Rome, 221
Roosevelt, Franklin D., 514
Rosenmueller, František, 530
Rössler, Emil Franz, 390
Rostislav, Prince, 93, 190
Rouček, Joseph S., 245, 282, 313, 314 n.; biography of, 646
Rousseau, Jean Jacques, 34, 127, 138, 383
Roussel, Albert, 130
Rovnianek, Peter V., 524, 534
Roy, Vladimír, 46
Royal Bohemian Learned Society (see Královská česká společnost nauk)
Royal orchestras in Prague, 122
Royal Society of London, 452
Rožmberk's Book (see Kniha Rožmberská)
Ruben, Christian, 149
Rubeš, František Jaromír, 39
Rudaves, 203
Rudé Právo, 425 n., 439 n., 443
Rudolf II, Emperor, 122, 147, 151, 484
Rumania, changes in, 324; probability of anti-Communist revolution, 322;
Ruralism, 76
Russek, Senator, 515
Russia, 257
Russian Orthodoxy, 256
Rutta, Charles D., 515
Ruzicka, Joseph F., 526
Ryba, Jan Jakub, 125
Rychnovský, Jiří, 122
Rychtera, 417 n.

Šafařík, Pavel Josef, 34, 94, 177, 196, 245, 268, 314, 385
Šafránek, Miloš, 139
St. Adalbert (Vojtěch), 30, 201, 383
St. Amand, 183 ff.; the mission of, in the 7th century, 183-201
St. Augustine, Bishop of Hippo, 242
St. Boniface, 187, 199
St. Columbanus, 187, 197, 201
St. Emmeram, 187, 198
St. Florian, 189
St. Gallus, 198
St. Ludmila, 29, 30, 111, 383
St. Martin, 197
St. Paul, 287
St. Rupert, 198, 199
St. Severinus, 189
St. Vitus, Cathedral of, 175; Madonna, 163
St. Wenceslaus, 29, 30, 111, 383

Šalda, František Xaver, 36, 41, 43 n., 75, 317
Salzburg, 186, 199, 200
Salzman, Eric, 131
Samo, 186, 190 n., 191, 195-7, 204-7; Samo's State, 204-6
Sand, George, 76
Sander, Fritz, 417 n.
Sapir, Edward, 98
Sartre, Jean Paul, 23
Šašek of Bířkov, Václav, squire, 483
Saturník, Theodor, 392
Saunders, R. L. de C., 467
Saussure, Ferdinand de, 98
Sava-Drava interfluvium, 204
Sborník věd právních a státních, journal, 391
Sborník Historický, 253
Scandinavia, 234; Scandinavians, 207
Schäffle, A. E., 336
Scheinpflug, Olga, 70, 74
Schiller, Friedrich von, 42, 43 n.
Schmidt, Jan Ferdinand, 388
Schneider, Joseph Z., 477; biography of, 646
Scholars, Czech, education of, 300; social status of, 300; examples of, 301; comparison with the French, 304; comparison with the American, 305; comparison with the German, 305; under the Communists, 306
Scholarship, Czech, character of, 297-306; under the Communist rule, 298, 306
Scholarship, in Slovakia, 298
Scholarship, teamwork in, 305, 306
Scholastik, John, 108
Schopenhauer, Arthur, 406-7, 413, 452, 454, 456
Schultz, A. H., 506, 509 n.
Schumpeter, J. A., 335, 337, 338 n.
Schuylkill River Treaty, 500
Schwarz, Ernst, 193
Schwartz-Markovič, Edward, 534
Schwarzenberg, František, 282
Schweiger, Hanuš, 150
Science, Czech, 39; (*see also* Scholarship)
Science, in Czechoslovakia, bibliography on, 609 ff.
Science and technology, in Czechoslovakia, 447 ff; the Purkinje effect in the evolution of scientific thought, 449-57; Jindřich Matiegka and the anthropometric approach to the study of body composition, 458-61; contribution to the change in concept of circulation of the blood, 462-70; Prokop Waldfogel of Prague and the 15th century printers, 471-6; engineering until the Second World War, 477-81; geography, exploration and cartography, 482-9; bibliography on, 609 ff.
Sclavini, 202
Sculpture, in Czechoslovakia, 175; during the reign of Charles IV, 175; Beautiful Madonnas, 176; Josef Václav Myslbek, and his school, 177 ff.; constructivist movement, 178; abroad, 178; under the Communists, 178 ff.
Sculpture in Czechoslovakia, bibliography on, 548-9
Šebor, Miloš, 482; biography of, 647
Seckenheim, Battle of, 238
Šedivý, B., 401 n.
Sedláček, August, 486
Sedláček, Vojtěch, 153
Sedlec Antiphonary, 142, 161
Seeger, Joseph, 123
Šejnoha, Jaroslav, 167; biography of, 647
Seligman, R. A. 338
Šembera, Alois Vojtěch, 58, 386
Sensory perception, 452
Serbs, 204
Serfdom, 402
Seton-Watson, R. W., 543
Severyn, J., 474
Sgall, Petr, 104
Shakespeare, William, 18, 24, 26, 28, 42
Shary, John H., 525
Shils, Edward, 309 n.
Shoe industry (*see* Baťa, Tomáš)
Shoe production, in Czechoslovakia, 481 (*see also* Baťa, Tomáš)
Sigismund, Emperor, 164, 166
Silone, Ignazio, 89, 90
Silvester, Pope, 220
Šíma, Josef, 152
Simmel, Georg, 406, 413
Škoda Works, 477, 479, 522
Skřivánek, John M., 510; biography of, 647
Škrach, Vasil K., 317
Škréta, Karel, 147
Škroup, František, 125
Škvor, Jiří (George), 29; biography of, 647

Sládek, Josef Václav, 35, 54
Sládkovič, Andrej, 45
Sladkovský, Karel, 256, 275 n.
Slančíková-Timrava, Božena, 46
Slavic colonization, 202
Slavic Congress, 35, 207
Slavic literary language, the first Moravian codification of, 105-11
Slavic settlements, 194, 203
Slavíček, Antonín, 150, 177
Slavický, Klement, 130
Slavie, Czech newspaper, 547
Slávik, Juraj, 44, 48; biography of, 648
Slavniks, 207
Slavonia, 204
Slavs, 184, 186, 197, 198; of the Danube, 195, 199
Slávy dcera, 35
Slovak literary language, development of, 44; (*see also* Literature, Slovak)
Slovak literature (*see* Literature, Slovak)
Slovak National Council, 275
Slovak State, 397
Slovakia, under the Avars, 204; under the Mojmírs, 206
Slovaks, 207, 397; abroad (*see* Czechs and Slovaks abroad); political thinking of, 270 n., 271 n., 271
Slovan, 51-3
Slovenes, 184, 186-9, 196, 199, 200, 204
Slovenia, 185
Slovenská Jednota, periodical, 541
Slovenské Noviny, periodical, 537, 541
Slovenskje Národňje Noviny, periodical, 533
Slovenský Denník, 534
Slovenský Lud, 536
Slovenský Národ, 540
Slovník naučný, 56-7; (*see also Ottův slovník naučný*)
Slovo a slovesnost, 97, 101, 104
Slowan, periodical, 530
Slowan Amerikánský, 530, 547
Smetana, Augustin, 314
Smetana, Bedřich, 121, 125, 133, 177
Šnajdr, Václav, editor, 550
Sobota, Emil, 279, 281
Social Institute, Prague, 317
Social legislation, in Czechoslovakia, 365-6
Social sciences, in Czechoslovakia, bibliography on, 589 ff.
Social status of Czech scholars, 300

Social structure, 297
Socialism, 398, 403
Socialist realism, 18, 26, 77
Sociální revue, 317
Société d'Anthropologie de Paris, 505
Society, Czechoslovak, economic and social structure of, 359-72
Society, Czechoslovak, the role of intelligentsia in the development of, 307-12
Society of Czechoslovak Engineers, 479
Society of Jesus, Province of the Kingdom of Bohemia, 517
Sociologická revue, 317, 318
Sociologický sborník, 317
Sociology, in Czechoslovakia, 295 ff.; the development of, before World War II, 313-8; the character of Czech scholarship-contribution to the sociology of knowledge, 297-306; the role of the intelligentsia in the development of the Czechoslovak society, 307-12; anticipated changes in Czechoslovakia, 319-25
Sociology, in Czechoslovakia, bibliography on, 589-92
Sociology in Czechoslovakia, development of, 313-18; early ideas and concepts, 313 ff.; Tomáš G. Masaryk, 314 ff.; Eduard Beneš, 315; Inocenc A. Bláha, 316; other outstanding sociologists, 316 ff.; sociological periodicals, 317; under the Communists, 318
Sociology of knowledge, contribution of Czech scholarship to, 297-306
Socrates, 291
Sokol gymnastic movement, 207, 273
Solnař, Vl., 427 n., 428 n.
Sorabicus limes, 194
Šourek, Otakar, 133
Sova, Antonín, 35
Sovereignty, concept of, 410
Soviet constitution, 399-400
Soviet legislation, influence of, on Czechoslovak legislation, 426, 429, 441
Soviet Union, desirability of anti-Communist revolution, 321 n.; desirability of democratization, 323 n., probability of anti-Communist revolution, 321, 324; probability of democratization, 323-4; Soviet-Chinese schism, 324
Soviet-Chinese Schism, 324
Spahn, O., 336
Špála, Václav, 152

Spinka, brewmaster, 480
Spinka, Matthew, 493; biography of, 648
Spławinski, 207
Spranger, B., 147
Spring of Nations, 35
Spulber, Nicholas, 397 n.
Stability, 324-5; of technologically advanced satellites, 325
Stádnik, Miloš, 373
Stahel, Konrad, printer in Brno, 474
Stalin, Josef V., 104
Staller, George J., 376, 377
Stamic, Jan Václav, 124, 135, 136
Stamic, Johann Anton, 136
Stamic, Karl, 136
Stammler, R., 336
Stansel, Valentin, 519
Stašek, Antal, 54
State of necessity in justifying abortion, 427-8, 431, 432 n.
Statuta ducis Conradi, oldest code of laws in Moravia, 381, 384, 386-7
Štědroň, Bohumír, 133
Štefánek, Anton, 310 n., 311 n., 312 n., 317
Štefánik, Milan R., 207, 521
Steinach, W., 462
Štěpánek, Vladimír, 21
Štern Evžen, 317
Štetina (*see* Bakalář, Mikuláš)
Stewart, T. D., 505, 509 n.; biography of, 649
Stich, Jan Václav (Giovanni Punto), 138
Stieber, Miroslav, 392
Stiegler, G. J., 336
Stile rappresentativo, 122
Štítný of Štítný, Thomas, 31
Štorch, Karel, 314
Stravinsky, Igor, 130
Stretti-Zamponi, 150
Stříbrný, Jiří, 417 n.
Stříbrný, Zdeněk, 18, 24, 25, 28
Stricker, Salomon, 462
Strnadel, Antonín, 153
Strnadt, J., 194, 198
Strozzi, 148
Structural linguistics, 98, 99, 104
Štúr, L'udovít, 44, 45, 275 n., 533
Sturm, Rudolf, 51; biography of, 649
Štursa, Jan, 177
Stuyvesant, Peter, 502, 503
Suchoň, Eug., 129
Sudeten Germans, industries of, 363

Sugar, refining of, 479
Suk, Josef, 128
Šulák, L. J., 514
Sulfuric acid, Czech, production of, 479
Sully, Duke of, French statesman, 230
Supreme Court of Czechoslovakia, decisions of, 427 n., 433
Surrealism, 87, 88, 152; in Slovak literature, 46
Šusta, Josef, 260, 261
Švabinský, Max, 150, 151
Švambera, Václav, 485, 487
Svatopluk, Prince, 108
Svejda, Norma, 500, 504; biography of, 649
Světlá, Karolina, 35
Švihovský, Věnceslav, 540
Svoboda, weekly, 514
Svoboda, Emil, 279
Svoboda, V. A., 255
Svobodný Zítřek, periodical, 540
Svod zákonův slovanských, 425 n.
Svolinský, Karel, 153
Svornost, newspaper, 533, 548, 524
Swift, Jonathan, 62
Swiss Criminal Code of 1937, 427 n.
Sychra, Vladimir, 153
Sychrava, Lev, 539
Symbolism, 151
Syntax, 101, 102

Tabor, 210, 212, 214-7, 219-20, 222-3
Taborites, 212, 218
Táborský, Edward, 277, 281, 282, 398 n., 417 n., 418 n.; biography of, 650
Tabula iuris publici Marchionatus Moraviae, by J. V. Monse, 383
Tacitus, 187
Tadeáš of Hájek, 484
Tatbestand, 409
Talich, Václav, 131
Technical schools, in Czechoslovakia, 478
Technology, in Czechoslovakia, bibliography on, 618-20; (*see also* Engineering)
Teleology, 406-7, 411, 412
Telos (see Economic theory and teleological knowledge)
Ten Eyck, Andrew, 251
Tetzel, Gabriel, 483
Teutonic knights, Order of the, 225
Texas, Czechs in, 510-5
Texas, University of, 514, 515

Texaský Rolník, newspaper, 515
Textor, Lucy, E., 367, 370
Theodore, Carl, Elector of Pfalzbayern, 135
Theodoric, Master, 144
Theory of "two sides" of the state, 409
Thirty Years War, 493, 498
Thompson, Dorothy, on Karel Čapek, 62
Thomson, J. J., 454
Thun, Lev, 250
Thuroczy, Joannes, 475
Tichý, František, 153
Tisa-Danube mesopotamia, 203
Tkadleček, 114
Tkadlík, František, 149
Tobolka, Zdeněk, 278, 472
Tocqueville, Alexis de, 51, 54
Tokaj, 206
Tolstoy, Lev, 25, 313
Toman, Karel, 36
Tomaschek, Johann Adolf, 388
Tomášek, Jan Václav, 124, 129, 139
Tomaso da Modena, 144
Tomek, Václav Vladivoj (Wácslav Wladivoj), 248, 249-50, 252, 253, 258
Toscanini, A., 131
Tours, 197
Tovačovský of Cimburk, Ctibor, 32
Travaux du Cercle Linguistique de Praque, 97, 99, 101, 102
Trávníček, František, 104
Třeboň, Master, 145, 163
Triepel, 417 n.
Triner, James, 525
Trnka, Bohumil, 101, 102
Trnka, Jiří, 153, 179
Trnobranský, 417 n.
Trubetzkoy, Nicholas, 97, 99-101
Tschermak-Seysenegg, Armin, 456
Tulka, Josef, 150
Tůma, František (Francis), 123, 139
Tumlíř, Jan, 83; biography of, 650
Turgenev, Ivan, 25
Turks, 227, 228, 233, 234, 236, 237, 240-2
Turnovský, Jan Trojan, 122
Tvorba, political revue, 104
Tyl, Josef Kajetán, 22, 23, 40, 43 n., 53-4; and Karel Havlíček Borovský, 53; opinion of the United States by, 53
Tyrol, 186
Tyrš, Miroslav, 207

Ukraine, 202

Ullík, Hugo, 150
Umělecká Beseda, association of artists, 151
Uncle Tom's Cabin, 54, 55
UNESCO, 498
Unification of Czechs and Slovaks, 311
Union of Bohemian Brethern, 268, 269; (*see also* Unitas Fratrum)
Unitas Fratrum, 32, 33, 258, 268, 269, 493, 499
United Nations, 236, 498
United States, Czechs and Slovaks in, bibliography on, 620-3; (*see also* Czechs and Slovaks abroad)
United States, Czech opinion of, 51-9
U.S. National Museum, 505
Unity of the Brethern, in Texas, 513, 515; (*see also* Unitas Fratrum)
Universitas Carlo-Ferdinandea, in Prague, 385, 390, 392; (*see also* Prague, University of)
Universitas Carolina, in Prague, 392; (*see also* Charles University)
Upper Austria, 186, 188, 190, 193, 194, 198, 200, 201
Upper Silesia, 226
Úprka, Joža, 153
Urban, Milo, 47
Utraquist Church, 224, 225

Václav, Svatý (*see* St. Wenceslaus)
Vančura, Vladislav, 18, 23, 27, 82
Vančura, Zdeněk, 18, 23, 27
Vaněček, V., 425 n.
Vaňhal, Jan Křtitel, 139
Vaníček, Bedřich, 152
Vansová, Terezia, 45
Vascular tree, differences from elastic tubing, 463; in skeletal muscle, 467; responses of, 463; intrinsic disease of, 469
Vašica, Josef, 108, 109
Vavřinec of Rokycany, 474
Vavřínek, František, 279
Veblen, Thorstein, 335
Veigl, 178
Velislav Bible, 143
Verlett, Janetje, 502
Venice, Republic of, 226, 229 n., 231-2, 238-9
Vermeiren, Louise, 157
Vespucci, Amerigo, 516
Věstník, newspaper, 515
Via lucis, by Comenius, 494

Index

Vidal, G., 427 n.
Vienna, 205; Vienna School of Jurisprudence, 405-7, 413
Villen, Jacques, 170
Vinsalvo, Galfred de, 113
Vintíř (see Günther, German hermit)
Virgil, 199
Virginia, Czech immigrants in, 501
Virginia, map of, by Augustine Heřman, 503
Vistulan state, 206
Vitalis, Manaud, 472
Vitásek, František, 487
Vlach, Jan, 178
Vlček, Jaroslav, 39, 43 n., 50
Vlchek, Frank, J., 525
Vltava, river, 204
Vočadlo, O., 317
Vodička, Felix, 18
Vodňanský, Jan, 33
Vogl Garrett, Edith, 134; biography of, 650
Voigt, M. A., 384
Voix libre de la Bohême, La, 544
Vojtěch, Svatý (see St. Adalbert)
Volné Směry, art periodical, 151
Voltaire, 34, 134, 138
Voříšek, Czech composer, 139
Votruba, František, 49
Vratislav of Mitrovice, Václav, 484
Vráz, E. Stanislav, 486, 520
Vráz, Vlasta, 546; biography of, 650
Vrchlický, Jaroslav, 127, 177
Všehrd, organization of law students in Prague, 388
Vycpálek, 130
Vyšehrad, 206; *Vyšehrad Codex*, 142
Vyšší Brod Madonna, 144, 164

Wachau, 193
Wagner, Richard, 127
Waitz, 250
Waldes, Henry, manufacturer of zippers, 525
Waldfogel, Jiří, 471
Waldfogel, Prokop, 471-3
Waldhauser, Conrad (Konrad), 31, 114
Waldron, Resolved, 503
Wallachia, Principality of, 227
Wallenstein, 259
Warner, Cayrus, 526
Washington, George, 52, 57

Waskovich, George, 245; biography of, 651
Weber, M., 288 n., 307 n., 336
Weingart, 103
Weiske, J., 391
Weiszäcker, C. F. von, 456
Wellek, René, 11, 14, 17, 20, 65, 102; biography of, 651
Wells, Herbert George, 62
Wenceslaus II, King of Bohemia, 387
Wenceslaus IV, King of Bohemia, 145, 156, 157, 163
Wenceslaus Bible, 158
Wends, the, 186
Werunsky, E., 391
Western civilization, 201
Weyr, František, 317, 331 n., 405-8, 409, 413
White Mountain, Battle of, 122, 124, 217, 247, 252, 275, 384, 500, 517
Whitesuntide Prague revolution, 275
Wieser, F. v., 336, 338, 338 n.
Williams, R. M., 305 n.
Windischgrätz, 275
Wingart, Miloš, 110
Wittelsbach, dynasty of, 232
Wocel, Jan Erazim, 387
Wogast, 191
Wolfskron, A. R. Ritter, 387
Wollin Czechs, in Poland, 541, 542
World Council of Churches, 498
World War I, 257
Worms, the city of, 191
Wundt, Wilhelm Max, 332 n., 406, 413
Wurmser of Strassburg, Nicholas, 142, 144
Würtemberg, 185, 186
Wycliffe, John, 201, 210, 211, 216, 259, 301, 313
Wycliffism, 210, 211
Wyman, Hans, 526

Yared, Gerazim, monk, 262
Young Czechs Party, 278
Yugoslavia, 204

Zaborski, Jerzy, 202, 203 n., 207 n., 209 n. biography of, 652
Zach, Jan, 123, 175, 178; biography of, 652
Zadkine, Osip, 178
Zahradníček, Jan, 36
Zahraniční Politika, journal, 280

Zakon sudnyj ljudem, 108
Záruba-Pfefferman, Quido, 487
Zator, Duchy in Upper Silesia, 226
Zauberman, Alfred, 376
Záviš, Magister, 121
Zbrojovka Works, 477
Zbyněk of Hasenburg, Archbishop, 145
Zdrůbek, František, 548, 550
Zelenka, Jan Dismas, 123
Želibský, Ján, 153
Zell, Ullrich, 474
Zemské desky (The Land Register), 387
Ženíšek, František, 150
Zeyer, Julius, 82
Zhdanov, Andrey, 23
Zíbrt, Čeněk, 472

Zikmund of Puchov, 484
Žilka, F., 317
Zlatoústý, Jan (John Chrysostom), 32
Žižka of Trocnov, John, 213, 259; military strategy and use of weapons by, 477
Zlín, 343, 347, 481
Zoshchenko, Mikhail, 23
Zosima, monk, 24
Zprávy SVU, a monthly Bulletin, published by the Czechoslovak Society of Arts and Sciences, 11
Zrzavý, Jan, 152, 153
Zubatý, Josef, 102
Zubina, M., 401 n.
Zycha, Adolf, 391

DATE DUE			
D8	Fordham Equip. Co.		